Do More with SOA Integration: Best of Packt

Integrate, automate, and regulate your business processes with the best of Packt's SOA books

Series Editor

Carl Jones

[PACKT] PUBLISHING enterprise
professional expertise distilled

BIRMINGHAM - MUMBAI

Do more with SOA Integration: Best of Packt

First published: December 2011

Production Reference: 1141211

Published by Packt Publishing Ltd.
Livery Place,
35 Livery Street,
Birmingham B3 2PB, UK.

ISBN 978-1-84968-572-6

www.packtpub.com

Cover Image by Tina Negus (tina_manthorpe@sky.com)

Credits

Series Editor

Carl Jones

Contributors

Antony Reynolds

Arun Poduval

Daniel Liebhart

David Salter

Doug Todd

Frank Jennings

Guido Schmutz

Harish Gaur

Jason Williamson

Jeremy Bolie

Jerry Thomas

Kevin Geminiuc

Lawrence Pravin

Marcel Krizevnik

Markus Zirn

Matjaz B. Juric

Matt Wright

Michael Cardella

Peter Welkenbach

Poornachandra Sarang

Praveen Ramachandran

Ramesh Loganathan

Sean Carey

Stany Blanvalet

The Hoa Nguyen

Todd Biske

Tom Laszewski

Yves Coene

Technical Editor

Lubna Shaikh

Production Coordinator

Arvindkumar Gupta

Cover Work

Arvindkumar Gupta

About the Contributors

Antony Reynolds has worked with Oracle BPEL from the days before Oracle acquired Collaxa in 2004 and with it the product now known as the Oracle BPEL Process Manager. Since then Antony has been a keen evangelist of the power of SOA and has worked with key European customers to help them realize the power of the Oracle SOA Suite within their own organizations. Prior to joining Oracle, Antony was a system architect working on the Galileo Computerized Reservation System. With more than 20 years of IT experience Antony has always focused on secure, high-volume systems on the leading edge of the technology curve and is now a leading proponent of business-focused SOA at Oracle.

Arun Poduval works as a Technical consultant at Midwave Corporation, specialized in SOA/Middleware.

Daniel Liebhart has over 20 years of experience in the information technology field, which has culminated in a broad technical and business know-how, which comprises the engineering, realization, and operation of complex and internationally operated IT systems for the Telecommunication, Finance, Logistic, and Chemical industries, as well as for public services. He has authored three books for Hanser Publications, is a passionate computer science engineer, has won several awards, and has worked for Trivadis, a leading independent IT service company operating in Germany, Austria, and Switzerland. He works as an assistant professor at the University of Applied Science in Zurich.

David Salter is an enterprise software architect who has been developing software professionally since 1991. His relationship with Java goes right back to the beginning, using Java 1.0 for writing desktop applications and applets for interactive web sites. David has been developing Enterprise Java Applications using both the J2EE standards and open source solutions for the last five years. David runs the Java community web site `Develop In Java`, a web site for all levels of Java developers.

Doug Todd is CTO of Enterra Solutions in Yardley, PA. He has more than 20 years of experience in systems architecture, applications architecture, systems integration, and applications integration with major corporations. Todd is responsible for Enterra's overall IT strategy and tactical implementation, enterprise information architecture, and technology product offerings.

Frank Jennings works in the Information Products Group of Sun Microsystems Inc. He has more than nine years of experience in Java, SOA and System Design. He is an Electronics Engineer from Madras University and has worked for several open source projects. Frank has written regular columns for leading Java journals including Java Developer's Journal and Linux Developer's Week. He holds a Post Graduate Diploma in Computer Science and an Advance Diploma in Computer Integrated Management from University of Indianapolis, and his blog can be read at `http://blogs.sun.com/phantom`.

Guido Schmutz is an Oracle ACE director for Fusion Middleware and SOA and works for the Swiss Oracle Platinum Partner Trivadis. He has more than 20 years of technology experience ranging from mainframes, integration, and SOA technologies in financial services, government, and vendor environments. Currently, he is focusing on SOA and application integration projects using the Oracle SOA Suite.

Harish Gaur has more than 13 years of experience in the enterprise software industry including more than seven years at Oracle. He is currently the Director of Product Management for Fusion Middleware at Oracle. In his current role, he works closely with strategic customers implementing SOA & BPM using Oracle Fusion Middleware. He is co-author of BPEL Cookbook (2007) and Fusion Middleware Patterns (Sept 2010). Harish holds an engineering degree in Computer Science and is an MBA from Haas School of Business, UC Berkeley.

Jason Williamson has over 17 years of experience in technology and business execution, from software development, product marketing, and management, to entrepreneurial enterprises. During his tenure with Oracle, he has been responsible for helping to develop and implement Oracle's strategy around legacy and business systems transformation. He now serves as a special advisor to Oracle's premier customers in the financial services industry. Jason spends his free time with his wife Susan and four children. He serves as a coach for youth sports and is involved in advocacy, fundraising, and speaking for Spina Bifida awareness.

Jeremy Bolie is a Senior IT Manager at QCT, managing the custom applications and Documentum development team. Jeremy has over 10 years of experience with Java and Oracle technologies, and has been involved with web services and Service-Oriented Architectures since the late 1990s.

Jerry Thomas is Chief Architect at CenterStone Software, which helps many of the world's largest organizations automate and manage their real estate, facilities, personnel, assets, leases, and workplace operations more efficiently. Thomas focuses on CenterStone's enterprise workplace management product and web services, BPEL, and system infrastructure. Prior to CenterStone, Thomas worked as a consultant and held principal development positions at Riverton, ONTOS, and Hewlett-Packard.

Kevin Geminiuc currently works as a senior software architect in Denver. Over the last 15 years, Kevin has worked as a systems architect, technical manager, developer, and hardware engineer. Kevin's technical interests include SOA, RFID, AVL, and genetic software.

Lawrence Pravin is the Product Manager, Process Integration Packs, Sierra Atlantic Inc. Process Integration Packs deliver end-to-end business process integration solutions between enterprise applications. He has over 10 years of rich experience in packaged applications, and has deep integration expertise with Oracle, PeopleSoft, Siebel, and SAP applications.

Marcel Krizevnik is a researcher at the University of Maribor where he is preparing a Ph.D. in computer and information science. Marcel started his career as a software developer of chemistry information systems. Now, his main research areas are service-oriented architecture and cloud computing. He is also a member of SOA Competency Center and Cloud Computing Center. In the last three years, he has been involved in several SOA technology projects.

Markus Zirn is a Senior Director of Product Management for Oracle Fusion Middleware. In this role, he heads the Strategic Customer Program, where he works with Oracle's leading and most innovative middleware customers. He has been part of the Enterprise Software industry for more than 10 years, including roles as Vice President of Product Marketing and part of the founding team of QUIQ and as a Management Consultant of Booz Allen & Hamilton's Silicon Valley High Tech Practice. Markus' passion for Service-Oriented Architecture (SOA) and BPEL stems both from practical experience designing and optimizing business processes as part of process reengineering projects and from being part of the advent of "software as a service" before web services became mainstream. He holds a Masters of Electrical Engineering from the University of Karlsruhe and is an alumnus of the Tripartite program, a joint European degree from the University of Karlsruhe, Germany, the University of Southampton, UK, and ESIEE, France.

Matjaz B. Juric holds a Ph.D. in computer and information science. He is a full-time professor at the university and head of the Cloud Computing and SOA Competence Centre. Matjaz is Java Champion and Oracle ACE Director. He has more than 15 years of work experience. He has authored/coauthored Business Process Driven SOA using BPMN and BPEL, Business Process Execution Language for Web Services (English and French editions), BPEL Cookbook: Best Practices for SOA-based integration and composite applications development (award for best SOA book in 2007 by SOA World Journal), SOA Approach to Integration, Professional J2EE EAI, Professional EJB, J2EE Design Patterns Applied, and .NET Serialization Handbook. He has published chapters in More Java Gems (Cambridge University Press) and in Technology Supporting Business Solutions (Nova Science Publishers). He has also published in journals and magazines, such as SOA World Journal, Web Services Journal, Java Developer's Journal, Java Report, Java World, eai Journal, theserverside.com, OTN, ACM journals, and presented at conferences such as OOPSLA, Java Development, XML Europe, OOW, SCI, and others. He is a reviewer, program committee member, and conference organizer. Matjaz has been involved in several large-scale projects. In cooperation with IBM Java Technology Centre, he worked on performance analysis and optimization of RMI-IIOP, integral part of the Java platform. Matjaz is also a member of the BPEL Advisory Board.

Matt Wright is a director at Rubicon Red, an independent consulting firm helping customers enable enterprise agility and operational excellence through the adoption of emerging technologies such as Service-Oriented Architecture (SOA), Business Process Management (BPM), and Cloud Computing. Matt holds a B.Sc. (Eng) in Computer Science from Imperial College, University of London.

Michael Cardella is a Staff Engineer at Qualcomm CDMA Technologies (QCT). Michael works in the custom applications development team, primarily on web-service- and business-process-related applications. Previously he served as Principal Architect for a leading web services security and management product.

Peter Welkenbach works as a consultant, senior architect, and trainer in the fields of requirement engineering, object-oriented methodologies, software engineering, and quality management. He has more than 20 years' experience of designing and implementing complex information systems for banks, automotive manufacturers, and pharmaceutical companies. Peter Welkenbach is a course developer, author of numerous publications, and speaker at JAX and international Oracle conferences.

Poornachandra Sarang, Ph.D., is CEO of ABCOM Information Systems and is currently a visiting professor for Post-Graduate Computer Science courses at the University of Mumbai. Dr. Sarang provides consulting services to worldwide clients in architecting and designing IT solutions based on Java, CORBA, and Microsoft platforms. He has authored/co-authored several books on Java, C++, J2EE, e-Commerce, and .NET.

Praveen Ramachandran works as a Technical Consultant for Midwave Corporation focusing on BPEL and other EAI technologies. Midwave is a rapidly growing firm that specializes in building highly available and highly secure information technology systems for medium to large companies and government agencies in seven midwestern states. Midwave is an Oracle Partner.

Ramesh Loganathan has 16 years of Systems engineering and R&D management experience in technology-intensive product development organizations. Ramesh has full life-cycle experience setting up and managing product development organizations and motivating high-caliber engineering teams. He has strong insight into Systems software, Middleware-technology, Database internals, Internet Architectures, and frameworks. Ramesh is now VP-Middleware Technologies at Pramati, driving the product direction and setting up a new Technology Consulting business around Middleware Systems.

Sean Carey is a Software Architect at SPS Commerce, a leader in hosted EDI. Sean has over seven years of experience in mission-critical e-commerce implementations, and 15 years of industry experience in software design.

Stany Blanvalet is a BPEL and J2EE consultant. Previously, working as a Java EE architect, Stany introduced and administered Belgacom's BPEL-based DSL provisioning application, a mission-critical BPEL production system. He is a contributor to the Jaisy-ORABPEL Interface project , an open-source JMX monitoring tool for Oracle BPEL Process Manager.

The Hoa Nguyen currently works for the SDC subsidiary of SpaceBel SA in Brussels as senior software engineer. His main interests are J2EE, web services, and workflow development with BPEL. Since 2001, he has been one of the lead engineers of the SSE project team at SpaceBel and is also in charge of SSE software releases and on-site SSE software installations at ESA.

Todd Biske is a Senior Enterprise Architect with Monsanto in St. Louis, Missouri. He has over 15 years of experience in Information Technology, both as a corporate practitioner and as a consultant, working with companies involved with Agriculture, Atmospheric Sciences, Financial Services, Insurance, and Travel and Leisure. He has an M.S. degree in Computer Science from the University of Illinois at Urbana-Champaign, is a member of the SOA Consortium, is a frequent conference presenter, and writes a popular blog on strategic IT topics at `http://www.biske.com/blog/` .

When Todd isn't working or blogging, he spends the vast majority of his time enjoying life with his wife Andrea, and their three children, Elena, Spencer, and Maria.

Tom Laszewski has over 20 years of experience in databases, middleware, software development, management, and building strong technical partnerships. He is currently the Cloud Migration Director in Oracle's Server Technology organization. Most recently, Tom is spending a significant amount of his time enabling Cloud computing service providers on the Oracle software and hardware stack. This involves architecting future-proof cloud infrastructure solutions utilizing Oracle Exadata, Oracle Exalogic, Oracle Virtual Server, Sun Blade Servers, Oracle Database, Oracle Fusion Middleware, and Oracle Enterprise Linux. Tom holds a Master of Science in Computer Information Systems from Boston University.

Yves Coene currently works for SpaceBel SA in Brussels as Project Manager. He has 15 years of experience in aerospace software projects such as Ariane 5, the International Space Station, F16 MLU, and various other projects for the European Space Agency. Since 2001, he and his team have been responsible for the SSE project for ESA in Frascati, Italy.

Table of Contents

Preface

A Packt Compendium is a book formed by drawing existing content from several related Packt titles. In other words, it is a mash-up of published Packt content – *Professional Expertise Distilled* in the true sense. Such a compendium of Packt's content allows you to learn from each of the chapters' unique styles and Packt does its best to compile the chapters without breaking the narrative flow for the reader.

Please note that the chapters in this compendium were originally written and intended as a part of various separate Packt titles, so you might find that the information included in this instance is more akin to that of a stand-alone chapter, rather than creating step-by-step, continuous flowing prose. We are sure that you will find this medley a useful and valuable resource with which you can benefit from a range of Packt books - and their authors' expertise!

Do more with SOA Integration: Best of Packt is a medley of eight separate titles from Packt's existing collection of excellent SOA books:

1. BPEL cookbook
2. SOA Approach to Integration
3. Service Oriented Architecture: An Integration Blueprint
4. Building SOA-Based Composite Applications Using NetBeans IDE 6
5. Oracle SOA Suite Developer's Guide
6. WS-BPEL 2.0 for SOA Composite Applications with Oracle SOA Suite 11g
7. Oracle Modernization Solutions
8. SOA Governance

Dismantling SOA Hype

Service-Oriented Architecture (SOA) has long since attracted a lot of buzz from every realm of the IT industry, and it remains a rapidly emerging technology. However, there is still some level of fear and anxiety among the IT community about SOA. Is SOA real? Do I need SOA? How is it done? You will be happy to know that SOA is a reality; it exists and you can do it as well.

New technology, after being adopted by"technology enthusiasts" and"visionaries" is adopted by"pragmatists". Technology Acceptance Model is one of the most influential models to explain the process of technology adoption. According to TAM, SOA has to prove itself on two terms—perceived usefulness and perceived ease of use—for SOA to successfully cross the chasm and be adopted more widely. We think SOA has proven its effectiveness on both these fronts. Not only can SOA deliver on its promises of reusability and agility (usefulness) but it can also reduce the overall cost of ownership through the standards-based approach (ease of use). That is precisely the reason why SOA enables organizations to cut the cost of IT dramatically and use the resulting savings in building other innovations.

As organizations increase their SOA footprint, IT Managers, Architects, and developers are starting to realize that the impact of SOA on IT and business operations can be immense. After having gained confidence with web services, they want to take it to the next level. However, adopters are challenged with some basic questions: How do I SOA-enable my existing integration investment? Can I build flexible and agile business processes? How can I administer my SOA environment without spending a fortune? There have been various best practices defined around SOA. However, missing from the map is the real-world flavor. People want to learn from people. The IT community is looking for real-world examples; examples to gain an understanding of how other companies are embarking on an SOA initiative and apply industry learning to their projects.

What this book covers

The book begins with a refresher of SOA and the various types of integration available, and then delves deeper into integration best practices with XML, binding components and web services from Packt titles like "Oracle SOA Suite Developer's Guide " and "BPEL Cookbook". Along the way you'll also learn from a number of real world scenarios. By the end of "Do more with SOA Integration: Best of Packt" you will be equipped with knowledge from a wide variety of Packt books and will have learnt from a range of practical approaches to really get to grips with SOA integration.

Chapter 1: Basic Principles, covers the fundamental integration concepts. This chapter is intended as an introduction for specialists who have not yet dealt with the subject of integration.

Chapter 2: Integration Architecture, Principles, and Patterns, is an overview of the challenges in integration and why integration is one of the most difficult problems in application development. We will identify the best strategies for SOA-based integration and discuss top-down, bottom-up, and inside-out approaches. You will learn about different types of integration, such as data-level integration, application integration, business process integration, presentation integration and also, B2B integrations.

Chapter 3: Base Technologies, describes a selection of base technologies. By far the most important of these are transaction strategies and their implementation, as well as process modeling. In addition, Java EE Connector Architecture (JCA), Java Business Integration (JBI), Service Component Architecture (SCA), and Service Data Objects (SDO) are explained. Many other base technologies are used in real-life integration projects, but these go beyond the scope of this book.

Chapter 4: Best Practices for Using XML for Integration, discusses various design anomalies that may arise while designing XML schemas. Some of the broad categories covered in this chapter are design recommendations for architecting domain-specifi c XML schemas, tips for designing XML schemas with examples, using XSL effectively for translating Infosets from one form to another, securing XML documents with encryption and digital signature, and XML serialization and the differences between SAX, DOM, and StAX.

Chapter 5: Extending Enterprise Application Integration, This chapter focuses on very common business problem i.e. siloed applications and segregated data glued together using proprietary integration solution. How can we best leverage SOA to add value on top of existing integration infrastructure? By service-enabling existing data-integration processes, business processes could be easily automated by orchestrating underlying services. Infosys, a leading systems integrator, has helped many of its customers leverage their existing EAI investment, and explains you how to do exactly this. This chapter takes an example of broken customer data synchronization between Siebel and SAP, and outlines a strategy to automate this process by integrating with proprietary integration solutions like TIBCO and webMethods.

Chapter 6: *Service-Oriented ERP Integration*: Driven by the business requirements of different departments, countries, and subsidiaries, many organizations end up with multiple ERP systems. The result is data fragmentation and manual processes. This, in turn, leads to poor customer service and loss of revenue. The problem is how to address this problem without re-architecting the entire solution. Sierra Atlantic, a leading consulting firm specializing in integration technologies, encountered a similar issue with its client. In this chapter, Lawrence Pravin, Architect at Sierra Atlantic, takes an example of a broken sales order creation process. He walks you through a step-by-step approach to automate it across PeopleSoft HR and Oracle E-Business Suite using BPEL in a service-oriented approach.

Chapter 7: *Service Engines*, provides an overview of Java Business Integration (JBI) and the Enterprise Service Bus (ESB). You will learn about JBI Service Engines and how they are supported within the NetBeans IDE.

Chapter 8: *Binding Components*, introduces JBI Binding Components and how they provide protocol independent communication between JBI components. You will also learn about the support that the NetBeans IDE provides for Binding Components.

Chapter 9: *SOA and Web Services Approach for Integration*, discusses the architecture of web services and their benefits. This chapter provides an in-depth coverage of the various patterns that can be applied while creating SOA using web services. You will learn the essential differences between EAI and B2B and how to apply SOA integration techniques in this space. The chapter also discusses several guidelines for creating interoperable web services. Finally, a complete, albeit trivial, example of creating web services on the .NET and Java EE platforms is discussed.

Chapter 10: *Service- and Process-Oriented Approach to Integration Using Web Services*, takes a look at how ESB provides a concrete infrastructure for SOA, extending the simple services model to include a robust services bus with extensive mediation functionality.

Chapter 11: *Loosely-coupling Services*, describes how we can use the Oracle Service Bus to build services that are implementation agnostic. Doing so allows us to change the service location, communication protocol, or even replace a service implementation with another, with no impact on the client.

Chapter 12: *Integrating BPEL with BPMN using BPM Suite*, presents an interesting new feature provided by Oracle Business Process Management Suite 11g (Oracle BPM Suite 11g) - the BPMN 2.0 service engine. It allows direct execution of BPMN 2.0 processes, without the need to transform them to BPEL. The chapter discusses Oracle BPM Suite architecture and features, and demonstrates how both, BPMN and BPEL processes can be used inside a single SOA composite application.

Chapter 13: SOA Integration – Functional View, Implementation, and Architecture, focusses to place SOA in the context of Modernization. SOA Legacy Modernizaton will bring you legacy IT infrastructure into the world of World Wide Web, Web 2.0, and all the other latest Internet-based IT architectures. Within days, a legacy system can be accessed via a web browser. Your time-to-market using the Legacy SOA Integration approach is weeks, instead of months or years for some other modernization options.

Chapter 14: SOA Integration – Scenario in Detail, is an SOA Integration hands-on example using web enablement of mainframe COBOL/VSAM. We will use Java Server Pages (JSP), Java Database Connectivity (JDBC), the Oracle Legacy Adapter, Oracle Application Server, Java EE Connector API, and XA transaction processing to show a two-phase commit across an Oracle database and VSAM on the mainframe.

Appendix A: Establishing SOA Governance at Your Organization, provides a detailed overview of both the techniques explored in the Advasco story, as well as other options available to you and your organization.

Conventions

In this book, you will find a number of styles of text that distinguish between different kinds of information. Here are some examples of these styles, and an explanation of their meaning.

There are three styles for code. Code words in text are shown as follows:"We can include other contexts through the use of the `include` directive."

A block of code will be set as follows:

```
WhereCondition where = WhereConditionHelper.whereInstancesStale();
      IInstanceHandle[] instances = getLocator(domainId,
domainPassword).listInstances(where);
           for(int i=0; i<instances.length; i++){
               instances[i].delete();
       }
```

When we wish to draw your attention to a particular part of a code block, the relevant lines or items will be made bold:

```
WhereCondition where = WhereConditionHelper.whereInstancesStale();
      IInstanceHandle[] instances = getLocator(domainId,
domainPassword).listInstances(where);
           for(int i=0; i<instances.length; i++){
               instances[i].delete();
       }
```

New terms and **important words** are introduced in a bold-type font. Words that you see on the screen, in menus or dialog boxes for example, appear in our text like this:"clicking the **Next** button moves you to the next screen".

> Warnings or important notes appear in a box like this.

> Tips and tricks appear like this.

Reader Feedback

Feedback from our readers is always welcome. Let us know what you think about this book, what you liked or may have disliked. Reader feedback is important for us to develop titles that you really get the most out of.

To send us general feedback, simply drop an email to `feedback@packtpub.com`, making sure to mention the book title in the subject of your message.

If there is a book that you need and would like to see us publish, please send us a note in the **SUGGEST A TITLE** form on `www.packtpub.com` or email `suggest@packtpub.com`.

If there is a topic that you have expertise in and you are interested in either writing or contributing to a book, see our author guide on `www.packtpub.com/authors`.

Customer Support

Now that you are the proud owner of a Packt book, we have a number of things to help you to get the most from your purchase.

Downloading the Code for the Book

Visit `http://www.packtpub.com/support`, and select this book from the list of titles to download any example code or extra resources for this book. The files available for download will then be displayed.

> The downloadable files contain instructions on how to use them.

Errata

Although we have taken every care to ensure the accuracy of our contents, mistakes do happen. If you find a mistake in one of our books—maybe a mistake in text or code—we would be grateful if you would report this to us. By doing this you can save other readers from frustration, and help to improve subsequent versions of this book. If you find any errata, report them by visiting `http://www.packtpub.com/support`, selecting your book, clicking on the **Submit Errata** link, and entering the details of your errata. Once your errata have been verified, your submission will be accepted and the errata added to the list of existing errata. The existing errata can be viewed by selecting your title from `http://www.packtpub.com/support`.

Questions

You can contact us at `questions@packtpub.com` if you are having a problem with some aspect of the book, and we will do our best to address it.

1 Basic Principles

This chapter describes the fundamental concepts of integration, and is intended as an introduction to integration technology and terminology. You will:

- Learn the basic concepts, which are often used in the context of integration architecture
- Grasp an overview of the different architecture variants, such as point-to-point, hub-and-spoke, pipeline, and **service-oriented architecture** (**SOA**)
- Learn about service-oriented integration with an explanation of both the process and the workflow integration patterns
- Understand the different types of data integration and the accompanying patterns
- Gain an understanding of **Enterprise Application Integration** (**EAI**) and **Enterprise Information Integration** (**EII**), and an indication of how direct connection, broker, and router patterns should be used
- Understand developments in SOA resulting from the introduction of enterprise-wide events
- Understand the integration technologies of the future: grid computing and **extreme transaction processing** (**XTP**)

Integration

The term *integration* has a number of different meanings. A fundamental knowledge of the terms and concepts of integration is an essential part of an integration architect's toolkit. There are many ways of classifying the different types of integration. From an enterprise-wide perspective, a distinction is made between **application-to-application** (**A2A**), **business-to-business** (**B2B**), and **business-to-consumer** (**B2C**) integration. Portal, function, and data integration can be classified on the basis of tiers. Another possible grouping consists of integration based on semantics.

Fundamental integration concepts include **Enterprise Application Integration (EAI)**, **Enterprise Service Bus (ESB)**, middleware, and messaging. These were used to define the subject before the introduction of SOA, and still form the basis of many integration projects today. EAI is, in fact, a synonym of integration. In David Linthicum's original definition of EAI, it means *the unrestricted sharing of data and business processes among any connected applications*. The technological implementation of EAI systems is, in most cases, based on middleware. The main base technology of EAI is messaging, giving the option of implementing an integration architecture through asynchronous communication, using messages which are exchanged across a distributed infrastructure and a central message broker.

The fundamental integration architecture variants are:

- point-to-point
- hub-and-spoke
- pipeline
- service-oriented architecture

A point-to-point architecture is a collection of independent systems, which are connected through a network.

Hub-and-spoke architecture represents a further stage in the evolution of application and system integration, in which a central hub takes over responsibility for communications.

In pipeline architecture, independent systems along the value-added chain are integrated using a message bus. The bus capability is the result of interfaces to the central bus being installed in a distributed manner through the communication network, which gives applications local access to a bus interface. Different applications are integrated to form a functioning whole by means of distributed and independent service calls that are orchestrated through an ESB and, if necessary, a process engine.

A fundamental technique for integration is the usage of **design patterns**. These include process and workflow patterns in a service-oriented integration, federation, population, and synchronization of patterns in a data integration, and direct connection, broker, and router patterns, which form part of EAI and EII. It is important to be familiar with all of these patterns, in order to be able to use them correctly.

The most recent integration architectures are based on concepts such as event-driven architecture, grid computing, or **extreme transaction processing (XTP)**. These technologies have yet to be tested in practice, but they are highly promising and of great interest for a number of applications, in particular, for corporate companies and large organizations.

Concepts

The Trivadis Integration Architecture Blueprint applies a clear and simple naming to each of the individual layers. However, in the context of integration, a wide range of different definitions and terms are used, which we will explain in this chapter.

- **Application to Application (A2A)**: A2A refers to the integration of applications and systems with each another.
- **Business to Business (B2B)**: B2B means the external integration of business partners', customers', and suppliers' processes and applications.
- **Business to Consumer (B2C)**: B2C describes the direct integration of end customers into internal corporate processes, for example, by means of Internet technologies.
- **Integration types**: Integration projects are generally broken down into integration portals, shared data integration, and shared function integration. Portals integrate applications at a user interface level. Shared data integration involves implementing integration architectures at a data level, and shared function integration at a function level.
- **Semantic integration**: One example of a semantic integration approach is the use of model-based semantic repositories for integrating data, using different types of contextual information.
- **Enterprise Application Integration (EAI)**: EAI allows for the unrestricted sharing of data and business processes among any connected applications.
- **Messaging, publish/subscribe, message brokers, and messaging infrastructures**: These are integration mechanisms involving asynchronous communication using messages, which are exchanged across a distributed infrastructure and a central message broker.
- **Enterprise Service Bus (ESB)**: An ESB is an integration infrastructure used to implement an EAI. The role of the ESB is to decouple client applications from services.
- **Middleware**: The technological implementation of EAI systems is, in most cases, based on middleware. Middleware is also described as communication infrastructure.
- **Routing schemes**: Information can be routed in different ways within a network. Depending on the type of routing used, routing schemes can be broken down into **unicast** (1:1 relationship), **broadcast** (all destinations), **multicast** (1:N), and **anycast** (1:N—most accessible).

A2A, B2B, and B2C

Nowadays, business information systems in the majority of organizations consist of an application and system landscape, which has grown gradually over time. The increasing use of standard software (packaged applications) means that information silos will continue to exist. IT, however, should provide end-to-end support for business processes. This support cannot, and must not, stop at the boundaries of new or existing applications. For this reason, integration mechanisms are needed, which bring together individual island solutions to form a functioning whole. This happens not only at the level of an individual enterprise or organization, but also across different enterprises, and between enterprises and their customers. At an organizational level, a distinction is made between A2A, B2B, and B2C integration (Pape 2006). This distinction is shown in the image below. Each type of integration places specific requirements on the methods, technologies, products, and tools used to carry out the integration tasks. For example, the security requirements of B2B and B2C integrations are different from those of an A2A integration.

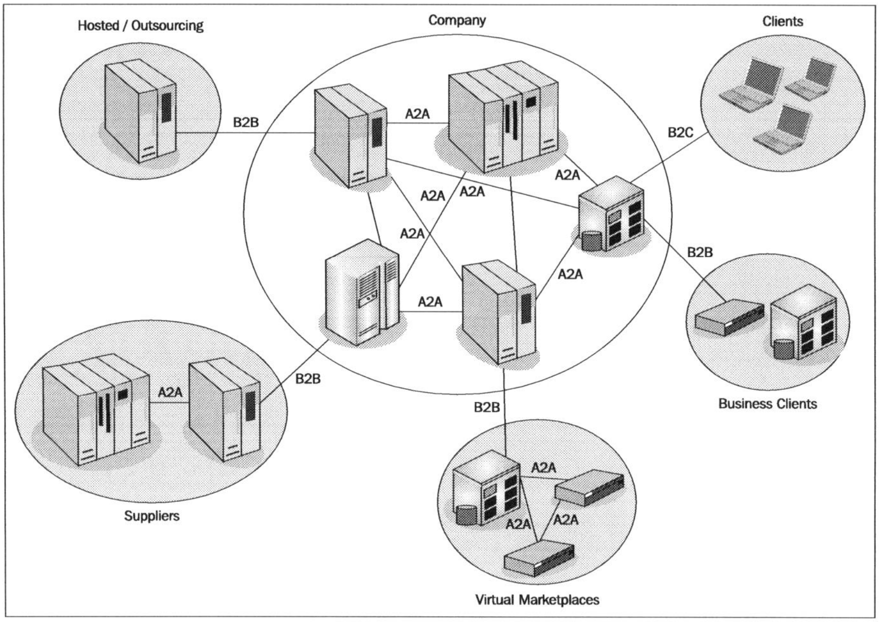

Modern concepts such as the **Extended Enterprise** integration across organizational boundaries, (Konsynski 1993) and the **Virtual Enterprise** (Hardwick, Bolton 1997) can be described using a combination of the different integration terms.

Integration types

Integration projects are generally broken down into information portals, shared data integration, and shared function integration. Portals integrate applications at a user interface level. Shared data integration involves implementing integration architectures at a data level, and shared function integration at a function level.

Information portals

The majority of business users need access to a range of systems in order to be able to run their business processes. They may need to be able to answer specific questions (that is, a call center taking incoming customer calls must be able to access the latest customer data) or to initiate or implement certain business functions (that is, updating customer data). In these circumstances, employees often have to use several business systems at the same time. An employee may need to access an order system (on a host) in order to verify the status of a customer order and, at the same time, may also have to open a web-based order system to see the data entered by the customer. Information portals bring together information from multiple sources. They display it in one place so that users do not have to access several different systems (which might also require separate authentication) and can work as efficiently as possible (Kirchhof et al. 2003). Simple information portals divide the user's screen into individual areas, each of which displays the data from one backend system independently, without interacting with the others. More sophisticated systems allow for limited interaction between the individual areas, which makes it possible to synchronize the different areas. For example, if the user selects a record in one area, the other areas are updated. Other portals use such advanced integration technology that the boundaries between the portal application and the integrated application become blurred (Nussdorfer, Martin 2006).

Shared data

Shared databases, file replication, and data transfers fall in the category of integration using shared data (Gorton 2006).

- **Shared databases**: Many different business systems need to access the same data. For example, customer addresses may be required in an order system, a CRM system, and a sales system. This kind of data can be stored in a shared database in order to reduce redundancy and synchronization problems.
- **File replication**: Systems often have their own local data storage. This means that any centrally managed data (in a top-level system) has to be replicated in the relevant target databases, and updated and synchronized regularly.
- **Data transfers**: Data transfers are a special form of data replication in which the data is transferred in files.

Shared business functions

In the same way that different business systems store redundant data, they also have a tendency to implement redundant business logic. This makes maintenance and adapting to new situations both difficult and costly. For example, different systems must be able to validate data using predefined, centrally managed business rules. It makes sense to manage such logic in a central place.

- **EAI**: The term EAI is generally used to describe all the methods which attempt to simplify the process of making a connection between different systems, in order to avoid a type of "spaghetti architecture" which results from the uncontrolled use of proprietary point-to-point connections. The systems are linked together with EAI solutions, instead of a single proprietary application programming interface (API).
- **SOA**: Service-oriented architecture is a term used to describe one way of implementing an enterprise architecture. SOA begins with an analysis of the business, in order to identify and structure the individual business areas and processes. This allows for the definition of services, which implement individual areas of business functionality. In an SOA, technical services are the equivalent of the specialist business areas, or functionality, in the business processes. This represents a major conceptual difference when compared with classic EAI solutions, which have a quite different focus. Their approach involves the simple exchange of data between systems, regardless of the technical semantics, and independently of any technical analysis of the processes.

Differences between EAI and SOA

In many cases, EAI solutions have only been able to fulfill the expectations placed on them to either a limited extent, or in an unsatisfactory way. This is, among other things, due to the following factors (Rotem-Gal-Oz 2007):

- EAI solutions are generally data oriented and not process oriented.
- EAI solutions do not address business processes. Instead, they are defined independently.
- EAI solutions are highly complex, and because of their use of proprietary technologies, do not allow for long-term protection of investments, which is possible when using open standards.
- EAI solutions need product-specific knowledge, which is only relevant in an EAI context, and cannot be reused in other projects.
- In the long term, EAI solutions are almost as costly to operate as the previously mentioned "home-made" spaghetti architectures.

If EAI solutions are used in combination with web services to link systems together, this is still not the equivalent of an SOA. Although the number of proprietary connection components between the systems being linked are reduced by the use of open **WS-*** standards, a "real" SOA involves a more extensive architectural approach, based on a (business) process-oriented perspective on integration problems.

While EAI is data driven and puts the emphasis on application interface integration, SOA is a (business) process-driven concept, which focuses on integrating service interfaces in compliance with open standards encapsulating the differences in individual integration approaches. As a result, it removes the barrier between the data integration and application integration approaches. However, SOA has one significant problem, which is that of semantic integration. Existing web services do not provide a satisfactory answer to this problem, but they do allow us to formulate the right questions in order to identify future solutions.

Semantic integration and the role of data

The challenge represented by semantic integration is based on the following problem:

- The representation of the data and the information contained in the data are often closely interlinked, and not separated into user data and metadata.
- The information suffers from the missing data context; there is no meta information defining how the data needs to be interpreted.

This means that the data structure and data information (its meaning) are often not the same thing and, therefore, have to be interpreted (Inmon, Nesavich 2008).

The following example will help to make this clearer:

A date, such as "7 August 1973," forms part of the data. It is not clear whether this information is a text string or in a date format. It may even be in another format and will have to be calculated on the basis of reference data before runtime. This information is of no relevance to the user.

However, it might be important to know what this date refers to, in other words, its semantic meaning in its reference context. Is it a customer's birthday, or the date on which a record was created? This example can even be more complex.

Another example that can be interpreted differently in different contexts is the term *Caesar*, for instance. Depending on the context, it could be the name of a pet or the name of pet food, a well-known salad, a gambling casino, or the name of a Roman emperor.

It is clear that data without a frame of reference is lacking any semantic information, causing the data to be ambiguous and possibly useless. Ontologically-oriented interfaces, as well as adaptive interfaces, can help to create such semantic reference and will become increasingly important in the field of autonomous B2B or B2C marketplaces in the future.

One semantic integration approach is, for example, the use of model-based semantic repositories (Casanave 2007). These repositories store and maintain implementation and integration designs for applications and processes (Yuan et al. 2006). They access existing vocabularies and reference models, which enable a standardized modeling process to be used. Vocabularies create a semantic coupling between data and specific business processes, and it is through these vocabularies that the services and applications involved are supplied with semantic information in the surrounding technical context. The primary objective of future architectures must be to maintain the glossary and the vocabularies, in order to create a common language and, therefore, a common understanding of all the systems and partners involved. Semantic gaps must be avoided or bridged wherever possible, for example transforming input and output data by using canonical models and standardized formats for business documents. These models and formats can be predefined for different industries as reference models [EDI (FIPS 1993), RosettaNet (Damodaran 2004), and so on]. Transformation rules can be generated and stored on the basis of reference models, in the form of data cards and transformation cards. In the future, there will be a greater focus on the declarative description (*what?*) and less emphasis on describing the concrete software logic (*how?*) when defining integration architectures. In other words, the work involved in integration projects will move away from implementation, and towards a conceptual description in the form of a generative approach, where the necessary runtime logic is generated automatically.

Enterprise Application Integration (EAI)

The term Enterprise Application Integration (EAI) has become popular with the increased importance of integration, and with more extensive integration projects. EAI is not a product or a specific integration framework, but can be defined as a combination of processes, software, standards, and hardware that allow for the end-to-end integration of several enterprise systems, and enable them to appear as a single system (Lam, Shankararaman 2007).

> **Definition of EAI**
>
> The use of EAI means the unrestricted sharing of data and business processes among any connected applications (Linthicum 2000).

From a business perspective, EAI can be seen as the competitive advantage that a company acquires when all its applications are integrated into one consistent information system. From a technical perspective, EAI is a process in which heterogeneous applications, functions, and data are integrated, in order to allow the shared use of data and the integration of business processes across all applications. The aim is to achieve this level of integration without major changes to the existing applications and databases, by using efficient methods that are cost and time effective.

In EAI, the focus is primarily on the technical integration of an application and system landscape. Middleware products are used as the integration tools, but, wherever possible, the design and implementation of the applications are left unchanged. Adapters enable information and data to be moved across the technologically heterogeneous structures and boundaries. The service concept is lacking, as well as the reduction of complexity and avoidance of redundancy offered by open standards. The service concept and the standardization only came later with the emergence of service-oriented architectures (SOA), which highlighted the importance of focusing on the functional levels within a company, and its business processes.

Nowadays, software products which support EAI are often capable of providing the technical basis for infrastructure components within an SOA. As they also support the relevant interfaces of an SOA, they can be used as the controlling instance for the orchestration, and help to bring heterogeneous subsystems together to form a whole. Depending on its strategic definition, EAI can be seen as a preliminary stage of SOA, or as a concept that competes with SOA.

SOA is now moving the concept of integration into a new dimension. Alongside the classic "horizontal" integration, involving the integration of applications and systems in the context of an EAI, which is also of importance in an SOA, SOA also focuses more closely on a "vertical" integration of the representation of business processes at an IT level (Fröschle, Reinheimer 2007).

SOAs are already a characteristic feature of the application landscape. It is advisable when implementing new solutions to ensure that they are SOA-compliant, even if there are no immediate plans to introduce an integration architecture, or an orchestration layer. This allows the transition to an SOA to be made in small, controllable steps, in parallel with the existing architecture and on the basis of the existing integration infrastructure.

Levels of integration

Integration architectures are based on at least three or four integration levels (after Puschmann, Alt 2004 and Ring, Ward-Dutton 1999):

- **Integration on data level**: Data is exchanged between different systems. The technology most frequently used for integration at data level is File Transfer Protocol (FTP). Another widespread form of data exchange is the direct connection of two databases. Oracle databases, for example, exchange data via database links or external tables.
- **Integration on object level**: Integration on object level is based on data-level integration. It allows systems to communicate by calling objects from outside the applications involved.
- **Integration on process level**: Integration on process level uses workflow management systems. At this level, communication between the different applications takes place through the workflows, which make up a business process.

Messaging

Message queues were introduced in the 1970s as a mechanism for synchronizing processes (Brinch Hansen 1970). Message queues allow for persistent messages and, therefore, for asynchronous communication and the guaranteed delivery of messages. Messaging decouples the producer and the consumer with the only common denominator being the queue.

The most important properties of messaging, quality attributes of messaging, are shown in the following table:

Attribute	Comment
Availability	Physical queues with the same logical name can be replicated across several server instances. In the case of a failure of one server, the clients can send the message to another.
Failure handling	If communication between a client and a server fails, the client can send the message via failover mechanisms to another server instance.

Attribute	Comment
Modifiability	Clients and servers are loosely coupled by the messaging concept, which means that they do not know each other. This makes it possible for both clients and servers to be modified without influencing the system as a whole. Another dependency between producer and consumer is the message format. This dependency can be reduced or removed altogether by introducing a self-descriptive general message format (**canonical** message format).
Performance	Messaging can handle several thousands of messages per second, depending on the size of the messages and the complexity of the necessary transformations. The quality of service also has a major influence on the overall performance. Non-reliable messaging, which involves no buffering provides better performance than reliable messaging, where the messages are stored (**persisted**) in the filesystem or in databases (local or remote), to ensure that they are not lost if a server fails.
Scalability	Replication and clustering make messaging a highly scalable solution.

Publish/subscribe

Publish/subscribe represents an evolution of messaging (Quema et al. 2002). A subscriber indicates, in a suitable form, its interest in a specific message or message type. The persistent queue guarantees secure delivery. The publisher simply puts its message in the message queue, and the queue distributes the message itself. This allows for many-to-many messaging:

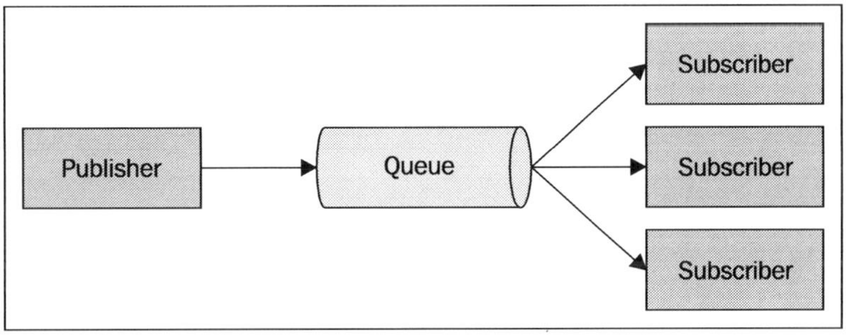

The most important properties of publish/subscribe, quality attributes of publish/subscribe, are listed in the following table:

Attribute	Comment
Availability	Physical topics with the same logical name can be replicated across several server instances. In the case of the failure of one server, the clients can send the message to another.
Failure handling	In the case of the failure of one server, the clients can send the message to another replicated server.
Modifiability	The publisher and the subscriber are loosely coupled by the messaging concept, which means that they do not know each other. This makes it possible for both publisher and subscriber to be modified without influencing the system as a whole. Another dependency is the message format. This can be reduced or removed altogether by introducing a self-descriptive, general message format (canonical message format).
Performance	Publish/subscribe can process thousands of messages per second. Non-reliable messaging is faster than reliable messaging, because reliable messages have to be stored locally. If a publish/subscribe broker supports multicast/broadcast protocols, several messages can be transmitted to the subscriber simultaneously, but not serially.
Scalability	Topics can be replicated across server clusters. This provides the necessary scalability for very large message throughputs. Multicast/broadcast protocols can also be scaled more effectively than point-to-point protocols.

Message brokers

A message broker is a central component, which is responsible for the secure delivery of messages (Linthicum 1999). The broker has logical ports for receiving and sending messages. It transports messages between the sender and the subscriber, and transforms them where necessary.

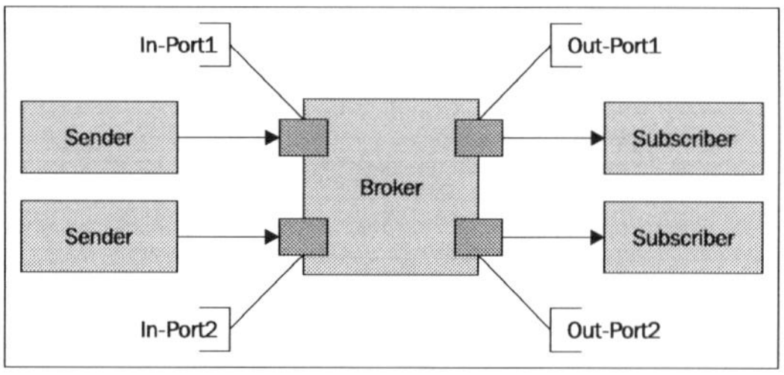

The most important tasks of a message broker, as shown in the preceding diagram, are implementing a hub-and-spoke architecture, the routing, and the transformation of messages.

- **Hub-and-spoke architecture**: The broker acts as a central message hub with the senders and receivers arranged like spokes around it. Connections to the broker are done through adapter ports that support the relevant message format.
- **Message routing**: The broker uses processing logic to route the messages. Routing decisions can be hardcoded, or can be specified in a declarative way. They are often based on the content of the message (content-based routing) or on specific values or attributes in the message header (attribute-based routing).
- **Message transformation**: The broker logic transforms the message input format into the necessary message output format.

The most important properties of a message broker, quality attributes of a message broker, are listed in the following table:

Attribute	Comment
Availability	To provide high availability, brokers must be replicated and operate in a clusters.
Failure handling	Brokers have different types of input ports that validate incoming messages to ensure that they have the correct format, and reject those with the wrong format. If one broker fails, the clients can send the message to another replicated broker.
Modifiability	Brokers separate transformation logic and routing logic from one another and from senders and receivers. This improves modifiability, as the logic has no influence on senders and receivers.
Performance	Because of the hub-and-spoke approach, brokers can potentially be a **bottleneck**. This applies in particular in the case of a high volume of messages, large messages and complex transformations. The throughput is typically lower than with simple reliable messaging.
Scalability	Broker clusters allow for high levels of scalability.

Messaging infrastructure

A messaging infrastructure provides mechanisms for sending, routing, and converting data, between different applications running on different operating systems with different technologies, as shown in the following diagram (Eugster et al. 2003):

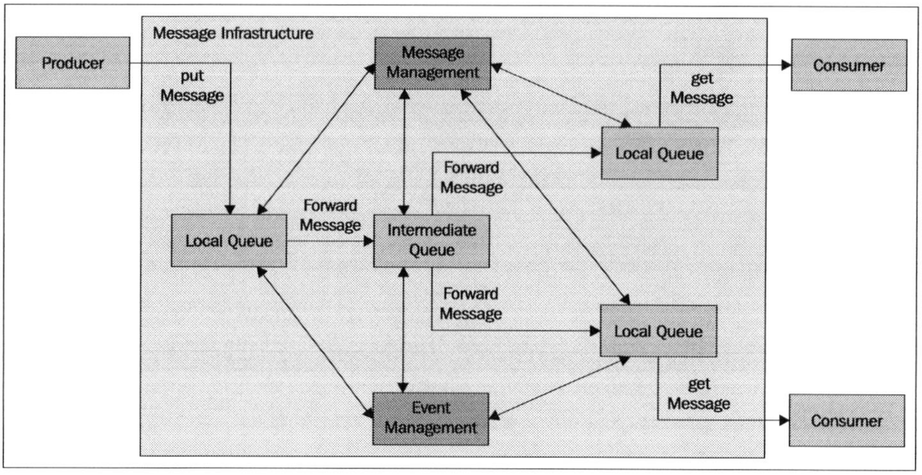

A messaging infrastructure involves the following parties/components:

- **Producer:** An application which sends messages to a local queue.
- **Consumer:** An application which is interested in specific messages.
- **Local queue**: The local interface of the messaging infrastructure. Each message sent to a local queue is received by the infrastructure and routed to one or more receivers.
- **Intermediate queue**: In order to ensure that messages are delivered, the infrastructure uses intermediate queues, in case a message cannot be delivered, or has to be copied for several receivers.
- **Message management**: Message management includes sending, routing, and converting data, together with special functions, such as guaranteed delivery, message monitoring, tracing individual messages, and error management.
- **Event management**: The subscription mechanism is controlled through special events.

Enterprise Service Bus

An Enterprise Service Bus is an infrastructure that can be used to implement an EAI. The primary role of the ESB is to decouple client applications from services, as shown in the following diagram (Chappell 2004):

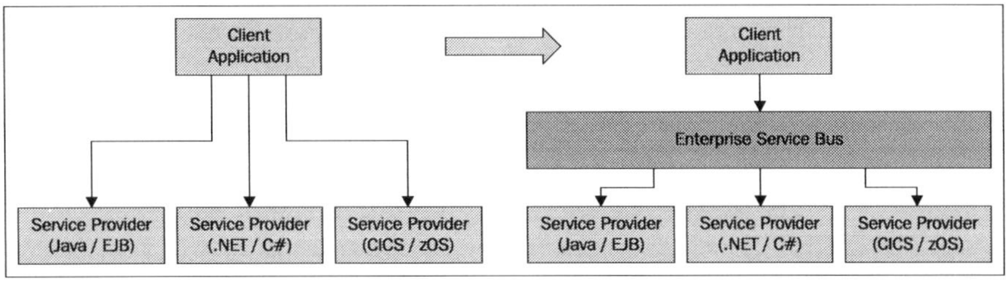

The encapsulation of services by the ESB means that the client application does not need to know anything about the location of the services, or the different communication protocols used to call them. The ESB enables the shared, enterprise-wide, and even intra-enterprise use of services and separate business processes from the relevant service implementations (Lee et al. 2003).

The core functions of an ESB

The major SOA vendors now offer specific Enterprise Service Bus products, which provide a series of core functions in one or another form, shown in the following diagram:

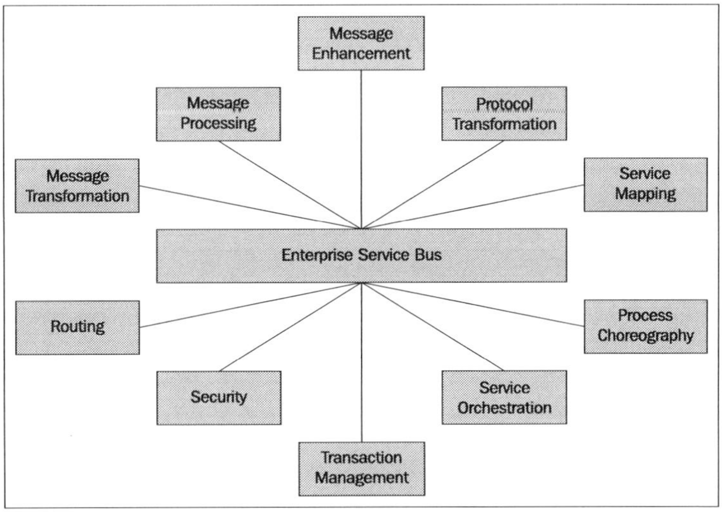

The structure of an ESB

The following diagram shows the basic structure of an ESB in a vendor-neutral way:

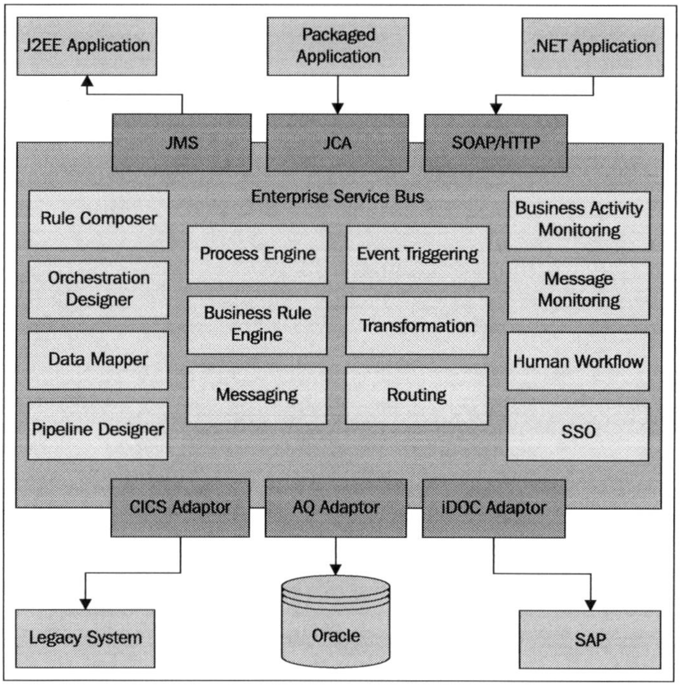

The naming for the single components used by the different vendors of SOA products will vary from those shown in the above diagram, but the products provide the following functions as a minimum (Craggs 2003):

- Routing and messaging as base services
- A communication bus, which enables a wide variety of systems to be integrated using predefined adapters
- Transformation and mapping services for a range of different conversions and transformations
- Mechanisms for executing processes and rules
- Monitoring functions for a selection of components
- Development tools for modeling processes, mapping rules, and message transfers
- A series of standardized interfaces, such as JMS (Java Messaging Specification (Hapner et al. 2002)), JCA (Java Connector Architecture (JCASpec 2003)), and SOAP/HTTP

Middleware

In most cases the technological realization of EAI systems is done through what is commonly termed **middleware**. Middleware is also described as a communication infrastructure. It allows communication between software components, regardless of the programming language in which the components were created, the protocols used for communication, and the platform on which the components are running (Thomson 1997). A distinction is made between the different types of middleware according to the methods of communication used, and the base technology.

Middleware communication methods

Communication methods for middleware can be broken down into five categories:

- **Conversational (Dialog-Oriented)**: The components interact synchronously with one another. They always react instantly to the information being exchanged. This type of communication is generally used in real-time systems.
- **Request/reply**: This is used when an application needs to call functions from another application. It corresponds to a call to a subroutine, with the important difference that the communication can take place over a network.
- **Message passing**: This enables information to be exchanged in a simple and well-directed way using messages. Communication takes place in one direction only. If an application wants to react to an incoming message, its response must be placed in another message.
- **Message queuing**: Information is exchanged in the form of messages which are sent through a queue, in other words, indirectly. Queuing allows the secure, planned, and prioritized delivery of messages. It is often used for the near real-time exchange of information between loosely coupled systems.
- **Publish/subscribe**: Two roles are involved in non-directed communication: the publisher of a message sends the message only to the middleware. The subscriber subscribes to all the types of message that are of interest to him or her. The middleware ensures that all subscribers receive the corresponding messages from a publisher.

Middleware type	Communication	Relationship	Synchronous/ asynchronous	Interaction
Peer-to-peer, API	Conversational	1:1	Synchronous	Blocking
Database gateways	Request/reply	1:1	Synchronous	Blocking
Database replication	Request/reply/	1:N	Synchronous	Blocking
	Message queue	1:N	Asynchronous	Non-blocking
Remote procedure calls	Request/reply	1:1	Mostly synchronous	Mostly blocking
Object request brokers	Request/reply	1:1	Mostly synchronous	Mostly blocking
Direct messaging	Message passing	1:1	Asynchronous	Non-blocking
Message queue systems	Message queue	M:N	Asynchronous	Non-blocking
Message infrastructure	Publish/ subscribe	M:N	Asynchronous	Non-blocking

Middleware base technologies

Middleware can be broken down into the following base technologies:

- **Data-oriented middleware**: The integration or distribution of data to different RDBMS using the appropriate synchronization mechanisms.
- **Remote procedure call**: The implementation of the classic client/server approach.
- **Transaction-oriented middleware**: The transaction concept (ACID—Atomicity, Consistency, Isolation, Durability) is put into effect using this type of middleware. A transaction is a finite series of atomic operations which have either read or write access to a database.
- **Message-oriented middleware**: The information is exchanged by means of messages, which are transported by the middleware from one application to the next. Message queues are used in most cases.
- **Component-oriented middleware**: This represents different applications and their components as a complete system.

Routing schemes

Information can be routed in different ways within a network. Depending on the type of routing used, routing schemes can be broken down into the following four categories:

- Unicast (1:1 relationship)
- Broadcast (all destinations)
- Multicast (1:N)
- Anycast (1:N, most accessible)

Unicast

The unicast routing scheme sends data packages to a single destination. There is a 1:1 relationship between the network address and the network end point:

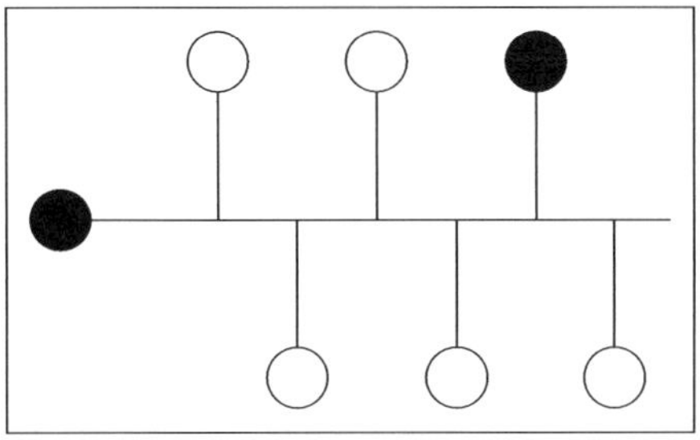

Broadcast

The broadcast routing scheme sends data packets in parallel to all the possible destinations in the network. If there is no support for this process, the data packets can be sent serially to all possible destinations. This produces the same results, but the performance is reduced. There is a 1:N relationship between the network address and the network end point.

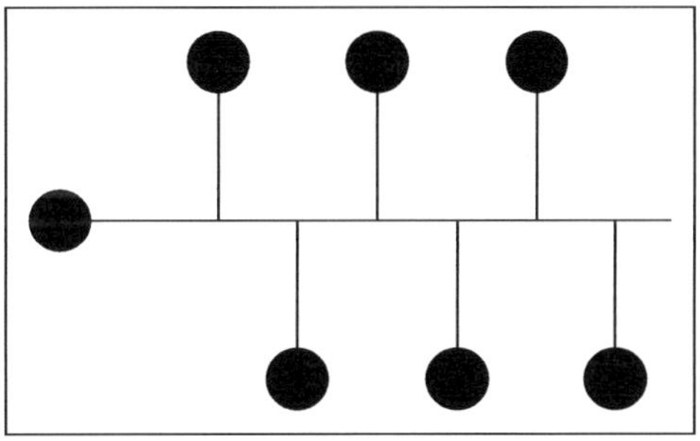

Multicast

The multicast routing scheme sends data packets to a specific selection of destinations. The destination set is a subset of all the possible destinations. There is a 1:N relationship between the network address and the network end point:

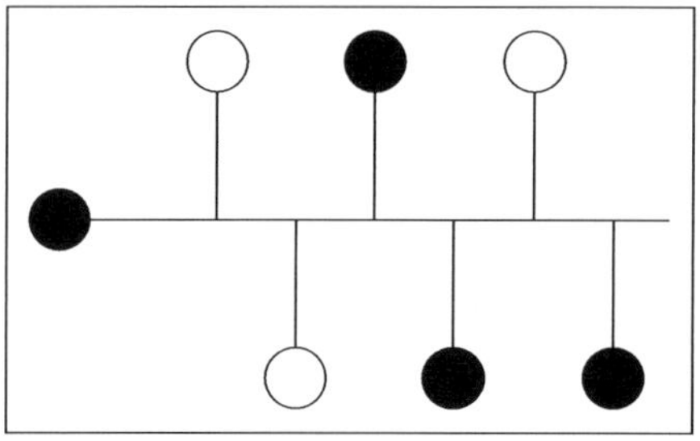

Anycast

The anycast routing scheme distributes information to the destination computer which is nearest, or most accessible. There is a 1:N relationship between the network address and the network end point, but only one end point is addressed at any given time for the purpose of routing the information.

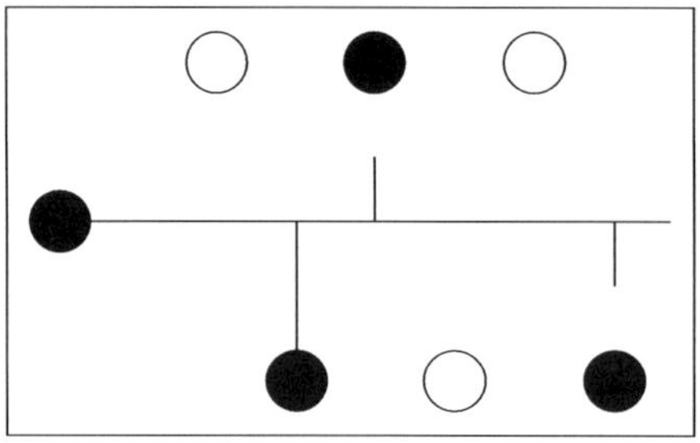

Integration architecture variants

The fundamental integration architecture variants are:

- **Point-to-point architecture**: A collection of independent systems which are connected through a network.
- **Hub-and-spoke architecture**: A further stage in the evolution of application and system integration, in which a central hub takes over responsibility for communications.

- **Pipeline architecture**: In pipeline architecture, independent systems along the value-added chain are integrated using a message bus. The bus capability results in the distribution of the interfaces to the central bus throughout the communication network, which gives applications a local access to a bus interface.
- **Service-oriented architecture**: The integration of different applications to form a functioning whole by means of distributed and independent service calls, which are orchestrated through an ESB and, if necessary, a Process Engine.

Point-to-point architecture

A point-to-point architecture is a collection of independent systems which are connected through a network. All the systems have equal rights, and can both use and provide services (Lublinsky 2002). This architecture can be found in many organizations, where application islands that have grown through time have been connected directly to each other.

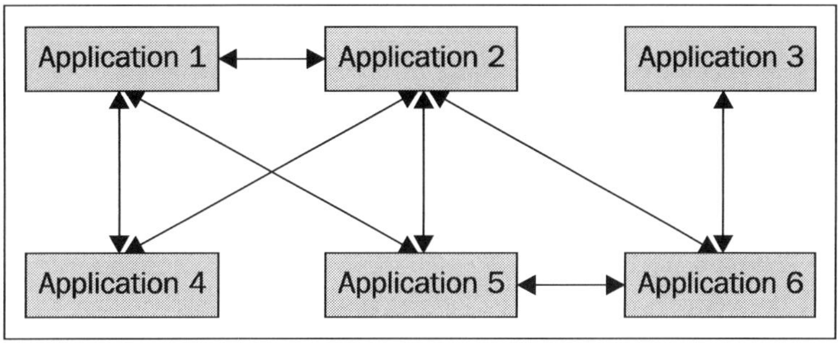

As shown in the above diagram, in this architecture, there is no central database—each system has its own data storage.

New systems are connected directly with the existing ones, which over time leads to a highly complex set of interfaces. A point-to-point architecture with n applications can in theory have n*(n-1)/2 interfaces.

It is easy to imagine how complex, error-prone, and difficult it can be to maintain such an architecture as more and more applications are added. Expanding the system is costly and, as the number of interfaces grows, operation becomes increasingly time consuming and expensive. A SWOT analysis is shown in the following table:

Strengths	Weaknesses
• Low startup and infrastructure costs • Autonomous systems	• Only practical if there are a few systems and a few connections • Replacing individual systems is a highly laborious and costly process • Very inflexible, not the base for an SOA and, therefore, it is difficult to represent business processes • No overview of data • Limited reusability of components • Time consuming and costly operation
Opportunities	**Threats**
• Functions within the systems can be rapidly adapted to meet new requirements	• High follow-up costs • Lack of standardization

Hub-and-spoke architecture

Hub-and-spoke architecture represents a further stage in the evolution of application and system integration, as shown in the following diagram (Gilfix 2003):

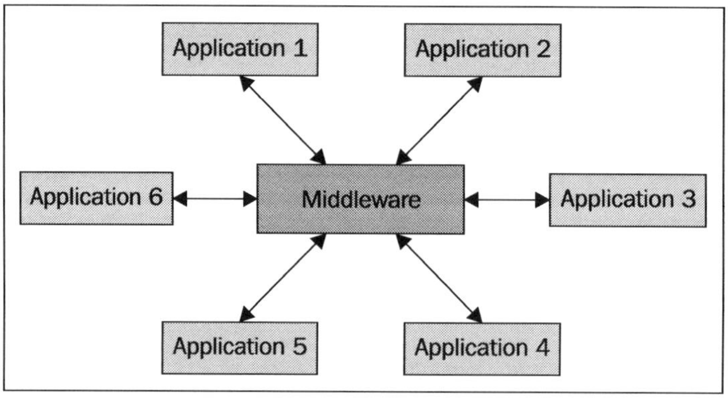

Its objective is to minimize the growing interface complexity by using a central integration platform to exchange messages between the systems. The central integration platform can transform messages, route them from one application to the next, and change the content of the messages. This architecture is often used for complex data distribution mechanisms. A SWOT analysis is shown in the following table:

Strengths	**Weaknesses**
• Reduction of the interface problem • Low follow-up costs • Compliance with standards • Autonomous systems • Simplified monitoring	• High startup and infrastructure costs
Opportunities	**Threats**
• Individual systems can be integrated/replaced easily	• With high transfer volumes, the central hub could become a performance bottleneck • Single point of failure

Pipeline architecture

In a pipeline architecture, independent systems along the value-added chain are integrated using a message bus, as in the following figure. The implementation of this architecture corresponds to that of the hub-and-spoke architecture, as the corresponding middleware products are normally installed and operated on central servers. The bus capability results in the distribution of the interfaces to the central bus throughout the communication network, which generally also gives applications local access to a bus interface (Ambriola, Tortora 1993).

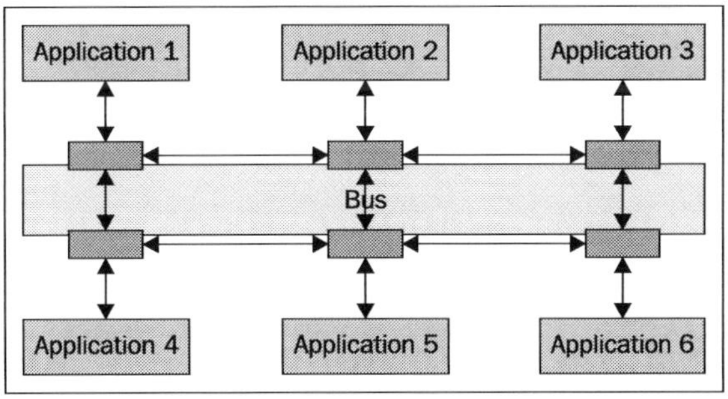

Similarly to the hub-and-spoke architecture, this architecture also keeps interface problems to a minimum. The use of appropriate middleware components allows the communication between the systems to be standardized. The bus system is responsible for message distribution. The transformation and routing rules are stored in a central repository. Depending on the middleware product in use, business functions and rules can also be represented. A SWOT analysis is shown in the following table:

Strengths	Weaknesses
• Low follow-up costs • Very flexible architecture • Compliance with standards • Autonomous systems	• High startup and infrastructure costs
Opportunities	**Threats**
• Individual systems can be integrated/replaced easily	• With high transfer volumes, there is the risk of a performance bottleneck, if it is not separated from normal traffic (for example, separate bulk channel)

This form of architecture is ideal for:

- Very high performance requirements (event-driven architecture)
- 1:N data distribution (for example, broadcasting)
- N:1 database (for example, data warehouse)

Service-oriented architecture

The core of a service-oriented architecture, and the main distinction between this form of architecture and those described earlier, is the fact that business processes and applications are no longer coded as complex program structures, but are orchestrated as independent, distributed service calls.

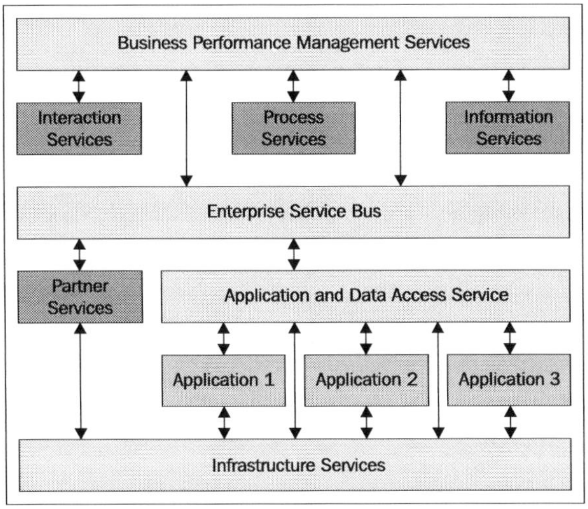

An ESB is used as the central integration component for service calls. It has similar properties to those of the integration platform in hub-and-spoke architecture, or of the bus in pipeline architecture. A SWOT analysis is shown in the following table

Strengths	Weaknesses
• Low follow-up costs • Very flexible architecture • Compliance with standards • Supported by all major software houses	• High startup and infrastructure costs • Requires a comprehensive SOA strategy and governance
Opportunities	**Threats**
• Individual systems can be implemented and orchestrated easily	• Lack of focus on relevant business processes

Patterns for EAI/EII

Three basic patterns are used for the implementation of EAI and EII platforms:

- Direct connection
- Broker
- Router

Direct connection

Direct connection represents the simplest type of interaction between two applications and is based on a 1: N topology, in other words, an individual point-to-point connection. It allows a pair of applications within an organization to communicate directly. Interactions between the source and the target applications can be as complex as necessary. Additional connection rules are defined for more complex point-to-point connections. Examples of connection rules include data mapping rules, security rules, and availability rules.

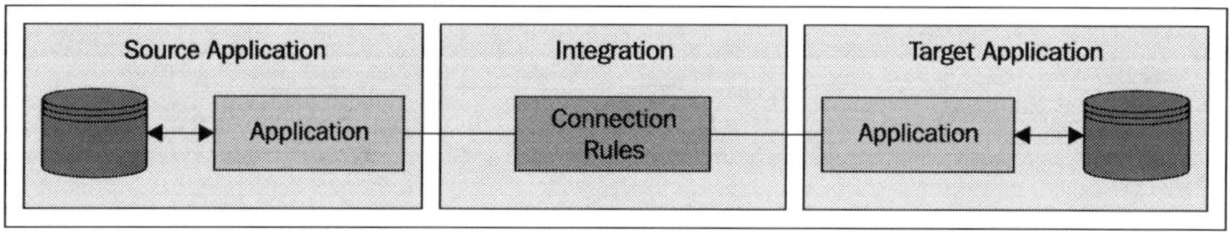

The direct connection pattern can be broken down into the following logical components:

- The source applications consist of one or more applications, which want to initiate interaction with the target applications.
- The connection is the line between the source and the target application, and represents a point-to-point connection between the two applications.
- Connection rules are the business rules which relate to the connection, such as data mapping and security rules.
- The target application is a new or existing (modified or unmodified) application, which provides the necessary business services.

The advantages and disadvantages of the direct connection pattern are shown in the following table:

Advantages	Disadvantages
• Functions well in the case of applications with simple integration requirements and only a few backend applications • Loose coupling • Receivers do not need to be online	• Results in several point-to-point connections between each pair of applications, and therefore, to spaghetti configurations • Does not support the intelligent routing of queries • Does not support the decomposition/ re-composition of queries

Uses

Direct connection is used for the following purposes:

- Reducing the latency of business events
- Supporting the structured exchange of information within an organization
- Supporting real-time one-way message flows
- Supporting real-time request/reply message flows
- Continued use of legacy investments

Broker

The broker pattern is based on the direct connection pattern, and extends it to a 1: N topology. It allows an individual request from a source application to be routed to several target applications, which reduces the number of 1:1 connections required. The connection rules take the form of broker rules. This allows the distribution rules to be kept separate from the application logic (**Separation of Concerns** principle or **SoC**). The broker is also responsible for the composition and decomposition of interactions. The broker pattern uses the direct connection pattern for the connection between the applications. The broker pattern forms the base for the publish/subscribe message flow:

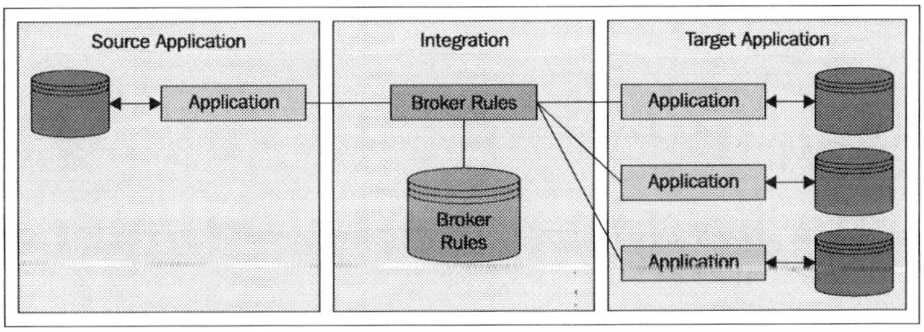

The broker pattern can be broken down into the following logical components:

- The source applications consist of one or more applications which want to interact with the target applications.
- The broker component keeps the number of direct connections to a minimum. It also supports message routing, message enhancement, and the transformation, decomposition, and re-composition of messages.
- The target applications consist of both new and existing (modified or unmodified) applications. These applications are responsible for implementing the necessary business services.

The advantages and disadvantages of the broker pattern are shown in the following table:

Advantages	Disadvantages
• Allows for the interaction of several different applications. • Minimizes the impact on existing applications. • Makes routing services available, so that the source application no longer needs to know the target applications. • Provides transformation services, which enable the source and target applications to use different communication protocols. • Decomposition/re-composition services are available to allow a single request to be sent from one source to several target applications. • The use of the router keeps the number of necessary modifications to a minimum when the location of the target application is changed.	• Logic has to be implemented on the broker for routing and decomposition/re-composition tasks.

Uses

Broker is used for the following purposes:

- An individual application should be able to interact with one or more target applications.
- A hub-and-spoke architecture reduces complexity when compared with a point-to-point architecture.
- The externalization of the routing, decomposition, and re-composition rules increases maintainability and flexibility.
- Broker pattern is important when a request is processed from a source application and results in several interactions with the target systems.
- The source system is decoupled from the target applications, and there is no dependency on the interfaces of these target applications.

Router

The router pattern is a variant of the broker pattern with several potential target applications, in which the message is always routed to only one target application. The router decides which target application will receive the interaction. While the broker pattern supports 1:N connections, the router pattern only allows 1:1 connections, as the router rules determine the target application in each case.

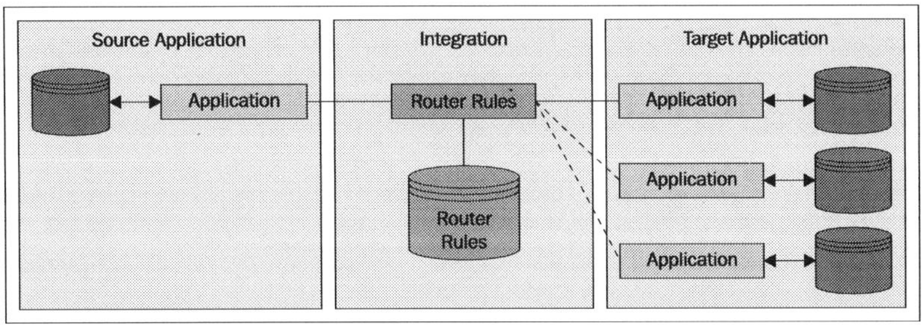

The router pattern as shown in the diagram can be broken down into the following logical components:

- The source applications consist of one or more applications that want to interact with the target applications.
- The router component provides all the business rules needed for processing the message, such as routing and transformation. It receives requests from several source applications, and routes them intelligently to the correct target application. The resulting integration is, in fact, a point-to-point connection between the source and the target.
- The target applications consist of both new and existing (modified or unmodified) applications. These applications are responsible for implementing the necessary business services.

The advantages and disadvantages of the router pattern are shown in the following table:

Advantages	Disadvantages
• Allows for the interaction of several different applications. • Minimizes the impact on existing applications. • Makes routing services available, so that the source application no longer needs to recognize the target applications. • Provides transformation services which enable the source and target applications to use different communication protocols. • The use of the router keeps the number of necessary modifications to a minimum when the location of the target application is changed.	• No decomposition and re-composition of messages. • No possibility of sending several simultaneous requests to the target applications on the basis of the incoming request.

Uses

Router is used for the following purposes:

- An individual application should be able to interact with one of several target applications
- A hub-and-spoke architecture reduces complexity when compared with a point-to-point architecture
- The externalization of the routing, decomposition, and re-composition rules increases maintainability and flexibility
- Router pattern is important when a request is processed from a source application and results in an interaction with only one of several potential target systems
- As with the Broker pattern, the source system is also decoupled from the target applications, and has no dependency on the interfaces of these applications

Patterns for data integration

Data integration is implemented using three fundamental patterns:

- Federation
- Population
- Synchronization

Federation

The federation pattern is a simple data integration pattern that provides access to different data sources, and gives the calling application the impression that these sources are a single, logical data source. This is achieved as follows:

1. Expose a single consistent interface to the application.
2. Translate the interface to whatever interface is needed for the underlying data.
3. Compensate for any differences in function between the different data sources.
4. Allow data from different sources to be combined into a single result set that is returned to the user.

This is illustrated in the following diagram:

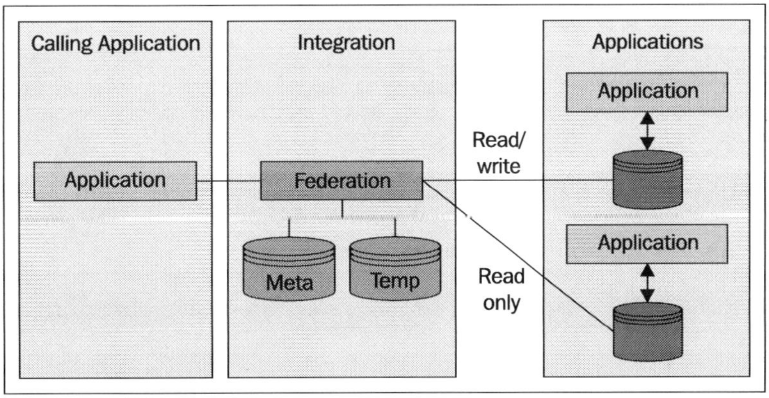

The federation pattern as shown in this diagram can be broken down into the following logical building blocks:

- The calling applications have the need for information, but they don't possess the information.

- The federation building block uses metadata to determine where the data required is stored, and in what format. The metadata repository allows the decomposition of a single query executed against the federation building block, into individual requests to different data sources. To the user (the calling application), the information model appears to be a single virtual repository. The data is accessed via suitable adapters for each target repository. The federation component sends an individual result to the calling application, and integrates several different formats into a shared federated schema.
- The source applications have the information that is important for the calling applications.

The federation pattern supports structured and unstructured data, together with read-only and read/write accesses to the underlying data sources. Read/write accesses should be limited, wherever possible, to a single data source, as otherwise a two-phase commit is needed, which can be difficult in distributed databases.

Uses

Federation is used for the following purposes:

- The data needed by an application is distributed across different databases (for historic, technical, or organizational reasons)
- Federation is more effective than other data integration technologies, when:
    - Near real-time access is needed for rapidly changing data
    - Making a consolidated copy of the data is not possible for technical, legal, or other reasons
    - Read/write access must be possible
    - Reducing or limiting the number of copies of the data is a goal
- It is possible to continue to make use of existing investments

Population

The population pattern has a very simple model. It gathers data from one or more data sources, processes the data in an appropriate way, and applies it to a target database. In its simplest form, the population pattern is based on the read dataset-process data-write dataset model. This corresponds to the classic ETL (Extract, Transform, and Load process.

This is illustrated in the following diagram:

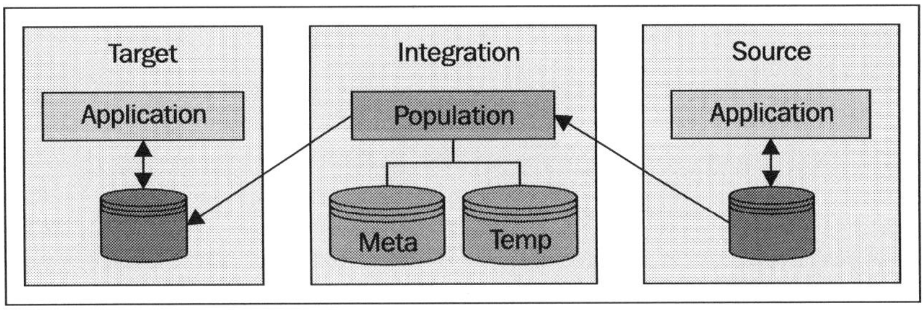

The population pattern can be broken down into the following logical components:

- The target applications have a need for information, which they do not possess. Therefore, a copy from another data source in a source application is required.
- The population component reads one or more data sources in the source application, and writes the data to a data source in the target application. The rules for extracting data from the source application can be as complex as necessary. They range from simple rules, such as *read all data*, to more complex rules where only specific fields in specific records can be read under certain conditions. The loading rules for the target database can vary from a simple overwrite of the data, to a more complex process of inserting new records and updating existing ones. The metadata is used to describe these rules.
- The source applications have the important information needed by the target applications.

Uses

Population is used for the following purposes:

- A specialized copy of existing data (derived data) is needed:
    - Subsets of existing data sources
    - A modified version of an existing data source
    - Combinations of existing data sources
- Only read access to the derived data in the target application is possible (or only a few write accesses).
- In the case of a significant number of write accesses, the two-way synchronization pattern should be used.

- The user must be provided with quick access to the information required, instead of being bombarded with too much, irrelevant, incorrect, or otherwise useless misinformation.
- However, IT drivers often dictate the use of the population pattern. In other words, the copies of data are made for technical reasons. These drivers include:
  - Improved performance of user access
  - Load distribution across systems

Synchronization

The synchronization pattern (also known as the **replication** pattern) enables bidirectional update flows of data in a multi-copy database environment. The "two-way" synchronization aspect of this pattern is what distinguishes it from the "one-way" capabilities provided by the population pattern.

This is illustrated in the following diagram:

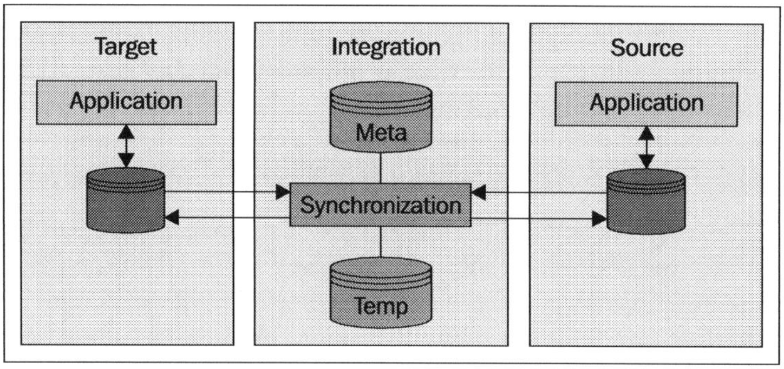

The synchronization pattern shown in this diagram can be broken down into the following logical components:

- The target applications have a need for information, which they do not possess. Therefore, a copy from another data source in a source application is required.
- At a simplistic level, the synchronization component can be compared to the population pattern, with the only difference being that the data flows in both directions. If the data elements flowing in both directions are fully independent, then two-way synchronization is no more than two separate instances of the population pattern. However, it is more common to find some overlap between the datasets flowing in either direction. In this case, conflict detection and resolution are needed.

- The source applications have information which is relevant to the target applications.

Uses

Synchronization is used for the following purpose:

- A specialized copy of existing data (derived data) is needed. This copy can take different forms:
    - Subsets of existing data sources
    - A modified version of an existing data source
    - Combinations of existing data sources

Multi-step synchronization

There is one variant of the synchronization pattern: the multi-step variant. The multi-step variant of the two-way synchronization pattern makes use of one instance of the population pattern, with its gather, process, and apply functions, for each of the two synchronization directions. An additional "reconcile" function is placed between the two data flows, and guarantees that there are no conflicts in the updates. If the opportunities for conflicts are minimal, this pattern can be constructed from existing population components. However, a specialized solution should be used for more complex situations.

The following diagram illustrates the "reuse" of the population pattern, once for each direction with the additional "reconcile" component in the middle.

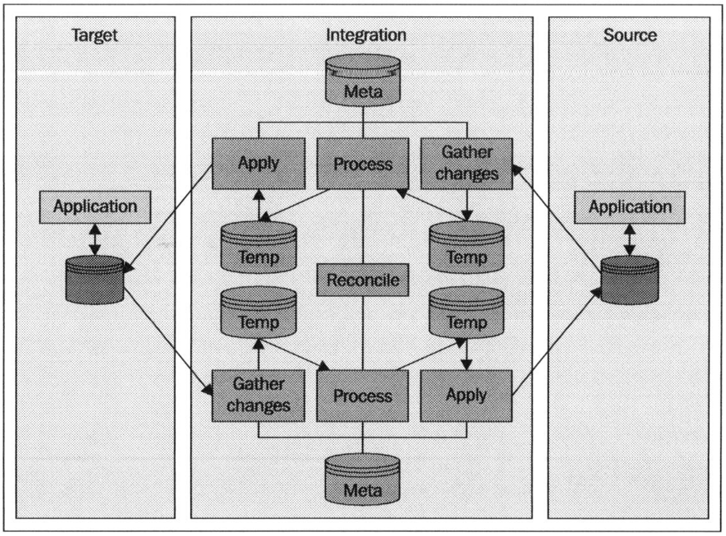

Patterns for service-oriented integration

Service-oriented integration is based on two fundamental patterns:

- **Process integration**: The process integration pattern extends the 1: N topology of the broker pattern. It simplifies the serial execution of business services, which are provided by the target applications.
- **Workflow integration**: This is basically a variant of the serial process pattern. It extends the capability of simple serial process orchestration to include support for user interaction during the execution of individual process steps.

Process integration

The process integration pattern extends the 1: N topology of the broker pattern seen in EAI. It simplifies the serial execution of business services, which are provided by the target applications, and therefore enables the orchestration of serial business processes, based on the interaction of the source application. The serial sequence is defined using process rules, which allows for decoupling from the process logic (flow logic and the domain logic) of the individual application. The rules define not only the control and data flow, but also the permitted call rules for each target application. Interim results (process data) are stored in individual results databases.

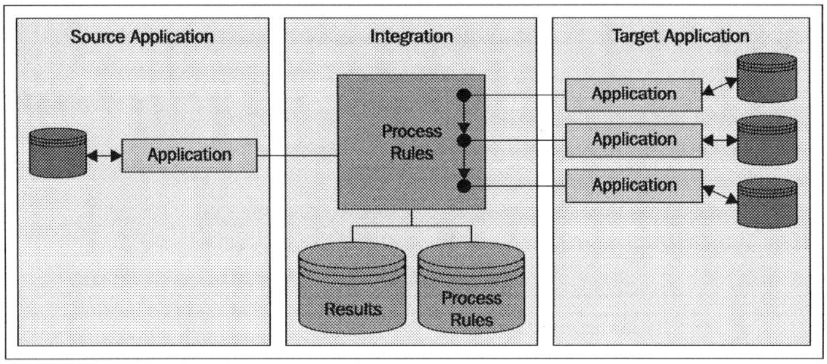

The process integration pattern can be broken down into three building blocks:

- The source applications consist of one or more applications that want to interact with the target applications.
- The serial process rules support the same services as the broker in the broker pattern, including routing queries, protocol conversion, message broadcasting, and message decomposition and re-composition. In addition, externalization of the process flow logic from the individual applications is also supported. The process logic is determined by serial process rules which, together with the control and data flow rules, define the execution rules for each target application. These rules are stored in a process rules database.

- The target applications consist of both new and existing (modified or unmodified) applications. These applications are responsible for implementing the necessary business services.

The advantages and disadvantages of the process integration pattern are shown in the following table:

Advantages	Disadvantages
• Improves the flexibility and responsiveness of an organization by implementing end-to-end process flows and externalizing process logic from individual applications. • Provides a foundation for Business Process Management that enables the effectiveness of business processes to be monitored and measured.	• Only direct, automatic processing supported. No user interaction is possible (refer to the workflow variant). • No parallel processing possible.

Uses

Process integration is used for the following reasons:

- Support for end-to-end process flows which use the services provided by the target applications
- Improves the flexibility and responsiveness of IT by externalizing process logic from individual applications

Variants

There are two variants of this pattern:

The **parallel process** pattern extends the simple serial process orchestration provided by the serial process patterns, by supporting concurrent execution and orchestration of business service calls. The concurrent execution of sub-processes requires the sub-steps to be split up and brought together, so that they can be executed in parallel. Different patterns are available for this purpose at an implementation level (for example, patterns for parallel computing and different architecture styles (for example, pipes-and-filters architectures). The interim results of a sub-step may or may not influence the overall results. It is also possible for the interim results of a sub-step to influence the execution of other sub-steps.

The **external business rules** variant adds the option of externalizing business rules from the serial process, into a business rule engine, where they can be evaluated. The process only reacts to the responses of the rule engine. The complex rule evaluations are carried out by the specialized rule engine. Externalizing the rules improves flexibility and responsiveness, because the business rules can be adapted much more easily and quickly.

Workflow integration

The workflow integration pattern represents an extension of the process integration pattern, as illustrated in the following diagram:

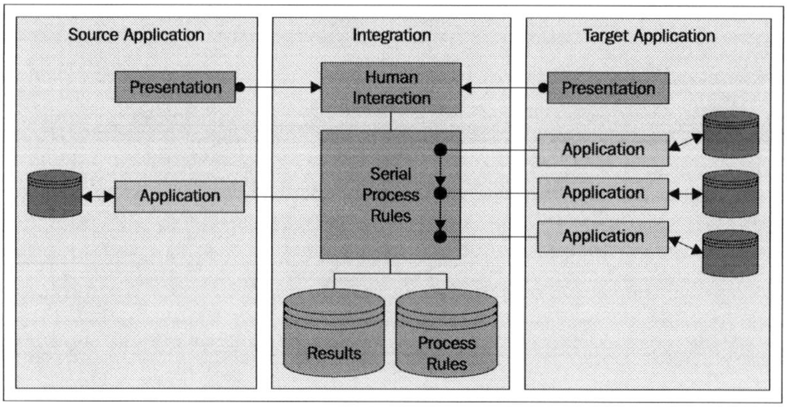

It extends the capability of simple serial process orchestration to include support for user interaction during the execution of individual process steps. As a result, it supports a classic workflow.

Variants

The **parallel workflow** integration pattern is a variant of the workflow integration pattern, and corresponds to the parallel process integration pattern which forms part of the process integration pattern. It extends the capability of **parallel process orchestration** to include support for user interaction during the execution of individual process steps. As a result, it supports a parallel workflow.

Event-driven architecture

Event-driven architecture (**EDA**) is one of the hot topics of the industry. These architectures are often wrongly referred to as the successors to SOAs (Mühl et al. 2006). In fact, the concepts involved in EDA are as old as IT itself. In addition, EDAs are growing rapidly in popularity, together with the integration architectures of SOA. However, both types of architecture can be used completely independently of one another, and can be combined orthogonally. From the perspective of integration, two aspects of EDA are of particular interest:

- The symbiosis between EDA and SOA that has already been referred to, which allows SOA domains to be linked/integrated together on an event-driven basis.
- The technology offered by EDA which enables events from one or more event streams on the data integration level to be consolidated into new information.

Introducing EDA

According to a study by Gartner (Gartner 2006), the success of companies such as Dell and Google is due to the fact that these organizations are able to identify market factors or market events in the global marketplace at an early stage, and follow them up consistently and quickly. Both examples are very close to the picture drawn by Gartner of an ideal organization: the **real-time enterprise** (**RTE**). An RTE is characterized by its highly-automated business processes and the shortest possible process runtimes (Nussdorfer, Martin 2003).

While SOA concepts within IT structures form the basis for the automation of business processes, the second step, which relates to the ideal image of the RTE, involves processing more fine-grained information about changes in the state of these business processes. The complexity of these state changes is increasing noticeably, in the same way that the number of reaction interfaces in the business processes is. This is where the significance of EDA lies, because the observable changes in the state of the business processes can be modeled as events. Classic integration architectures, such as **OLTP (Online Transaction Processing)**) or **OLAP (Online Analytical Processing)** are no longer able to meet the requirements for rapid and consistent action on the basis of event analyses (Zeidler 2007).

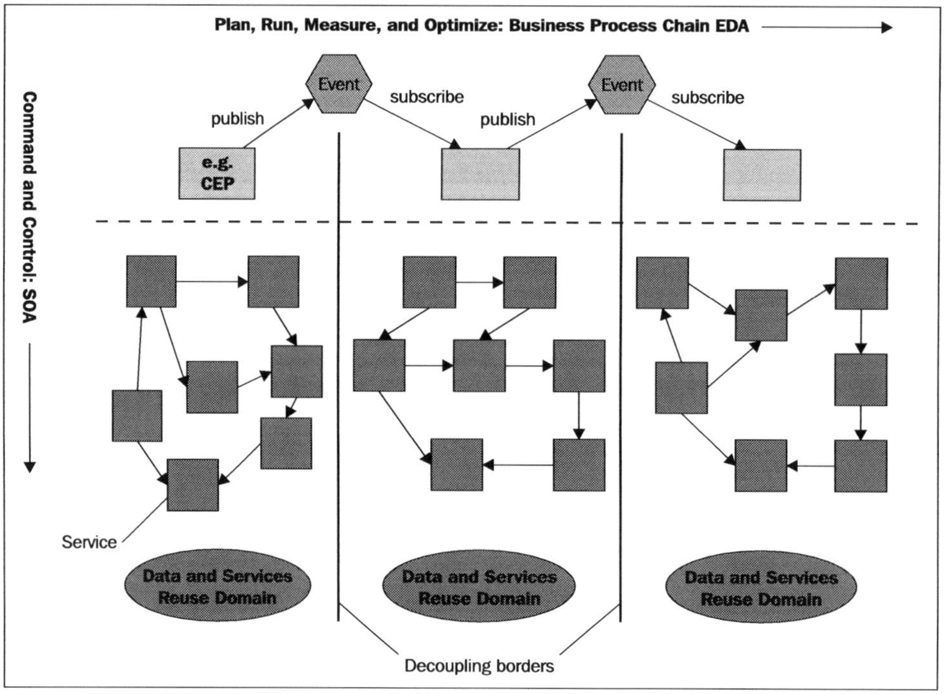

The above diagram illustrates the symbiosis between EDA and SOA, which is often referred to as **SOA 2.0** (Carter 2007) or **Next Generation SOA** (Luckham 2002). An SOA or an SOA domain provides the technical services, independently of consumers. These services can be combined or orchestrated, and they form the building blocks for the business processes. If a service of this kind triggers an event, for example because of a change in its state, an orthogonal EDA extension can activate a new SOA domain. As a result, a service becomes an event-producing building block in an EDA. In contrast to the typical producer/consumer patterns of an SOA, the EDA largely uses a publish/subscribe mechanism. An event processor processes the events as they occur, and publishes the processed results via an event channel, which triggers the services of other SOA domains. Various types of event processor are used depending on the type of event processing required. These include **Complex Event Processors** (**CEP**), for example, which are described later in this chapter.

The SOA domains (to be integrated) should ideally be defined in such a way that they represent reusable services which can be used several times in business process chains of any length. The principle of loose coupling for the formation of such flexible business process chains is of decisive importance in the EDA, in the same way as it is in the SOA.

Event processing

The second aspect of integration that we want to highlight is of a more technical nature. It concerns the possibilities for event processing within an EDA concept, as shown in the following figure:

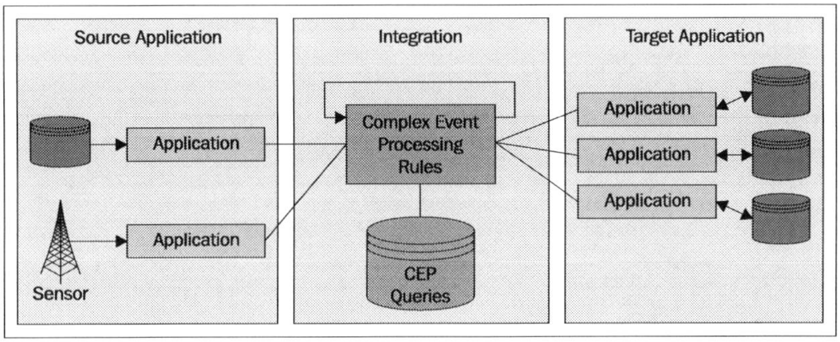

Event-processing technologies have been in day-to-day use in many industries for several years. Examples include algorithmic trading in stock markets and **Radio Frequency Identification** (**RFID**) in road charging systems.

There are three fundamental types of event processing:

- **Simple Event Processing** (**SEP**)
- **Event Stream Processing** (**ESP**)
- **Complex Event Processing** (**CEP**)

Simple Event Processing (SEP)

Events occur either individually, or in streams. Single events can be regarded as an important change in state in a message source and, in particular, in a business event. Events of this kind typically trigger processes in the systems which receive the message. This form of event processing corresponds exactly with the specification of the **Java Messaging Service** (**JMS**). Therefore, a typical example of SEP is JMS.

Event Stream Processing (ESP)

ESP involves processing streams of incoming messages or events. Typical ESP systems have sensors which channel a large number of events, and use filters and other processing methods to influence the stream of messages or events. Individual events are less important, and instead the focus is on the event stream. Well-known examples include the systems which track stock market prices: one single fluctuation in prices is generally not particularly significant. A more informative overall trend can only be determined from several events.

Complex Event Processing (CEP)

The third form of event processing is Complex Event Processing, which is part of ESP. In CEP there is a strong focus on identifying patterns in a large number of events and their (message) contents, which may be distributed across different data streams.

The CEP funnel model is illustrated in the following figure:

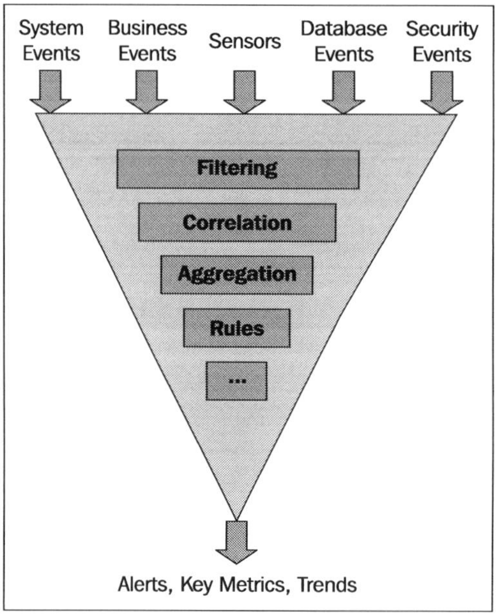

The CEP funnel model illustrates the process of compressing (large) volumes of events to produce compressed information. The source of the events includes business events (Viehmann 2008). One of the classic uses of CEP is in tracing credit card fraud. In the case of two transactions using the same credit card, which were made within a short period of time, in locations a long distance apart, this type of geographical and chronological pattern indicating the possibility of fraud, can easily be applied to the model. Systems of this kind, which correlate thousands of events in order to filter out the few cases of fraud or misbehavior, are more and more frequently in use.

Grid computing/Extreme Transaction Processing (XTP)

Grid computing and XTP are the new integration technologies, which are likely to become increasingly popular over the next few years.

- **Grid computing**: An infrastructure for the integrated, collaborative use of resources. Grids can be broken down into Data Grids, In-Memory Data Grids, Domain Entity Grids, and Domain Object Grids on the basis of their primary functionality, and are used in a wide range of applications.
- **XTP**: This is a distributed storage architecture, which allows for parallel application access. It is designed for distributed access to large, and very large, volumes of data.

Grid computing

Grid computing is the term used to describe all the methods that combine the computing power of a number of computers in a network, in a way that enables the (parallel) solution of compute-intensive problems (distributed computing), in addition to the simple exchange of data. Every computer in the grid is equal to all the others. Grids can exceed the capacity and the computing power of today's super computers at considerably lower cost, and are also highly scalable. The computing power of the grid can be increased by adding computers to the grid network, or combining grids to create meta grids.

> **Definition of a grid**
>
> A grid is an infrastructure enabling the integrated, collaborative use of resources which are owned and managed by different organizations (Foster, Kesselmann 1999).

The following diagram illustrates the basic model of grid computing, with the network of computers forming the grid in the middle:

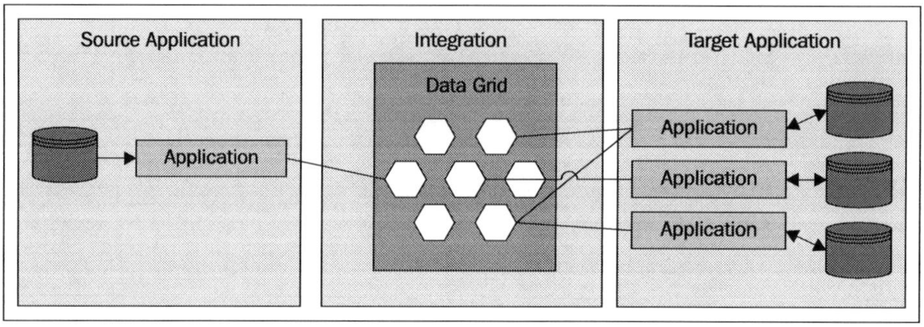

The main tasks of grids are:

- **Distributed caching and processing**: Data is distributed across all the nodes in a grid. Different distribution topologies and strategies are available for this purpose. A data grid can be divided into separate sub-caches, which allows for the use of more effective access mechanisms involving pre-filtering. The distribution of the data across different physical nodes guarantees the long-term availability and integrity of the data, even if individual nodes fail. Automatic failover behavior and load balancing functionality are part of the grid infrastructure. Transaction security is also guaranteed throughout the entire grid.
- **Event-driven processing**: The functionality of computational grids. Computing operations and transactions can take place in parallel across all the nodes in a grid. Simple event processing, similar to the trigger mechanism of databases, ensures that it is possible for the system to react to data changes. Individual pieces of data in the grid can be joined together to form more complex data constructs using the "in-memory views" and "in-memory materialized views" concepts.

Grids have the following features which allow more sophisticated **Service Level Agreements** (**SLA**) to be set up:

- Predictable scalability
- Continuous availability
- Provision of a replacement connection in the case of a server failure (failover)
- Reliability

Grids can be broken down into data grids, in-memory data grids, domain entity grids, and domain object grids on the basis of their primary functionality.

Data grids

A data grid is a system made up of several distributed servers which work together as a unit to access shared information and run shared, distributed operations on the data.

In-memory data grids

In-memory data grids are a variant of data grids in which the shared information is stored locally in memory in a distributed (often transactional) cache. A distributed cache is a collection of data or, more accurately, a collection of objects that is distributed (or partitioned) across any number of cluster nodes, in such a way that exactly one node in the cluster is responsible for each piece of data in the cache, and the responsibility is distributed among the cluster nodes.

Competitive data accesses are handled cluster-wide by the grid infrastructure, if a specific transactional behavior is required. The advantages include the high levels of performance possible as a result of low latency memory access. Today's 64-bit architectures and low memory prices allow larger volumes of data to be stored in memory where they are available for low latency access.

However, if the memory requirements exceed the memory available, "overflow" strategies can be used to store data on a hard disk (for example, in the local filesystem or local databases). This will result in a drop in performance caused by higher latency. The latest developments, such as solid state disks, will in future allow a reasonable and cost-effective compromise in this area, and will be an ideal solution in scenarios of this kind.

Data loss caused by a server failing and, therefore, its area of the memory being lost, can be avoided by the redundant distribution of the information. Depending on the product, different distribution topologies and strategies can be selected or enhanced.

In the simplest case, the information is distributed evenly across all the available servers.

An in-memory data grid helps the application to achieve shorter response times by storing the user data in memory in formats which are directly usable by the application. This ensures that storage accesses with low latency and complex, time-consuming transformations and aggregations when the consumer accesses the data can be avoided. Because the data in the grid is replicated, buffering can be used to accommodate database failures, and the availability of the system is improved. If a cluster node in the data grid fails, the data is still available on at least one other node, which also increases availability. Data will only be lost in the case of a total failure, and this can be counteracted by regular buffering to persistent storage (hard disk, solid state disk, and so on).

Domain entity grids

Domain entity grids distribute the domain data of the system (the applications) across several servers. As these are often coarse granular modules with a hierarchical structure, their data may have to be extracted from several different data sources before being made available on the grid across the entire cluster. The data grid takes on the role of an aggregator/assembler which gives the consumers cluster-wide, high-performance access to the aggregated entities. The performance can be further improved by the grid by initializing the domain data before it is actually used (pre-population).

Domain object grids

A domain object grid distributes the runtime components of the system (the applications) and their status (process data) across a number of servers. This may be necessary for reasons of fail-safety, and also because of the parallel execution of program logic. By adding additional servers, applications can be scaled horizontally. The necessary information (data) for the parallelized functions can be taken from shared data storage, (although this central access can become a bottleneck, which reduces the scalability of the system as a whole) or directly from the same grid or a different grid. It is important to take into account the possibilities of individual products or, for example, to combine several products (data grid and computing grid).

Distribution topologies

Different distribution topologies and strategies are available, such as replicated caches and partitioned caches (Misek, Purdy 2006).

Replicated caches

Data and objects are distributed evenly across all the nodes in the cluster. However, this means that the available memory of the smallest server acts as the limiting factor. This node determines how large the available data volume can be.

Advantages:

- The maximum access performance is the same across all the nodes, as all the nodes access local memory, which is referred to as **zero latency access**.

Disadvantages:

- Data distribution across all the nodes involves high levels of network traffic, and is time consuming. The same applies to data updates, which must be propagated across all the nodes.
- The available memory of the smallest server determines the capacity limit. This node places a limit on the size of the available data volume.

- In the case of transactionality, if a node is locked, every node must agree.
- In the case of a cluster error, all the stored information (data and locks) can be lost.

The disadvantages must be compensated for as far as possible by the grid infrastructure, and circumvented by taking appropriate measures. This should be made transparent to the programmer by using an API which is as simple as possible. The implementation could take the form of local read-only accesses without notification to the other cluster nodes. Operations with supervised competitive access require communication with at least one other node. All the cluster nodes must be notified about update operations. An implementation of this kind results in very high performance and scalability, together with transparent failover and failback.

However, it is important to take into consideration that replicated caches requiring a large number of data updates do not scale linearly in the case of potential cluster growth (adding nodes), which involves additional communication activities for each node.

Partitioned caches

Partitioned caches resolve the disadvantages of replicated caches, relating to memory and communications.

If this distribution strategy is used, several factors must be taken into account:

- **Partitioned**: The data is distributed across the cluster in such a way that there are no overlaps of responsibility with regard to data ownership. One node is solely responsible for a specific part of the data, and holds it as a master dataset. Among other things, this brings the benefit that the size of the available memory and computing power increases linearly as the cluster grows. In addition, compared with replicated caches, it has the advantage that all the operations which are carried out on the stored objects require only a single network hop. In other words, in addition to the server that manages the master data, only one other server needs to be involved, and this stores the accompanying backup data in the case of a failover. This type of access to master and backup data is highly scalable, because it makes the best possible use of point-to-point connections in a switched network.

- **Load-balanced**: Distribution algorithms ensure that the information in the cache is distributed in the best possible way across the available resources in the cluster, and therefore provide transparent load balancing (for the developer). In many products, the algorithms can be configured or replaced by in-house strategy modules. However, depending on the distribution and optimization strategy, this approach also has disadvantages. The dynamic nature of data distribution may cause data to be redistributed when the optimization strategy is activated, if another member is added to the cluster. In particular, in environments where temporary cluster members are highly volatile, frequent recalculations of the optimum distribution characteristics, and physical data redistribution with its accompanying network traffic, should be avoided. This can be achieved by identifying volatile cluster nodes within the grid infrastructure, and ensuring that they are not integrated into distribution strategies.
- **Location transparency**: Although the information about the nodes in the cluster is distributed, the same API is used to access it. In other words, the programmer's access to the information is transparent. He does not need to know where the information is physically located in the cluster. The grid infrastructure is responsible for adapting the data distribution as effectively as possible to access behavior. Heuristics, configurations, and exchangeable strategies are used for this purpose. As long as no specific distribution strategy needs to be created, the way in which the strategy functions in the background is unimportant.

Agents

Agents are autonomous programs that are triggered by an application, and are executed on the information stored in the grid under the control of the grid infrastructure. Depending on the product, specific classes of programming APIs may need to be extended or implemented for this purpose. Alternatively, declarative options allow agent functionality of this kind to be established (for example, using aspect-oriented methods or pre-compilation steps). Predefined agents are often provided with particular products.

Execution patterns

Let's take a brief look at these execution patterns:

- **Targeted execution**: Agents can be executed on one specific set of information in the data grid. The information set is identified using a unique key. It is the responsibility of the grid infrastructure to identify the best location in the cluster for the execution, on the basis of the runtime data available (for example, load ratios, node usage, network loads).

- **Parallel execution**: Agents can be executed on a specific group of information sets, which are identifiable by means of a number of unique keys. As with the target execution, it's the responsibility of the grid infrastructure to identify the best location in the cluster for the execution, on the basis of the runtime data available (for example, load ratios, node usage, network loads).
- **Query-based execution**: This is an extension of the parallel execution pattern. The number of information sets involved is not specified by means of the unique keys, but by formulating one or more filter functions in the form of a query object.
- **Data-grid-wide execution**: Agents are executed in parallel on all the available information sets in the grid. This is a specialized form of the query-based execution pattern in which a NULL query object is passed, in other words, a non-exclusive filter condition.
- **Data grid aggregation**: In addition to the scalar agents, cluster-wide aggregations can be run on the target data, so that computations can be carried out in (near) real-time. Products often provide predefined functionality for this purpose, including count, average, max, min, and so on.
- **Node-based execution**: Agents can be executed on specific nodes in the grid. An individual node can be specified. However, agents can also be run on a defined subset of the available nodes, or on all the nodes in the grid.

Uses

Grid technology can be used in a variety of different ways in architectures:

- **Distributed, transactional data cache (domain entities)**: Application data can be stored in a distributed cache in a linear scalable form, and with transactional access.
- **Distributed, transactional object cache (domain objects)**: Application objects (business objects) can be stored in a distributed cache in a linear scalable form and with transaction security.
- **Distributed, transactional process cache (process status)**: Process objects and their status can be stored in a distributed cache in a linear scalable form, and with transaction security.
- **SOA grid**: This is a specialized form of the previous scenario. **Business Process Execution Language** (**BPEL**) processes are distributed in serialized form (hydration) throughout the cluster, and can be processed further on another server following de-serialization (dehydration). This results in highly scalable BPEL processes.

- **Data access virtualization**: Grids allow virtualized access to distributed information in a cluster. As already mentioned, the location of the data is transparent during the access, regardless of the size of the cluster, which can also change dynamically.
- **Storage access virtualization**: Information is stored in a distributed cache in the format appropriate for the application, regardless of the type of source system and its access protocols or access APIs. This is particularly advantageous in cases where the information has to be obtained from distributed, heterogeneous source systems.
- **Data format virtualization**: Information is stored in a distributed cache in the format appropriate for the application, regardless of the formats in the source system. This is particularly advantageous in cases where the information has to be obtained from distributed, heterogeneous source systems.
- **Data access buffers**: The access to data storage systems (such as RDBMSs) is encapsulated and buffered so that it is transparent for the application. This allows any failover actions by the target system (for example, Oracle RAC) and the necessary reactions of the application to be decoupled. As a result, applications no longer need to be able to react to failover events on different target systems, as this takes place at grid level.
- **Maintenance window virtualization**: As already described, data grids support dynamic cluster sizing. Servers can be added to and removed from the cluster at runtime. This makes it possible to migrate distributed applications gradually, without significant downtimes for the application, or even the entire grid. A server can be removed from the cluster, the application can be migrated to this server, and the server can then be returned to the cluster. This process can be repeated with every other server. Applications developed in future on the basis of open standards will reduce this problem.
- **Distributed master data management**: In high-load environments, unacceptable bottlenecks may occur in central master data applications. Classic data replication can help to resolve this problem. However, it does involve the use of resources, and is not suitable for (near) real-time environments. Another solution is to distribute the master data across a data grid, provided that there is enough storage.
- **High performance backup and recovery**: It is possible to perform long-running backups in several stages in order to improve performance. The data can be written in stages to an in-memory cache, and then at delayed intervals to persistent storage.
- **Notification service in an ESB**: Grid technology replaces the message-based system used for notification in a service bus.

- **Complex real-time intelligence**: This combines the functionality of CEP and data grids, and therefore enables highly scalable analysis applications which provide complex pattern recognition functions in real-time scenarios, to be made available to the business. In its simplest form, this is an event-driven architecture with CEP engines as consumers, in which the message transport and the pre-analysis and pre-filtering of fine granular individual events is based on grid technology. The infrastructure components of the grid are also responsible for load balancing, fail-safety, and the availability of historic data from data marts in the in-memory cache. The combination of a grid and CEP makes it possible to provide highly scalable, but easily maintained, analysis architectures for (near) real-time business information.

XTP (Extreme Transaction Processing)

As a result of the need for complex processing of large and very large volumes of data (for example, in the field of XML, importing large files with format transformations, and so on.), new distributed storage architectures with parallel application access functions have been developed in recent years.

A range of different cross-platform products and solutions is available, also known as "extreme transaction processing" or XTP. The term was coined by the Gartner Group, and describes a style of architecture which aims to allow for secure, highly scalable and high-performance transactions across distributed environments on commodity hardware and software.

Solutions of this kind are likely to play an increasingly important role in service-oriented and event-driven architectures in the future. Interoperability is a driving force behind XTP.

Distributed caching mechanisms and grid technologies with simple access APIs form the basis for easy, successful implementation (in contrast to the complex products widely used in scientific environments in the past). Although distributed cache products already play a major role in "high-end transaction processing" (an expression coined by Forrester Research), their position in the emerging **Information-as-a-Service** (**IaaS**) market is expected to become more prominent.

New strategies for business priority have been introduced by financial service providers in recent years. Banks are attempting to go beyond the limits of their existing hardware resources and develop increasingly high-performance applications, without having to invest in an exponential increase of their hardware and energy costs.

The growth of XTP in areas such as fraud detection, risk computation, and stock trade resolution is pushing existing systems to their performance limits. New systems which should implement this challenging functionality require new architecture paradigms.

It is clear that SOA, coupled with EDA and XTP, represents the future for financial service infrastructures as a means of achieving the goal of running complex computations with very large volumes of data, under real-time conditions. XTP belongs to a special class of applications (extreme transaction processing platforms) that need to process, aggregate, and correlate large volumes of data while providing high performance and high throughput. Typically, these processes produce large numbers of individual events that must be processed in the form of highly volatile data. XTP-style applications ensure that transactions and computations take place in the application's memory, and do not rely on complex remote accesses to backend services, in order to avoid communication latency (low latency computation). This allows for extremely fast response rates while still maintaining the transactional integrity of the data.

The SOA grid (next generation, grid-enabled SOA) is a conceptual variant of the XTPP (Extreme Transaction Processing Platform). It provides state-aware, continuous availability for service infrastructures, application data, and process logic. It is based on an architecture that combines horizontally scalable, database-independent, middle-tier data caching with intelligent parallelization, and brings together process logic and cache data for low latency (data and process affinity). This enables the implementation of newer, simpler, and more efficient models for highly scalable, service-oriented applications that can take full advantage of the possibilities of event-driven architectures.

XTP and CEP

XTP and CEP are comparable, in that they both consume and correlate large amounts of event data to produce meaningful results.

Often, however, the amount of event data that needs to be captured and processed far exceeds the capacity of conventional storage mechanisms ("there just isn't a disk that can spin fast enough"). In these cases, the data can be stored in a grid. CEP engines can be distributed across this data and can access it in parallel. Analyses can be carried out, and business event patterns can be identified and analyzed in real-time. These patterns can then be processed further and evaluated using **Business Activity Monitoring** (**BAM**).

Solid State Disks and grids

Solid State Disk (**SSD**) technology is developing at high speed. Data capacities are increasing rapidly and compared with conventional drives, the I/O rates are phenomenal. Until now, the price/performance ratio per gigabyte of storage has been the major obstacle to widespread use. It is currently a factor of 12 of the cost of a normal server disk, per gigabyte of storage. The major benefit for data centers is the very low energy consumption, which is significantly less than that of conventional disks.

Because of their low energy requirements, high performance, low latency, and the expectation of falling costs, SSDs are an attractive solution in blades or dense racks. One interesting question concerns the influence which SSDs may have on data grid technology.

Disk-based XTP systems can benefit from the introduction of an SSD drive However, SSDs currently have a much lower storage capacity (128 GB versus 1 TB) than conventional disks. Nevertheless, this is more than the capacity of standard main memory, and SSDs are also less costly per gigabyte than memory. The capacity of SSDs is lower than that of conventional disks by a factor of 10, and higher than the capacity of memory by a factor of 8.

SSDs bridge the gap between memory-based and disk-based XTP architectures. SSD-based architectures are slightly slower than memory-based systems, but significantly faster than the fastest disk-based systems. The obvious solution is, therefore, to provide a hierarchical storage architecture in XTP systems, where the most volatile data is stored in memory, data accessed less often is stored on SSDs, and conventional disk-based storage is used for long-term persistent data. It also seems reasonable to store memory overflows from memory-based caching on SSDs.

Summary

At this point in time, you should have a basic understanding of the fundamental concepts of integration, and the terminology used with it. You should now understand:

- The basic concepts used in the context of integration architecture
- The different architecture variants, such as point-to-point, hub-and-spoke, pipeline, and SOA
- What service-oriented integration is and why it is important
- The different types of data integration and the accompanying patterns

- The difference between Enterprise Application Integration (EAI) and Enterprise Information Integration (EII)
- The concept of Event Drive Architecture (EDA) and the different types of Event Processing and why they play an important role in integration
- The integration technologies of the future: grid computing and extreme transaction processing (XTP)

2

Integration Architecture, Principles, and Patterns

The growing needs for information availability and accessibility present new challenges for application development. Stand-alone applications cannot fulfill the growing needs anymore. There are two forces working in parallel with regard to the need for integration. First, it is necessary to allow for application integration within an enterprise, and second, there are growing needs to ensure inter-enterprise or "business-to-business" integration.

The majority of companies, however, still have existing legacy applications, developed using different architectures and technologies, which have usually not been designed for integration. Companies cannot afford to write off or replace them over night, because they are mission critical; also they cannot afford to develop their entire information systems from scratch in today's business environment.

In addition, companies will undoubtedly need to introduce new applications and systems from time to time. New solutions are usually based on modern architectures, which differ significantly from architectures used by existing legacy applications. These new applications also have to be integrated with existing applications; and existing applications have to be integrated with each other to fulfill the information availability and accessibility goals. To make things even more difficult, there is often a significant investment already in place for a variety of application integration technologies.

We can see that integrating applications is a difficult task, maybe even one of the most difficult problems facing enterprise application development. To fulfill these integration objectives, several methods, techniques, patterns, and technologies have been developed over the years, ranging from point-to-point integration over enterprise application integration (EAI) and business process management to service oriented architectures (SOA).

In this chapter, we will look at the integration challenges, become familiar with different architectures and principles, and will take a quick overview of integration patterns. We will look at:

- Integration challenges
- Requirements and common strategies
- Integration architectures
- Types of integration
- Integration infrastructure
- Integration technologies
- The Integration process
- Integration patterns

Integration Challenges

The ability to instantly access vital information that may be stored in a variety of different applications may influence the success of a company. For each company, the presence of effective information infrastructure that avoids the need for employees to perform numerous manual tasks like filling in paper forms, and other bureaucracy, is very important. Employees should not have to contend with such inefficiencies and 'irritations' such as switching between different applications to get their work done, reentering the same data more than once in different applications, or waiting for data to be processed. Ideally, a well-integrated system should offer end-to-end support for business processes with instant access to information, no matter which part of the system is used. Similar consideration hold true for companies that want to be successful in e-business or those that want to improve their position in the virtual world.

Companies are realizing the importance of integration at different speeds. Some of them are already fully involved in integration projects with many solutions already working, as they have seen the advantages of integration and understand how to achieve successful integration. Other companies are aware that integration is important but, although they may have started integration projects, they do not have the results yet, mainly because the integration projects have not been successful. Further still, some companies are only now realizing the importance of integration, and this could in fact be too late for them. Such companies may be looking for ways to achieve integration fast, without spending too much money, and without assigning too many staff members to the integration project. But cutting corners and attempting to implement only the most needed parts of integration in the shortest possible time will most likely result in only partially working solutions at best.

The problem that makes things worse is the fact that managers are often not familiar with all the complexity hidden behind the integration process. Sometimes, even the "IT people", the architects and developers, do not fully understand the traps behind integration. Most importantly, managers might not understand that integration is a topic that is related to the company as a whole, and not with the IT department only.

Another scenario that leads to the same disorganized approach is when the management of a company does not see the need for integration yet, but the IT department is aware that integration is needed and should be initiated as soon as possible. Therefore, the integration team starts to build a partial solution to solve the most urgent problems. As the integration is not approved from the top, the IT sector does not get enough resources, it does not have enough time and money, and, most significantly, it does not have authorization to start to solve the integration problem globally. Most developers will agree that these are all-too-familiar situations.

Integration seems to be one of most important strategic priorities, mainly because new innovative business solutions demand integration of different business units, enterprise data, applications, and business systems. Integrated information systems improve the competitive advantage with unified and efficient access to the information. Integrated applications make it much easier to access relevant, coordinated information from a variety of sources. In effect, the total becomes more than the sum of its parts. It's easy to see that integration can be an important and attractive strategic priority.

Current Situation

Typical companies that have existed more than just a few years rarely have integrated information systems. Rather they are faced with a disparate mix of heterogeneous existing systems. Companies will typically have different applications, developed over time. These include:

- Applications developed inside the company
- Custom-built but outsourced solutions
- Commercial and ERP applications

These applications have typically been developed on different platforms, using different technologies and programming languages. Because they have been developed over time, different applications use different programming models. This is manifested through:

- Combinations of monolithic, client/server, and multi-tier applications
- Mix of procedural, object-oriented, and component-based solutions
- Mix of programming languages
- Different types of database management systems (relational, hierarchical, object) and products
- Different middleware solutions for communication (message-oriented middleware, object request brokers, remote procedure calls, etc.)
- Multiple information transmission models, including publish/subscribe, request/reply, and conversational
- Different transaction and security management middleware
- Different ways of sharing data
- Possible usage of EDI, XML, and other proprietary formats for data exchange

Another important aspect is the integration that has already been implemented between the existing applications. This includes everything from simple data exchange to use of middleware products. In addition to all this diversity of architectures, technologies, platforms, and programming languages the companies have kept introducing new applications—and with new applications they have introduced modern application architectures too.

Effective Information Systems

Ultimately, the driving force behind all these situation is an effective information system. The important point here is that an information system is, by definition, only as effective as the integration between different applications. Applications developed in the past have usually not been designed for integration. This is why in the majority of older applications no or only very limited ways exist to achieve interoperability with other applications. There is often little, if any, documentation relating to their development and processes. Even today, some applications are developed with little or no concern given to how to connect them with other systems. For these reasons, integration is as relevant to existing legacy systems as it is to modern solutions.

The reason for integration lies in business expectations. From the business viewpoint, the goal is to maximize the benefits of each application and the information system as the whole. Particularly, end-to-end support for business processes and an efficient way of user interaction are important. Separate applications cannot fulfill the requirements anymore. The data is partitioned among different applications; each has its own view on the data, which makes joining it a difficult problem. Therefore users often cannot obtain the global picture, and valuable information is locked in these applications that could be shared and distributed to all new groups of information consumers: remote employees, business partners, and customers, to name just a few of them. In addition, separate applications are also highly unsuitable for supporting modern front-end applications, such as web access, business-to-business and business-to-customer collaborations—for example integrating back-office applications with a front-end customer web-order system.

[Integrated information systems seamlessly support business processes.]

In order to stay competitive, companies must modernize and improve the functionality of their information systems. Managers see an information system as a tool through which they can maximize the company benefits. They are prepared to invest in them because they know what return of investment they can expect; they can foresee the efficiency increase and the productivity boost.

Replacing Existing Applications

Improving the functionality of an information system is possible in several ways. The most obvious way is to replace the old applications with a freshly developed solution. Even if, at first sight, this seems like an attractive solution, we can easily see why it is inapplicable in most cases. Developing and deploying new software overnight is impossible; also, migration of live (in-use) systems can incur significant costs.

If we were able to develop an integrated information system that would cover all the requirements, this would perhaps offer the ultimate solution. Unfortunately, there are several factors that prevent us from doing this.

First of all, to develop new information system from scratch requires time and resources that in most cases, we simply cannot afford. There have been many years of development invested into the existing applications, and re-implementing all of this functionality would require a lot of knowledge, time, and resources. It is very unlikely that this would be possible in a reasonable or acceptable time. The existing systems also contain a lot of knowledge that we would have to recapture.

Likewise, it is infeasible to introduce commercial solutions, like ERP systems, in any great hurry. In a sense, each company evolves like a living organism, with a lot of specialties and a distinctive way of doing business. All these properties have to be reflected in a business's information systems. Adapting commercial solutions requires time, and in the eyes of managers, time is money.

Companies today are also so complex that ERP systems could not cover all possible needs. Research from leading consulting companies suggests that ERP can only account for 30% to 40% of information needs. The remainder has to be covered by custom solutions. This is also the reason why the majority of ERP suppliers, such as SAP, or Oracle, have introduced interoperability interfaces into their products.

Even if we could develop the new information system in a reasonable amount of time, we would still need to deploy it, to transfer all data, and to teach the users how to use the new system. These are some of the reasons why there will be only a few companies that will attempt to replace their entire information systems. Such companies will soon realize that the replacement is more complicated, more complex, more time consuming, and more costly than even their worst-case scenarios could have predicted.

Replacing existing systems with new solutions therefore almost always requires more time and more money than previously planned, even in the most pessimistic scenarios. Incorporating all the peculiarities and special cases in the software requires time and knowledge. It depends on the company if it has business processes well documented, but there are few companies with detailed documentation for all the business processes that would need to be developed. For those that do not have all the necessary documentation, it is even more difficult. Often, there is no single person that understands the entire process.

It is clear that replacing existing systems with new solutions will often not be a viable proposition. Too much time and money has been invested in them and there is too much knowledge incorporated in these systems. Therefore a standard ways to reuse existing systems and integrate them into the global, enterprise-wide information system must be defined.

Requirements and Strategies

To be successful with integration, companies must have an integration strategy. Management must support the integration process and provide the necessary priorities to enable a centralized control and management of the integration. There must be clear requirements specifying what is expected from an integrated system and goals have to be defined. Integration is today best seen as an ongoing process. Two important goals for integrated information systems that should be fulfilled are single data input and information access with low latency.

Single Data Input

Single data input ensures that data is entered into the information system only once. Although this sounds like an obvious goal, it is very difficult to achieve it 100% in the real world. Entering the data only once means that we have to provide a level of integration where the user does not have reenter the same data again for no matter what purpose. This might not be so difficult to achieve for main, or primary applications. But don't forget that the users often use many subsidiary applications as well, which provide solutions to some every day problems. This includes everything from serial mail printing to analysis of business data. For these operations, they typically use productivity tools and transfer the data from the information system to these tools. Those users that are not very familiar with the technology end up retyping the same data.

It is obvious that a single data input guarantees data consistency and minimizes the mistakes that are provoked by data retyping and managing local stores of enterprise data. Let us look at the example of serial letters.

In a non-integrated system, the user would probably reenter the data to some specialized, self-developed solution, in the 'Office' style product of a word processor. Very rarely will the user be so familiar with the technology as to be able to implement an automatic data transfer. If the user on the other hand, is somewhat familiar with the technology, he or she will do the data transfer manually, which will still require a lot of effort. He or she will extract data for the information system application that takes care of customer management and then change the format manually, probably using an editor and a filter tool to import the data into the word processor. When he or she has to do the serial letter again, it is likely that he or she will use the old data and hope that not too much has changed. Doing the whole data transfer all over again will probably be too time consuming and the user will think twice before doing it. Rather he or she will risk not including the recent changes in the addresses. As a result, some new customer might not get the correspondence, and for some existing customers it may be sent to old addresses. Remember also, that the user will typically guess how many modifications have been done to the original data, because an analysis would take too long and would be too difficult to do (based on the fact that the user would have to implement it himself or herself).

Information Access with Low Latency

The other important goal is data access with low latency, sometimes also called data access without latency. Information access with low latency ensures that the changes made in one part of the information system become visible in all related parts immediately—or in the shortest possible time. Achieving this can be a very complicated task even in a smaller information system. If we imagine a distributed information system, this can get considerably more complicated.

On the other hand, is achieving low latency very important for today's online systems? Imagine an information system that enables users to book coach tickets over the phone. The clerk on the phone will enter the destination and the dates that the customer wants to travel on. Using a low latency information system, the clerk will be able to answer the question if the seats are available for a given destination at a given time. Otherwise, this information will have to be mailed to the customer, complicating the process and making it more costly. Introducing this latency will also mean that the company will not be able to sell all the seats but will always need a certain number of seats reserved just in case. We could find many similar examples; therefore, a general answer is that low latency is very important for today's information systems.

It is only a small step from the mentioned scenario to the e-business example where the customers access the information system themselves through a web-based interface. The customers expect that they will get information immediately; however, the information given to customers also has to be reliable.

Achieving low latency in front-end systems requires there to be a low latency strategy implemented in the back-end systems; this means in the integrated enterprise information system.

The main reason why low latency is difficult to achieve is because the functionality required to perform business tasks is dispersed across different applications. Additional to this, is the physical distribution of applications and communication links that do not provide enough throughput and reliability.

Solving the problem of the dispersion among applications can be achieved in a number of different ways. Historically, this problem has been addressed at the data level only. The typical solutions include building consolidated databases and data warehousing.

These techniques have to take snapshots of the data from time to time and store them in the central data storage in a format that is suitable to do analysis and other ways of validating and analyzing it. This approach was, however, not very good at achieving low latency, because in the real world the data transfers can be run only a few times a day. To be fair, we have to mention that data warehouses were never intended to solve the low latency problem.

Direct access to data in real time is much harder to implement, particularly if we have to deal with many distributed data sources. Real-time access has several performance and scalability limitations. The most efficient way to access data is through application logic.

> Both requirements, single data input and information access with low latency, are related to the ultimate objective of integration—end-to-end support for business processes provided by the information system, which can be relatively easily adapted to the changes in business processes.

Importance of a Centrally Managed Integration Project

It should be clear that integration is not only a technical problem. Rather, it also requires a good level of organization and management in order to be successful. Ultimately, it requires support from the senior management. Senior managers have to recognize the need for integration first, and that this integration must take place on an enterprise-wide scale. For successful integration, it is crucial that the company initiates the integration project with enough resources, priorities, and authorizations to be able to achieve the coordination of all involved parties.To achieve this, there are several possibilities.

If a company has a centralized IT department, then it can take over the responsibility for integration too. However, we have to be careful to ensure that there are actually enough staff members available for the task at hand. One, two, or three persons with part-time responsibilities are not enough to make the integration project take off. Obviously, this will depend on the size of a company and the number of application domains, but often this is another area where management and reality do not agree.

It will also depend on the planned schedule. Although integration today is one of the main priorities of companies, it is still worth mentioning that planning a very long schedule for integration will probably result in a lack of success. The business and its requirements are prone to rapid changes, and an integration architecture that is defined over a long period of time will be unable to incorporate such changes.

Of course, a centralized IT department is not always the case. Often, companies will have IT departments (or similar structures) distributed all over the company. This can be a consequence of merging or even a consequence of the past needs because of the size of the company. Still, we have to identify somebody who will be responsible for the integration and who will be able to coordinate all the involved parties. Assigning the responsibility to one of the IT departments would be unwise because this would place this IT department above the others. This can lead to the other IT departments being unwilling to fully cooperate—and this can be enough to make integration unsuccessful.

It is a much better idea to introduce and organize a new central body that we will call an integration service, responsible for integration. The integration service should have three major responsibilities:

- Definition of integration architecture
- Selection of integration infrastructure and technologies
- Development and maintenance of integration documentation

Responsibility to Define Integration Architecture

The first function of the integration service is the operational responsibility of defining the integration architecture. This includes the identification of architectural and semantic questions regarding the integration. The major responsibility of the integration service is to define logical, high-level integration architecture.

As we will see later in this section, the top-down approach has to provide a sort of 'city plan', which will show us the available 'roads' and allow us to place individual 'houses'. The city plan represents a high-level integration architecture. It would be best if the integration architecture models the integrated information system as it should be, that is, as we would like it to be. Such architecture would, however, also need to enable reuse of at least some of the existing applications and to minimize the dependencies between applications. This last requirement will enable us to replace existing applications with new systems.

The integration service should also resolve the important semantic issues that have to be centrally implemented. This includes unification of the data model, issues regarding the interfaces between applications, the format of messages sent between applications, and so on.

Responsibility to Select Integration Infrastructure and Technologies

Another important responsibility is to identify, select, deploy, and maintain a consistent integration infrastructure, based on a set of interoperable technologies. Particularly, the identification and selection of integration infrastructure should be a coordinated effort and the integration service must take into account all aspects for existing applications and try to find an optimal solution. Consistent technology for integration is important.

It is not necessary that the integration service selects only one technology for integration. It may well be that there is no single technology that would be able to incorporate all of the applications. If we select more than one technology, we should provide instructions on how to achieve interoperability between them and make these instructions available to all parties involved.

Development and Maintenance of Integration Documentation

The third responsibility of the integration service is the development and maintenance of the integration documentation. Typically, the documentation consists of a set of interface models that describe the communication between the application domains and applications. These models will be realized from the integration design. The technology selection will also have influence on the how these interfaces are implemented.

The integration service will have to take care that the project teams follow the integration guidelines and that they modify their applications to accommodate the interfaces and technology necessary for integration. They should also include the support for new software that they develop.

Further, the integration service should contact the application vendors that have developed and supplied applications used in the company. They should find out how to incorporate the necessary solutions and technology into their applications and should also define the schedules.

We have to be aware that for successful integration, the answers to the technology questions alone are not sufficient. Today, there are practically no technological barriers for integration. It would be very difficult to find platforms, operating systems, or applications that would be impossible to integrate.

However, there can be significant difficulties when integrating two applications on a single operating system, written in the same programming language, and using the same database management system, because we have to solve many semantic differences between them. Integration is dependent on the application architecture and to the interoperability interfaces, particularly their availability. A technology cannot avoid organizational problems. From this perspective, a solid organizational structure for existing systems integration is essential and is a key success factor.

Integration Architecture Steps and Approaches

Integration is not an easy task, and to succeed, we will have to plan and design it carefully. Therefore, we first have to select the applications that we will include in integration. Applications in each company can be put into the following two classes:

- Primary applications, which are important for the whole company and used by a large number of employees. These applications have been either developed either in-house, outsourced, or bought and are under the control of IT department.
- Subsidiary applications often used by a single employee. Most likely they have been developed without the knowledge of the IT department by the user himself or herself in a productivity tool, like office applications and similar. These subsidiary applications ease the every day work of this employee and implement the tasks that this employee has to perform, but are not supported by the primary applications. Examples include printing circular letters, generating specific reports, etc.

When designing the integration architecture, it is very important that we include both the primary and the subsidiary applications. The users have developed subsidiary applications because they need them, and they will not want to live without them. If we do not implement them as a part of integrated information system, the users will continue to use these self-developed solutions. This will result in several problems, including manual transfers of data between the primary and subsidiary applications and important data being stored on local computers in a variety of formats, like word processors, spreadsheets and similar. Accessing this data will be very difficult and the objectives of integration will not be met.

Therefore, before we begin with integration, we should do an analysis of all the applications that have been used in a company from large company-wide applications to the small personal solutions of individual employees. After we have selected the applications, we have to choose the approach to integration. We will look at two different approaches to integration and discuss their advantages and disadvantages:

- Bottom-Up Approach
- Top-Down Approach

Let's look at the bottom-up approach first.

Bottom-Up Approach

The bottom-up approach to integration focuses on individual problems that arise because of the lack of integration between applications. It solves the individual problems through uncoordinated integration projects, without building the global integration architecture.

In order to define the bottom-up approach to integration, let's consider an example of a mobile phone operator that has several separate applications that do not communicate. These applications are:

- An application for customer management
- Two different applications for accounting the domestic and international calls
- An application that manages the accounts of customers
- An application that prints invoices
- An application that handles the tariffs and costs of calls

To keep the example simple, let's suppose that there are no connections between the applications. However, it is obvious that there should be many. Due to the lack of integration, users have to reenter the same information two or three times, which not only makes the work take longer than necessary, but also introduces an element of human error through typing mistakes. These can be difficult to track down, thus losing additional time. The IT department and the users of these applications are fully aware that integration would bring important benefits. At the very least, connections are required between the invoice printing applications, both call accounting applications, the customer management application, and the account management application.

Let's also presume that in this particularly company, the IT department does not have the authority to make independent decisions and cannot convince the upper management of the necessity of integration. The users of these applications also don't have important positions in the company because they are mostly clerks.

Due to regulations, competition between the mobile phone operators is not a serious issue, so management does not prioritize the need for complex analysis and other up-to-date information. They are satisfied with information that is several days old, which can therefore be prepared manually.

In this particular scenario, it is easy to see that convincing management of the need for integration would be a difficult, if not an impossible, task. Now, we may wonder why management does not see the need for integration. Unfortunately, too often a business must feel pain before management gives attention to a problem—this is reactive rather than proactive management, and, unfortunately, is very typical. In our scenario, things have not developed far enough for this to happen.

In our case, the IT department can wait until management experiences the negative effects of their inefficient systems, and then starts to look towards integration. Or, the IT department can take things into their own hands and try to implement the most needed integration parts between the applications. Unfortunately, both approaches will ultimately lead into the same problems.

If the IT department waits and does nothing regarding the need for integration, the time will come when management start to feel that there is a problem that can be solved with integration. In our scenario, this will most likely be the situation when competition in the market starts to increase. At this point, management will look for ways in which to minimize costs; they will initially identify the lost hours of the workforce, because of the unnecessarily repetitive nature of some of the tasks (for example, reentering the data, manually changing the structure of the data, and so on). They will also feel the need for accurate and on-time information, which can only be effectively produced by an integrated information system.

Given the example, it will likely be a little too late by the time management senses the problem. Therefore, management will ask for the IT department to implement the fastest possible scenario to get results as soon as possible. Almost definitely, management will not take the time to understand everything that they need from the information system. They will see a subset of problems, most likely the most obvious one. In our example, this would be, say, the potential integration between the invoice printing, call accounting, customer, and account management applications mentioned previously. Furthermore, management will probably not consider anything beyond what will satisfy their own narrow view of the problem.

Now most IT departments, because they don't have a choice anyway, will agree and try to implement the connections between applications that they need most and that can be built in the quickest time. They will start to look for solutions on how to integrate the relevant applications in the easiest way. Let's say that in our present example not all applications have been developed within the company. Some of them are commercial applications, and some of them have been outsourced.

The IT department therefore is not familiar with the finer details of all the applications. To apply changes to the applications, the IT department in our scenario would again have to contract external companies. This would result in additional costs and would almost certainly extend the schedule. This option will, therefore, most likely be dismissed.

So, the IT department will search for ways in which to integrate their applications without modifying them (or at least that minimize the amount of modification). The most obvious potential solution is to use data-level integration. The IT department could choose to simply move the data between the databases of different applications. It is, however, important to recognize the basis of this decision, and the fact that we do not blame the IT department in such cases. Indeed, if an IT department were to consult an external expert, this consultant would almost certainly make the same decision, given the facts and the requirements defined by the management. The challenge thus now becomes how to bridge different databases.

Let us look at a possible outcome of this potential solution. The IT department would probably first implement the data transfer from customer management application to the invoice printing application. Then, they might implement the data transfer from the domestic and international call accounting applications to the tariff and cost management application. The data transfer that had previously been done manually would simple port this data to the tariff and cost management application, which would then return the actual consumption in currency. The same approach would then be applied to other connections too.

After implementing all necessary data transfer connections between the applications, it could seem like the integration problem had been solved. However, the success would only be true on the surface, and new problems would soon emerge. If the IT department follows this pattern of implementing partial solutions, it will soon lead to a system of applications that will have several dependencies that they will not even be aware of.

In the proposed scenario, almost every application would have to be connected to all the others. This might not seem a lot when connecting two or three applications, but if we consider (more typically) twenty to fifty or more applications, it clearly leads to an exponential increase in complexity. Small changes to one application could require modifications to all the data transfer bridges to other applications. In fact, the maintenance of an integrated system will be more time consuming and costly than the maintenance of the applications themselves, which will make the benefits of integration less obvious.

This approach to integration also soon limits how far we can go, and has several other disadvantages. Here we will consider just two:

- We access the databases directly, bypassing the business logic. This makes it necessary to duplicate any business logic in all data transfer bridges, making the maintenance even more difficult. Accessing the database directly is risky because it is easy to break the business rules (and therefore the overall integrity).
- The integration based on data exchange between applications requires that a process that transfers data runs from time to time. We can do this every day, every hour, or even every few minutes, but we can hardly implement it continuously, because this would require too many resources.

Numerous examples for similar integration attempts can be found. Let us consider the demand for web-based customer front ends that have been and still are very popular. Basically, this was the attempt to provide Internet access to existing systems, often to more than one. Expressed in other words, this is nothing else but an integration project to integrate the newly developed front end with existing back-end applications. More explicitly, integration between existing systems is the foundation for implementing this kind of application. However, companies didn't have time to wait for the integration to be done first. Rather, they needed a web-based front end "over night". Companies that were late in identifying this need were in a particularly bad position.

Given that most companies did not have the integration solved in time, they again searched for fast solutions that were not based on solid foundations. It is most likely, such web-based front-end systems were implemented with point-to-point links to each existing application without a global understanding of the problem. Again, this solution looked successful for a short period of time, but a second look tells us otherwise—here we also see a point-to-point solution, which requires a lot of maintenance. Additionally, this time we also had to modify existing systems a little. We will talk more about this later when we consider extensions to existing systems.

What was not done in this project was to take the time to get a global understanding of the integration, the challenges, and the requirements that an integrated system has to fulfill. Rather, the integration was attempted with an ad hoc solution, without planning and architecting, and the data structures have remained separate and inconsistently defined. Enhancements to the systems will dispose of the management problems, and security questions will become important, not to mention other questions—transactional behavior, lifecycle, naming, and so on.

Actually, this is an interesting situation. Remember that the need for integration is primarily a consequence of the lack of global architecture and planning in the past. Thus, implementing the integration without planning is a choice only the most optimistic people will select—or people who are given little choice, because the management has made a decision. Management sometimes sees the purpose of the IT department to provide the solution in the minimum of time that is cost effective in the short term. Such management will often not want to hear that a longer term total integration solution would provide much better long-term results.

> It is not reasonable to expect that attempting integration in the same way that has brought us un-integrated systems will this time result in usable integration architecture and solutions.

The complicated thing is that the company will probably not realize this early enough and will continue to support other projects in the same way. Soon the point of no return will be reached when additional layers are patched on top. The system will reach an unmanageable level of complexity where it will be impossible to modify them because a small modification will provoke the need for changes in so many tightly coupled parts.

This is why the bottom-up approach to integration will most likely bring the company a step forward at first, but soon the company will regret it, needing to go two or three steps backward. An information strategy that focuses on individual, uncoordinated integration projects will, over time, introduce even more problems into the company's information infrastructure. Thus, attempting to perform integration from the bottom-up approach is highly discouraged. In the following section, we'll see why the top-down approach is much better.

Top-Down Approach

Lack of planning and architecting was one of the principal reasons why many of today's companies have different applications running on different systems that are not interoperable in any ideal way. As such, it is unreasonable to expect that we can achieve an efficient level of integration without precise planning and designing.

Information system building is essentially an engineering discipline. Therefore, let's consider taking a hint from civil engineering, defining the architecture before we begin. To use an analogy, we wouldn't start to build a house without plans, except maybe for a dog kennel! Indeed, there is no real damage done if a dog kennel falls down; it is not even a major problem if the dog does not like the house (we can always replace the dog!).

Extending our analogy further, let's consider the construction of a whole community of houses. When we start building a house in civilized surroundings, like in a city or a town, we cannot simply build the house anywhere we would like to. We have to position it according to environmental plans and designs. We also cannot build connecting roads to other houses in any random way we like. This would result in one-to-one communications between houses that would be unmanageable; it would be almost impossible to oversee their construction and navigate between them. Rather, we again have to stick to a global design where it has been chosen how the roads will be positioned and interconnected.

It is a similar situation in application integration. We cannot simply start to connect the existing applications without a good plan and architecture. This would almost certainly result in a large number of point-to-point connections that are very difficult to manage and maintain. Rather, we have to define the architecture of the integrated system first, and only then start to look at the existing applications and decide how they can fit into the integration architecture. This approach has several advantages and will enable us to build an architecture into which the existing applications will fit as well as new-generation systems. It will also enable us to replace and re-engineer existing systems with new developments. This way of thinking is known as the top-down approach to integration.

The top-down approach is nothing but a defined approach for defining global integration architecture. An integration architecture should, by definition, be comprehensive and define all foreseeable aspects of the business problems that can occur on the macro or micro scale. This effectively strengthens the integrity and consistency of integration throughout the whole company. The integration architecture should also recognize the dependencies between applications and the application development. It should provide guidelines and priorities by which the management will plan and schedule the tasks and requirements addressed to the IT department and the information system. It is infeasible, for example, to start to build a business-to-business integration before we have realized an adequate integration within our existing applications.

The top-down approach focuses on integration as a global activity. It defines a comprehensive integration architecture that defines all foreseeable aspects of the business problems related to integration, analyzes existing dependencies, sets guidelines, and defines priorities. It manages integration as a large coordinated project and gathers the efforts of all involved parties.

> In real-world cases, often bottom-up and top-down approaches are used together, where the best practices of both are combined. Such an approach, often called an inside-out approach, reflects the requirements of the integration project and takes into account various criteria, including the existing applications, architectures, and requirements related to the new, integrated system.

Sound Integration Architecture Benefits

Sound integration architecture usually provides the following benefits:

- Reusability: Services perform a set of operations that are described and accessed through an interface. The interfaces enable the interoperability between services and promote the reuse of functionality.
- Encapsulation: Services on each tier are strongly encapsulated. The only way to access the service is through the interface. The client of the service does not know and does not have to know the internal details of a service. The encapsulation enables replacing the implementation of a service without influencing the rest of the system as long as the interface and the functionality remain unchanged.
- Distribution: The access to services is not limited to a single computer or even a single process. They can be distributed (and/or replicated) among computers without modifications in the source code of clients. Communication details are handled by the middleware layer, thus achieving location transparency.
- Partitioning: Putting the functionality in the appropriate tiers enables us to build thin clients, put the business logic into the middle tier, and solve the persistence in the back-end. By using the abstraction layers, we can achieve flexible deployment options and configurations.
- Scalability: Matching the capacity of the middle tier to the client demands by implementing performance optimization techniques in the middle tier and the ability to physically distribute and replicate the critical services enables good control over the scalability over a long time period.
- Enhanced performance: Applications can take advantages of server-side optimization techniques, like multiprocessing, multithreading, pooling, resource and instance management, and thread management, without changing code and allowing dynamic configuration changes.
- Improved reliability: Single points of failure, as well as bottlenecks, can be eliminated using replication and distribution.

- Manageability: With the separation in multiple tiers, it is much easier to locate the services that need to be modified. Most frequent are changes in the business logic that is located in a separate tier. The changes there do not require costly and time-consuming reinstallations. Rather, they can be managed centrally.
- Increased consistency and flexibility: As long as the interfaces between the tiers and the interfaces inside the tier stay unchanged, the code can be modified without impact to other parts of the system. In multi-tier architectures, it is much easier to adapt the information system to the changing business needs. A change in the business tier services will consistently effect all applications.
- Support for multiple clients: Different kinds of clients can access the business logic through the same interface.
- Independent development: Services can be developed independently of other services. Interfaces between services define the contract between them that enables independent development (as long as the contracts are respected).
- Rapid development: Application developers can focus on rapidly developing and deploying the business functionality, while remaining transparent to the underlying infrastructure. Services can be used in unpredictable combinations to form applications.
- Composition: Services can be composed in a variety of ways, which provides great flexibility and support for business processes.
- Configurable: Different implementations of the same service can be readily interchanged at run-time, enabling you to provide the capabilities that you need without redesigning applications.
- Security: Caution has to be taken that measures are applied to address different aspects of security, such as authorization, authentication, confidentiality, non-repudiation, etc.

Types of Integration

Integration architecture is usually built systematically in several layers. The idea behind this is to break the problem into several smaller problems and solve each sub-problem step by step (similar to, for example, the way in which network architecture is broken up into layers, as defined by ISO OSI). Therefore, today integration can be seen in several layers. We usually start building the integration architecture at the lowest layer and climb gradually. Omitting a layer is a short-term solution to speed up the process, but we will almost certainly have to pay back this time later. The most important types of integration are:

- Data-level integration
- Application integration
- Business process integration
- Presentation integration

These types of integration refer to integration within the enterprise as well as to the integration between enterprises (B2B). Let's now examine these types of integration individually.

Data-Level Integration

Data-level integration focuses on moving data between applications with the objective of sharing the same data among these different applications. It is often the starting point where a company starts to work on integration.

From a technical perspective, data-level integration is a relatively simple approach that is well understood by most developers. Accessing databases is relatively easy and there are several tools available that make the data sharing easier and faster. Also, data-level integration does not require changes to the applications. The following figure shows data-level integration.

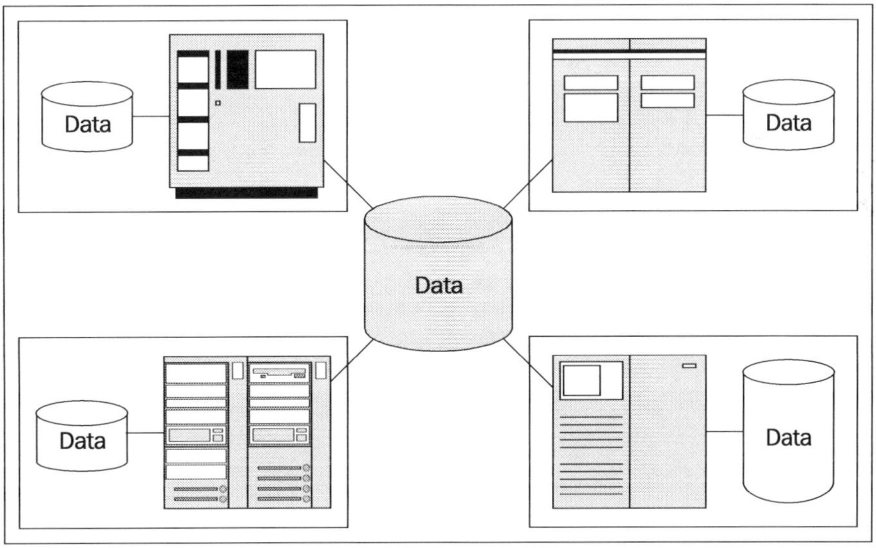

Although the technology for accessing databases is well understood and not too difficult, the whole task of implementing data-level integration is not easy at all.

The problem lies in the complexity of the databases and in their number. To move the data between databases, it is not enough to be familiar with the technology. We also have to understand what data is stored in which database and in what form. We have to know when and how we can extract the data. Even more important is to be familiar with the type and structure of the destination database. Only then will we be able to store data in the database in a format that is understood by all the applications that use this database and that doesn't break the consistency of the database.

It is the semantics of the databases that is the most difficult part of data-level integration. It is not unlikely that we will have to deal with several hundred different databases. Some of them will belong to legacy applications, some of them to newer applications. Probably we will not be familiar with all of the applications. This also means that we will not be familiar with the structure of all of the data involved and the way they are stored.

Sometimes we will have limited access to the databases because of contract restrictions. Then we will have to find other possibilities to access the data, for example using application programming interfaces (APIs), which we will discuss in the next section. If this is not applicable, we might be able to access flat files containing exported data and to add information using flat files that are imported by the target application. This, however, adds another layer of complexity to data-level integration.

Application Integration

Application integration focuses on sharing functionality—business logic; and not just pure data as in data-level integration. Application integration is usually achieved through the use of application programming interfaces (APIs). Applications that expose their functionality through APIs enable access to the functionality in a programmatic way without using the user interface.

Previously, developers did not realize the usefulness of APIs. Therefore most older applications do not have them. Since then, most newer applications have accepted the concept of services that an application can provide to other applications. In newer existing applications, it will be more likely to find APIs. Through the use of APIs, we can access the functionality of existing systems. However, the APIs exposed by different existing applications will differ in the way we have to access them and which technology we have to use to access them.

The objective of application integration is therefore twofold: to understand and use APIs for accessing the required functionalities; and to mask the technology differences between different technologies used for APIs and their access. The later is achieved using services, which expose the interfaces (APIs), as shown in the following figure.

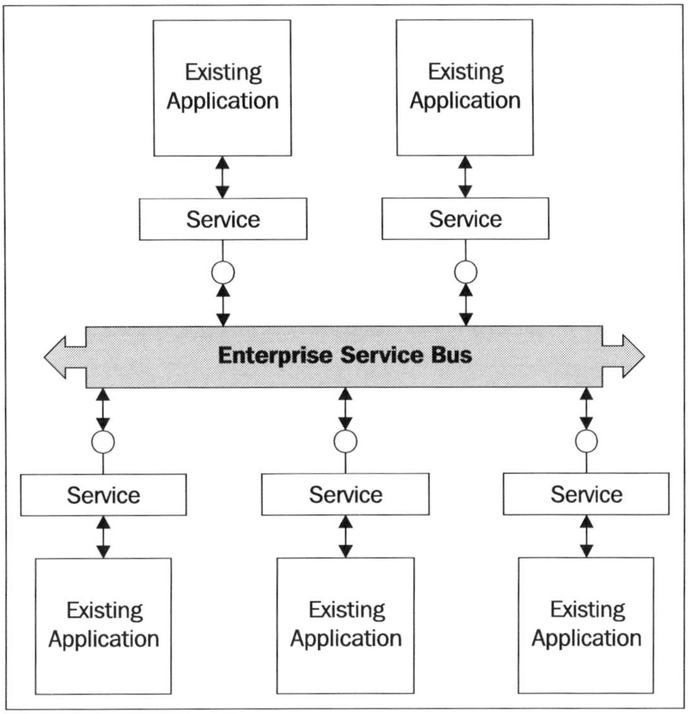

Please notice that the interfaces provide the contract between the applications. As long as the interfaces stay unchanged, this means that the contracts have not been changed. But it also means that the interfaces are the entities that tie different parts of the information system together. Nobody cares how the interfaces are implemented, or what applications actually execute in the background. We can change the applications that implement a certain interface without influencing the whole information system or partial applications—as long the interface stays unchanged.

Therefore, great care has to be taken in the definition of interfaces. Today, we understand good interfaces as those that are loosely coupled. This can be achieved primarily by sharing data only, without behavior; structuring the data; and using open standard technologies.

Business Process Integration

Business process integration enables non-compromise support for business processes in the enterprise where existing solutions take part in distinctive steps of the business process. It exposes the functionality as abstractions of business methods through interfaces.

Business process integration presents the enterprise-wide information system as we would like to have it—or as we would build it if we could build it anew, with clear requirements for what we would like to get from the integrated system and with the knowledge and support of modern technologies. This means that the information system interfaces are based on a new designed architecture. However, the functionalities are not re-implemented; rather, they use existing applications. Those existing applications are remodeled in a way that they expose the functionality of the business process tier and fit into the modern application architecture. Finally, the different pieces are glued together, usually by using a business process modeling and execution language, such as BPEL (Business Process Execution Language), as shown in the following figure.

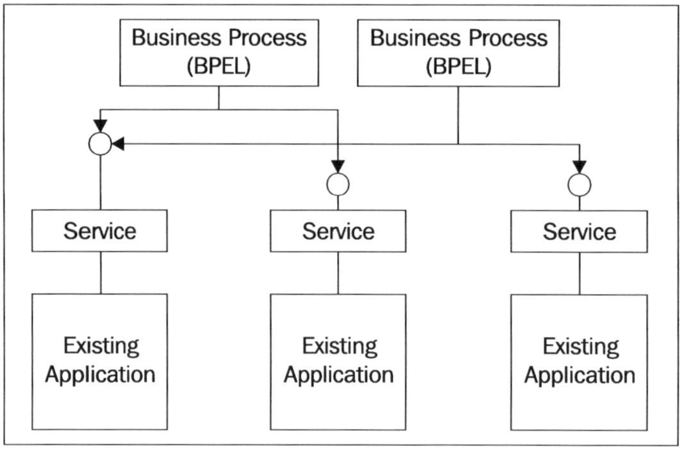

SOA, BPEL, and related technologies today provide new opportunities for making integrated information systems more flexible and adaptable to business process changes. This way our information systems can get more agile, provide better support for changing requirements, and align closer to business needs. We have to be aware that achieving business process integration is often connected with business process reengineering and is not a sole technical problem. It, however, requires the implementation of several technical layers as the foundation and integrates applications at a higher-level of abstraction.

Presentation Integration

Often, after achieving business process integration, we will continue with the presentation integration. Because existing applications are now remodeled and encapsulated on the middle tier, where they expose their services through high-level interfaces, it becomes crucial that the user gets a unified view of the information system as well. As long as the user has to switch between legacy applications, they should be fully aware that they are using old applications.

Presentation integration results in an integrated system that provides a unified presentation layer, through which the users can access the functionality of the integrated system. Because they use the newly developed presentation layer, they are not aware of the diversity of existing applications that are executing in the background. The presentation layer also accesses the functions through common interfaces, provided by business tier, developed in the business process integration phase. Therefore, the presentation layer is decoupled and not aware of the details of existing applications.

With the development of a unified presentation tier, we hide the fact that in the background different applications, some legacy and other new developed, are executing. This way, we improve the efficiency of end users and provide a way to replace parts of legacy systems in the future without influencing the other parts of the system.

We will consider presentation integration as a step in which we define and implement a common user interface—usually a portal—for the business-method-level integrated information system, such that the user interface will provide the illusion of a new system, and add the missing piece to the multi-tier integration architecture. We should not look at presentation integration as simple user interface integration, adding web or graphical user interfaces, which we may have covered by application extension. We should also not consider presentation integration only as a way to extract the data from existing applications through the user interfaces.

Business-to-Business Integration

Today, the integration of applications inside a company is not sufficient. There are growing needs to enable inter-enterprise integration, often referred to as business-to-business (B2B) integration, or e-business. E-Business places particular new challenges for an information system. The requirements today are very high and gone are the days when a company could just publish off-line catalogs on its web pages. What is expected is online, up-to-date information, efficiency, reliability, and quality. Even well known names from traditional business cannot expect that their position will be maintained in an e-business environment without effort.

Of course, the prerequisite for efficient e-business or B2B integration is an integrated enterprise information system, possibly on the business-process level, which must be at both ends. Only this level of integration enables on-demand processing of requests. Customers today are expecting immediate response and are not satisfied with batch processing and several days of delays in confirming orders, for example. However, this is often the case, when e-business is not backed by an efficiently integrated enterprise information system. Immediate responsiveness, achieved by highly coupled integration of back-end (enterprise information) and front-end (presentation) systems is a key success factor.

Although this sounds obvious, research from leading consulting companies like Gartner Group shows that today there are very few front-end systems that are efficiently integrated with the back end. Most of these non-integrated applications will fail to meet the business expectations. The primary reason is the lack of enterprise integration, which is the most important prerequisite for both a successful e-business and an efficient company.

Another important fact is that most front-end applications can use existing and legacy systems as back-end solutions. Making the integration between such systems efficient will be the key success factor. In particular, immediate response and immediate propagation of data to all related applications will be the major problem. Front-end applications not efficiently supported by back-end systems will certainly fail to meet all requirements.

Integration Infrastructure

Let us now focus on the required infrastructure services for integration. We will identify the services from a high-level perspective and separate them into the horizontal and vertical layers. The services in horizontal layers will provide basic infrastructure services useful for the majority of existing and new-generation applications. The vertical layer services will provide functionalities related to a specific task within infrastructure that can span through several horizontal layer services.

The services on the horizontal layer include:

- Communication
- Brokering and routing
- Transformation
- Business intelligence

The vertical layers are:

- Transactions
- Security
- Lifecycle
- Naming
- Scalability
- Management
- Rules

The relations between the services are shown in the following figure:

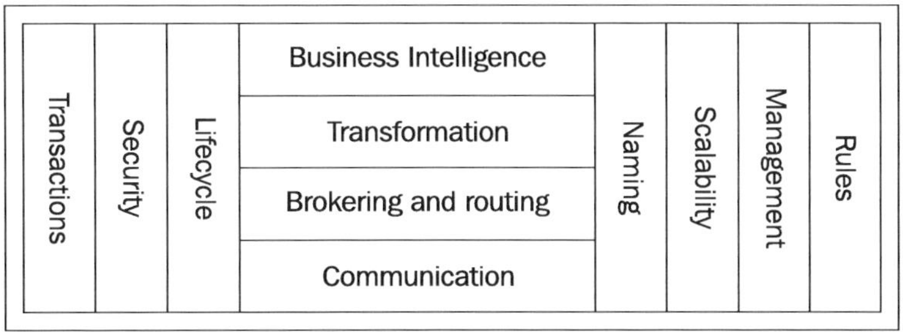

Let's now examine these services in finer detail, starting with the four horizontal layers that we've mentioned above.

Communication

The primary responsibility of the communication service is to provide the abstraction for communication details. It provides the transparency for accessing different remote systems and unifies the view on them. This ensures that the developers do not have to deal with the low-level communication details. As the communication layer does not execute business logic, it enables the separation of business logic and the communication services, but allowing communication between them.

Different types of middleware provide different communication layer services. The most commonly used for application integration are the database access technologies, like JDBC, that provide the data-layer abstraction to access different databases through a unified view. Message-oriented middleware (MOM) provides asynchronous communication through sending and receiving messages through a message queue or a message channel. The remote procedure call provides communication services for synchronous, procedural-oriented communication. Somewhat similar are the object request brokers, which provide an object-oriented view on the distributed entities. Enterprise services busses (ESB) are the latest reincarnation of the integration broker targeted to fulfill the objectives of SOA.

Typically, all mentioned middleware uses certain standard or custom protocols to achieve communication. These protocols include SOAP (Simple Object Access Protocol), HTTP, TCP/IP, IIOP (Internet Inter-ORB Protocol), but also proprietary protocols.

The communication layer can also provide location transparency. This means that the actual location is managed separately from the application logic. This enables flexibility through deployment and configuration. The location transparency functionality is often connected with the introduction of the naming and directory services, which are then used as a repository for storing such information.

Brokering and Routing

The brokering and routing layer takes care of implementing the technical side of integration. No matter what type of integration we use, this layer should adapt the communication between applications in such way that all participating applications will be able to interoperate. This layer is essential for integration and actually has a number of responsibilities.

First, it has to provide the way to gather the required data from multiple sources, most likely existing and new-generation application and/or data stores. This responsibility is called aggregation, because data is gathered from different sources to represent a business concept, like an invoice or order.

Then, this data will have to be processed. Again, we will use a mix of existing and new-generation systems. Each of these applications will probably have its own interfaces and message syntax. Therefore, the brokering and routing layer will have to transform the data and messages into suitable parts that can be processed by individual applications.

Finally, this layer will have to gather the results of all applications and present them consistently. This part is called synthesis, meaning combining of results into a meaningful business notion.

To achieve these three steps automatically, the brokering and routing layer will need metadata information that will define the participating applications, methods, messages, and interfaces, and the sequence of operations involved. This layer also has to provide a means of handling events, making it appropriate for a declarative environment. Usually, it will associate events with certain operations that have to be performed.

Transformation

Transformation of data structures, their representations, and technologies has always been very important. In the past, small, custom-written programs that have read the source and transformed it to the destination format have usually solved the problems related to the transformation. With the advent and global use of markup languages, particularly XML, which has become the de-facto standard for data exchange, transformations have achieved a new level of maturity.

Therefore, transformation is today considered as a service that has to be provided by the integration infrastructure. Transformation engines are usually based on XSLT (Extensible Stylesheet Language for Transformations), which allows a relatively easy specification of data and schema transformations, and even allows specifying transformation rules as templates in a declarative way. Another advantage is that XSLT transformations can be executed on any XSLT engine, making transformation independent of the programming language, platform, and other restrictions.

Usually, XSLT transformation is made easier with the support of several tools, which provide graphical editors that allow us to graphically construct transformations using drag-and-drop techniques. These tools are becoming part of development environments on one hand, and part of integration technologies, such as ESBs on the other hand, which further simplifies transformations.

Business Intelligence

The business intelligence layer is responsible for presenting the high-level interface to access business information to other applications and to the users. The business-intelligence layer presents data to users in an understandable form. With the growth of e-commerce, the business-intelligence layer also takes some responsibilities for B2B integration.

Today, the business-intelligence layer is supported by a flexible unified presentation tier, most likely in the form of personalized portals. Personalized portals enable the delivery of valuable personalized business data and content directly to employees, business partners, and customers.

In addition to data and content delivery, the business-intelligence layer is often connected with data-processing technologies like Online Analytical Processing (OLAP), data mining, decision-support systems, and executive-information systems. These sources analyze enterprise data and provide information like estimation, forecasting, time-series analysis, and modeling.

Next, we'll turn our attention to the vertical service layers that define the integration infrastructure.

Transactions

The integration infrastructure has to provide the means for carrying out the business operations in a transactional manner. Therefore, it has to be able to invoke several operations on different existing and new-generation systems. It has to support the atomic ACID transaction model and long-running transactions with compensation semantics, usually referred to as business activities.

So, adherence to the transactional semantics means that any operation performed on one or more applications that causes a state change or changes to permanent data has to be performed as operation that guarantees that the consistency of the system is preserved. It also has to isolate the operation from other operations to a certain degree and guarantee that the outcomes of operations are written to the persistent storage.

Security

The integration infrastructure has to provide ways to constrain access to the system. Similarly, as the integration infrastructure horizontal services define a unified way to access the different applications, they should also define a way in which to manage security, possibly in a declarative way. The security should include all four horizontal layers. It should be able to reuse the existing application security, and base the security on roles that are defined with a single user log in. The security system should not be based on different passwords for different applications or even parts of applications. It should relate to all the important aspects, like communication channel encryption, authentication, authorization, and auditing.

Lifecycle

The integration infrastructure should provide ways to control the lifecycle of all applications involved. It should enable existing applications to be replaced one by one or even by parts without having influence on the other applications in the integrated system. The replacement should be possible step by step, when business needs dictate it and when enough resources are available. It should also provide ways to do the replacement while the system stays online. This functionality is often achieved by minimizing the dependencies between applications and specifying ways for the applications to interoperate.

Naming

A unified naming service will allow for the implementation of location transparency and will enable the replacement of one resource with another if this is required. The naming service in usually implemented with a naming and directory product that enables storing and looking for name-related information. Ideally, the naming service is unified and provides one logical picture of the enterprise, although it is physically implemented using replication and distribution to avoid a single point of failure.

Scalability

The integration infrastructure should be designed with scalability in mind. It has to access information about clients and provide concurrent access to the applications. It has to incorporate solutions that will enable enough room for extending the load demands on the system. Achieving scalability in an integrated system can be a difficult problem because we have to take into account existing applications that probably have not been designed for the kind of scalability that we would like to achieve. Particularly, the requirements for the number of concurrent clients probably have not been so strict. Therefore, we should think of scalability and probably implement some prototypes to test what levels of performance we can expect. We should also the load testing tools that will enable us to simulate high loads and assess the relevant performance criteria.

The integration infrastructure, however, cannot fully compensate for bad application architecture and design. Therefore, we will have to asses the architecture of existing applications to discover how well they scale. For newly developed applications, on the other hand, we should follow sound design and performance-related practices to achieve the best possible scalability.

Management

We also have to provide ways to manage the integration infrastructure. Many solutions, particularly custom applications, leave this out, which results in difficulties at the maintenance stage. The management layer should provide methods and tools to manage horizontal and vertical services. It should provide easy configuration and version management. A declarative management system enables access for changing and updating the parameters without needing to modify the source code and re-deploy the solutions. Remote management enables the infrastructure management to be carried out from remote locations, which minimizes the need for trained personal on site.

Rules

The horizontal services require specific rules for performing communication, brokering, routing, and business-intelligence tasks. These rules should not be hard-coded into applications, but should rather be declaratively specified inside the integration infrastructure. This includes the definitions, data formats, data transformations and flows, events, information processing, and information representation. Often these rules are stored in a repository, which provides a centralized storage to avoid duplication and inconsistencies.

Integration Technologies

Comprehensive enterprise-wide integration infrastructure usually requires more than one technology. Typically, also, because of the existing technologies, we will have to use a mixture of technologies. When selecting and mixing different technologies, we have to focus on their interoperability.

Interoperability between technologies will be crucial because we will use them to implement the integration infrastructure. Achieving interoperability between technologies can be difficult even for technologies based on open standards. Small deviations from standards in products can deny the "on-paper" interoperability. For proprietary solutions, interoperability is even more difficult. It is not only the question of if we can achieve interoperability, but also how much effort we have to put in to achieve it. Technologies used for integration are often referred to as middleware.

Middleware is system services software that executes between the operating system layer and the application layer and provides services. It connects two or more applications, thus providing connectivity and interoperability to the applications. Middleware is not a silver bullet that will solve all integration problems. Due to over-hyping in the 1980s and early 1990s, the term "middleware" has lost popularity, but is coming back in the last few years. The middleware concept, however, is today even more important for integration, and all integration projects will have to use one or many different middleware solutions. Middleware is mainly used to denote products that provide glue between applications, which is distinct from simple data import and export functions that might be built into the applications themselves.

All forms of middleware are helpful in easing the communication between different software applications. The selection of middleware influences the application architecture, because middleware centralizes the software infrastructure and its deployment. Middleware introduces an abstraction layer in the system architecture and thus reduces the complexity considerably. On the other hand, each middleware product introduces a certain communication overhead into the system, which can influence performance, scalability, throughput, and other efficiency factors. This is important to consider when designing the integration architecture, particularly if our systems are mission critical, and are used by a large number of concurrent clients.

When speaking of middleware products, we encompass a large variety of technologies. The most common forms of middleware are:

- Database access technologies
- Message-oriented middleware
- Remote procedure calls
- Transaction processing monitors
- Object request brokers
- Application servers
- Web services
- Enterprise service buses
- Several hybrid and proprietary products

Database Access Technologies

Database access technologies provide access to the database through an abstraction layer, which enables us to change the actual DBMS without modifying the application source code. In other words, it enables us to use the same or similar code to access different database sources. Therefore, database access technologies are useful for extracting data from different DBMSs. The technologies differ in the form of interfaces to the database they provide. They can offer function-oriented or object-oriented access to databases. The best known representatives are Java Database Connectivity (JDBC) and Java Data Objects (JDO) on the Java platform, and Open Database Connectivity (ODBC) and Active Data Objects (ADO.NET) on the Microsoft platform.

Message-Oriented Middleware

Message-oriented middleware (MOM) is a client/server infrastructure that enables and increases interoperability, flexibility, and portability of applications. It enables communication between applications over distributed and heterogeneous platforms. It reduces complexity because it hides the communication details and the details of platforms and protocols involved. The functionality of MOM is accessed via APIs. It typically resides on both ends, the client and the server side. It provides asynchronous communication and uses message queues to store the messages temporarily. The applications can thus exchange messages without taking care of the details of other applications, architectures, and platforms involved. The messages can contain almost any type of data, asynchronous nature of communication enables the communication to continue even if the receiver is temporary not available. The message waits in the queue and is delivered as soon as the receiver is able to accept it. But asynchronous communication has its disadvantages as well. Because the server side does not block the clients, they can continue to accept requests even if they cannot keep pace with them, thus risking an overload situation. The basic architecture is shown in the following figure.

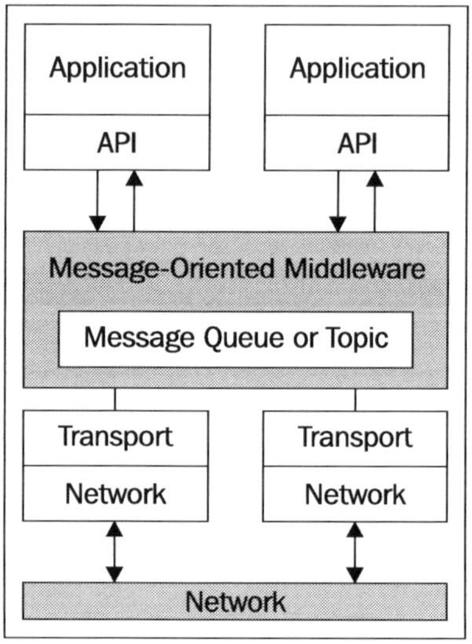

MOM products are proprietary products and have been available from the mid eighties. Therefore, they are incompatible with each other. Using a single product results in dependence on a specific vendor; this can have negative influence on flexibility, maintainability, portability, and interoperability. MOM product must specifically run an each and every platform being integrated. Not all MOM products support all platforms, operating systems, and protocols. We will, however, see that the Java platform provides ways to achieve relatively high independence from a specific vendor through a common interface, used to access all middleware products—the Java Messaging Service (JMS).

Remote Procedure Calls

Remote procedure calls are also a client/server infrastructure intended to enable and increase interoperability of applications over heterogeneous platforms. Similar to MOM, it enables communication between software on different platforms and hides almost all the details of communication. RPC is based on procedural concepts—developers use remote procedure or function calls. The first implementations date back to the early 1980s.

The main difference between MOM and RPC is the manner of communication. While MOM supports asynchronous communication, RPC promotes synchronous, request-reply communication (sometimes referred to as "call/wait"), which blocks the client until the server fulfills its requests. The next figure shows two applications communicating using RPC. To achieve remote communication, applications use procedure calls. RPC middleware hides all communication details, which makes using remote procedure calls very similar to local procedure calls.

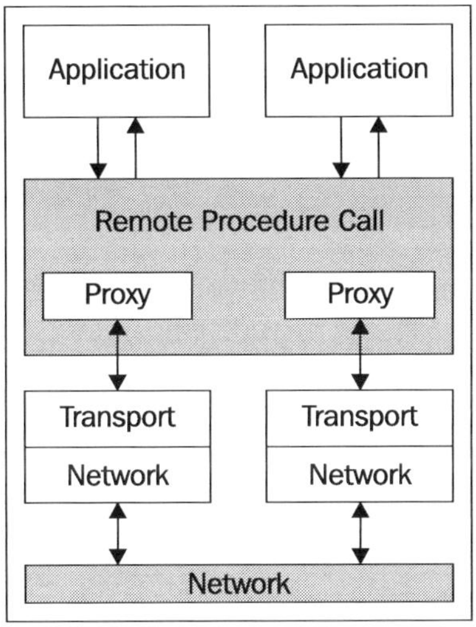

RPC guards against overloading a network, unlike the asynchronous mechanism, MOM. There a few asynchronous implementations available, but they are more the exception than the rule. RPC increases the flexibility of architecture by allowing a client of an application to employ a function call to access a server on a remote system. RPC allows the remote access without knowledge of the network address or any other lower-level information. The semantics of a remote call is the same whether or not the client and server are collocated. RPC is appropriate for client/server applications in which the client can issue a request and wait for the server to return a response before continuing with its own processing. On the other hand, RPC requires that the recipient is online to accept the remote call. If the recipient fails, the remote calls will not succeed, because the calls will not be temporarily stored and then forwarded to the recipient when it is available again, as is the case with MOM.

RPC is often connected with the Distributed Computing Environment (DCE), developed by the Open Systems Foundation (OSF). DCE is a set of integrating services that expand the functionality of RPC. In addition to RPC, the DCE provides directory, time, security, and thread services. Over these fundamental services, it places a layer of data-sharing services, including distributed file system and diskless support.

Transaction Processing Monitors

Transaction processing (TP) monitors are important middleware technology in mission-critical applications. They represent the first generation of application servers. TP monitors are based on the concept of transactions. They monitor and coordinate transactions among different resources. Although the name suggests that this is their only task, they have at least two very important additional roles: providing performance management and security services. They provide performance management with load balancing and resource pooling techniques, which enable efficient use of computing resources and thus a larger number of concurrent clients. TP monitors map client requests through application service stateless routines to improve system performance. They can also take some application transition logic from the client. They also provide security management where they enable or disable access of clients to certain data and resources. TP monitors can be viewed as middle-tier technology and this is why they are predecessors of todays application servers.

TP monitors have been traditionally used in legacy information systems. They are based on the procedural model, use remote procedure calls for communication between applications, and are difficult to program because of complex APIs through which they provide the functionality. In spite of that, they have been successfully used for more than 25 years. TP monitors are proprietary products, which makes migration from one product to another very difficult.

Object Request Brokers

Object request brokers (ORBs) are a middleware technology that manages and supports the communication between distributed objects or components. ORBs enable seamless interoperability between distributed objects and components without the need to worry about the details of communication. The implementation details of ORB are not visible to the components. ORBs provide location transparency, programming language transparency, protocol transparency, and operating system transparency.

The communication between distributed objects and components is based on interfaces. This enhances maintainability because the implementation details are hidden. The communication is usually synchronous, although is can also be deferred synchronous or asynchronous. ORBs are often connected with location services that enable locating the components in the network. ORBs are complex products but they manage to hide almost all complexity. More specifically, they provide the illusion of locality—they make all the components appear to be local, while in reality they may be deployed anywhere in the network. This simplifies the development considerably but can have negative influence on performance. A basic outline of ORB architecture is shown in the next figure:

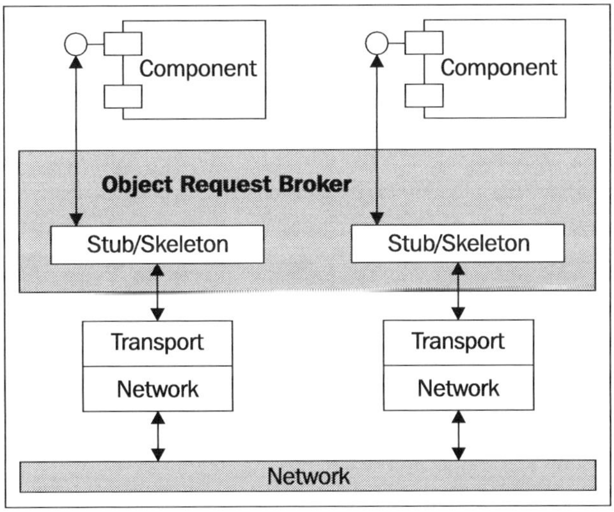

ORB products may choose different scenarios as to how and where to implement their functionality. They can move some functions to the client and server components or they can provide them as a separate process or integrate them into to the operating system kernel. There are three major standards of ORBs:

- OMG CORBA ORB compliant
- Java RMI and RMI-IIOP
- Microsoft COM/DCOM/COM+/.NET Remoting/WCF

There are many ORB products compliant with the CORBA ORB specifications and various implementations of RMI and RMI-IIOP. Particularly, RMI-IIOP is important, because it uses the same protocol for communication between components as the CORBA ORB, namely the IIOP (Internet Inter-ORB Protocol). This makes RMI-IIOP interoperable with CORBA.

Application Servers

Application servers handle all or the majority of interactions between the client tier and the data persistence tier. They provide a collection of already mentioned middleware services, together with the concept of a management environment in which we deploy business logic components—the container. In the majority of application servers, we can find support for web services, ORBs, MOM, transaction management, security, load balancing, and resource management. Application servers provide a comprehensive solution to enterprise information needs. They are also an excellent platform for integration. Today, vendors often position their application servers as integration engines, or specialize their common purpose application severs by adding additional functionality, like connections to back-end and legacy systems and position their products as integration servers. Although such servers can considerably ease the configuration of different middleware products, it is still worth thinking of what is underneath.

Whether used for integration or new application development, the application servers are software platforms. A software platform is a combination of software technologies necessary to run applications. In this sense, the application servers, or more precisely the software platforms that they support, define the infrastructure of all applications developed and executed on them. Application servers can implement some custom platform, making them the proprietary solution of a specific vendor (these are sometimes referred to as proprietary frameworks). Such application servers are more and more rare.

On the other hand, application servers can support a standardized, open, and generally accepted platform, such as Java enterprise Edition. The following lists the most important aspects of a platform:

- Technical aspects define the software technologies that are included in the software platform, the architecture of the applications developed for that platform, interoperability, scalability, portability, availability, reliability, security, client contracts, possibilities to grow and accommodate new solutions, and so on. In terms of integration, a very important aspect is the interoperability with other systems.
- Openness enables the application server vendors and third-party companies to have some possibility of influencing the development of the platform. Different solutions exist, from fully closed platforms that bind us to a certain vendor, to the fully open platforms, for example the open-source initiative, where everything, even source code, is free and can also be freely modified. Open platforms are often defined with specifications. These are documents that strictly define the technologies included in the platform and enable different vendors to implement the platform (as application servers for example). A tight specification guarantees consistency and a platform defined in terms of specifications can also have a reference implementation and a set of compatibility tests.
- Interoperability among platform implementations is crucial for the adoption of a certain platform. Particularly, the way the platform regulates additions and modifications is crucial. The stricter a platform is with the implementation of the core specification, the better chances it has to be successful and to gain a large market share. Each platform, however, has to provide ways for application servers to differentiate their product, possibly through implementing some additional functionality.
- Cost of the platform is also an important factor and it is probably the most difficult to assess because it includes the cost of the application server and other development software, the cost of hardware, the training, and the cost of the maintenance of the applications through their lifecycle.
- Last (and perhaps least important) is maturity, from which we can predict how stable the platform is. The more mature the platform is, the more it has been tested and the more has been proved that it is suitable for large scale applications.

Web Services

Web services are the latest distributed technology. They provide the technological foundation for achieving interoperability between applications using different software platforms, operating systems, and programming languages. From the technological perspective, web services are the next evolutionary step in distributed architectures. Web services are similar to their predecessors, but also differ from them in several aspects.

Web services are the first distributed technology to be supported by all major software vendors. Therefore, it is the first technology that fulfills the universal interoperability promise between applications running on disparate platforms. The fundamental specifications that web services are based on are SOAP (Simple Object Access Protocol), WSDL (Web Services Description Language), and UDDI (Universal Description, Discovery, and Integration). SOAP, WSDL, and UDDI are XML based, making web services protocol messages and descriptions human readable.

From the architectural perspective, web services introduce several important changes compared to earlier distributed architectures. They support loose coupling through operations that exchange data only. This differs from component and distributed object models, where behavior can also be exchanged.

Operations in web services are based on the exchange of XML-formatted payloads. They are a collection of input, output, and fault messages. The combination of messages defines the type of operation (one-way, request/response, solicit response, or notification). This differs from previous distributed technologies. For more information, please refer to WSDL and XML Schema specifications.

Web services provide support for asynchronous as well as synchronous interactions. They introduce the notion of end-points and intermediaries. This allows new approaches to message processing. Web services are stateless and utilize standard Internet protocols such as HTTP (Hyper Text Transfer Protocol), SMTP (Simple Mail Transfer Protocol), FTP (File Transfer Protocol), and MIME (Multipurpose Internet Mail Extensions). So, connectivity through standard Internet connections, even those secured with firewalls, is less problematic.

In addition to several advantages, web services also have a few disadvantages. One of them is performance, which is not as good as distributed architectures that use binary protocols for communication. The other is that plain web services do not offer infrastructure and quality of service (QoS) features, such as security, transactions, and others, which have been provided by component models for several years. Web services fill this important gap by introducing additional specifications:

- WS-Security: Addresses authentication and message-level security, and enables secure communication with web services.
- WS-Coordination: Defines a coordination framework for web services and is the foundation for WS-AtomicTransaction and WS-BusinessActivity.
- Transaction specifications (WS-AtomicTransaction and WS-BusinessActivity): specify support for distributed transactions with web services. AtomicTransaction specifies short duration, ACID transactions, and BusinessActivity specifies longer running business transactions, also called compensating transactions.

- WS-Reliable Messaging: Provides support for reliable communication and message delivery between web services over various transport protocols.
- WS-Addressing: Specifies message coordination and routing.
- WS-Inspection: Provides support for dynamic introspection of web service descriptions.
- WS-Policy: Specifies how policies are declared and exchanged between collaborating web services.
- WS-Eventing: Defines an event model for asynchronous notification of interested parties for web services.

Enterprise Service Buses

An Enterprise Service Bus (ESB) is a software infrastructure acting as an intermediary layer of middleware that addresses the extended requirements that usually cannot be fulfilled by web services, such as integration between web services and other middleware technologies and products, higher level of dependency, robustness, and security, management, and control of services and their communication.

An ESB addresses these requirements and adds flexibility to communication between services, and simplifies the integration and reuse of services. An ESB makes it possible to connect services implemented in different technologies (such as EJBs, messaging systems, CORBA components, and legacy applications) in an easy way. An ESB can act as a mediator between different, often incompatible, protocols and middleware products.

The ESB provides a robust, dependable, secure, and scalable communication infrastructure between services. It also provides control over the communication and control over the use of services. It has message interception capabilities, which allow us to intercept requests to services and responses from services and apply additional processing to them. In this manner, the ESB acts as an intermediary.

An ESB usually provides routing capability to route the messages to different services based on their content, origin, or other attributes and transformation capability to transform messages before they are delivered to services. For XML-formatted messages, such transformations are usually done using XSLT (Extensible Stylesheet Language for Transformations) or XQuery engines.

An ESB also provides control over the deployment, usage, and maintenance of services. This allows logging, profiling, load balancing, performance tuning, charging for service use, distributed deployment, on-the-fly reconfiguration, etc. Other important management features include the definition of correlation between messages, definition of reliable communication paths, definition of security constraints related to messages and services, etc.

An ESB should make services broadly available. This means that it should be easy to find, connect, and use a service irrespective of the technology it is implemented in. With broad availability of services, an ESB can increase reuse and can make the composition of services easier. Finally, an ESB should provide management capabilities, such as message routing, interaction, and transformation, which we have already described.

The Integration Process

Integration problems are usually very complex. Just imagine how many different people have to take part and on how many different levels. The business units have to coordinate the integration efforts, and define the information exchange and technical baselines. The information provided by all business units should also be consistent. Redundancies in the data model have to be identified, and removed on a company-wide level. Physical and electronic supply chains should be based on the same data views and all business units should behave to a common pattern, giving the same answers to the same questions.

Choosing the Steps and Defining the Milestones

Integration can be seen as a rather special software development project, because a lot of attention will have to be put on existing applications. Unfortunately, it is not a simple or small project, but usually a large project that will need a relatively long time to finish. During its course, it will consume a lot of resources, like developer time and money, so it is important that integration is done and managed in a defined and consistent way. In other words, the integration project has to follow sound software development practices.

Therefore, the integration project should be started and managed similarly to a large software development project. The integration project, however, in some aspects differs considerably from software development projects that do not have to take existing applications into account.

> The quality of an information system is only as good as the architecture that underlies it. The investment in information system development will have a much greater long-term payback when we consider the needs of a family of problems rather than just the problem of the moment.

Before we continue the discussion of the integration project, let's consider what the possible roles are we will most likely find ourselves in:

- We might be employed in the IT department of a large company that needs to integrate its existing systems into a global, integrated information system. In this case, the major responsibility will fall on the IT department, which will be responsible for realizing the integration project.
- We might be part of a software company that is hired to do the integration for a certain company. The responsibility for successfully realizing the integration will be on the software company completely.
- The third possibility is that we will be hired by a company that is performing the integration, only to modify some existing application for the purposes of integration. In this case, we will not be responsible for the whole integration, but only for the application that we have to modify.

From these three roles, the third scenario is obviously the easiest. If we are responsible for a single application only, then we will be involved in integration only partially. Setting up the integration project, defining the integration architecture, infrastructure, and most other difficult tasks will be performed by the company that has hired us. We will have to follow the specifications that we receive to help to modify the existing application in order to fit into the integration architecture.

The first scenario, where the IT department takes over the integration project for its company, is more difficult. The responsibilities of the IT department will be large and will include setting up the integration project, designing the integration architecture, selecting the infrastructure, analyzing the existing applications, developing the integrated information system, etc. The IT department will usually be familiar with existing applications that the company has. It will also have direct contact to employees, which will simplify a little finding out the requirements. In contrast, for the IT department this is very likely the first integration project, therefore the experience is minimal.

The second scenario is the most difficult one. If we are a software company that takes over the integration project, we will have similar responsibilities to the IT department. That is, setting up the integration project, designing the integration architecture, selecting the infrastructure, analyzing the existing applications, developing the integrated information system, etc. The software company will also not be familiar with the existing applications, with their functionality, and all finer details. Getting this information might be difficult if the employees are not cooperative in the company for which we perform the integration. However, on the plus side, we will probably have a lot of experience from previous integration projects, and experience with many different middleware technologies.

Sound Practices

The integration process defines the sequence of activities that have to be done in a disciplined manner in order to successfully develop an integrated information system. The goal of an integration process is to guarantee high quality of the integrated solution that will satisfy the customer and will be done on schedule and within the allocated financial resources. An integration project is based on an integration process. A well-managed integration project, based on the proposed integration process outline, will provide the basis for us to plan, implement, and finish the integration successfully.

The integration process is tightly connected to the software development process, with which it shares several activities. Each company that develops software has defined a software development process. The software development process quality and maturity (as assessed with the Capability Maturity Model (`http://www.sei.cmu.edu/cmm/cmm.html`), for example) will have impact on the ability to accomplish the integration successfully. A better defined development process will reach a higher maturity level, and the chances that the integration will be successful will become much better.

Before we look into the details of integration process activities, let's first look at the sound development practices that are particularly important for integration. There are four important practices that should be considered in each integration project:

- Iterative development
- Incremental development
- Prototyping
- Reuse

Let's take a closer look at each of these considerations, in turn.

Iterative Development

We have already identified that the integration project will be a very large project that will require a lot of time and resources to finish. On the other hand, we have also seen that no company will be willing to wait too long (for example a year or more) from the initiation of the integration project until the usable integrated solutions are deployed. Iterative development solves this problem.

When using iterative development, we do not look at the integration as one large whole, but rather partition it into several small pieces, which we implement step by step.

Instead of waiting for the solution until the end of the project, we are able to deliver intermediate results. When developing iteratively, we can evaluate the results of every iteration, and improve them in the next iterations (look also at incremental development). This also enables us to assess the progress level.

Iterative development is a good practice also when the requirements are not completely defined. As we will see, today it is practically impossible to define the requirements at the beginning of integration and not to change or modify them later. With iterative development, we can relatively easily adapt to changing requirements, because we can apply changes to the intermediate releases.

Although iterative development is more difficult to manage for the project manager, it allows us to build a trust relationship between the developers and the customers. Customers will be able to see and use intermediate results. However, it might be difficult to assess how many iterations we will need, and limiting the number of iterations is not the correct solution to reduce the schedule.

Incremental Development

With iterative development, we have partitioned the integration into several smaller tasks that will deliver some usable products. However, it is unlikely that we will solve each task in our first attempt adequately. Usually, we learn from our own mistakes and improve ourselves. In other words: "Before we make things right, we make them wrong."

Incremental development is a strategy to improve in small steps to finally reach the stated goals. This requires that we partition the problem into sub-problems (iterative development). Incremental development enables us to work faster and to return to the same problem later to improve it.

Although incremental and iterative development strategies are commonly used together, they are actually two different strategies. Iterative development partitions the problem into sub-problems, while incremental development supplements and improves partial solutions step by step. Iterative and incremental development strategies are important to integration and enable us to partition the integration into several sub-problems and allow us to manage the changing requirements. If possible, they should be used combined for integration projects.

Prototyping

Prototyping is a strategy that enables us to find the correct solutions for a given problem without spending too much time and money on the problem. With prototyping, we can build pilot solutions to integration challenges and assess whether they can be developed in the way we would like to and with the technologies we would like to use. Prototyping is commonly used to assess, verify, and validate chosen architectures and solutions for integration. Often prototyping is used to verify the requirements and the performance and scalability as well.

Reuse

Reuse is the ability to develop new applications with the use of existing solutions. This is also the exact goal of integration; to develop an integrated information system via the reuse of existing applications, without modifying them too much. The problem is that to achieve reuse we must have software components that have been developed specifically for this purpose. The majority of existing systems are not designed with this in mind, so we will have to search for solutions that will make existing systems reusable. When discussing the practice of reuse, we should also mention reuse of a higher abstraction layer—the reuse of ideas and sound solutions in the form of pattern reuse.

Following these practices will enable us to achieve integration successfully and deliver partial results quickly. This is an important fact, because companies that start integration are not able to wait a long time (it can take a few years in a large company) to get the whole integrated system at once. They need partial results that solve their most urgent needs for integration. These most urgent needs will influence the decision what to do first and how to partition the integration into smaller tasks. However, a disciplined development path is still needed to effectively solve even the partial needs. Ad hoc solutions, although faster at first sight, will not fulfill the long-term integration needs.

Integration Process Activities and Phases

Integration requires that we analyze existing applications, design the integration architecture, select the integration infrastructure, design the solution, implement the integration, etc. All these are activities of an integration process and they have to be performed step by step. Here, we will classify these activities more strictly and define the sequence in which they should be performed. In general, we can partition the activities into technical and supporting activities. Technical activities include:

- Requirements gathering
- Analysis of existing applications

- Selection of integration infrastructure
- Problem domain analysis
- Design
- Implementation
- Testing
- Deployment

In addition to technical activities, we will also need support activities. The important support activates are:

- Project management
- Configuration and change management
- Communication with the environment

Integration is usually achieved in four phases which are:

- Data-level integration
- Application integration
- Business process integration
- Presentation integration

Data-level integration focuses on moving data between applications with the objective of sharing the same data among these different applications. Application integration focuses on sharing application functionality—business logic; and not only pure data as in data-level integration. Business process integration focuses on end-to-end support for business processes, both private (within organizations), public (between two or more organizations). Presentation integration focuses on a common user interface (typically a portal) for the integrated information system.

The four integration phases are usually done step by step, although not necessarily. Sometimes, we can skip a phase. The question is how to connect the activities and the phases of an integration process. The answer is that we will perform the activities for each integration phase. The technical activities that will not differ from phase to phase are the first three activities: requirements gathering, analysis of existing applications, and selection of integration infrastructure. We will have to perform these activities before a distinction between the four integration phases will be made. We will also perform all support activities equally for all phases.

The rest of the technical activities will be tied to the integration phase. These activities will differ in data-level integration, in application integration, business process integration, and presentation integration.

Integration Patterns

At first glance, concrete integration problems and the corresponding solutions are seldom identical. However, after working on several integration projects, we can see that problems and the solutions can be classified into common categories—integration patterns. Integration patterns will help us to understand the different solutions and methods for integration and allow us to choose the best solution for our problem. They allow us to look at integration problems from a certain abstraction level.

Integration patterns describe proven methods and processes used for integration within the enterprise or beyond. They emerge from classifications of common integration solutions. Each integration pattern defines a common integration problem and a sound solution. The most important integration patterns include:

- Integration broker pattern (also known as integration messenger)
- Wrapper pattern (integration adapter, integration connector)
- Integration mediator pattern
- Single-step application integration
- Multi-step application integration
- Virtual service (integration façade)
- Data access object (DAO) (Data exchange pattern) pattern
- Data mapping pattern
- Direct data mapping
- Multi-step data mapping
- Process automator pattern

For more information on integration patterns, please look at the various pattern catalogs and books, such as *J2EE Design Patterns Applied*, from Wrox Press.

Summary

In this chapter, we have overviewed the integration challenges and figured out that integration is one of the most difficult problems in application development. Therefore, it has to be planned carefully, it has to be based on sound integration architectures, on selected infrastructure and technologies, and managed according to integration process best practices.

We have seen that integration is not a solely technical problem, although technologies play an important role. Therefore, we have overviewed integration technologies and middleware products, ranging from data access technologies over remote procedure calls, message-oriented middleware to web services and enterprise services buses. We have also identified the best strategies for integration and discussed top-down, bottom-up, and inside-out approaches.

We have overviewed different types of integration, such as data-level integration, application integration, business process integration, presentation integration, and also B2B integrations. We have seen that the ultimate goal of each company is to have an information system, which not only provides end-to-end support for business processes, but is also easy adaptable to reflect the changes in business processes quickly and efficiently.

Achieving such integrated information systems is not an easy task. Today, we believe that Service-Oriented Architectures (SOA) and the related technologies, processes, and patterns provide ways to develop such information systems.

3
Base Technologies

This chapter describes a selection of the base technologies related to the implementation of solutions based on the Trivadis Integration Architecture Blueprint. It will:

- Cover transactions and transaction strategies
- Contain a description of **Open Grid Services infrastructure** (**OGSi**), a dynamic, hardware-independent software platform
- Consider **Java Connector Architecture** (**JCA**), which is a general architecture for connecting heterogeneous systems
- Explain **Java Business Integration** (**JBI**) as a standardized description of the functions of an **Enterprise Service Bus** (**ESB**)
- Describe **Service Component Architecture** (**SCA**) in terms of a model for developing applications and systems based on a Service-Oriented Architecture (SOA)
- Present **Service Data Objects** (**SDO**) as a Disconnected Data Architecture
- Cover process modeling, including a description of the most important standards for modeling business processes

The base technologies that currently play a role in the implementation of integration solutions include transactions and standards such as OGSi, JCA, JBI, SCA, and SDO, all of which we will cover in this chapter.

Transactions and transaction strategies have a central function in every type of architecture. Knowledge of the options available, and the differences between the options, is essential when choosing suitable data access strategies. Important aspects include transactional systems, isolation levels, two-phase commit, and global (XA) transactions (a transaction that may span multiple resources, also known as a **Distributed Transaction**).

Open Grid Services infrastructure (**OGSi**) is a hardware-independent, dynamic software platform which simplifies the process of modularizing distributed applications and their services, and managing them throughout their entire life cycle. The OSGi platform requires a Java Virtual Machine (JVM) and provides a framework on the basis of the JVM. The most important features of OSGi are the OSGi architecture, the component model (the bundles), and the collaborative model.

Java Connector Architecture (**JCA**) is a general architecture in the Java Enterprise Edition (JEE) environment used to connect heterogeneous systems, such as legacy applications, through a standardized interface in the form of a resource adapter. Other standardized interfaces defined by the JCA specification allow for collaboration with other system components.

The **Java Business Integration** (**JBI**) specification describes the functionality of a standardized ESB. JBI can also be regarded as a service-oriented meta-container that implements a component architecture. JBI uses two types of containers: service engines and binding components. The service engines contain the business logic, while the binding components merely act as a proxy for the service users.

Service Component Architecture (**SCA**) is a collection of specifications that describe a model for developing applications and systems on the basis of an SOA. SCA models solutions as groups of service components that provide services and include references to other services. Functionality is made available externally as a service in the form of interfaces. Service components have properties that describe the specific characteristics of the components and are used to configure them.

Service Data Objects (**SDO**) offer a consistent model for managing data, regardless of its source system and source format. SDO makes use of a Disconnected Data Architecture. Although SCA and SDO can be used independently of one another, a combination of the two specifications represents a powerful and flexible tool for developing distributed applications.

One important base technology used in the majority of integration projects consists of business process modeling tools. The modeling process is always done using graphical tools. The Trivadis Integration Architecture Blueprint envisions the usage of graphical tools that support a clearly defined modeling notation. A number of these notations are available. The most important ones are **Business Process Modeling Notation** (**BPMN**), **Event-Driven Process Chain** (EPC), and **Business Process Execution Language** (**BPEL**).

Transactions

Transactions and transaction strategies play a central role in every architecture. A knowledge of the options available and the differences between them is essential when choosing suitable data access strategies. This section covers the aspects relating to integration. These include transactional systems, isolation levels, two-phase commit, and XA transactions.

- **Transactional systems**: These allow for controlled "all-or-nothing" data manipulation.
- **Isolation levels**: These levels coordinate data access by parallel transactions and, depending on the level, determine the visibility of the manipulated data. There are four different isolation levels:
    - serializable
    - repeatable read
    - read committed
    - read uncommitted
- **Two-phase commit**: The two-phase commit is the algorithm on which transactions are based. It requires all the systems participating in a transaction to commit to the successful completion of the transaction.
- **XA transactions**: An XA transaction is a standardized, global transaction that can span several (heterogeneous) resources. XA uses a two-phase commit to ensure that all resources either commit, or rollback, any particular transaction simultaneously.

Transactional systems

Transaction processing systems and the theoretical concepts that lie behind them have existed in one form or another since the 1970s and were developed by database guru Jim Gray (Lindsay 2008).

The purpose of transactions and of the infrastructure components that support them is "all-or-nothing" data manipulation within a unit of work (Gray, Reuter 1993).

The following brief example will help to make this clearer:

Say you want to make a bank transfer. This involves debiting the amount from your account and crediting it to another account. The bank transfer process, its sub-activities (debiting and crediting), and the data manipulation involved (deducting the amount from the first account, adding it to the second account) represent a unit of work. This takes place within one transaction to ensure that none of the sub-activities are carried out individually, for example, a debit without a credit or vice versa. The two processes are only valid in combination, even if system errors occur. This consistency is made possible by the use of transactions.

All the operations in a transaction are enclosed within a transaction boundary, as shown in the following figure. It contains all the individual operations, which make up the transaction.

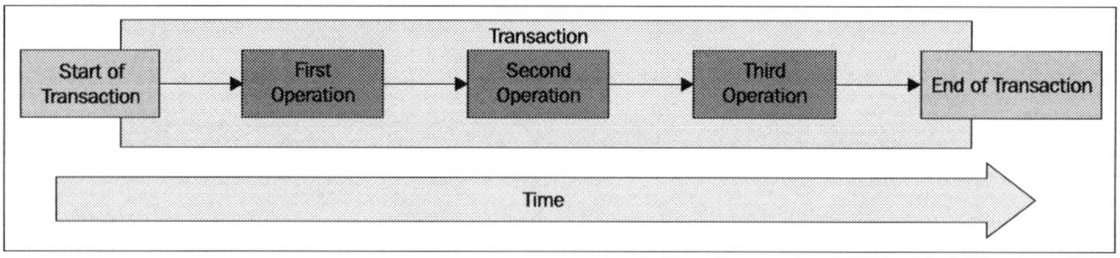

Transactions can be completed in one of two ways:

- Successful—commit
- Unsuccessful—rollback

In the case of a commit, all the changes made during the transaction are reflected in the system. As transactional systems are generally databases or other persistent components, the state changes made in a commit are saved permanently. In the event of a rollback, all the state changes are reversed. Atomic transactions can be nested, but many systems do not support this. In this case, sub-transactions (nested transactions) are provisional, and are only completed when the top-level transaction is completed (commit or abort).

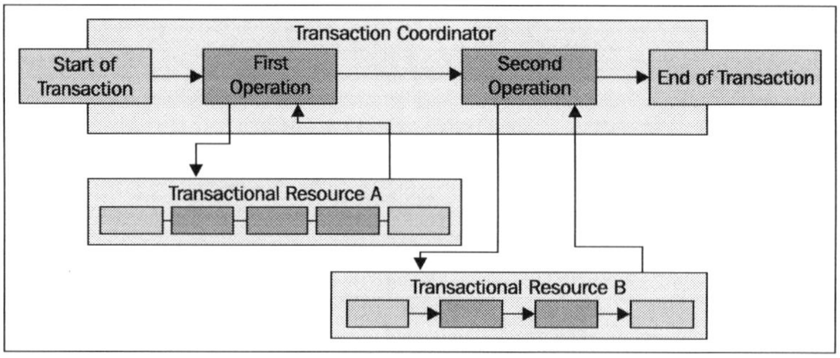

A transaction coordinator is always associated with transactions, as shown in this figure. This infrastructure component manages, monitors, and coordinates the transactions. A coordinator can take the form of an independent component or, for performance reasons, can be part of the application. The coordinator communicates with participants assigned to the transaction (for example, a database and the application which is accessing it) and controls the necessary termination actions, in other words, the commit or the rollback. Different transaction types and mechanisms have different forms of communication and participants (local, remote, distributed, homogeneous, heterogeneous, and so on). The XA protocol for global transactions is often used in distributed environments with several heterogeneous transactional resources (for example, an RDBMS and an XML database).

In many systems, a transaction manager is responsible for managing the transaction coordinators, which coordinate large numbers of transactions. The initiating resource starts the transaction in the transaction manager, and a coordination manager is assigned to the transaction.

Atomic transactions have the following properties, which are also known by the acronym ACID:

- **Atomicity**: The transaction can be successfully completed (commit) or can be unsuccessful as a result of system errors or program crashes (abort). In the first case, all the changes to the data are implemented as if the changes had taken place in one single (atomic) step. In the event of an abort, all the changes made up to this point in the transaction are reversed (rollback), and the system is returned to its status before the transaction started. Atomic transactions cannot be broken down. If an abort occurs, the system is unchanged. Otherwise, all the changes (not just part of them) are implemented.
- **Consistency**: Transactions produce consistent results. As a result, they guarantee that the application and the business logic have a well-defined status.
- **Isolation**: When concurrent transactions are processed, the interim results that occur during the transaction are not visible to other transactions, as long as this transaction is not yet completed. If several transactions are executed simultaneously, they must not influence each other.
- **Durability**: The system status created by a successful transaction completion (commit) is guaranteed to be durable.

Isolation levels

There are four different transaction isolation levels, or, in other words, states that are recognized separately by different parallel transactions. A partial breakup of strict isolation is permitted in many scenarios to improve performance. In order to provide the highest level of process isolation (serializable), data must be blocked. The process that initiates the transaction puts locks on the data. The result is a reduction in the possible process concurrency, in other words, the possible parallelization. Transactions represent a processing bottleneck. The aim of the additional, more relaxed isolation levels is to improve performance compared to strict serialization, by making optimistic assumptions.

In descending order of isolation properties, that is, with increasing visibility and the related possibility of data inconsistencies, the four isolation levels of the ANSI/ISO SQL standard are:

- Serializable
- Repeatable read
- Read committed
- Read uncommitted

Serializable

All the transactions are completely isolated from each other. They appear to take place serially, one after another. So-called **phantom reads**, which will be explained later in the chapter, cannot occur, as shown in the following diagram:

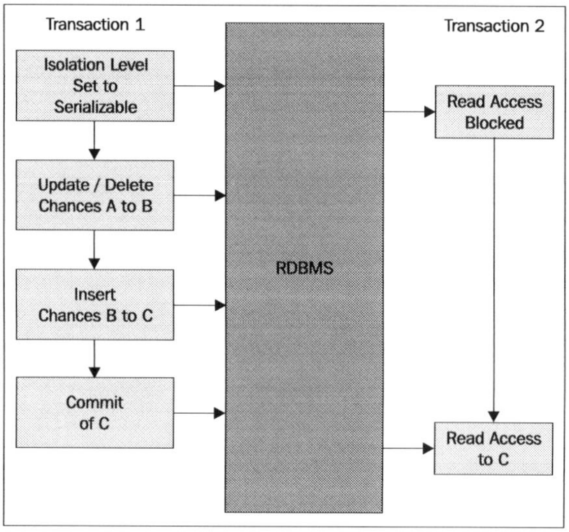

Repeatable read

Data that has been read (in an RDBMS with a `SELECT`, for example) cannot be changed. On this isolation level, read locks are required on all data that has been read. However, range locks are not needed, as shown in the following diagram:

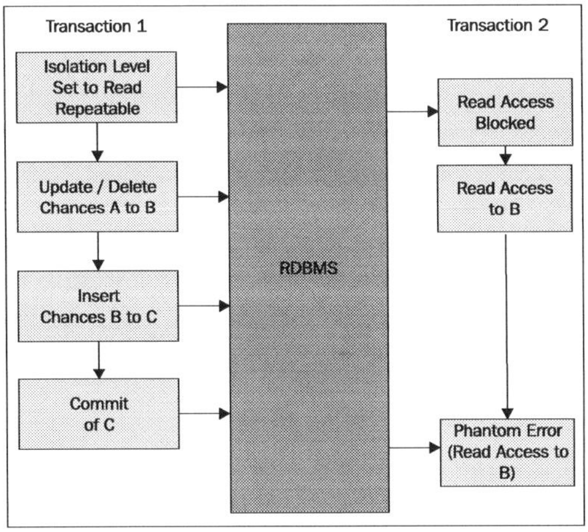

Read committed

Data that has been read (for example with a `SELECT`) can be changed by other transactions in the background. Read locks are released immediately after the read process has been completed. In contrast, write locks are only released at the end of the transaction, as shown in the following diagram:

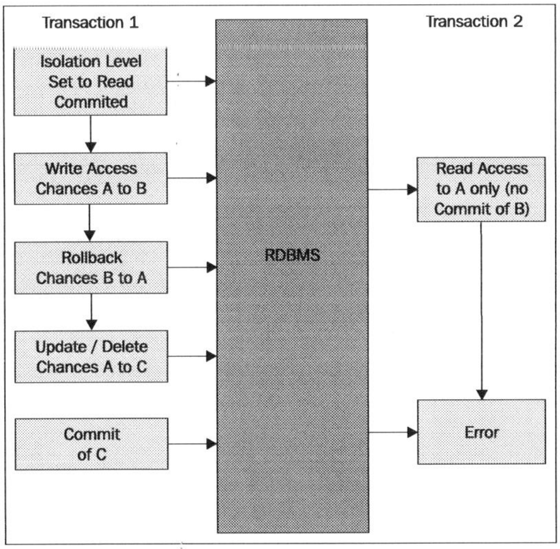

Read uncommitted

On this isolation level, so-called **dirty reads** are possible. Data in **transaction 1** is visible to **transaction 2**, although **transaction 1** has not yet been successfully completed (committed).

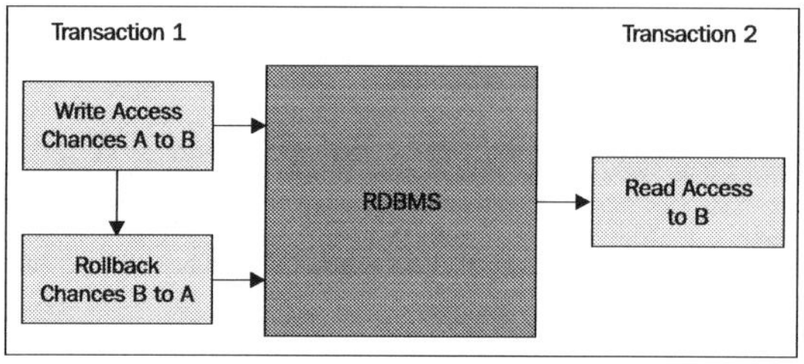

Phantom reads

A phantom read occurs when **transaction 2** can read data created by **transaction 1**, but **transaction 1** has not yet been completed with a commit. Phantom reads can take place in the following ANSI/ISO SQL standard isolation levels:

- Repeatable read
- Read committed
- Read uncommitted

Phantom reads are not possible in the serializable isolation level. The following table gives an overview of this:

Isolation level	**Behavior**		
	Dirty read	**Non-repeatable read**	**Phantom read**
Serializable	No	No	No
Repeatable Read	No	No	Yes
Read Committed	No	Yes	Yes
Read Uncommitted	Yes	Yes	Yes

Different products use the possible isolation levels and the standardized versions in very different ways. In many cases, only a subset of the four options is supported. In some products, additional product-specific syntax must be added to a `SELECT` to enforce a read lock.

Two-Phase Commit protocol (2PC)

The Two-Phase Commit is the basic mechanism for implementing global transactions. The Two-Phase Commit protocol is a distributed algorithm, which requires all the resources in a distributed system that are participating in a transaction to complete the transaction successfully (commit). The result is that all the resources complete the transaction with a *commit*, or reverse it with an *abort*. This is also guaranteed in the event of network errors and/or server failures. A server node takes on the role of coordinator. On each of the participating nodes, there must be the possibility of buffering the local transaction status in order to ensure that, if a server crashes, the transaction can be canceled and the log data is never lost or corrupted (except, of course, in the case of total failures). In addition, the participating nodes must be able to communicate with one another. In particular, where there is a heavy transaction load, the communication latency of the network can be a significant performance factor.

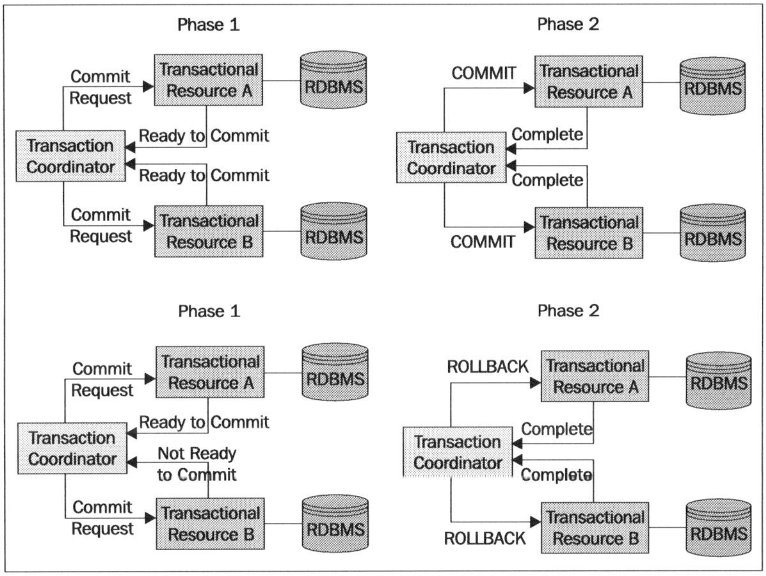

The concept of Two-Phase Commit is the result of implementing the algorithm, which can be divided into the commit request and the commit phases, as shown in this diagram.

- **Commit request**: The transaction coordinator asks the participating resources if they are prepared to commit. Depending on the local transaction results (commit or abort), the individual resources send a corresponding reply.
- **Commit**: On the basis of the result of the commit request phase, the transaction coordinator instructs the participating resources to implement a commit or abort locally.

This protocol is shown in the following diagram:

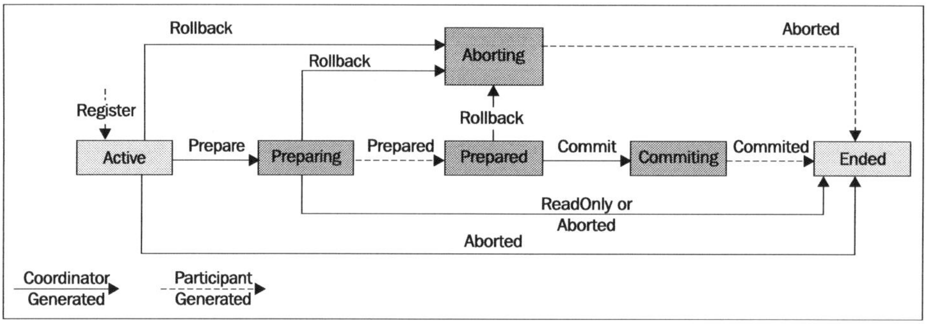

It is initiated by the transaction coordinator when the final step in the transaction is reached. A Two-Phase Commit is made possible by the bidirectional communication of the XA protocol. The Two-Phase Commit is not possible in non-XA transactions, as these protocols are unidirectional and the transaction manager cannot receive any responses from the resource manager. The majority of transaction managers communicate with the resource managers in phase 1 and 2 in parallel in multiple threads, in order to improve performance. By parallelizing communication, the resources can be released at the earliest possible point.

XA transactions

An XA transaction is a global (top-level) transaction, which can span several (heterogeneous) resources, as shown in the next diagram. A non-XA transaction only ever involves a single resource.

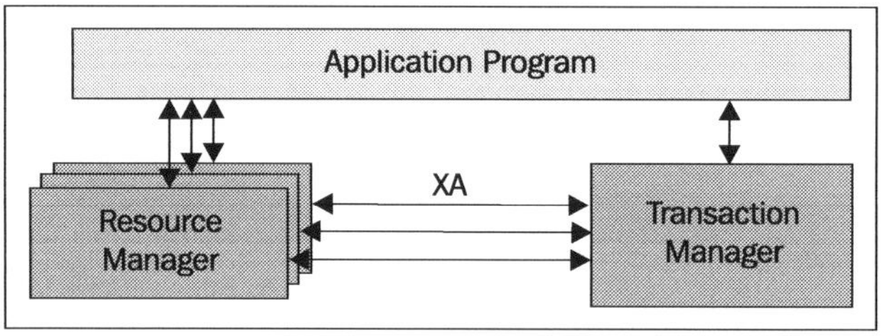

The **X/Open XA** specification describes a bidirectional interface at system level for a communication bridge between several local resource managers on the one hand, and a global transaction manager on the other (OpenGroup 1991). The transaction manager controls the transaction, manages the lifecycle of the transaction, and coordinates one or more resources. The resource manager is responsible for controlling and managing its assigned resource (for example, a database or a message queue).

Because of its bi-directionality, XA uses the Two-Phase Commit protocol. In comparison with atomic transactions, XA has a certain coordination overhead, which can have a negative impact on performance. For this reason, XA should only be chosen when multiple resources are being used simultaneously (in the same transaction context).

> XA is only needed if different resources (for example, two databases, not two tables) are accessed in the same transaction. This includes those scenarios where really only one single transaction is needed. As a result, read-only accesses that need no locks can be implemented without XA. (See also the information about transaction isolation levels.) However, XA supports read-only scenarios of this kind by means of optimizations and, therefore, in these cases the use of XA does not normally result in reductions in performance.

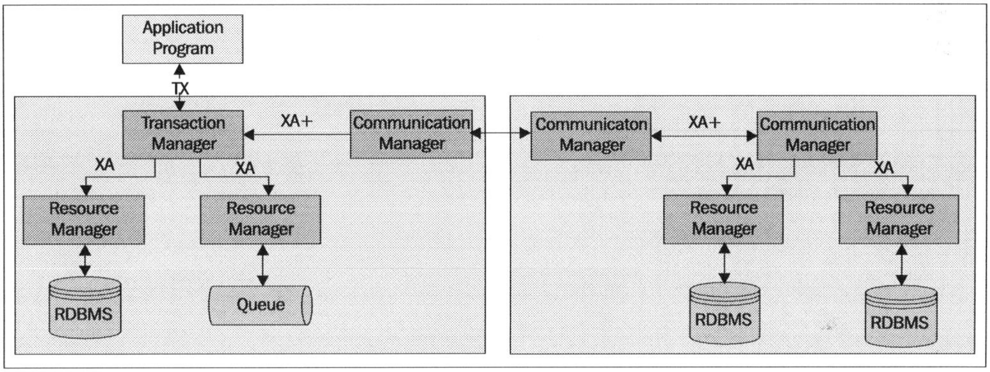

The most common scenario in which XA is used is the simultaneous update of a relational database and a message queue (or message topic) in one transaction, as shown in the preceding image. Other prevalent scenarios of this kind include accesses to two or more databases, or several messaging systems (Rahm 1994).

An XA transaction must coordinate all the participating resource types in the event of a rollback, and must isolate the updates from other transactions (see the information on transaction isolation). Without XA, messages that are sent to a queue or a topic may be read before the transaction is completed. If XA is used, the queue (or the topic) is only released when the transaction has been successfully completed, which means that other transactions do not have access to the message.

OSGi

OSGi is a hardware-independent, dynamic software platform that simplifies the process of modularizing distributed applications and their services, and managing them throughout their entire life cycle (Wütherich et al. 2008). The OSGi platform requires a Java Virtual Machine (JVM) and provides a framework on the basis of the JVM. The OSGi alliance (Open Service Gateway initiative) is an industry consortium consisting of a number of manufacturers from different sectors, which originally developed the platform for use in embedded systems. The most important features of OSGi are as follows:

- **OSGi architecture**: OSGi defines the following layers as its base architecture:
    - Execution environment
    - Module
    - Life cycle
    - Services
    - Security
    - Applications
- **Component model**: The fundamental component model consists of a **bundle**. In OSGi, bundles are also referred to as **services**, which are managed in a service registry. However, the concept of a service in OSGi has nothing in common with the concept of a service in an SOA. The specification of the OSGi service platform defines a runtime environment (container) based on a Java Virtual Machine and Java base architecture. OSGi focuses on the component, which is packaged as a bundle, and which can publish its interface through the service registry, making it available for use. A monitored life cycle is defined for such components.
- **Collaborative Software Environment**: OSGi bundles can collaborate through the OSGi service registry, in which the services a bundle provides are registered.

The specification of the OSGi service platform defines a runtime environment (container) based on a Java Virtual Machine (JVM). One of the important enhancements is the option of equipping the software bundles with independent class loaders and, therefore, running different versions of the same software in parallel on the same JVM. In addition, the OSGi container gives the bundles their own service life cycle, which enables services to be installed, started, stopped, removed, and updated at runtime. Both these factors—versioning and life cycle—are of particular interest in productive environments where high levels of availability are needed. OSGi is therefore ideal for integrating embedded systems, for example, as there is no maintenance window needed for upgrading components.

OSGi has published 4 specifications. The majority of OSGi implementations are based on the release 3 specification from 2003 (OGSi 2003). Well-known implementations include the Eclipse 3.0 platform (Gruber et al. 2005) and the "software in the car" platform developed by BMW (Saad 2003) and Daimler (Heinisch, Simons 2004). As of October 2009, there are five certified OSGi implementations for release 4.

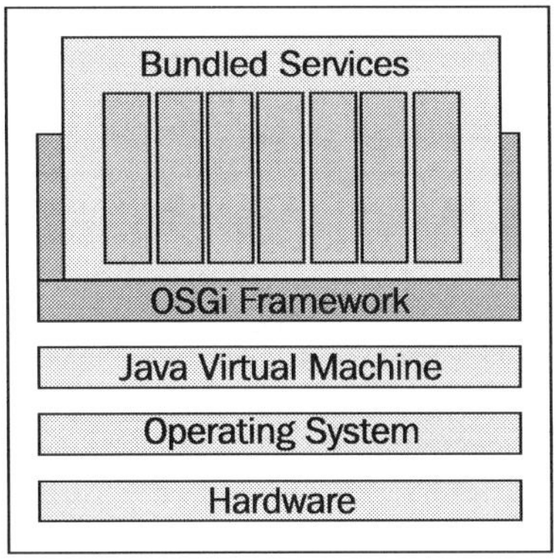

The architecture of the OSGi service platform enables a range of independent service modules to be run in parallel on the same JVM and allows them to be monitored, managed, and updated throughout the entire software life cycle, as shown in the preceding diagram. Remote maintenance is also possible. The interdependencies of bundles are resolved and managed by the OSGi container. The implementations and products that are currently available consist of the OSGi framework and a number of existing software bundles, which, because of their modular structure, can be dynamically added to or removed from a runtime environment.

The current OSGi specification focuses on the component, which is packaged as a bundle. A compoment can publish its interface using the service registry and make it available for use. Components of this kind have a monitored life cycle with options for (re)deployment.

The OSGi framework covers the following points:

- Applications can share one individual virtual machine
- Class loader problems
- The isolation and security of individual applications and services
- Controlled communication and collaboration between applications
- The use of shared resources (such as libraries)

- Life cycle management of applications and services (for example, versioning applications and services)
- Policies are offered by bundles

OSGi architecture

The most important layers of the OSGi architecture are the execution environment, modules, life cycle management, and service registry, as shown in the following diagram:

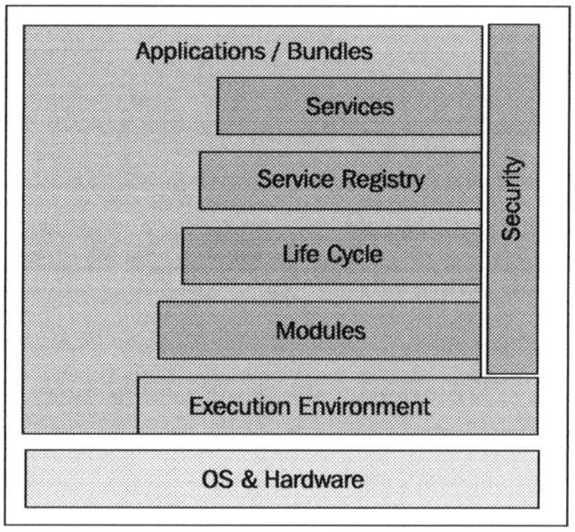

Let's have a look at these layers one by one:

- **Execution environment**: A Java environment, such as J2SE.
- **Modules**: All the classes and resources grouped together as bundles. A bundle can include entire applications, parts of applications, individual service components, and entire libraries. The starting point at runtime is the OSGi system bundle, which makes the OSGi software infrastructure available.
- **Life cycle management**: A defined life cycle for each bundle in the form of an API. This API has the following life cycle statuses, as shown in the following diagram:
    - install
    - resolve
    - start
    - stop
    - refresh
    - update
    - uninstall

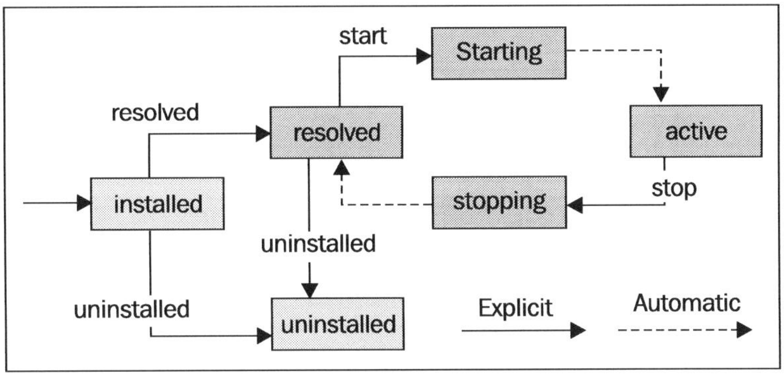

- **Service registry**: The management of all services. This includes identifying services on the basis of their interface definition or properties, and sending notifications between services. It also involves binding to one or more services using program controls, pre-defined standard behavior rules, and distribution configurations.

OSGi bundles

The OSGi component model consists of bundles. These are services, which are managed in a service registry. However, the OSGi service is nothing more than the general interface concept of a software component. It defines a decoupled component model that supports the reusability and the use of small components.

A bundle represents an application deliverable, which is similar to an application executable, in the form of a JAR file. A bundle registers one or more services. A service is specified in a Java interface and can be implemented by several bundles. Services are bound to the bundle life cycle. A query language can be used to search for services registered by other bundles.

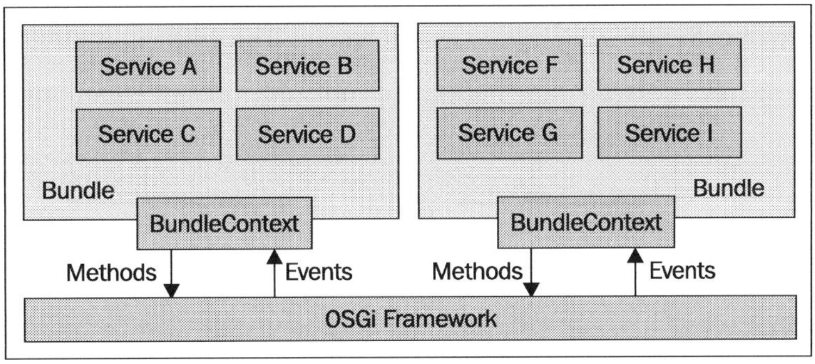

A bundle contains program code, additional resources (optional), and a manifest file that defines the bundle context. The OSGi framework reads the manifest and installs the code and resources in the OSGi runtime environment on this basis. Dependencies with other bundles and services are also resolved using the information in the manifest. At runtime, the framework starts the bundle via the bundle activator and manages the class path and the dependencies (references to other bundles and services). The framework can also stop a bundle by means of the bundle activator.

Collaborative model

Bundles can collaborate in two ways:

- Through service objects
- As shared bundles/packages (package sharing)

A dynamic registry allows a bundle to find other service objects. The framework manages the dependencies between the bundles and services transparently.

Java Connector Architecture (JCA)

JCA is a general architecture in the Java Enterprise Edition (JEE) environment used to connect heterogeneous systems, such as legacy applications, using a standardized interface in the form of a resource adapter. Agreements (contracts) laid down in the JCA specification guarantee collaboration with other system components (JCASpec 2003).

Uses

Java Connector Architecture (JCA) defines standards for connecting the Java Enterprise Edition platform with heterogeneous, distributed **Enterprise Information Systems (EIS)**. JCA enables EIS to be integrated with application servers and business applications as a result of its developer API and manufacturer API specifications. This guarantees that resource adapters are reusable. The manufacturer of a business application can be certain that the application will communicate in a uniform way with a different EIS. In the same way, the manufacturer of an EIS, which is supplied with a JCA adapter can be sure that the EIS can be addressed by all the applications on a Java EE application server, and that the EIS can be integrated into a Java EE architecture in compliance with Java standards. JCA adapters can also be used to integrate an EIS into an ESB or into a BPEL process server.

JCA supports the request/response model with transactions that are more or less short-lived, for example, those from a database environment. JCA does not support more complex, long-lasting transactions, such as those required in workflows and integration scenarios. Java Business Integration (JBI), covered later, which has a communication concept based on the mediated message exchange pattern, is intended to close this gap in the Java EE standard.

JCA components

Each of the components of JCA are detailed in the following figure:

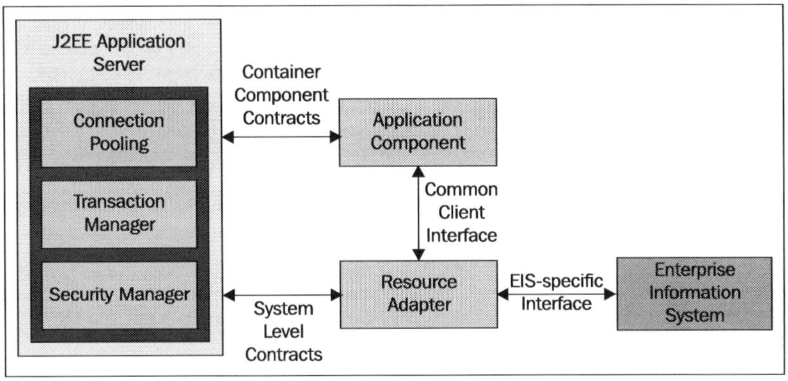

Let's take a look at these components one by one:

- **Resource adapter**: This is the core of the JCA functionality and contains the Java interfaces/classes in the form of the resource adapter archive. The resource adapter runs in an application server.
- **Common Client Interface (CCI)**: The CCI is the API for the resource adapter. It is used to implement the application contract. This is the API applications use to access the EIS.
- **Container-Component Contracts**: These link the application that uses a JCA adapter and the application server. They define the services provided by the component.
- **System-Level Contracts**: These link the application server and the EIS. They also extend the application server with regard to the EIS, so that connection pooling, transaction management, and security management can be used when accessing an EIS. They add connection pooling, transaction management, and security management functionality to the application server.
- **Enterprise Information System**: This is the system with which the connection is to be created using JCA.

Contracts

JCA defines a series of different system-level contracts (agreements), which determine the way in which the application server, JCA, EIS, and application work together:

- **Connection management**: This concerns managing the connection pool with the EIS. The application is provided with connections from this pool, and the application server is responsible for making valid connections available. The functionality for putting in place and testing the connection to the EIS must be in place.
- **Transaction management**: This allows the application server to use a transaction manager to support transactions across several resource managers. The contract also enables internal EIS transaction mechanisms to be used without the need for an external transaction manager.
- **Security management**: This supports a secure environment on the application server in order to protect valuable information provided by the EIS.

Optional system contracts are available covering life cycle management, work management, transaction inflow, and message inflow management, as detailed next:

- **Life cycle management**: This contract enables the application server to manage the life cycle of the resource adapter. It provides a mechanism for the application server to bootstrap a resource adapter during application server startup, or during the installation of the adapter. It also provides a means for the application server to notify the resource adapter instance when it is uninstalled, or when an orderly shutdown of the application server takes place.
- **Work management**: This contract ensures that the application manager is responsible for thread management and the thread pool. Resource adapters can transfer their activities (monitoring network end points, calling application components, and so on) as individual instances to the application server for execution. The adapter is no longer responsible for managing threads itself. Instead, the application server must create new threads for execution or take them from a pre-configured pool. However, the resource adapter continues to control the transaction context where the threads are executed under the control of the application server.
- **Transaction inflow management**: This contract enables the resource adapter to propagate a transaction imported from the EIS to the application server. It also ensures that the resource adapter transfers calls for transaction completion initiated by the EIS, or calls for crash recovery, to the application server to guarantee that the ACID properties of the transaction behavior are not lost.

ssage inflow management: This contract allows the resource adapter to vide asynchronous delivery of messages to the message end points of application server, regardless of the specific message style, semantics, l infrastructure. The contract also describes an option for expanding the plication server in order to integrate different message providers [Java ssaging Service (JMS), Java API for XML Messaging (JAXM)] using the cept of a resource adapter.

Java Business Integration (JBI)

The functionality of an ESB is described in general terms in the **Java Business Integration (JBI)** specification (Ten-Hove, Walker 2005). JBI implements a component architecture. JBI is based primarily on two constructs: service engines and binding components. The service engines contain the business logic, while the binding components merely act as a proxy for the service users (Wallrab 2005).

The tasks of a JBI component are as follows:

- Receiving and sending messages. In JBI this is carried out by the binding components.
- Providing interfaces for format conversions. The converter and the business logic needed to transform messages are referred to as the service engine in JBI.
- Installing components (binding component or service engine).
- Deploying components (binding component or service engine).
- Providing mechanisms for managing the life cycle of a component.
- Controlling and monitoring components.

Requests from one component to another are decoupled, and take the form of messages, which the JBI infrastructure passes to the recipients. JBI supports different message exchange patterns:

- **One-way**: The service consumer issues a request to the service provider. No path for reporting error messages is provided.
- **Reliable one-way**: Similar to the one-way pattern, but the provider can inform the consumer of a fault through a response path.
- **Request/response**: The service consumer issues a request to the service provider and waits for a response. In this case, the provider can also inform the consumer of a fault.
- **Request/optional response**: The service consumer issues a request to the service provider. A response is optional. Both the consumer and the provider can inform each other of faults.

JBI components

The most important JBI components are detailed in the following diagram:

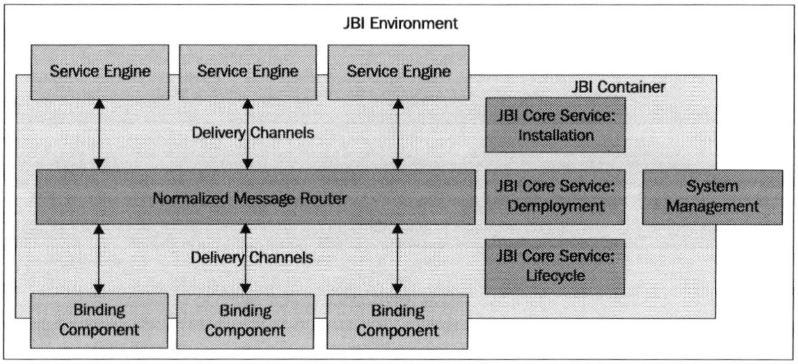

Let's take a look at these components one by one:

- **JBI environment**: A JBI environment is represented by an individual Java Virtual Machine. Therefore, JBI can take the form of an independent ESB, or can be integrated into an application server and its JVM. Where the environment is integrated into an application server, the **Enterprise JavaBean (EJB)** components installed on the server can function as service providers, or as consumers of the ESB.
- **JBI container**: This is comparable to the EJB container of a Java EE application server. The JBI environment itself is a container, which provides service engines and binding components.
- **Pluggable components**: Service engines (SEs) and binding components (BCs) are pluggable components. They are connected to the normalized message router through delivery channels, which allows them to communicate with one another.
- **Service engine (SE)**: These are service providers or consumers that are installed locally in a JBI environment. They represent the business components or the essential functionality that supports the business logic, such as **Extensible Stylesheet Language** (XSL) transformations or database accesses.
- **Binding components (BCs)**: These encapsulate the communications and decouple the communication functionality from the business components (SEs). Binding components allow remote access to distributed services, and also enable distributed services to access the JBI environment.
- **Normalized Message Router (NMR)**: This is the backbone of the JBI architecture. All communications between providers and consumers pass through this router. The NMR uses a canonical format.

- **Normalized message**: This type of message has two parts. There is the header, which contains the metadata (metadata in this context is also referred to as **message context data**), and the payload, in the form of an XML structure that contains the normalized message. The structure of the normalized message is comparable to that of XML messages from **Java Message Service** (**JMS**).
- **Delivery channel (DC)**: This connects a message source with a message target. A channel is a virtual construct that conceals the communication details from the providers and consumers and decouples them from the NMR. Delivery channels connect components (providers and consumers) to the NMR, which is responsible for coordinating communications. Channels are logical addresses in the ESB that encapsulate the physical addresses.

Service Component Architecture (SCA)

Service Component Architecture (**SCA**) is a collection of OASIS (a non-profit consortium driving the adoption of open standards for the global information society) specifications, which describe a model for developing applications and systems on the basis of an SOA (Edwards 2007). SCA models solutions as groups of service components that provide services and include references to other services. Functionality is made available externally as a service in the form of interfaces. Service components have properties that describe the specific characteristics of the components, and are used to configure them.

Services can be combined to form composites. A composite is a composition of SCA components that belong together. These components represent a coarse granular business function and form a separate, functional, reusable unit. Composite services can also contain components that are only used within these composites. The functionality of these internal components is not, however, made available externally as a service in the form of interfaces.

Bindings describe how a service can be accessed. SCA has declarative mechanisms for this purpose, which are based on open specifications. The specifications not only determine how the defined bindings that are currently available can be described, but also how extensions for new protocols should be implemented.

SCA specification

The SCA specification is made up of four parts, as detailed in the following diagram:

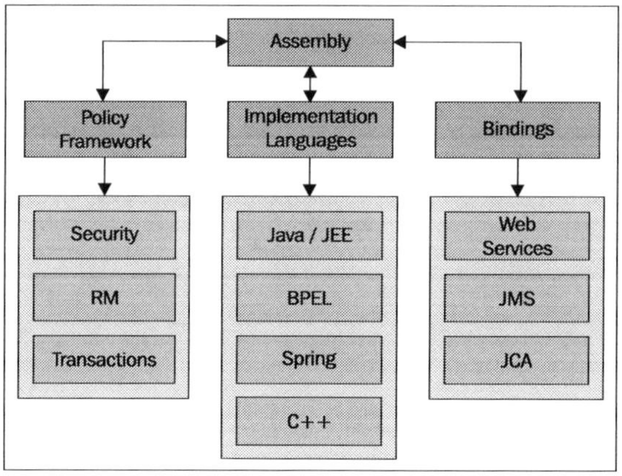

Let's discuss these four parts further:

- **SCA assembly model**: This describes how SOA applications are created with SCA. It also defines how individual modules, in the form of components, can be combined and integrated to produce more complex modules, and how these modules communicate.
- **SCA policy framework**: This defines how security, transaction behavior, message exchange, and reliable messaging can be specified declaratively for a service.
- **SCA client and implementation**: This defines how SCA components can be implemented in different programming languages and on different platforms (for example Java, .NET, C++).
- **SCA binding specification**: This describes how various access technologies and protocols (such as SOAP, JMS, RMI-IIOP, REST, HTTP) can be used.

SCA elements

SCA and SCA components include the elements detailed in the following diagram:

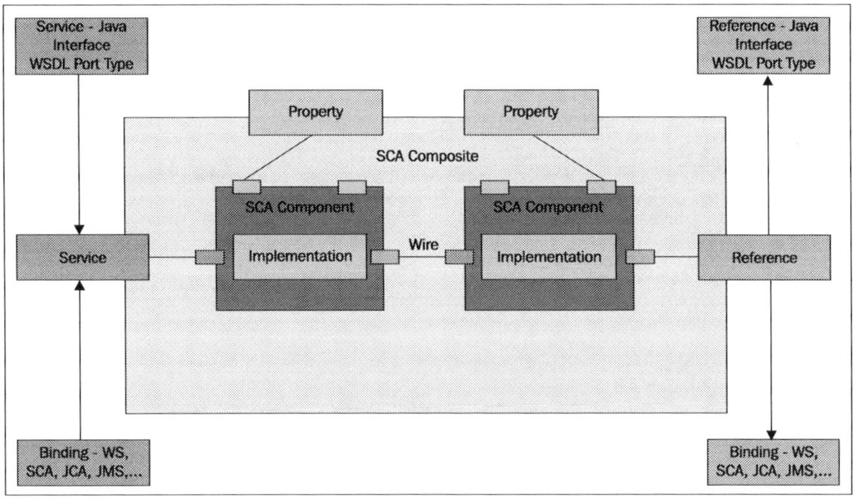

Here's a brief description of these elements:

- **Service**: A service represents the starting point for access to an SCA component or composite.
- **Reference**: A reference is a pointer to an external service.
- **Binding**: This is both an interface and a binding. In this case, an interface is an external declaration of the service, represented by a Java interface, a **Web Service Definition Language** (**WSDL**) port type, a **Business Process Execution Language** (**BPEL**) partner link, a C++ class, and so on. An interface binding can be bound to a service or a reference.
- **Property**: This is a type/value pair used to describe and configure specific characteristics of the component.
- **Implementation**: This defines the way in which an SCA component is implemented or, in other words, the form that the logic takes. The implementation types can be some Java code, for example, but can also be a human interaction.
- **Wire**: This is the mechanism that links two SCA components together. Normally, one component's reference is bound to the service offered by another component.

Composites

A composite component is a logical construct that consists of SCA components that can form part of a single process on a single computer, or can be distributed across several processes on several computers. An application can be created with a single composite. The individual SCA components that make up the composite can be implemented using the same or different technologies. SCA applications can be called by a non-SCA technology, such as a web service client or a **servlet**. They can also access external data sources and other applications.

An SCA composite is described by a configuration file. This uses an XML format, **Service Component Definition Language** (**SCDL**, or **Skiddle**), to describe the components and the details of their relationships with one another, and with other external components.

Composites and components are the core elements of every SCA application.

Service Data Objects (SDO)

Service Data Objects (**SDO**) offer a consistent model for managing data, regardless of its source system and source format (Beatty et al. 2003). SDO makes use of a Disconnected Data Architecture. SDO supports the management of data that has been decoupled from its source and transported across different systems and tiers, by subsequently synchronizing it with its source again. SCA and SDO can be used independently of one another, and their specifications have nothing in common. However, a combination of the two specifications represents a powerful and flexible tool for developing distributed applications.

The SDO specification was published jointly by BEA and IBM, standardized as **JSR 235,** and transferred to the **Open Service-Oriented Architecture (OSOA).** The current version of the specification is version 2.1 for Java, COBOL, C++, and C (Barber, Edwards 2007).

SDO architecture

SDO consists of data objects, data graphs, and data access services, as shown in the following diagram:

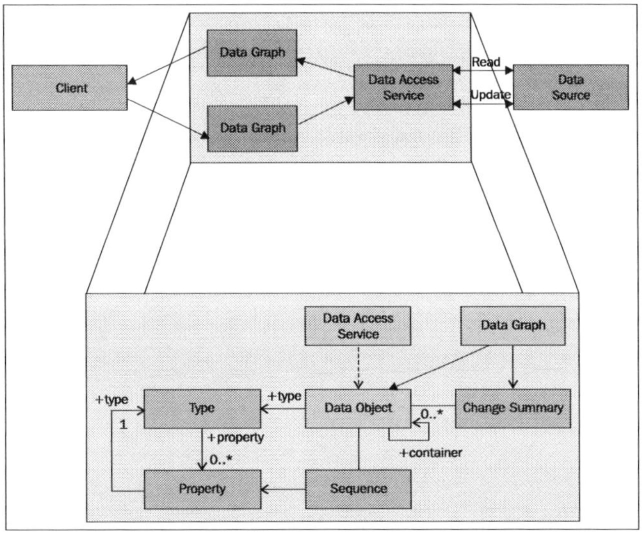

Now let's take a look at these three components:

- **Data object**: This is the object-oriented representation of the fundamental data. It encapsulates the data attributes in the form of simple values, as a reference to other objects and the descriptive metadata.
- **Data graph**: This represents a **Data Transfer Object** (DTO), which is transferred between the different tiers of an architecture. It can be made up of several individual data objects by using object graphs. These can include, for example, a master data set consisting of several detail data sets and their relationships to one another. In addition to the user data, changes to the object are included, or in other words, all the data objects that have been added, modified, and deleted are included.
- **Data access service**: This is the interface between the client and the data sources. The data access service is responsible for decoupling the applications from the physical accesses to the source systems, which hold the data. This service uses the data access object pattern.

SDO also provides metadata for describing data objects, including data types, relationships between data objects, and constraints. The metadata API is used by tools and other frameworks to simplify the development of applications that make use of SDO.

Implemented patterns

SDO implements a series of patterns, including:

- **Data Access Object** (**DAO**): The DAO encapsulates the calls to the data access layer.
- **Data Transfer Object** (**DTO**): The DTO is a transport container for data objects moving between different layers, tiers, or systems, and it reduces the number of method calls from remote interfaces.
- **Entity object** (**EO**): The EO is an object from the application domain. It represents entities from the business domain.
- **Disconnected data usage**: Data objects can be generated by data system accesses. The connection to the data system can be broken and recreated later, and changes to the data object can be propagated to the data system.
- **Optimistic concurrency semantics data access**: As a result of disconnected data usage, after the connection to the data system has been broken, the resources must be released for further accesses as part of the resource management process. An optimistic access strategy is put in place in order to maintain data consistency, despite competing accesses. When changes to data are propagated back to the data system once the connection has been re-established, the data in question is checked to determine whether it has been modified by another process in the meantime (after the initial query). This involves, for example, comparing the time stamps or counters. The original data set (the data that was read initially) may also be included with the modified data, and compared with the current data in the data system.

Process modeling

One important base technology used in the majority of integration projects consists of business process modeling tools. The modeling process is always done using graphical tools. The Trivadis Integration Architecture Blueprint envisages the usage of graphical tools that support a clearly defined modeling notation. A number of these notations are available. The most important are **Event-Driven Process Chain** (**EPC**), **Business Process Modeling Notation** (**BPMN**), and **Business Process Execution Language** (**BPEL**), which are all explained next:

Event-driven Process Chain (EPC)

The Event-driven Process Chain (EPC) is a model used to represent business processes in an organization, as part of business process modeling (Scheer, Werth 2005). The notation was developed as a part of the **Architecture of Integrated Information Systems** (**ARIS**) for modeling business processes, and is a central element of the ARIS concept (Scheer et al. 2006). An example of an EPC is shown in the following diagram:

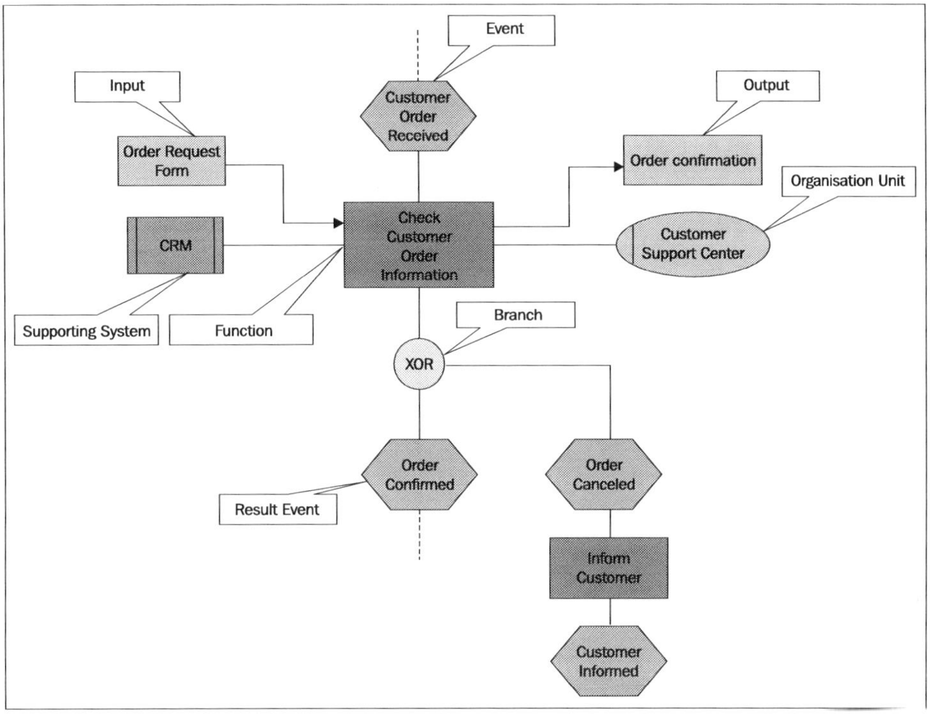

EPCs represent work processes in graphical form using semi-formal modeling language with syntax rules. This allows business processes to be systematized and parallelized, which saves time and money. As decisions are made within the process on the basis of conditions and rules, logical operators are used in the EPC (AND, OR, EXCLUSIVE OR). In addition to these operators, the basic model of the Event-Driven Process Chain includes events and functions. Objects are joined together in directional diagrams with lines and arrows in a 1:1 mapping (with the exception of logical links). In a chain of this kind, events and functions are alternate objects. This means that they form an alternating sequence, which results in a diagram being created. An important feature of the EPC is the representation of the functions that make up a process in a chronological and logical sequence.

Business Process Modeling Notation (BPMN)

The Business Process Modeling Notation (BPMN) is an OMG standard (OMG 2008). It provides symbols that enable technical and IT specialists to model business processes and workflows (White 2004). A BPMN example is shown in the following diagram:

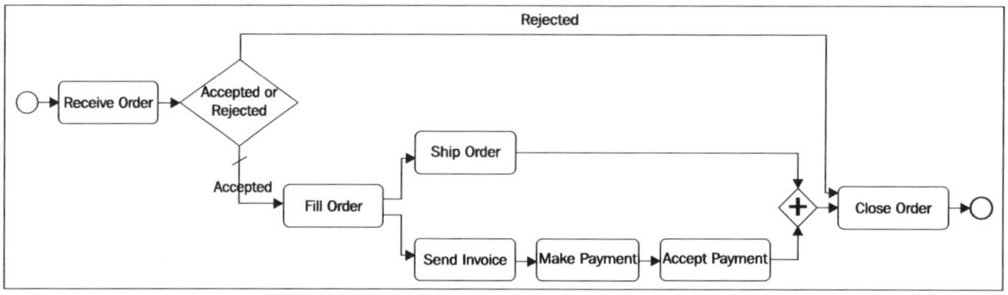

The BPMN is designed to represent business processes in graphical form. The BPMN standards document also defines the semantics, in other words, the meaning of the symbols, but it places less emphasis on this aspect and does not focus on formal definitions. BPMN diagrams are referred to as **Business Process Diagrams** (**BPD**), and are intended to provide support for experts who are representing or developing processes. The specification does not include a standardized format for storing and exchanging diagrams that are created using BPMN.

The BPMN standard defines how a BPMN diagram can be converted to BPEL, so that the processes described can be run by a software package. However, BPMN and BPEL are not able to express the same types of concepts.

> It is worth noting that BPMN models are generally underspecified, and lack some of the details required for execution.

The graphical elements of the BPMN can be broken down into:

- **Flow objects**: These are nodes in the business process diagram. Flow objects represent either an *activity* (a task to be completed), a *gateway* (decision point), or an *event*.
- **Connecting objects**: These are the links in the business process diagram. Connecting objects are either *sequence flows,* which link activities, gateways, and events, or *message flows,* which illustrate the movement of messages between different objects.
- **Swimlanes**: These are the objects used to represent participants and systems.
- **Artifacts**: Other elements such as *data objects* (the artifacts processed by a business process), *groups* (the option of creating groups to represent sub-processes), and *annotations* (comments) are referred to as artifacts.

Business Process Execution Language (BPEL)

The first versions of Business Process Execution Language (BPEL) and BPEL4WS for web services were developed by IBM, Microsoft, Siebel, BEA, SAP, and Oracle in 2002 (version 1.1 was issued in April 2003). XLANG (from Microsoft) and WSFL (from IBM) were integrated into BPEL (Andrews et al. 2003). The most recent version (version 2.0) was published in the form of a committee draft on January 31, 2007 (Alves et al. 2006).

BPEL allows a process to be described and represented. The description takes a graphical form and is created in a BPEL editor. However, other workflow modeling techniques can also be used. In contrast to the other methods, the modeled business process can directly generate the controls for the workflow engine (BPEL engine). BPEL enables various different services to be linked together to form a complete application.

BPEL distinguishes between two different types of business processes: business protocols and executable business processes. **Business protocols** are abstract process descriptions that act as interaction patterns for the **executable business processes**.

A BPEL process consists of a process interface and a process diagram. The process interface is formulated in WSDL, as every BPEL process is a web service. The process diagram defines the process flow (actions), the instancing method (correlation sets), the partners (partner link), and the fault management mechanisms (fault manager).

The process is structured using a combination of hierarchical blocks and diagrams. The blocks can be nested. In BPEL they take the form of structured activities, which are similar to the constructions of a structured programming language. One typical feature is the <switch> structured activity, which defines a conditional implementation. Structured activities control the flow of atomic activities and form the nodes of an execution tree. The atomic activities control the individual steps in a BPEL process, for example, <invoke> calls a web service.

The application of process modeling

Almost every integration project needs business processes and other workflows to be modeled. A service-oriented integration would be almost impossible without the use of BPEL. Data integrations are usually accompanied by modeling of Extract, Transform, and Load (ETL) processes. In addition, the majority of commercial ESB and middleware infrastructures use graphical tools to model the routing of messages, or have their own process modeling tools. This means that it is advisable for every integration architect to be familiar with the use of these tools. Currently, the most important process modeling notation is BPEL.

Summary

Having read this chapter, you should now have a better understanding of the base technologies related to the implementation of solutions based on the Trivadis Integration Architecture Blueprint. You should now be familiar with:

- Transactions and transaction strategies
- Open Grid Services infrastructure (OGSi)—the dynamic, hardware-independent software platform
- Java Connector Architecture (JCA)—the general architecture for connecting heterogeneous systems in the Java EE world
- Java Business Integration (JBI)—a standardization of the functions of an Enterprise Service Bus (ESB)
- Service Component Architecture (SCA)—a component model for developing applications and systems based on a SOA
- Service Data Objects (SDO)—supporting a Disconnected Data Architecture
- Process modeling and the most important standards for modeling business processes

We have now covered the fundamental concepts and technologies related to the implementation of integration solutions.

4

Best Practices for Using XML for Integration

When designing XML documents for integration, there are number of considerations to be aware of. Before designing the XML schema, it is necessary to understand the domain. You also need to consider how your application intends to receive and send documents, and how and when to go about validating those documents. It is also important to separate the XML document processing from the application's business logic processing.

The standard schemas for several vertical domains are easily available. Your first preference while designing a schema for your application is to look for a standard vertical schema. If a standard schema does not fully meet your requirements, you should consider extending a standard schema to meet your application requirements. Whether you design your own domain-specific schema or rely on standard vertical schemas, you still must understand the dynamics of mapping the application's data model to the schema. You also need to consider the processing model, and whether to use a document-centric model or an object-centric model.

Domain-Specific XML Schemas

Despite the availability of more and more vertical domain schemas, application developers still may have to define application-specific XML schemas that must be agreed upon, and shared between interoperating participants. With the introduction of modern schema languages such as XSD, which introduced strong data typing and type derivation, XML schema design shares many of the aspects of object-oriented design especially with respect to modularization and reuse.

The design of domain-specific XML schemas breaks down according to the definition of XML schema types, their relationship to other types, and any constraints to which they are subjected. The definitions of such XML schema types, relationships, and constraints are typically the result of the analysis of the application domain vocabulary (also called the business vocabulary). As much as possible, schema designers should leverage already-defined public vertical domain schema definitions to promote greater acceptance and interoperability among intended participants. The designers of new schemas should keep interoperability concerns in mind and try to allow for reuse and extensibility.

Generally, document schema design and the layout of document instances closely parallel object-oriented design. In addition, design strategies exist that identify and provide well-defined solutions to commonly recurring problems in document schema design.

Keep the following recommendations in mind when designing an XML schema:

- Adopt and develop design techniques, naming conventions, and other best practices similar to those used in object-oriented modeling to address the issues of reuse, modularization, and extensibility. Some of the common design techniques are discussed in the later sections.
- Leverage existing horizontal schemas, and vertical schemas defined within your industry, as well as the custom schemas already defined within your enterprise. You can check out `http://www.xml.org` for information on design guidelines specific to your industry like healthcare, defense, and insurance.
- Do not solely rely on self-describing element and attribute names. Comment and document custom schemas.
- Use modeling tools that support well-known schema languages such as XSD. Some of the tools are Netbeans 5.5 Enterprise Pack, Eclipse, and Visual Studio.NET. You may find many open-source tools listed at `http://xmlbeans.apache.org/docs/2.0.0/guide/tools.html`.

Keep in mind that reusing schemas may enable the reuse of the corresponding XML processing code.

Sending and Receiving XML Documents

XML schemas of documents to be consumed and produced are part of the overall exposed interface of an XML-based application. The exposed interface encompasses schemas of all documents passed along with incoming and outgoing messages regardless of the message-passing protocol—SOAP, plain HTTP, or message queuing.

Typically, an application may receive or return XML documents as follows:

- Received through a web service endpoint
- Returned to a web service client
- Through a message queue or topic when implementing a business process workflow or implementing an asynchronous web service architecture
- Exchanging XML documents through a plain-socket connection

Note that a generic XML-based application can additionally receive and return XML documents through a servlet over plain HTTP.

There are circumstances when a web service may internally exchange XML documents through a message queue or topic. When implementing an asynchronous architecture, the interaction layer of a web service may send XML documents asynchronously using messages to the processing layer. Similarly, when a web service implements a workflow, the components implementing the individual stages of the workflow may exchange XML documents using messages. From a developer's point of view, receiving or sending XML documents through a message queue or topic is similar in principle to the case of passing documents as SOAP message attachments. XML documents can be passed through a message queue or topic as text messages or in a serialized form.

Validating XML Documents

Once a document has been received or produced, a developer may—and most of the time must—validate the document against the schema to which it is supposed to conform. Validation, an important step in XML document handling, may be required to guarantee the reliability of an XML application. An application may legitimately rely on the parser to do the validation and thus avoid performing such validation itself.

However, a valid XML document may still be invalid in the application's domain. This might happen, for example, when a document is validated using DTD, because this schema language lacks capabilities to express strongly-typed data, complex unicity, and cross-reference constraints. Other modern schema languages, such as XSD, more rigorously—while still lacking some business constraint expressiveness—narrow the set of valid document instances to those that the business logic can effectively process. Regardless of the schema language, even when performing XML validation, the application is responsible for enforcing any uncovered domain-specific constraints that the document may nevertheless violate. That is, the application may have to perform its own business logic-specific validation in addition to the XML validation.

To decide where and when to validate documents, you may take into account certain considerations. Assuming a system—by system we mean a set of applications that compose a solution and that define a boundary within which trusted components can exchange information—one can enforce validation according to the following observations:

- Documents exchanged within the components of the system may not require validation.
- Documents coming from outside the system, especially when they do not originate from external trusted sources, must be validated on entry.
- Documents coming from outside the system, once validated, may be exchanged freely between internal components without further validation.

For example, a multitier e-business application that exchanges documents with trading partners through a front end enforces document validity at the front end. Not only does it check the validity of the document against its schema, but the application also ensures that the document type is a schema type that it can accept. It then may route documents to other applications or servers so that the proper services can handle them. Since they have already been validated, the documents do not require further validation. In a web service, validation of incoming documents is typically performed in the interaction layer. Therefore, the processing layer may not have to validate documents it receives from the interaction layer.

Some applications may have to receive documents that conform to different schemas or different versions of a schema. In these cases, the application cannot do the validation up front against a specific schema unless the application is given a directive within the request itself about which schema to use. If no directive is included in the request, then the application has to rely on a hint provided by the document itself. Note that to deal with successive versioning of the same schema—where the versions actually modify the overall application's interface—it sometimes may be more convenient for an application to expose a separate endpoint for each version of the schema.

To illustrate, an application must check that the document is validated against the expected schema, which is not necessarily the one to which the document declares it conforms. With DTD schemas, this checking can be done only after validation. When using DOM, the application may retrieve the system or public identifier (`SystemID` or `PublicID`) of the DTD to ensure it is the identifier of the schema expected, while when using SAX, it can be done on the fly by handling the proper event.

When relying on the schemas to which documents internally declare they are conforming (through a DTD declaration or an XSD hint), for security, and to avoid external malicious modification, you should keep your own copy of the schemas and validate against these copies. This can be done using an entity resolver, which is an interface from the SAX API (`org.xml.sax.EntityResolver`) that forcefully maps references to well-known external schemas to secured copies. An alternative to this would be to use Schematron—a simple and powerful Structural Schema Language that is not based on grammars but on finding tree patterns in the parsed document.

Mapping Schemas

After defining the application interface, and the schemas of the documents to be consumed and produced, the developer has to define how the document schemas relate or map to the data model on which the application applies its business logic. We refer to these document schemas as external schemas. These schemas may be specifically designed to meet the application's requirements, such as when no preexisting schemas are available, or they may be imposed on the developer. The latter situation, for example, may occur when the application intends to be part of an interacting group within an industry promoting standard vertical schemas (for example, UBL or ebXML schemas).

Choosing Processing Models

An XML-based application may either apply its business logic directly on consumed or produced documents, or it may apply its logic on domain-specific objects that completely or partially encapsulate the content of such documents. Domain-specific objects are Java objects that may not only encapsulate application domain-specific data, but may also embody application domain-specific behavior.

An application's business logic may directly handle documents it consumes or produces, which is called a document-centric processing model, if the logic:

- Relies on both document content and structure
- Is required to punctually modify incoming documents while preserving most of their original form, including comments, external entity references, and so forth

In a document-centric processing model, the document processing may be entangled with the business logic and may therefore introduce strong dependencies between the business logic and the schemas of the consumed and produced documents. Moreover, the document-centric processing model does not promote a clean separation between business and XML programming skills, especially when an application developer who is more focused on the implementation of the business logic must additionally master one or several of the XML processing APIs.

There are cases that require a document-centric processing model, such as:

- The schema of the processed documents is only partially known and therefore cannot be completely bound to domain-specific objects; the application edits only the known part of the documents before forwarding them for further processing.
- Because the schemas of the processed documents may vary or change greatly, it is not possible to hard-code or generate the binding of the documents to domain-specific objects; a more flexible solution is required, such as one using DOM with XPath.

A typical document-centric example is an application that implements a data-driven workflow: Each stage of the workflow processes only specific information from the incoming document contents, and there is no central representation of the content of the incoming documents. A stage of the workflow may receive a document from an earlier stage, extract information from the document, apply some business logic on the extracted information, and potentially modify the document before sending it to the next stage.

Generally, it is best to have the application's business logic directly handle documents only in exceptional situations, and to do so with great care. You should instead consider applying the application's business logic on domain-specific objects that completely or partially encapsulate the content of consumed or produced documents. This helps to isolate the business logic from the details of XML processing.

A pure object-centric processing model requires XML-related issues to be kept at the periphery of an application—that is, in the web service interaction layer closest to the service endpoint, or, for more classical applications, in the web tier. In this case, XML serves only as an additional presentation medium for the application's inputs and outputs.

Note that the object - and document-centric processing models may not be exclusive of one another. An application may be globally document-centric and exchange documents between its components, and some components may themselves locally process part of the documents using an object-centric processing model. Each component may use the most suitable processing model for performing its function. For example, consider an application in the automobile industry. An automobile manufacturing company may interact with its customers using a B2C model and at the same time integrate with its business partners using a B2B model. The customer interaction in this case may be document-centric, while the partner interaction that can be more tightly coupled could be object-centric.

Fragmenting Incoming XML Documents

When your service's business logic operates on the contents of an incoming XML document, it is a good idea to break XML documents into logical fragments when appropriate. The processing logic receives an XML document containing all information for processing a request. However, the XML document usually has well-defined segments for different entities, and each segment contains the details about a specific entity.

Fragmenting an incoming document can be viewed as a centralized implementation of the flexible mapping design. Fragmenting an incoming document, by suppressing redundant parsing of the incoming document and limiting the exchanges between stages to the strictly relevant data, improves performance over a straightforward implementation of flexible mapping. However, it loses some flexibility because the workflow dispatching logic is required to specifically know about (and therefore depend on) the document fragments and formats expected by the different stages.

Fragmenting a document has the following benefits:

- It avoids extra processing and exchange of superfluous information throughout the workflow.
- It maximizes privacy because it limits sending sensitive information through the workflow.
- It centralizes some of the XML processing tasks of the workflow and therefore simplifies the overall implementation of the workflow.
- It provides greater flexibility to workflow error handling as each stage handles only business logic-related errors while the workflow dispatching logic handles document parsing and validation errors.

Design Recommendations

When you design an XML-based application, specifically one that is a web service, you must make certain decisions concerning the processing of the content of incoming XML documents. Essentially, you decide the "how, where, and what" of the processing: You decide the technology to use for this process, where to perform the processing, and the form of the content of the processing.

In summary, keep in mind the following recommendations:

- When designing application-specific schemas, promote reuse, modularization, and extensibility, and leverage existing vertical and horizontal schemas.

- When implementing a pure object-centric processing model, keep XML on the boundary of your system as much as possible—that is, in the web service interaction layer closest to the service endpoint, or, for more classical applications, in the presentation layer. Map document content to domain-specific objects as soon as possible.
- When implementing a document-centric processing model, consider using the flexible mapping technique. This technique allows the different components of your application to handle XML in a way that is most appropriate for each of them.
- Strongly consider validation at system entry points of your processing model—specifically, validation of input documents where the source is not trusted.
- When consuming or producing documents, as much as possible express your documents in terms of abstract `Source` and `Result` objects that are independent from the actual XML-processing API you are using.
- Consider a "meet-in-the-middle" mapping design strategy when you want to decouple the application data model from the external schema that you want to support.
- Abstract XML processing from the business logic processing using the XML document editor design strategy. This promotes separation of skills and independence from the actual API used.

Tips for Designing XML Schemas

While designing an XML Schema, make sure that you design based on your system-specific requirements. There is more than one way of designing a schema and they all might fit your architecture. Even before you start designing your schemas, you should have the design objectives captured and documented for further reference.

Enumerating the design objectives is very important prior to designing your schema because you may or may not be able to refine your schema based on the inequity you discover later. The following sections discuss some of the common dilemmas of Schema design.

Default Namespace—targetNamespace or XMLSchema?

When designing a schema, you have three options pertaining to namespace. They are:

1. Making XMLSchema (1.http://www.w3.org/2001/XMLSchema) as the default namespace.
2. Making the targetNamespace (user defined) as the default namespace.
3. Not specifying the default namespace at all.

Which one of the above options is the best practice for designing your schema?

The XML Schema you design should have at least two namespaces (except for no-namespace schemas). They are:

1. XMLSchema namespace (1.http://www.w3.org/2001/XMLSchema)
2. targetNamespace

The possible case for designing your schema is restricted to the below mentioned options:

Case 1: Make XMLSchema the default namespace, and explicitly qualify all references to components in the targetNamespace.

The snippet below is from a sample purchase order schema, which explains the Case 1 usage.

```
<?xml version="1.0"?>
<schema xmlns="http://www.w3.org/2001/XMLSchema"
            targetNamespace="http://www.porder.org"
            xmlns:po=" http://www.porder.org"
            elementFormDefault="qualified">
   <include schemaLocation="po.xsd"/>
   <element name="purchaseOrder">
       <complexType>
          <sequence>
              <element name="shipTo">
                 <complexType>
                     <sequence>
                        <element ref="po:Address"
                           maxOccurs="unbounded"/>
                     </sequence>
                 </complexType>
              </element>
          </sequence>
       </complexType>
   </element>
</schema>
```

This schema includes the purchase order (`po.xsd`) schema, which contains the declaration of the `Address` element. The `Address` element is defined as follows:

```
<xs:complexType name="Address">
    <xs:sequence>
        <xs:element name="name"   type="xs:string"/>
        <xs:element name="street" type="xs:string"/>
        <xs:element name="city"   type="xs:string"/>
        <xs:element name="state"  type="xs:string"/>
        <xs:element name="zip"    type="xs:decimal"/>
    </xs:sequence>
    <xs:attribute name="country" type="xs:NMTOKEN"
     fixed="US"/>
</xs:complexType>
```

The schema shown in the first code snippet refers to the above schema's `Address` complex type.

Note that in this case, `XMLSchema` is the default namespace. That is the reason why we don't have namespace qualifiers for our components like `element`, `complexType`, and `sequence`.

From first code snippet, it is evident that the namespace prefix, '**po**' is associated with the `targetNamespace`. And any reference to the components in the targetNamespace is explicitly qualified by '**po**'.

Case 2: Make the `targetNamespace` the default namespace, and explicitly qualify all components from the `XMLSchema` namespace.

The snippet below is from a sample purchase order schema, which explains the current usage.

```
<?xml version="1.0"?>
<xsd:schema xmlns:xsd="http://www.w3.org/2001/XMLSchema"
            targetNamespace="http://www.porder.org"
            xmlns=» http://www.porder.org»
            elementFormDefault=»qualified»>
   <xsd:include schemaLocation=»po.xsd»/>
   <xsd:element name=»purchaseOrder">
        <xsd:complexType>
           <xsd:sequence>
              <xsd:element name="shipTo">
                 <xsd:complexType>
                    <xsd:sequence>
                       <xsd:element ref="Address"
                          maxOccurs="unbounded"/>
```

```
                    </xsd:sequence>
                </xsd:ComplexType>
            </xsd:element>
        </xsd:sequence>
    </xsd:complexType>
  </xsd:element>
</xsd:schema>
```

In the above snippet `xsd` points to `XMLSchema` namespace and the default namespace is `targetNamespace` and hence a namespace qualifier is not required for the 'Address' as Case 1.

Case 3: No Default Namespace—qualify both `XMLSchema` and `targetNamespace`.

The snippet below is from a sample purchase order schema, which explains the current usage.

```
<?xml version="1.0"?>
<xsd:schema xmlns:xsd="http://www.w3.org/2001/XMLSchema"
            targetNamespace="http://www.porder.org"
            xmlns:po=" http://www.porder.org"
            elementFormDefault="qualified">
   <xsd:include schemaLocation="po.xsd"/>
   <xsd:element name="purchaseOrder">
        <xsd:complexType>
           <xsd:sequence>
              <xsd:element name="shipTo">
                 <xsd:complexType>
                    <xsd:sequence>
                       <xsd:element ref="po:Address"
                          maxOccurs="unbounded"/>
                    </xsd:sequence>
                 </cxsd:omplexType>
              </xsd:element>
           </xsd:sequence>
        </xsd:complexType>
   </xsd:element>
</xsd:schema>
```

In the above snippet, `xsd` points to the `XMLSchema` namespace and `po` points to the `targetNamespace`. The `XMLSchema` elements are fully qualified along with reference to 'Address'.

The following table discusses the pros and cons of the cases discussed in the earlier sections.

Case	Pros	Cons
1	If your schema is referencing components from multiple namespaces then this approach gives a consistent way of referring to the components (i.e., you always qualify the reference).	Schemas that have no targetNamespace must be designed so that the XMLSchema components (element, complexType, sequence, etc.) are qualified. If you adopt this approach to designing your schemas then in some of your schemas you will qualify the XMLSchema components and in other schemas you won't qualify the XMLSchema components. Changing from one way of designing your schemas to another way can be confusing.
2	Schemas that have no targetNamespace must be designed so that the XMLSchema components (element, complexType, sequence, etc.) are qualified. This approach will work whether your schema has a targetNamespace or not. Thus, with this approach you have a consistent approach to designing your schemas —always namespace-qualify the XMLSchema components.	If your schema is referencing components from multiple namespaces then for some references you will namespace-qualify the reference, whereas other times you will not (i.e., when you are referencing components in the targetNamespace). This variable use of namespace qualifiers in referencing components can be confusing.
3	1. Schemas that have no targetNamespace must be designed so that the XMLSchema components (element, complexType, sequence, etc.) are qualified. With this approach, all your schemas are designed in a consistent fashion. 2. If your schema is referencing components from multiple namespaces then this approach gives a consistent way of referencing components (i.e., you always qualify the reference).	Very cluttered: being very explicit by namespace qualifying all components and all references can be annoying when reading the schema.

> This is a human readability issue as it does not affect the semantics of the XML schema at all. The cleanest and simplest (but not the most compact) approach is Case 2.
>
> If your schema has a suggested prefix (like `wsdl:` for the WSDL namespace) then use that prefix otherwise use "`tns`" which stands for Target Name Space.

Localize Namespace vs. Expose Namespaces

The namespaces of the elements and the attributes that a schema defines may be localized within the schema itself. The alternative to this would be to expose the namespaces in instance documents. We will compare and contrast the two approaches.

A typical schema will reuse elements and types from multiple schemas, each with different namespaces. A schema, then, may comprise components from multiple namespaces. Thus, when a schema is designed the schema designer must decide whether or not the origin (namespace) of each element should be exposed in the instance documents.

A binary switch attribute in the schema is used to control the hiding/exposure of namespaces: by setting `elementFormDefault="unqualified"` the namespaces will be hidden (localized) within the schema, and by setting `elementFormDefault="qualified"` the namespaces will be exposed in instance documents.

All Schemas must have a consistent value for `elementFormDefault`.

Be sure to note that `elementFormDefault` applies just to the schema that it is in. It does not apply to schemas that it includes or imports. Consequently, if you want to hide namespaces then **all** schemas involved must have set `elementFormDefault="unqualified"`. Likewise, if you want to expose namespaces then all schemas involved must have set `elementFormDefault="qualified"`.

Requirements for Localizing the Schema

There are two requirements on an element for its namespace to be localized (hidden) from instance documents:

1. The value of `elementFormDefault` must be "unqualified".
2. The element must not be globally declared. For example:

```
<?xml version="1.0"?>
    <xsd:schema ...>
       <xsd:element name="book">
       ...
    </xsd:schema ...>
```

The element `book` can never have its namespace hidden from instance documents, regardless of the value of `elementFormDefault`.

`book` is a *global* element (i.e., an immediate child of `<schema>`) and therefore must always be qualified. To enable namespace hiding, the element must be a local element.

> Whenever you create a schema, make two copies of it. The copies should be identical, except that in one copy you set `elementFormDefault="qualified"`, whereas in the other copy you set `elementFormDefault="unqualified"`. If you make two versions of all your schemas then people who use your schemas will be able to implement either design approach—hide (localize) namespaces, or expose namespaces. Note that exposing namespaces helps in avoiding name collisions.

Advantages of Localizing Component Namespaces within the Schema

The instance document is simple. It's easy to read and understand. There are no namespace qualifiers cluttering up the document, except for the one on the document element. The knowledge of where the schema got its components is irrelevant and localized to the schema.

Advantages of Exposing Namespaces in Instance Documents

If your company spends the time and money to create a reusable schema component, and makes it available to the marketplace, then you will most likely want recognition for that component.

Another case where it is desirable to expose namespaces, is when processing instance documents. Oftentimes, when processing instance documents the namespace is required to determine how an element is to be processed (e.g., "if the element comes from this namespace then we'll process it in this fashion, if it comes from this other namespace then we'll process it in a different fashion"). If the namespaces are hidden, then your application is forced to do a lookup in the schema for every element. This will be unacceptably slow.

Global vs. Local Declaration

A component (`element`, `complexType`, or `simpleType`) is "global" if it is an immediate child of `<schema>`, whereas it is "local" if it is not an immediate child of `<schema>`, i.e., it is nested within another component.

Below is a snippet of an XML instance document. We will explore the different design strategies using this example.

```
<Book>
   <Title>SOA and POA</Title>
   <Publisher>Packt</Publisher >
</Book>
```

Russian Doll and Salami Slice Designs

The Russian Doll design approach has a schema structure mirroring the instance document structure, e.g., declare a `Book` element and within it declare a `Title` element followed by a `Publisher` element:

```
<xsd:element name="Book">
   <xsd:complexType>
       <xsd:sequence>
          <xsd:element name="Title" type="xsd:string"/>
          <xsd:element name="Publisher" type="xsd:string"/>
        </xsd:sequence>
   </xsd:complexType>
</element>
```

The instance document has all its components bundled together. Likewise, the schema is designed to bundle together all its element declarations.

In Salami Slice design, we disassemble the instance document into its individual components. In the schema, we define each component (as an element declaration), and then assemble them together:

```
<xsd:element name="Title" type="xsd:string"/>
   <xsd:element name="Publisher" type="xsd:string"/>
   <xsd:element name="Book">
       <xsd:complexType>
           <xsd:sequence>
              <xsd:element ref="Title"/>
              <xsd:element ref="Publisher"/>
           </xsd:sequence>
       </xsd:complexType>
   </xsd:element>
```

Note how the schema declared each component individually (`Title`, and `Publisher`) and then assembled them together in the creation of the `Book` component.

> **Best Practice**
>
> Use Salami Slice design when your task requires that you make available to instance document authors the option to use element substitution. When minimizing size and coupling of components is of utmost concern then use the Russian Doll design.

Element vs. Type

When should an item be declared as an element versus when should it be defined as a type? XML Schema provides two constructs for tagging data in XML instances elements and types; which construct to employ is not always clear. While data can often be stored as attributes or elements, there are a number of constraints on attributes that generally impact one's decision.

Consider this example:

Should `Title` be declared as an element?

```
<xsd:element name="Title">
     ...
</xsd:element>
```

or as a type?

```
<xsd:complexType name="Title">
     ...
</xsd:complexType>
```

> **Best Practice**
>
> When in doubt, make it a type. You can always create an element from the type, if needed. With a type, other elements can reuse that type.

Example: If you cannot decide whether to make `Title` an element or a type, then make it a type:

```
<xsd:complexType name="Title">
...
</xsd:complexType>
```

If you decide later that you need a `Title` element, you can create one using the `Title` type:

```
<xsd:element name="Title" type="Title"/>
```

If the item is not intended to be an element in instance documents then define it as a type.

Example: If you will *never* see this in an instance document:

```
<Title>
<>
...
</Title>
```

then define `Title` as a `complexType`. If the item is intended to be used as an element in instance documents and other elements are to be allowed to substitute for the element, then it must be declared as an `element`.

Suppose that we would like to enable instance document authors to use interchangeably the vocabulary `Title` and `BookName`,

```
<xsd:Title>
...
</xsd:Title>
...
<xsd:BookName>
...
</xsd:BookName>
```

To enable this substitutable-tag-name capability, `Title` and `BookName` must be declared as elements, and made members of a `substitutionGroup`:

```
<xsd:element name="Title">
...
</xsd:element>
<xsd:element name="BookName" substitutionGroup="Title"/>
```

Zero, One, or Many Namespaces

In a project where multiple schemas are created, should we give each schema a different `targetNamespace`, or should we give all the schemas the same `targetNamespace`, or should some of the schemas have no `targetNamespace`? In a typical project, many schemas will be created. The schema designer is then confronted with this issue: "shall I define one `targetNamespace` for all the schemas, or shall I create a different `targetNamespace` for each schema, or shall I have some schemas with no `targetNamespace`?"

Here are the three design approaches for dealing with this issue:

1. Heterogeneous Namespace Design: Give each schema a different `targetNamespace`.
2. Homogeneous Namespace Design: Give all schemas the same `targetNamespace`.
3. Chameleon Namespace Design: Give the "main" schema a `targetNamespace` and give no `targetNamespace` to the "supporting" schemas (the no-namespace supporting schemas will take on the `targetNamespace` of the main schema, just like a Chameleon). When a schema uses Chameleon components those components become part of the including Schema's `targetNamespace`, just as though the schema author had typed the element declarations and type definitions inline. If the schema includes multiple no-namespace schemas then there will be a chance of name collisions. In fact, the schema may end up not being able to use some of the no-namespace schemas because their use results in name collisions with other Chameleon components.

> **Best Practices**
>
> When you are reusing schemas that *someone else* created you should `<import>` those schemas, i.e., use the Heterogeneous Namespace design. It is a bad idea to copy those components into our namespace, for two reasons:. soon your local copies would get out of sync with the other schemas, and you lose interoperability with any existing applications that process the other schema's components.

Use the Heterogeneous Namespace Design

1. When there are multiple elements with the same name (avoid name collision).
2. When there is a need to visually identify in instance documents the origin/ lineage of each element/attribute. In this design, the components come from different namespaces, so you have the ability to identify in instance documents that "element A comes from schema X".

Use the Homogeneous Namespace Design

1. When all of your schemas are conceptually related.
2. When there is no need to visually identify in instance documents the origin of each element/attribute. In this design, all components come from the same namespace, so you lose the ability to identify in instance documents that "element A comes from schema X".

Use the Chameleon Design

1. With schemas that contain components that have no inherent semantics by themselves.
2. With schemas that contain components that have semantics only in the context of an including schema.
3. When you don't want to hard-code a namespace to a schema, rather you want including schemas to be able to provide their own application-specific namespace to the schema.

Using XSL for Transformation

With the growing popularity of XML as a medium to interact with different systems, more and more organizations are turning to XML to solve their interoperability issues. And with architects trying to achieve a clear demarcation between display and business logic, XSL is gaining importance. XSL is basically an XML document tree conforming to a schema that is applied to a XML tree to produce an output tree.

XSL can be used to define how an XML file should be displayed by transforming the XML file into a format that is recognizable to a browser. One such format is HTML. Normally XSL does this by transforming each XML element into an HTML element.

XSL can also add completely new elements into the output file, or remove elements. It can rearrange and sort the elements, test and make decisions about which elements to display, and a lot more.

For more information on using XSL to transform XML documents, read the XML tutorial at `http://www.w3schools.com/xsl/`.

This section discusses a list of the best practices to be followed when writing XSL stylesheets.

xsl:import and xsl:include

The `xsl:include` instruction is similar to the `include` instruction available in several programming languages. The XSLT processor replaces it with the contents of the stylesheet named in the `href` attribute. For example, the following stylesheet includes the `attach.xsl` stylesheet for transformation processing.

```
<xsl:stylesheet xmlns:xsl="http://www.w3.org/1999/XSL/Transform"
     version="1.0">
  <xsl:include href="attach.xsl"/>
  <xsl:template match="po_name">
```

```
    <p><xsl:apply-templates/></p>
  </xsl:template>
</xsl:stylesheet>
```

If `attach.xsl` looks like this,

```
<xsl:stylesheet xmlns:xsl="http://www.w3.org/1999/XSL/Transform"
     version="1.0">
  <xsl:template match="emphasis">
   <b><xsl:apply-templates/></b>
  </xsl:template>
</xsl:stylesheet>
```

the XSLT processor will treat:

```
<xsl:stylesheet xmlns:xsl="http://www.w3.org/1999/XSL/Transform"
     version="1.0">
  <xsl:include href="attach.xsl"/>
  <xsl:template match="po_name">
   <p><xsl:apply-templates/></p>
  </xsl:template>
</xsl:stylesheet>
```

as:

```
<xsl:stylesheet xmlns:xsl="http://www.w3.org/1999/XSL/Transform"
     version="1.0">
  <xsl:template match="emphasis">
   <b><xsl:apply-templates/></b>
  </xsl:template>
  <xsl:template match="po_name">
   <p><xsl:apply-templates/></p>
  </xsl:template>
</xsl:stylesheet>
```

The included stylesheet must still be a complete and well formed XML document.

> An included stylesheet may in turn include other stylesheets, and they may include other stylesheets. There's no limit to the levels of inclusion that you can use, although the more you do it, the more complexity you have to keep track of.

The `xsl:include` element can be included anywhere you want in a stylesheet, as long as it's a top-level element, that is, a child of the `xsl:stylesheet` element that makes up the main body of the stylesheet.

Using `xsl:include` doesn't change XSLT's approach to multiple template rules that apply to the same node. If the XSLT processor can't find one template that is more specific than another for a particular source tree node, it's an error. Using `xsl:include` does increase the chance of this error happening, especially if you include stylesheets that include other stylesheets, because it's harder to keep track of the full collection of template rules being grouped together.

The `xsl:import` instruction is similar to `xsl:include` except that instructions in the imported stylesheet can be be overridden by instructions in the importing stylesheet and in any included stylesheet. For example, the following `makehtml2.xsl` stylesheet tells the XSLT processor to import the `attach.xsl` stylesheet.

```
<xsl:stylesheet xmlns:xsl="http://www.w3.org/1999/XSL/Transform"
     version="1.0">
  <xsl:import href="attach.xsl"/>
  <xsl:template match="po_name">
   <p><xsl:apply-templates/></p>
  </xsl:template>
</xsl:stylesheet>
```

If `attach.xsl` looks like this,

```
<xsl:stylesheet xmlns:xsl="http://www.w3.org/1999/XSL/Transform"
     version="1.0">
  <xsl:template match="po_name">
   <h1><xsl:apply-templates/></h1>
  </xsl:template>
</xsl:stylesheet>
```

the XSLT processor will treat:

```
<xsl:stylesheet xmlns:xsl="http://www.w3.org/1999/XSL/Transform"
     version="1.0">
  <xsl:import href="attach.xsl"/>
  <xsl:template match="po_name">
   <p><xsl:apply-templates/></p>
  </xsl:template>
</xsl:stylesheet>
```

as:

```
<xsl:stylesheet xmlns:xsl="http://www.w3.org/1999/XSL/Transform"
     version="1.0">

  <xsl:template match="po_name">
   <p><xsl:apply-templates/></p>
  </xsl:template>

</xsl:stylesheet>
```

The `attach.xsl` stylesheet's `"po_name"` template rule was ignored while importing because of the existing template rule with the same match.

> Whether you want to use `xsl:import` or `xsl:include` depends on whether you want to override some of the templates that are defined in the imported stylesheet: if you do, then use `xsl:import`, otherwise, use `xsl:include`. Use `<xsl:import>` to import common, general-purpose rules into a stylesheet designed to handle the specific transformation. If you can help it, don't `xsl:import` any more `xsl` than you need.

Securing XML Documents

In the last section, we discussed various best practices for designing your XML documents in web services. However, the web services model brings into the system unique security challenges because the business data in the form of XML documents may be required to travel across untrusted networks and has the chance of being manipulated by external systems.

Throughout the entire business transaction, different classes of users and systems need access to the entire business transaction. If any part of this chain is compromised, the whole business application deployed as a service will fail.

Web services are inherently about how to share the process of computing across a distributed network of systems. Web services' communication channel being XML, messages are text-based, readable, and self describing.

XML Security Threats

All the components in web services are described in XML. SOAP and all the WS -Security specifications are XML formats. Hence it just makes sense for expressing security data in XML format. Fortunately, there has been no need to invent new cryptography technologies for XML. The XML security standards have used existing cryptography directly. XML-based data transfer has emerged as the standard for organizations to exchange business data. As with all communications over the public Internet, XML-based transfers have their own set of vulnerabilities to confront. Like any other document exchange, XML document exchange must support the usual security measures which are Confidentiality, Integrity, Authenticity, and Non-Repudiation. The following list illustrates some specific XML security threats:

- **Schema Altering**—Manipulation of WS schema to alter the data processed by the application.
- **XML Parameter Tampering**—Injection of malicious scripts or content into XML parameters
- **Coercive Parsing**—Injection of malicious content into the XML
- **Oversized Payload**—Sending oversized files to create an XDoS attack
- **Recursive Payload**—Sending mass amounts of nested data to create an XDoS attack against an XML parser
- **XML Routing Detours**—Redirecting sensitive data within the XML path
- **External Entity Attack**—An attack on an application that parses XML input from suspicious sources using an incorrectly configured XML parser

These threats pose potentially serious problems to developers creating applications, components, and systems that depend on XML data. The solution for the above problems is XML Encryption.

XML Encryption

XML Encryption provides end-to-end security for applications that require secure exchange of structured data. XML itself is the most popular technology for structuring data, and therefore XML-based encryption is the natural way to handle complex requirements for security in data interchange applications.

XML Encryption is a process for encrypting and decrypting parts of XML documents. Most of today's encryption schemes use transport-level techniques that encrypt an entire request and response stream between a sender and receiver, offering zero visibility into contents of the interchange to intermediaries. Content-level encryption converts document fragments into illegible ciphertext, while other elements remain legible as plaintext.

Some features of XML encryption are:

1. The ability to encrypt a complete XML file
2. The ability to encrypt a single element of an XML file
3. The ability to encrypt only the contents of an XML element
4. The ability to encrypt binary data within an XML file

Encrypting an XML File

Here's a short sample XML file that can serve to demonstrate XML encryption:

```
<?xml version='1.0'?>
<POInfo xmlns='http://packtpub.com/payments'>
  <Name>FJ</Name>
  <Amount>125.00</Amount>
  <CreditCardNumber>1234-5678-4564-4321</CreditCardNumber>
  <Date>July 6, 2006</Date>
</POInfo>
```

When you encrypt an entire XML file, the process simply replaces the root element (`<POInfo>` in the sample) with an `<EncryptedData>` element that contains the encryption details, including the encrypted content.

Here is how the encrypted file will look:

```
<?xml version="1.0" encoding="UTF-8"?>
<xenc:EncryptedData
   xmlns:xenc="http://www.w3.org/2001/04/xmlenc#"
   Type="http://www.w3.org/2001/04/xmlenc#Element">
   <xenc:EncryptionMethod
      Algorithm="http://www.w3.org/2001/04/xmlenc#aes128-cbc"
      xmlns:xenc="http://www.w3.org/2001/04/xmlenc#"/>
   <ds:KeyInfo xmlns:ds="http://www.w3.org/2000/09/xmldsig#">
      <xenc:EncryptedKey
         xmlns:xenc="http://www.w3.org/2001/04/xmlenc#">
         <xenc:EncryptionMethod
            Algorithm="http://www.w3.org/2001/04/xmlenc#kw-tripledes"
            xmlns:xenc="http://www.w3.org/2001/04/xmlenc#"/>
         <xenc:CipherData
            xmlns:xenc="http://www.w3.org/2001/04/xmlenc#">
            <xenc:CipherValue
               xmlns:xenc="http://www.w3.org/2001/04/xmlenc#">
               MKeT0ZmHFLwnZaSXO+oZSxlSJ5/BqvblqG76B3nOMU0=
            </xenc:CipherValue>
         </xenc:CipherData>
      </xenc:EncryptedKey>
   </ds:KeyInfo>
   <xenc:CipherData
      xmlns:xenc="http://www.w3.org/2001/04/xmlenc#">
      <xenc:CipherValue
         xmlns:xenc="http://www.w3.org/2001/04/xmlenc#">
          +M/Tamk/62Lut4HqLpU/es9sdhnNTTpasbeszN8GN8EAJZsX0vvClcKEW
          UAgIdbvyJpprQ+jUIiWJKTz1X3L6VAefHqO963pU3bzmGMo
```

```
        pHLqS1Eg7iAPFhKV1PJclyswyyepEjyu+bOgqzgGnS1XA0/V
        NP7kLK70rB2Zb0DSbaCi+7HjTNGWF9YKtPIP5bvrs5xw+x
        HnKO++2EuqzK+deD7mCu8w6sG9vmRCrUR99Mx1QDZon9a2962ZD
        FSwoIJKg5I83GzOU+RObBBUme+yTf7UWybEiwtHp5ZgvuaQYJA=
      </xenc:CipherValue>
    </xenc:CipherData>
</xenc:EncryptedData>
```

Encrypting a Single Element

To encrypt a single element of an XML file, you specify the desired child element, rather than the root element of the input file as the element to encrypt. The following snippet shows the results of encrypting only the `<CreditCardNumber>` element of the sample file.

```
<?xml version="1.0" encoding="UTF-8"?>
<POInfo xmlns="http://jeffhanson.com/payments">
  <Name>John Doe</Name>
  <Amount>125.00</Amount>
  <xenc:EncryptedData
    xmlns:xenc="http://www.w3.org/2001/04/xmlenc#"
    Type="http://www.w3.org/2001/04/xmlenc#Element">
    <xenc:EncryptionMethod
      Algorithm="http://www.w3.org/2001/04/xmlenc#aes128-cbc"
      xmlns:xenc="http://www.w3.org/2001/04/xmlenc#"/>
    <ds:KeyInfo xmlns:ds="http://www.w3.org/2000/09/xmldsig#">
      <xenc:EncryptedKey
        xmlns:xenc="http://www.w3.org/2001/04/xmlenc#">
        <xenc:EncryptionMethod
          Algorithm=
            "http://www.w3.org/2001/04/xmlenc#kw-tripledes"
          xmlns:xenc="http://www.w3.org/2001/04/xmlenc#"/>
        <xenc:CipherData
          xmlns:xenc="http://www.w3.org/2001/04/xmlenc#">
          <xenc:CipherValue
            xmlns:xenc="http://www.w3.org/2001/04/xmlenc#">
             6zhAcEW7KIKrbSjEOkXDrVkmws5zhQQLDO4YYW+RfRY=
          </xenc:CipherValue>
        </xenc:CipherData>
      </xenc:EncryptedKey>
    </ds:KeyInfo>
    <xenc:CipherData
      xmlns:xenc="http://www.w3.org/2001/04/xmlenc#">
      <xenc:CipherValue
        xmlns:xenc="http://www.w3.org/2001/04/xmlenc#">
```

```
            JqsRmdSoS+PXqCe80Y8zNiQ49sHTLNaAgHX1Ja7d+u9fv
            TFBrkBMK7C7EHsQTglZ3yT9yCZDuFnjBoQTLULKqOy71Qw
            EPRPObtYLPIJgy1vUdNrw47uDmJ/R5r/B0SH37HN8mfNv
            i50zPt1qPxxRwA==
         </xenc:CipherValue>
      </xenc:CipherData>
   </xenc:EncryptedData>
   <Date>July 6, 2005</Date>
</POInfo>
```

Notice that the encryption process replaced the `<CreditCardNumber>` tag and its contents with an `<EncryptedData>` tag, while leaving the siblings of the `<CreditCardNumber>` element unaltered.

This type of encryption can be performed using XML Signature and Encryption. The interested reader may look up the implementation at the Apache site (`http://xml.apache.org/security/`).

Best practices for XML encryption, can be summarized as follows:

- It is good to have standard element tags for representing encrypted elements within the XML documents. This will enable parsers to better understand encrypted elements and data during the validation process.
- It is necessary to provide means for encrypting only the desired elements within an XML document instead of encrypting the whole document. This will pave the way for incorporating several confidential data elements that are intended for different recipients within a single XML document.
- There should be standard mechanisms for exchanging the secret keys used for encryption and decryption processes.
- The standard should allow encryption of different parts of the document with different keys, so that multiple recipients can decrypt only those portions that are intended for them.
- The standards should be adaptable to both ASCII and binary data.
- The standards should be adaptable to different cryptographic algorithms.
- The standards should work along with other XML security standards and specifications.

SSL versus XML Encryption

Why do we need exclusive standards and methodology for XML encryption when we already have established technologies like Secure Socket Layers (SSL) and Transport Security Layer (TSL), which also use cryptographic concepts to secure communications?

Although SSL and TSL are good for securing communications across two parties, they are not suitable for multi-party interactions, which is a typical characteristic of XML/web service interactions. Also, SSL and TSL do not have the capacity to encrypt only specific parts of the document or to encrypt different portions of the document using different keys—which are critical to XML encryption.

SSL guarantees security of payload during the transit. However, when the payload reaches a node, it is unprotected. Also, SSL is a point-to-point security mechanism where as XML encryption guarantees end-to-end security.

XML Signatures

XML Signature is a W3C recommendation that defines XML syntax for digital signatures. It is used by various web technologies such as SOAP, SAML, and others.

XML signatures will enable a sender to cryptographically sign data, and the signatures can then be used as authentication credentials or a way to check data integrity. This also guarantees non-repudiation.

XML signatures can be applied to any XML resource, such as XML, an HTML page, binary-encoded data such as a GIF file, and XML-encoded data. The primary feature of the XML digital signature is its ability to sign only specific portions of the XML document just like the encryption example we discussed in the previous section.

XML signatures can be broadly classified into three types:

1. Enveloped signature—An enveloped signature is the signature applied over the XML content that contains the signature as an element. The Signature element is excluded from the calculation of the signature value.
2. Enveloping signature—An enveloping signature is the signature applied over the content found within an Object element of the signature itself. The object or its content is identified through a Reference element by way of a Uniform Resource Identifier (URI) fragment identifier or transform.
3. Detached signature—A detached signature is the signature applied over the content external to the Signature element, and it can be identified by way of a URI or a transform. The signed XML resource can be present within the same document as the Signature element, or it can be external to the XML document.

Guidelines for Securing Your Services

Security testing, which is important for any software application, is even more crucial for web services. Web services' security architecture not only depends on the standard security measures, it also depends on the service scope and scale of deployment. For instance, security can either be enforced in the application server itself, or as a separate security appliance that can virtualize the service by sitting in the middle between the service and its consumers.

The points that you need to consider for securing your web services are:

1. Find suitable security architecture—Decide whether to implement the security on the transport layer or on the message layer. TLS (Transport Layer Security) is a mature technology so both standards and tools have already been developed. It also provides a good transition path for engineers who are somewhat familiar with transport-level security but are new to web services. On the other hand, TLS has inherent limitations that make it inappropriate when you desire an end-to-end security. Fortunately, message layer security provides an alternative solution for situations where TLS's limitations are troublesome.
2. Follow the standards religiously—publicly available, commonly used, well-analyzed cryptographic algorithms are the best choice, simply because they've already undergone a great deal of research and scrutiny since they were adopted by the industry.
3. Filter your XML—XML requires complex processing to ensure that transactions are known to be good before they penetrate deep into the enterprise. XML filtering offers a variety of functionality as complex rule sets can be built around network-level information, message size, and message content.
4. Prevent XML Denial-of-Service (XDos)—To protect against XDoS, implement reasonable constraints for all incoming messages. With the use of an XML security gateway as a proxy, you can configure simple settings on message size, frequency, and connection duration.

Securing your web services is a vital aspect of ensuring a successful deployment. When deployed externally for consumption by partners or customers, only secure web services can provide a justifiable integration solution. An interested reader may refer to the WS-Security standard for creating secured web services. WS-Security is a communications protocol originally developed by IBM, Microsoft, Verisign, and Forum Systems. It contains specifications on how integrity and confidentially can be enforced on web services messaging. It describes how to attach signature and encryption headers to SOAP messages. It also describes how to attach security tokens, including binary tokens such as X.509 certificates and Kerberos tickets, to XML messages.

XML Streaming and DOM

There are two programming models for working with XML documents i.e. document *streaming* and the *document object model* (DOM).

The *DOM* model involves creating in-memory objects representing an entire document tree and the complete document state. Once in memory, DOM trees can be navigated freely and parsed arbitrarily, and provide maximum flexibility. However, the cost of this flexibility is a potentially large memory footprint and significant processor requirements, as the entire representation of the document must be held in memory as objects for the duration of the document processing. This may not be an issue when working with small documents, but memory and processor requirements can escalate quickly with document size.

Streaming refers to a model in which XML documents are transmitted and parsed serially at application run time, often from dynamic sources whose contents are not precisely known beforehand. Moreover, stream-based parsers can start generating output immediately. While providing a smaller memory footprint, reduced processor requirements, and higher performance in certain situations, the primary trade-off with stream processing is that you can only see the document state at one location at a time in the document.

Streaming models for XML processing are particularly useful when your application has strict memory limitations, as in the case of hand held devices (PDAs, Smart phones) that run J2ME, Windows Mobile, and Symbian OS, or when your application needs to simultaneously process several requests, as with an application server.

Pull Parsing versus Push Parsing

Streaming *pull parsing* refers to a model in which a client application calls methods on an XML parsing library when it needs to interact with an XML document; the client only gets (pulls) XML data when it explicitly asks for it.

Streaming *push parsing* refers to a model in which an XML parser sends (pushes) XML data to the client as the parser encounters elements in an XML document; the parser sends the data whether or not the client is ready to use it at that time.

Pull parsing provides several advantages over push parsing when working with XML streams:

- With pull parsing, the client controls the application thread, and can call methods on the parser when needed. By contrast, with push processing, the parser controls the application thread, and the client can only accept invocations from the parser.

- Pull parsing libraries can be much smaller and the client code to interact with those libraries much simpler than with push parsing libraries, even for more complex documents.
- Pull clients can read multiple documents at one time with a single thread.

What is StAX?

The StAX project was started by BEA with support from Sun Microsystems, and the JSR 173 specification. The primary goal of the StAX API is to give "parsing control to the programmer by exposing a simple iterator-based API. This allows the programmer to ask for the next event (pull the event) and allows state to be stored in procedural fashion." StAX was created to address limitations in the two most prevalent parsing APIs, SAX and DOM.

> Note: On Microsoft's .Net platform, the equivalent to this is the `System.Xml.XmlReader` class.

StAX and Other JAXP APIs

As an API in the JAXP family, StAX can be compared, among other APIs, to SAX, TrAX, and JDOM. Of the latter two, StAX is not as powerful or flexible as TrAX or JDOM, but neither does it require as much memory or processor load to be useful, and StAX can, in many cases, outperform the DOM-based APIs.

StAX offers features that are beneficial in many cases; these include:

- StAX-enabled clients are generally easier to code than SAX clients. While it can be argued that SAX parsers are marginally easier to write, StAX parser code can be smaller and the code necessary for the client to interact with the parser simpler.
- StAX is a bidirectional API, meaning that it can both read and write XML documents. SAX is read only, so another API is needed if you want to write XML documents.
- SAX is a push API, whereas StAX is pull. The trade-offs between push and pull APIs apply here.

The following table compares the JAXP APIs.

Feature	StAX	SAX	DOM	TrAX
API Type	Pull, Streaming	Push, Streaming	In memory tree	XSLT Rule
Ease of Use	High	Medium	High	Medium
XPath	No	No	Yes	Yes
CPU & Memory Consumption	Good	Good	Differs	Differs
Forward Only	Yes	Yes	No	No
Read XML	Yes	Yes	Yes	Yes
Write XML	Yes	No	Yes	Yes
Create, Read, Update, and Delete.	No	No	Yes	No

Performance Considerations

It is important to consider performance when processing XML documents. XML document processing—handling the document in a pre- or post-processing stage to an application's business logic—may adversely affect application performance because such processing is potentially very CPU, memory, and input/output or network intensive.

There are factors with XML document processing that affect performance. Often, the physical and logical structures of an XML document may be different. An XML document may also contain references to external entities. These references are resolved and substituted into the document content during parsing, but prior to validation. Given that the document may originate on a system different from the application's system, and external entities—and even the schema itself—may be located on remote systems, there may be network overhead affecting performance. To perform the parsing and validation, external entities must first be loaded or downloaded to the processing system. This may be a network intensive operation, or require a great deal of input and output operations, when documents have a complex physical structure.

In summary, XML processing is potentially CPU, memory, and network intensive, for these reasons:

- It may be CPU intensive. Incoming XML documents need not only to be parsed but also validated and they may have to be processed using APIs that may themselves be CPU intensive. It is important to limit the cost of validation as much as possible without jeopardizing the application processing and to use the most appropriate API to process the document.

- It may be memory intensive. XML processing may require creating large numbers of objects, especially when dealing with document object models.
- It may be network intensive. A document may be the aggregation of different external entities that during parsing may need to be retrieved across the network. It is important to reduce as much as possible the cost of referencing external entities.

Following are some guidelines for improving performance when processing XML documents. In particular, these guidelines examine ways of improving the CPU, memory, and input/output or network consumption.

Limit Parsing of Incoming Documents

In general, it is best to parse incoming XML documents only when the request has been properly formulated. In the case of a web service application, if a document is retrieved as a source parameter from a request to an endpoint method, it is best first to enforce security and validate the meta information that may have been passed as additional parameters with the request.

In a more generic messaging scenario, when a document is wrapped inside another document (considered an envelope), and the envelope contains meta-information about security and how to process the inner document, you may apply the same recommendation: Extract the meta-information from the envelope, then enforce security and validate the meta-information before proceeding with the parsing of the inner document. When implementing a SAX handler and assuming that the meta-information is located at the beginning of the document, if either the security or the validation of the meta-information fails, then the handler can throw a SAX exception to immediately abort the processing and minimize the overall impact on performance.

Use the Appropriate API

It's important to choose the most appropriate XML processing API for your particular task. In this section, we look at the different processing models in terms of the situations in which they perform best and where their performance is limited.

In general, without considering memory consumption, processing using the DOM API tends to be slower than processing using the SAX API. This is because the DOM may have to load the entire document into memory so that the document can be edited or data retrieved, whereas SAX allows the document to be processed as it is parsed. However, despite its initial slowness, it is better to use the DOM model when the source document must be edited or processed multiple times.

When using higher-level technologies such as XSLT, keep in mind that they may rely on lower-level technologies like SAX and DOM, which may affect performance, possibly adversely.

Choosing Parser

Each parser and stylesheet engine implementation is different. For example, one might emphasize functionality, while another performance. A developer might want to use different implementations depending on the task to be accomplished. Consider using JAXP, which not only supports many parsers and stylesheet engines, but also has a pluggability feature that allows a developer to swap between implementations and select the most effective implementation for an application's requirements. If you are using Microsoft's .Net platform, look up System.Xml namespace for XML parsing classes.

Reduce Validation Cost

Not only is it important, but validation may be required to guarantee the reliability of an XML application. An application may legitimately rely on the parser's validation so that it can avoid double-checking the validity of document contents. Validation is an important step of XML processing, but keep in mind that it may affect performance.

Although you must validate external incoming XML documents, you can exchange freely—that is, without validation—internal XML documents or already validated external XML documents. In short, you need to validate only at the system boundaries, and you may use validation internally only as an assertion mechanism during development. You may turn validation off when in production and looking for optimal performance.

In other words, when you are both the producer and consumer of XML documents, you may use validation as an assertion mechanism during development, then turn off validation when in production. Additionally, during production validation can be used as a diagnostic mechanism by setting up validation so that it is triggered by fault occurrences.

Referencing External Entities

An XML document may be the aggregation of assorted external entities, and these entities may need to be retrieved across the network when parsing. In addition, the schema may also have to be retrieved from an external location. External entities, including schemas, must be loaded and parsed even when they are not being validated to ensure that the same information is delivered to the application regardless of any subsequent validation. This is especially true with respect to default values that may be specified in an incoming document schema.

There are two complementary ways to reduce the cost of referencing external entities:

1. **Caching using a proxy cache:** You can improve the efficiency of locating references to external entities that are on a remote repository by setting up a proxy that caches retrieved, external entities. However, references to external entities must be URLs whose protocols the proxy can handle.
2. **Caching using a custom entity resolver:** SAX parsers allow XML applications to handle external entities in a customized way. Such applications have to register their own implementation of the `org.xml.sax.EntityResolver` interface with the parser using the `setEntityResolver` method. The applications are then able to intercept external entities (including schemas) before they are parsed.

Dynamically Generated Documents

Dynamically generated documents are typically assembled from values returned from calls to business logic. Generally, it is a good idea to cache dynamically generated XML documents to avoid having to re-fetch the document contents, which entails extra round trips to a business tier. This is a good rule to follow when the data is predominantly read only, such as catalogue data. Furthermore, if applicable, you can cache document content (DOM tree or JAXB content tree) in the user's session on the interaction or presentation layer to avoid repeatedly invoking the business logic.

However, you quickly consume more memory when you cache the result of a user request to serve subsequent, related requests. When you take this approach, keep in mind that it must not be done to the detriment of other users. That is, be sure that the application does not fail because of a memory shortage caused by holding the cached results. To help with memory management, use soft references, which allow more enhanced interaction with the garbage collector to implement caches.

Using XML Judiciously

XML documents can enhance web service interoperability: Heterogeneous, loosely coupled systems can easily exchange XML documents because they are text documents. However, loosely coupled systems must pay the price for this ease of interoperability, since the parsing that these XML documents require is very expensive. This applies to systems that are loosely coupled in a technical and an enterprise sense.

Contrast this with tightly coupled systems. System components that are tightly coupled can use standard, non-document-oriented techniques (such as RMI or .Net Remoting) that are far more efficient in terms of performance and require far less coding complexity. Fortunately, with technologies such as JAX-WS and JAXB you can combine the best of both worlds. Systems can be developed that are internally tightly coupled and object oriented, and that can interact in a loosely coupled, document-oriented manner.

Generally, when using XML documents, follow these suggestions:

- Rely on XML protocols, such as those implemented by JAX-WS and others, to interoperate with heterogeneous systems and to provide loosely coupled integration points.
- Avoid using XML for unexposed interfaces or for exchanges between components that should be otherwise tightly coupled.

Summary

This chapter discussed various design anomalies that may arise while designing XML schemas. As mentioned in this chapter, there are several ways to design a schema that suits your architecture requirements. The suggestions given in this chapter are meant for consideration only when you already know your system very well.

Some of the broad categories covered in this chapter are enumerated as follows:

1. Design recommendations for architecting domain-specific XML Schemas
2. Tips for designing XML schemas with examples
3. Using XSL effectively for translating Infosets from one form to another
4. Securing XML documents with encryption and digital signature
5. XML serialization and the differences between SAX, DOM, and StAX
6. Some of the performance issues concerned with using XML as a medium of application integration

5

Extending Enterprise Application Integration

Leverage the orchestration capability of Oracle BPEL Process Manager to enable standards-based business process integration that complements traditional EAI middleware.

Most organizations have a highly disparate application infrastructure comprising a variety of applications from multiple vendors, running on different platforms, and created with completely different technologies. Traditional **Enterprise Application Integration** (**EAI**) products—from companies such as TIBCO, webMethods, Vitria, and SeeBeyond—have emerged in the last decade to tackle these integration challenges. Over the last few years, many organizations have made significant investments in these EAI solutions. As a result, business integrations in the EAI space tend to be locked into a single vendor, and the integration components are tightly coupled.

The cost of maintaining these proprietary integration links is a significant burden. Specialized skills are required, exacerbating the cost and stability concerns. Furthermore, ripping and replacing existing EAI solutions is not a plausible alternative for an organization protecting massive investments in EAI.

BPEL addresses all these problems by delivering a standards-based, platform-neutral solution. The loosely coupled BPEL process eliminates vendor lock-in, reduces integration costs, and provides interoperability; it also adds a sophisticated layer of security, exception management, and logging. Most important, companies can leverage their existing infrastructure, service-enable it, and orchestrate it using BPEL.

In this chapter we will present an architectural blueprint for leveraging Oracle BPEL Process Manager to develop new integration solutions as well as interface with existing ones. It includes a case study in which orchestrated web services must be integrated with existing heterogeneous EAI solutions based on TIBCO BusinessWorks and webMethods.

Furthermore, because any business process implementation is incomplete without a carefully designed error management, security, and logging framework, we'll explain how BPEL scopes and compensation handlers can make this process more robust and fault-tolerant, as well as how to secure the BPEL process and participating services.

Case Study Background

EAI is an excellent driver for service-enabling existing applications; existing middleware processes can be exposed as web services, which are then orchestrated via BPEL.

The following diagram illustrates a generic approach in which Oracle BPEL Process Manager is used to orchestrate existing EAI interfaces as well as to integrate new applications. This approach assumes that the middleware can expose the business processes as web services and that the application servers themselves have web service interfaces.

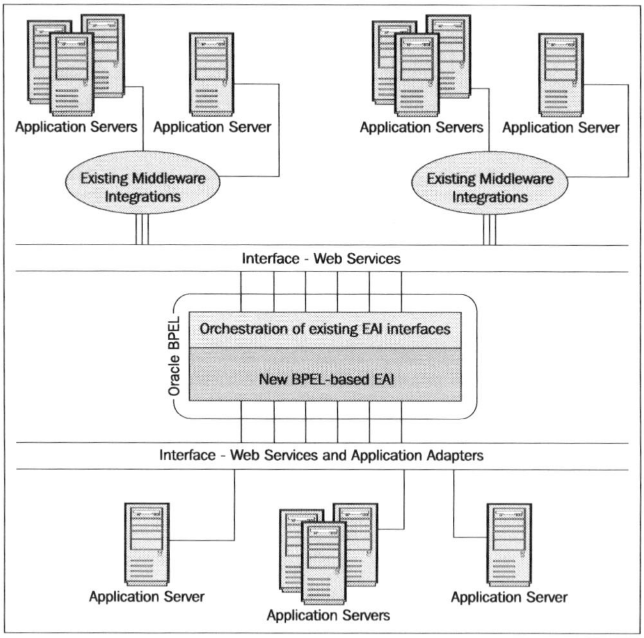

An analysis of a specific case study involving two traditional EAI middleware products demonstrates how BPEL can play an important role in integrating the two products.

In many organizations, changes made in one customer "system of record" are not propagated to the other systems in which customer data is maintained. Consider a scenario in which an enterprise, for various business reasons, ends up using two middleware products from different vendors, such as Siebel CRM integrated with TIBCO BusinessWorks and SAP R/3 integrated with webMethods.

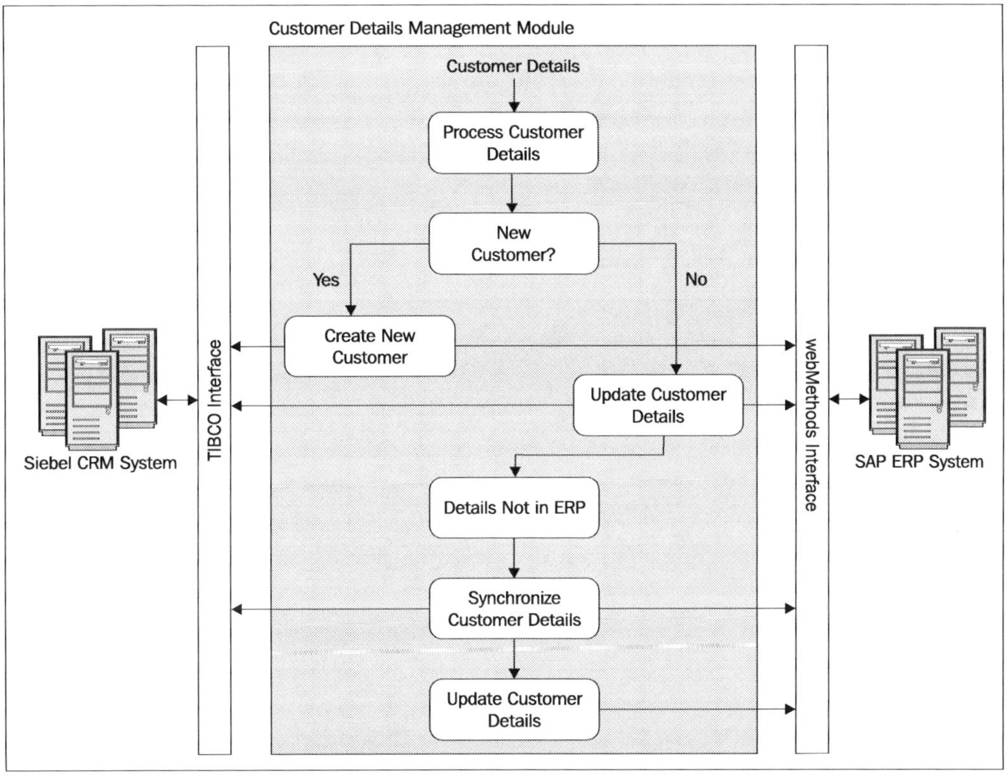

In this model, inconsistent customer data across the SAP and Siebel systems can adversely affect customer service levels and can drive down department and organization revenues. Rather, consistency can be maintained through a common Customer Details Management Module that has multiple interfacing points with the TIBCO and webMethods integrations. For example, when Siebel receives customer data, it checks whether the customer is a new or existing one, and then either adds new data to SAP or updates existing customer data in both apps.

You could use the existing middleware tools (TIBCO and webMethods) to achieve this integration, but doing so would simply increase the footprint of proprietary integration and vendor lock-in. This situation represents an excellent opportunity to service-enable the applications, thereby achieving a standards-based, vendor-agnostic solution.

The first step toward achieving a standards-based interface in EAI is to expose the process as a web service. Most middleware platforms can talk to each other through web services, but the scenario becomes complex when a set of interfacing services must be glued together with appropriate business logic.

You could use another middleware process or even complex Java code to orchestrate web services. However, the process would have to provide following capabilities:

- Parallel web service invocations
- Asynchronous web service invocations
- Loose coupling between services and portability
- Exposing the whole orchestration with standards-based interfaces
- Orchestration monitoring

As shown in the following figure, a prefabricated standards-based orchestration solution based on BPEL can address these issues:

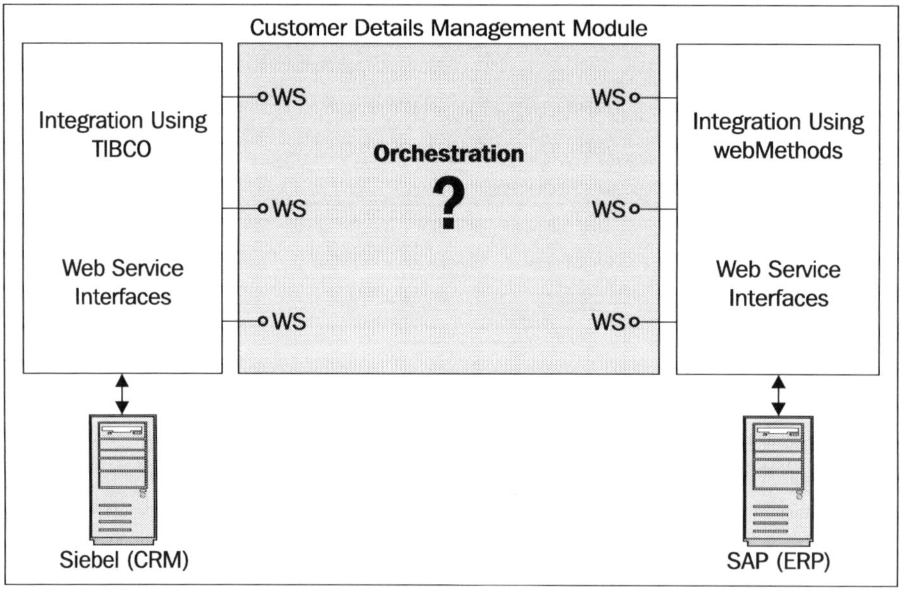

Introducing BPEL into this scenario has the following potential advantages:

- BPEL supports loosely coupled web service orchestration.
- Business logic (even parallel flows!) can be represented in simple XML tags.
- Data can be easily routed among services with simple `assign` (`copy` rules) and `invoke` statements.
- The Customer Details Management Module can be invoked as an independent web service component from another orchestration, middleware tool, or web application.
- Processes can be managed via a simple GUI, such as with Oracle BPEL Process Manager.

Most middleware tools can expose their business processes as web services, making it easier to bridge existing integrations with BPEL orchestrations. In fact, you can use a common message format for all the middleware service interfaces involved.

Now let's consider how Oracle BPEL Process Manager can be used to achieve this synchronization of customer data across SAP and Siebel.

Implementing the Customer Details Management Module

BPEL plays an instrumental role in automating the customer data synchronization process between SAP and Siebel. The steps involved in implementing this BPEL process are:

1. Expose TIBCO and webMethods processes as web services.
2. Orchestrate web services using a BPEL process.
3. Add exception-management capability to the BPEL process.
4. Secure communication between Oracle BPEL Process Manager, application adapters, and the EAI tool.
5. Centralize the logging and notification process.

Step 1: Expose TIBCO and webMethods Processes as Web Services

Customer information is represented in a canonical format and contains fields needed for both SAP and Siebel. If you're passing this generic format across TIBCO and webMethods, these platforms will convert the canonical format into Siebel and SAP customer records, respectively.

Here are the steps you would take to expose the BusinessWorks process as a web service:

1. Analyze the functionality offered by your BusinessWorks process, to determine whether it can be an independent component in the integration scenario.
2. Determine the input and output of the process.
3. If input and output are complex, use W3C XML schemas (XSDs) to define them. You can use XSDs to define your custom fault schema as well.
4. Create the WSDL, using the WSDL palette, and define input and output message formats (associate them with predefined XSDs, if required). You can import existing WSDL as well.
5. Configure an HTTP Connection resource.
6. Use a SOAP Event Source as the first activity, followed by business logic, and then use a SOAP Send Reply to expose the process as a service.
7. Associate the HTTP Connection resource with the Event Source.
8. Associate WSDL and Send Reply with the Event Source.
9. Handle possible exceptions, and use SOAP Send Fault for sending exceptions to the service client.
10. If your machine name is **mymachine**, the port used for the HTTP Connection resource is 8000, and the process name is **SOAPService**, your service can be accessed using the URL `http://mymachine:8000/SOAPService`.
11. Get the final WSDL of the service from the **WSDL** tab of the Event Source activity.

Here's how you would do the same with webMethods:

1. Check whether your webMethods Flow Service can be an independent component in the integration scenario.
2. Specify **Execute ACL to Anonymous** under the **Permissions** tab if you want to invoke this web service from outside the webMethods environment without any authentication.
3. Select the Flow Service in webMethods Developer, and click on **Generate WSDL** from the **Tools** menu.
4. While generating the WSDL document, specify the protocol (SOAP-RPC/SOAP-MSG/HTTP-GET/HTTP-POST) and transport mechanism (HTTP/HTTPS).
5. Define the target namespace for the WSDL document.
6. Enter the IP address or name of the machine where webMethods Integration Server is hosted in the **Host** field.
7. In the **Port** field, enter the port number to be used for connecting to the current Integration Server.
8. Save the WSDL document to the local file system. You can find the service endpoint in the generated WSDL document.

> webMethods Integration Server sends predefined SOAP faults for certain error conditions. If you have to send custom SOAP faults, you should use a custom SOAP processor. You should also use a wrapper service or a custom SOAP processor to expose the service as a document/literal web service.

Now, suppose you have the following three TIBCO web services (implemented with TIBCO BusinessWorks processes and TIBCO Adapter for Siebel):

- Siebel Add
- Siebel Update
- Siebel Query

Similarly, you have the following webMethods web services deployed (using webMethods Integration Server and webMethods SAP R/3 Adapter):

- SAP Add
- SAP Update

The solution architecture can be summarized as follows:

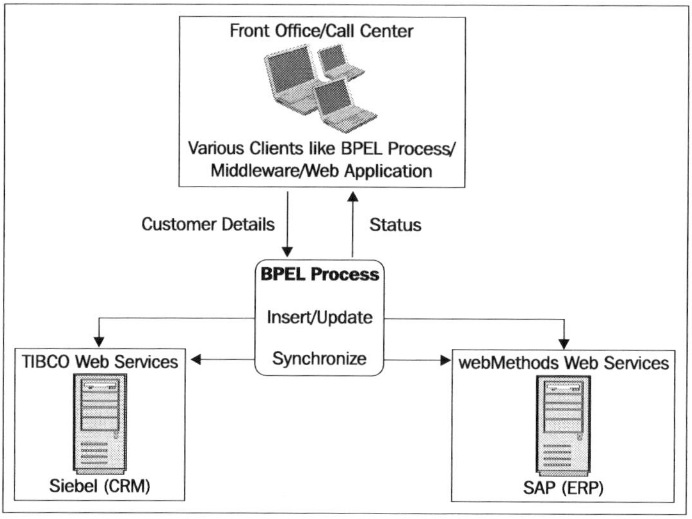

As seen in the figure, the BPEL process brokers the conversation between the front-office call center and back-end SAP and Siebel CRM applications via EAI tools.

Here are some best practices for exposing middleware processes as web services:

- Adhere to WS-I standards whenever possible.
- Try to expose services in "document" style with literal encoding. If that option is not available, use "RPC" style with literal encoding. Although either is recommended by WS-I, you will find document style easier, at least when you create `copy` rules for a BPEL `assign` activity—with RPC style, all the schema elements come as separate message parts, whereas with document style, the entire message is delivered in one part. You can use a single `copy` rule to copy the entire schema, thereby easing the development effort, and verify the style and encoding in the final WSDL document.
- Avoid the use of SOAP encoding; the SOAP Action attribute of WSDL is an empty string.
- Confirm that the middleware uses WSDL 1.1 to describe the interface of the web service.
- Use HTTP binding of SOAP.
- Make sure that all XSDs used for describing the schema conform to the XML schema specification proposed by the W3C. For example, global element declarations should not use references to other global elements; that is, use the `type` attribute instead of the `ref` attribute.

Step 2: Orchestrate Web Services

Having exposed middleware processes as web services, you can then orchestrate them using Oracle BPEL Process Manager, which has a powerful, GUI-based BPEL-authoring interface.

Previously, we mentioned that an important aspect of the Customer Details Management Module is that it synchronizes customer data between SAP and Siebel. This process is visually created in BPEL Designer as shown in the following figure:

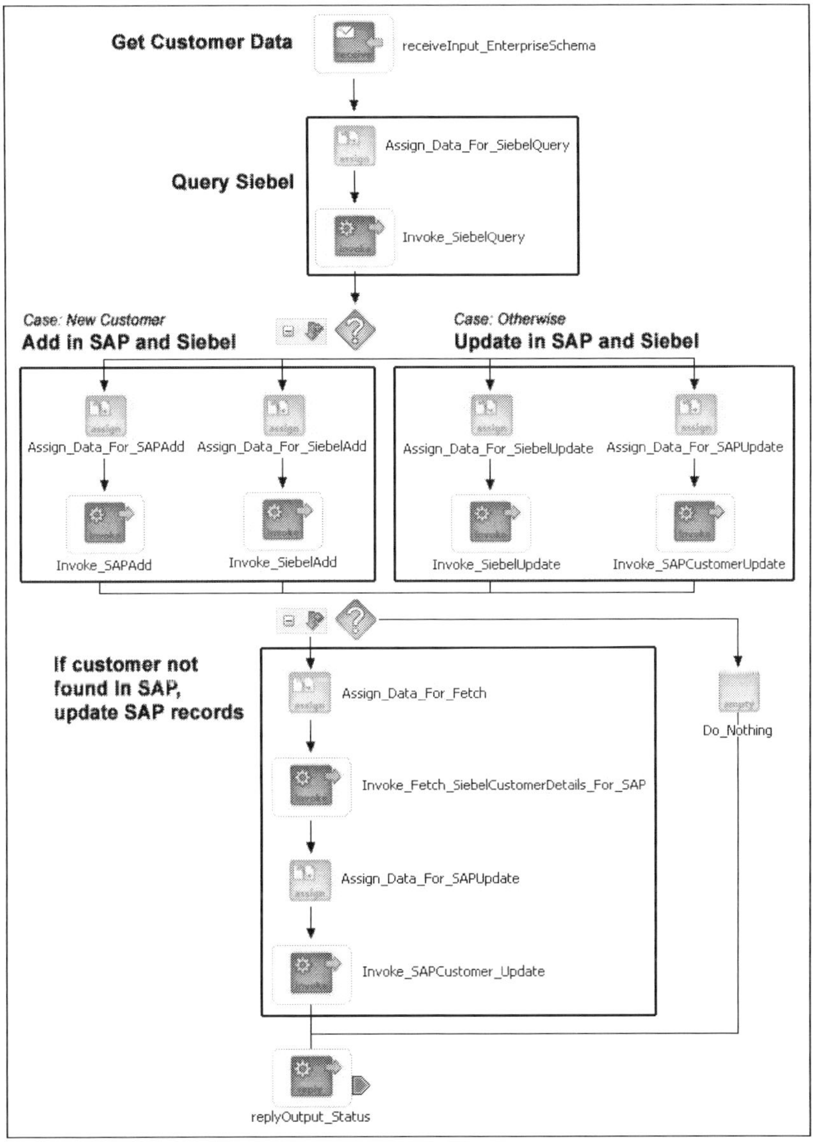

The BPEL Processes Images in this chapter have been edited for clarity purposes. Actual BPEL process will look slightly different in BPEL Designer (Partners Links are not shown in this BPEL process).

Here's a summary of this process flow:

1. A `receive` activity accepts the customer details (enterprise schema).
2. Details are passed to Siebel through `assign` and `invoke` (Siebel Query service) activities.
3. Via a `pick` activity, the Siebel Query result is used to determine whether the customer is existing or new.
4. If the customer is new, parallel execution is invoked, with `flow` activity adding the customer in both Siebel and SAP; otherwise, another parallel flow updates customer details in both applications.
5. If the customer details are not present in SAP, those fields are fetched from Siebel by Siebel Query. This and the other SAP fields to be updated are passed to SAP Update, possibly via a set of `assign copy` rules.
6. The final status of Customer Update/Addition is returned by use of an explicit `reply` activity.

As you can see, on either side of the business process are web services for adding and updating Siebel and SAP data. These web services, which we designed in Step 1, internally invoke EAI processes.

This BPEL process addresses the business requirements of customer management, but it still can't handle exceptions. For example, what would happen if a customer was added successfully in Siebel but addition failed in SAP? To address that issue, you need to enable exception management in your business process.

Step 3: Add Exception Management Capability

Exception management allows a BPEL process to handle error messages or other exceptions returned by outside web services and to generate error messages in response to business or run-time faults.

The following table contains exceptions that need to be handled to make the customer management BPEL process more robust.

No.	Case	Resolution
Case 1	Siebel Query fails	Terminate the process; retry
Case 2	Siebel Add fails; SAP Add succeeds	Compensate to remove SAP record; retry
Case 3	Siebel Add succeeds; SAP Add fails	Normal flow; retry
Case 4	Siebel Add fails; SAP Add fails	Normal flow; retry
Case 5	Siebel Update succeeds; SAP Update fails	Normal flow; retry
Case 6	Siebel Update fails; SAP Update succeeds	Compensate to roll back SAP record; retry
Case 7	Siebel Update fails; SAP Update fails	Normal flow; retry

Cases other than 1, 2, and 6 (discussed later) needn't be handled explicitly to keep the data consistent.

It is necessary to track the status of the web service to catch exceptions and take appropriate actions. Before a discussion of how cases 1, 2, and 6 are handled, let's see how the status of a specific web service is tracked.

The entire BPEL process has these reply schema attributes:

- `Siebel_Add_Status`
- `Siebel_Update_Status`
- `SAP_Add_Status`
- `SAP_Update_Status`

All these attributes can have the values `Failed`, `Success`, or `NA`, which can be set by the BPEL process at various points. To set the `Failed` status, the process can catch the SOAP faults thrown by target web services (use a catch handler with each `invoke` activity). The client invoking the Customer Details Management Module can resend the details in case of any failures.

Now, let's see how exceptions are managed:

Case 1

If the Siebel query itself fails, the process should be terminated, and the invoking client can retry.

Case 2

When customer-details insertion fails in Siebel and succeeds in SAP (they occur in parallel), data consistency will be lost. Moreover, in the case of a retry, the following problems may occur:

- If you try to invoke the BPEL process to insert customer details into Siebel, customer details may be duplicated in SAP.
- If you try to invoke the BPEL process to update customer details, update in Siebel will fail, because there is no corresponding record.

To handle the situation, you have to delete the SAP customer record before a retry takes place, using another webMethods web service with a BPEL compensation handler and scopes.

The scope and compensate activities are key BPEL development tools. A *scope* is a container and context for other activities; a *scope activity* is analogous to a { } block in a programming language. A scope simplifies the BPEL flow by grouping functional structures, and provides handlers for faults, events, and compensation as well as data variables and correlation sets.

Oracle BPEL Process Manager provides two constructs for handling compensation:

- **Compensation handler**: This handler is the business logic for achieving rollbacks. Handlers can be defined for processes and scopes.
- **Compensate activity**: This activity invokes the compensation handler on an inner scope activity that has already successfully completed, and it can be invoked only from within a fault handler or another compensation handler.

Exceptions are caught at the scope level via catch handlers. Catch handlers, in turn, use the compensate activity to invoke the compensation handler for the inner scope. The compensation handler will perform the required rollbacks.

Returning to our example, let's assume that our BPEL process has two scopes: an inner one and an outer one. Invoke activities for SAP Add and Siebel Add services come under outer scope, but only SAP Add comes under the inner scope. A compensation handler can be associated with the inner scope, and the compensation handler will contain an invoke activity for the SAP Delete service.

You have to associate a catch block with the outer scope so that a `SiebelAddfault` sent by the BusinessWorks web service can be caught. Whenever a `SiebelAddfault` occurs, a compensate activity compensates the inner scope, and the SAP customer record is deleted. Note that compensate will be successful only if *all* the activities in the inner scope have been successful.

A modified BPEL process with scopes and compensation handlers is shown in the figure below:

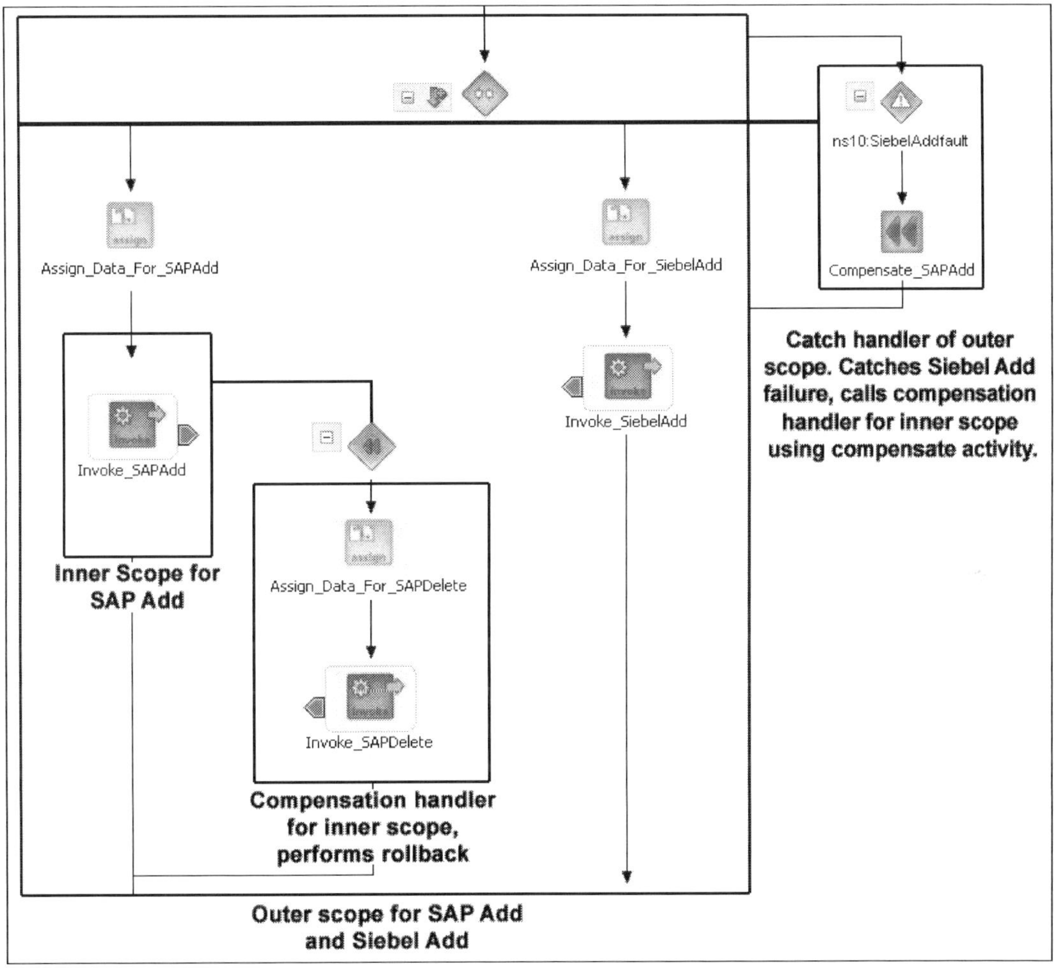

Case 6

The transaction also fails if the Siebel update fails and the SAP update succeeds. This leads to data inconsistency; thus, you have to use compensation logic to roll back the transaction that occurred in SAP. The compensation handler is associated with the SAP Update service and will invoke the SAP Rollback service. Modification of the BPEL process will adhere to the guidelines identified earlier.

The ability to explicitly invoke the compensate activity is the underpinning of the error-handling framework of BPEL. Unlike traditional EAI compensation mechanisms, BPEL offers a standardized method of dealing with rollbacks.

Having created a BPEL process to orchestrate TIBCO and webMethods web services, let's see how we can make the communication between BPEL, adapters, and EAI tools more secure.

Step 4: Secure Business Communication

Security can be enabled at two levels: outbound (invoking secure TIBCO and webMethods services) and inbound (securing the BPEL process).

Outbound Security

TIBCO and webMethods services need to be secured to prevent unauthorized access. Oracle BPEL Process Manager supports HTTP basic and WS-Security authentication for calling external services. This example focuses on how to secure the TIBCO and webMethods services and mechanisms to call them from the BPEL process, using HTTP authentication.

Web services deployed in TIBCO BusinessWorks and webMethods Integration Server support HTTP basic authentication. While designing the TIBCO web service, check the **Use Basic Authentication** checkbox on the **Transport Details** tab of the SOAP event source activity. While deploying the web service by using TIBCO Administrator, you can set service access levels for different users/roles. When designing the web service with webMethods Developer, you can set the ACL (Access Control List) for different operations.

If you use basic authentication while deploying the TIBCO and webMethods services, the services, on each invocation, will expect credentials, and these should be passed by the BPEL process. This task can be achieved by setting two "partner link" properties: `httpUsername` and `httpPassword`. The value of these properties can be set statically as follows:

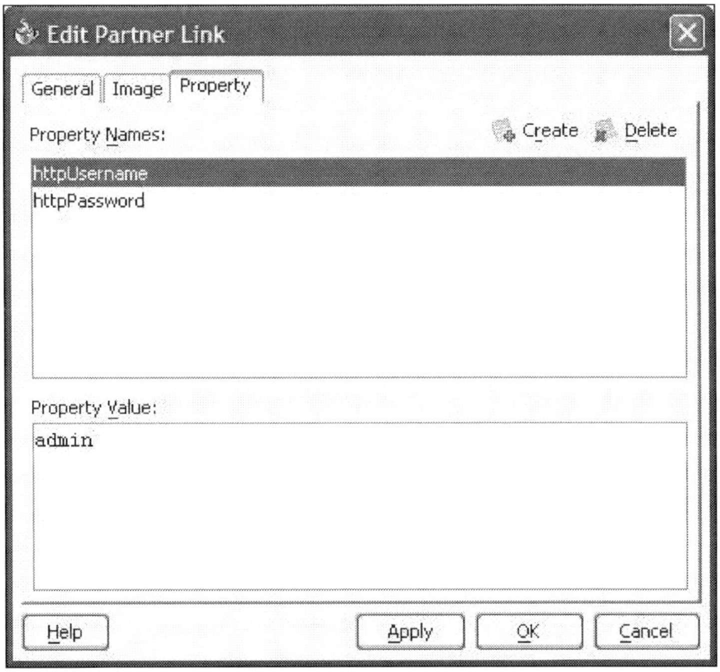

To pass the credentials dynamically, use a `copy` rule.

```
<copy>
  <from variable="varUsername"/>
  <to partnerLink="p1" bpelx:property="httpUsername"/>
</copy>
```

In addition, you can secure TIBCO and webMethods services by using WS-Security. BPEL processes can pass WS-Security authentication headers to WS-Security-secured web services. You need to define the WS-Security headers that the service supports in the WSDL document for the service. These header fields can then be manipulated as variables in the BPEL process, just like message-body data elements. You can find more details about WS-Security authentication in the HotelShopFlow example, downloadable from the OTN at `http://www.oracle.com/technology/products/ias/bpel/files/hotelshopdemostandalone.zip`.

Inbound Security

BPEL processes can be secured from invocation by unauthorized users using HTTP authentication; it is also possible to set different credentials for different BPEL processes.

To enable this security, HTTP basic authentication has to be enabled at the application-server level. Credentials can then be extracted in the BPEL process and passed to TIBCO and webMethods web services as "partner link" properties.

For more details about BPEL security, listen to the "**Securing BPEL Processes & Services**" Webinar on OTN.

Step 5: Centralize Logging and Error Handling

Your business processes are now secure and robust, but it is equally important to build logging and notification capability into them. Building a centralized logging and error-handling framework will make the application even more robust, increase reusability, and reduce development costs. You can build such a framework by using a web service from the BPEL process as well as from middleware. Via Oracle BPEL Process Manager, you can add logging to this service with the file adapter and require that an email notification be sent in case of error.

The following sample schema can be used for the framework:

Schema Element	Description
`ROLE`	Roles such as `ERROR`, `DEBUG`, `WARNING`, and `INFO`
`CODE`	Error code
`DESCRIPTION`	Error description
`SOURCE`	Source of error
`EMAIL`	Email ID to which notification has to be sent

This BPEL process can be exposed as an asynchronous one-way web service, which makes the clients of this service continue operations without any delay. The centralized logging and notification process **LogNotify** is shown in the following figure (Partners Links are not shown in this BPEL process for clarity purpose):

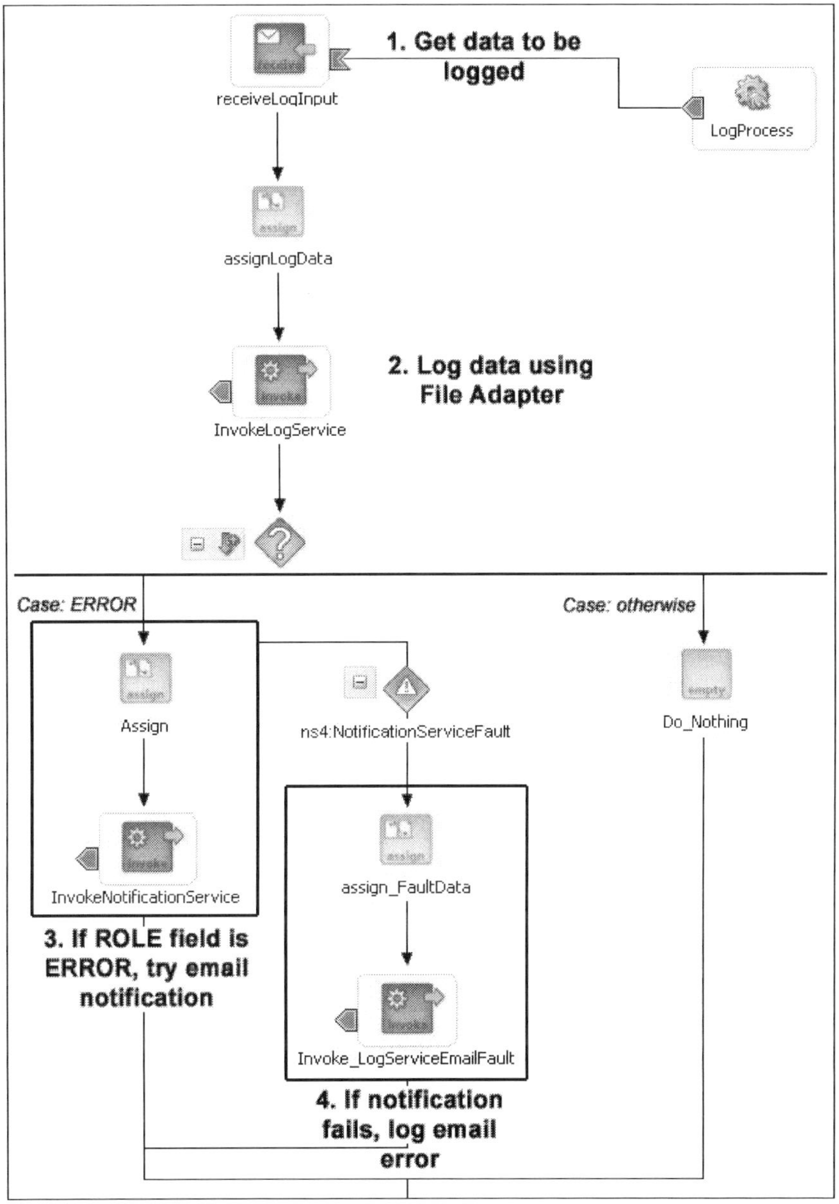

As shown in the figure above, the LogNotify process does the following:

1. Receives information to be logged from an external process.
2. Invokes Log Service to write this data into a log file. Log Service leverages the file adapter for this purpose.

3. If logging is successful, the process completes. In addition, if the `ROLE` field contains `ERROR`, the service will notify the relevant person via email. Email information is retrieved from the original message received (see the sample schema).
4. If notification fails, the process ends after the notification error has been logged in a file.

Each `invoke` activity in our main BPEL process can have a separate `try-catch` block. SOAP faults sent by the middleware process (which may even include exceptions thrown by the end application) are handled in the `catch` block and routed to the common logging and error-handling framework.

The figure below shows how the LogNotify process is invoked when Siebel Add fails:

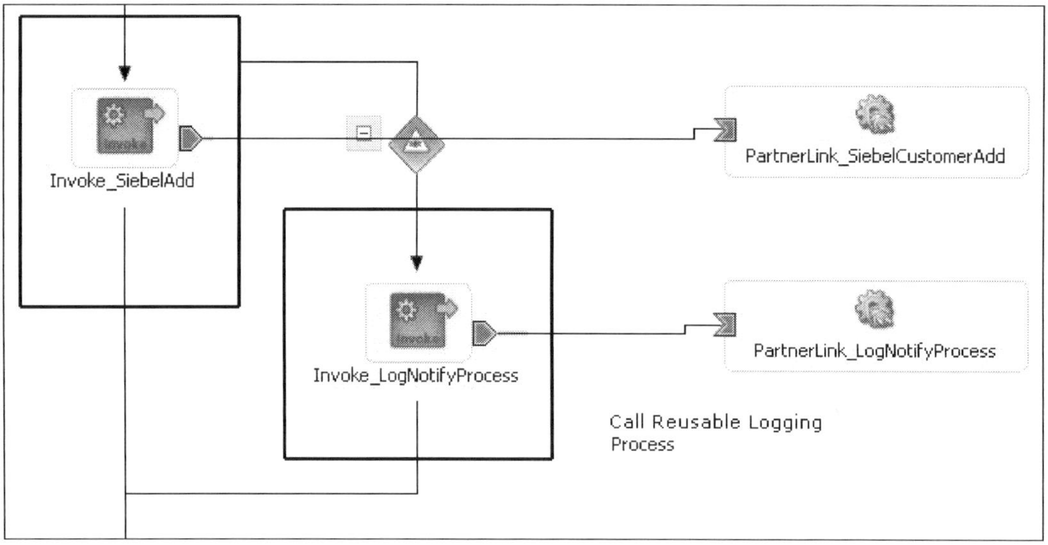

Summary

The integration market is flooded with powerful EAI products, with which lots of integration has already been done. BPEL represents a unique choice for service-enabling these existing EAI solutions. By exposing existing middleware processes as web services and orchestrating them with Oracle BPEL Process Manager, organizations can embark on the route of SOA.

6
Service-Oriented ERP Integration

A step-by-step approach for integrating PeopleSoft 8.9 CRM with Oracle Applications 11i using BPEL.

Many organizations have heterogeneous application portfolios that cross different departments, geographic locations, or subsidiaries. While multiple ERP systems may be necessary to meet the requirements of the business unit, they essentially result in data fragmentation. Integration of these systems is complex and traditionally handled in a proprietary manner; nevertheless, companies invest significant energy in integrating information spread across multiple ERP systems to make better business decisions.

BPEL provides a standard, process-centric way to integrate disparate systems. Oracle's BPEL Process Manager, a key tool in Oracle Fusion Middleware for delivering service-oriented architecture (SOA), supports the industry-standard BPEL specification backed by Microsoft, IBM, SAP, and BEA, and is widely recognized as an enterprise blueprint for reducing the cost, complexity, and inflexibility of integration projects.

In this chapter we'll present an approach for integrating PeopleSoft 8.9 CRM (PeopleTools 8.46) with Oracle Applications 11i using BPEL. Specifically, via a sample business scenario, you'll learn how PeopleSoft is configured to expose its modules as web services and how the BPEL Applications adapter is configured to interact with Oracle apps.

Functional Scenario

In a typical order-management business scenario, an order is entered into the CRM system, and fulfillment occurs through the back-office ERP. In this example, we are using PeopleSoft as the front-office application to manage marketing, sales, and service operations and Oracle E-Business suite for ERP (order management, inventory, and financials). The business process considered here is the **Quote-to-Order** process.

One part of this business process—quote and order entry—is executed in the CRM system, while order fulfillment is performed in the ERP system. To optimize internal operations, the entire cross-application Quote-to-Order business process needs to be automated.

Here is the functionality available in this business process integration:

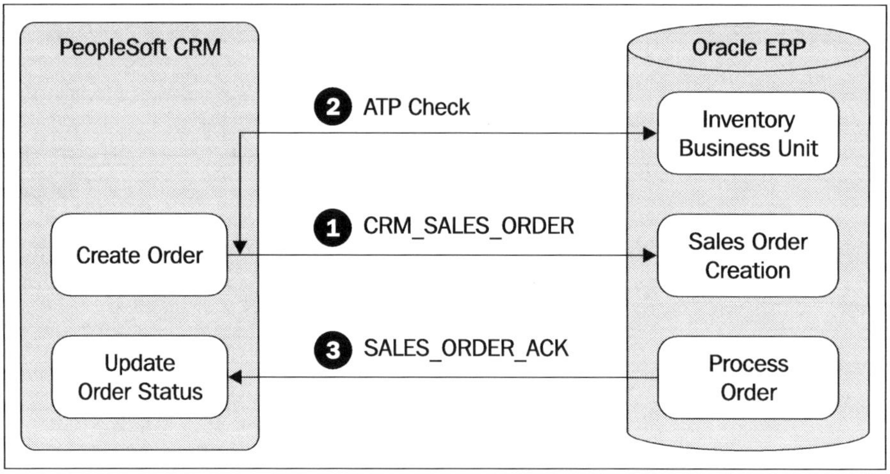

Step 1: Sales orders creation in PeopleSoft:

- A sales order in PeopleSoft can be created either by converting a quote into a sales order, or directly through the **Order Capture** screen.
- Upon submission, the system will check for the required information and change the status to"Open"; otherwise the status will be"Hold".
- This sales order process will invoke and submit the order information to the Integration process. This in turn will invoke BPEL Process Manager.

- BPEL Process Manager converts the messages data into the format required by the Oracle ERP Order Management module.
- The sales order creation takes place in the Oracle ERP application, and the order acknowledgment is propagated to PeopleSoft.

Step 2: ATP check in Oracle ERP:

- During the order creation process, the salesperson may wish to check the availability of the material to promise the delivery date.
- PeopleSoft CRM will make a synchronous call to the ERP application to get the on-hand available quantity using the Item/Product Availability inquiry component.
- BPEL Process Manager will transmit this ATP check request to Oracle ERP.
- Oracle ERP will check the available quantity for the specific item from the inventory. It will send back the relevant availability details to BPEL Process Manager.
- BPEL Process Manager will pass on this ATP response information to PeopleSoft CRM. Based on this operation, the customer will be promised the actual delivery date.

Step 3: Propagation of order status updates from Oracle ERP to PeopleSoft CRM:

- After propagating the sales order to the ERP application, the order is booked in ERP, the acknowledgment is sent to the BPEL process, and in turn is propagated to PeopleSoft CRM system, where the order status will be changed to"In Process".
- Oracle ERP will propagate the changes to the order status from time to time. This status from ERP is mapped to equivalent status in CRM.

Here we will focus on the order creation step. The design-time viewlet at `http://www.oracle.com/technology/pub/articles/bpel_cookbook/files/configuration_setup_viewlet_version3.0_viewlet.html` illustrates the configuration and execution in action. For further details about other steps in this process, please refer to the *Oracle Apps Integration Cookbook* at `http://download.oracle.com/otndocs/products/integration/oracle_apps_integration_cookbook.pdf`.

Solution Overview

Now that you understand the functional business process, let's see how it's accomplished at the architecture level. The following figure provides a high-level overview of the participating components for a typical integration between PeopleSoft CRM and Oracle Applications with Oracle BPEL Process Manager as the integration platform:

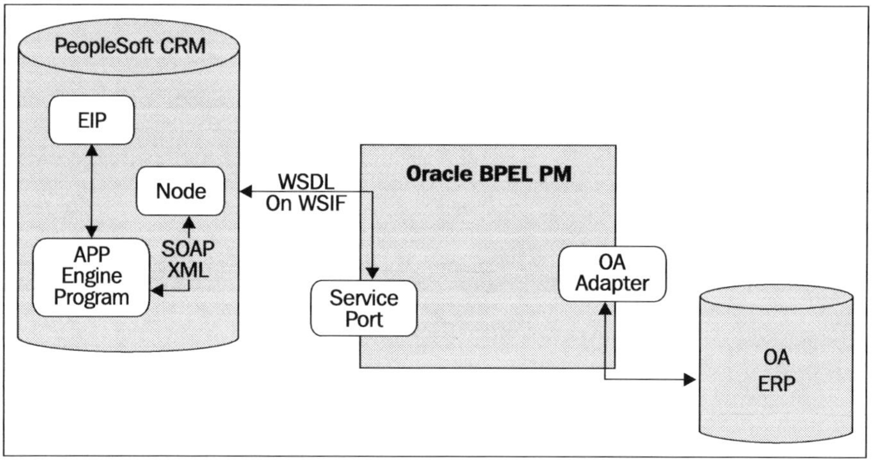

Enterprise Integration Points (EIPs) are web service connections that allow PeopleSoft applications to work smoothly with third-party systems and other PeopleSoft software. Upon submission of an order in PeopleSoft CRM, an EIP in PeopleSoft transforms it to XML format. This Order XML is then passed on to the attached PeopleCode method (`WSDL_ORDER`). (PeopleCode is the PeopleSoft programming language for enforcing business rules or performing other customizations.) `WSDL_ORDER` will convert the received Order XML into SOAP XML and will send this request to the PeopleSoft remote node. The **remote node** is what handshakes with a configured web service in BPEL Process Manager.

A web service can be invoked from PeopleSoft by mapping the remote node to the WSDL using **Web Service Invocation Framework (WSIF)** binding, which is strongly supported by BPEL Process Manager. Upon receiving this SOAP XML, the PeopleSoft node will invoke the web service based on the WSDL imported and configured to this node. The web service is invoked and executed in BPEL Process Manager.

BPEL Process Manager processes the order data as SOAP XML and sends it to Oracle Applications; it internally leverages the Oracle Applications (OA) Adapter to communicate with 11i. The OA Adapter is a pure JCA 1.5 Resource Adapter that can be used to send and receive messages from E-Business Suite. Oracle Applications exposes some of the seeded API and table to external applications via this adapter.

Oracle Applications processes the order and sends the acknowledgment; BPEL Process Manager receives this response and forwards it to the PeopleSoft node. The node will then respond to the PeopleCode that requested the web service. The latter will retrieve the XML data and submit it to the configured component interface in PeopleSoft. A **component interface** is what exposes PeopleSoft components for synchronous access from another application (written in Java or PeopleCode).

That's the high-level flow of Order data from PeopleSoft to Oracle Applications and back. In the next section, you'll learn how to expose PeopleSoft CRM modules as web services, build a BPEL process, and configure the OA Adapter.

Integrating PeopleSoft CRM with Oracle ERP

Once the order is submitted in PeopleSoft CRM, order information needs to be passed to Oracle Apps. There are three key steps in this process.

1. Design the business process in Oracle BPEL Process Manager.
2. Configure the OA Adapter.
3. Configure PeopleSoft.

Let's take a deep drive into each of these steps.

Step 1: Design the BPEL Process

In this step, we will use BPEL Designer to create a process. BPEL Process Manager will receive the SOAP XML containing sales order information from PeopleSoft and transform it to the OA Adapter's XML format. (The schema will be generated by the OA Adapter automatically when the partner link is created for the calling API.) Then, the OA Adapter partner link will be invoked and transformed and the Order XML submitted to Oracle Applications. The Oracle API will process the order and return the order number in output acknowledgment XML.

BPEL Process Manager handles remote and binding faults. When a connection is not available, it retries five times and then throws an exception. When a binding exception occurs, the binding fault will be handled.

A typical example of an integration business process designed for BPEL Process Manager is shown in the following figure (*This figure has been edited for clarity purposes. Actual BPEL process will look slightly different in BPEL Designer. Partners Links are not shown in this BPEL process*):

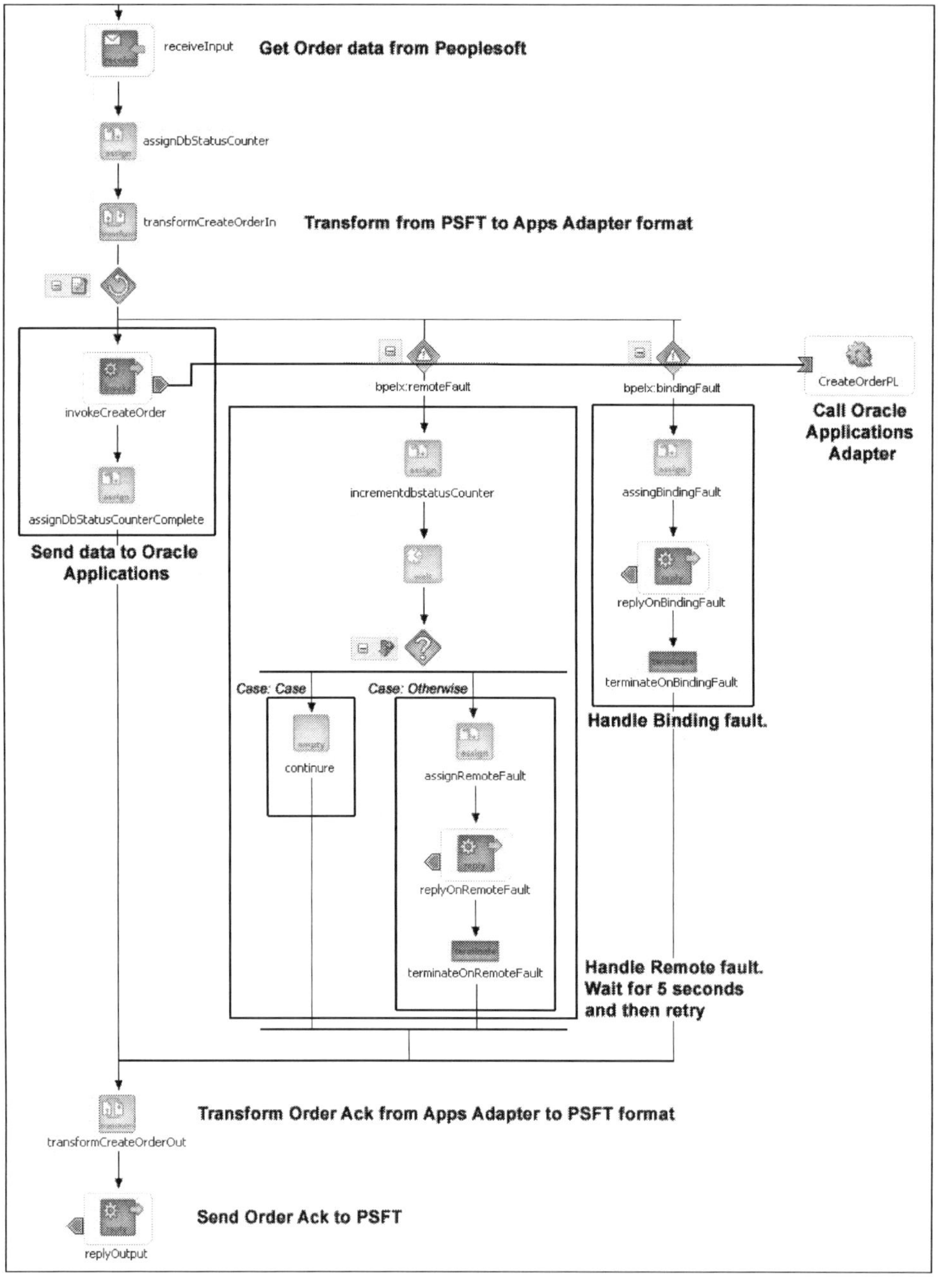

The critical activities in the process would be:

1. Select **Applications | New Application Workspace | New Project | BPEL Process Project**.
2. Import the schema to define the input and output variables of the BPEL process.
    - From the structure window select **project schemas | import Schema**. Enter the input schema name (**createorder.xsd**).
    - From the structure window, select **Message Types**.
        - Select **CreateOrderRequestMessage** and map the `CreateOrderIn` root element of `createorder.xsd`.
        - Select **CreateOrderResponseMessage** and map the `CreateOrderOut` root element of `createorder.xsd`.
    - From the structure window, select **Variables**.
        - Confirm that `InputVariable` is mapped to `CreateOrderRequestMessage`.
        - Confirm that `OutputVariable` is mapped to `CreateOrderResponseMessage`.
3. Create the partner link for OA Adapter.
    - Add a partner link activity from the component palette to the CreateOrder process and name it CreateOrderPL.
    - Click on **Define Adapter Service**.
    - Configure BPEL Process Manager and OA Adapter for the partner link (more on that in the *Step 2: Configure OA Adapter* section).

4. Add an `invoke` activity to call OA Adapter.
   - Drag and drop the `invoke` activity to the process and double-click on it.

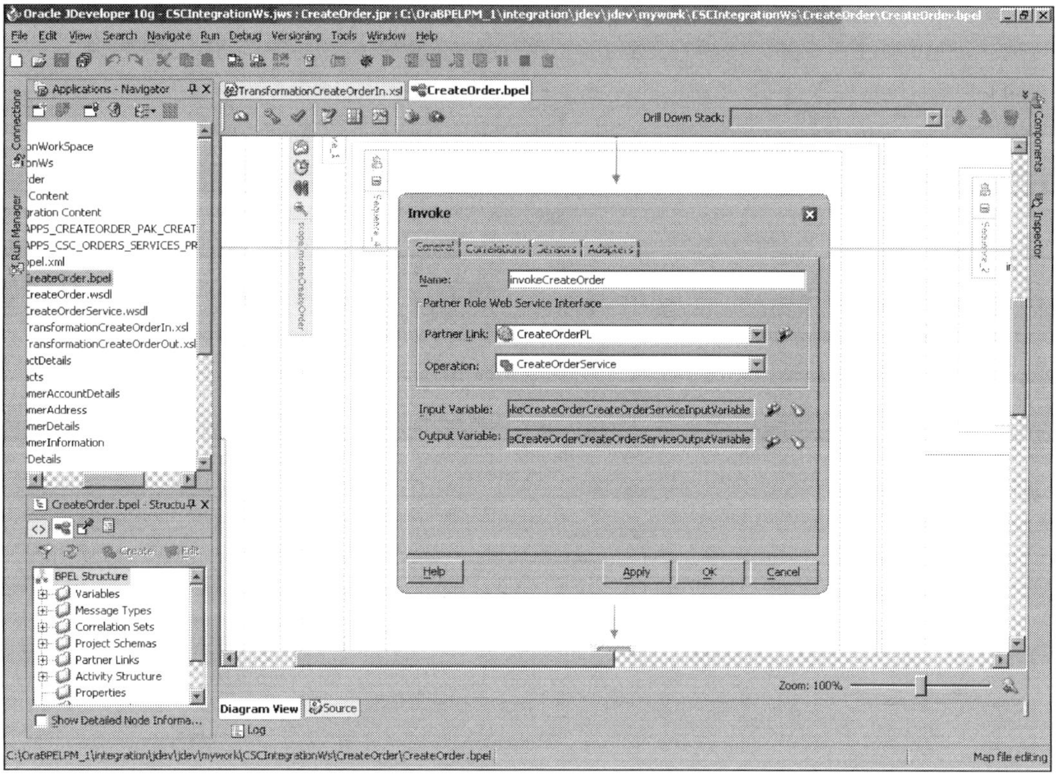

   - Map the partner link to `CreateOrderPL` and create the input and output variables.
5. Add a `transform` activity above the `invoke` activity for transforming PeopleSoft outbound XML to Oracle Apps inbound XML.
   - Double-click on the `transform` activity. Select **inputVariable** as **Source Variable**, **invokeCreateOrderInputVariable** as **Target Variable**, and click on the create mapping icon as shown:

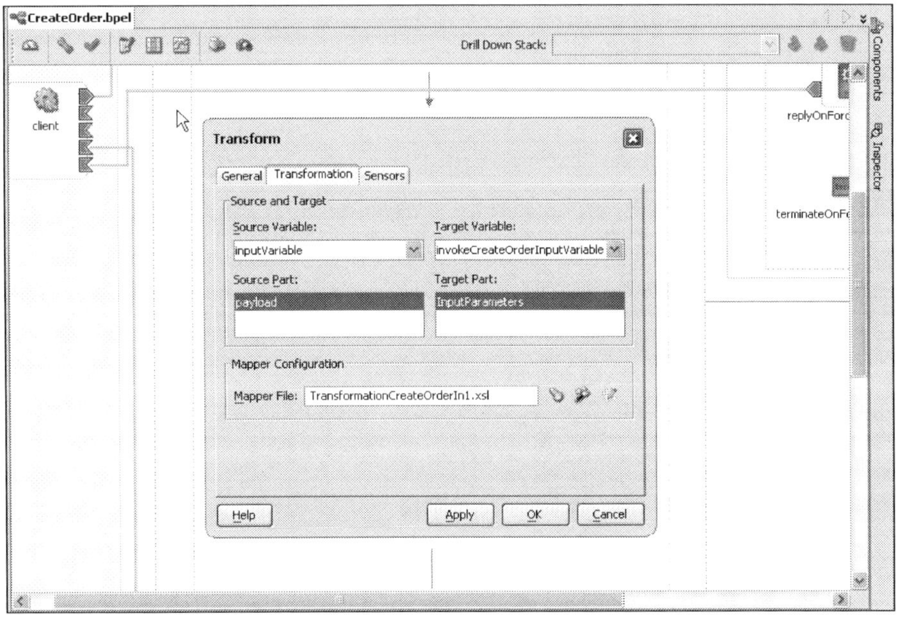

- Map the source and target schemas as shown in the following screenshot:

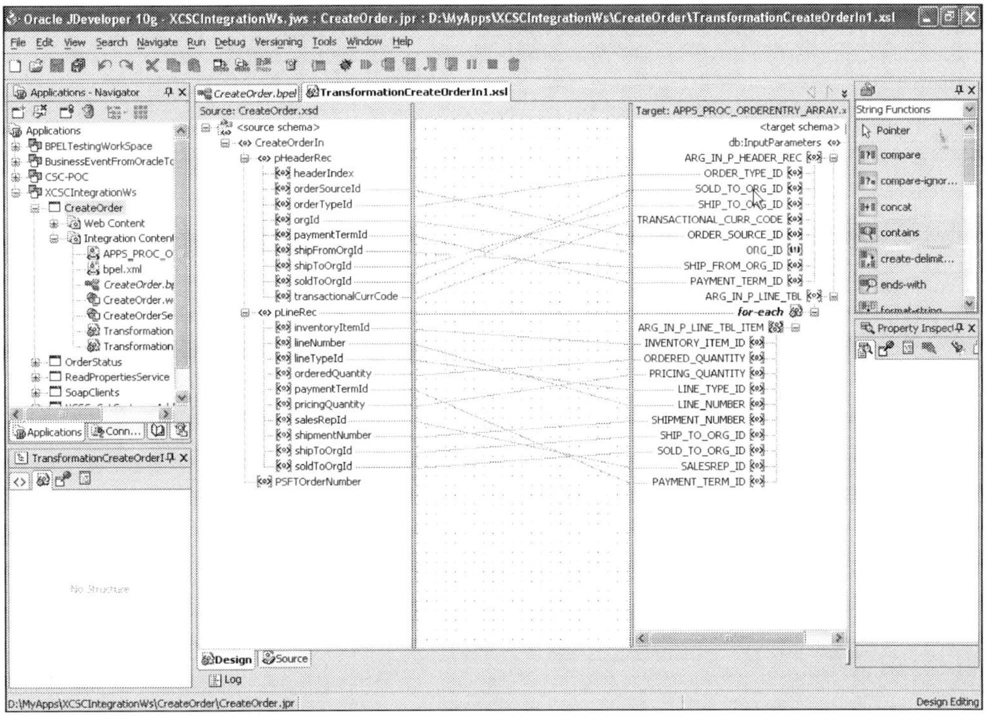

6. Add another `transform` activity below the `invoke` activity for transforming Oracle Apps outbound XML to PeopleSoft inbound XML.

   - Double-click on the `transform` activity. Select **invokeCreateOrderOutputVariable** as **Source Variable**, **outputVariable** as **Target Variable**, and click on the create mapping icon as shown.

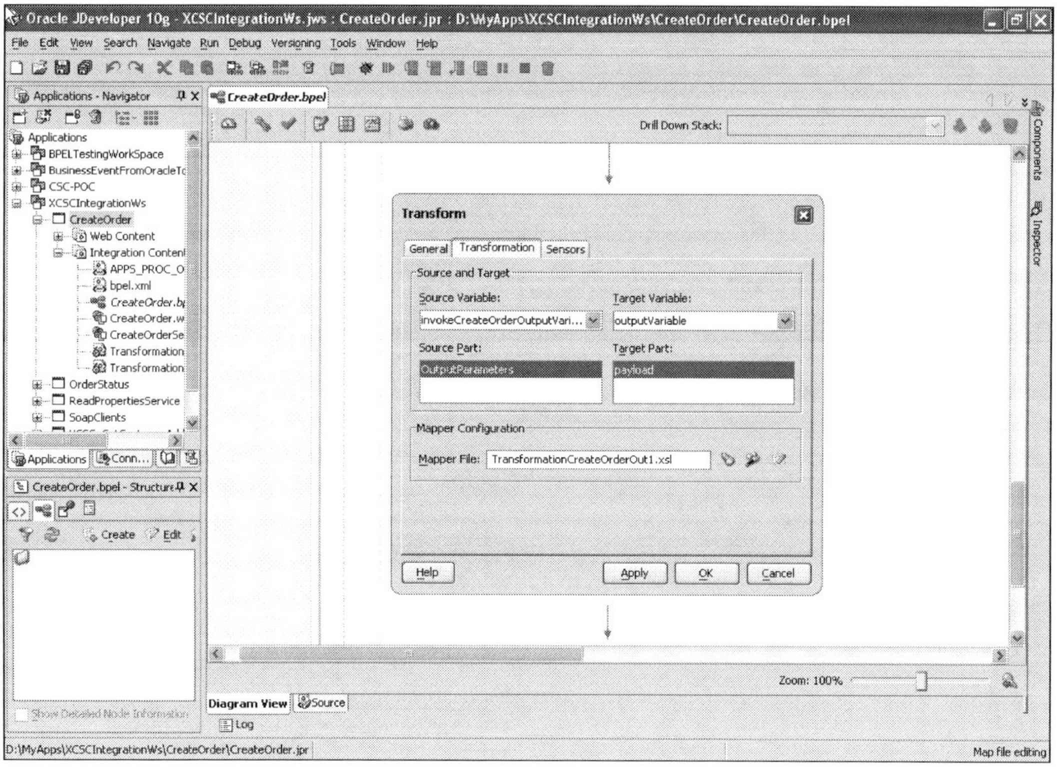

   - Map the source and target schemas, as shown in the following screenshot:

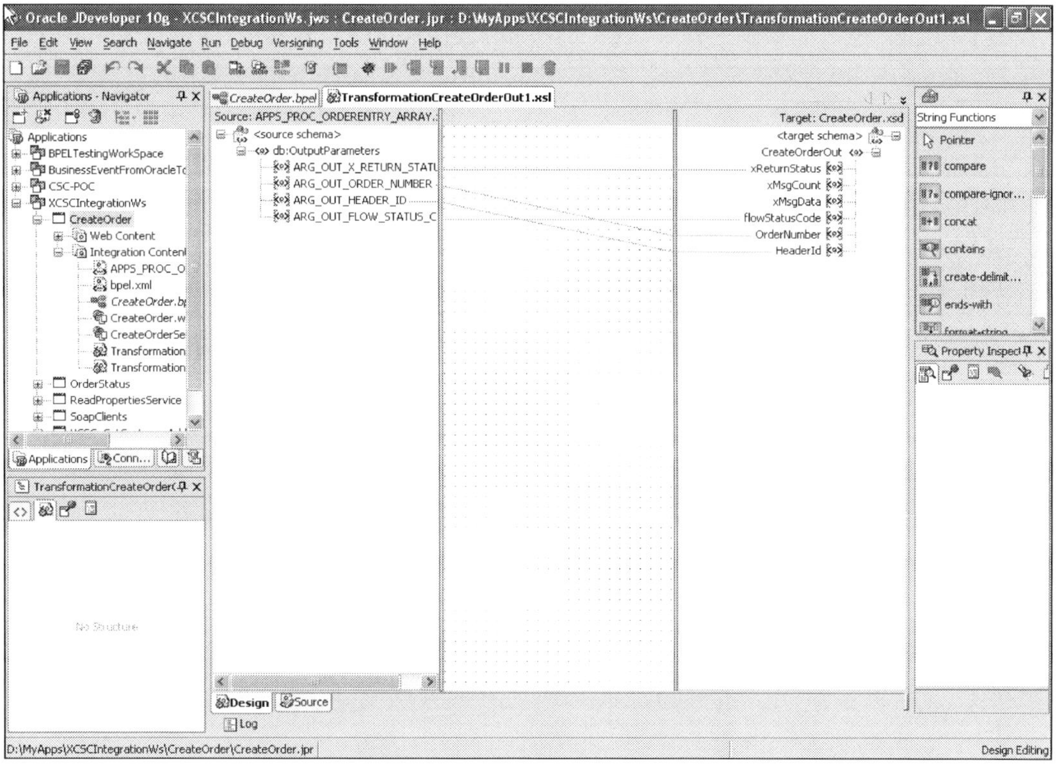

The following files, all available in the sample code download, will recreate the process described in BPEL Designer.

`Bpel.xml`	The deployment descriptor file that defines the locations of the WSDL files for services to be called by this BPEL process flow.
`CreateOrder.xsd`	The schema for the input XML submitted by the PeopleSoft application.
`CreateOrder.bpel`	The process source file containing process flow, partner links, data variables, and necessary fault handlers.
`CreateOrder.wsdl`	The WSDL client interface, which defines the input and output messages for this BPEL process flow, the supported client interface and operations, and other features. This functionality enables the BPEL process flow to be called as a service.

You have now completed the design of the BPEL process. Next, we'll take a detailed look at configuring the OA Adapter, followed by the configuration at the PeopleSoft end.

Step 2: Configure OA Adapter

OA Adapter is deployed in Oracle Containers for J2EE in managed mode. It can be used to send and receive messages from E-Business Suite. Here are the steps involved in configuring the adapter:

1. Define an Adapter Service and select **Oracle Applications** adapter.

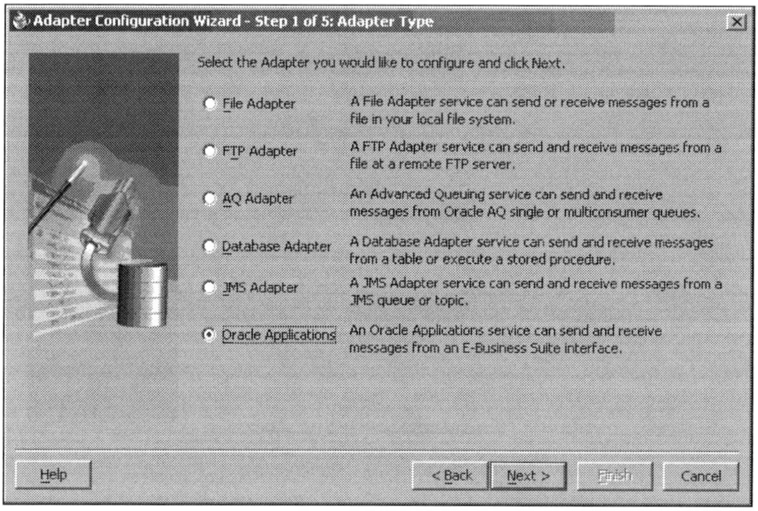

2. Enter a service name. This name will be used as the web service for the selected API/table.

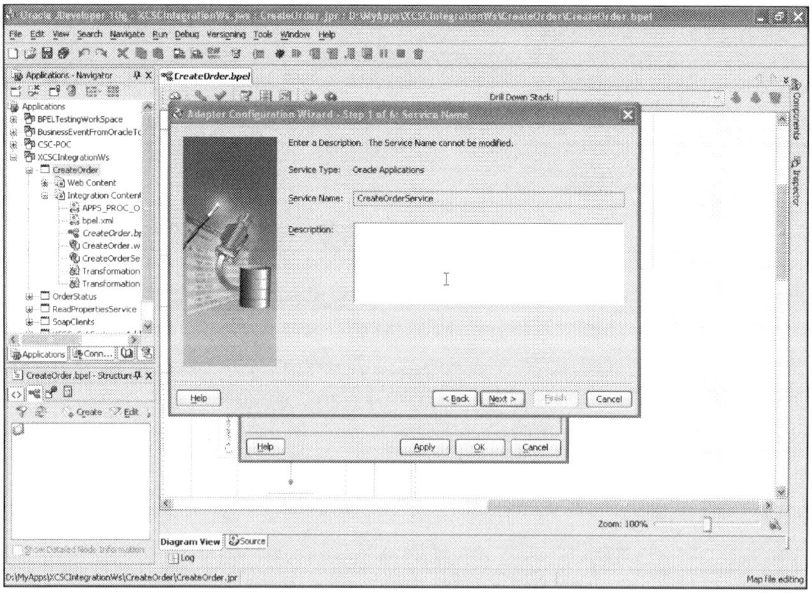

3. Select a database connection that is defined in the project. If there is no database connection available, click on **New** and follow the wizard.

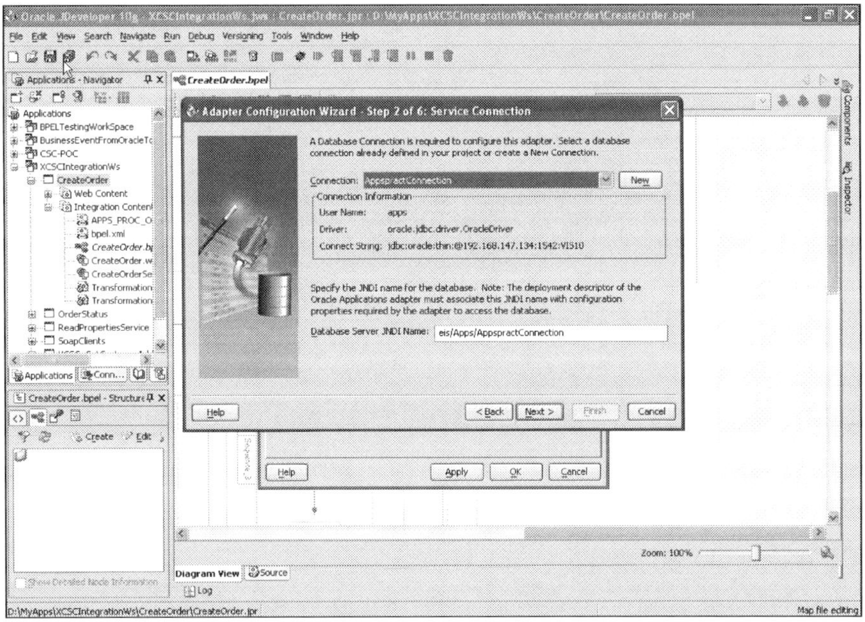

4. Select the **Table/Views/APIs** interface to the **Oracle Application Data**.

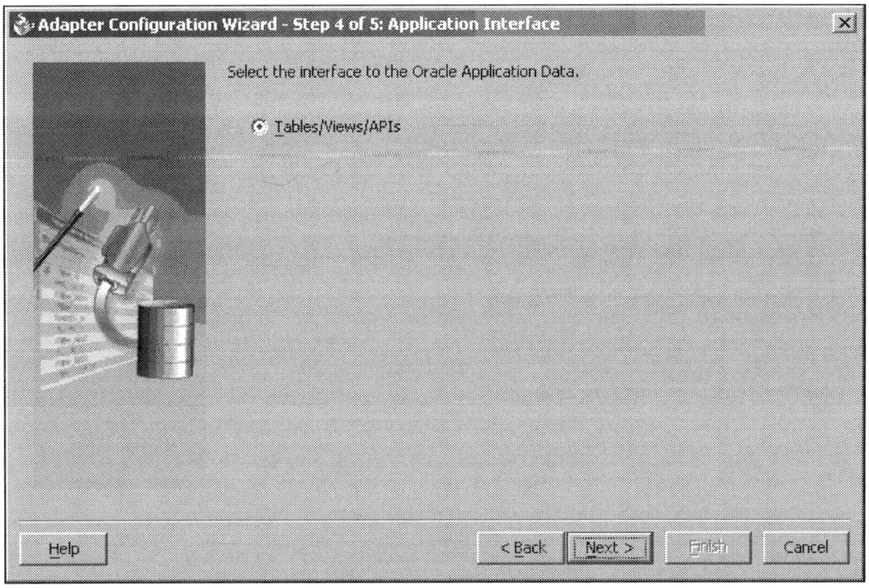

5. Search for and select the `PROC_ORDERENTRY_ARRAY` API that is to be invoked from the BPEL process.

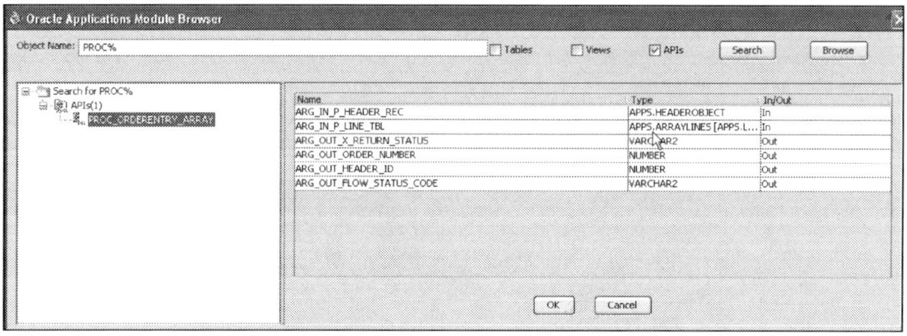

In this case, `PROC_ORDERENTRY_ARRAY` is the wrapper API written for the `PROCESS_ORDER` pre-seeded API because BPEL Process Manager will not support the oracle record type. Instead, you will use object types in a wrapper procedure similar to the record types used in `PROCESS_ORDER`. This interface is responsible for processing the sales order in Oracle Apps.

6. The API will be added to the Adapter Service.

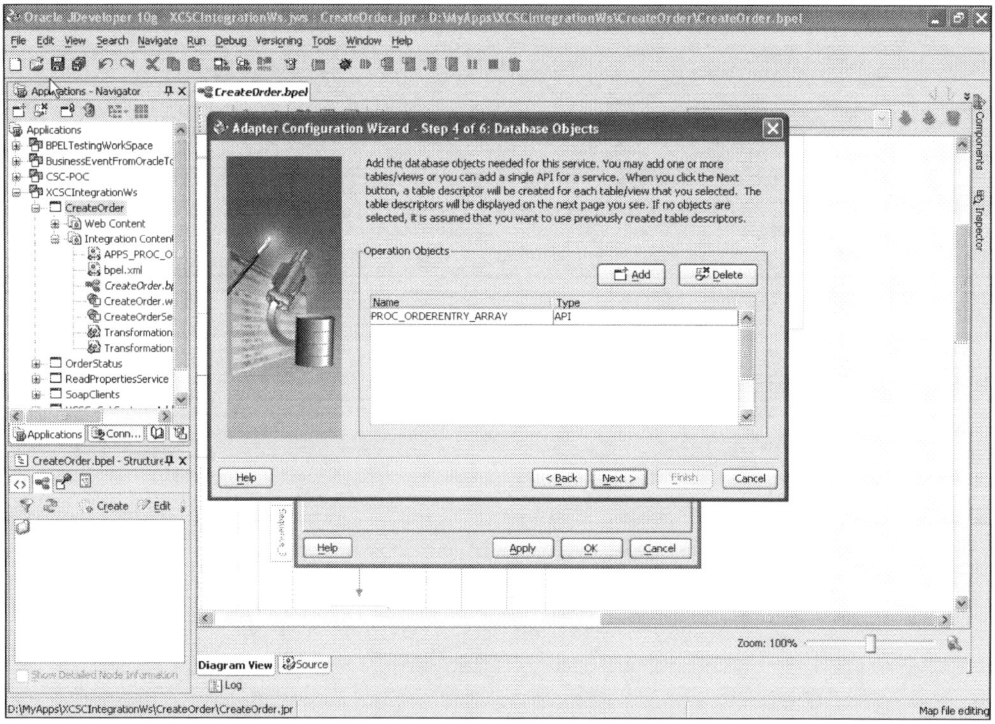

7. The Oracle Applications partner link will be added to the BPEL process, and `APPS_PROC_ORDERENTRY_ARRAY.xsd` will be created.

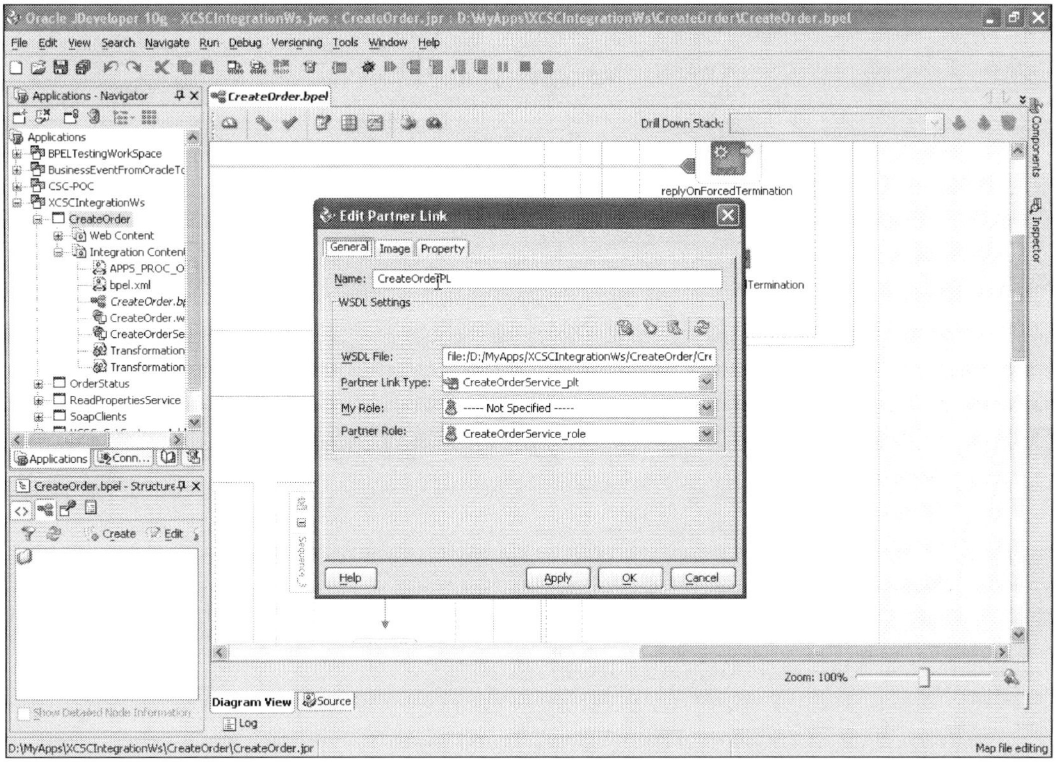

A WSDL file will be created by the Adapter Service for the `PROC_ORDERENTERY_ARRAY` API, which behaves like a web service and binds to the ERP using WSIF.

The following files in the sample code download will help you configure the OA Adapter in BPEL Designer:

`Proc_orderentry_array.sql`	Custom wrapper API to invoke OA seeded `Process_Order` API.
`Create_ObjectScript.sql`	Contains the"Creation of Objects" script used in the `PROC_ORDERENTERY_ARRAY` custom API.
`CreateOrder.bpel`	The process source file containing process flow, partner links, data variables, and necessary fault handlers.
`CreateOrder.wsdl`	The WSDL client interface, which defines the input and output messages for this BPEL process flow, the supported client interface and operations, and other features. This functionality enables the BPEL process flow to be called as a service.

This completes the design of the BPEL process and the configuration of OA Adapter. Next (and finally), we'll configure PeopleSoft.

Step 3: Configure PeopleSoft

Now that you have created the BPEL process, let's look at the four-step process in configuring PeopleSoft.

- In Step 1, import the BPEL process WSDL into PeopleSoft. You will then use the imported WSDL to configure a node. This node will eventually communicate with the BPEL process.
- In Step 2, configure the Sales Order EIP to invoke this node whenever a new sales order is created.
- Finally, before the node sends the order information to BPEL process, you would need to transform it into a SOAP XML. Hence, in Step 3 and 4, you will write a small PeopleCode function to perform this transformation and establish its relationship with the node.

Let's drill down into each of these steps.

Configure the PeopleSoft Node to Interact with the BPEL Process

In this step, we will configure a node to interact with the BPEL process. We will define the request and response messages and channels on which these messages will travel.

First, import `CreateOrder.wsdl` (created previously) into PeopleSoft using the URL option. This identifies CreateOrder as the process, that will be invoked when an order is created in PeopleSoft. Upon importing the WSDL into PeopleSoft, the Integration Broker adds it to the WSDL repository.

To import `CreateOrder.wsdl`, select **PeopleTools | Integration Broker | Web Services | Import WSDL**.

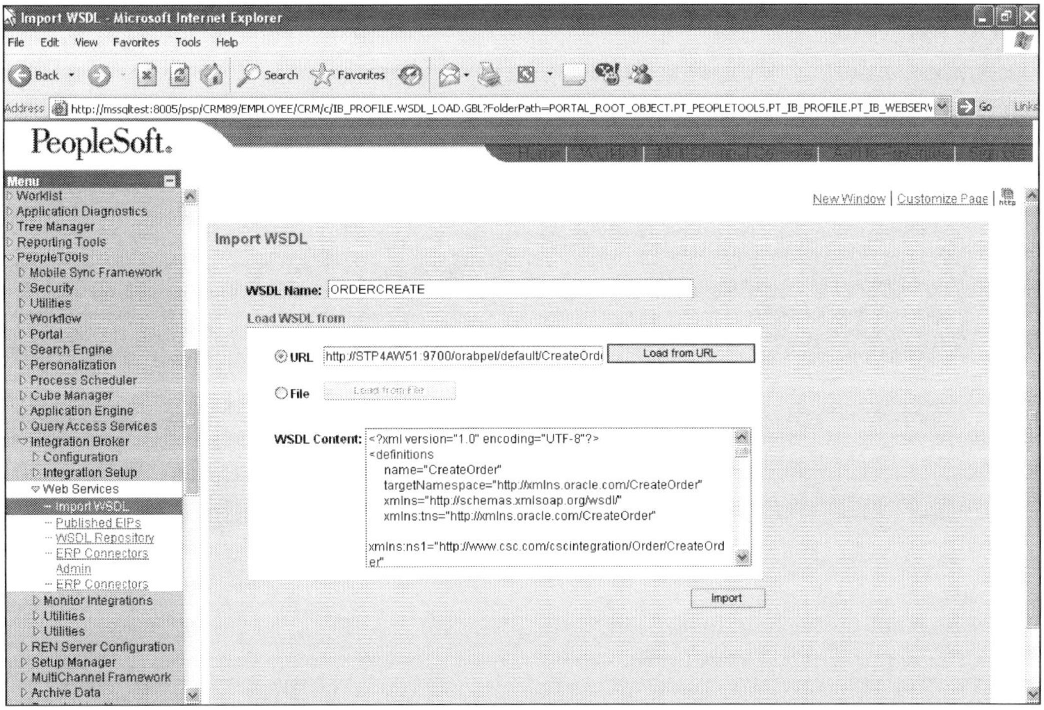

You can now access the WSDL in the WSDL repository using the **WSDL Repository** page.

Once the CreateOrder WSDL is imported into PeopleSoft, a remote node has to be configured to communicate with the BPEL process. To define this communication, you have to add the corresponding *request message*, *response message*, and *message channel*.

To create a new remote node:

1. Select the **Create a New Node Definition** option.

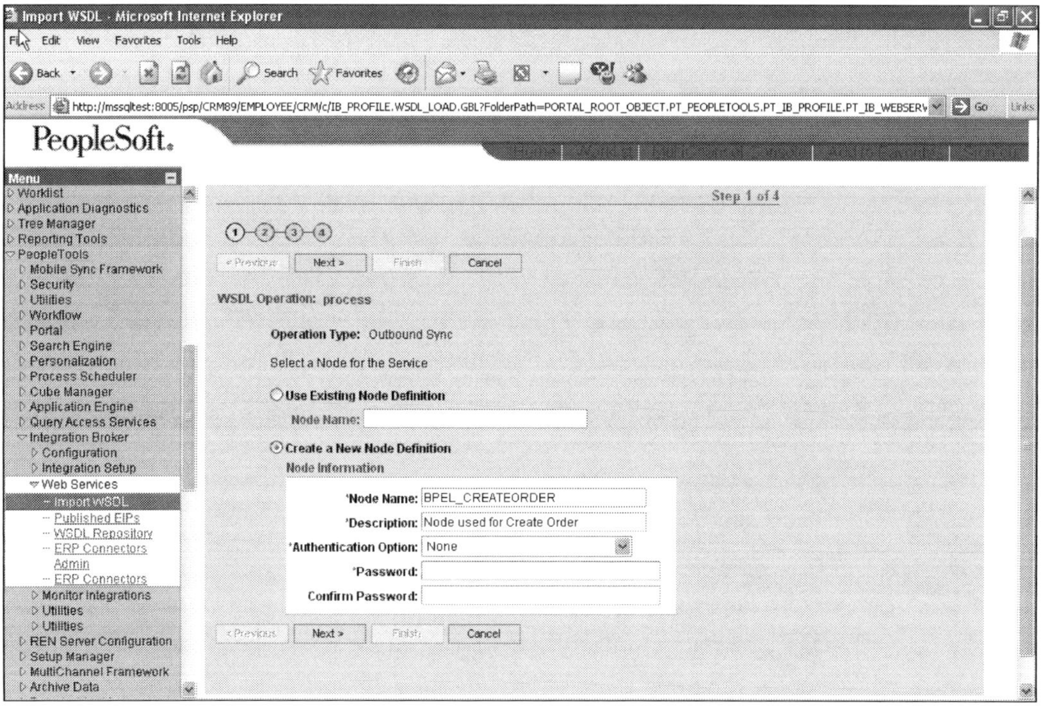

2. In the **Node Name** field, enter **BPEL_CREATEORDER** for the new node definition.
3. In the **Description** field, enter a descriptive name for the node.
4. From the **Authentication Option** drop-down list, select an authentication method. The valid options are **None** (the default), **Certificate**, or **Password**.
5. In the (optional) **Password** field, enter a password.
6. In the (optional) **Confirm Password** field, re-enter the password.

Click on the **Next** button to proceed to the next page in the WSDL Operation Wizard, where you select request and response messages for the service. Request and response messages are unstructured messages that you create in PeopleSoft to represent SOAP `Request` and `Response` messages.

To create a new request or response message:

1. Select the **Create a New Message** option in the appropriate section.
2. To create a new request message, select the option in the **Request Message** section. Enter **BPEL_ORDER_REQ** in the **Message Name** field.
3. To create a new response message, select the option in the **Response Message** section. Enter **BPEL_ORDER_RES** in the **Message Name** field.
4. Newly created messages default the message version to **VERSION_1**. PeopleSoft Integration Broker populates the **Message Version** field with this value.

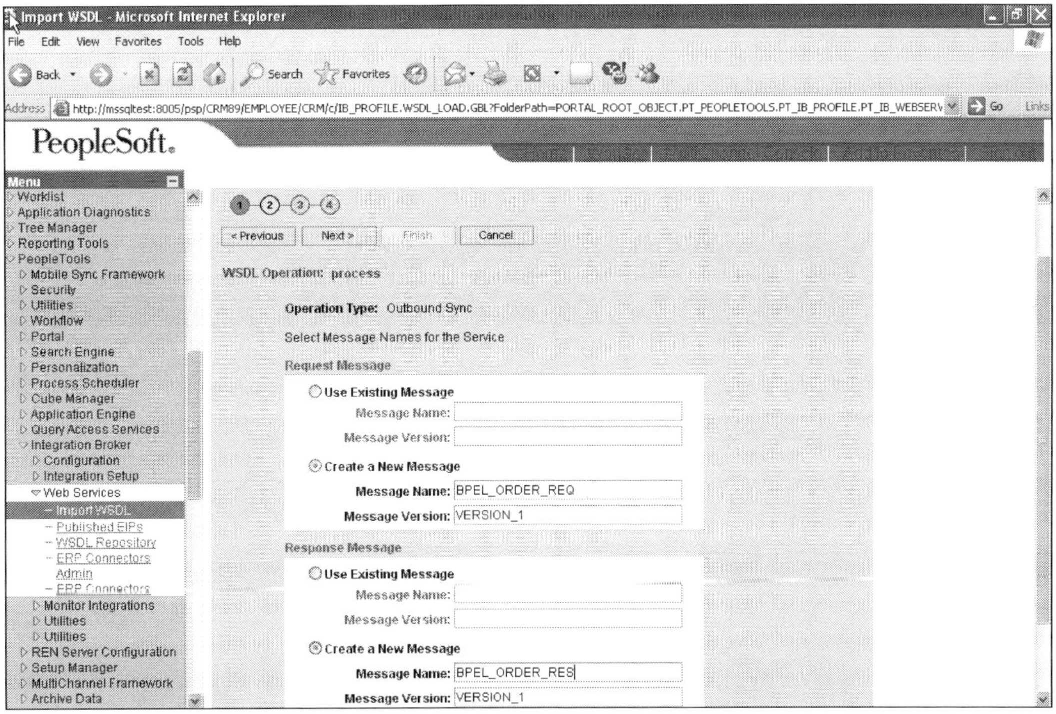

PeopleSoft Integration Broker automatically assigns the new message to the new message channel. At the end of the wizard configuration, the outbound synchronous transaction is created on the node using the new messages.

5. Enter the new message channel name in the **Channel Name** field as **BPEL_SERVICES**.

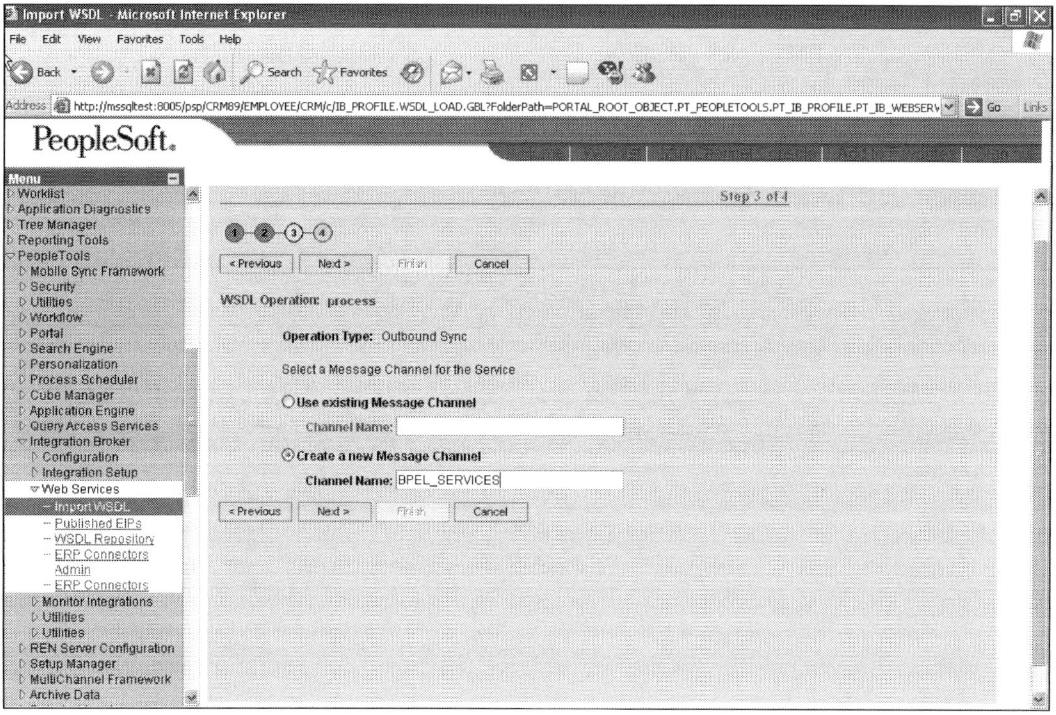

This completes Step 1 of configuring PeopleSoft. You imported the WSDL to tell PeopleSoft which web service to call. You also defined node, messages, and channels to pass information to the web service (BPEL process CreateOrder). In the next step, you will establish a relationship between the Sales order EIP and this newly configured node.

Establish Relationship between EIP and Node

This step will create a link between the `CRM_SALES_ORDER` EIP and the new node. When the `CRM_SALES_ORDER` EIP is published to the Integration Broker, the link that we just created will send the `CRM_SALES_ORDER` message to the remote node we just created, as a request message.

1. Select **Node Definition** from the **People Tools | Integration Setup**; search for the **BPEL_CREATEORDER** node.

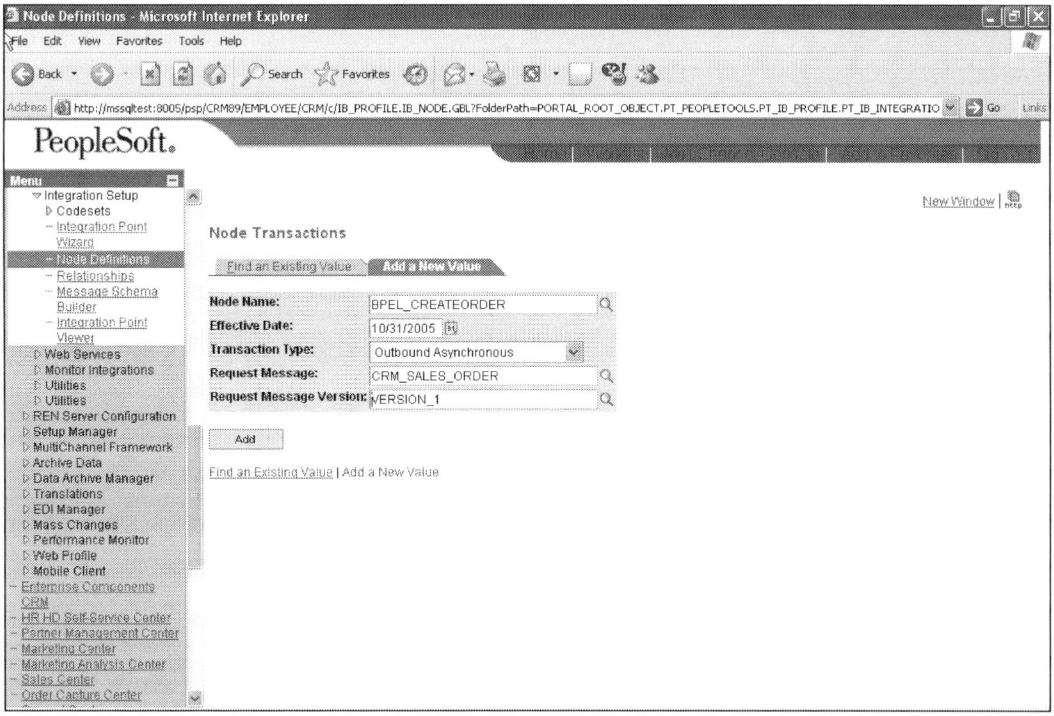

2. In this selected node, change the **Transaction Type** to **Outbound Asynchronous**, and enter **CRM_SALES_ORDER** as **Request Message**.

Create Transformation Code

In this step, you will create the Application Engine program `WSDL_ORDER`. (Application Engine is the PeopleSoft high volume application processor. Application Engine programs are developed with the Application Designer and can leverage common PeopleTools objects such as records, PeopleCode, and SQL objects.) `WSDL_ORDER` will transform the sales order message received from the EIP to a BPEL request (SOAP message) and publish the transformed message on the node channel.

Add the following code to transform and send the request to the node we created earlier. Once the request is submitted to the node, the node will invoke the web service configured to it. The web service will be invoked and the response is sent back to the node, which sends the XML message to the PeopleCode method.

```
/* Get the data from the AE Runtime */
Local TransformData &transformData = %TransformData;

Local File &logFile = GetFile("TestSyncReqResStep3.log","W",
%FilePath_Absolute);

Local string &destNode = &transformData.DestNode;

&logFile.WriteLine("DestNode:" | &destNode);

/* Set a temp object to contain the incoming document */
Local XmlDoc &xmlDoc = &transformData.XmlDoc;

Local string &xmlStr = &xmlDoc.GenXmlString();

&logFile.WriteLine("Transformed XML :" | &xmlStr);

/* Maps the &xmlDoc  to the BPEL_ORDER_REQ and
   publish to the BPEL_CREATEORDER node.
   Node will invoke BPEL CreateOrder process.
   Response will be assigned to &response variable. */

Local XmlDoc &response = SyncRequestXmlDoc(&xmlDoc, Message.BPEL_
ORDER_REQ, Node.BPEL_CREATEORDER);

&logFile.WriteLine("Response XML Data:" | &response.GenXmlString());

&logFile.Close();
```

Linking WSDL_ORDER Apps Engine Program with the Node

In this step, you will relate the transformation code to the CreateOrder node. Hence, whenever BPEL Process Manager is invoked, this transformation code will be executed.

Create a new relationship WSDL_ORDER and map it to the `WSDL_ORDER` node. To do that:

1. Select **Relationships** from the **People Tools | Integration Setup** and select **Add New Value.**
2. Map the initial node as **BPEL_CREATEORDER, Request Message Name** as **CRM_SALES_ORDER , Transaction Type** as **OA , Result Node** as **BPEL_ CREATEORDER**, and **Request Message Name** as **CRM_SALES_ORDER** and their versions will be selected by default. Then click on **Add**.

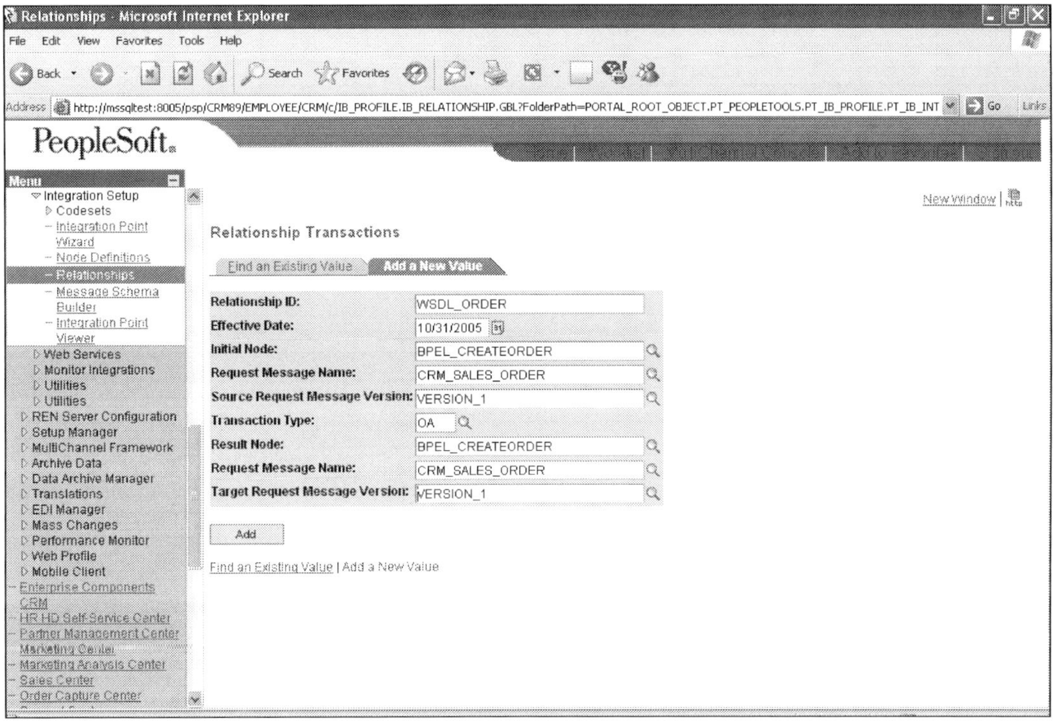

3. Map the transformation **Request** as **WSDL_ORDER**.

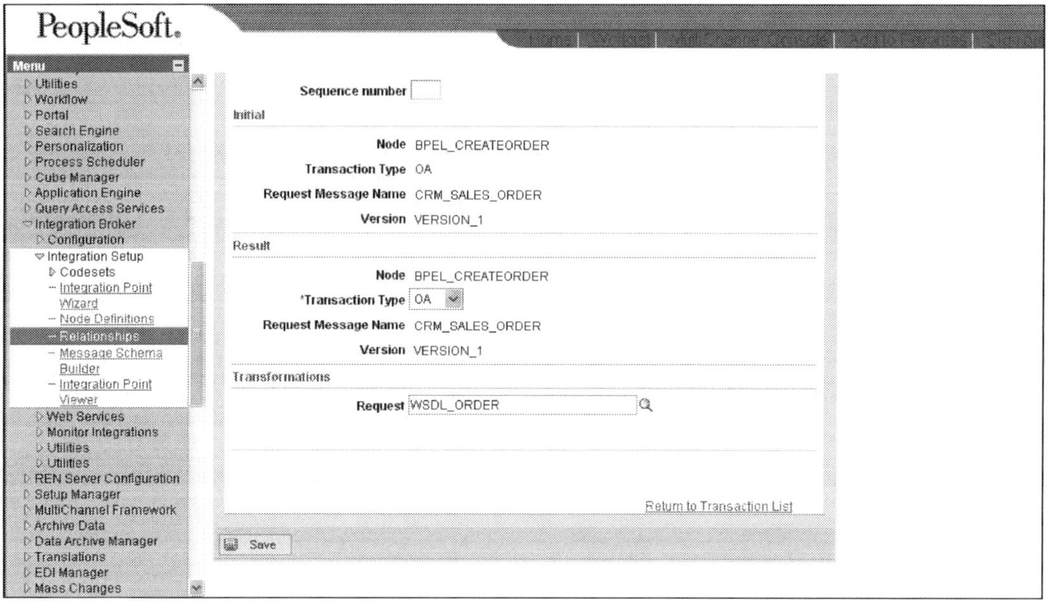

This completes the sales order creation steps. Again, watch the design time-viewlet (`http://www.oracle.com/technology/pub/articles/bpel_cookbook/files/configuration_setup_viewlet_version3.0_viewlet.html`) to see how all these steps are configured; in the run-time viewlet (`http://www.oracle.com/technology/pub/articles/bpel_cookbook/files/psft_bpel_oracle_ordercreation_2.0.html`), you will actually see a sales order being submitted from PeopleSoft and traveling to Oracle Apps.

Summary

With heterogeneous applications across multiple different business units, organizations have challenges aggregating information. Integrating these systems represents a huge investment. Now, as demonstrated here, such organizations have a choice to easily integrate such applications using standards like BPEL.

7
Service Engines

This chapter will introduce the JBI Service Engine and how it is supported within the NetBeans Enterprise Pack.

In this chapter, we will discuss the following topics:

- Need for Java Business Integration (JBI)
- Enterprise Service Bus
- Normalized Message Router
- Introduction to Service Engines
- NetBeans Support for Service Engines
- BPEL Service Engine
- Java EE Service Engine
- SQL Service Engine
- IEP Service Engine
- XSLT Service Engine

Need for Java Business Integration (JBI)

To have a good understanding of Service Engines (a specific type of JBI component), we need to first understand the reason for Java Business Integration.

In the business world, not all systems talk the same language. They use different protocols and different forms of communications. Legacy systems in particular can use proprietary protocols for external communication. The advent and acceptance of XML has been greatly beneficial in allowing systems to be easily integrated, but XML itself is not the complete solution.

When some systems were first developed, they were not envisioned to be able to communicate with many other systems; they were developed with closed interfaces using closed protocols. This, of course, is fine for the system developer, but makes system integration very difficult. This closed and proprietary nature of enterprise systems makes integration between enterprise applications very difficult. To allow enterprise systems to effectively communicate between each other, system integrators would use vendor-supplied APIs and data formats or agree on common exchange mechanisms between their systems. This is fine for small short term integration, but quickly becomes unproductive as the number of enterprise applications to integrate gets larger. The following figure shows the problems with traditional integration.

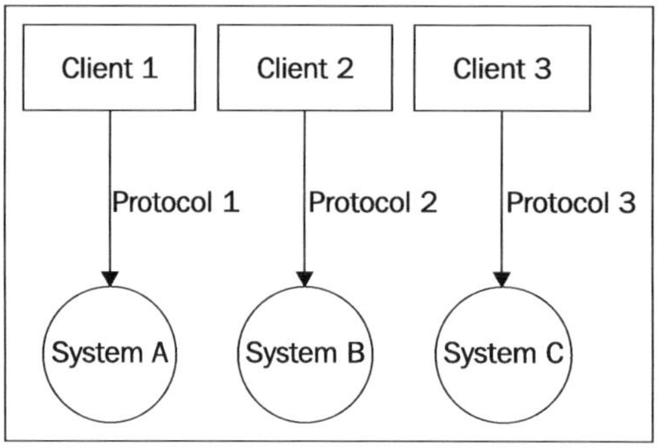

As we can see in the figure, each third party system that we want to integrate with uses a different protocol. As a system integrator, we potentially have to learn new technologies and new APIs for each system we wish to integrate with. If there are only two or three systems to integrate with, this is not really too much of a problem. However, the more systems we wish to integrate with, the more proprietary code we have to learn and integration with other systems quickly becomes a large problem.

To try and overcome these problems, the Enterprise Application Integration (EAI) server was introduced. This concept has an integration server acting as a central hub. The EAI server traditionally has proprietary links to third party systems, so the application integrator only has to learn one API (the EAI server vendors). With this architecture however, there are still several drawbacks. The central hub can quickly become a bottleneck, and because of the **hub-and-spoke** architecture, any problems at the hub are rapidly manifested at all the clients.

Enterprise Service Bus

To help solve this problem, leading companies in the integration community (led by Sun Microsystems) proposed the Java Business Integration Specification Request (JSR 208) (Full details of the JSR can be found at `http://jcp.org/en/jsr/detail?id=208`). JSR 208 proposed a standard framework for business integration by providing a standard set of service provider interfaces (SPIs) to help alleviate the problems experienced with Enterprise Application Integration.

The standard framework described in JSR 208 allows pluggable components to be added into a standard architecture and provides a standard common mechanism for each of these components to communicate with each other based upon WSDL. The pluggable nature of the framework described by JSR 208 is depicted in the following figure. It shows us the concept of an Enterprise Service Bus and introduces us to the Service Engine (SE) component:

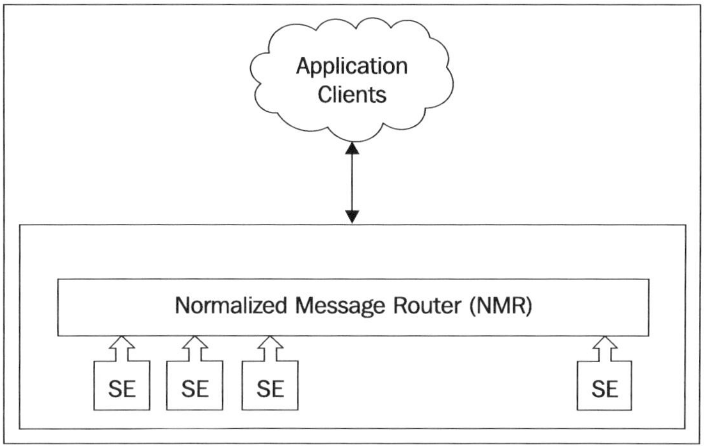

JSR 208 describes a service engine as a component, which provides business logic and transformation services to other components, as well as consuming such services. SEs can integrate Java-based applications (and other resources), or applications with available Java APIs.

> Service Engine is a component which provides (and consumes) business logic and transformation services to other components. There are various Service Engines available, such as the BPEL service engine for orchestrating business processes, or the Java EE service engine for consuming Java EE Web Services. We will discuss some of the more common Service Engines later in this chapter.

The Normalized Message Router

As we can see from the previous figure, SE's don't communicate directly with each other or with the clients, instead they communicate via the NMR. This is one of the key concepts of JBI, in that it promotes loose coupling of services.

So, what is NMR and what is its purpose? NMR is responsible for taking messages from clients and routing them to the appropriate Service Engines for processing. (This is not strictly true as there is another standard JBI component called the Binding Component responsible for receiving client messages. Again, this further enhances the support for loose coupling within JBI, as Service Engines are decoupled from their transport infrastructure).

NMR is responsible for passing normalized (that is based upon WSDL) messages between JBI components. Messages typically consist of a payload and a message header which contains any other message data required for the Service Engine to understand and process the message (for example, security information). Again, we can see that this provides a loosely coupled model in which Service Engines have no prior knowledge of other Service Engines. This therefore allows the JBI architecture to be flexible, and allows different component vendors to develop standard based components.

> Normalized Message Router enables technology for allowing messages to be passed between loosely coupled services such as Service Engines.

The figure below gives an overview of the message routing between a client application and two service engines, in this case the EE and SQL service engines.

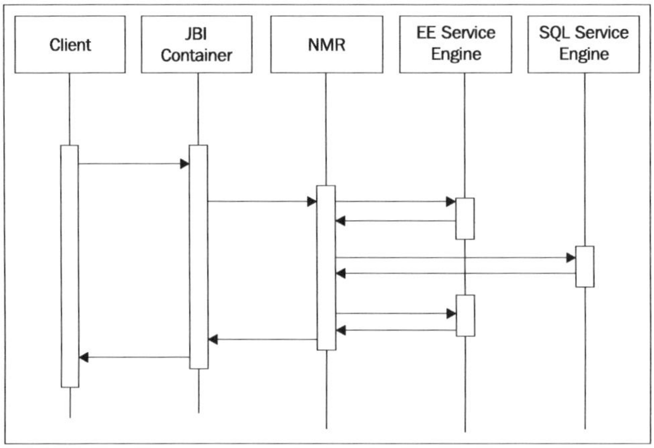

In this figure, a request is made from the client to the JBI Container. This request is passed via NMR to the EE Service Engine. The EE Service Engine then makes a request to the SQL Service Engine via NMR. The SQL Service Engine returns a message to the EE Service Engine again via NMR. Finally, the message is routed back to the client through NMR and JBI framework. The important concept here is that NMR is a message routing hub not only between clients and service engines, but also for intra-communication between different service engines.

The entire architecture we have discussed is typically referred to as an Enterprise Service Bus.

> *Enterprise Service Bus (ESB)* is a standard-based middleware architecture that allows pluggable components to communicate with each other via a messaging subsystem.

Now that we have a basic understanding of what a Service Engine is, how communication is made between application clients and Service Engines, and between Service Engines themselves, let's take a look at what support the NetBeans IDE gives us for interacting with Service Engines.

Service Engine Life Cycle

Each Service Engine can exist in one of a set of predefined states. This is called the Service Engine life cycle.

- Started
- Stopped
- Shutdown
- Uninstalled

The figure below gives an overview of the life cycle of Service Engines:

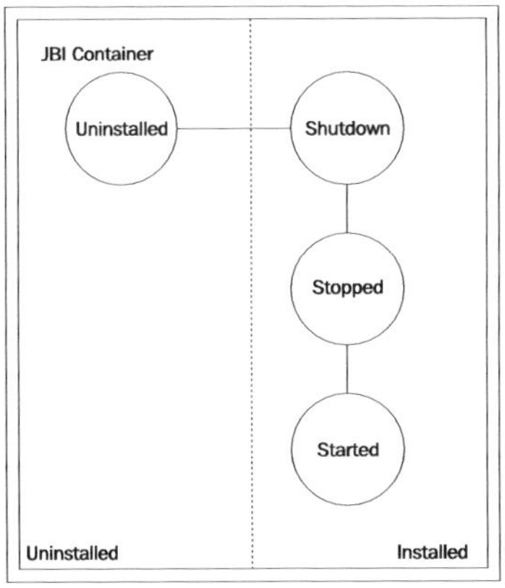

Service Engines can be managed from the command line utility, `asadmin`, that is supplied as part of the Sun Java System Application Server. The table below shows some of the common commands that can be used to manage Service Engines:

`asadmin list-jbi-service-engines`	Obtains a list of installed Service Engines
	`$>./asadmin list-jbi-service-engines`
	`sun-aspect-engine`
	`sun-bpel-engine`
	`sun-dtel-engine`
	`sun-etl-engine`
	`sun-iep-engine`
	`sun-javaee-engine`
	`sun-script-engine`
	`sun-sql-engine`
	`sun-wlm-engine`
	`sun-xslt-engine`
	`Command list-jbi-service-engines executed successfully.`

`asadmin show-jbi-service-engine`	Shows the status of an installed Service Engine
	`$>./asadmin show-jbi-service-engine sun-bpel-engine`
	`Component Information`
	`---------------------`
	`Name        : sun-bpel-engine`
	`State       : Shutdown`
	`Description : This is a bpel service engine.`

`asadmin start-jbi-component`	Starts a Service Engine
	`$>./asadmin start-jbi-component sun-bpel-engine`
	`Started component sun-bpel-engine.`

`asadmin stop-jbi-component`	Stops a Service Engine
	`$>./asadmin stop-jbi-component sun-bpel-engine`
	`Stopped component sun-bpel-engine.`

Service Engines can also be managed from within the NetBeans IDE instead of using the `asadmin` application. We will look at that in the next section.

Service Engines in NetBeans

The NetBeans Enterprise Pack provides a version of the Sun Java System Application Server 9.0 which includes several Service Engines from the Open ESB project.

All of these Service Engines can be administered from within the NetBeans IDE from the **Services** explorer panel. Within this panel, expand the **Servers | Sun Java System Application Server 9 | JBI | Service Engines** node to get a complete list of Service Engines deployed to the server.

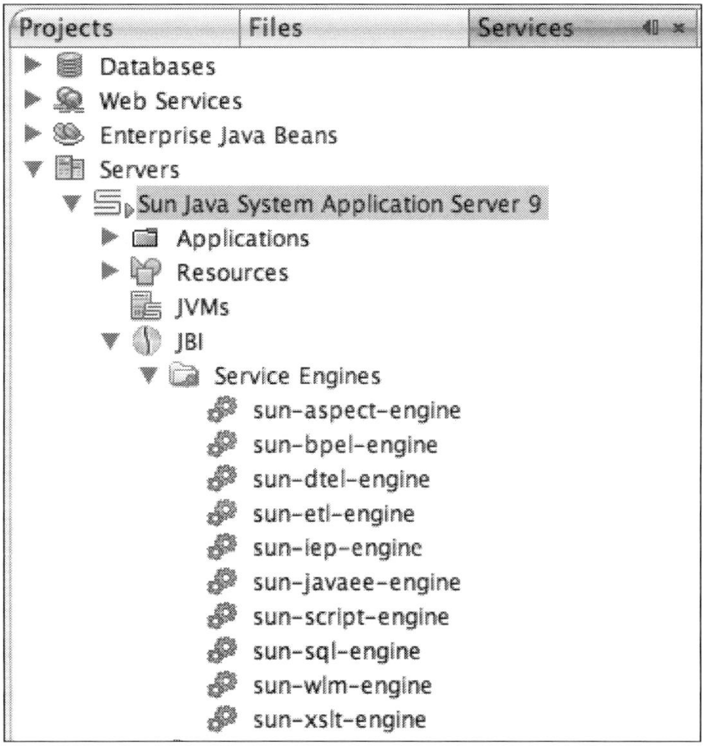

The NetBeans Enterprise Pack 5.5 and the NetBeans 6.0 IDE have different **Service Engines** installed. The following table lists which Service Engines are installed in which version of the NetBeans Enterprise Pack:

Service Engine Name	Description	NetBeans 6.0	NetBeans 5.5
sun-aspect-engine	Aspect Service Engine	Yes	No
sun-bpel-engine	BPEL Service Engine	Yes	Yes
sun-dtel-engine	DTEL Service Engine	Yes	No
sun-etl-engine	ETL (Extract, Transform and Load) Service Engine	Yes	No
sun-iep-engine	IEP (Intelligent Event Processor) Service Engine	No	No
sun-javaee-engine	Java EE Service Engine	Yes	Yes
sun-script-engine	Scripting Service Engine	Yes	No
sun-sql-engine	SQL Service Engine	Yes	No
sun-wlm-engine	WLM (Work List Manager) Service Engine	Yes	No
sun-xslt-engine	XSLT Service Engine	Yes	No

In the previous section, we discussed the life cycle of Service Engines and how this can be managed using the `asadmin` application. Using the NetBeans IDE, it is easy to manage the state of a Service Engine. Right-clicking on any of the **Service Engines** within the **Services** explorer shows a menu allowing the life cycle to be managed as shown in the figure below:

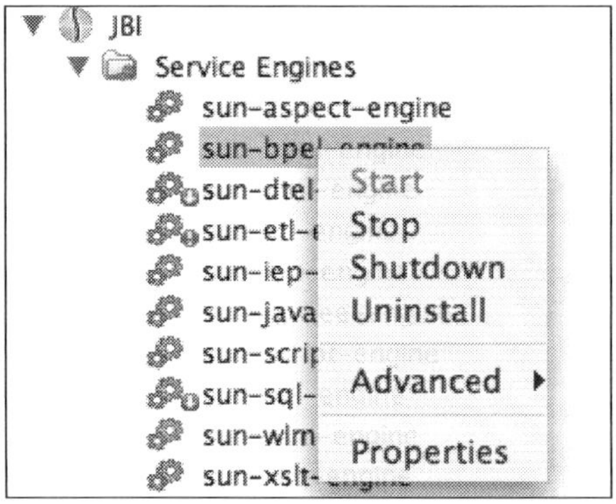

To illustrate the different states in a Service Engine life cycle, a different icon is displayed:

Start	
Stop	
Shutdown	
Uninstalled	The service engine is not displayed in the list.

Now that we have a good understanding of what Service Engines are, and what support the NetBeans IDE provides, let's take a closer look at some of the more common Service Engines provided with the NetBeans Enterprise Pack.

BPEL Service Engine

Similar to all the other Service Engines deployed to the JBI Container within the Sun Java System Application Server and accessible through NetBeans, the BPEL Service Engine is a standard JBI Compliant component as defined by JSR 208.

The BPEL Service Engine enables orchestration of WS-BPEL 2.0 business processes. This enables a work flow of different business services to be built as shown in the following figure:

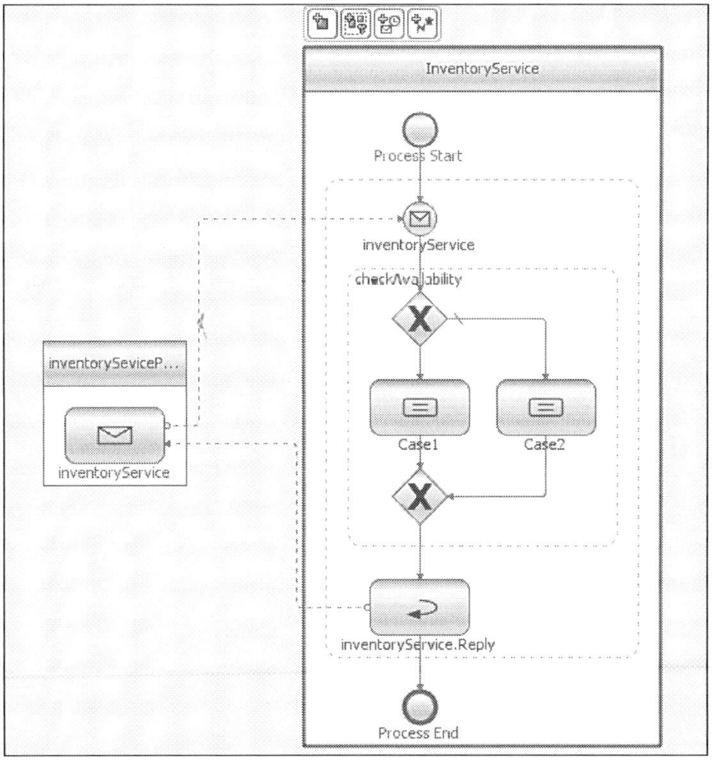

Within NetBeans, we can create BPEL modules which consist of one or more BPEL processes. BPEL modules are built into standard JBI component, and then deployed to the JBI container where the BPEL Service Engine allows the processes within the module to be executed. In JBI terms, this is called a Service Unit.

> A *Service Unit* is a deployable component (jar file) that can be deployed to a Service Engine.

New BPEL modules are created in NetBeans by selecting the **File | New Project** menu option and then selecting **BPEL Module** from the **SOA** category as shown in the following figure:

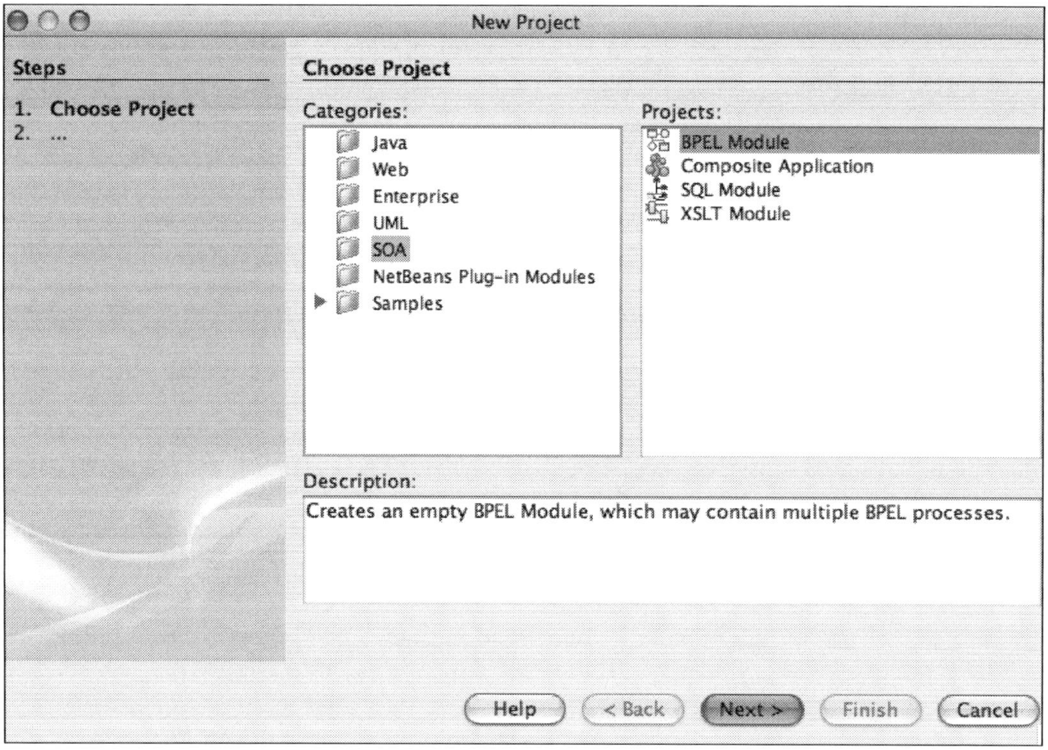

Within a BPEL module project, we add **BPEL Processes**. These processes describe the orchestration of different services.

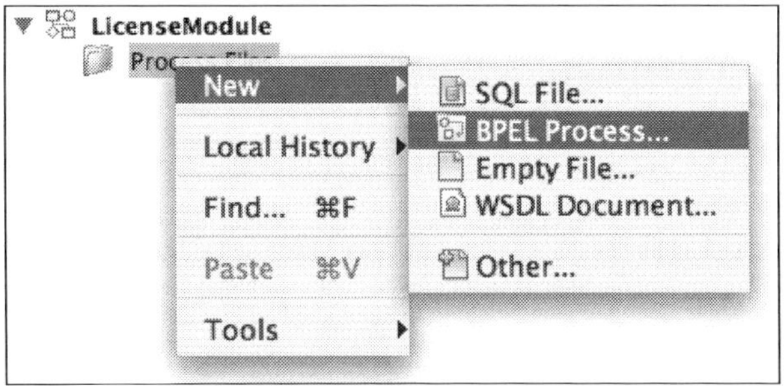

All the standard operations specified by WS-BPEL 2.0 Specification (like Providing and Consuming Web Services, Structuring the processing logic, and performing basic activities such as assignments and waiting) are available within the BPEL Service Engine. The NetBeans designer provides simple drag-and-drop support for all of these activities.

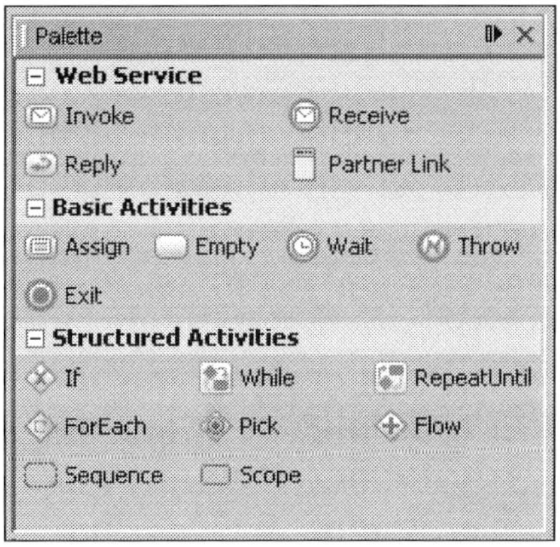

Consider, for example, a service for generating license keys for a piece of software. In a Service Oriented Architecture, our system may consist of two services:

1. A Customer Service: this service would be responsible for ensuring that license requests are only made by valid customers.
2. A License Generation Service: this service would be responsible for generating valid license keys.

Within NetBeans, we can create a BPEL process that ties these services together allowing us to return valid license keys to our customers and details of purchasing options to non-customers.

Java EE Service Engine

The Java EE service engine acts as a bridge between the JBI container allowing Java EE web services to be consumed from within JBI components. Without the Java EE service Engine, JBI components would have to execute Java EE Web Services via remote calls instead of via in-process communication. The Java EE Service Engine allows both servlet and EJB-based web services to be consumed from within JBI components.

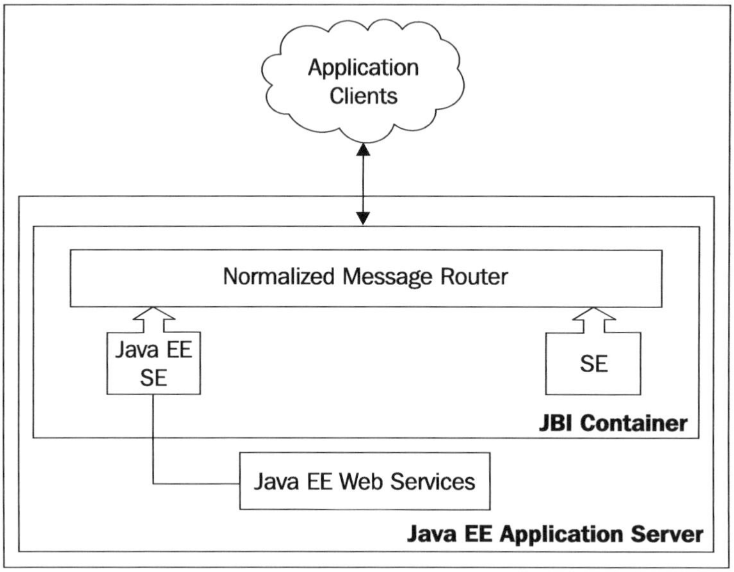

The Java EE Service Engine provides several benefits when executing Java EE Web Services.

- Increased performance
- Transaction support
- Security support

These are explained in the following subsections.

Increased Performance

Using the Java EE service engine enables Java EE web services to be invoked in process within the same JVM, as the services are running. This eliminates the need for any wire-based transmission protocols and provides increased performance.

Transaction Support

Using an in-process Communication Model between Java EE Application Server and JBI container allows both web services and JBI modules to use the same transaction model. Through multiple web service calls and calls to other JBI modules. For example, BPEL processes can all use the same transaction.

Security Support

When executing Java EE Web Services from within the JBI container, the Java EE Service Engine allows security contexts to propagate between components. This removes the need to authenticate against each service.

SQL Service Engine

SQL service engine allows SQL statements to be executed against relational databases and allows the results of SQL statements to be returned to the client application or other Service Engines for further processing.

SQL service engine allows SQL DDL (Data Definition Language), SQL DML (Data Manipulation Language), and stored procedures to be executed against a database. This, therefore, allows different scenarios to be executed against the database. For example, obtaining a customer's address or the number of outstanding invoices a customer may have.

Within NetBeans, the SQL module is used to interact with the SQL Service Engine. The SQL module project consists of three artifacts as follows:

- configuration xml file (`connectivityInfo.xml`)
- one or more SQL files containing distinct SQL statements
- WSDL file describing the SQL operations.

SQL Modules are created by choosing **File | New Project** and then selecting the **SQL Module** option from within the **SOA** projects category.

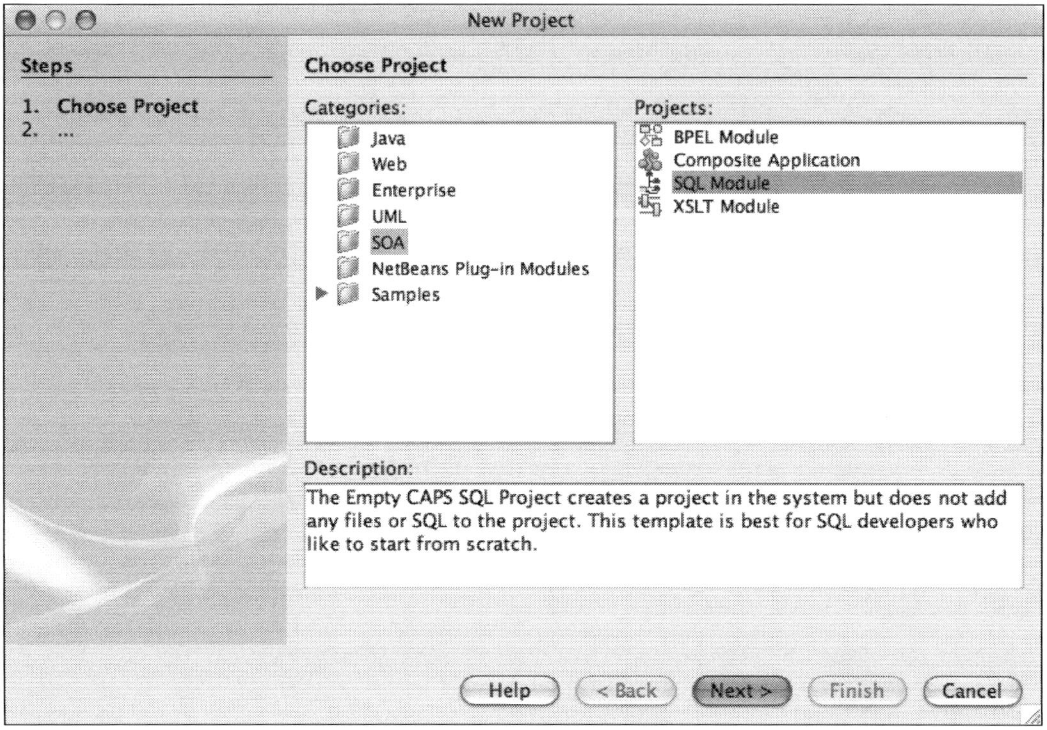

Within a **SQL Module**, there is a configuration file called `connectivityInfo.xml` which contains connection details for the database. This can either be specified as a driver connection or as a JNDI name for a data source.

```
<?xml version="1.0" encoding="UTF-8"?>
<connection>
    <database-url value='jdbc:derby://localhost:1527/db_name'/>
    <jndi-name value=''/>
</connection>
```

Each SQL statement that is to be presented to client applications as a new operation must be stored in a separate SQL file. Using the example scenarios above, we would have two SQL files with contents shown in the following table:

`customer_address.sql`	`select address1, address2, zip from customer where customer_id=?`
`outstanding_invoices.sql`	`select count(*) from invoices where customer_id=? and isPayed='n'`

In order for other JBI components to be able to access our SQL module, we must have a WSDL file which describes the operations we have defined (`customer_address.sql` and `outstanding_invoices.sql`). NetBeans will generate this file for us when we select the **Generate WSDL** option from right-clicking on the project in the **Projects** explorer.

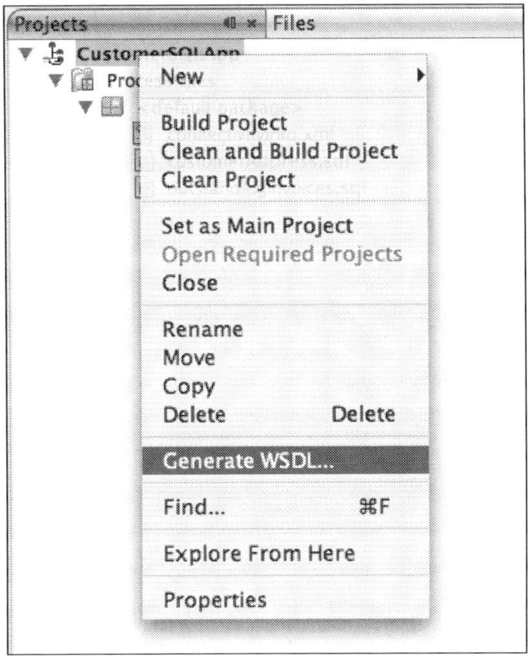

SQL Service assembly units cannot be executed directly from within the JBI container. To execute the SQL Service Unit, it needs to be added as part of a composite application. This is then called a Service Assembly.

> *Service Assembly*: a deployable component (jar file) that consists of a collection of Service Units.

IEP Service Engine

The Intelligent Event Processing service engine allows data to be read from an input source and then processed into a format that can be used for a variety of different purposes such as reporting or business intelligence information.

For example, an IEP project could be created that takes sales information from a retail system, collects all information made over the last hour, and then outputs it to a database table for reporting purposes. This would enable fast reporting based upon a periodically updated subset of the business data. Any reporting queries performed would therefore be "off-line" to the business database. This way different reporting queries could be performed as and when necessary without any performance impact on the business database.

Depending on the version of NetBeans that you have installed, you may not automatically have support for creating and editing IEP projects. If you do not have IEP project support within NetBeans, both the IEP service engine and NetBeans editor support for IEP projects can be downloaded from `http://www.glassfishwiki.org/jbiwiki/attach/IEPSE/InstallationGuide.zip`.

New IEP modules can be created within NetBeans by selecting the **File | New Project** menu option and then selecting the **Intelligent Event Processing Module** option within the **SOA** category as shown in the following figure:

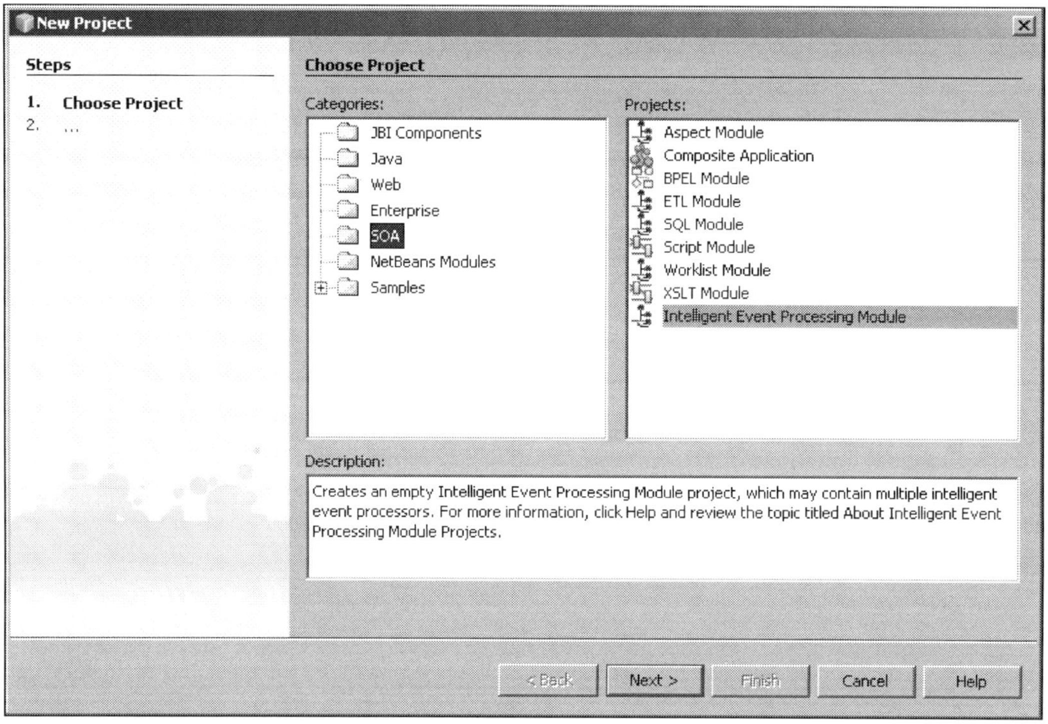

After making the above selections, the second stage of the **New Project** wizard allows the **Project Name** and the **Project Location** to be specified.

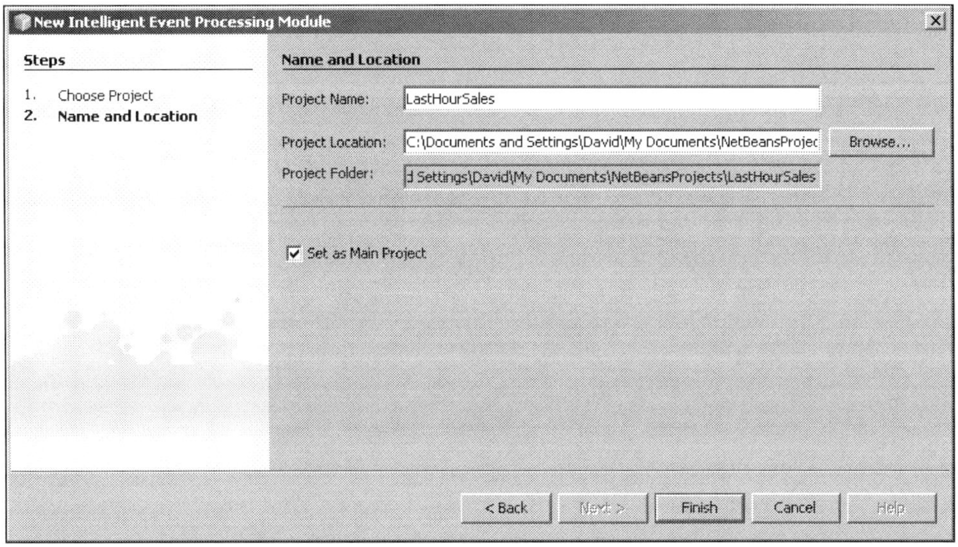

Finally, after creating the new IEP module, new Intelligent Event Processors can be added to the project. This is achieved by right-clicking on the newly created IEP project within the NetBeans **Project** pane and selecting the **New | Intelligent Event Processor** menu option. Selecting this option displays the **New Intelligent Event Processor** wizard which includes one page allowing the IEP **File Name** and **Folder** to be specified.

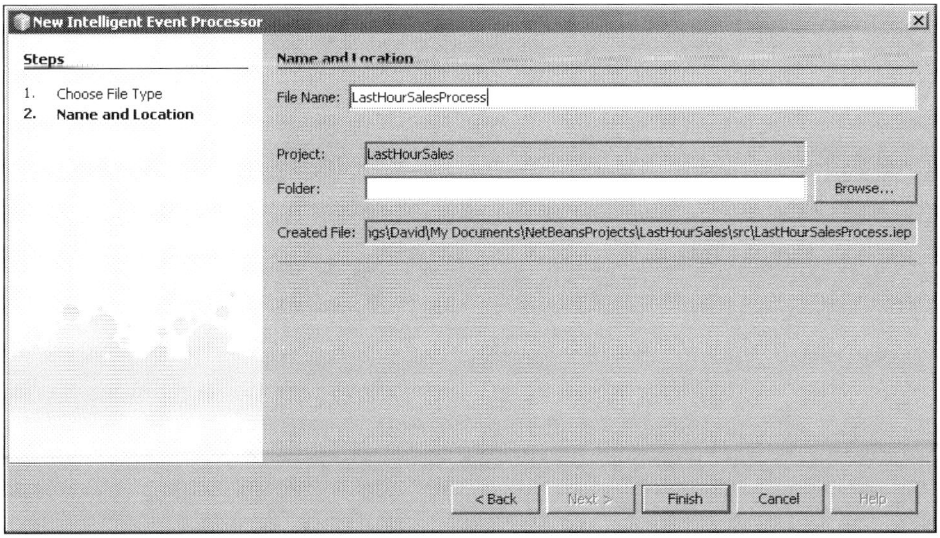

The IEP Process Editor within NetBeans allows many different processing actions to be performed on data. IEP Processes are defined using a drag-and-drop editor. The **Palette**, which shows all of the operations that can be performed on data, is shown in the following figure:

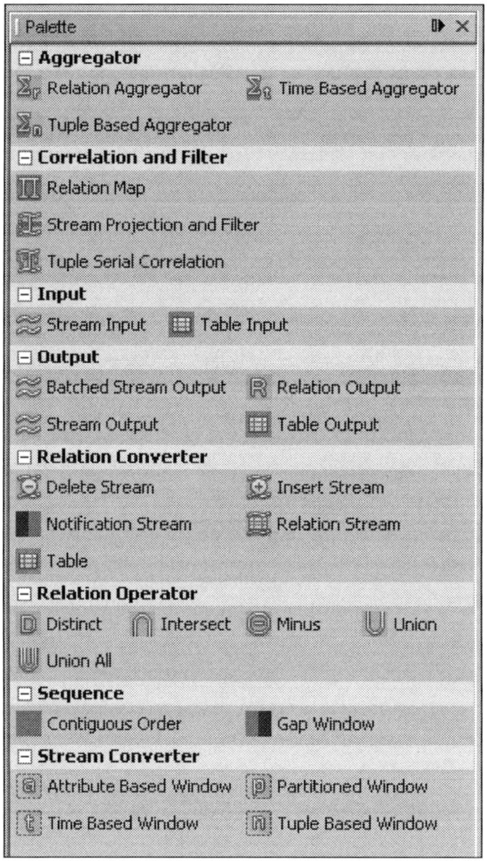

IEP Processes (Service Assemblies) cannot be executed directly from within the JBI container. To execute IEP Processes, they need to be deployed into a Service Assembly and added as part of a composite application.

XSLT Service Engine

XSLT Service Engine enables transformations of XML documents from one format to another using XSL stylesheets. The service engine allows XSL transformations to be deployed as web services which can then be used by external clients.

New XSLT modules can be built to run against the XSLT service engine by selecting the **File | New Project** menu option and then selecting the **XSLT Module** option from within the **SOA** category as shown in the following figure:

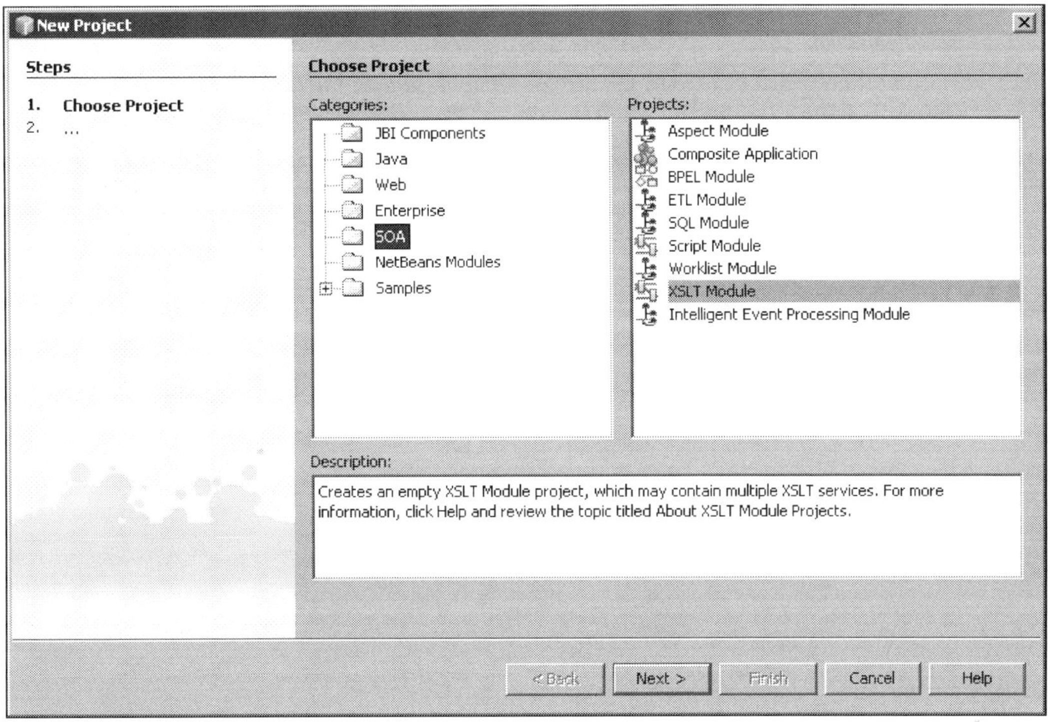

Several different types of files can be created within an **XSLT Module** to allow the service engine to transform XML files from one format to another. XML Schema files can be used to define XML within the transformation process. WSDL files are used to define the operations that are transformed within the service engine. We won't discuss how WSDL files and XML Schema files are created and maintained in this chapter.

The final type of file that can be specified within an **XSLT Module** is an XSLT Service. These types of files can be created by right-clicking on the **XSLT Module** within the **Project** explorer in NetBeans and selecting the **New | XSLT Service** menu option. The result is shown in the next screenshot.

When creating an XSLT Service Unit, two different processing modes (**Service type**) are available:

- Request-Reply Service
- Service Bridge

The **Request-Reply Service** mode enables an XML message to be received from a client, transformed, and then sent back to the original client.

The **Service Bridge** mode enables an XML message to be received from a client and transformed into a different format. The transformed message is then used as an input for invoking a service. The output of this service is then transformed using a second **XSL** stylesheet and returned to the original caller. The **Service Bridge** mode is therefore acting as a bridge between two services. This is an implementation of the Adapter Pattern as defined in Design Patterns—Elements of Reusable Object-Oriented Software by Erich Gamma, Richard Helm, Ralph Johnson, and John Vlissides.

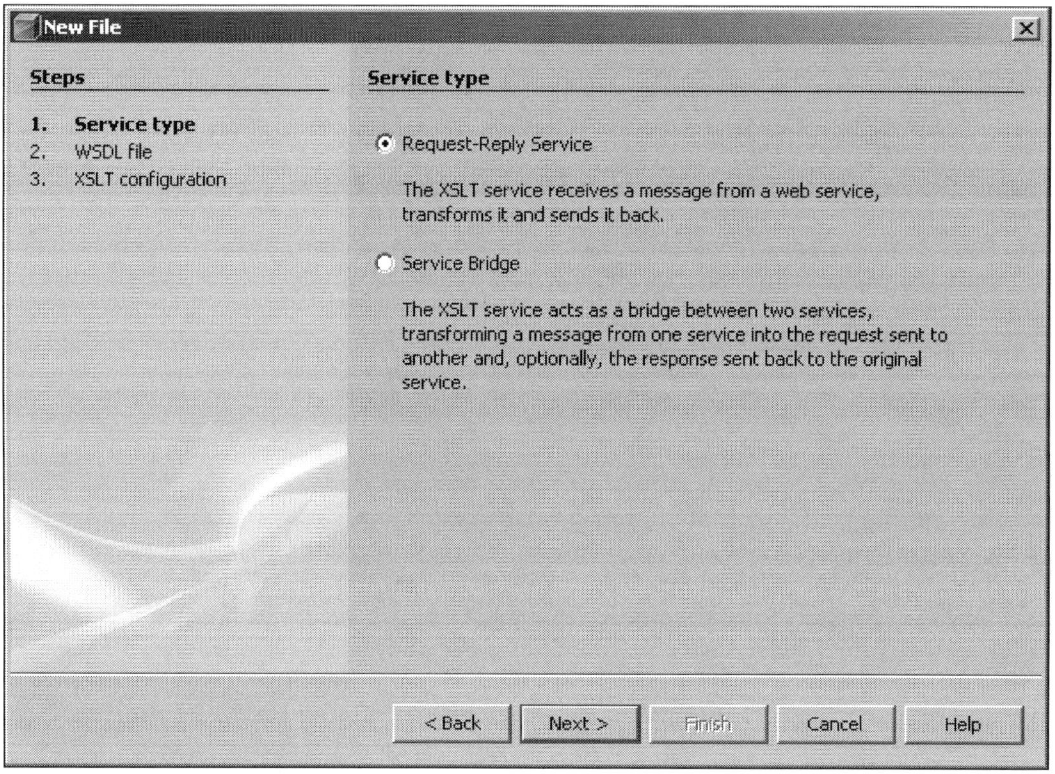

When creating a **Request-Reply Service**, the **New XSLT Service** wizard allows the web service for the XSLT transformation to be specified including details of the port, the operation being executed and the input and output types of the operation as shown in the following two screenshots:

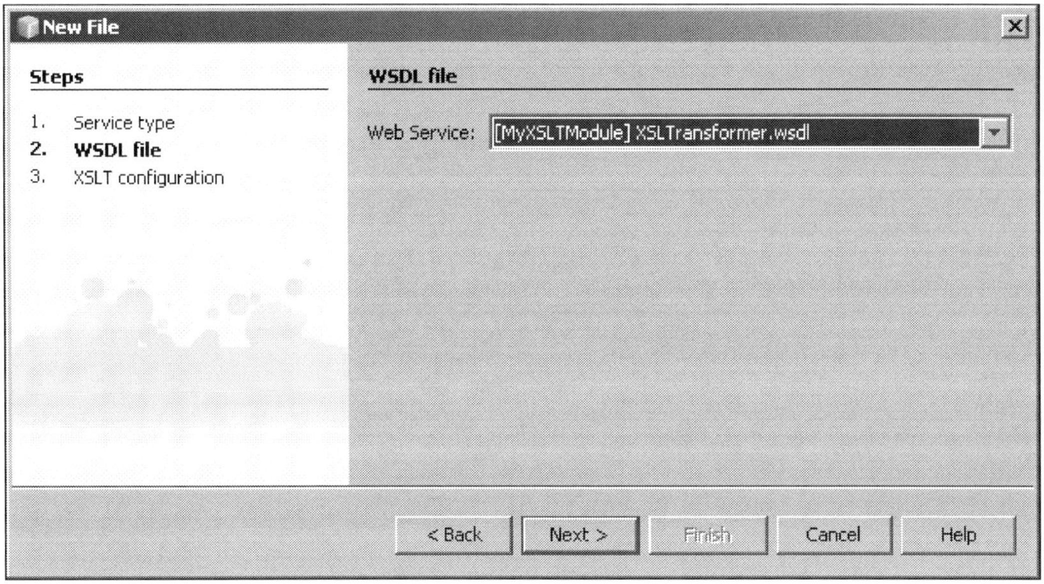
New File
Steps
1. Service type
2. WSDL file
3. XSLT configuration
WSDL file
Web Service:
[MyXSLTModule] XSLTransformer.wsdl
< Back
Next >
Finish
Cancel
Help

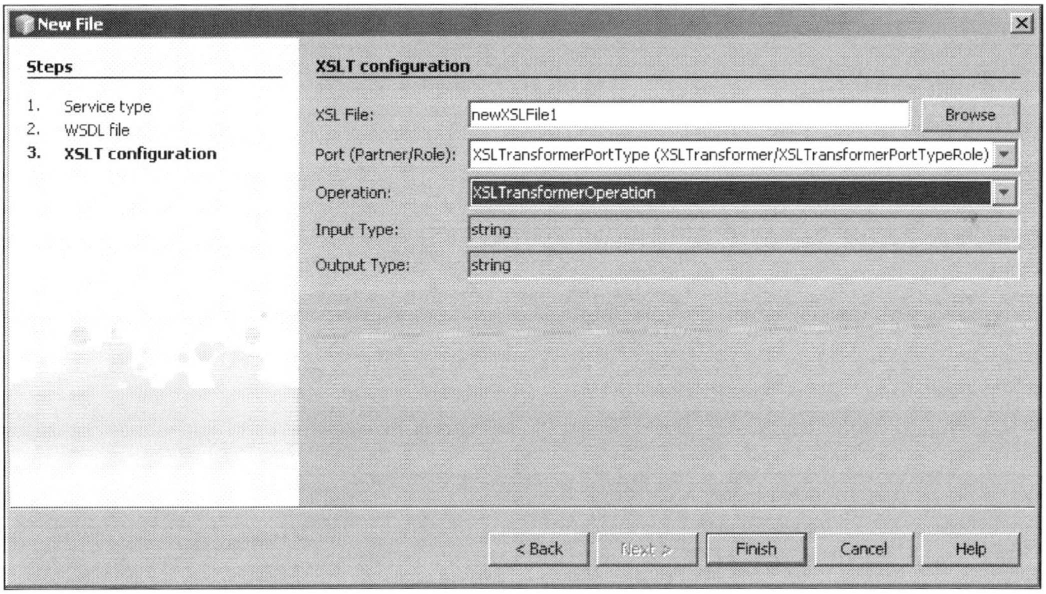
New File
Steps
1. Service type
2. WSDL file
3. XSLT configuration
XSLT configuration
XSL File:
newXSLFile1
Browse
Port (Partner/Role):
XSLTransformerPortType (XSLTransformer/XSLTransformerPortTypeRole)
Operation:
XSLTransformerOperation
Input Type:
string
Output Type:
string
< Back
Next >
Finish
Cancel
Help

When creating a **Service Bridge** service, the two web services to be bridged are specified by first selecting the WSDL for the implemented web service and then for the invoked web service.

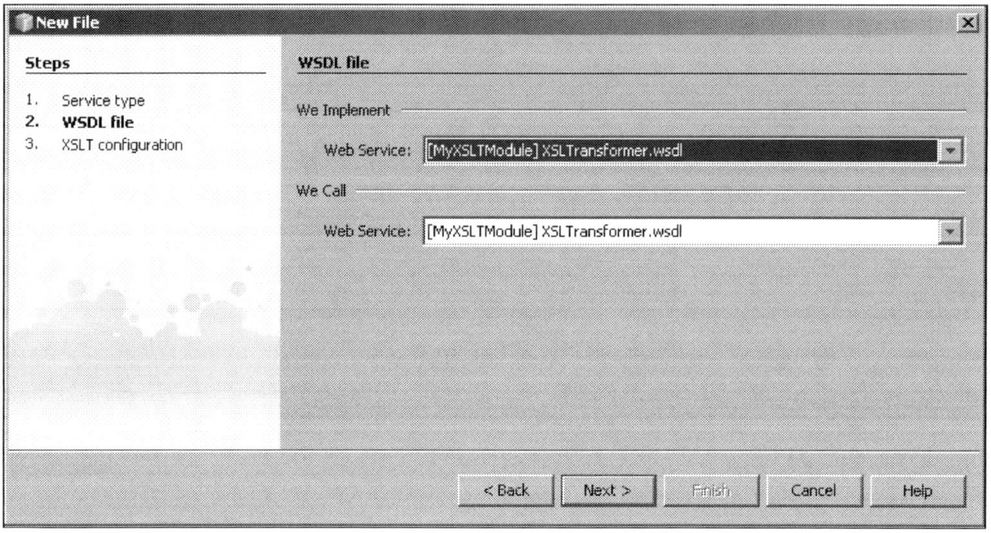

Having selected the web services to bridge, the wizard allows the implemented and invoked web services to be fully specified. Here we need to specify the operation from our implemented service and the operation to call on the invoked service.

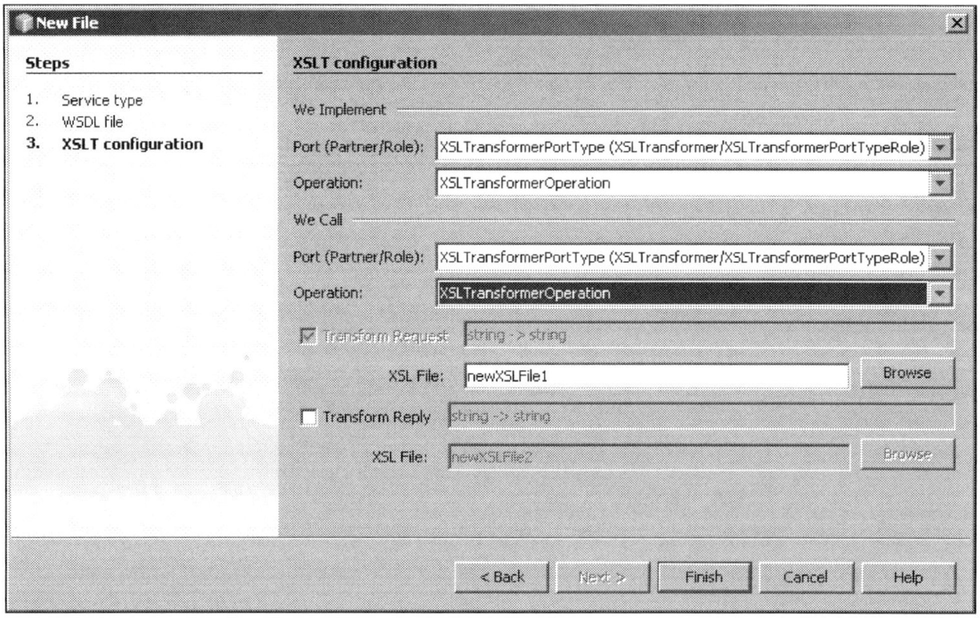

Summary

In this chapter, we have introduced the concept of a Service Engine and given an overview of the Service Engines installed with the NetBeans Enterprise Pack (the BPEL, Java EE, SQL, IEP, and XSLT Service Engines). We've learned that Service Engines:

- Provide business logic functionality to their clients
- Can be consumers and/or providers
- Run within a Java Business Integration (JBI) Server
- Expose their interfaces via WSDL
- Communicate within an Enterprise Service Bus via messaging

We've also discussed some basic concepts about JBI such as the Normalized Message Router, Service Assemblies, and Service Units. We have a good understanding of JBI, some of the problems with Enterprise Application integration and why JBI is useful.

8
Binding Components

In this chapter, we will take a closer look at JBI components, discuss binding component (BC), and look at the support that NetBeans Enterprise Pack provides for these components.

In this chapter, we will discuss:

- The role of binding components in JBI Container
- NetBeans Support for binding components
- File BC
- SMTP BC
- SOAP BC
- JDBC BC
- JMS BC
- FTP BC

Binding Components

Binding components are standard JSR 208 components that plug in to NMR and provide transport independence to Normalized Message Router (NMR) and Service Engines. The role of binding components is to isolate communication protocols from JBI container so that Service Engines are completely decoupled from the communication infrastructure. For example, BPEL Service Engine can receive requests to initiate BPEL process while reading files on the local file system. It can receive these requests from SOAP messages, from a JMS message, or from any of the other binding components installed into JBI container.

[*Binding Component* is a JSR 208 component that provides protocol independent transport services to other JBI components.]

The following figure shows how binding components fit into the JBI Container architecture:

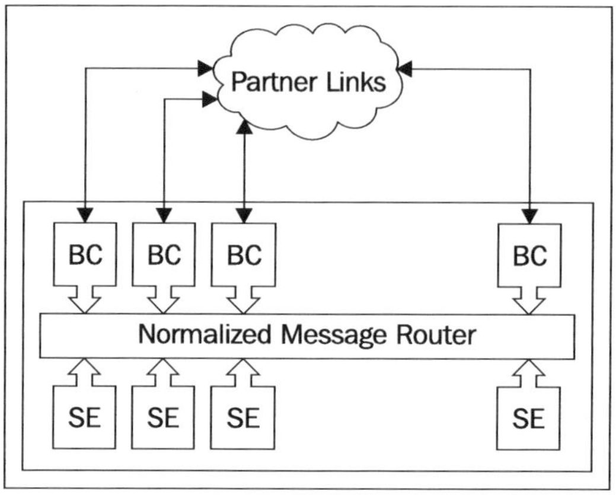

In this figure, we can see that the role of **BC** is to send and receive messages both internally and externally from **Normalized Message Router** using protocols, specific to the binding component. We can also see that any number of binding components can be installed into the JBI container. This figure shows that like Service Engines (**SE**), binding components do not communicate directly with other binding components or with Service Engines. All communication between individual binding components and between binding components and Service Engines is performed via sending standard messages through the **Normalized Message Router**.

NetBeans Support for Binding Components

The following table lists which binding components are installed into the JBI container with NetBeans 5.5 and NetBeans 6.0:

Binding Component	NetBeans 5.5	NetBeans 6.0
File BC	No	Yes
HTTP BC	No	Yes
JDBC BC	No	No
JMS BC	No	Yes
SOAP BC	Yes	No
SMTP	No	No

As is the case with Service Engines, binding components can be managed within the NetBeans IDE. The list of **Binding Components** installed into the **JBI** container can be displayed by expanding the **Servers | Sun Java System Application Server 9 | JBI | Binding Components** node within the **Services** explorer.

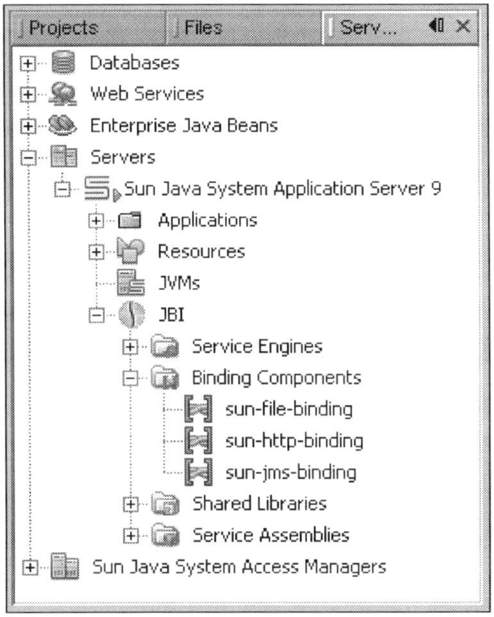

The lifecycle of binding components can be managed by right-clicking on a binding component and selecting a lifecycle process—**Start**, **Stop**, **Shutdown,** or **Uninstall**.

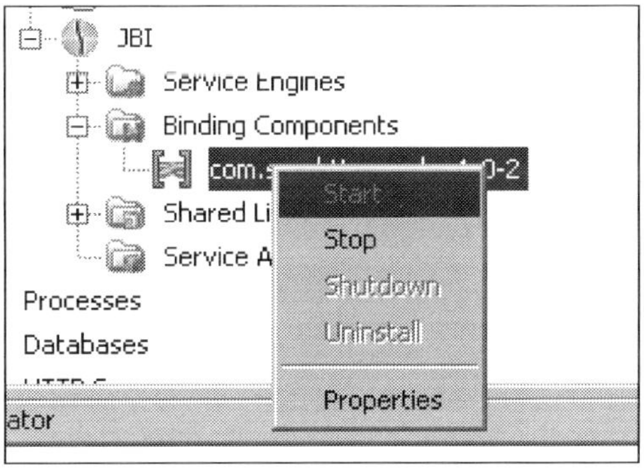

The properties of an individual binding component can also be obtained by selecting the **Properties** menu option from the context menu as shown in the following figure.

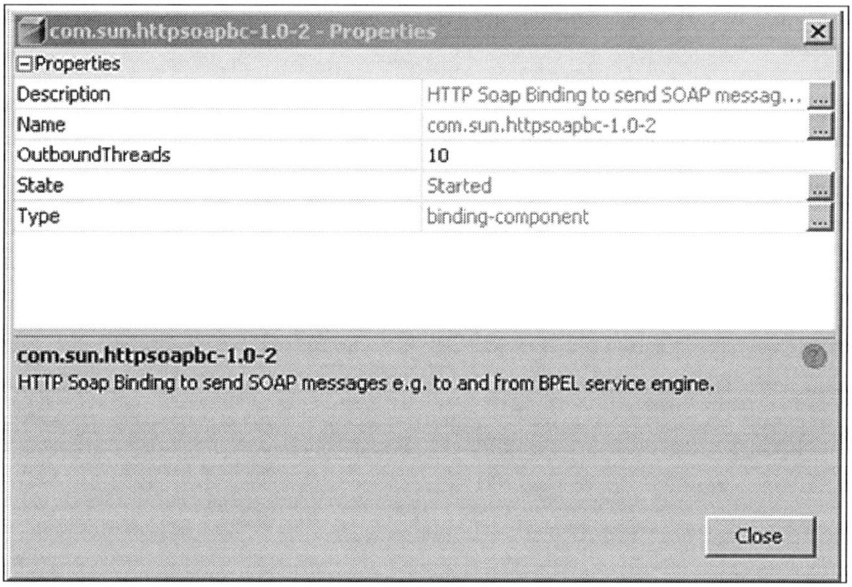

Now that we've discussed what binding components are, and how they communicate both internally and externally to the Normalized Message Router, let's take a closer look at some of the more common binding components and how they are accessed and managed from within the NetBeans IDE.

File Binding Component

The file binding component provides a communications mechanism for JBI components to interact with the file system. It can act as both a **Provider** by checking for new files to process, or as a **Consumer** by outputting files for other processes or components.

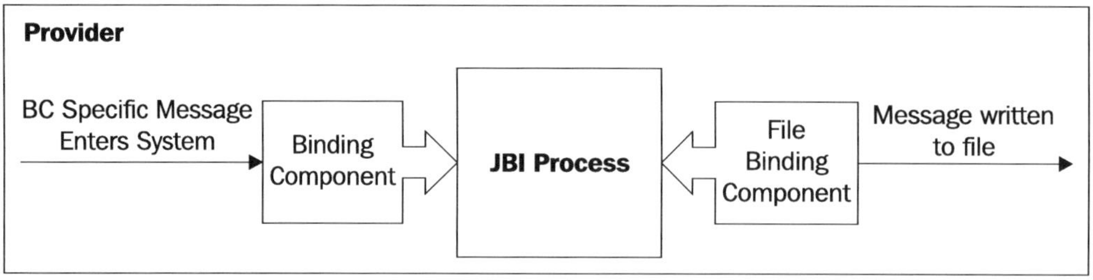

The figure above shows the file binding component acting as a **Provider** of messages. In this scenario, a message has been sent to the JBI container, and picked up by a protocol-specific binding component (for example, a SOAP message has been received). A **JBI Process** then occurs within the JBI container which may include routing the message between many different binding components and Service Engines depending upon the process. Finally, after the **JBI Process** has completed, the results of the process are sent to **File Binding Component** which writes out the result to a **file**.

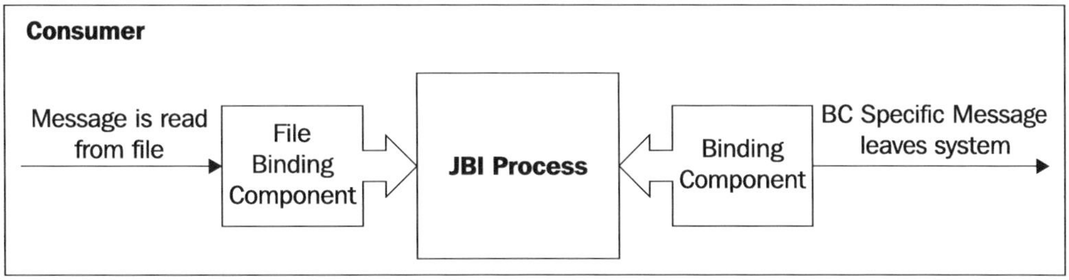

The figure above shows the file binding component acting as a **Consumer** of messages. In this situation, the **File Binding Component** is periodically polling the file system looking for files with a specified filename pattern in a specified directory. When the binding component finds a file that matches its criteria, it reads in the file and starts the **JBI Process**, which may again cause the input message to be routed between many different binding components and Service Engines. Finally, in this example, the results of the **JBI Process** are output via a **Binding Component**.

Of course, it is possible that a binding component can act as both a provider and a consumer within the same JBI process. In this case, the file binding component would be initially responsible for reading an input message from the file system. After any JBI processing has occurred, the file binding component would then write out the results of the process to a file.

Within the NetBeans Enterprise Pack, the entire set of properties for the file binding component can be edited within the **Properties** window. The properties for the binding component are displayed when either the input or output messages are selected from the WSDL in a composite application as shown in the following figure. (Don't worry if you don't understand the WSDL editor and its role in SOA applications yet.

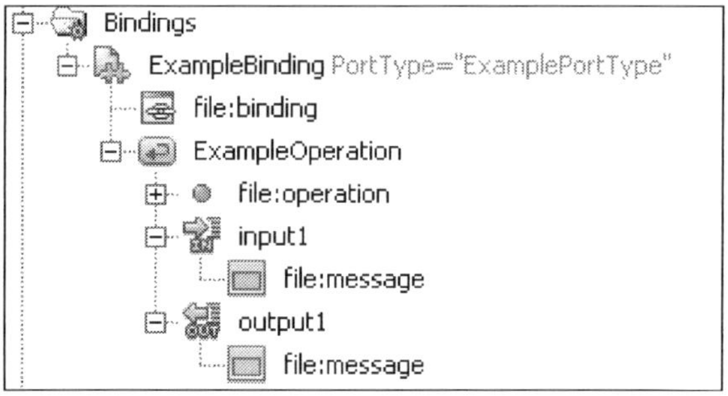

The entire set of properties that are configurable for an instance of a file binding component is shown in the next screenshot. You probably won't need all of the properties within your applications, so we've described some common properties that you will probably need to access in applications where you use file binding components.

- *fileName*: Specifies the input or output filename (depending on whether the binding component is acting as a consumer or a provider). If the **fileNameIsPattern** property is set to true, the markers `%d`, `%u` and `%t` can be specified within the filename to represent numbers, uuid's, and date and times respectively. These file patterns act differently when the file binding component is being used in a consumer or provider capacity.

	Consumer	Provider
%d	Pattern matches any integer number.	Replaced by sequential integer starting at 0.
%u	Pattern matches any string.	Replaced by a generated UUID
%t	Pattern matches any date and time (yyyyMMdd-HH-mm-ss-SSS)	Replaced by current timestamp (yyyyMMdd-HH-mm-ss-SSS)

- *pollingInterval*: Specifies the time in milliseconds between polling the file system when acting as a consumer. The default time is always set to 1s.

- *multipleRecordsPerFile*: When acting as a consumer, the property specifies whether there are multiple messages in the input file. When acting as a provider, this property specifies whether multiple output messages will be stored within the output file by appending messages to the output file every time they are generated.
- *archive*: Specifies whether input messages are archived to the **archiveDirectory** after being processed.

SMTP Binding Component

The SMTP Binding Component provides email services to the JBI Server and can act as either a provider by receiving inbound SMTP messages or as a consumer by sending SMTP email to external email addresses.

Neither NetBeans Enterprise Pack 5.5 nor the NetBeans 6 SOA pack provide inbuilt support for the SMTP binding component. This support can be downloaded from the OpenESB project website (`http://open-esb.dev.java.net/Downloads.html`).

To add support for the SMTP binding component, the following packages need to be downloaded:

- **smtpbc.jar**: The actual SMTP binding component.
- **org-netbeans-modules-wsdlextensions-smtp.nbm**: NetBeans Module Support allowing SMTP binding editing for WSDL files.
- **javax-mail.nbm**: NetBeans Modules Support for email.

`Smtpbc.jar` can be downloaded from the **Components** section of the **OpenESB** project website, whereas the NetBeans modules can be downloaded from the **Developer Tools** section.

Install the binding component (`smtpbc.jar`) into the application server by right-clicking on **Servers | Sun Java System Application Server 9 | JBI | Binding Components** and selecting the **Install New Binding Component** menu option.

After installing the SMTP binding component into the application server, we can install developer support into the NetBeans IDE. This is done by installing the two new NetBeans modules (`org-netbeans-modules-wsdlextensions-smtp.nbm` and `javax-mail.nbm`) through the **NetBeans Update Manager or Plugin Manager**. This developer support allows SMTP to be chosen as the Binding Type for WSDL bindings.

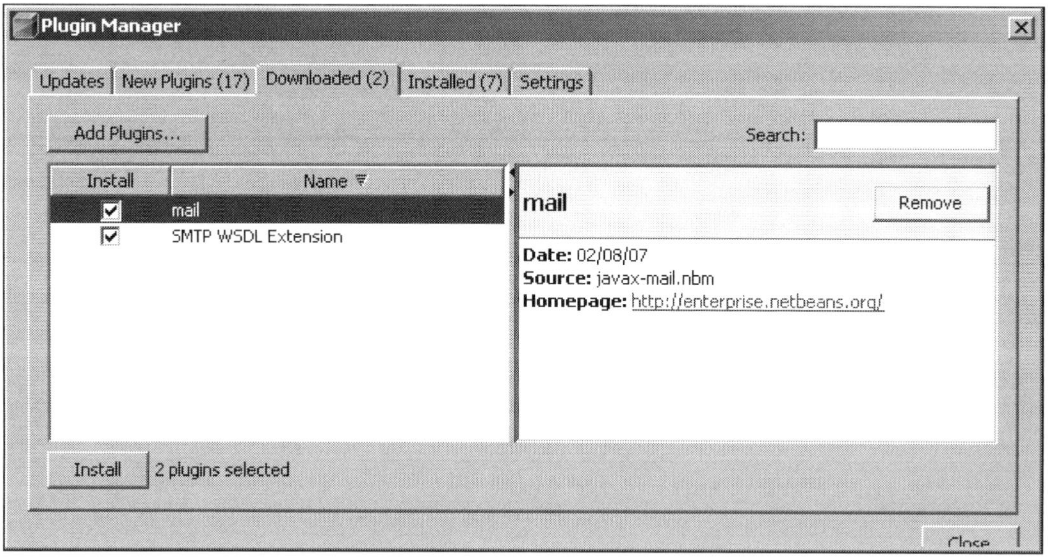

When the binding component is acting as a **Provider**, standard properties (such as who the message is from, who it is addressed to, the subject and body of the message) can be read from the message and converted into a WSDL message. This then allows any of these properties to be used within a JBI process. For example, an input message sent via an email could be processed differently depending on who it is addressed to or what the subject of the email is. If the design time support for the binding component is installed into NetBeans (as discussed earlier in this section), then all of these email properties can be edited as part of the WSDL message structure, shown as follows:

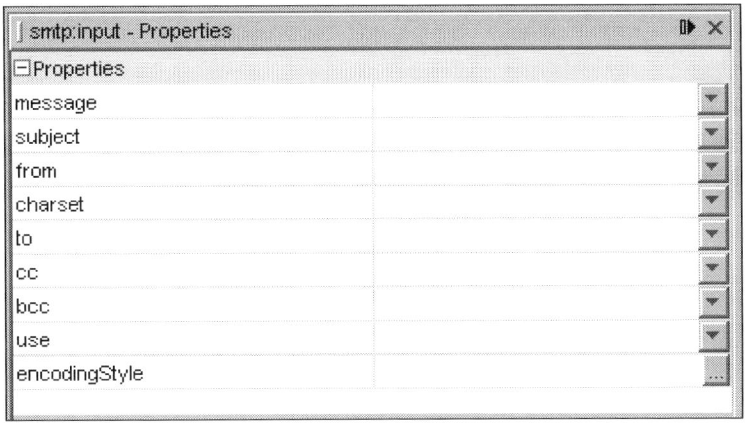

If the binding component is acting as a **Consumer**, it is responsible for sending emails via SMTP. In this situation, the `mailto: protocol (RFC 2368)` is fully supported. This allows emails to be sent to specified email addresses and also sent to **cc** and **bcc** addresses. Support is also provided for SMTP servers that require authentication (in the form of the **username** and **password** parameters). SSL Support is also provided (**useSSL**) for situations where the remote email server requires the secure sockets layer.

When the design time modules for the binding component are installed into NetBeans, then the properties for outgoing SMTP messages can be edited within the WSDL message structure, shown as follows:

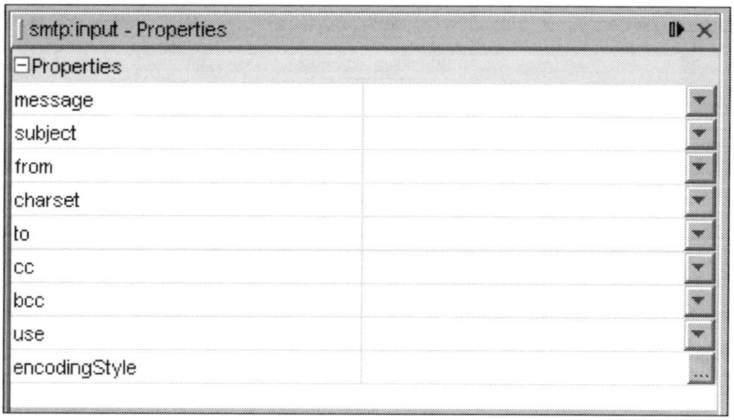

FTP Binding Component

The FTP binding component provides FTP transport services to the JBI container allowing messages to be received and sent via the FTP protocol. The component can act as a consumer or a provider and supports the FTP protocol as described by RFC 959.

When the binding component is acting as a consumer, it functions in a similar fashion to the file binding component in that it polls periodically for files based upon a given file name or file name pattern. The difference however, is that the FTP binding component polls specified FTP sites rather than the local file system. After a file is polled by the binding component, the contents of the file are routed as a standard message into the JBI framework. These inbound messages are then routed via the Normalized Message Router to other binding components and/or Service Engines as defined by the JBI process.

The binding component can also act as a provider and in this instance it is responsible for routing JBI messages to a specified FTP address. Depending upon the complexity of your JBI process, the FTP binding component can act as both a consumer and provider all within the same service assembly.

If you are running your SOA application behind a firewall, the FTP binding component can be configured to use a proxy server to allow access outside the firewall. The binding component supports SOCKS4 and SOCKS5 proxy servers. The proxy server support for the binding component is defined at a global level against the binding component itself, rather than defined within the WSDL bindings within a service assembly. The proxy is configured within NetBeans by setting the **Proxy URL**, **Proxy User ID,** and **Proxy User Password** properties on the binding component.

In addition to setting the proxy details, you can specify the maximum number of simultaneous threads the binding component can use. This can be done by using the **Outbound Threads Number** property. The default value for the number of threads is 10, but you will need to configure this value depending on the number of users accessing your SOA application, and the number of times that the FTP binding component is called.

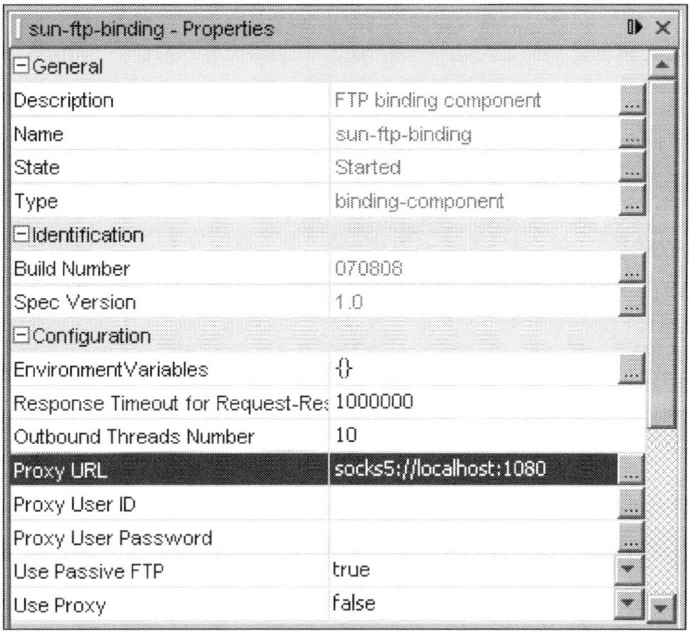

Neither the FTP binding component nor the support for FTP binding within the WSDL editor is provided, by default, within the NetBeans 5.5 Enterprise Pack, or NetBeans 6 SOA pack. To add support for these components, the following files need to be downloaded from the OpenESB project website and installed in the same way that we installed the SMTP binding component earlier in this chapter (that is, to install the binding component into the application server and to install the FTP Binding support into the WSDL editor as a NetBeans plugin).

- `ftpbc.jar`: The actual FTP Binding Component.
- `org-netbeans-modules-wsdlextensions-ftp.nbm`: NetBeans Module Support allowing FTP binding editing for WSDL files.

Once we have installed these components into the Application Server and the NetBeans IDE, we can start using the FTP Binding Component. Within a service assembly, we can specify the WSDL binding to use the FTP binding component. The properties window within the IDE allows us to modify the properties for the FTP binding, enabling the connection details of the FTP connection to be specified, shown as follows. The **url** property allows the address of the FTP server to be specified in the standard `ftp://username:password@host` format. Several other properties are available to control the connection, however, the most common that you will probably need to modify are the **dirListStyle** and **mode** properties which allow the host type and connection mode (**Binary** or **ASCII**) to be set.

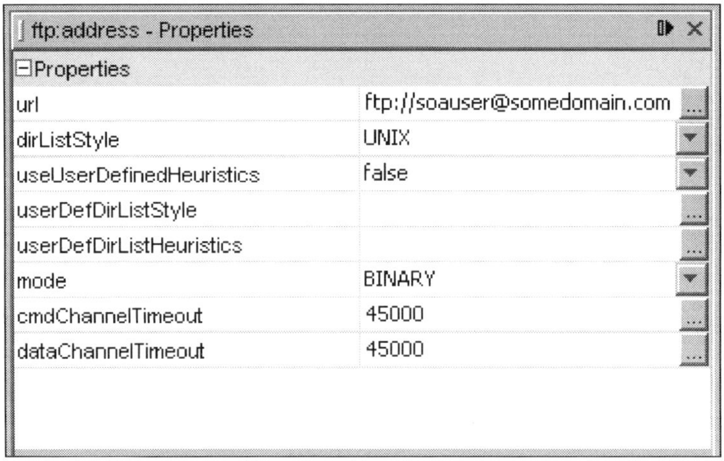

The FTP message properties within a WSDL message are displayed in the IDE properties window by selecting the operation within the WSDL bindings section of the WSDL editor. This property window allows the message properties to be set.

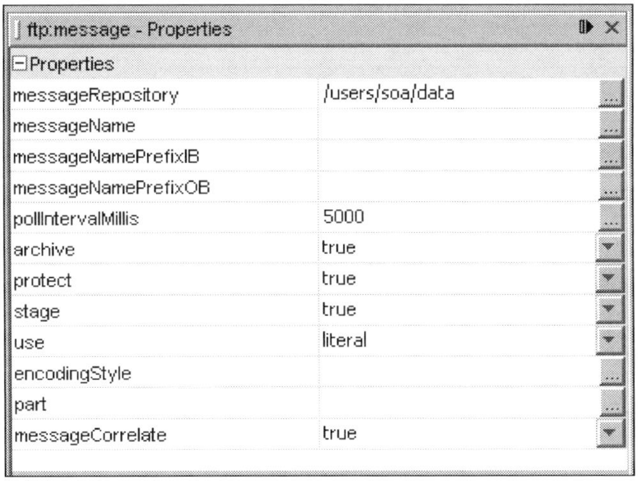

The common properties that you will probably need to set when using the FTP Binding Component are:

- **messageRepository**: directory name where messages are stored within the FTP server. This base directory must have an additional directory structure underneath it to enable the binding component to perform its processing. The following sub-directories must be available:
    - **/inbox**: directory where inbound messages are stored.
    - **/instage**: directory where inbound messages are stored before they are fully uploaded to the FTP server.
    - **/inprotect**: directory where inbound messages are stored to stop them from being overwritten.
    - **/inarchive**: directory where inbound messages are stored after they have been processed.
    - **/outbox**: directory where outbound messages are stored.
    - **/outstage**: directory where outbound messages are stored before they are fully uploaded to the FTP server.
    - **/outprotect**: directory where outbound messages are stored to stop them from being overwritten.
    - **/outarchive**: directory where outbound messages are stored after they have been processed.

- **messageName**: The name of the message file created within the **messageRepository**. Inbound messages are prefixed by the value held in the **messageNamePrefixIB** property, whilst outbound messages are prefixed by the value held in the **messageNamePrefixOB** directory.
- **pollIntervalMillis**: The time between polls of the FTP server in milliseconds.
- **archive**: Boolean indicating whether messages are archived or removed after being processed.
- **protect**: Boolean indicating whether existing messages are moved to a protected area before the current message is processed hence stopping the existing message from being overwritten.

SOAP Binding Component

The SOAP binding component (also known as the HTTP binding component) allows JBI messages to be sent and received using SOAP over HTTP and HTTPS. The component supports RPC Literal, RPC Encoded, and Document Literal encoding schemes.

The component can act as a consumer providing HTTP SOAP 1.1 Services externally. This is achieved by using the embedded Grizzly HTTP connector.

The component can also act as a provider and in this situation is capable of invoking external web services. The WSDL Editor within NetBeans provides support for editing the WSDL bindings and allows the address of remote SOAP servers to be specified.

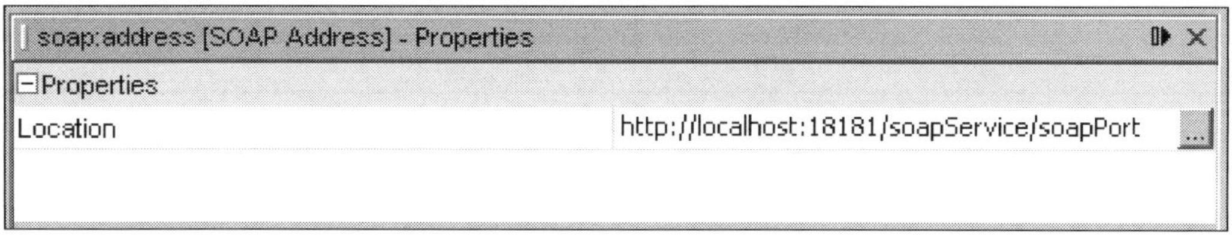

In situations where the JBI container is running inside a firewall, the SOAP binding component can be configured to use a proxy server to enable remote web services outside the firewall to be accessed.

Many of the properties of the SOAP binding component are global to all service assemblies within the JBI container that make use of the binding component. NetBeans provides support for editing these properties directly within the IDE.

The most common properties that you will probably need to configure in your applications are:

- **Default HTTP Port Number**: The port number for inbound SOAP requests when the binding component is acting as a consumer of SOAP requests. The default port is **9080**.
- **Default HTTPS Port Number**: The port number for inbound SOAP requests when HTTPS is being used as the transport mechanism instead of HTTP. The default port is **9181**.
- **Non proxy hosts**: This is a pipe | separated list that contains all the hosts that will be contacted directly instead of through a proxy server if a proxy is enabled.
- **Proxy Host**: The specifies the name of the proxy server for outbound SOAP requests. If the proxy server requires authentication, then the **Proxy user name** and **Proxy user password** properties can be specified. The port number of the proxy server can be specified using the **Proxy port** property.

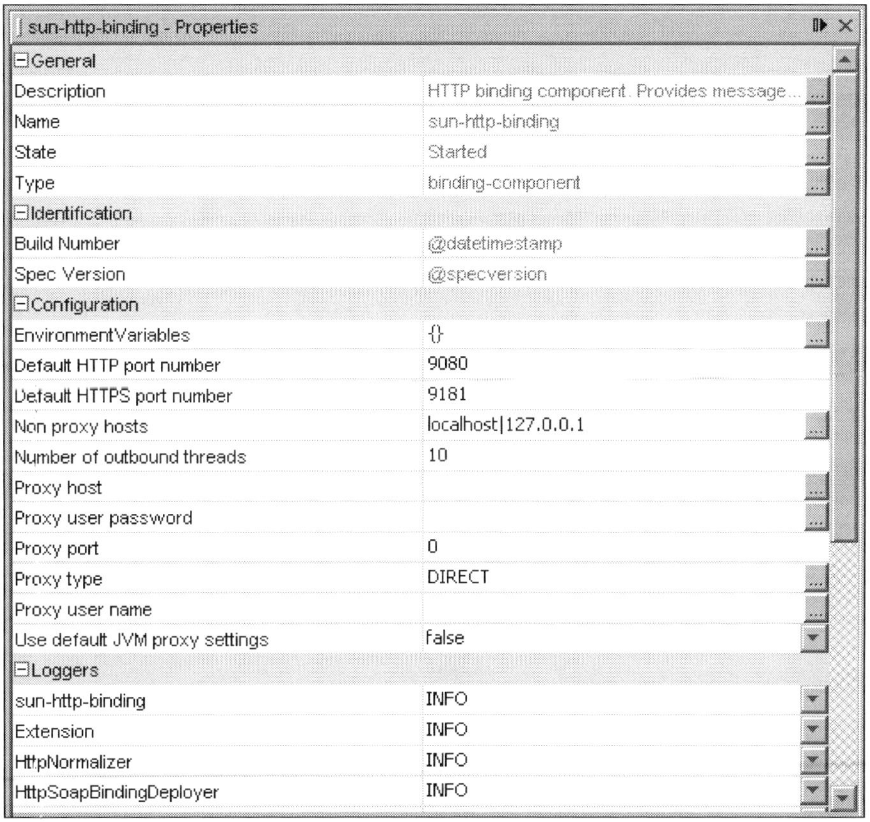

JDBC Binding Component

In some situations, you will find that you need to interact with a database as part of your JBI applications. When interacting with the database, we can use the SQL Service Engine. Alternatively, if you have more limited database needs, you can use the JDBC binding component.

The JDBC binding component can act as a provider or a consumer. When acting as a provider, the component can issue these different DML commands to the database either to select information from the database or to change data:

- Select
- Insert
- Update
- Delete

When acting as a consumer, the component can poll specified tables on the database to find newly inserted data. When new data is identified by the component, this data can be routed into the JBI framework as a standard WSDL message to other components. The JDBC Binding Component can connect to any database that conforms to the JDBC 3.0 specification and can be accessed via a JNDI datasource lookup.

The JDBC Binding Component is not supplied with the NetBeans 5.5 Enterprise Pack or with the NetBeans 6.0 SOA pack, and must be downloaded separately from the Open ESB project (`http://open-esb.dev.java.net/Downloads.html`). Similarly, WSDL editor support can be downloaded from the open ESB project website. To fully support the JDBC Binding Component, the following files must be downloaded:

- `jdbcbc.jar`: The actual JDBC binding component.
- `org-netbeans-modules-wsdlextensions-jdbc.nbm`: NetBeans Module support allowing JDBC binding editing for WSDL files.

These additional components can be installed into NetBeans in the same way we installed the SMTP binding component and WSDL support earlier in this chapter.

After installing the WSDL extensions for the JDBC Binding Component, you will find that visual editing is provided within NetBeans for both consumer and provider instances. The properties of the WSDL binding can be seen in the following figure:

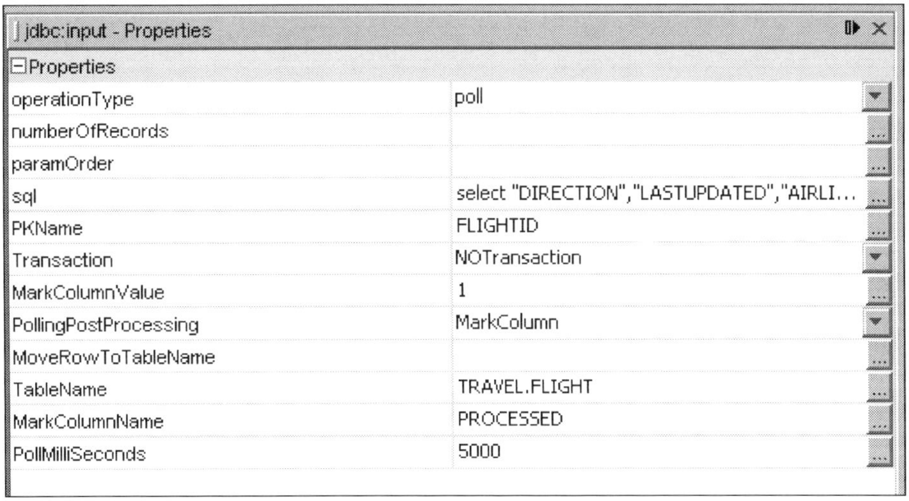

The WSDL editor provides support for editing the different properties that can be specified for the binding component. The major properties that you will probably need to edit when using this component are described as follows:

- **operationType**: specifies what operation the binding component is performing—**poll**, **insert**, **update**, **find**, or **delete**.
- **sql**: sql that will be executed against the database. If the sql is a **select** statement, then the **numberOfRecords** property specifies how many rows are retrieved from the database.
- **PollingPostProcessing**: After the database has been polled for new records, the binding component can be requested to perform post processing on the rows that have been polled. The **PollingPostProcessing** property can be set to several different values:
    - **Delete**: polled rows are deleted after polling.
    - **MarkColumn**: The column specified by the **MarkColumnName** property on the polled rows will be updated to hold the value specified in the **MarkColumnValue** property. This property can be checked when the database is polled to ensure the existing data is not continually re-polled.
    - **MoveRow**: polled rows of data are moved to the table specified by the **MoveRowToTableName** property.
    - **CopyRow**: polled rows of data are copied to the table specified by the **MoveRowToTableName** property.

- **PollMilliSeconds**: time period in milliseconds between individual polls of the database.
- **TableName**: name of the database table that is being accessed in the binding operation.

JMS Binding Component

The final binding component we are going to discuss in detail is the JMS Binding Component.

The JMS Binding Component allows the JBI container to communicate with JMS message queues and topics. The component can act as a provider and/or as a consumer of JMS messages, and as such can subscribe to a topic and wait for JMS messages, or it can send messages to a predefined Queue or Topic.

> A JMS Queue allows messages to be consumed by only one client and is a point to point type of messaging. A JMS Topic allows messages to be consumed by any number of clients and is a publish or subscribe type of messaging.

The binding component can send and receive JMS TextMessage's and MapMessage's.

The NetBeans Enterprise Pack provides design time support for the JMS Binding Component and allows the binding attributes to be defined graphically within the WSDL editor. The connection details of the JMS Message Server can be specified within the *service* of the WSDL file.

- **connectionURL**: This property allows the base address of the message server to be specified. This can be in the format `mq://` for the Sun Java Message Queue system, or in the more generic `jndi://` format where the message queue is obtained via a JNDI lookup. The **username** and **password** properties enable the connection details to be specified for the message server.
- **connectionFactoryName**: If JNDI is being used to look up the message server, then the **connectionFactoryName** property specifies the JNDI name of the connection factory to use. The **initialContextFactory** and **providerURL** properties provide the standard lookup configuration parameters for JNDI lookups. If access to the message server is secured using JAAS, then the **securityPrincipal** and **securityCredential** properties can be used to specify the caller.

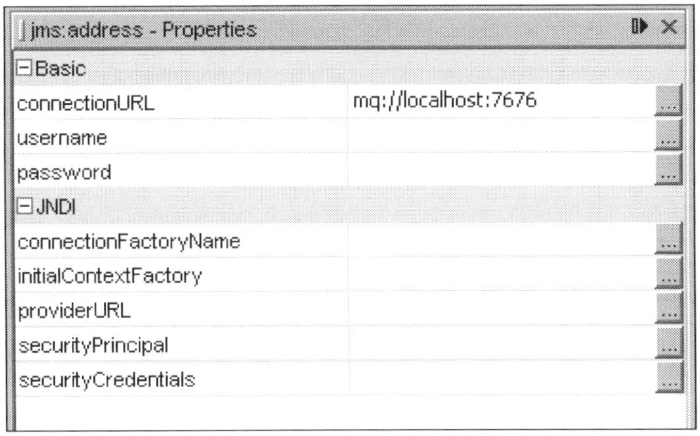

For a specific JMS operation, it is necessary to specify whether the binding component is connecting to a queue or a topic and whether transaction support is to be used for the connection.

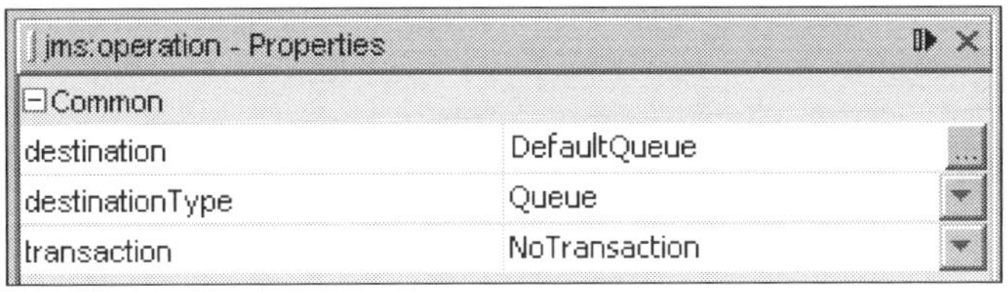

NetBeans provides editor support to enable these properties to be configured:

- **destination**: name of the queue or topic that the binding component is to receive messages from or send messages to.
- **destinationType**: indicates whether the destination is a **Queue** or a **Topic**
- **transaction**: specifies whether the JMS conversation will use **NoTransactions** or whether it will be enrolled in a **XATransaction**. XA transaction support is only enabled when the binding component is acting as a **Consumer** and is receiving inbound messages.

Finally, the payload and type of a JMS message can be configured for a given WSDL operation.

- **messageType**: type of the message being sent or received from the specified **Queue** or **Topic**. The **messageType** can be either **TextMessage** (for `javax.jms.TextMessage` type messages) or **MapMessage** (for `javax.jms.MapMessage` type messages).

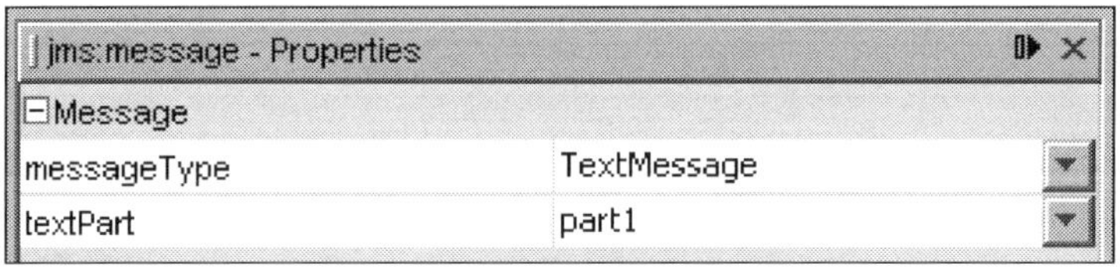

Other Binding Components

Due to the standardized nature of the JBI Framework and JBI components, many other JBI binding components have been written by the developer community, all of which can be deployed to the Sun Java System Application Server or the GlassFish Server. One such source of JBI components can be found in the OpenESB project (`https://open-esb.dev.java.net`). The OpenESB project provides many different binding components such as:

- CICS Binding Component
- MSMQ Binding Component
- LDAP Binding Component

The full list of binding components available from the OpenESB project can be found at `https://open-esb.dev.java.net/Components.html`.

Summary

In this chapter, we have discussed the JBI framework, Binding Components and their role within the JBI Container. We've seen how the Binding Component provides transport and protocol independence for other JBI components. We've seen how this enables the JBI container to provide a highly decoupled framework allowing developers and integrators to build resilient SOA applications.

We continued to discuss the different binding components (namely file, FTP, SOAP, JDBC, JMS and SMTP) that are either installed into the application server with the NetBeans Enterprise pack or can be downloaded directly from the OpenESB project web site. We also discussed that because binding components are developed to a standard set of interfaces, any JBI compliant binding component can be installed into the Application Server.

9

SOA and Web Services Approach for Integration

Intergration may be restricted within an Enterprise or may involve third parties (B2B or B2C). Service-Oriented Architectures are complex. Most SOA implementations do not take off because most of the time it is not clear when, where, and how to begin. In this chapter, you will learn many useful tricks and tips to successfully apply SOA techniques for application integration within and outside your enterprise.

You will learn the following in this chapter:

- Designing Service-Oriented Architectures: Here, you will first learn the concepts behind Service-Oriented Architectures, why and how SOA helps in building more flexible solutions, followed by the design patterns for SOA and the guidelines for creating them.
- Designing Web Services: In this section, you will learn how to create web services for implementing SOA. The various patterns discussed in the SOA section will now be covered in depth in the context of SOA implementation using web services.
- Differences between B2B and EAI Web Services: SOA can be used for B2B or EAI kind of applications. In this section, we will study the implications of using web services in these two scenarios.
- Interoperable WSDL: A WSDL (Web Services Description Language) document describes the interface to a web service and the binding information. Typically, SOA may be used in a scenario where applications running on disparate platforms need integration. In such cases, the WSDL documents that describe the web services interfaces to different applications must provide compatibility for integration. This section describes how to create interoperable WSDL documents.

- Interoperability Challenges in Web Services: An SOA might use several web services deployed on disparate platforms and technologies. These web services must interoperate with each other. Several specifications have come up to achieve this interoperability. In this section, you will study these specifications and their use in creating interoperable web services.
- Developing Interoperable Web Services: In this section, we will look at a complete application that shows how to create web services for the .NET and J2EE platforms that interoperate with each other.

Designing Service-Oriented Architectures

Over the last several decades, corporations have developed applications based on a wide range of systems and technologies. Though these systems are componentized, the integration of these systems poses a challenge due to their heterogeneity. The need for integration arises due to globalization and a wide acceptance of e-business. Globalization has increased the competition. The customer pressure keeps continuously increasing to provide a better quality of service. Customer needs change more often due to the offerings made by competitors over the Internet. Today's IT infrastructure must adapt to these demanding changes.

SOA Evolution

In the 1980s, applications were mostly vertical, built to meet the customer requirements in a vertical market segment. The software solutions were sufficient to meet the needs of a vertical industry. For example, an automobile industry never felt the need for interacting with its suppliers by electronic means. The same was true in the case of most other industries. Very rarely there was a need to communicate with other businesses. This is shown in the following figure:

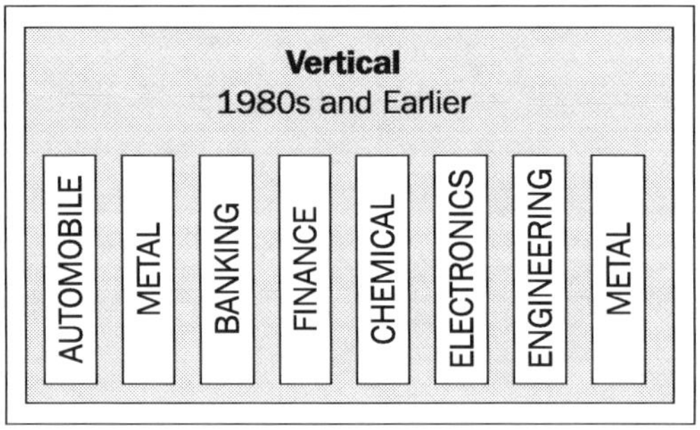

In the late '80s and early '90s, we saw the need for business applications to grow horizontally to cooperate with business partners. The industry saw the evolution of B2B (Business-to-Business) collaborations through components now spreading across several industry verticals. These components were now distributed giving rise to an extended supply chain, providing customers and business partners access to services. This is illustrated in the following figure.

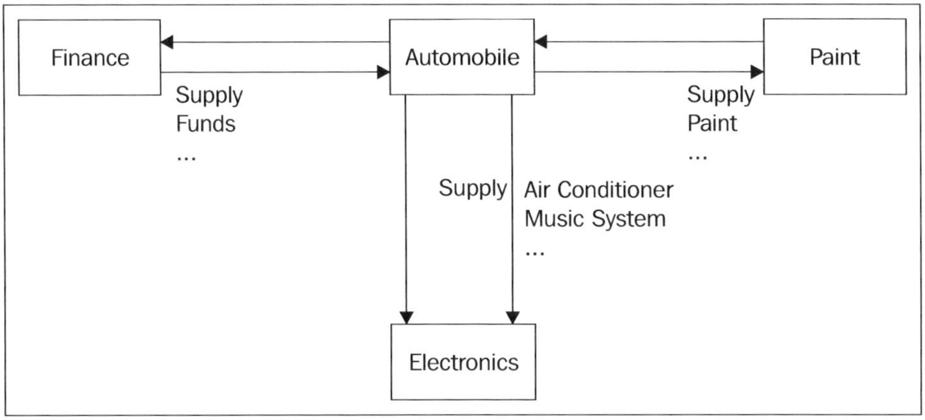

In today's world, the way that businesses operate has changed tremendously. Businesses not only want interaction with their partners, but they allow their customers and employees to access their business services electronically. Today, we talk about B2C (Business-to-Customer), whereby customers have a direct access to the services offered by businesses. Exposing the business logic to an untrusted user base poses its own challenges in terms of security, integrity, and so on. Besides, such services must be user friendly and must hide the complexities of the internal business processes from the end customer. This is where the true need for Service Oriented Architecture is felt. Businesses should offer services rather than an interface to their business logic. The business logic is implemented in several components—exposing the interface to these components results in tight coupling with the business logic. A client application consumes the service through a well-defined interface to the service and does not care about how it is implemented.

Such interactions are depicted in the following figure of today's complex IT requirements.

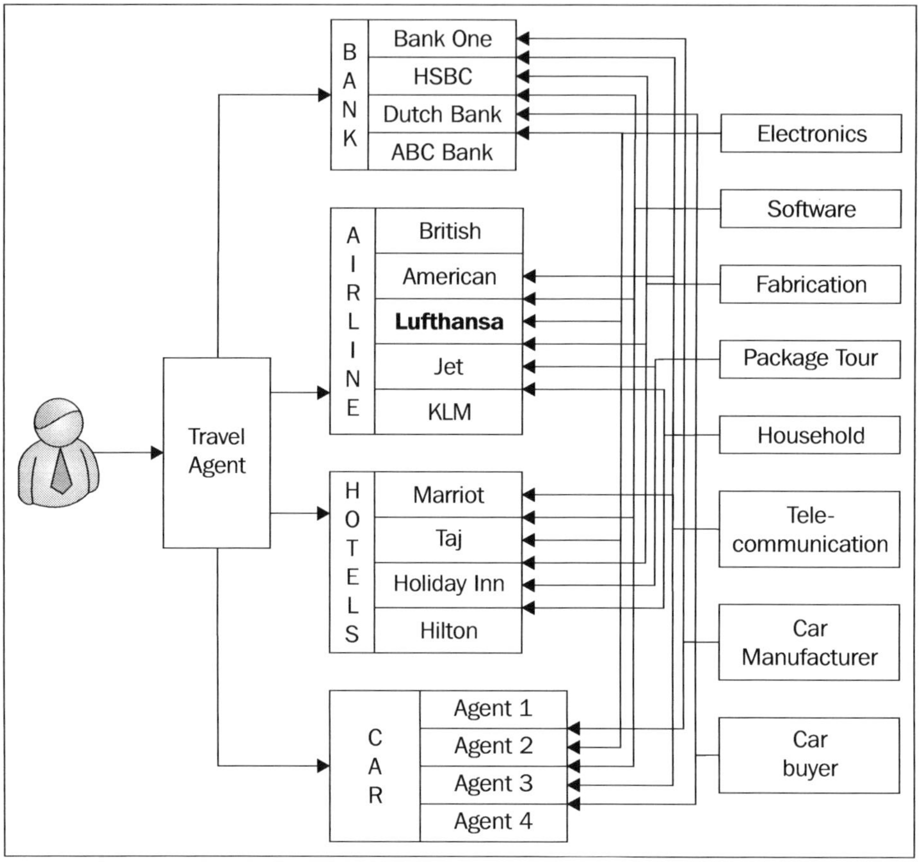

The above figure illustrates a typical Travel Agency scenario. A traveler interacts with the travel agency. The travel agency interfaces with several airlines, hotels, and car rental companies. It also interfaces with several banks for online payments, accounting, etc. Each of these organizations in turn interfaces with several other businesses. The total network soon becomes complex. However, this is the requirement of today's businesses and as IT professionals, we are supposed to provide solutions to these demanding requirements.

IT Evolution

Looking at current business needs, the IT environments in today's world need to be more flexible, and must quickly adapt to the constantly changing business requirements. The applications running on heterogeneous environments must communicate and integrate seamlessly. IT environments have been evolving along the lines of business requirement evolution as illustrated in the following figure.

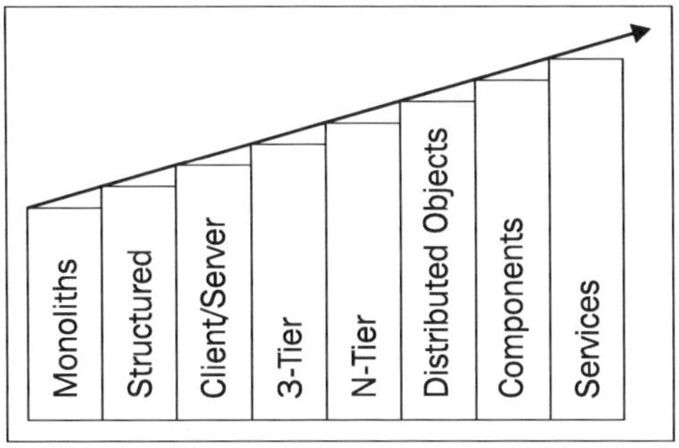

In the early years of computing, we had only monolithic applications running on stand-alone machines. From the monolithic systems of early '60s, the industry saw the development of structured, client/server, 3-tier, N-tier, distributed systems, and finally the service-oriented architectures of the modern age. The service-oriented architectures attempt to meet today's business requirements. They are loosely coupled, location transparent, and protocol independent. SOA hides the underlying technology architectures from the service consumer. The service implementation may be on a Java EE (earlier J2EE) or .NET platform, or it may even be a legacy application running on an IBM mainframe. The service consumer need not know the platform on which the service is running; the service implementation is totally transparent to the consumer.

While implementing such complex systems based on SOA, the use of patterns plays an important role in success. Patterns provide the solutions to well-known problems solved by others over many years. Patterns at the code and architecture levels have been well documented, well accepted, and almost standardized. The patterns for creating Service-Oriented Architectures (SOA) are still evolving. There are many who have identified and published their findings, but a standard catalog of these patterns is yet to come. In this chapter, we will look at the patterns documented by IBM for creating SOA applications.

Patterns

Patterns are based on the proven successful experiences of the past. The various patterns for e-business as suggested by IBM are shown in the following figure of the hierarchy of patterns.

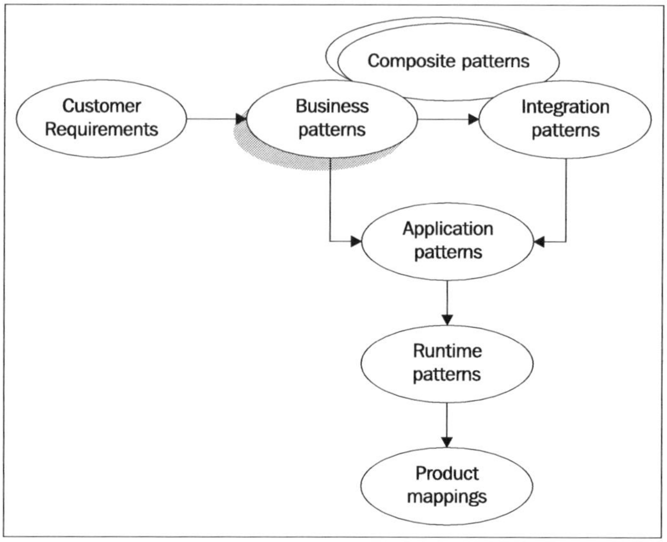

These patterns are briefly discussed in the following paragraphs. We will discuss a few of the important patterns in the context of SOA in the next section.

Business Patterns

At the top, we start with Business patterns. These define the interface to consumers that include customers, employees, and business partners. The business patterns arrange the various business assets for the interaction with consumers. The following are the four business patterns:

- Self-Service
- Collaboration
- Information Aggregation
- Extended Enterprise

The business patterns provide the most abstract view of the business services to the consumer. They define the interaction between the various business assets to provide a very high-level view of the business service. These patterns are explained in later sections.

Integration Patterns

Sometimes, a single business pattern may not be sufficient to meet the customer requirements. In such cases, we apply integration patterns that tie together multiple business patterns to achieve the desired output. The integration patterns differ from the business patterns in that they do not solve a specific business problem on their own. Rather, they facilitate a more advanced business function by gluing one or more business patterns together. They also help in the feasibility of the composite patterns. The following are the two integration patterns:

- Access Integration
- Application Integration

The Access Integration patterns define how the business services are accessed and the Application Integration patterns define how the applications interoperate with each other. These patterns are discussed in more detail in the next section.

Composite Patterns

Composite patterns combine business and integration patterns. Like other patterns, they provide solutions to recurring problems. There can be numerous combinations of business and integration patterns used to solve a specific business problem. However, problems that recurrently occur across industries can be solved with the use of a specific combination of business and integration patterns and are documented as composite patterns. These are listed below:

- e-Marketplace
- Electronic Commerce
- Portals
- Account Access

For example, creating an e-Marketplace such as ebay.com requires interactions with a wide range of customers. Here, several business services from different industries need to collaborate to provide a business service to an end customer. Such business services involve auction, banking, shipping and delivery, and so on. The composite pattern combines business and integration patterns to achieve this.

Application Patterns

The application patterns define the interaction between the various application components. These are more abstract than the architectural patterns you may have studied elsewhere. In the case of architectural patterns, the interaction between the components is defined. In the case of application patterns, we define the interaction between the applications. Such applications may be internal applications within an enterprise or may involve third-party applications.

Runtime Patterns

Runtime patterns describe the IT infrastructure. They defines the logical middleware components and their interactions with each other. We will discuss the following runtime patterns later in the chapter.

- Direct Connection
- Runtime patterns for Broker

The runtime patterns define the arrangement of nodes and how they connect to each other.

Product Mappings

Finally, the product mappings define the known software products for implementing the runtime patterns. The IBM catalog documents the mappings of IBM's various products such as IBM Websphere, DB2, and so on to implement the runtime patterns. An interested reader may refer to the IBM site (`http://www.ibm.com/redbooks`) for further details.

Guidelines

The application of these patterns requires a careful study of a business problem. For example, you may be developing a Portal. You will have to decide who are the users of this portal? What business services need to be offered to these clients, who are the business partners, and what kinds of interactions with the system they require, based on the answers to these questions, you will create a list of business assets needed to provide the services to clients. These assets are then arranged in well-known patterns to achieve the desired business results. This results in creating enterprise architecture. We will not discuss the guidelines for the use of specific patterns here as we discuss them in more depth later in the chapter.

Designing Sound Web Services for Integration

The Web Services technology plays an important role when applying the concepts of Service-Oriented Architectures. The web services technology is based on open standards such as:

- XML—eXtensible Markup Language
- SOAP—Simple Object Access Protocol
- WSDL—Web Services Description Language
- UDDI—Universal Description, Discovery, and Integration

The use of open standards enables the interoperability between different vendor solutions. The existing solutions can be wrapped as web services and new services can be developed without the need to know who the consumer is. The consumer can consume any web service irrespective of the platform on which it is running using the standard web protocols. This enables the just-in-time integration of the applications and allows the business to establish new partners on the fly. Thus, the web services technology is the right candidate for creating SOA.

Web Services Architecture

The web services architecture is shown in the following figure.

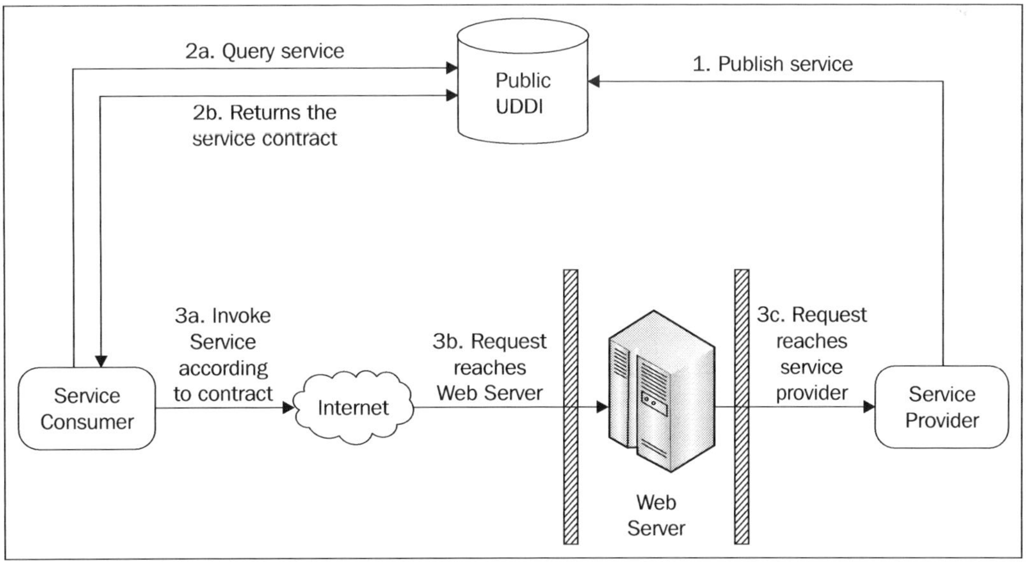

A service provider creates the service and publishes it on a UDDI registry for consumers to discover it. A consumer queries the registry and obtains a reference to the service interface from the registry. After the interface is obtained, the consumer creates a programming interface to the service. The consumer then consumes the service using standard SOAP protocols. The request is directed through a web server protected by firewalls to the service provider. This is one way of invoking the service. Another way of invoking the service would be to use a messaging server in place of a web server.

Web Services Benefits

The approach of building your SOA with web services as the means of implementation offers several benefits as listed here:

Self-Contained

Web services are self-contained in the sense that they do not require any components to be installed on the client side. On the server merely a Servlet engine, an EJB container, or a .NET runtime is required for deploying the service. When the service is deployed and ready to run, a client can consume the service without the need for any software installations on its machine. You can contrast this with other technologies such as DCOM, or RMI where the client stub must be installed on the consumer machine before the client can access the service.

Self-Describing

Web services are self-describing. An interface to a (web) service is published through a WSDL document. Such a WSDL document defines the format for the message exchange and the data types used in messages. To consume a service, the client needs to know only about the format and contents of a request and response message.

Modular

Web services provide a further abstraction on the existing component technologies based on J2EE, CORBA, DCOM, and so on. Using these various technologies, we create components. The web services compose these components to offer a service to the client. The interface to the components is not exposed to the client. This results in a modular software development resulting in creating a more abstract view of a business service.

Accessible Over the Web

Web services are published, located, and invoked over the Web. Web services use standard web protocols. The service description is published using WSDL; the service is located with the help of a UDDI registry and it is invoked using SOAP. All these protocols are web-based.

Language, Platform, Protocol Neutral

As web services are based on open XML standards, they are language neutral; a client written in any language can access a web service written in any other language. Web services are platform neutral; the consumer and service may be running on two independent platforms. Web services are transport neutral; the service can be invoked using any standard network protocol.

Open and Standards-Based

The web services technology is based on open standards making web services easily interoperable with other web services. These standards are XML-based and are SOAP, WSDL, and UDDI.

Dynamic

Web services can be discovered and consumed at run time, without the need to have any compile-time knowledge of them. In most other technologies, the client needs compile-time knowledge of the component interface. An exception to this is CORBA (Common Object Request Broker Architecture), which provides a DII (Dynamic Invocation Interface) for run-time discovery and invocation of the service. A similar dynamic invocation interface is also available in the Java and .NET platforms.

Composable

Web services can be aggregated into a larger service. We can use orchestration engines for composing web services into a larger service. Such orchestration can be coded using well-accepted BPEL (Business Process Execution Language).

Having considered the benefits of web services, we will now look at the patterns that may be applied while creating web services to implement SOA.

Patterns

In the previous section, we looked at the various patterns for e-business. We will now study these patterns in more depth in the context of an SOA implementation. In an SOA approach, the focus is on creating and reusing loosely coupled services rather than creating coarse-grain applications. The building blocks are services, which can be composed to meet the business needs. Such services are self-contained, modular, and composable into larger services Applications on the other hand are usually large and inflexible. We will now describe the various patterns in the context of SOA.

Self-Service Business Pattern

The self-service business pattern captures direct interaction between the business user and the service provider. The user may be a customer, an employee, a business partner, or a stake-holder in the company. The service provider is the business that is providing the desired service to the consumer. Thus, the self-service business pattern nicely fits into the SOA paradigm where the main building block is the **service**.

The architecture of a self-service business pattern is shown in the following figure.

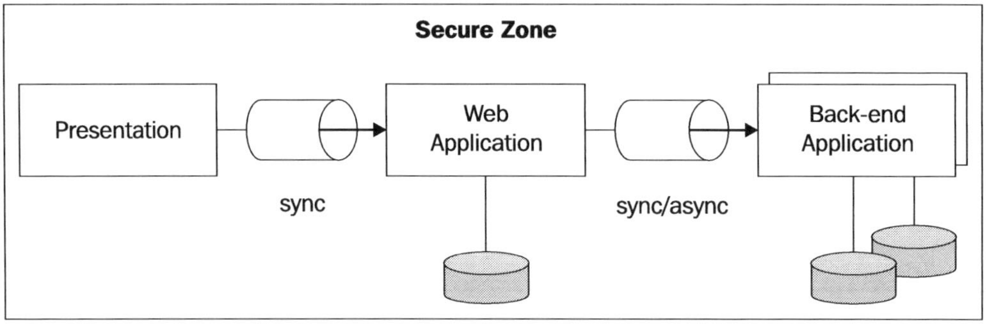

In this pattern, the presentation tier consumes the service provided by the web tier, which in turn consumes the service provided by the back end. This provides the direct interaction between the service consumer and the service provider with the help of services invoked in a chain-like fashion.

Guidelines

To apply the Self-Service business pattern, analyze the business requirement to assimilate what can be offered as a service. An example could be that employees need to look up salary benefits. Usually, these benefits do not get modified over a very long period of time. A list of benefits may be made directly accessible to the employees so as to eliminate repetitive requests made to the payroll department. You may provide a secured web page to employees for viewing the list of benefits. The web page may also provide querying facilities on the benefits database.

Another example is reserving a seat on an airplane. A few years ago, tele-check-in facilities were not available. A traveller had to check-in well in advance at the airline's counter to get a good seat. With the introduction of tele-check-in you can now reserve the seat couple of days in advance. However, this still requires human intervention. Recently, many airlines have started offering this as an online service to the customers. The seating map of the airplane is made directly accessible to the customer over Internet. The customer can select the seat of her or his choice and gets an online confirmation of the reservation. The application of the Self-Service pattern fits perfectly in such a situation.

Extended Enterprise Business Pattern

The previous pattern (Self-Service) provided an interaction between the consumer and the service. In the extended enterprise business pattern, the interaction between the two partner businesses is explored. The collaborative businesses expose their functionality as services. A business can access the service exposed by its partner through a programmatic interface. A business may act as a service consumer, a service provider, or both. The architecture for this pattern is illustrated in the following figure.

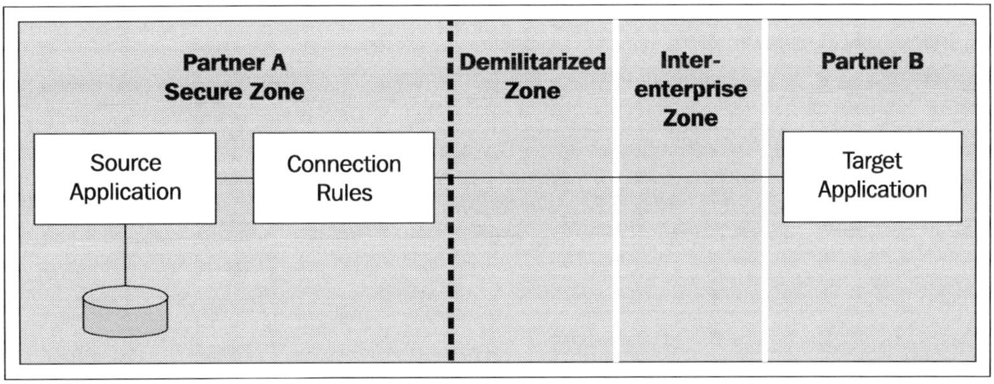

This pattern essentially is a manifestation of application integration pattern. However, due to SOA implementation based on open standards, such integration is loosely coupled. The loose coupling also facilitates the integration of disparate technologies. In the case of application integration, the coupling may not be always possible and is usually tightly coupled. The application of SOA also mandates meeting additional QoS (Quality of Service) requirements such as security, performance, and availability.

Guidelines

Consider the case of the automobile industry. An automobile manufacturing company depends on several other manufacturers for its spare parts. The company maintains its inventory of spare parts and when it runs low on stocks, a new order is placed with the supplier. A few years ago, the access to the entire inventory was closely guarded and the suppliers had to wait for a physical intimation from the company. A part of the inventory may now be exposed directly to the supplier. The supplier can monitor the inventory levels and supply the goods to the company when a threshold low is reached. Rather than exposing the application interface to the inventory management system, this may be implemented as SOA. The desired service is defined and coded to expose the relevant inventory status to individual suppliers. The Direct Connection pattern for the Extended Enterprise fits perfectly in this scenario. It involves the interaction between the two cooperating (partner) businesses. To expose the inventory to the associated business partners may require a tight implementation of security.

Application Integration Pattern

The application integration patterns capture the best practices in integrating the back end applications and data. They are observed in the EAI (Enterprise Application Integration) space and are helpful in defining process automation and workflows. Process integration help companies connecting applications and its users together within and across enterprise boundaries. Such interactions may be serial or parallel. A serial interaction is classified as a series of 1-to-1 interactions between a source and multiple targets in a time-sequenced manner. In the case of parallel interaction, such interactions between the source and multiple targets are concurrent. Using both serial and parallel together, you can classify the interactions in four categories as follows:

- No Serial, No Parallel—Here the messages are transported on a single path to a single target and this is the simplest connection.
- Serial, No Parallel—A single series of operations is done on multiple targets sequentially.
- No Serial, Parallel—Messages are switched, split, and joined on multiple paths to multiple targets.
- Serial, Parallel—Multiple series of operations are done on multiple targets by splitting and joining.

Application Integration Patterns

The patterns for Application Integration are classified further as Process- or Data-focused depending on what they perform. A Process-focused integration patterns defines the functional process flow between the applications and services. A Data-focused integration pattern defines the logical integration of the information or the data used by the applications.

The Process-focused integration patterns are further classified into the following four categories:

- Direct Connection application pattern
- Broker application pattern
- Serial Process application pattern
- Parallel Process application pattern

When applied to the Extended Enterprise domain, these are classified as:

- Exposed Direct Connection application pattern
- Exposed Broker application pattern: Router variation
- Exposed Serial Process application pattern

We will now discuss each of these patterns.

Direct Connection Application Pattern

This is the simplest pattern and defines a 1-to-1 interaction between a pair of applications. These interactions may be complex, which might be broken down into multiple elementary interactions. The pattern addresses these connections. The following figure illustrates this pattern.

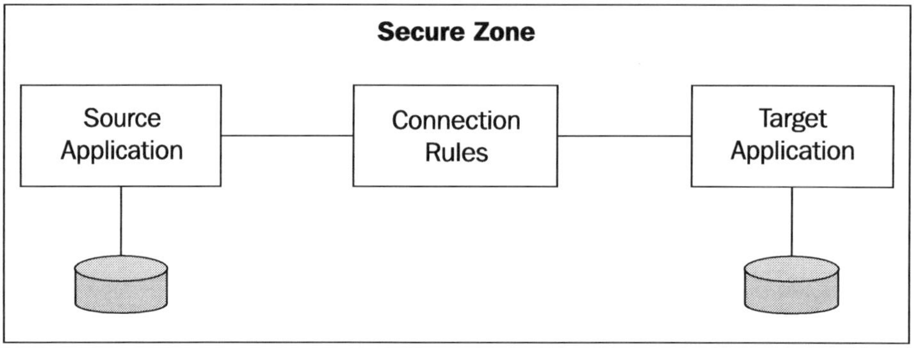

The connections may require the application of certain business rules such as data mapping rules, security rules, and so on. The connection may be message or call oriented. These are further classified as synchronous or asynchronous. Generally, the call-oriented connection is synchronous while the message-oriented connection is asynchronous—whether it is synchronous or asynchronous is decided by the integration needs.

In the case of an Extended Enterprise domain, the **Exposed Direct Connection** application pattern allows the applications to communicate directly across the enterprise boundaries. Thus, this can be applied only in the case of trusted patterns and requires a highly secure channel for communication across the enterprise boundary.

Guidelines

The Direct Connection application pattern maps perfectly into the SOA paradigm. There is a 1-to-1 connection between a service consumer and a provider. The services may be classified based on the functionality and QoS (Quality of Service). The connection rules may be modeled on these factors. A consumer may discover a desired service from the registry. Thus, the application of this pattern fits perfectly in the SOA domain.

The connection may be defined logically rather than physically. This result in creating a **Service Bus**, which is a subset of the **Enterprise Service Bus**.

Broker Application Pattern

The Broker application pattern is based on 1-to-N connections. A single interaction initiated by a source application is distributed across multiple target applications. This is illustrated in the following figure.

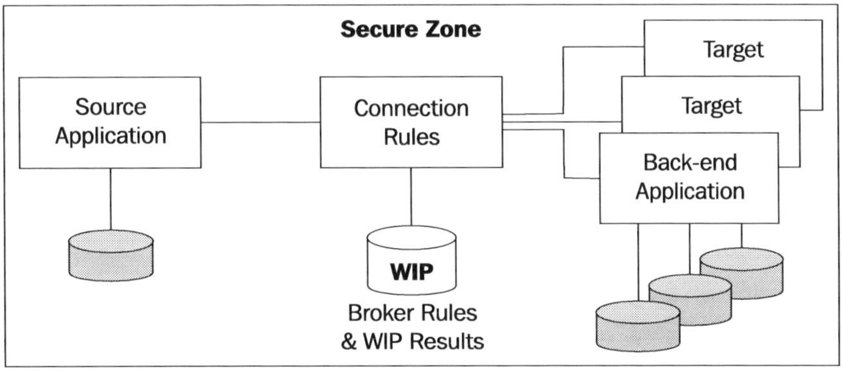

This pattern helps in reducing the clutter of point-to-point connections between the applications. Among the several target applications, the applications that require a common interaction with the source application are isolated and grouped together. The interaction rules are defined in the Broker Rules tier. The decomposition and composition of interactiond are managed by the broker rules.

The pattern may have another variation based on how the interaction is routed. This is illustrated in the following figure.

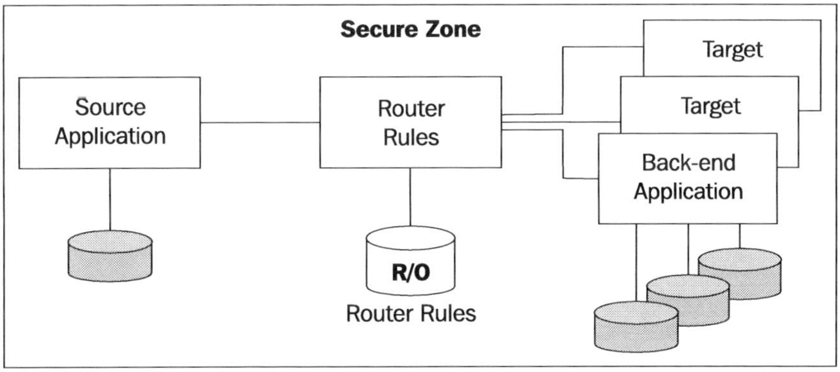

In this case, the rules for routing the interaction request are defined in the Router Rules tier. The interaction is routed to a single target application from a logical group of applications. The route is decided by the routing rules.

In the case of an Extended Enterprise domain, this pattern defines the interaction between a source application and the multiple target partner applications.

Guidelines

The Broker application pattern facilities SOA. Legacy applications can be wrapped as services. A Service Broker provides a desired service to a service consumer. The type of service and its composition and decomposition are decided at run time providing a very flexible solution in application integration.

Serial Process Application Pattern

This is an extension of the broker application pattern discussed in the previous section. In this case, a source application initiates an interaction with multiple target applications as in the case of a broker application pattern. However, the interaction, which is essentially a consumption of a service, now consists of invoking a series of business processes serially in a desired sequence. Basically, it facilitates the orchestration of several business processes for the desired interaction by the source application. This is illustrated in the following figure.

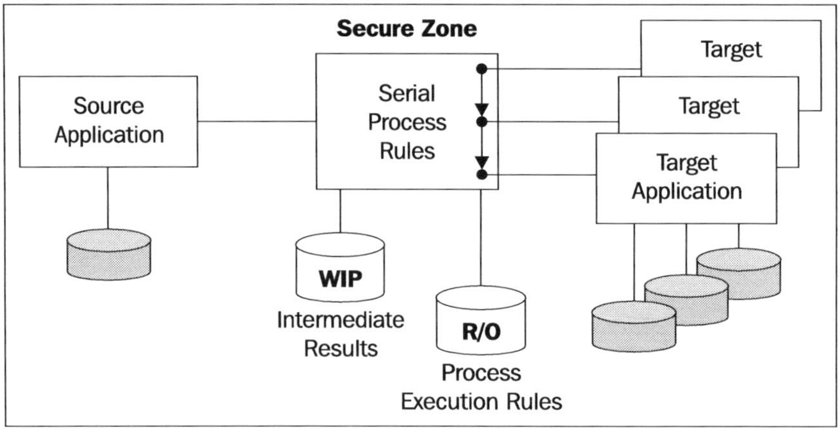

The Serial Process application pattern facilitates the separation of process flow logic from the logic of the individual applications. The flow is controlled by the Serial Process Rules tier. These rules not only define the control and data flow rules, but also define the execution rules for each target application. The intermediate results are stored in a WIP (Work-in-progress) database. The execution rules are stored in a registry.

In the case of an Extended Enterprise domain, the pattern defines the interaction of a source application with the series of target partner applications in a pre-determined sequence.

Guidelines

The Serial Process application pattern fits perfectly in the SOA paradigm. The businesses provide autonomous services. A consumer requires a series of services to be executed in a desired sequence. The orchestration flow may be defined at run time. The consumer requests a certain kind of business service that is decomposed into smaller services and executed sequentially on a set of target applications.

An example of this can be a travel reservation. A traveller desires a hotel and a car reservation besides her air travel reservation. These services are offered, obviously, by different business. Hotel, car, and airlines reservations operate independently of each other. The traveller initiates a reservation request for desired travel dates. The request is split into multiple service requests that are executed sequentially by partner businesses. When all the partner requests are processed, the reservation confirmation or non-availability is communicated to the consumer.

The practical implementation of this pattern is seen in the case of orchestration servers based on BPEL (Business Process Execution Language). The reader may also refer to a Packt book on BPEL (*Business Process Execution Language for Web Services, Second Edition,* ISBN 978-1-904811-81-7).

Parallel Process Application Pattern

This is an extension of the Serial Process application pattern where the sub-processes are executed concurrently on multiple targets. This is illustrated in the following figure.

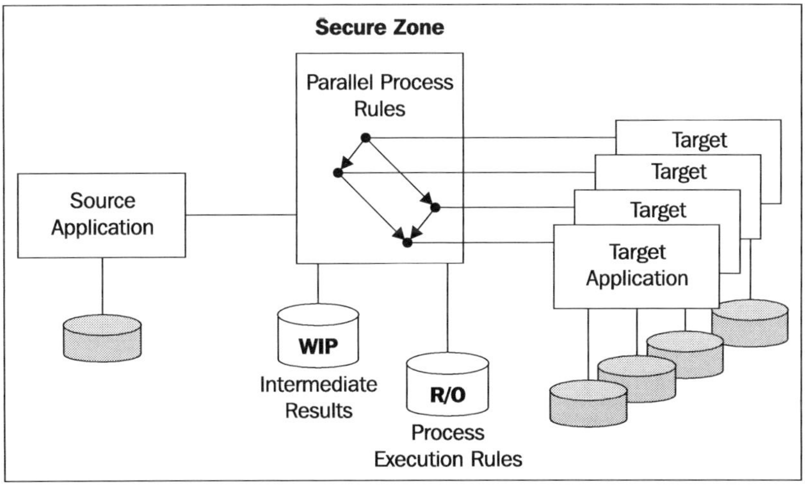

The concurrent execution of sub-processes requires a more sophisticated execution engine. The processes must be split, executed, and joined properly. The final result depends on the success/failure of each process. The consumer request may require an intermediate splitting and joining of a business operation. In such cases, the intermediate results dictate the further execution of the consumer request. Thus, the execution unit shown in the Parallel Process Rules tier can be very complex.

Guidelines

This pattern is observed in the implementation of a BPEL engine. Considering our example of a traveller in the previous section, the reservation request for a hotel, car and airlines may be executed in parallel as these are independent of each other. Depending on the outcome of each reservation, the ultimate confirmation or denial is communicated to the requester. The implementation of this pattern is best done with the use of a commercial off-the-shelf orchestration engine. Such engines typically use BPEL for creating business processes. The use of BPEL results in ease of defining and modifying the processes. Applying this pattern on custom-built application components is too complex and should be avoided.

Runtime Patterns

The application patterns discussed so far overlay the runtime patterns. The runtime pattern uses a set of nodes to group functional and operational components. The nodes are interconnected to form a pattern. The business logic of the application is deployed on nodes.

Nodes

We consider the following definitions for nodes in the context of runtime patterns:

Application Server/Services

An application server may consist of a servlet or EJB container. It typically hosts web applications and does not generally support HTTP connections. The HTTP requests from the presentation tier are redirected through a web server redirector.

Rules Repository

The rules repository, as the name suggests, stores the rules for controlling the mode of operation of an interaction. The rules, as seen earlier, may consist of data mapping rules, security access rules, availability rules, and so on. The use of a repository node is optional.

Router

The Router node is similar to the Broker node discussed earlier. It is responsible for routing a request to one of the appropriate target nodes. The router rules provide separation of the application logic from the distribution logic.

Protocol Firewall Node

A firewall controls the flow of information between an internal secured application and an external unsecured consumer. A firewall controls the traffic flow with the help of filters. Though generally this is considered as a first line of defence, it may be combined with comprehensive security systems that provide message encryption, content filtering, and intrusion detection. A firewall may be of two types: a protocol firewall or a domain firewall. A protocol firewall is a typical IP router.

Domain Firewall Node

A domain firewall is implemented generally as a dedicated server node. With the help of a domain firewall, we create a demilitarized zone for added security.

Connectors

In addition to the nodes, some connector definitions are important to us in the context of runtime patterns. A connector facilitates the interaction between two components. Depending on the required level of detail, a connector may be classified as follows:

- Primitive connector—represents a simple connection between the two components. This is considered an un-modeled connector as it does not provide any functionality other than a simple connection between the components.
- Component connector—provides an additional functionality in the connection between two components. This is also called a modeled connector.

A connector may be an Adapter connector, Path connector, or both.

Adapter Connector

An Adapter connector contains some business logic that transforms the messages and the data between the consumer and the source blocks to match the data and protocol requirements of each side. Thus, it enables the logical connectivity between the source and target components.

Path Connector

A Path connector provides a physical connectivity between the components. It may be as simple as a wired connection between the components or may be as complex as an Internet.

We will now study runtime patterns for integration.

Direct Connection Runtime Pattern

The Direct Connection pattern is depicted in the following figure.

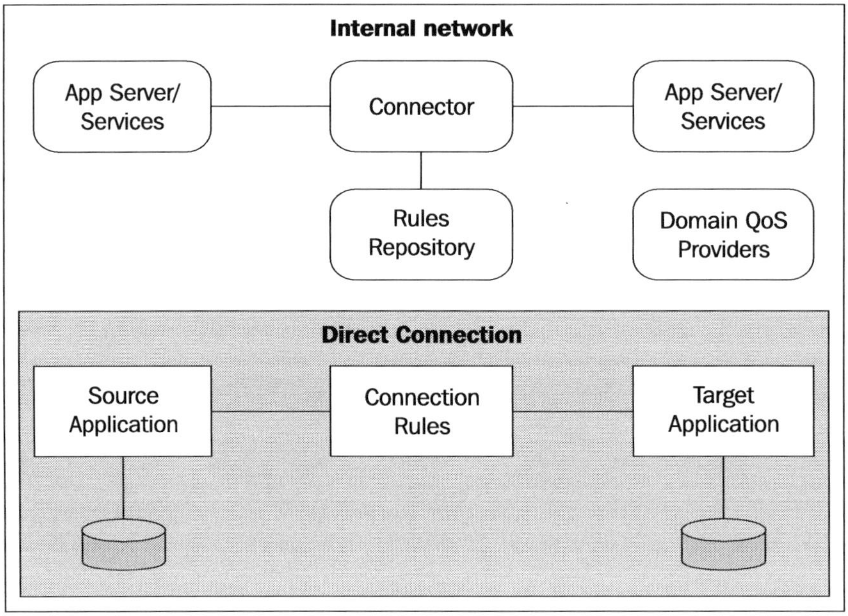

In this pattern, a source application connects directly to a target application using a connector. The connector itself may be explicitly or implicitly modeled. Depending on the connector and interaction variation, the connector may be classified as follows:

- Adapter Connector
- Path Connector
- Message Connector
- Call Connector
- Call Adapter Connector

The Adapter and Path connectors are explained previously. The connector is called a message connector whenever we use messaging services for connection. The Call Connector indicates a direct call to the service, while a Call Adapter Connector indicates a call through an adapter.

The source and target applications are modeled using the **Application Server/ Services** node. The **Rules Repository** and **Domain QoS Providers** are optional and need not be shown in the pattern artefact. As discussed earlier, the Rules Repository contains the rules for connection. The QoS Provider defines the various Quality-of-Service attributes for the connection.

In SOA, a rules repository may be implemented as a service registry.

This pattern provides a direct connection between a service consumer and a service provider with the help of connectors. The pattern is classified into the following categories depending on the connector used:

- Single Adapter connector
- Coupling Adapter connector
- Service Bus

Each of these is discussed further.

Direct Connection Pattern using Single Adapter

This pattern is depicted in the following figure.

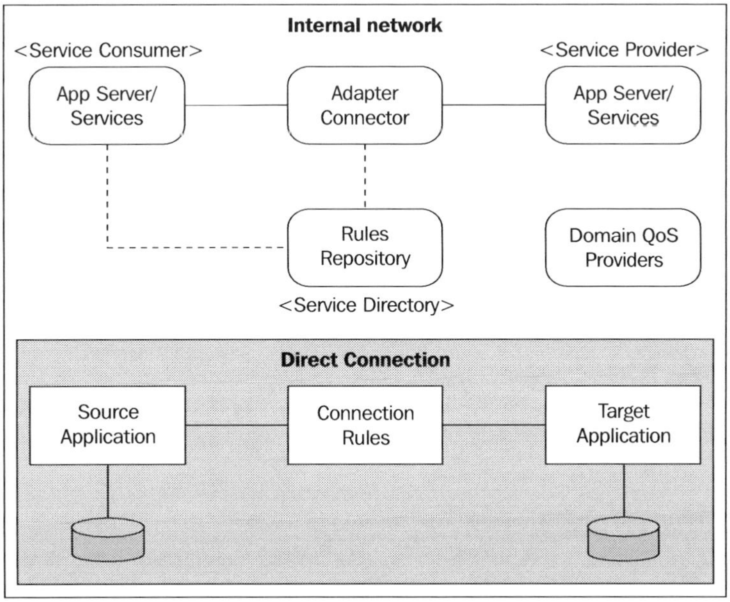

The Basic Direct Connection pattern uses a single adapter to connect a service consumer to a service provider. The adapter provides message and data transformation to match the different protocol requirements of the consumer and the provider. This is a very important pattern in the implementation of service-oriented architecture. This is typically used for providing a service-oriented interface to a legacy application. The Rules Repository node shown in the pattern models the service directory. The consumer looks up the directory to discover services and select an appropriate service to use.

Direct Connection using Coupling Adapter

This pattern is depicted in the following figure.

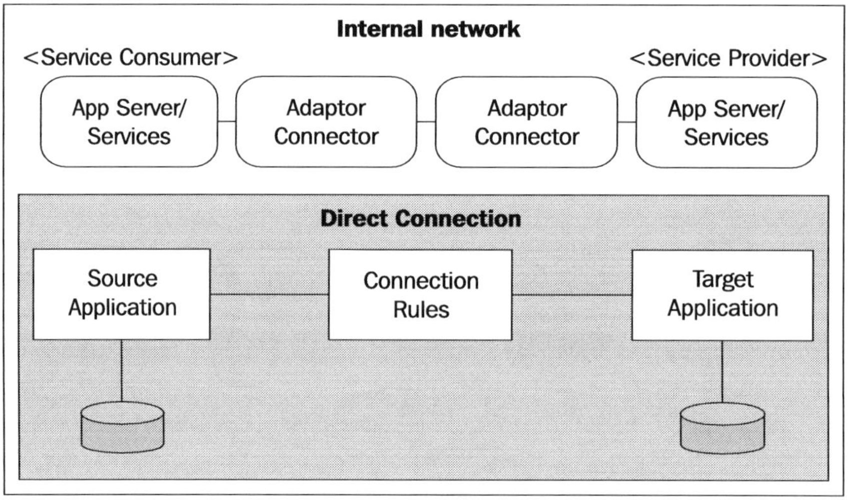

In this case, multiple adapters are coupled to achieve the desired transformation. This improves the adapter reusability in multiple point-to-point connections. The coupled adapters together support the transformation of request and response between the consumer and the provider.

Direct Connection using Service Bus

This pattern is depicted in the following figure.

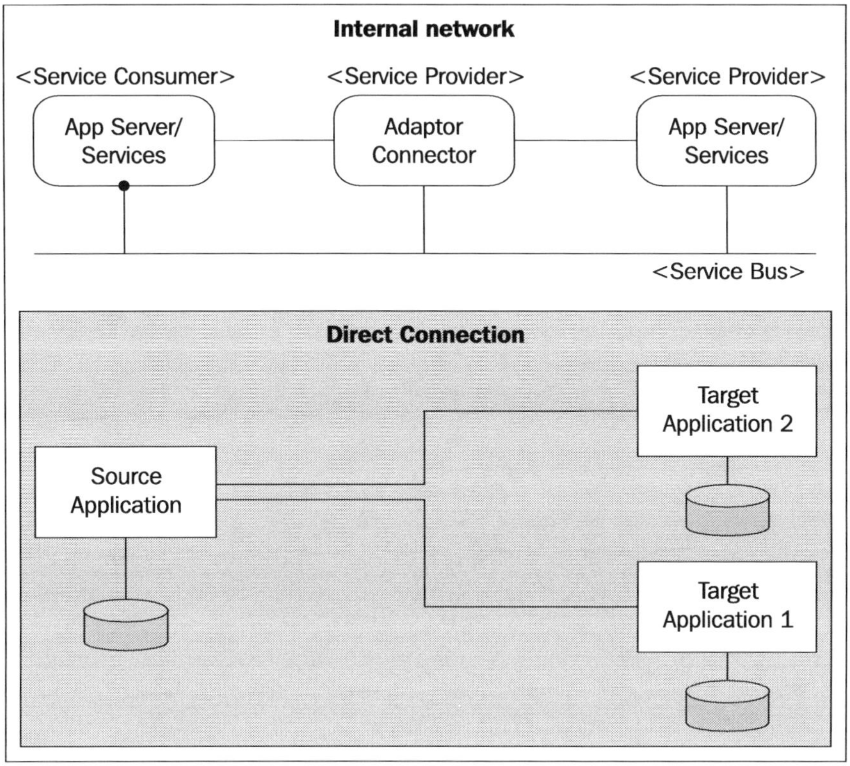

In this case, we assume that the various Application Server nodes are connected using a common Service Bus. A Source application connects to a desired Target application using this service bus. A source application may connect to more than one target application as depicted in the previous figure. Each connection may use a different connection pattern.

In the pattern diagram, the model adapter connectors and connection rules node are not shown. This is to emphasize the use of the service bus. The service bus minimizes the number of adapters required for each point-to-point connection and is an extension of the Direction Connection with coupling adapter runtime pattern.

Along with the service bus, the adapter connectors may be explicitly modeled as shown in the following figure.

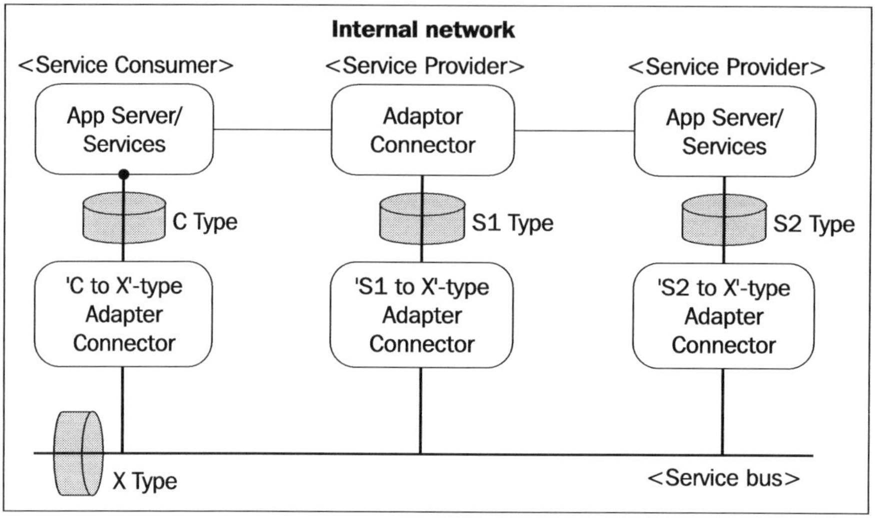

Here, the service bus is said to be of **X-type** as each of the application services connects to this X-type connector. An example of such an X-type service bus could be an HTTP service bus or a JMS (Java Messaging Service) service bus. The X-type adapter connectors bridge the service consumers and providers of different types to the underlying service bus. The service bus itself may span across multiple tiers, and may even cross enterprise boundaries.

A rules repository node may be added to the above pattern to enable the consumers to search for the services with desired characteristics. Such services may be offered within the enterprise or outside the enterprise. The service bus shown is a subset of the Enterprise Service Bus.

Runtime Patterns for Broker

As in the case of application patterns discussed earlier, a broker may be introduced in the runtime nodes, which will act as a message distributor. A source application connects to many target applications through a broker. A typical configuration for this pattern that uses a router to connect to multiple target applications is shown in the following figure.

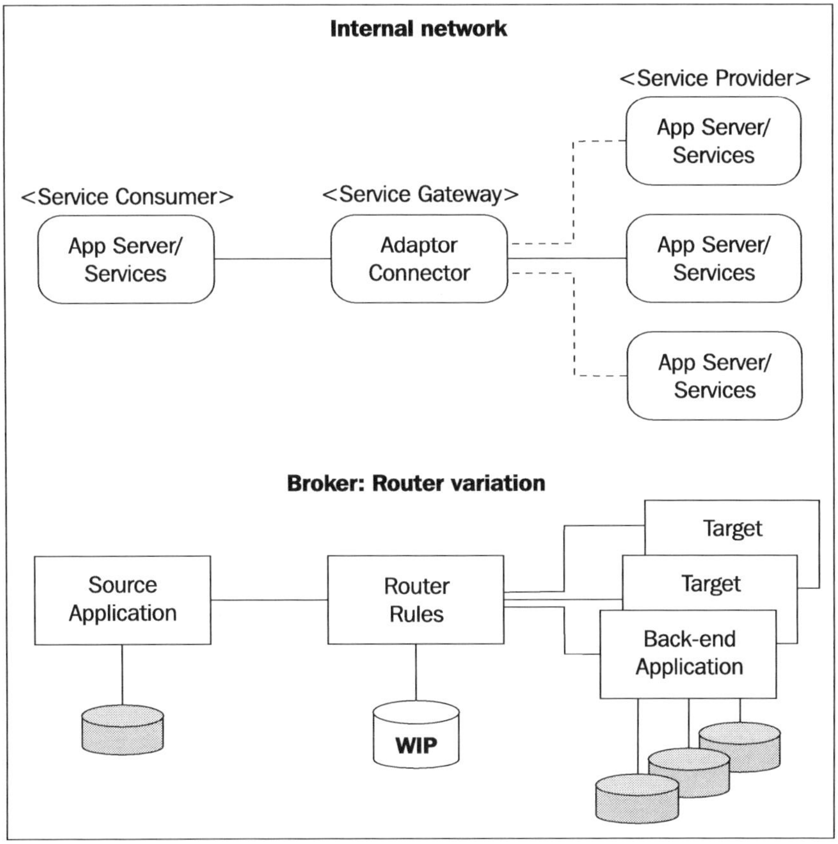

As in the case of application patterns, the router defines the rules for routing the consumer requests to one of the target applications. During the call, the router converts the transport protocols between the consumer and the provider. It also transforms the message formats between the two parties.

Another variation of this pattern is shown in the following figure.

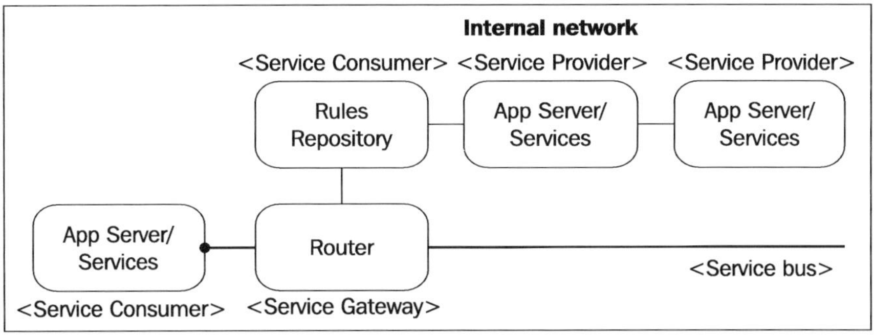

In this case, the router connects to the service bus and is responsible for transforming a service request from one protocol to another. For example, an HTTP call may be converted to a JMS call or an RMI-IIOP call.

Again, a service registry may be implemented by creating a Rules Repository node for clients to discover the services.

Having studied the various business and application patterns for SOA implementation, we will now look at the implementation of SOA in B2B and EAI domains.

Differences between B2B and EAI Web Services

Let us first look at the differences between B2B and EAI. The major differences may be listed as follows:

1. EAI as the name suggests acts within an enterprise to solve a local problem, while B2B as the name suggests acts across the enterprises.
2. EAI aims at integration of application and data sources within an enterprise, while businesses integrate for purposes such as a supply chain or collaborating on a common product design.
3. B2B mandates implementations of community management, user profile management, and sophisticated security management, while such services are not required for EAI.
4. B2B may require a deep support for standards such as OBI (Open Buying on Internet), XML, cXML (Commerce XML), and EDI (Electronic Data Interchange), while EAI has no requirement for such standards.
5. The connectivity to a single application in EAI is relatively small, while in the case of B2B the number of partner connections can be large. Also, the connectivity is unpredictable in B2B.

Having considered the differences between EAI and B2B, let us look at the differences in SOA implementation in the two cases.

Interface Design

As EAI is within an enterprise, the restrictions on the interface design can be relaxed as compared to B2B. You may use the SOA approach for exposing the services. However, you may decide not to use standard web protocols while implementing SOA. The protocols may be totally proprietary if it eases the integration. Secondly, the protocols don't need to be web-based as there may not be a need to access the service over the Web. An example of one such protocol is OpenEAI Message Protocol. This is a messaging protocol that expresses all actions on enterprise data objects in terms of request/reply and publish/subscribe messaging models. It also includes administrative information required for implementing security, routing, logging, and auditing. Other protocols are Omri and Indigo; these are recognized by Microsoft for B2B applications.

Compare this with the B2B situation in which the interface has to be exposed using standard web protocols as the service will be invariably accessed over the Web potentially even by unknown users. Even in the case of known users, there could be differences in the platform and technologies used by the consumer and the server. Thus, the use of standard web protocols becomes a mandatory requirement in order to make your service universally accessible.

The other factor that needs to be considered during the interface design is the security implementation. The messages must be protected and the data integrity must be guaranteed. This is a mandatory requirement in case of B2B, while in case of EAI this may be relaxed. The security can be easily compromised in the case of EAI as the interaction is restricted only within the organization. As a matter of fact, in most of the EAI situations, the security is totally discarded. This is mainly due to the complexities involved in implementing and managing security. Also, the secured channel reduces the system performance.

Now, we will look at the need for and use of a service registry in these two cases.

Use of a Service Registry

The service registry stores the information about the various services. In the case of EAI, as the services are offered and consumed locally, the use of a service registry is not recommended. Only in the case of large enterprises, where the number of services could be large, is a service registry suggested. If the number of services is small, it will be easier to publish them by other means such as paper or electronic documents rather than storing them in service registries.

In the case of B2B, the use of service registries becomes a mandatory requirement. In a B2B situation, it is important that the business must make its services publicly known. An unknown consumer can look up the service registry for a desired service. Once a desired service is identified, the consumer can obtain its interface and bind to the service provider to consume the service.

Using a service registry also requires an additional effort in coding the client applications and managing the registry. It also results in additional processing time. In the case of EAI as the services are available locally, these overheads are unjustifiable. In the case of B2B, there is no option other than to bear these overheads.

Writing Interoperable WSDL Definitions

As seen from the discussions in the earlier sections, web services technology can easily be used to implement SOA and to integrate applications running on different platforms. Every platform has its own data representation format and data type system. A web service must provide a universally accepted data type system to take care of the disparities in data types of various platforms. WSDL too, which is a grammar to describe the web service interface, must support interoperability. Although WSDL is not a mandatory requirement in the implementation of web services, it is widely supported. Thus, it is very important for us to understand how to create interoperable WSDL. To create an interoperable WSDL, the developer needs to create a WSDL that is compliant with the Basic Profile defined by WS-I (Web Service Interoperability Organization). The Basic Profile is discussed in the next section. The problem is that in many cases WSDL is created easily with the vendor tools and this WSDL may not truly comply with the Basic Profile.

To create a WSDL compliant to the WS-I Basic Profile, you will need to code it by hand and then verify it with the WS-I provided tools. Writing WSDL by hand is not only time consuming but it is also error prone. Thus, most times it is easier to use vendor-specific auto-generated WSDL. This WSDL may then be modified to remove any platform-specific idiosyncrasies.

The following Listing gives a template for WSI Basic Profile-compliant WSDL. You may use this template to easily create a compliant WSDL for your web services.

```
<?xml version="1.0" encoding="utf8"?>
<wsdl:definitions targetNamespace="http://www.mycompany.com"
                  xmlns:tns="http://www.mycompany.com"
                  xmlns:wsdl="http://schemas.xmlsoap.org/wsdl/"
                  xmlns:soap="http://schemas.xmlsoap.org/wsdl/soap/">
    <wsdl:types xmlns:xsd="http://www.w3.org/2001/XMLSchema" >
        <xsd:schema elementFormDefault="qualified"
                    http:= "http://www.mycompany.com"
```

```
                targetNamespace=" ">
        <xsd:element name="MyElement1" type="tns:Element1Type"/>
        <xsd:complexType name="Element1Type">
            <xsd:sequence>
                <xsd:element name="First" type="xsd:int"/>
                <xsd:element name="Second" type="xsd:int"/>
            </xsd:sequence>
        </xsd:complexType>
        <xsd:element name="MyElement2" type="tns:Element2Type"/>
        <xsd:complexType name="Element2Type">
            <xsd:sequence>
                <xsd:element name="First" type="xsd:int"/>
                <xsd:element name="Second" type="xsd:int"/>
            </xsd:sequence>
        </xsd:complexType>
    </xsd:schema>
</wsdl:types>
<wsdl:message name="InputMessage">
    <wsdl:part name="InputDocument" element="tns:MyElement1"/>
</wsdl:message>
<wsdl:message name="OutputMessage">
    <wsdl:part name="OutputDocument" element="tns:MyElement2"/>
</wsdl:message>

<wsdl:portType name="MyWebServicePortType">
    <wsdl:operation name="requestResponseMyServiceOperation">
        <wsdl:input message="tns:InputMessage"/>
        <wsdl:output message="tns:OutputMessage"/>
    </wsdl:operation>
    <wsdl:operation name="oneWayOperation">
        <wsdl:input message="tns:InputMessage"/>
    </wsdl:operation>
</wsdl:portType>

<wsdl:binding name="MyWebServiceSoap"
              type="tns:MyWebServicePortType"
              xmlns:http="http://schemas.xmlsoap.org/wsdl/http/"
              xmlns:soapenc=
                       "http://schemas.xmlsoap.org/soap/encoding/"
              xmlns:mime="http://schemas.xmlsoap.org/wsdl/mime/">
    <soap:binding transport="http://schemas.xmlsoap.org/soap/http"
                  style="document"/>
    <wsdl:operation name="requestResponseMyServiceOperation">
```

```
            <soap:operation
                soapAction="http://www.mycompany.com/OutputMessage"
                style="document"/>
            <wsdl:input>
                <soap:body use="literal"/>
            </wsdl:input>
            <wsdl:output>
                <soap:body use="literal"/>
            </wsdl:output>
        </wsdl:operation>
        <wsdl:operation name="oneWayOperation">
            <soap:operation
                soapAction="http://www.mycompany.com/InputMessage"
                style="document"/>
            <wsdl:input>
                <soap:body use="literal"/>
            </wsdl:input>
        </wsdl:operation>
    </wsdl:binding>

    <wsdl:service name="MyWebService">
        <wsdl:port name="MyWebServiceSoap" binding="tns:
MyWebServiceSoap">
            <soap:address
                location="http://localhost/WebApplication1/
MyWebService.asmx"/>
        </wsdl:port>
    </wsdl:service>
</wsdl:definitions>
```

The template shown in the above listing contains a single request/response operation and a single one-way operation. The template also defines two types and the two corresponding elements `MyElement1` and `MyElement2`. You may modify the template and add more operations and types as required by your service. Using this template, you can now easily create an interoperable WSDL that is compliant to the Basic Profile by following the simple steps listed next:

1. Replace all occurrences of `MyWebService` with the name of your web service.
2. Replace all occurrences of `http://www.mycompany.com` with the namespace of your service.

3. Define the complex data types required by your service by modifying the code shown below. Assign an appropriate name for your data type and create the desired sequence of data types for your desired new complex data type.

```
<xsd:element name="MyElement1" type="tns:Element1Type"/>
<xsd:complexType name="Element1Type">
    <xsd:sequence>
        <xsd:element name="First" type="xsd:int"/>
        <xsd:element name="Second" type="xsd:int"/>
    </xsd:sequence>
</xsd:complexType>
<xsd:element name="MyElement2" type="tns:Element2Type"/>
<xsd:complexType name="Element2Type">
    <xsd:sequence>
        <xsd:element name="First" type="xsd:int"/>
        <xsd:element name="Second" type="xsd:int"/>
    </xsd:sequence>
</xsd:complexType>
```

4. Define input and output messages for your service. We assume a document-centric service here. Assign the desired name for the messages and select the appropriate data types. You can do so by replacing the attribute values for the `name`, `part`, and `element` tags in the code below:

```
<wsdl:message name="InputMessage">
    <wsdl:part name="InputDocument" element="tns:MyElement1"/>
</wsdl:message>
<wsdl:message name="OutputMessage">
    <wsdl:part name="OutputDocument" element="tns:MyElement2"/>
</wsdl:message>
```

5. In the `portType` tag you will need to set the operations required by your web service. This may be one-way or request/response type. In the code below two operations are shown. The first one is of type request/response and the second one is of type one way. Modify this code to assign the desired names for the operations and assign the appropriate input and output messages defined earlier in your WSDL schema.

```
<wsdl:portType name="MyWebServicePortType">
    <wsdl:operation name="requestResponseMyServiceOperation">
        <wsdl:input message="tns:InputMessage"/>
        <wsdl:output message="tns:OutputMessage"/>
    </wsdl:operation>
    <wsdl:operation name="oneWayOperation">
        <wsdl:input message="tns:InputMessage"/>
    </wsdl:operation>
</wsdl:portType>
```

6. Assign the desired name and type for the binding in the `wsdl:binding` tag.

```
<wsdl:binding name="MyWebServiceSoap"
               type="tns:MyWebServicePortType"
```

7. In the operation tag set the desired operation `name`, specify the desired `soapAction` and the `input` and `output` by modifying the following lines of code. This code represents the request/response type of operation.

```
<wsdl:operation name="requestResponseMyServiceOperation">
     <soap:operation
         soapAction="http://www.mycompany.com/OutputMessage"
         style="document"/>
     <wsdl:input>
         <soap:body use="literal"/>
     </wsdl:input>
     <wsdl:output>
         <soap:body use="literal"/>
     </wsdl:output>
</wsdl:operation>
```

8. For one-way operation, make modifications similar to the previous bulleted item in the code lines below:

```
<wsdl:operation name="oneWayOperation">
    <soap:operation
        soapAction="http://www.mycompany.com/InputMessage"
        style="document"/>
    <wsdl:input>
        <soap:body use="literal"/>
    </wsdl:input>
</wsdl:operation>
```

9. Finally, modify the following line in the service tag to specify the URL for your service.

```
<soap:address location="http://www.yourCompany.com/
              WebApplication1/MyWebService.asmx"/>
```

Validating Interoperable WSDL

As we have hand-coded the interoperable WSDL in the previous section, there is no guarantee that it can be implemented as the platforms may not support all the features specified in the WSDL. To ensure that the WSDL is valid and can be implemented use the following steps:

1. Create a test web service for your platform. While creating a test web service, implement all the web service's methods by creating a test code. Ensure that all the input and output documents are covered in the test code.
2. Create client code for testing your web service. Call all the service methods of the test service. Ensure that all the defined messages are exchanged between the client and the web service. Validate the results of each service call.
3. Create a test client on another platform and do a similar testing to that suggested in step 2. If the platform choice for your web service is Java EE, then create a client on the .NET platform to verify the interoperability. If your test web service is on the .NET platform, use Java for creating a test client. Minimally, test the interoperability between these two popular platforms, .NET and Java EE.
4. Now, create a test web service for the other platform and do a cross testing across different platforms as in steps 2 and 3 above.
5. If any of these tests require you to modify the WSDL, do so and iterate through all the steps above until your WSDL is finalized.
6. Once you thoroughly test the implementation of your WSDL, publish it in a UDDI directory.

Interoperability Challenges in Web Services

As seen clearly from the ongoing discussions so far, the introduction of web services provided an elegant solution to integrate the diverse applications existing in this world. Before the introduction of web services, several technologies were available for remote invocation of services. These included, but were not limited to, DCE (Distributed Computing Environment), RPC (Remote Procedure Calls), CORBA IIOP (Common Object Request Broker Architecture Internet InterOperable Protocol), Java RMI (Remote Method Invocation), and Microsoft DCOM (Distributed Common Object Model). Web services differ from these technologies on the following grounds:

- Programming Language Independence
- Platform Independence
- Broad Industry Support

These benefits provided a great business value as the applications written in one programming language could now be easily accessed over the web by a client written in an altogether different language. Also, the existing applications need not be reengineered; they simply need to be wrapped as a web service.

Thus, with the introduction of web services, everybody jumped on the bandwagon quickly and as a result the implementations did not quite adhere to the specifications. Thus, we had several web services that were aimed at interoperability, but did not meet the requirements as the underlying protocol implementations did not match the specifications one hundred percent. The specifications are a number of XML standards, which are widely supported. These are:

- SOAP (Simple Object Access Protocol), used for invoking web services.
- WSDL (Web Services Description Language), used for describing the interface to a web service.
- UDDI (Universal Description, Discovery, and Integration), a service registry for publishing information about web services.

The above specifications came into existence at the beginning of this century. The first one was SOAP. SOAP 1.1 was published as a W3C note on Nov 8, 2000. It provided an envelope to encapsulate the following:

- Application messages
- Encoding rules for data types
- Conventions for representing remote procedure calls

The WSDL 1.1 specification was published on March 15, 2001. WSDL provided a convention for defining application messages, operations, and bindings to SOAP, HTTP, and MIME. The UDDI version 2 was published in July 2002.

Due to a sudden rush to implement these specifications, especially the most important one, which is SOAP, the market saw the SOAP specification published even before the finalization of the XML schema. The then published SOAP specification had its own type system called SOAP Encoding. Eventually, when the XML schema specifications were published, SOAP specifications needed modifications.

WSDL had its own problems. WSDL is more suitable for machines than human-beings. WSDL is difficult to understand and implement due to the many layers of abstraction defined in it.

UDDI comparatively suffered less than these other two specifications. The use of a service registry is not mandatory for implementing and using web services. Thus, this specification was the last one to get published and thus faced lesser issues on interoperability.

The market rushed to implement these various specifications from the notes published by W3C even before the standardization work was completed.

WS-I Specifications

To resolve these issues, finally the Web Services Interoperability Organization (WS-I) was formed in 2002 with the help of SAP, IBM, Microsoft, and others. The main purpose of WS-I was to bring the vendors and customers together to resolve the issues of interoperability. A working group called the Basic Profile WG was formed for this purpose. The working group delivered the Basic Profile (BP) 1.0 in August 2003.

The SOAP Encoding was disallowed in a BP-compliant web service. The committee also published a BP-conformant real-world Supply Chain Management application. It also identified and documented common usage patterns of web services. It also published a test tool for verifying service artefacts for BP conformance. The success of BP 1.0 was demonstrated by a sample application created with the joint efforts of 10 different vendors including BEA, IBM, Microsoft, Oracle, SAP, and SUN.

We will now discuss different versions of the Basic Profile and the modifications made in each of these.

WS-I Basic Profile 1.0

The key features of BP 1.0 are as follows:

- Use of SOAP, a lightweight XML-based messaging protocol. SOAP is used for transferring information through web service request and response messages.
- SOAP encoding is prohibited. The use of XSD data types is mandated.
- The use of HTTP binding with SOAP is necessary.
- Requires the use of HTTP 500 status response for faulty SOAP messages.
- The HTTP POST method must be used instead of any other HTTP methods.
- WSDL 1.1 specification is used to describe the web service interface.
- Necessitates the use of rpc/literal or document/literal forms of WSDL SOAP binding.
- Prohibits the request-response and notification style operations.
- WSDL SOAP binding extension with HTTP is used as a transport rule.
- Requires WSDL descriptions for UDDI.

The above list essentially summarizes the key features of BP 1.0. Thus, to create an interoperable web service, you must adhere to the listed rules to make the service BP 1.0 compliant. Failing this, the service may not interoperate with other services.

WS-I Basic Profile 1.1

WS-I Basic Profile 1.1 brought about further changes in the specifications. These are summarized below:

SOAP Changes

In SOAP, the following changes were made:

- Disallowed constructs:
  - An ENVELOPE SHOULD NOT contain the namespace declaration `xmlns:xml="http://www.w3.org/XML/1998/namespace"`.
  - A DESCRIPTION SHOULD NOT contain the namespace declaration `xmlns:xml="http://www.w3.org/XML/1998/namespace"`.
- Attributes on SOAP1.1 elements:
  - The `soap:Envelope`, `soap:Header`, and `soap:Body` elements in an ENVELOPE MUST NOT have attributes in the namespace `"http://schemas.xmlsoap.org/soap/envelope/"`.
- SOAP action HTTP header:
  - A RECEIVER MUST NOT rely on the value of the `SOAPAction` HTTP header to correctly process the message.

WSDL Changes

In WSDL, following changes were made:

- XML Namespace declarations:
  - A DESCRIPTION SHOULD NOT contain the namespace declaration `xmlns:xml=http://www.w3.org/XML/1998/namespace`.
- WSDL documentation element:
  - In a DESCRIPTION the `wsdl:documentation` element MAY be present as the first child element of `wsdl:import`, `wsdl:part` and `wsdl:definitions` in addition to the elements cited in the WSDL1.1 specification.

- Bindings and Parts:
    - An ENVELOPE MUST contain exactly one part accessor element for each of the `wsdl:part` elements bound to the envelope's corresponding `soapbind:body` element.
    - In a doc-literal description where the value of the parts attribute of `soapbind:body` is an empty string, the corresponding ENVELOPE MUST have no element content in the `soap:body` element.
    - In an rpc-literal description where the value of the parts attribute of `soapbind:body` is an empty string, the corresponding ENVELOPE MUST have no part accessor elements.
- Part Accessors:
    - The part accessor elements in a MESSAGE described with an rpc-literal binding MUST have a local name of the same value as the `name` attribute of the corresponding `wsdl:part` element.

WS-I Basic Profile 1.2

The following changes were made in BP 1.2.:

SOAP Changes

- XML Envelope Serialization:
    - An ENVELOPE MUST be serialized as XML 1.0.
- Unicode BOMs:
    - A RECEIVER MUST accept envelopes that include the Unicode Byte Order Mark (BOM).
- XML declarations:
    - A RECEIVER MUST accept messages with envelopes that contain an XML Declaration.
- Character Encodings:
    - A RECEIVER MUST ignore the encoding pseudo-attribute of the envelope's XML declaration.

- SOAP Envelope Structure:
  - An ENVELOPE MUST conform to the structure specified in SOAP 1.1 Section 4, "SOAP Envelope".
  - An ENVELOPE MUST have exactly zero or one child elements of the `soap:Body` element.
- SOAP Defined Faults Action URI:
  - An ENVELOPE MUST use the `http://www.w3.org/2005/08/addressing/soap/fault` URI as the value for the `wsa:Action` element when present, for either of the SOAP1.1 defined `VersionMismatch` and `MustUnderstand` faults.
- SOAP `MustUnderstand` or `VersionMismatch` fault Transmission:
  - A RECEIVER that receives a SOAP envelope that generates either a SOAP `MustUnderstand` or `VersionMismatch` fault SHOULD transmit such a fault on the HTTP response message, regardless of the value of the `wsa:ReplyTo` or `wsa:FaultTo` SOAP headers present in the message.
- Use of `wsa:Action` and WS-Addressing WSDL Binding:
  - An ENVELOPE that includes a `wsa:Action` SOAP header block and which is described using WSDL 1.1 description MUST conform to WS-Addressing WSDL Binding, Section 5.1.
- Understanding WS-Addressing SOAP Header Blocks:
  - When a message contains multiple WS-Addressing SOAP header blocks with at least one of those header blocks containing a `soap:mustUnderstand='1'` attribute, then a RECEIVER MUST understand all the WS-Addressing SOAP header blocks or none of them.
- Valid Range of Values for `SOAPAction` when WS-Addressing is used:
  - When `wsa:Action` MAP is present in an envelope, the containing MESSAGE MUST specify a `SOAPAction` HTTP header with either a value that is an absolute URI that has the same value as the value of the `wsa:Action` MAP, or a value of "" (empty string).

- Use of Non-Anonymous Response EPR in a Request-Response Operation:
    - If an INSTANCE sends a `MustUnderstand` or `VersionMismatch` fault generated as a result of an invocation of a Request-Response WSDL operation, it MUST send that fault in the entity body of HTTP response using the same HTTP connection as the request message of that operation.
    - If an INSTANCE sends a response, which is neither a `MustUnderstand` nor `VersionMismatch` fault, as a result of an invocation of a Request-Response WSDL operation and the response EPR has a non-anonymous `wsa:Address` value, then the response MUST be sent in the entity body of an HTTP request in a separate HTTP connection specified by the response EPR using the SOAP 1.1 Request Optional Response HTTP binding.

WSDL Changes

- WSDL and Schema Import:
    - In a DESCRIPTION, the namespace attribute of the `wsdl:import` MUST NOT be a relative URI.
- WSDL documentation Element:
    - In a DESCRIPTION the `wsdl:documentation` element MAY be present as the first child element of `wsdl:import`, `wsdl:part` and `wsdl:definitions` in addition to the elements cited in the WSDL1.1 specification.
- Multiple GED Definitions with the same QName:
    - A DESCRIPTION SHOULD NOT contain multiple global element declarations that share the same qualified name.
- Multiple Type Definitions with the same QName:
    - A DESCRIPTION SHOULD NOT contain multiple type definitions that share the same qualified name.

WS-I Basic Security Profile 1.0

The Basic Security Profile was created to address the interoperability issues of secured web services. The profile addresses several key areas listed next:

- Transport Layer Security
- SOAP Message Security

- Username Token Profile
- X.509 Certificate Token Profile
- XML-Signature
- XML Encryption, Algorithms
- Relationship of Basic Security Extension Profile to Basic Profile
- Attachment security

The security profile does not completely guarantee interoperability. However, it addresses the most common problems experienced in practical implementations to increase the probability of interoperability.

The focus is laid on the interoperability characteristics of two main technologies:

- HTTP over TLS—technology that protects the confidentiality of all information that flows over an HTTP connection
- SOAP Message Security

It does not prohibit the use of any encryption algorithms; however, it recommends some TSL & SSL cipher suits.

It is a requirement that the partners exchanging the messages must agree on the following:

- Which elements must be signed and/or encrypted
- Which elements may be signed and/or encrypted
- Which security tokens must be present
- Which security tokens may be present

The profile puts the following conditions on the applications:

- The `Envelope`, `Header`, or `Body` elements must not be encrypted. Encrypting these elements breaks the SOAP processing model and is therefore prohibited.
- A SOAP intermediary INSTANCE MUST NOT remove or modify any HEADER_ELEMENT unless that SOAP intermediary is acting in the role specified by the S11:actor attribute of that HEADER_ELEMENT.
- Messages may be signed and encrypted, potentially by multiple entities signing and encrypting overlapping elements. A signature applied before encryption has different security properties than encryption applied before a signature.
- SOAP Message Security defines a Timestamp element for use in SOAP messages. (Time stamp must contain only one `CREATED` & `EXPIRES` element)

Thus, to create interoperable secured web services, the conditions just listed must be satisfied. Note that the list is by no means complete, and the reader is referred to the WS-I site (`http://www.ws-i.org`) for full coverage of the security profile. The previous discussions merely give an overview of what is required to create secured interoperable web services.

Guidelines for Creating Interoperable Web Services

Fundamentally, web services are interoperable. Thus, regardless of the client's hardware and software, it should be able to run a web service. The functionality of the web service should remain independent of the following:

- Application platform such as Weblogic server, SunOne App Server, .NET Server, and so on
- Programming language such as Java, C++, C#, Visual Basic
- Hardware such as PC, PDA, Mainframes
- Operating systems such as Unix, Linux, Windows, and so on
- Application data models

However, we have seen previously that due to differing implementations of the specifications by different vendors, some web services may not correctly interoperate with others. To create interoperable web services the following tips may be useful.

Avoid using Vendor-Specific Extensions

Some vendors may extend certain specifications such as SOAP and WSDL. Avoid using such extensions in your applications.

Use the Latest Interoperability Tests

WS-I publishes the tools for interoperability tests. Use the latest version of these tools while testing for interoperability. This will ensure the BP conformance of your web services.

Understand Application Data Models

When you integrate two applications, it is most likely these two applications will be using different data models though they may be providing similar functionality such as accounting. Understand carefully the data models of the two interacting applications and reconcile them in a common model.

Understand Interoperability of Data Types

All the data types of the two interacting applications may not be compatible to each other. Thus, when you pass parameters and receive the resulting values from a method call, if these data types are not compatible, the two applications will not interoperate correctly.

Having considered the various aspects of implementing SOA, the requirements for creating interoperable web services and various standards for interoperability, we will now take a practical approach to learning by demonstrating the creation of interoperable .NET and J2EE web services in the next section.

Java EE and .NET Integration using Web Services

So far, we have looked into the various aspects of interoperability between web services deployed on disparate platforms. If the web services follow the compliance requirements of the Basic Profile discussed earlier, they can interoperate easily. Fortunately for us, most of the vendors have updated their development platforms to meet the WS-I compliance requirements for creating web services. In this section, we will look at the integration of web services deployed on two popular platforms, Java EE and .NET.

Sample Integration Scenario

We will develop a .NET web service that will be deployed on a .NET server. We will also develop a Java web service that is deployed on a Sun Application Server. We will then write a C# console application that calls both the services and prints the results of the two web service calls on the user console. The application architecture is illustrated in the following figure.

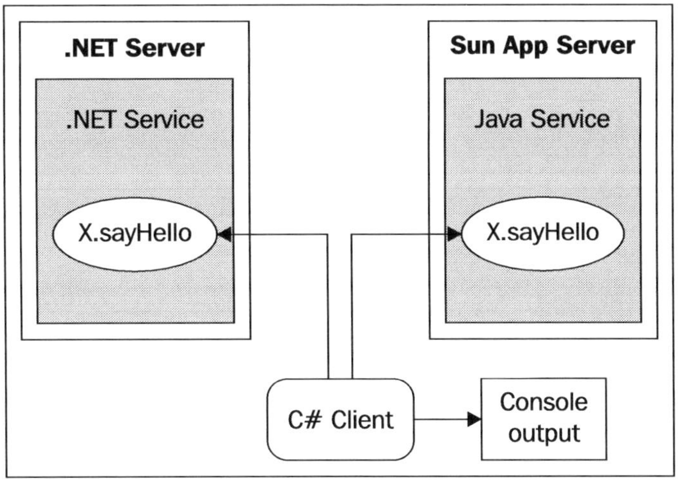

I have kept this application very simple so that we can focus more on the compliance requirements. The service methods on both the web services simply return a greeting message to the caller.

Developing the Java Web Service

First, we will develop a Java web service. Creating a Java web service on the latest Java EE platform is an easy task. Write a simple Java class as shown in the following listing.

```
package endpoint;

import javax.jws.WebService;

@WebService
public class Hello
{
    public String SayHello()
    {
        return "\nHello from Java Service!";
    }
}
```

You need to import the `javax.jws.WebService` package as seen in the listing. The `Hello.java` file contains a public class `Hello`. To convert this into a component that can be deployed as a web service, simply annotate the class with the `@WebService` attribute. The deployment tool then provides the required plumbing to expose this class as a web service. In the class, we write the service methods that can be invoked by a service consumer. We write a single method in this class called `SayHello` that returns a greeting message to the caller.

Deploying the Service

The easiest way to build and deploy the web service is to use a vendor-supplied IDE. You may use Java Studio Enterprise or NetBeans IDE to build and deploy the service. I used NetBeans 5.5 IDE to deploy the service. The NetBeans 5.5 version provides a template for creating web services. This template creates EJB components for service objects. As I said, to keep the things simple, I avoided using this template. Rather, I used the **ant Build** to compile and deploy the project. You will find the sample `build.xml` file in your NetBeans installation. This file is also available in the code download for this book.

NetBeans IDE can be configured for deployment to any server. I used SunOne Application Server PE 9 for testing. NetBeans also comes with a bundled Tomcat server. You may use this for deployment. If you decide to use Sun App Server for deployment, you will have to add the server in the NetBeans configuration. Incidentally, the Sun Application Server is installed on your machine as a part of Java EE installation.

Once you deploy the service, you can verify it by examining the WSDL generated during the deployment process. To look up the WSDL, type the following URL in your browser:

```
http://localhost:8080/Hello/HelloService?WSDL
```

This will show the generated WSDL in the browser window. We will now examine this WSDL to verify that this is BP compliant.

WSDL for Java Web Service

The WSDL is shown in the following listing.

```
<definitions targetNamespace="http://endpoint/" name="HelloService">
    <types>
        <xsd:schema>
            <xsd:import namespace="http://endpoint/"
schemaLocation="http://DRSARANG:8080/Hello/HelloService/__container$pu
blishing$subctx/WEB-INF/wsdl/HelloService_schema1.xsd"/>
```

```
        </xsd:schema>
    </types>
    <message name="SayHello">
        <part name="parameters" element="tns:SayHello"/>
    </message>
    <message name="SayHelloResponse">
        <part name="parameters" element="tns:SayHelloResponse"/>
    </message>
    <portType name="Hello">
        <operation name="SayHello">
            <input message="tns:SayHello"/>
            <output message="tns:SayHelloResponse"/>
        </operation>
    </portType>
    <binding name="HelloPortBinding" type="tns:Hello">
        <soap:binding transport="http://schemas.xmlsoap.org/soap/http"
style="document"/>
        <operation name="SayHello">
            <soap:operation soapAction=""/>
            <input>
                <soap:body use="literal"/>
            </input>
            <output>
                <soap:body use="literal"/>
            </output>
        </operation>
    </binding>
    <service name="HelloService">
        <port name="HelloPort" binding="tns:HelloPortBinding">
            <soap:address location="http://DRSARANG:8080/Hello/
HelloService"/>
        </port>
    </service>
</definitions>
```

If you examine this document carefully against the BP conformance requirements, you will find that this file is 100% BP compliant. Thus, to import this as a reference in the .NET client, when we develop it later, would be very easy.

Developing the .NET Web Service

Creating a .NET web service using Visual Studio IDE is as simple as creating a Java web service using NetBeans IDE. I used Visual Studio 2005 for creating the web service and the test client application. The IDE provides a template for creating an ASP.NET Web Service. Follow the default project options while creating the web service. I used the **NetService** as the name for my project and selected C# as the development language. The wizard generates a default class for the web service with a default service method. I modified this service method to send a greeting message to the caller. The modified source file is shown in the following listing.

```
using System;
using System.Web;
using System.Web.Services;
using System.Web.Services.Protocols;

[WebService(Namespace = "http://tempuri.org/")]
[WebServiceBinding(ConformsTo = WsiProfiles.BasicProfile1_1)]
public class Service : System.Web.Services.WebService
{
    public Service () {

        //Uncomment the following line if using designed components
        //InitializeComponent();
    }

    [WebMethod]
    public string SayHello() {
        return "\nHello from .NET service";
    }

}
```

As can be seen from the listing, the `Service` class inherits from the `System.Web.Services.WebService` class. The class is attributed with two attributes `WebService` and `WebServiceBinding`. The `WebService` attribute specifies the namespace for the defined web service. The `WebServiceBinding` attribute defines the conformance target. In our example, the conformance target is Basic Profile 1.1 as specified by the constant from the `WsiProfiles` class. Within the class definition, each desired method that is to be invoked as a web service method should be annotated using the `WebMethod` keyword. In our example, the `SayHello` method is declared as a web method that can be invoked using SOAP.

Deploying the .NET Web Service

Once you write the code for the web service, it can be deployed using the wizard provided in the VS.NET IDE. You may now look up the generated WSDL by opening the following URL in your browser:

```
http://localhost:20278/NetService/Service.asmx?WSDL
```

Note that you will need to set up the appropriate port number in the above URL. The generated WSDL is shown in following listing.

```
<wsdl:definitions targetNamespace="http://tempuri.org/">
   <wsdl:types>
   <s:schema elementFormDefault="qualified" targetNamespace="http://
tempuri.org/">
   <s:element name="SayHello">
<s:complexType/>
</s:element>
   <s:element name="SayHelloResponse">
   <s:complexType>
   <s:sequence>
<s:element minOccurs="0" maxOccurs="1" name="SayHelloResult" type="s:
string"/>
</s:sequence>
</s:complexType>
</s:element>
</s:schema>
</wsdl:types>
   <wsdl:message name="SayHelloSoapIn">
<wsdl:part name="parameters" element="tns:SayHello"/>
</wsdl:message>
   <wsdl:message name="SayHelloSoapOut">
<wsdl:part name="parameters" element="tns:SayHelloResponse"/>
</wsdl:message>
   <wsdl:portType name="ServiceSoap">
   <wsdl:operation name="SayHello">
<wsdl:input message="tns:SayHelloSoapIn"/>
<wsdl:output message="tns:SayHelloSoapOut"/>
</wsdl:operation>
</wsdl:portType>
   <wsdl:binding name="ServiceSoap" type="tns:ServiceSoap">
<soap:binding transport="http://schemas.xmlsoap.org/soap/http"/>
   <wsdl:operation name="SayHello">
<soap:operation soapAction="http://tempuri.org/SayHello"
style="document"/>
   <wsdl:input>
```

```
<soap:body use="literal"/>
</wsdl:input>
   <wsdl:output>
<soap:body use="literal"/>
</wsdl:output>
</wsdl:operation>
</wsdl:binding>
   <wsdl:binding name="ServiceSoap12" type="tns:ServiceSoap">
<soap12:binding transport="http://schemas.xmlsoap.org/soap/http"/>
   <wsdl:operation name="SayHello">
<soap12:operation soapAction="http://tempuri.org/SayHello"
style="document"/>
   <wsdl:input>
<soap12:body use="literal"/>
</wsdl:input>
   <wsdl:output>
<soap12:body use="literal"/>
</wsdl:output>
</wsdl:operation>
</wsdl:binding>
   <wsdl:service name="Service">
   <wsdl:port name="ServiceSoap" binding="tns:ServiceSoap">
<soap:address location="http://localhost:20278/NetService/Service.
asmx"/>
</wsdl:port>
   <wsdl:port name="ServiceSoap12" binding="tns:ServiceSoap12">
<soap12:address location="http://localhost:20278/NetService/Service.
asmx"/>
</wsdl:port>
</wsdl:service>
</wsdl:definitions>
```

If you compare this WSDL against the BP conformance requirements, you will find that this is indeed BP 1.1 conformant.

Developing the Test Client

We will now develop a C# console application for consuming the previously created web services. Use the project wizard in VS.NET to create a console application. Follow the default while creating the application. I used **TestClient** as the name for my project. The wizard generates the skeleton code for a console application. You will need to add code to this skeleton to invoke the two web services. Before you do so, you will need to add web references to the two services. The IDE provides a menu for adding these references. Use the WSDL URLs specified earlier for locating the web services. Once you complete adding the web reference, you can modify the client code. The intelli-sense feature in the IDE will now resolve the references correctly.

The modified code is shown in the following listing.

```
using System;
using System.Collections.Generic;
using System.Text;

namespace TestClient
{
    class Program
    {
        static void Main(string[] args)
        {
            String str =
                        "Testing .NET, Java Web Services Integration";
            NetService.Service service1 = new NetService.Service();
            str += service1.SayHello();
            JavaService.HelloService service2 =
                        new JavaService.HelloService();
            str += service2.SayHello();
            Console.WriteLine(str);
            Console.ReadKey();
        }
    }
}
```

The application obtains the reference to the `NetService` by instantiating the `Service` class. The code then calls the service method on the obtained object reference. Similarly, a reference to the `JavaService` is obtained by instantiating the `HelloService` class. The `SayHello` method is invoked on the obtained object reference. Finally, the application prints the two greeting messages on the user console. Note that when you invoke the service method, the binary method call gets converted into a SOAP call. Similarly, the response from the web service is returned to the application as a SOAP response. The underlying runtime transforms the binary call to SOAP and the SOAP response to the C# return type as defined by the method.

Summary

SOA has become a buzz word in today's IT industry. From the component-oriented approach, we have now moved into the service-oriented approach. Businesses publish the offered services rather than the interfaces to their components. While designing SOA for an enterprise application, the study of patterns plays a vital role in the success of SOA implementation. In this chapter, the various SOA patterns and guidelines for applying those in real-life situations were covered.

The web services technology perfectly complements the creation of SOA. The chapter discussed the architecture of web services and its benefits. It covered the various patterns that can be applied while creating SOA using web services in depth.

Web services may be used in both EAI and B2B problem spaces. The chapter covered the essential differences between EAI and B2B and how to apply SOA integration techniques in these spaces.

Merely exposing your application as a web service is not sufficient. Any client should be able to use your service with ease. Web services are inherently interoperable. However, due the varying implementations of the web service specifications, usually these are not interoperable. To make web services interoperable, a consortium called the Web Services Interoperability (WS-I) organization was formed. The working group of WS-I created several documents for defining the requirements of creating interoperable secured web services. This chapter discussed these specifications. If you create a web service that is BP (Basic Profile) compliant, it will be interoperable with other services.

The chapter also discussed several guidelines for creating interoperable web services. Finally, a complete trivial example of creating web services on two popular platforms, .NET and Java EE, was discussed. We demonstrated by writing a .NET client that these services are interoperable.

10

Service- and Process-Oriented Approach to Integration Using Web Services

In this chapter we will discuss the more evolved SOA infrastructure option—Enterprise Service Bus. This is a technology for the infrastructure that spans service provider, communication infrastructure, transformation, and routing services and the integration client applications/business processes.

SOA fits into the Integration space and the various technology options available for SOA, including Web Services and ESB. An underlying driver in all technologies is the pervasive usage of XML and the sheer simplicity it offers to exchange data and information between systems. This is further fuelled by the strong support for the Web Service standards in all technologies. In this standards context, the difference between the various options will be in their abilities to handle different services topologies and any additional services-centric functionality that they offer.

In the current global business environment, as enterprises spread across the world, the demands on IT have changed. With increasing complexity of businesses and business relationships, it is imperative that the IT infrastructure scales up with them. This will require additional facilities in the infrastructure such as reliable and scalable communications and high availability of services, and manageability of the services infrastructure. As the services become more widespread in any enterprise, hosting and accessing services will place demands far beyond the connectivity that Web Services offer, or abilities to host the services that Application platforms such as Java EE (hitherto called J2EE) and .NET provide.

In SOA infrastructure, normally a high level of emphasis is placed on the connectivity and service description protocols. While the protocols and the services execution are necessary, the infrastructure that connects the service clients to the service execution environment is equally important, even if there may not be too many standards or specifications in this space. SOA as a concept will work just as well with any of the technologies. However, in a widely distributed enterprise, a higher level of performance and scalability may be expected from the platforms.

Providing a well performing services environment in such distributed enterprises will involve an operating infrastructure that both provides the services runtime and connects the various service providers, service consumers, and processes. Once there is an infrastructure that connects the various ends in the enterprise services environment, one could look at more capabilities such an infrastructure could provide beyond the basic services connectivity.

The Enterprise Service Bus is one such Infrastructure. A technology for the infrastructure that spans service provider and the integration client applications/ consumer ends. In this chapter, we will discuss the Enterprise Service Bus in more detail.

From Just Services to an Enterprise Bus

Market dynamics today causes the landscape of any enterprise to be very dynamic. Even in an organization located physically in a single location with a single data center, this co-location may not remain so for long given the immense M&A activity underway in businesses today. New companies would be acquired, and existing companies merged to create new entities. This results in very fluid organizations. The services infrastructure should be in a position to adapt to this fluidity. The peer-to-peer (P2P) integration solutions such as simple Web Services are probably best suited for organizations with not too many systems talking to each other with low volume of services traffic, in a single or just few locations. The moment that these assumptions are no longer valid, peer-to-peer (P2P) services infrastructure such as Web Services or EAI may not suffice. They are likely to face these constraints:

- It will be difficult to assure reliability across WANs, as network performance may be unpredictable.
- RPCs, being synchronous in nature, may face failures/timeout issues servicing service requests due to high latencies.
- In simple point to point connectivity, each request gets its own connection from the origin system to the provider system, which could result in a large number of connections in high services traffic environments.
- Scalability and reliability could come under stress.

"Services" or business components used over the network have come to mean Web Services, mostly. Web Services, as we know today, emerged rapidly with XML and SOAP over HTTP, gaining mainstream traction in IT.

The advent of XML opened up a very different front in approaches to integrating applications—which hitherto was done either using shared databases or EDI solutions. Now XML was a simple, elegant, and portable mechanism to represent data, with XML Schemas providing a powerful mechanism to describe and validate the structure of XML documents. Soon, SOAP followed—a brilliant middleware approach built around XML, using XML to not only represent business data, but also to represent the actual middleware plumbing metadata.

XML is used to represent information that identifies the specific service method to be executed, and the input parameters to that request. Web Services is now the suite of standards and approaches that are built around SOAP for systems to talk to each other.

The most common use of Web Services is for simple services (shown in the following figure)—the point-to-point interactions to "execute" remote services. A service provider makes its service available, and a service consumer accesses the service—by directly connecting to the service provider, say, via SOAP over HTTP. Here the focus is more on connectivity and service access, and not so much on the scalability of the solution space and flexibility in the infrastructure between the service provider and the integration application that accesses the service.

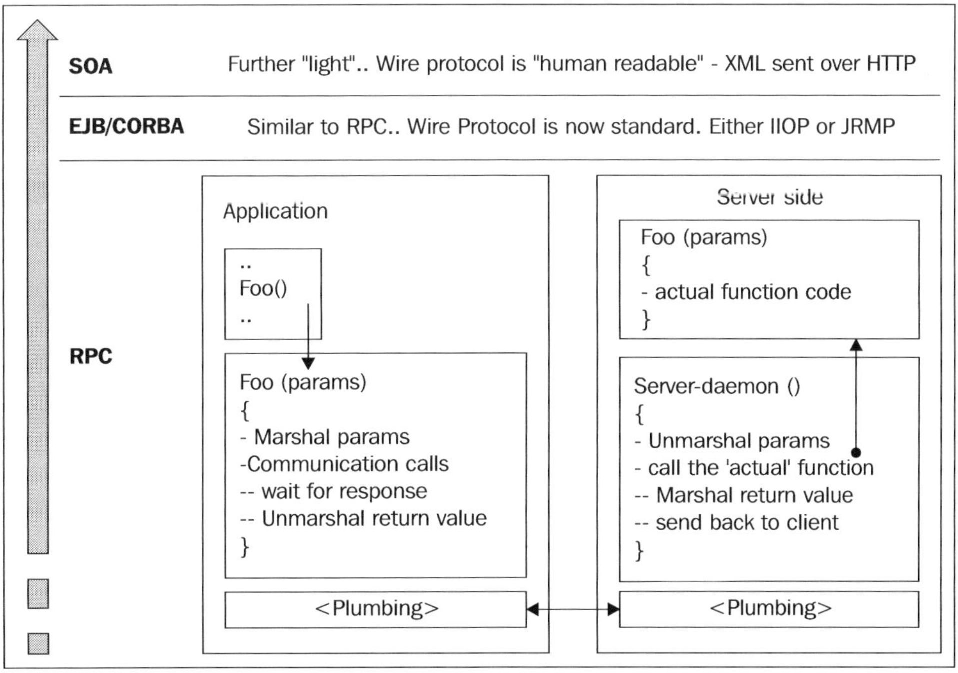

Web services, and the traditional middleware systems such as Java EE (EJB) and .NET, focused on a client application accessing services provided by the Application Server; mostly in a P2P mode. Though distributed services, wherein the application services are distributed across multiple servers and instances, were supported, the fundamental access model was still point-to-point. Even if one of the server instances were to access another server instance, the lowest-level connection is again point-to-point, with one server instance communicating with another.

Consider a simple example, say an Order Processing System that is a Java EE application needs to access a Warehouse application, which is another Java EE application. In this case, an Enterprise Java Bean (EJB) component in the Order application will access another EJB in the Warehouse application. Though order application is a Java EE application itself, for the Warehouse application it is just another client, just like a simple Java program that may access this EJB. The assumption is a simple point-to-point connectivity. Every accessing program/application must be aware of exactly where and how the "service providing" application can be accessed. The coupling is very tight—from protocols through the physical address to which the communication sockets are established.

As integration requirements rapidly spread beyond simple homogenous application environments, the environment is rapidly becoming heterogeneous and distributed. In contemporary IT architectures, there is a wide range of application platforms and environments. An added complexity is introduced when they are physically and geographically distributed. In such environments, the spaghetti links for integrating the large number of solution islands become a major performance and scalability challenge.

To address such wide-scale integration scenarios, there need to be additional infrastructure components that sit in between the two service ends. This would involve services being "available" on this infrastructure and accessed from this infrastructure. This infrastructure will extend across the organization and all existing solution islands can be made available on this common infrastructure. The business processes and integration applications will also be on the same infrastructure as "consumers" of the available services. If such infrastructure leverages the XML-based wire protocols that are popular in Web Services, then the services requests flow through the infrastructure as XML documents. As a large number of services become available and get accessed, this infrastructure will start looking like a "bus" transporting these XML documents. A bus, that enables "services"—a Service Bus.

The service bus provides the necessary abilities to host services, provide effective communication infrastructure where the notion of services is well understood as a first-class-artifact, and abilities to access the services through this infrastructure. Additionally, the bus can provide the abilities to manage the services and their access. This might include providing abstractions of services such that the location of the services is hidden from the consuming applications and process engines. The infrastructure will take on the responsibility of locating and routing the request to the right location. The difference between Services and a Service Bus is highlighted in the following figure.

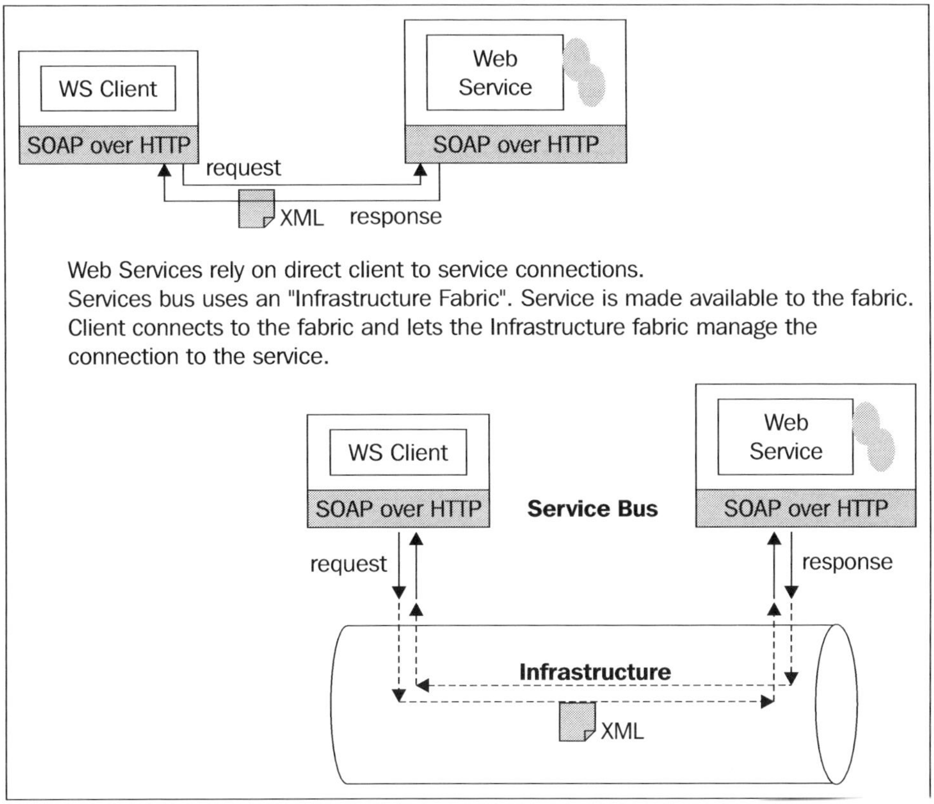

One important point to note is that even though the service bus provides additional capabilities, the capabilities only add to the existing service mechanism between service providers and consumers. The service description and request/response representation protocol can remain the same. Additional capabilities are built on this basic protocol. These protocols are well defined by the various Web Services standards. They are also very widely accepted and understood.

The application's view of the bus is based entirely on the omni-present Web Services standards. The services are described using WSDL, and the service requests may be in SOAP. It is just that the bindings used in the SOAP interactions may be different from simple HTTP or even JMS—even though standard bindings are preferable. The bindings specific to the middleware platform, enable the infrastructure to provide value additions in the service bus.

This "Service bus" provides the required infrastructure abstractions. So the applications can still be written assuming the Web Services-like application interface abstractions. Given the flexibility provided in the binding layer of Web Services via the Bindings, the communication layer need not be just HTTP or JMS connections. This layer can be replaced, transparent to the services and the integration applications, by a more powerful distributed services "bus" framework.

We Need Web Services and More

Why do simple Web Services and environments like EAI not provide a service bus? Both of these are inherently peer-to-peer models—Web Services in a pure point-to-point interaction model, and EAI in a hub-and-spoke model where one consuming end can access one or more legacy back ends, but each links in a point-to-point mode. While this serves the basic peer-to-peer connectivity and integration requirement very well, it doesn't provide for the enterprise-grade services scenario—where typically a plethora of connections would exist across a multitude of systems dispersed across geographies. In such widely distributed environments, a different higher performing and more scalable and reliable approach may be needed.

Web Services initially started as a point-to-point approach for integration, where one application can talk to another application in an SOA environment using a simple direct HTTP connection as the primary communication channel. SOAP provides the representation of the request and response that are sent on this channel. Over the years, WS standards have evolved. The WS standards provide a very powerful mechanism to describe any service, regardless of the protocol to be used for communication and also the bindings used to represent the inputs/outputs.

In Web Services, the focus is primarily on connecting two ends—peer-to-peer. All the standards in this space are directed towards this primary objective. In general, though, the interactions in enterprises are not simply P2P, they are more many-to-many. There are many systems and applications in the enterprise, and Business processing will require each application talking to one or more applications—with each application providing services that are accessed by one or more other applications/systems.

In such a widely distributed services environment, loose binding between the various applications is very important to get a successful organization-wide integration. The basic abstractions for the loose coupling are well provided by the various Web Services standards. Beyond this, even the infrastructure layers need to be loosely bound. This is where Web Services, EAI, and Application Platforms like Java EE and .NET fail to provide the needed flexibility.

Added to this, is an interesting natural interaction model between departments in an enterprise. In distributed organizations, the natural interaction between departments and locations is to send "business documents" to a mailbox and get those documents "processed". The business documents could be forms or documents that describe a business requirement or inputs. This is well understood by end users and business analysts, as it fits into the natural interaction models within an organization. In an automated interaction, these documents may very well be XML documents. The widespread acceptance of XML as a document representation format, with most organizations having well defined schemas to represent business document structures and document exchanges already happening in XML lays a very good foundation for alternative services interaction models.

In effect, flip the view from services "invoked" with documents passed in as arguments, to "sending" a document to an address or endpoint and getting the document "processed". This is a subtle, but very clear difference, resulting in a fundamentally different approach to the services infrastructure.

Enter Enterprise Service Bus (ESB)

The Enterprise Service Bus is a very strong technology option for high-end enterprise-wide SOA environments. ESB inherently provides the service-bus functionality described above.

There are simple Web Service-based integration options, and there are massively distributed integration platforms. The distributed services platform, while supporting Web Service standards, will have a highly scalable runtime and communication environment. The latter is an Enterprise Services platform and the former is just a simple point-to-point services solution.

ESB Architecture

ESB, as a technology for Enterprises Services, provides the necessary infrastructure to host/access the services and provides the required service bus functionality such as scalable communications and mediation and control of the services. While there are no authoritative definitions of ESB yet, there is a common ground that is rapidly evolving: a defined set of platform attributes with a clearly emerging architecture, from hosting or enabling access to services through mediation services and process engines.

Defining ESB

An ESB makes it easy to dynamically connect, mediate, and control services and their interactions. An Enterprise Service Bus, as the name suggests, is an enterprise-wide distributed common infrastructure for hosting, managing, and accessing the services.

The defining concepts of an Enterprise Service Bus are:

- An ESB provides an **enterprise-grade** service execution environment:

  Services need to run in a services operating environment that will ensure reliability, fault-tolerance, and security of the services. These will be inherent properties of the service binding, provided for by the ESB platform. Services themselves delegate the security, reliability, and communication to the ESB infrastructure; they need not implement low-level communications themselves. In cases where the actual service is running in an external SOA-aware service container, the ESB may delegate some of this processing to such containers.

- **Services** on the ESB are all first-class citizens:

  Services are not just protocol handling layers that help in un-marshaling the requests coming over protocols such as SOAP. In ESB, Services are broadly available and configured for mediated interaction with any other service or processes. The only programming required is the actual service implementation. No other code is needed either to access or to control the services. This would be provided by the ESB infrastructure. Though Web Services will naturally be supported, the ESB will also provide connectivity to a broad range of technologies such as Java EE and .NET components, bespoke applications, and legacy MOM systems.

- An ESB provides a **service bus** to make services broadly available for use across the enterprise:

  The bus is essentially a framework that provides a transparent entity on which services will be available. The service consumers, using this same entity, also access the services. The bus is a topology of "nodes" that forms this transparent and uniform "single" services framework. The bus will be able to scale to connect and host distributed applications and infrastructure services in an arbitrarily large deployment. Other integration technologies typically support hub-and-spoke or star topologies and usually rely on a single central broker. While these may be sufficient for managing a few resources inside a single LAN, they are unsuitable for a broad-scale SOA deployment across WANs and extended enterprises. The bus provides a logically continuous service infrastructure that enables other capabilities such as mediation of the service requests, transformation and routing of data, and control of the services environment.

The Enterprise Service Bus will provide the complete infrastructure from Service Containers and Communication Infrastructure to the Control and Management of the Services. Services may be hosted directly in the ESB environment or it may just provide the plumbing to access the services running in external legacy systems or application servers. Some of the key constituents of an Enterprise Service Bus are:

- XML-based backbone
- Framework to host and run services, or access services running externally
- Highly scalable communication ensuring quality of services
- Capability to connect heterogeneous systems
- Privision of mediation and control of services
- Support for content based routing and transformations
- Support for "orchestration" of services (can integrate with external process engines as well)
- Framework for events and notifications

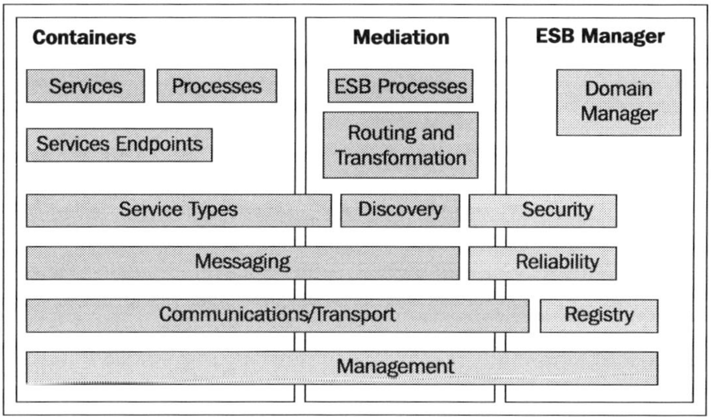

While, at the time of writing this book, there are still no common "standard" definitions of ESB, clearly ESB is evolving into a tangible infrastructure for SOA. Some critics show ESB systems to be just a mechanism to host services and discover the services, based on a registry of services and Web Services-based standards for defining service interfaces and actual access mechanisms. Now, surely, and ESB is not just a service repository, and it is also not just a framework that supports standard services runtime where there are some standards for services assembly and deployment. ESB is far more than that (see the above figure of the functional overview of ESB)—it is a middleware integration fabric for services. ESB provides an Enterprise Services platform in a Bus that connects all the services available in the enterprise to the business processes and services that need to "consume" these services—an enterprise-wide middleware for Services.

Middleware for Middleware Technologies

Extending the existing services platforms such as Web Services and filling in the missing links in the platform, the emphasis is on the infrastructure that "connects" various services and the consumers in the enterprise on a single infrastructure platform. The services themselves may typically have back-end applications that may be hosted on traditional middleware systems such as Java EE and .NET.

Are Java EE and .NET middleware platforms or just application servers? Surely, they are more application platforms with their primary function being to host and run applications. However, they also provide distributed processing functionality via being able to access the functional layer from other applications or application servers. This aspect of the platform is conventional middleware functionality, and when ESB infrastructure connects such platforms, a few technologists refer to ESB as a Middleware for Middleware systems (see the following figure of middleware for middleware technologies).

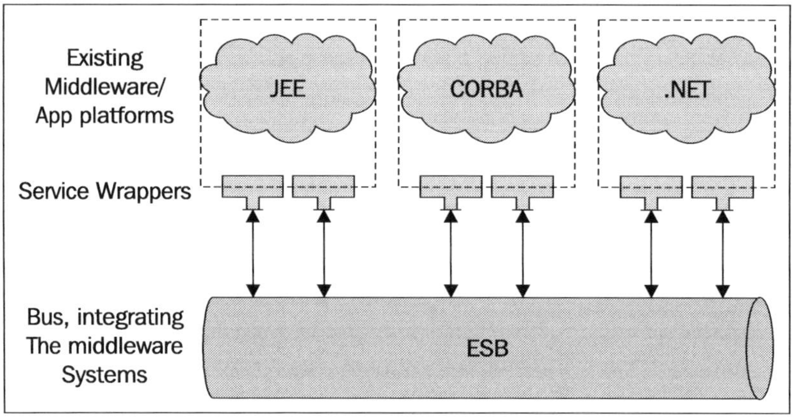

The services in ESB essentially conform to a common services model. The service implementation will hide the specific platform dependencies of the back-end applications that it may be accessing. Regardless of the platforms behind the service layer, the services themselves will be available in a common way on the ESB. The services in an ESB can be considered to be available on an ESB "address" often also called a service endpoint. Any consumer of the services needs to connect to the underlying framework in a standard way. Once connected, the consumer can access any service in the domain using the same "connection". In essence, each consumer and producer will "talk" only to the framework directly. The framework/runtime will take care of "delivering" the request to the relevant endpoint—very much like normal Messaging systems such as MS MQ, Websphere MQ, and TIBCO. Sonic ESB is one such product that supports this abstraction out of the box—built entirely on an underlying robust messaging infrastructure.

The middleware functionality of the platform is driven by the aspect that all services are available in a common manner. Any consumer of the service need only "connect" to the bus, and once connected can access any services that is available on the bus. While not necessary, ESB platforms typically do this by leveraging a message platform at the lowest level. A service invocation translates to a message being composed and "sent" to that endpoint. Unlike in simple integration solutions, a service or process that needs to access multiple services need not establish connections to each of the service endpoints—an optimal situation for extensive and distributed SOA environments.

Taking the notion of middleware systems a little further, is it likely that there will be multiple ESB platforms in an organization that need to be integrated as well? This is quite possible and will be challenge in the absence of ESB standards. The basic interoperability of ESB systems will itself be possible through simple gateways or adapters. However, ensuring that the benefits from the ESB platform over other SOA infrastructure continue in this integrated multiple ESB environment may be a challenge.

As often pointed out, there certainly is a risk of "locking" the application to one vendor's ESB leading to a likely need for integrating multiple "proprietary ESB systems", but this risk can easily be mitigated by ensuring the vendors have a commitment to the various standards that are emerging in the SOA space.

When considering applications on ESB, it may help to look for these attributes:

- The key application "assets" in an ESB environment are the service implementations/wrappers and the Business Process. Rest of the plumbing is a pure runtime configuration and setup. The latter can be vendor specific, the former should, to the extent possible, be vendor neutral.
- When defining services consider ESB vendors supporting standards.
- In the Java world, consider standards such as Java Business Integration (JBI) and WSDL2. If a Java service is written as per JBI or even just WSDL2, the application artifact (asset) may still be "portable" to other ESB/SOA runtimes with minimal effort. (In the .NET world, as it is a homogenous single-vendor technology environment, there will be no issues with respect to standards.)
- Business processes should be in standard languages (such as BPEL). At the least, the ESB vendor should support "exporting" the Business Process to BPEL. Then, even the Business Process becomes portable.

On a related note, there is a lot of talk and buzz around the standards to extend WS to support reliable messaging etc., but these may exist in localized implementations. To extend this to the extended enterprise, a common communication infrastructure like HTTP over Internet that supports Reliable Messaging and Routing will need to first come up. Even messaging systems such as JMS (the Java Messaging Service, a standard in the Java space) may not suffice for an extended enterprise, as there is no good interoperability across JMS implementations yet—just as there is no interoperability to other platforms such as .NET. Until then the solutions will be limited to those supported by a single vendor that can be used in closed environments alone. Outside this environment, gateways will need to be used (either via regular WS/HTTP or other such mechanisms).

Modeling the Enterprise Document Flows

ESB being the infrastructure sitting in the middle, between the service and its consuming integration applications, it is well placed to provide intermediary functions; functions that could be provided when the request for a service is on its "way" to the actual service running in its execution environment. Now, here, it is interesting to draw parallels between ESB and the way enterprises process business documents—on how the business processes are document centric. Documents flow through the business interactions, among various departments of an organization.

In an organization, all departments work towards serving the organization's business purpose. The business processes that span departments typically will involve a business document or data that is exchanged between departments to get processed. The business document could be, say, a manufacturing work order or a shipping request. When the document is received by a department, the information in the document is processed as per the established business processes and flows in the organization. The function of a department is here modeled by the structure of the information to be sent to the department, and an "address" to which the business document must be sent. Prior to automation, this "document" would have been a paper-based form and the address would be a mail stop or an address. The "integration" of these departments happened via the information flows. Say, a PO is given to the manufacturing department, which will manufacture per the details in the PO. In short, in enterprises business documents flow and get processed (see the following figure).

With automation coming in place, the departments each have their own business application that helps with the departmental business processes and functioning. And more recently, with the Web Services and SOA catching up, all these various departmental applications and solutions are now getting integrated organization-wide. The same document flow between departments could now be an electronic exchange of data between automated business applications, with the data sent to an "electronic address" such as the URL of service.

When integrating the departments, in homogenous technology environments, such as when all applications are either Java EE or .NET, there could be technology-specific mechanisms to access the various departmental services—for example, order processing department could explicitly "invoke" the processPO method in the manufacturing application—but this is a very tight integration where there is a binding to technology, service, method name and parameters, and the actual programming constructs to invoke the service. This, however, does not simulate the "normal" flow across departments in any organization, where data flow is the focus, rather than the "procedure invocation".

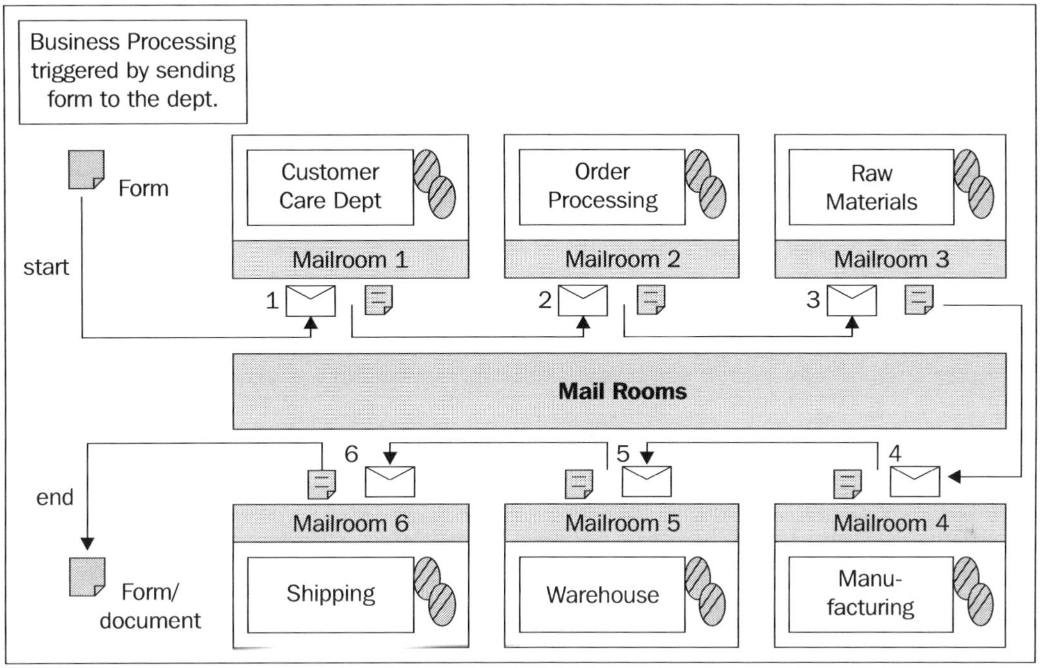

The loosely connected departments can be better integrated by keeping the internal details hidden—including what method to invoke. The intuitive integration lays emphasis on the information flows; the assumption being when a document comes in, it gets processed. Exactly what the process internals are, should be immaterial to the originating point. Surprisingly, this was the approach to integration in the days of EDI. Even if the technology was very minimal, the focus in EDI is on the data flowing rather than the actual processing.

The difference between data being "sent" to get processed and "invoking" a process with data as "input arguments" is very subtle. At the end of both modes, the "processing" of the "data" is what is expected. It is just that in one case the data coming in as a single document is the focus, and in the other case the method invocation is the focus. The crux here is that in loosely coupled environments, the "contract" between the departments is easily described if it is just the structure of the data and a location to deliver the data—and not in a tighter bound method with input parameters. This is consistent with a pre-integration organizational structure, where forms or printed documents "flow" between departments and get processed. Such loose coupling serves the significant purpose of keeping the binding between the departments to the minimum.

Extending this further, often there are cases where a single form gets processed in a "workflow" mode. Initially, it contains the input data that triggers the process. Say, it is an insurance claim form in an insurance company's claim process. This form goes from department to department, where it gets processed and annotated with additional information notes and decisions. For example, an investigative officer will validate the genuineness of the claim, and an appraising officer might verify the value of the claim, and so on. The form goes from department to department until it is paid and settled, when it gets filed. In effect, the document flows and gets processed. The specific steps in the processing, and "mail stops" along the way are dictated by established business processes in the organization.

Imagine if this were how business processes could be executed in an SOA environment! Business data is captured as a business document, and the document flows from one application to another through the service containers of the SOA infrastructure. As it flows through the SOA infrastructure, it gets updated with additional information at each step. And the sequence of processing, defined by the business processes, is also "attached" to the same document—like a processing schedule or an itinerary.

This idea of a document flowing and getting processed forms the basis for several additional ESB mediation functions such as transformations and content-based routing, that we will discuss later in this chapter.

Service: Procedure Centric or Document Centric?

Should services be procedure centric or document centric?

Services in the Web Services framework allow two modes: RPC (Remote Procedure Call) Invocation or Doc-literal, with clear, albeit subtle, differences. The difference between the two modes is about how a service on the "bus" can be accessed. There are two abstractions:

- Access the service as a traditional RPC—wherein the service is invoked and the input parameters sent, and as per the service interface there is a known response that is expected. The caller waits for the response and then proceeds.
- The service is triggered by sending ONE document, of probably a well-defined structure (say a schema or a WSDL type), which is processed and a response document is returned. This is also called doc-literal.

Now, do you think these don't look too different? Consider the example illustrated in the following figure, a service that expects a customer name and a Purchase Order as inputs. Regardless of how the inputs are sent (as a single document or as RPC parameters), the input required to execute the service will remain the same. For the service to be executed it must be triggered and the inputs provided—in the example here, the service must have both the customer name and the PO. In the RPC model, the application (client) invokes the service by passing in these two arguments. In the Document approach (Doc-literal—a SOAP term), the client has to put the customer name and the PO in a single XML document and send it across to an "address"—typically a Web Services URL. At that address, there is a service that expects the single document as input.

It may seem like it is just a subtle play on who does what, between the client application, the middleware (SOA infrastructure), and the actual service implementation! Skimming the surface, the difference is essentially in the application design abstractions in massively distributed environments—which are the typical target scenarios for SOA and ESB (incidentally, ESB is a technology for SOA infrastructure). In such environments, assuming there is a service that is defined, what will be the usage scenarios? In the RPC-type definition, the client application will need to know the various arguments, its types and the order of the arguments. In the Doc-Literal-type definition, there is a single document that is expected. Any required information needs to be modeled in this XML document.

Clearly in the latter case, the information binding needed to understand and use the service (on the client application side) is simpler. The name and IP/port are always needed, but to construct the input, in the latter case it is just a document with a well defined structure. In most SOA scenarios, these will be business documents, probably already well defined and understood within the entire organization. In the former case, regardless of the information model of the Business data/documents in the organization, one will need to know exactly how many and of what type are the input parameters, and extract the data from existing Business data/documents and then invoke the service.

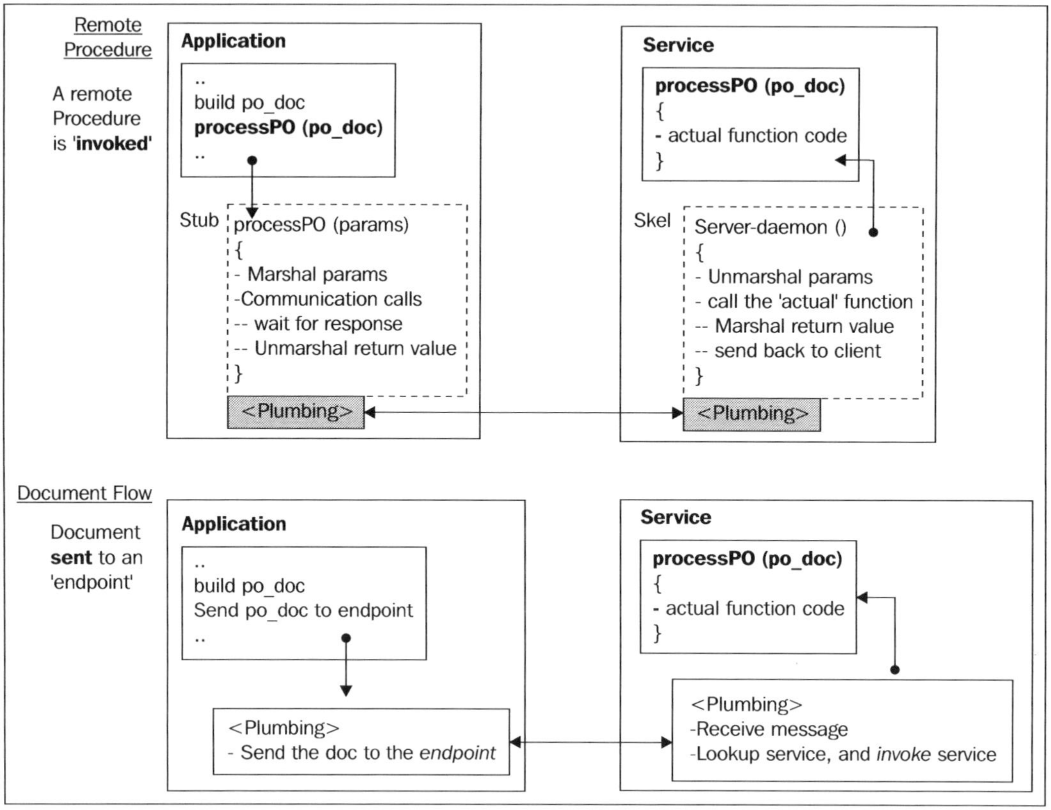

The RPC model is well suited in application environments where data exists in a relatively arbitrary and less structured form. Here, each application is defining its own form and structure. The doc-literal approach is more contemporary and aligned with the emerging Services-Oriented IT infrastructure. In organizations that are consciously and actively working towards an integrated "service-oriented" IT infrastructure, there is a strong push towards well defined business data structures and schema definitions. These will be followed and used throughout the organization for the inter-departmental IT systems' interactions. Business Documents are composed and "sent" to the required department's electronic address. In such scenarios, the application architecture to enable defining and using services becomes quite simplified:

- Locate the service endpoint (binding, IP, port)
- Compose the business document needed by the service, and send the document to the endpoint

The service definition also follows the same model. Based on the service functionality needed, identify a well-defined business document as its input, and in the service implementation, process that document by extracting any needed arguments from it. So, a well known set of business documents and schemas now becomes the key component of service descriptions. With this in place, service definitions and consumption become very simple and we will need very little information to either describe a service or to use a service.

XML Fits in Nicely in the Bus

XML is omnipresent today. So, it is little surprise that XML is at the core of most ESB functions as well, from the wire representation of requests to modeling all information flows as XML documents.

In ESB, Services are essentially business-functions that could either run self-contained (say, their logic is in Java) or are "wrappers" for back-end legacy processing—like say an SAP or Baan or on a mainframe or even Java EE/.NET. The primary objective of ESB here is to enable simple "integration" of various IT systems in the enterprise: enable systems to "talk" to each other and also enable simple business processes that "orchestrate" these services to provide some aggregate business logic. (For more complex business processes, full-fledged Orchestration servers may be used or even made available as part of the ESB platform. If ESB vendors themselves provide all the power of such Orchestration servers or support standards such as BPEL remains to be seen.)

At the center is the communication of data between systems and services. Now, while the communication could be based on a good Messaging backbone, the actual messages that flow may be service requests, most likely represented in SOAP, which is an XML document format. A further amplification of XML usage is that the service parameters are also in general one or more XML documents. The request parameters and responses also are XML documents.

In effect, information flows between systems as XML. Service requests and responses also are using XML as the exchange mechanism. And soon there are a large number of IT applications/solutions in the organization that talk to each other and integration is widely used—such that even simple operations performed on any system may involve accesses through ESB to multiple other systems, kind of like how widely prevalent DB usage is today.

Once XML becomes the key form for information flows through the systems, then additional needs immediately crop up, say like XML transformations. For example, a Purchase Order in the ERP system may have different fields, when compared to how the OrderProcessingApp understands a PO. And when a PO is sent from one to the other, somewhere it must be transformed from one structure to the other, so XSLT or XQuery comes into play. And once XML documents are flowing, one can quickly think of cases where the "processing" of the document is "attached" to the document, rather than passing the document as an input to a "process". In the mode where processing is "attached" to the document, what actually happens is that the ESB infrastructure handles the document and its processing through the various ESB containers/nodes, passing the document from one processing "step" to the other. In such a processing environment, smart "routing" comes into play. This is basically content-based routing of the document—wherein, based on the document contents, the document is sent to a particular processing "step" (service endpoint or container).

ESB Services: Built on Documents/Messages

Doc-literal opens up a new abstraction for services. Tracking the document-flow based enterprise that we discussed above, unlike the conventional middleware systems, where the remote processing is generally triggered via procedure-like semantics, the document flow abstraction is central to ESB systems. The services now take on a different form—abstracted behind endpoints that serve as an "address", to which a well-defined document needs to be "sent" for the service to be invoked.

Drawing upon the Web Services' doc-literal approach, ESB services are typically built around documents or messages being sent to a service "address".

Abstracting the Service Location with Endpoints

In describing the service, apart from the service interface, the bindings and the "address" are also key components. This address is normally the specific IP and port of the Web Service. In ESB, this is an abstract "address". The service can have the semantics of Web Services, with a well-defined interface that may include a set of related operations. Each operation has an expected input document and a return document. The fault responses are also defined for each operation. The bindings will provide the necessary information to "construct" a SOAP document, at run time, when the service needs to be accessed. The endpoint may be represented as a URL in a WSDL that may define the service.

At the time of writing this book, there is no standard definition of ESB endpoints. The basic service endpoint can be defined using W3C definitions. This, however, doesn't distinguish the various types possible in ESB. Based on common ESB use cases, endpoints could be of these types:

- Service
- Process
- Message Router
- Transformation
- Simple Message Destination (with no other value-added ESB handling)

In ESB systems, if a service execution essentially involves a document or message that is sent to an endpoint, then there is a lot value-added smart processing possible as a result of such usage:

- The documents could be "smartly" routed. Based on routing rules defined, the document could be sent to different endpoints based on its content.
- Documents could be transformed based on business requirements. Transformations can be for the structure, or even for content.
- The document could be processed in the ESB fabric as a process (ESB Itineraries)—the document gets sent to one endpoint, which actually represents a Business Process (and not just a service). This process will involve multiple steps (service invocations)—the business document along with process state data "flows" through the fabric from one service container to the other (per the process definition—itinerary), at each step getting "processed" by a service—as opposed to the less-efficient alternative model for the same, wherein one process engine "invokes" services in the bus in a hub and spoke model—each service request originating from the process engine.

Documents—Route, Transform, and Process

As documents or messages "flow" in an enterprise and "get processed" along the way—by the IT solutions of various departments—additional possibilities crop up.

Given that each IT solution would evolve by itself, regardless of other departments in the organization, it is quite likely that the information models used in the various solutions are different from each other. For example, the Purchase Order as represented in the Order-Processing system may be different from the PO represented in the ERP system. There may be additional or a reduced set of fields in the PO. So when exchanging data between these systems, the information from one system will need to be "transformed" to the form understood by the other system.

Such transformation could be done by the integration application—it extracts info from the first system, converts it to the required format, and then sends it to the second system. This is fine in P2P-based solutions, where the service-consuming application is tightly coupled to the service-providing application. However, in more loosely coupled integration environments such as the Service bus (ESB), such tight couplings are not desirable.

This is where more transparent transformation comes in. Each application is aware of its data formats alone. And in the integration environment, say in a Business Process, the required transformations are performed independently. In a more evolved SOA-based enterprise, it is quite likely that there is a corporate type repository, where all information models are described. In such cases, the PO in the Order system and the ERP system will be described in the type library and it can extend a bit further, to also include canned transformations that will transform the PO from the Order-system format to the ERP format.

A good Service Bus can leverage such type libraries and further add value to the platform by helping with the transformations, both during design time (by helping with the XSLT/XQuery needed for the transformation) as well as during run time (by picking up the latest transformation definitions from the central type library).

Once transformed, the document needs to be delivered to the service. As the document is now being managed by the ESB fabric, it is possible that the document can now be "routed" to a specific processing endpoint based on the contents in the document. The routing could be based on application-defined rules. (See the following figure).

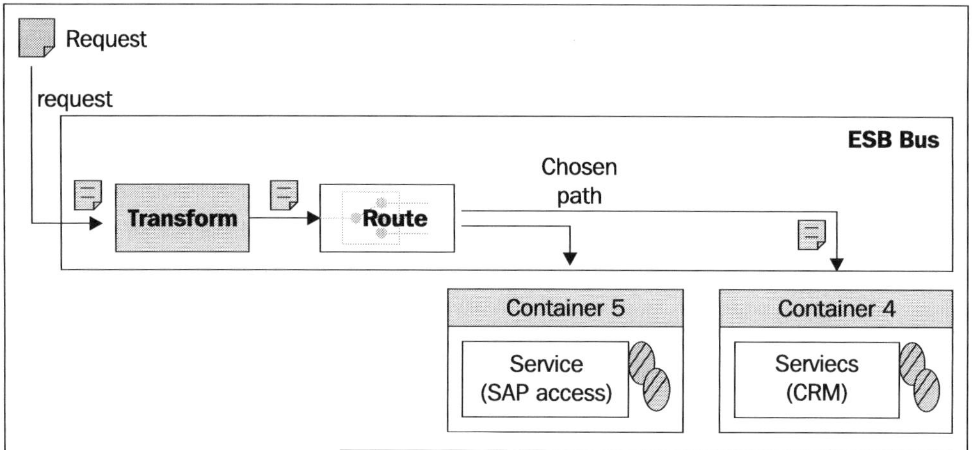

An incoming request, arrives into the ESB fabric. Endpoint is a logical address. The document can get "transformed" and "routed" to an endpoint before getting "processed"

One could also conceivably look at documents flowing from step to step, and getting processed much like a document processing schedule—a sequence of "mail-stops". The document "workflow" will not be too different from the business processes—with inputs, process flow control, steps, decision points, and an exit. This gets into the bus, forming the input here and the sequence of steps are attached as an "itinerary" to the document. It "flows" through the ESB system getting processed as needed.

ESB Infrastructure Components

ESB is an architecture approach that addresses most of the infrastructure complexities of SOA—from representing the services and executing the services to mediating between the services, the actual communication between the service client or process engine, and the service implementation. Broadly, the Services Runtime Environment and the Bus form two key components of an ESB infrastructure. And then, there are a set of additional services and capabilities, as shown in the following figure of ESB infrastructure.

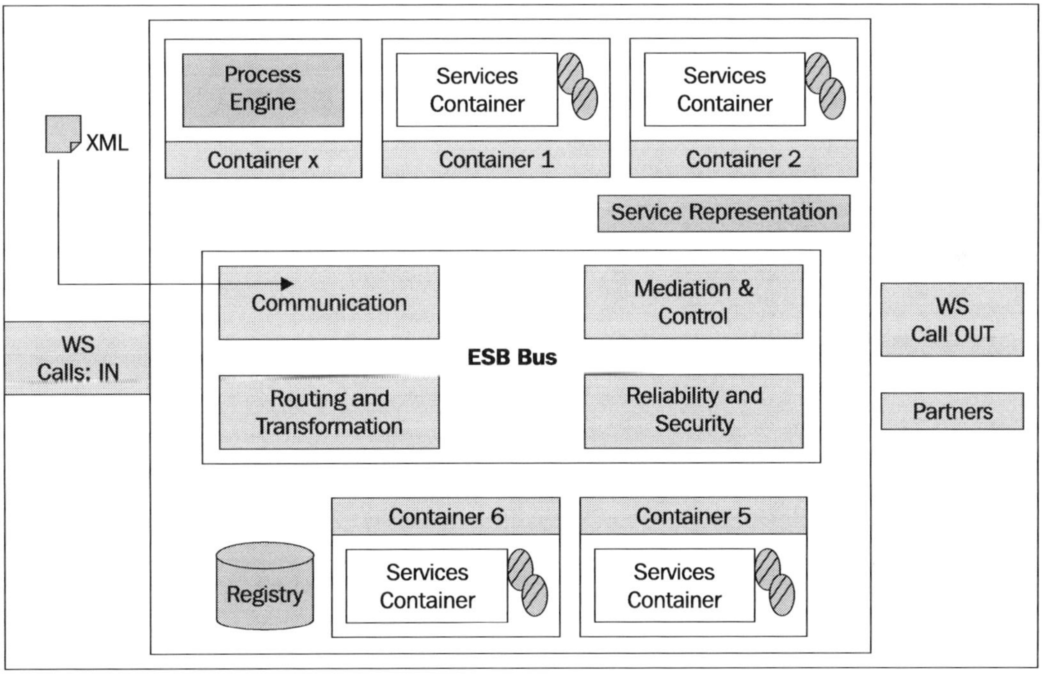

Common ESB terminology includes terms such as Services, Service Types, Service Containers, Service Descriptions, Transformations, Content-based Routing, Bindings and Binding Components, Service Interfaces, Service Registries and extensive XML handling.

Services are the lowest-level individual components in an ESB infrastructure. Every business function that needs to be executed on the bus will be a service. Services have a handling or processing logic within, to provide their business functionality. Services could be custom written, or could be service instances of a well-defined type—often referred to as a Service Type, and have the handling logic written once and multiple services configured that all use this same logic.

Service types define a specific "behavior". Each service type will have a definitive interface and processing semantics. The Service type is like an abstract definition, and the Service instances are the concrete instances of that "behavior" that are accessible by the consumers of the service.

Service containers in an ESB environment, shown in the following figure, provide the execution environment for the services, with a set of containers forming the ESB domain. Service containers may be provided by the ESB platform, or could be application servers that are "plugged" into the ESB platform. Services can be configured to run on one or more containers for scalability and load distribution. Services are generally of a given service type. Containers provide the necessary middleware plumbing that includes the communication layers, protocol handling, ESB services such as transformation and routing, security, and management functions. The service containers use Binding Components or Protocol Handlers to abstract the protocol handling from the services. This also enables service containers to transparently support multiple protocols—say invoking services via HTTP or a more native Messaging protocol.

Services, in an application-server context, may be application functional-tier components such as Java EE's Enterprise Java beans or .NET services. When such functionality is available in an ESB environment, it will need to be "wired" into the ESB platform. This is typically done by using "glue" services, which are essentially wrapper-services with the logic needed to access the functionality in the application server. The ESB services are generally implemented in a common way per some platform integration semantics defined by the ESB platform. In the Java world, this would be implementing a well-defined Java interface provided by the ESB platform. Services in ESB are independent of the specific functionality they provide or any back-end systems they may access—regardless of whether it is more contemporary application servers or any legacy systems. (Now, here they are quite conceivable that the application servers may themselves provide this glue without needing any "wrappers". This may happen as more standards evolve in the service definition and runtime space.)

Services need definition for consuming applications to understand the interface and the operation details. These definitions use standard interface languages such as WSDL. The primary description is the service's behavioral contract—on the operations it provides, the inputs and outputs from each operation, the message type definitions for the messages/parameters used in inputs and outputs. The specifics are—what URL to use, the protocol to use for communication, the specific bindings—on how each input and output is represented on the wire. These very exact definitions are very important to ensure that both ends of a service invocation speak the same language. The request is represented by the invoking end in exactly the same manner as how it is understood by the service-providing end.

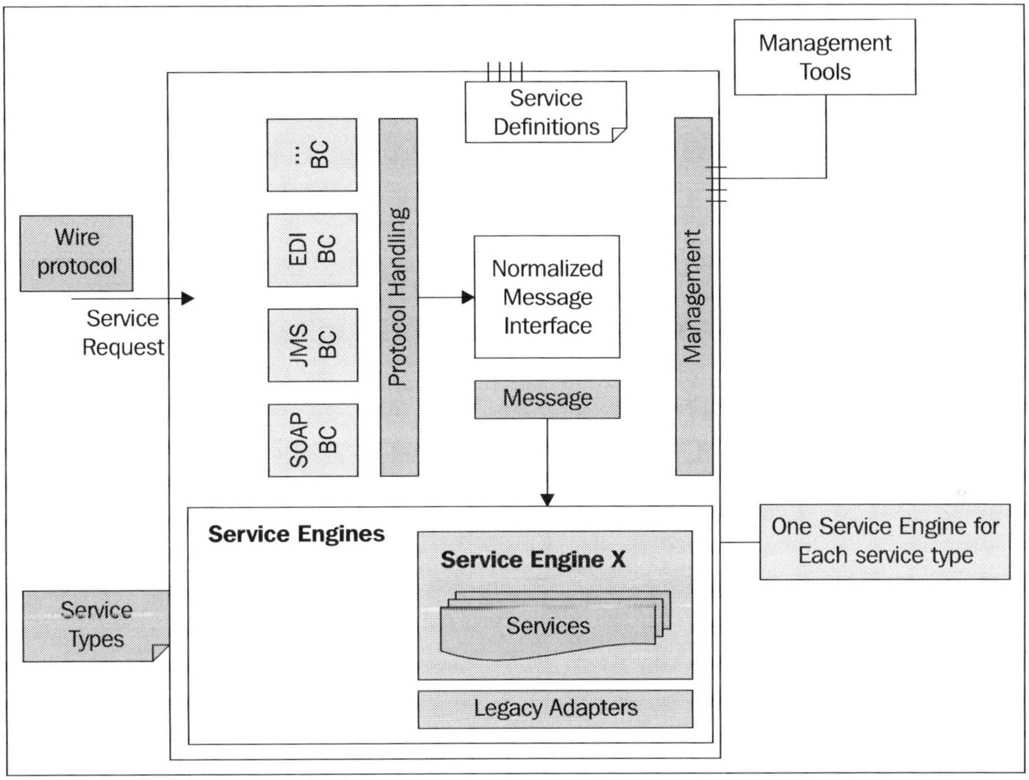

The **Registry** of services provides the capability to discover services available on the bus. ESB implementations may use standards such as UDDI or go proprietary. Registries become an even more relevant function in widely distributed integration environments such as those where ESB plays an important part. In an ESB environment, the registry of services is an important enabler for mediation of services. This will be useful for application developers to query on the services that are currently available on the platform. This is also equally useful for the functioning of ESB infrastructure—for the validations and execution at run time. The mediation and control services will extensively rely on the registry for keeping track of the various containers, service types, and service instances. Further, each service instance may be available on multiple containers—with the same access "endpoint" but multiple instances of the same endpoint available to provide for higher availability and concurrent load.

The Security, Transformation, and **Routing** services are provided by the ESB infrastructure. ESB infrastructure is inherently built to handle XML extensively. Apart from handling XML for the basic communication protocols, such as SOAP, XML documents are dealt with in the process of handling services and service requests.

XML handling will include transformations (XSLT) and XML Querying (XQuery). ESB environments could have an inbuilt XML Database as well—though such functionality can be equally effective with external XML databases that are available on the bus. Either way, having it on the bus enables more transparent access to the XML database when processing XQuery.

The Communication layer of ESB enables the notional Distributed "Service Bus". The transparent enterprise backbone should aim at leveling the distributed nature of the organization, by hiding the specific locations and connectivity of each department or organizational component/application. All the systems and locations should be available on a homogenous communication backbone.

Mediation and Control is a primary function of the bus infrastructure that helps abstract the exact location of the services and the mechanics of the services access. This involves late binding of the service physical address and protocols, also strong support in managing these services and their deployment and configuration. The services framework on the bus should abstract the specific location of the service instances. The whole service producer-consumer relationship should be based on a well-defined contract (possibly in a WSDL document) and an abstract location such as a named "endpoint" or a simple URL. At the endpoint or the URL, there should be the ESB plumbing that dynamically locates the service on the fly and directs the request to the service.

This indirection immediately enables additional infrastructure capabilities—with respect to mediation and control. As the location of the service is transparent, and only a logical "address" is available outside, the service location can be very dynamic. As load increases, the service can be started on additional service-containers (servers)—ensuring high scalability. When any container goes down for any reason, the next request will be routed to one of the other instances running—ensuring high uptime.

Mediation essentially is the system plumbing that sits between the consumer (that originated the service request) and the actual service—along the way, providing value-added system services such as validation, security, transformation of the data inputs, smart business-rules-based request routing, and handling any mismatch in the invocation abstractions or data models (as there would be in the case of a simple Web Service request made to a non WS services framework in the back end).

The ESB Communication Infrastructure connects all the service containers on the ESB platform to each other and to other infrastructure components of the platforms.

Communication and Interoperability are sometimes confused with each other. Interoperability across systems and services is a functionality provided by ESB platforms. A good ESB platform should allow Legacy Applications, Java EE, .NET, Databases, etc., to be part of an orchestrated business processes. Now, this has nothing directly to do with what the actual ESB runtime is, and what specific transport it uses as its backbone. The interoperability requirement ends just with stating that it should be able to connect the last mile to the service endpoint in its native transport—which any good ESB platform provides. From the service wrappers, through connectors, it would be able to connect to any back end and use any last-mile transport. Once a service requests lands in the ESB runtime fabric, how it delivers the request to the service container and service wrapper that access the last mile is purely transparent to the actual transport used by the legacy back end.

With the primary purpose of ESB being the ability to provide and consume services, the business processes are the most important "consumer" of services. These will need to run in Process Engines. In ESB, they would be like any other Orchestration Server, with an additional attribute that these may be in a services container in the ESB domain. Basically, processes in the process engine are also available as a "service". The process could be running on any orchestration engine, including BPEL engines. The requirement is that this engine be available on the bus, just as any other service is.

Built on Web Services Standards

ESB draws heavily upon the standards in the Web Services space, even though some of the extensions such as intelligent routing or mediation still do not have any standards foundation yet.

In ESB infrastructure, the key pieces in the infrastructure are Service Containers, Service Representation, Communication Frameworks, Wire Protocols, Transformation, Routing, Mediation and Control, Process Engines, and ESB Itineraries. Here there are parts that belong in the applications realm and some in the infrastructure realm. Service representations, business processes, and definition of transformations are part of the SOA application—its "source code". ESB implementations support standards in such areas that form SOA Applications.

In ESB, service representations and business process definitions rely on standards. Services are represented using WSDL, and processes by and large are based on BPEL. Additionally, WS-RM and WS-S are used for security and reliability—specifically for the SOA applications to specify the security and RM requirements.

Where there is no standardization yet, is the internal guts of the ESB—communication protocols and some of the emerging functionality such as mediation and control. The ESB Itineraries is essentially an internal execution mechanics like say another process engine. The process that runs as an itinerary may be coded in BPEL as well.

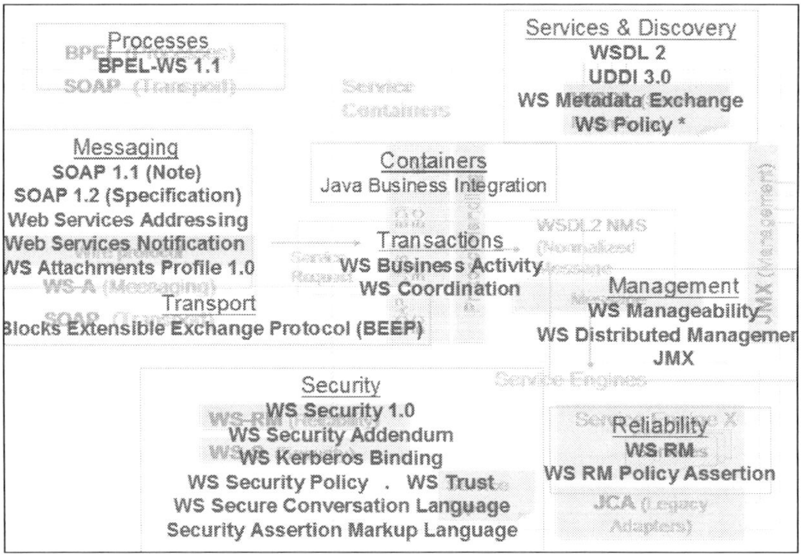

Referring again to the figure on ESB Infrastructure, of the areas listed there the ESB Bus functionality is the area with no standards in place. The service representations, bindings and protocols have well defined standards. While ESB systems do not have to support all the standards, many vendors do support all standards that come into play in application interaction layers—like service description—or in interoperability and communication layers—like reliability and security.

Description and Discovery: Like any reusable programming construct, the services also need a well-defined mechanism to describe the service details and also provide for "discovering" the services from a common services registry. Potential users may find information sufficient to enable their access and execution. The focus of these specifications and standards is the definition of a set of services supporting the description and discovery of businesses, organizations, and other web services providers; the web services they make available; and the technical interfaces that may be used to access those services.

Reliability: Given the widely distributed nature of services and consumers in an SOA environment, the reliability of the interactions between the service consumers and the providers becomes critical. It is not possible to solve business issues if the participants are unable to be sure of the completion of message exchanges. Reliable messaging, which allows messages to be delivered reliably between distributed applications in the presence of software component, system, or network failures, is therefore critical to Web Services.

Transactions: Transactions are a fundamental concept in building reliable distributed applications. A web-service environment requires coordination behavior provided by a traditional transaction mechanism to control the operations and outcome of an application. The conventional transaction models, the ACID semantics and two-phase commit protocols, assume a much tighter coupling with the operating environment for the resources participating in the transaction. In ESB, given the loosely coupled and very widely distributed nature of the transactions, approaches beyond conventional transaction and two-phase commit protocols are needed. Some of the emerging standards such as WS-Coordination, WS-AtomicTransaction, and WS-BusinessActivity are steps in this direction.

Security: An elaborate set of specifications are either already defined or in the process of being defined that addresses various aspects of security in an SOA environment. Several WS-* standards are in the works. Using these security specifications, applications can engage in secure communication designed to work with the general Web Services framework. Standards include WS-Security, WS-SecurityPolicy, WS-Trust and Security Assertion Markup Language.

Business Processes: A business process specifies the sequence of steps involved in a business operation. This includes the execution order of operations from a collection of web services, the data flowing/shared across these service invocations and the handling of exceptions. In extended business processes, the definition also includes which partners are involved and how they are involved in the business process, and other issues involving how multiple services and organizations participate. BPEL specifies business processes and how they relate to Web Services.

Transports: BEEP, the Blocks Extensible Exchange Protocol (formerly referred to as BXXP), is a framework for building application protocols. It has been standardized by IETF and does for Internet protocols what XML has done for data. MTOM is another specification that is gaining support.

Messaging: The messaging standards and specifications are intended to give a framework for exchanging information in a decentralized, distributed environment. SOAP defines the primary protocol for representing the requests and responses. WS-Addressing defines a standard mechanism to identify WS addresses, used in asynchronous operations and for notifications and acknowledgements. In the

Java world, Java Messaging Service provides a good programming abstraction for working with messages, though the standard falls short of specifying interoperability across different vendor's JMS implementations.

Management: Web services manageability is defined as a set of capabilities for discovering the existence, availability, health, performance, usage, as well as the control and configuration of a web service within the Web Services architecture. As web services become pervasive and critical to business operations, the task of managing and implementing them is imperative to the success of business operations.

Events: What about events? Are events also important? Particularly in the sense of EDA-Event Driven Architecture as proposed by Gartner? ESB and various Web Service standards do support building distributed applications that rely on events and notifications. The extent of usage remains to be seen.

Service Containers—The Primary Tier of the Bus

The ESB platform provides the services middleware and runtime. The middleware is the primary function of ESB that enables accessing services on the bus—from a variety of back-end systems and platforms. The service runtime provides a generic mechanism to run the services. In the minimum, this would be light-weight "wrappers" that enable accessing back-end systems. In more evolved usage scenarios, this could enable full-fledged application functionality that is run in this environment. This latter use case is in some ways replacing what Application Servers do today.

The functionality to enable running services is realized by the infrastructure component—Service Containers. These are essentially a run-time environment to run the individual services. In any ESB domain, there will be multiple Service Containers. Each container will run multiple services. Services may be of multiple service types. Depending on the capabilities of the ESB platform, services may also be clustered—the same service running on multiple containers for high availability and higher load handling.

Services have an "external" view in terms of their contract and addressability—on how they can be accessed. Then, the actual service implementation and its runtime artifacts—the classes/files/binaries, libraries, configuration etc. The service's internal implementation is often abstracted in a reusable service type. Service types include clear definition of the following:

- The interface for the service
- The actual implementation "code"
- Packaging, distribution and deployment onto the ESB platform
- Service instances can be configured of the service types.

Services that are accessed are service instances of a given service type. While service instances are the actually accessible and executable services, the service types enable the capability for reuse. We have one definition for a service type of all artifacts and its deployment configuration, out of which multiple logically different services can be configured, by creating instances, each with some different environment or initialization parameters, thus providing a different business services, out of the same development artifacts (in the service type).

The key steps inside a Service Container, in processing a service request will be:

- Protocol layer (understand the "bindings"): The first step in a service execution cycle is to understand the wire protocol and "un-marshal" the request. For example if the wire protocol used is SOAP, then the SOAP protocol must be understood in order to extract the vital request details including the service being accessed and the input parameters. These protocol adapters are also referred to as Binding Components.
- Extract Request details: The request inputs or messages are a key part of any service request. Most middleware technologies represent this in proprietary manners. There are also emerging standards such as WSDL2's Normalized Messages that have a standardized representation for any service request's inputs.
- Service instance: A service instance is a named instance that provides a specific Business Service. These are the end services in any SOA environment. These would form a "step" in any Business Process that uses the services. Each service is explicitly addressable. Each service is described by its interface and binding details. The interface defines the "contract" exposed by the service. Binding gives the specific invocation details such as protocols and physical wire representations of the input parameters and such.
- Service types: A service type can be broadly described as a class of services, with a common behavior and probably a common execution mechanism. In the spirit of reuse, these are made available as a service type.
- Service Execution Engines: Each service type would have a service engine that embodies all the execution logic required to run any instance of this service type. Any service will be executed in a service engine that can execute service instances of that type.

Inside the Container

Service containers, sitting on the peripheries of the ESB platform, form the leaf nodes of the Service Bus. They host the services provided by the applications. This is one clear part of an ESB platform where the SOA application comes in contact with the infrastructure. The services are defined by the SOA developers and deployed and configured onto the ESB domain and the individual containers. Considering that there is the application code involved, it is highly desirable that this be based on standards. This ensures that the application is not locked into a single vendor. Some of the key constituents of a Service Container are highlighted in the following figure.

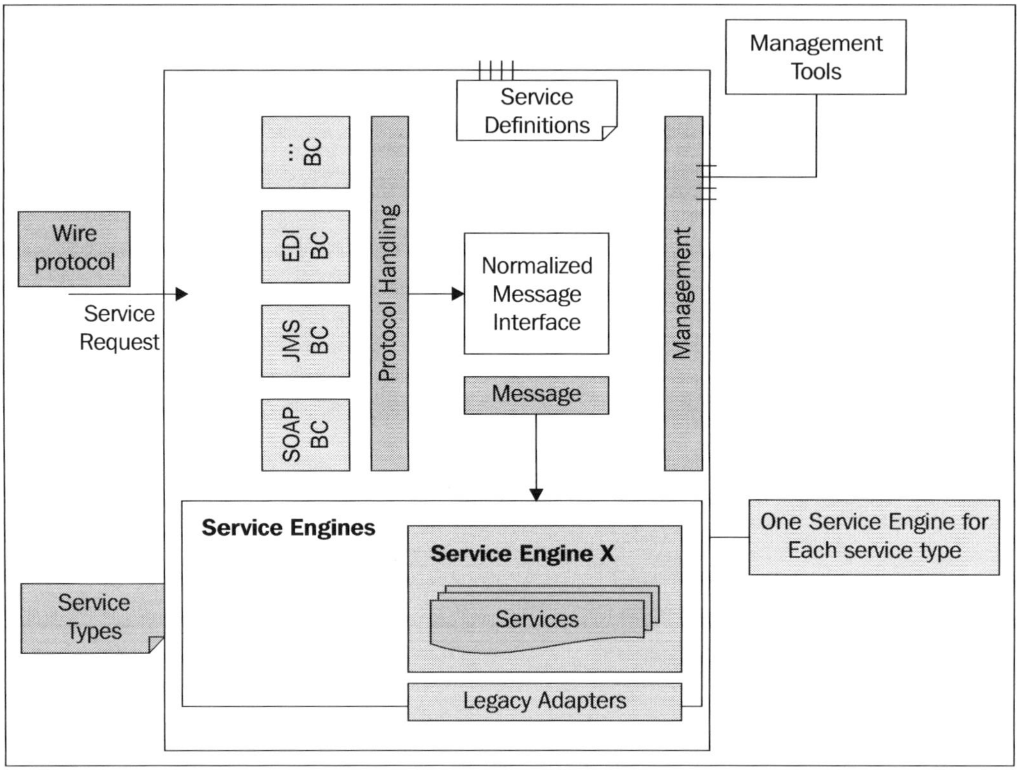

Service Containers will include mechanisms to define service types, configure service instances, describe the service interface and access details, manage the services and the container, and handle various wire protocols and connectivity to legacy systems.

In the case of Services, the service implementation is possibly in Java, C#, or any other language that is supported by the platform. The services platform could be an Application Server as well—so long as the ESB platform can access the service running in the application server. Given the portability of the language, Java is probably a better cross-platform option today, while C# would be a good choice on Windows-centric environments.

Services could either be written to be fully self contained, or could be written in a more generic manner to allow configuring multiple services with a similar behavior. This generic behavior is referred to as a Service Type. To configure any service, the service type that has all the required execution handling for a given service is to be written and deployed. The service type essentially defines a "class" of services. This definition includes the necessary processing code. Once the service type is defined and available on the platform, the individual service instances need to be defined. Depending on the service type, the service instance configuration may be different. Say for an SAP-ABAP access service, the specific SAP access handling is probably built into the service type. Configuring the individual service instances may involve essentially giving say an SAP ABAP function name. Each SAP function can now be defined as an explicitly named service, even though the actual handling logic is defined once for the whole class in the service type.

In implementing the handling for a service, one key aspect that comes into play is the back-end connectivity—given that ESB essentially solves the enterprise integration problem today. The specifics of what back end is connected to and how, is completely internal to the service implementation. The ESB platform may be expected to provide sufficient enabling pieces to help with this connectivity. Here again, there are integration standards at play such as JCA.

With the service definition in place, the immediate next requirement is the service description—needed to be able to communicate to consumers of the services. In a loosely coupled environment such as an enterprise-wide ESB platform, the definition has to be common across all services regardless of service type and the specific containers on which they run. WSDL describes the services. WSDL2, the current version of the standard, has a better definition of the wire formats, normalized messages, interfaces, and bindings. The NMS part of WSDL2 defines the input documents.

WSDL provides a clear structure for defining the operations and interfaces of a service. WSDL2 also defines the notion of a Normalized Message Service. The service implementation will expect just a Normalized Message as an input. This further simplifies the service or service type implementation. The service code will work off the simple document that comes in as the input. Likewise, the service implementation code need not have any handling for the protocol as well. The Service Container performs the protocol handling such as processing and un-marshaling the SOAP request.

WSDL2 also includes the detailed definition of the protocol bindings. The protocols are the actual wire protocols of the service requests. The primary input to any service invocation will be a document. The structure of the document will be well described by its schema.

Service containers will need a Service Engine to execute the services. This will be aware of the Service Type and any other common handling that the Services may expect. The Service Engine will be the component in the Services Container that will provide the interfaces with the various other components in the Service Container such as the protocol handler, adapters, management framework, and other system resources made available to the services by the container.

Being complex infrastructure components, Service containers need good management solutions. This will include configuring the containers, deploying Service Types, configuring services, monitoring and managing the services, and managing the start and stop of containers and services.

Why Standards?

Talking about the standards, one will realize that all good ESB solutions have to provide support for the various WS-* standards rapidly emerging—not much value in recreating anything new here. More importantly, from an SOA customer's standpoint, the security and flexibility (to choose different vendors) that standards provide is a very important factor. This is the interface/contact layer of the whole solution—be it WSDL for describing services, WS-R for specifying reliability requirements, WS-S for security, or soon JBI for service containers in the Java world! By 'interface/contact' layer, I mean any part of the solution that an application's artifact/code comes in direct touch with.

Under this layer, what the infrastructure does is totally transparent to the application's code. But as an infrastructure decision, this is one of the most important factors! The specific approach for the infrastructure determines a lot of the performance, reliability, and scalability abilities. And taking it a step further, this is what an ESB vendor must provide. Else, it is just a bunch of WS-* API handling layers. In short, both the standards-based application interface layers, and the high-performing and reliable infrastructure plumbing underneath are important in a platform choice. The former ensures that the application is not locked into a single vendor's platform, and the latter ensures that the platform chosen scales and delivers the organizational computing need.

It is often argued whether ESB needs a backbone infrastructure or if it could leverage existing infrastructure. ESB is about a Services backbone. Now if there is an ESB solution that does not include a backbone, then what exactly does it consist of? It is more of a simple integration solution that enables services. The communication backbone enables other things beyond just services' access—like mediation, control, and routing services. In the absence of this layer, one will need a proxy service to perform these functions—in a rather inefficient manner.

External View of Services: Documents Sent to Abstract "Endpoints"

In ESB, a service is identified by a document of a specific structure (schema) that is to be sent to an address or an "endpoint". SOA defines the notion of a service, from a normal procedure call with parameters or arguments, to a document "sent" to a specific place for "processing". The document is defined by its schema, and the address by an "endpoint".

An endpoint is a location. That location may be a simple URL that directly represents the host and port at which the service is available or may be an infrastructure component that will redirect the request to the right location after performing the systems plumbing.

This is not too different from the mail flow of some years or decades back—where forms were filled up and sent to various "departments" for processing. There is a clearly defined business process, even if not well documented, on the processing steps for any form. The form gets sent to the next "mail-stop". At that mail-stop there is someone or a department that processes the form, updates the form or appends the form with additional information or status or reference, and sends it across to the next department. At that department the same form is processed, with the department being fully "informed" of the original inputs and any additional information or statuses that were added to the form as it got processed until that point. The continues until the end of the Business Process, where the form may get eventually "closed". A customer care call is an example of this, shown in the following figure.

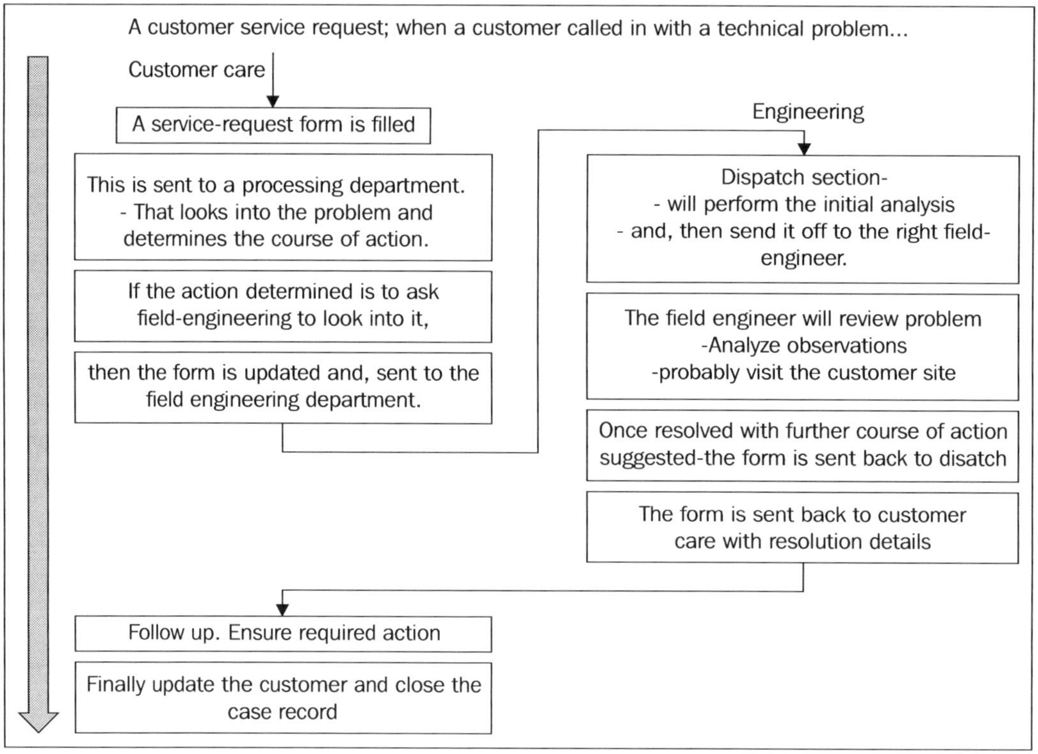

This is a potential real-life example of a workflow. While there are many ways for the information to flow, and there could be many ways each department may store its info, the requirement for the customer-service work request above is that all the relevant info up to that point for the work request be available at all points.

In the absence of centralized IT solutions, each department probably maintains the information in its own ledgers and probably maintains copies of each work request processed, but the main work request that contains all additional processing info, status, and observations flows to the next processing step.

In SOA-based environments, this is probably not too different. The services being integrated are generally departmental services—a service provided by a departmental self-contained application. As these are departmental applications, other departments may not have direct access to the data maintained in these systems. To perform cross-departmental functions such as above, a simple approach could be to expose services that provide access to data as needed. That would mean that a lot of the data-access logic would now need to reside in the Business Processes. An alternative, a better one, is to exactly "mimic" the manual processes that might have existed prior to IT—where the "form" along with all information updates "flows".

At each step in the process, it is essentially a "document" that is sent to a "location". Each functional processing has a well-defined location or endpoint and a well-defined document structure it might expect. Just send the document to that location, and it gets processed. Along with this, the document itself could contain the processing sequence or the itinerary for that document's processing—which department/location does what when.

An endpoint is an abstract named entity that represents the location at which a service is available. The endpoint is represented by a name defined using a simple string. The internal meaning of this name, and how it maps to a physical address, is internal to the ESB implementation. From an SOA application viewpoint, a service is available at that logical address, represented by an endpoint.

An endpoint translates to a physical address, by the configuration process supported by the ESB implementation. In Messaging system-based implementations, an endpoint may translate to a Message destination—Queue or Topic. The configuration of a service will then involve setting up the service type that will include getting the required files, classes/JARs/libraries, and other execution-time requirements to be made available in the service runtime environment. Create a service instance of this type. Create a Message destination, say a Queue. Create a new endpoint that is attached to this destination. Finally, associate this endpoint with the created service instance. When using this service, a message is sent to the endpoint, which internally will translate into a Message sent to the Message system destination—the new Queue that was created and attached to the endpoint.

JBI—A Standard Container to "host" Services

While there are several standards to describe services and represent service requests and responses on the "wire", the standards for actually hosting services is still emerging. JBI (Java Business Integration) is evolving as a standard framework for hosting and running services in the Java space. Having a standard framework to run services is important to avert vendor lock-ins. Standards-based services containers would mean that the services are built and deployed in a standard way, using mechanisms described by the standards to deploy the service engines and service types.

Service implementation and service invocation are both directly dependent on the chosen platform for hosting the services. Given that SOA is just a concept, just about any server-side infrastructure could be used to host the services. These include custom Java/C++ programs, Java EE, .NET, and CORBA. The mechanics of invoking a service are shown in the following figure.

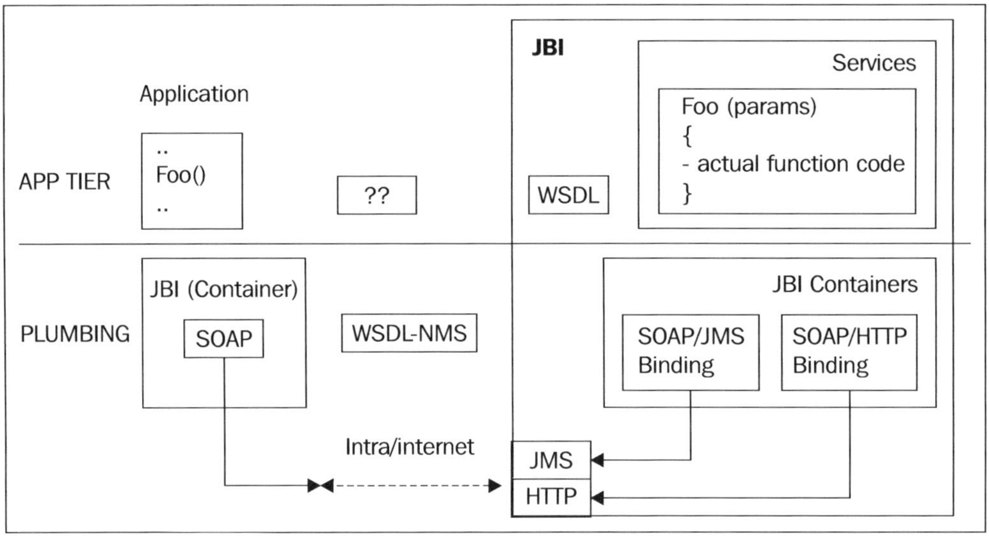

JBI (Java Business Integration) is an attempt from the Java Community, through the JCP, to solve the services container problem. A generic framework is being evolved to provide a runtime environment for the services. A Service can be written in a generic way, and be hosted on a JBI-compliant container from any vendor. This is not possible in a simple WS environment. WS standards only describe how a request is represented over the wire they don't provide for any mechanism to "host" services. JBI tries to fill this gap. See the following figure.

JBI architecture is modeled very closely on the actually processing involved in any service container. Given the flow of a service request and execution, JBI constituents are modeled very closely on these lines.

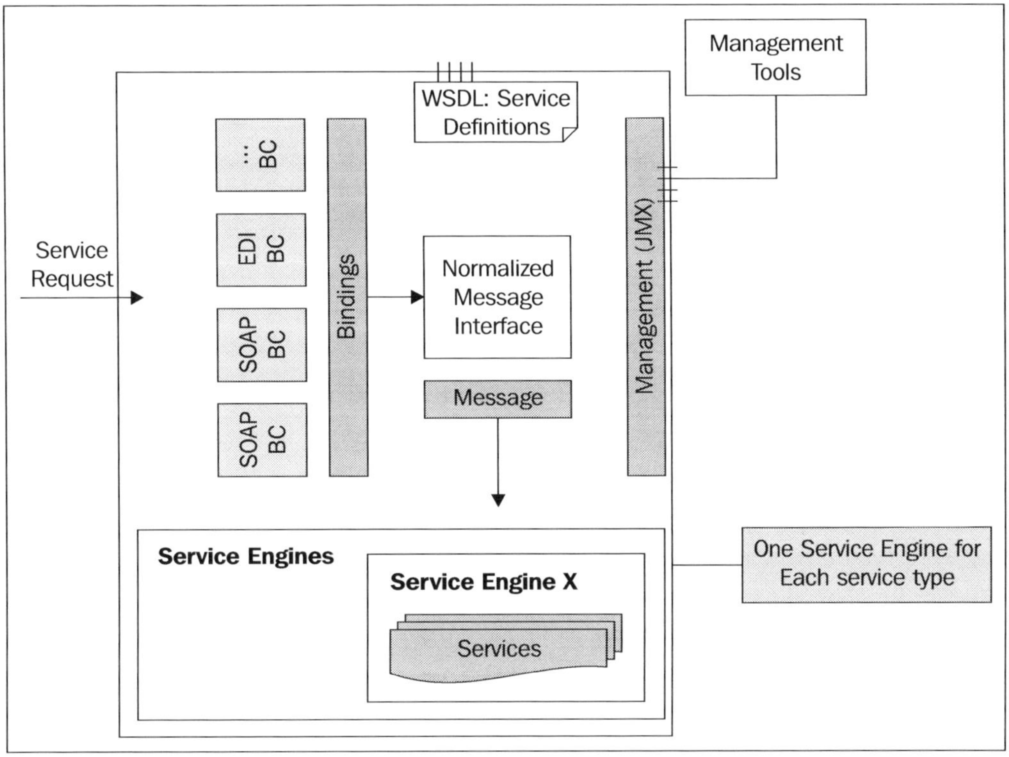

The JBI Constituents are:

Service Engines: JBI envisions specific runtime handling for various service types. Service types could be a "class" of services with the actual execution of such services abstracted by the service type's implementation. The service itself will then be a simple artifact. An example could be an XML-Transformation service. Each XSLT file may be a service instance. But the engine to run the XSLTs could be common, represented by a service type. When setting up a service, the service type is chosen first, and then any additional information such as the name of the XSLT file is provided as service properties. The end result is a specific transformation service. Say, if there is an XSLT to extract an address from an order (Order-to-Addr), I can set up a service instance using this XSLT file for extracting the billing address from an order and call the service instance ExtarctBillingAddressFromOrder. This will be a service of type TransformationService, with the Order-to-Addr.xslt as the XSLT file to be used. The TrasformationService type expects this as one of the service properties.

Binding Components: The binding components are the protocol adapter layers. There is one binding component per protocol. Say, one for SOAP, and one for JCA.

Normalized Message Service (NMS): Normalized messages play a key role in separating the service implementations from the Containers. Any service implementation can expect the request inputs/parameters to arrive in a standard manner via the Normalized Messages, regardless of which protocol the request came on, or which binding component processed it. Regardless of any other mechanics of the services container, the inputs arrive at the service execution layer in the exact same manner. This is very important to ensure portability of a service implementation—the service engine. The Normalized Message Router routes the message to the right execution engine.

Services: Services are the specific service instances. Services are the actual end service instances expected by any application or business processes in the SOA environment. Each service (instance) serves a specific business purpose or functionality. Each service will expect the inputs per the NMS, and the service implementation will rely on a specific service engine for its execution.

Service Definition: Each service in the system will need to be described, to enable the "consumption" of the service. The services in JBI will be described via the WSDL2 standards. WSDL2 improves upon earlier version of WSDL by clearly separating the interface and binding parts of any service definition.

Management: In the Java world, the omnipresent management standard is JMX (Java Management Extension). JBI also specifies the use of JMX for the management of the JBI Service containers.

Communication Infrastructure

ESB provides communication infrastructure as a core part of the platform. ESB is not about just two systems talking to each other. That is the turf of simple integration solutions like Adapters and "SOAP over HTTP"-type P2P invocation mechanisms. ESB is more about large-scale enterprise-wide services infrastructure involving a large number of service containers, invocations, transformations, routing, and orchestration, all in a highly scalable manner with good business responses. Applications and processes using services could become as common as DB access today is. As SOA takes off as a paradigm with good infrastructure support, the number of SOA service invocations will increase. Performing any user operation in an application may involve several back-end SOA service calls. This surely runs the risk of choking the networks. Such large-scale integration is practically feasible only with a very good high-performance backbone. Simple P2P integration mechanisms such as WS-over-HTTP will not suffice at all! Good ESB implementations will become imperative!

ESB systems, even though they are built around XML and Web Services, overcome the limitations of typical Web Service platforms by providing significant communication layers. Technologies such as messaging, under the covers, enable this scalability. SOAP over Messaging is one of the accepted bindings that enable supporting Standard Web Services as the applications' view of the services and their consumption, but the infrastructure could still transparently use Messaging to provide the lower-level communication. Messaging is at the same level as HTTP here, and is at a layer below the main WS abstractions.

In effect, WS and Messaging are complementary in ESB. WS over JMS actually adds significantly to scalability. Now, we are not talking about a simple WS request made over the network; we are talking about an enterprise-wide integration scenario, where many applications/systems in the enterprise talk to many other applications—enterprise wide, geographically distributed, over both high-speed LANs and not-so-high-speed WANs. Unlike simple Web Services, the ESB platform manages the communication.

Bus Services—Mediation, Transformations, and Process Flows

The Service Bus provides critical integration handling capabilities en route to a service's execution from a requesting application or process. These mediation functions, provided for by intermediary components of the ESB, include protocol handling, routing, transformation, security, and management.

ESB services and bus functionality hover around this aspect of "document flows" in an organization, which in the ESB context can also be seen as a message flow. With ESB modeled on such flows, the information now flows as documents or messages rather than as procedure requests. With ESB now acting as an intermediary between the service requester and the service provider, additional infrastructure services are possible in this mode, while propagating the request to the service implementation. The infrastructure has clear "insight" into the message contents unlike simple P2P services interaction. This is useful in providing services such as routing, automatic transformation, security, quality of service assurances, etc. All of these can happen transparently, without interfering with the actual service's execution or imposing any additional programming requirements on the service.

Why Mediation?

Mediation provides the transparency needed for the service consumers on exactly where the consumed services are and how they are executed. This is essential to ensure a loose coupling. Mediation is provided by the ESB platform, which acts as an intermediary between the service provider and the consumer—along the way providing key platform services. Without an intermediary, a requester has to know the service address and access it directly. With the ESB, the requester delegates the mechanics of making the call to the ESB. This includes handling the details of locating the service, invoking the service, or routing the message. This makes services and the code that invokes them simpler and easier to maintain.

In addition to the late discovery of the service, additional infrastructure functions would also need to be provided by some component. These include such functions as protocol handling, security, transactions, and data format transformations. Most of these will need a functional component between the client integration application and the service being accessed. The following figure shows the pre-processing in the bus prior to executing the service.

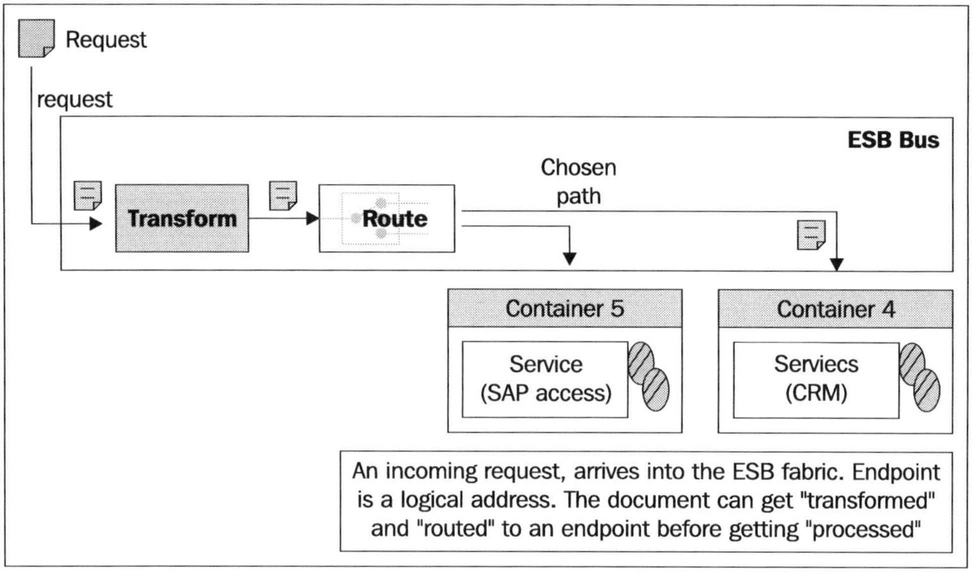

Mediation essentially is the system plumbing that sits between the consumer (that originated the service request) and the actual service. Along the way there can be value-added system services such as validation, security, transformation of the data inputs, smart business-rules-based request routing, and handling any mismatch in the invocation abstractions or data models (as would be in the case of a simple Web Service request made to a non-WS services framework in the back end).

Mediation functions eliminate the need for additional infrastructure and protocol handling functions to be built into the integration applications. The more contemporary SOA infrastructure provides this in a more generic manner. For instance, handling data model mismatches isdone more declaratively and across the enterprise. Global transformation rules are defined, where a given source document can be automatically transformed to specific target documents. When a service request is made, the mediation layer checks the document type expected by the actual service implementation and if the input document is of a different type, then applies the transformation rules specified to convert the input document to the form expected by the actual service.

This is done transparently even to the service deployment and configuration process. When defining the service there is no need to neither code for nor mention all document types that may be expected as input and what the transformation needed is. The various document types and transformations are globally defined and the rules applied automatically by the mediation layer.

Likewise, protocol mismatch is another common integration issue. The request arrives in a given protocol, but the service is deployed in a different protocol. An example is any ESB implementation such as Sonic ESB. Here the high-performing back end is JMS-based using proprietary wire protocols in the back-end bus. However, the request may come in from outside the ESB domain as a standard web service request. Now the service running in the ESB domain will expect the requests per its specific internal protocol. The service definition and the expected inputs are as per the specific formats.

Now, if the same service also has to be accessed from outside the domain as web services, and if to support this the programmers are asked to "code" the web service access as well, then the value from the platform is greatly diminished. The expectation is that the "same" service or process is "available" as a web service with some facilities provided by the SOA infrastructure—such services would normally be provided by the mediation layer. Based on some rules and protocol handling definitions, a SOAP request could be converted to an internal protocol and likewise on the response path, the internal response is converted to a SOAP response and sent back to the caller.

Physical Address Indirection Enables Mediation

Service lifecycle is the transitions from getting a service deployed and configured to starting and stopping the service. Service lifecycle typically determines the availability of a service. In hard-wired accesses, where the service specific connection details are exposed, anytime this service goes down, the service-becomes unavailable. If this can be abstracted behind a logical "address" or "endpoint", then the service lifecycle can be managed without always affecting its availability.

The services framework on the bus should abstract the specific location of the service instances. The whole service producer-consumer relationship should be based on a well-defined contract (possibly in a WSDL document) and an abstract location such as a named "endpoint" or a simple URL. At the endpoint or URL, the ESB plumbing will dynamically locate the service on the fly and direct the request to the service.

This indirection only enables mediation and control. As the location of the service is transparent with only a logical "address" available outside, the service location can be very dynamic. As load increases, the service can be started on additional service-containers (servers)—ensuring high scalability. When any container goes down for any reason, the next request is routed to one of the other instances running—ensuring high uptime.

Infrastructure Mediation

Infrastructure mediation is functionality that is void of any business logic or application inputs. It is about more environmental considerations such as the protocols, security, and service registries (see the following figure).

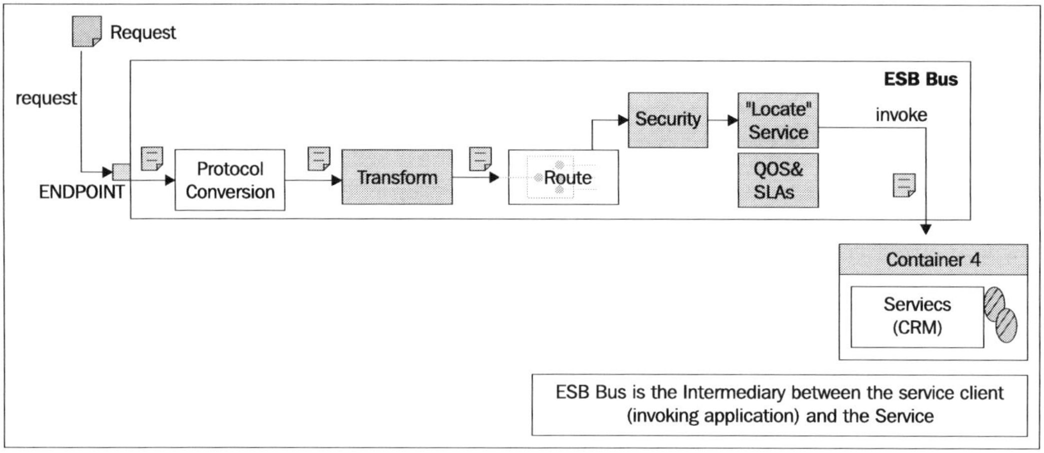

Protocol handling: Multiple protocols will exist in an enterprise. Even so, individual services may be available only on specific protocols. In this environment, requests may arrive on a certain protocol while the actual service is available on some other—such protocol mismatches can be handled transparently by the mediation layer when passing the request to the service. This may need support for multiple communication abstractions, such as event-driven publish-and-subscribe, synchronous and asynchronous invocation, and others.

Request routing and version resolution: This is the physical indirection handling, where the physical location of a service is determined by the mediation layer, and the request routed to the container running that service. In doing so, the infrastructure also can manage versions of the service artifacts. This will allow more advanced service upgrade management. There can be non-infrastructure routing possible such as subject-based, content-based, and even itinerary-based routings.

Security: The Mediation layer can enforce security policies regarding service usage. This requires additional infrastructure for defining and managing these policies, and for managing the identity of service requesters. Or the ESB may just hook into existing security infrastructure for identification, authorization, access control, and others as required.

Quality of service: The ESB can persist requests to message queues and retry service operations when failures occur, implement failover to alternative servers, and other steps to ensure that otherwise unreliable networks and services can be made to provide the quality of service required by the requester. More sophisticated implementations will interact with the environment to provision additional service instances to handle increased request volume, so that SLAs can still be met.

Service registry: The service registry will hold the information on the services, their current physical locations, and status information. This is used for service discovery and routing. When maintaining a namespace (service discovery), the ESB may extend the service metadata; this requires a specification (such as WSDL), to enable services to be classified to ease searching for reuse.

Message enrichment: This is a special case of semantic mapping, where the input data is tagged with additional information fetched from a database or other sources of information. Such enrichment enables the input document or message to emerge from the bus richer with data than when it arrived. In the example shown in the following figure, a service implementation expects a PO to include customer details, and if a PO arrives without the details, this message could be appended with the customer details loaded from the database.

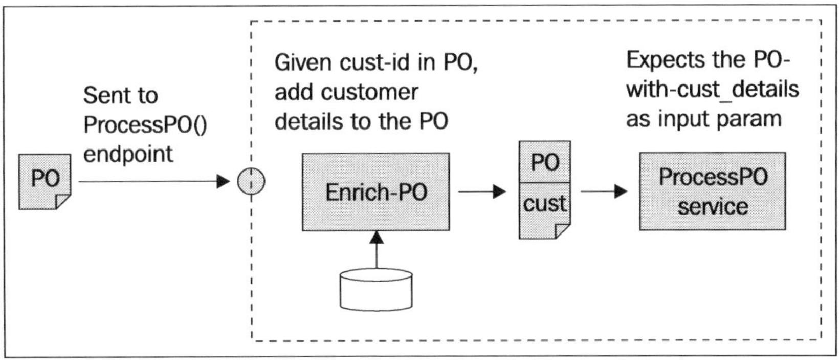

Intelligent Content-Based Routing

One defining attribute of ESB is that documents and messages flow through the bus and get processed along the way. One such processing is the content-based routing that the Bus provides. This is like conditional single-step itineraries—meaning, based on the content of the document it may take different paths. Say the document is a customer-order, and based on the part type, either it has to go to the manufacturing system (that is used for managing the operations of building 'custom built' products) or to the warehouse system (that is used for pre-built stocked products). Normally, some application would execute this check and logic. But in a smart document-flow-based organization, it is conceivable that content-based routing is possible—where routing rules are set up on various document types—and whenever the "router" is reached, it inspects the contents and applies the routing rules and picks a path. This can happen, independent of any other steps in the processing of the document or any other process-flow semantics. Routing happens in the ESB fabric, as shown in the following figure.

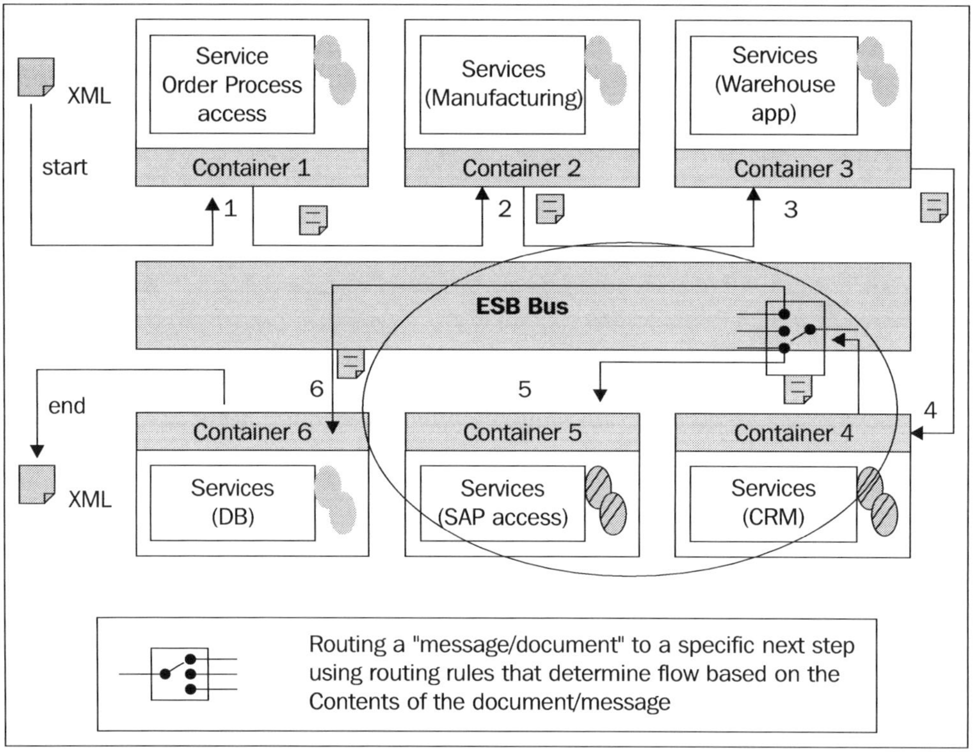

The routing rules are platform specific at this point. Each vendor has its own mechanism and possibly language—even in cases where pluggable rules engines are used, there are no portable standards. This will include support for accessing the input documents and the contents in the documents, and using this in defining the rules. For each rule defined, there will be an "endpoint" that is specified to which the input document or message is to be sent when the rule evaluates to true at run time. This rule evaluation will happen in the ESB fabric in the intermediary layers—either using native rules engines or embeddable external rules engines.

Content-based routing (CBR), under the hood, is essentially a simple rules engine. The CBR will get an input document(s), and the rules are based on the contents of this document(s), and will evaluate to a "destination" to which the input document(s) need to be routed or forwarded.

Transformation Services

As documents flow through the ESB system, getting processed along the way, it is quite possible that there is a need to transform the document structure along the way. One common need for this is when a service that is being accessed expects the information in a format that is different from the input document.

There may be several different types of transformation, like request, response, format mismatch, explicit conversion, extract parts from input document, and more. The document that flows and gets processed is essentially a superset document—it may need to be subsetted for each service along the way.

In a hub-spoke model, these transformations are explicit steps in a process, before the step that needs the modified document is executed. In an ESB system, the transformation is available as a system service, and so can be executed any place—it doesn't have to run in a Process Server alone, it can happen anywhere, and in-place!

The Need to Transform

Once we accept that documents "flow" in an enterprise and "get processed" along the way by the IT solutions of various departments, then additional requirements crop up.

Given that each IT solution would evolve by itself, regardless of other departments in the organization, it is quite likely that the information models used in the various solutions are different from each other. For example, the purchase order as represented in the Order-Processing system may be different from the PO represented in the ERP system. There may be additional or a reduced set of fields in the PO. So when exchanging data between these systems, the information from one system will need to be "transformed" to the form understood by the other system.

Such transformation could be done by the integration application: extract info from the first system, convert to the required format, and then send it to the second system. This is fine in P2P-based solutions, where the service-consuming application is tightly coupled to the service-providing application. However, in more loosely coupled integration environments such as the Service bus (ESB), such tight couplings are not desirable.

This is where more transparent transformation comes in. Each application is aware of its data formats alone, and in the integration environment, say in a Business Process, the required transformations are performed independently. In a more evolved SOA-based enterprise, it is quite likely that there is a corporate type repository, where all information models are described. In such cases, the PO in the Order system and the ERP system will be described in the type library. And it can extend a bit further, to also include canned transformations that will transform the PO from the Order-system format to the ERP format. In such cases, the ESB environment can automatically transform the document to the format needed before actually sending the document to the service that is being invoked.

A good Service Bus can leverage such type libraries and further add value to the platform by helping with the transformations, both during design time (by helping with the XSLT/XQuery needed for the transformation) as well as during run time (by picking up the latest transformation definitions from the central type library).

The transformations may be explicit transformations programmed in the application, or implicit auto-transformations based on type libraries. Type libraries are corporate schema repositories that provide additional information on the various XML document schemas used in the organization. This information will include conversion or transformation rules to get the data from other schema types to the required schema type. This will help automate mapping the information from the message or document to what the service requires, and so on all without the service implementer or the consumer application needing to code for any of this.

Transformation using XSLT

XSLT is part of XSL (eXtensible Stylesheet Language). XSL consists of two parts: XSL Transformations XSLT and XSL Formatting Objects.

XSLT files, often called stylesheets, are themselves XML documents defining a transformation for a class of XML documents. The basic design is that XSLT is declarative and based on pattern-matching and templates (see the following figure). XSL Formatting Objects is the "second half" of XSL. It is an *XML vocabulary* for specifying formatting in a more low-level and detailed way than is possible with HTML and CSS.

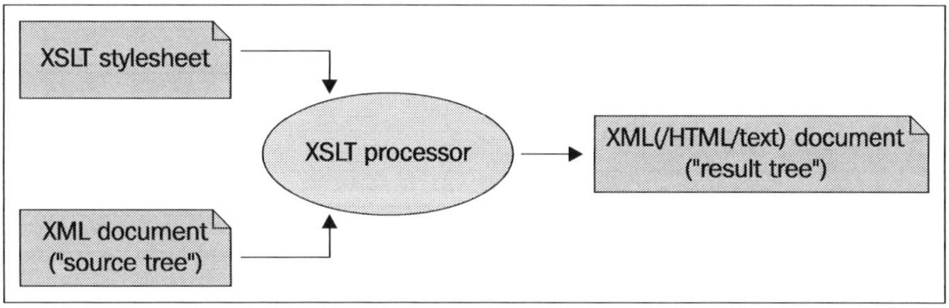

XQuery for More Complex XML Document Manipulation

With XML being omnipresent in enterprises, and more so in an ESB bus, other XML-centric processing quickly emerges as a need. As documents flow through the bus and get processed, there could be cases where the documents need to be saved in a document repository or database for subsequent retrieval and processing. Once documents get into a repository, when a business need to retrieve and process arises, there will be use cases where multiple documents need to be retrieved, possibly based on some query criteria, and then processed.

XQuery is a standard mechanism available to realize the XML querying and handling. A set of XML documents could be retrieved, and then filters and rules applied to the set of documents, and finally the output document(s) composed from this set by extracting and massaging data from the XML documents as needed.

ESB systems should support XML querying within the infrastructure. This will pre-suppose that there is the ability to store XML documents in a repository or database. XQuery could be a step in a business process, where this step returns multiple documents based on its rules and transformation definition. The process will then use each of these documents in its subsequent steps—probably in a loop with the same set of steps repeated for each document. In effect, we have now converted a business process into a batch processing mechanism. The process may still get its input document, which may represent the criteria for extracting the required XML documents and then processing the resultant set as defined in the process definition.

ESB Processes: Extending the WS Process Model

Business Processes are an inherent part of any SOA-based infrastructure. One primary purpose of embarking upon SOA-based infrastructure would be to enable the integration of the several systems in the organization to provide automated business processes that span accesses to these systems. The most common processes approach is a hub-and-spoke model where the processes run in a process engine. This is very much possible in ESB where the process engine is running in a container on the bus. Additionally, ESB enables an alternative model that closely mimics the document-flows-and-gets-processed model in manual organizational business process flows that we discussed earlier in this chapter. These are often referred to as "ESB Processes".

Processes—n the "Fabric"

The distributed process execution model can be extended further where the process view is flipped. From being a sequence of steps, it is a document flowing through a sequence of service executions—with the same document as "input" to all the services in the flow path.

Document Itineraries are ESB Processes

Once a document arrives at an endpoint in an ESB system, the document is processed by a Service—a service may be a business logic chunk or a process. Considering the document flow model of enterprises, the enterprise workflows involving a form or a document getting processed by various departments as it flows through the organization can be automated. In ESB, these are called Itineraries. When there is a document that needs to be processed, the processing steps are attached to this document—much like a business process.

The document and the process along with the state information on what has transpired so far with that document "hops" from one container to another in the bus as it gets processed by various steps of the process definition that is attached to the process. From an application standpoint, the process definition is all that matters and the expected end behavior is the same regardless of whether this process runs in a process server/engine or runs as an ESB Itinerary on the bus. The difference is only in the internal execution.

On the lines of a document flowing and getting processed in an organization, the ESB processes have a process state that "flows" and gets processed in the "fabric". This is shown in the following figure. Instead of the process running in a process server, the process input document and process state "hop" from one service container to another to execute the steps of the process. After executing one step, the infrastructure inspects the process and identifies where the next step must execute, and "sends" the process input and state to that container, where the next step is executed and the state updated. And that container sends the process to the next "step".

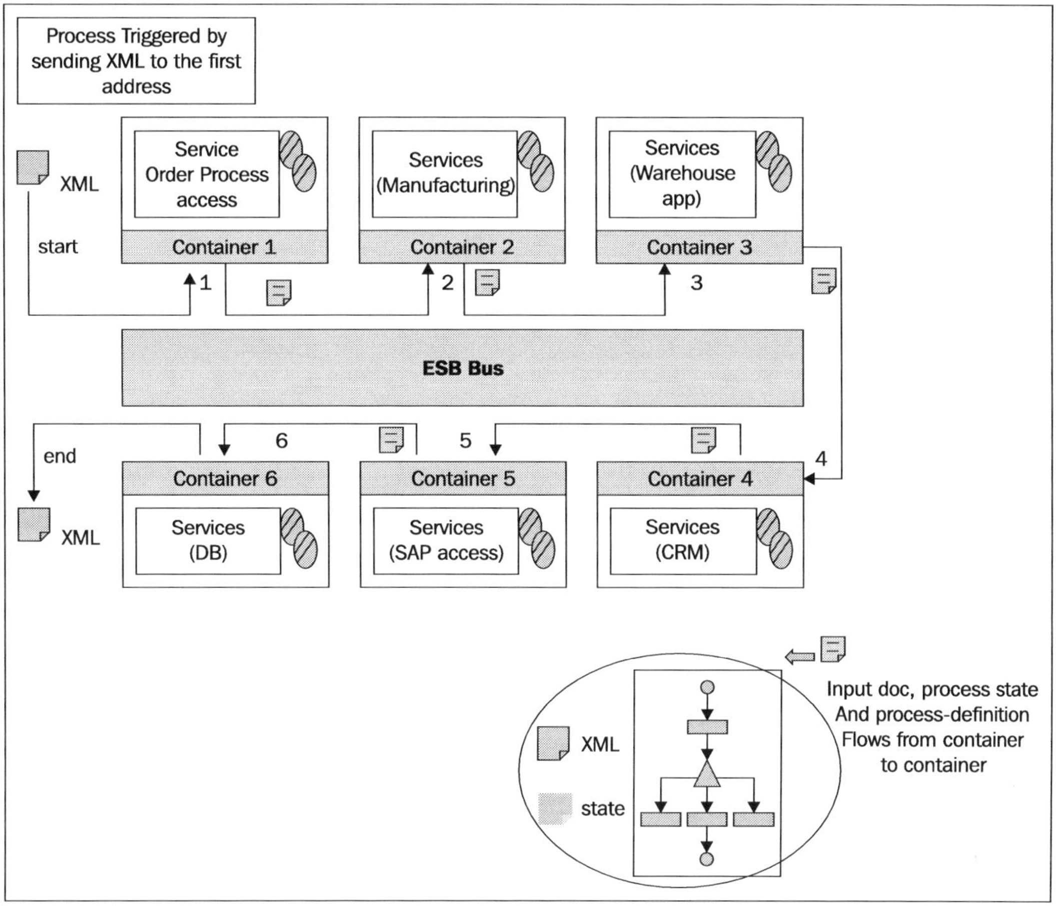

Consider a work-order query process, where an Order Processing application is accessed to get a work-order detail; this work order is checked for build status from the Manufacturing application, then there is a Shipping status check in the warehouse application, followed by an update to a customer record in the CRM application and then SAP is accessed for the shipping and logistics module and finally a DB update is performed before the order status details are sent out of the process exit. Now each of the six steps is a service in the SOA system, each running on a different container—each container containing services accessing a certain back-end/legacy system. The input document "flows" from one container to the other and gets processed. Each container "sends" the document to the next step. And the last step sends the output document out of the process environment.

Here the process essentially runs in the ESB fabric, as opposed to a normal process that runs in a process engine or orchestration server. In the two cases though, the process programming definition is not different, other than possibly a restriction that there be only one document input in one case, and no such restriction in the other. Otherwise, the process has inputs, processing steps, and flow constructs in both cases, possibly written in a business process programming language such as BPEL. In effect, the application developer's view of the process is independent of the specific process execution environment and mode. Whether it runs in a Process Server or runs as an ESB process in a distributed fabric, the process definition remains the same, say, a BPEL program.

The runtime differences are modeled into the deployment step that the platform may support, that will be used when taking the project artifacts such as a BPEL program and configuring the run-time behavior—say at this point choosing to have the process be available as an ESB process as opposed to having it run in the Process engine, assuming both options are available in the chosen ESB platform.

Itineraries—Processing Schedules for Business Documents

ESB Processes may be represented at run time as a process document with a processing itinerary attached to the document—and this is "executed" in the ESB environment with the document being sent along with its state and itinerary from one step to the other. The document or message, and the itinerary, "flow" and get processed as per the itinerary.

In traditional organizations, there is always a concept of a mail flow where a document or docket has a flow path or itinerary. Based on the document type, this gets set and then flows per that process, with each recipient along the way "processing" the document and adding any additional info or status/updates to the docket/document/form as it flows. ESB Processes follow this same model.

ESB Processes or Itineraries are a key component of the process in the fabric model, wherein, along with the input document, a schedule of processing is attached. The schedule is the process definition—the series of steps that need to be executed as part of the processing. The series of steps can also be seen as a processing "itinerary"—the order of steps that will be executed.

All the steps will get the input document and additional process state that flows along with the document and the itinerary. The process engine is now a distributed engine, where there is an itinerary-handling component in each container. It executes the service step to be run in that container and does the necessary housekeeping to locate the next step in the process (itinerary) and ship the request including the input document, process state, and the itinerary (process definition) to the service container that can run the next step.

ESB Process vs. Orchestrated Process

ESB Processes or Itineraries are still an emerging concept. Processes have so far been known to run only in an Orchestration server or a central process engine. Most vendor implementations support this model. A few ESB vendors are now beginning to support a distributed process execution framework wherein the processes run in the fabric. As Orchestration servers run in a hub-and-spoke model, there will be a performance overhead due to the additional network roundtrips involved with each request and response flowing as opposed to the ESB process model where the requests and responses are always local within the container and the network flows are essentially a single hop between requests where the process state and other information flows between containers.

Orchestration servers, however, do provide for centralized housekeeping, which will allow for tracking all process instances. Work lists or user interactions amidst process steps are another capability that is easily provided by Orchestration servers. For an ESB process to support this functionality, it will need a centralized administrative server that will be notified of process state transitions and work list requests. This will take away some of the performance benefits from running the processes in the fabric in a distributed environment.

Security and Transactions

Continuing the discussions on the security and transactions standards in the SOA space, we will now see how these apply to ESB. The requirements are essentially the same in an ESB environment as well. After all, ESB is a technology for SOA. Security and transactions are realized by a combination of handling built into the application and capabilities provided by the infrastructure. The infrastructure capabilities are available out-of-the-box for use by the SOA applications. In some cases, the usage is realized by explicitly programming for the security or transaction handling.

The ideal case, though, is when this is available declaratively, without needing any programming in the services or the processes. The required behavior is triggered by the deployment-time setup or the run-time configurations. We will now see how ESB provides for the security and transactions per the relevant Web Service standards.

Security Considerations in Integration Architecture

SOA-based integration environments are back-end systems that provide programmatic access to other systems—and not for end users as in a normal web application. Security models in such environments will be a little different from normal authentication that web applications will require, ranging from simple trust-based access, where unlimited access is provided for specific applications or network addresses to more complex security tokens. Apart from secure communications, the infrastructure will need to be able to secure the services being built, have mechanisms to get user login credentials, and be able to propagate the authentication details across the ESB domain, between service containers—and along the way, manage the privacy and trust, as shown in the following figure.

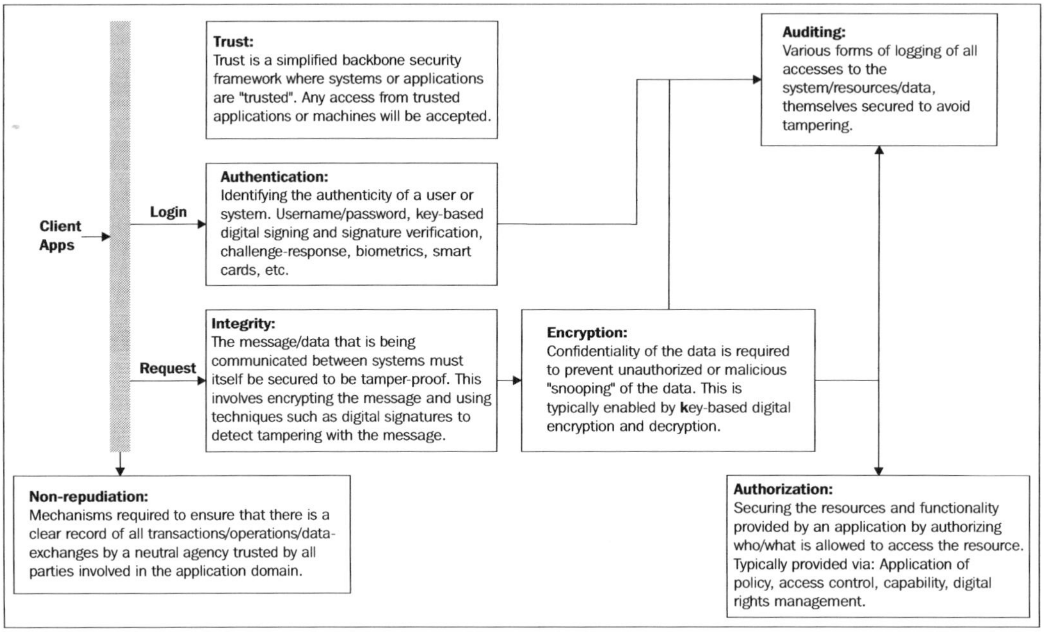

In a simple integration environment, which is essentially in a P2P mode, the security provided for by the legacy application can be directly supported in the integration application, without necessarily requiring any common security infrastructure across all legacy systems.

Building on Application Platforms Security (.NET & Java EE)

When the services infrastructure is built on Application Platforms, the security infrastructure provided by the platforms could be used. Both the popular application platforms, Java EE and .NET, provide extensive services frameworks ranging from Secure Socket communications (SSL), to elaborate authentication and authorization frameworks.

The Java EE platform provides for a highly evolved Security framework via JAAS (Java Authentication and Authorization Services) and other constituent specifications. This is in addition to the very flexible declarative application security model for both Web and ESB application modules.

When developing Web Services in Java EE, the service implementations will either be Servlets, or Session Beans or Message Driven Beans. All the three have security semantics that could be defined even when they are to be accessed as a Web Service.

For Web Services built on the .NET platform, the .NET security infrastructure can be used. This includes the capabilities provided by ASP.NET and IIS.

Since Web Services are part of ASP.NET, and these are hosted by the ASP.NET runtime, the security support provided by ASP.NET will also be available for Web Services. ASP.NET works with IIS and the Windows operating system in order to implement the security services. In ASP.NET, most of the IIS settings have been replaced with configuration files. However, security settings made in IIS are still valid in some areas because IIS is still handling the process of accepting users' requests. In fact, whenever IIS receives requests for some ASPX page, ASMX Web Service, or any other resource that is associated with ASP.NET, it uses the IIS applications mappings to send the request to ASP.NET.

ESB Security—Built on WS-Security

Security includes the message privacy/integrity to ensure tamper-proof communications and the authentication and authorization for access to the bus and the services. The security in ESB systems builds on prevailing Web Services security standards.

WS-Security and Related Specifications

The security standards that are coming up to address various aspects of the security infrastructure include WS-Security, WS-Trust, and WS-SecurityPolicy.

WS-Security includes authentication, integrity (via Digital Signatures) and privacy (via Encryption). WS-Trust provides a framework for trusted exchange of messages, where the sending entity is trusted by the receiving entity. The web service security model defined in WS-Trust relies on services specifying the requirements and an incoming message will have to prove a set of claims (e.g., name, key, permission, capability, etc.). If a message arrives without having the required proof of claims, the service will ignore or reject the message. A service can indicate its required claims and related information in its policy as described by WS-Policy and WS-PolicyAttachment specifications.

Security across the Enterprise

ESB in many respects adopts the various Web Services standards. Security in an ESB platform can be both native and driven by standards. ESB security has two distinct manifestations:

- Security for accessing services and processes from within the ESB domain (internal accesses)
- Security for accesses to the service or processes from outside the ESB domain (say, as standard web services)

Security and reliability for external accesses should be provided by a standards-compliant platform using the WS-S and WS-RM standards. Internal security also should be defined by using the same standards. In effect, the contract of a service includes its security and reliability assertions that the ESB platform will honor in both its internal and in its external accesses.

Additional internal accesses could leverage any proprietary security infrastructure. For example, in JMS-based ESB implementations, the JMS security infrastructure could be used as is. This should not be preferred by SOA application developers though, as this introduces a potential vendor lock-in.

One important consideration for applications is that the security should be non-programmatic. This ensures that the application program artifacts such as the services and business processes themselves are not locked into any vendor-specific support. The security should be declaratively available. Preferably the requirements should be specified in standard ways such as using WS-Security in the service WSDLs.

ESB can support security at multiple levels including transport layer, messaging layer, service containers, and Web Services gateways with the Domain server at the core of security services.

The transport layer security assures the privacy and integrity of the communications. These can be controlled by the SOA integration application via the WS-Security policy assertions. The ESB platform will honor the assertions and ensure that all communications conform to these assertions. While the specification of the integrity requirements is based on the standards, the actual implementation is platform specific and is built into the lowest communication layers.

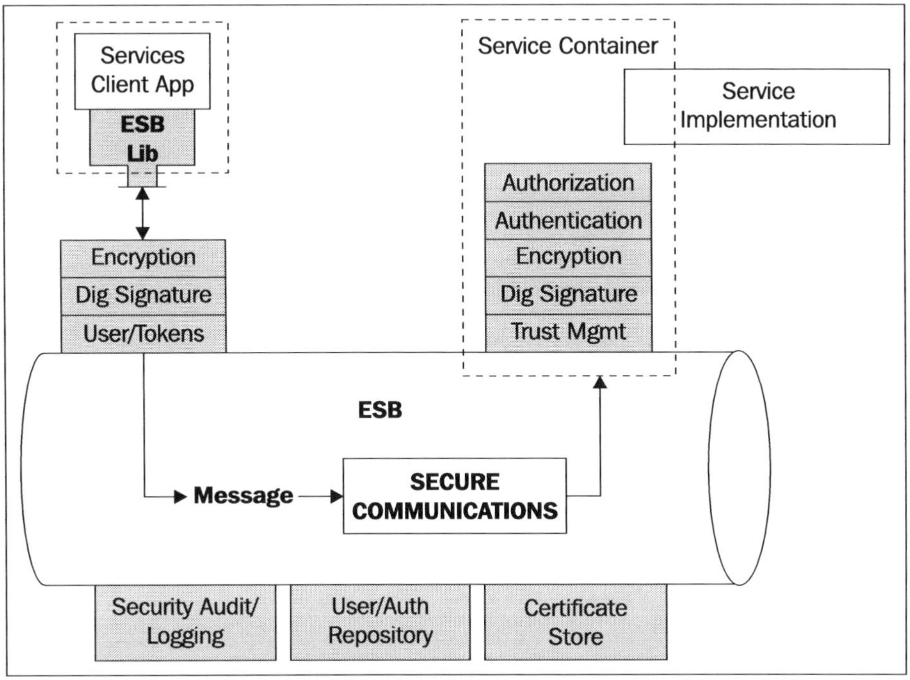

Message-layer security will rely on the messaging platform—most ESB solutions may rely on a messaging platform. Messaging platforms, either based on the Java standards or otherwise, have a clearly defined notion of connections, sessions, and the actual sending/receiving of messages. Security is built at all levels. The user credentials are generally provided when establishing connections to the messaging platform. The integrity and privacy is built into the transport layer of the messaging solution, the need for which is specified as a connection property. Access control is built into the destinations. For each destination, the allowed users and roles are specified, which are used to authorize access to any destination, either for sending messages or receiving messages. When an ESB platform is built on an underlying messaging solution, the well-defined security infrastructure of the messaging platform can be leveraged. This will involve delegating a lot of the security handling to the messaging layer. For instance, all access control could be delegated to the message layer's access control for the destinations—wherein, a service endpoint is translated into a messaging destination.

A more elaborate services-level security is possible in an ESB given the extensive mediation infrastructure that ESB platforms include. This could involve complete support for WS-Security including integrity via digital signatures, confidentiality via encryption, and user authentication using passwords or security tokens. Unlike the messaging layer security support, this layer could be based on more generic transport and communication layer-independent approaches. When a service is set up with WS-S policy assertions, the ESB platform will enforce all security assertions even when accessed from outside the ESB domain via regular SOAP over HTTP.

Transaction Semantics for Enterprise Integration

Business applications typically perform aggregate operations wherein one business function is performed by invoking multiple operations underneath. Due to various validations, business logic, and rules, operations could fail. Say when reserving inventory for an order, there might be insufficient inventory quantities. When while executing a series of operations an operation fails, the expectation is that the whole business operation has to fail, and all the state and data in the system be restored to what it was prior to the start of the business function.

We are quite familiar with this requirement in monolithic applications that work off a database. Database Servers and database access mechanisms provide very good support for this via transaction boundaries and abilities to commit or roll back a transaction. With the broad penetration of Application Servers and platforms, inherently applications now started accessing multiple data repositories (databases or the resources). This brought forth the need for distributed transactions. Platforms such as Java EE and .NET have implicit support for distributed transactions—mostly built on the established technologies such as the two-phase commit.

In an SOA or ESB environment, the business function is essentially a business process, and the operations accessed as part of this process are the various services available on the platform. Once these business processes start servicing serious business requirements, it will be inevitable that this will come with a strong need for transactions.

In the Web Services world, the connectivity to the various systems was the focus. Most accesses might be local to one system or a tightly knit domain that probably has a good distributed transaction backbone, and only few sporadic accesses happen to external Web Services. Here the need for tight transactions might not be high; and any transaction semantics can be explicitly programmed for. For example, the compensating operation for a reserveInventory (part number, quantity) function would be a function unReserveInventory (partNumber, quantity). The former function reserves a specified quantity of inventory. The latter function releases the given quantity—explicitly, as part of the rollback operation.

Now, with SOA platforms becoming more widespread and starting to serve as first tier application platforms, the transaction requirements change. The expectation may be that the same declarative transaction capabilities that are available in database and application-server platforms, where transaction semantics can be got without actually programming for rollback operations or compensating business operations, will be available here as well. This is easier said than done. Today, even ESB systems rely on long-running transaction models discussed below.

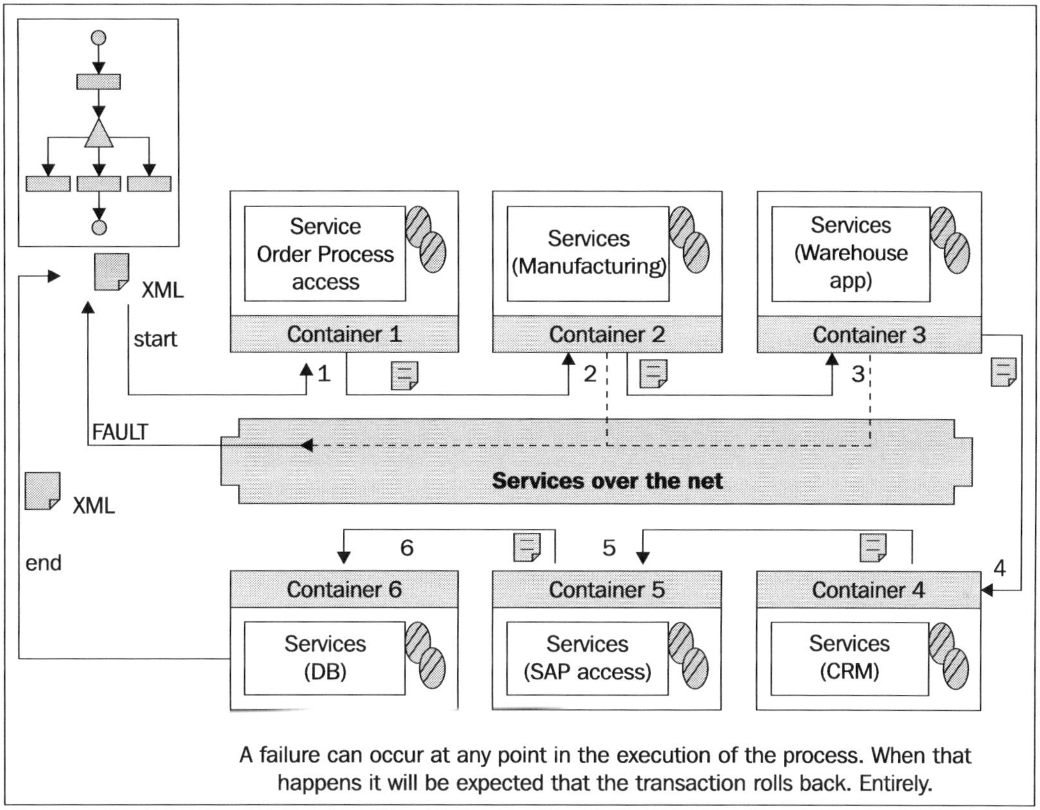

In a widely distributed setup such as a typical SOA environment, where the service containers may be geographically distributed over a WAN, the infrastructure for transactions becomes a little bit of a challenge (see the above figure). Even so, the minimal transaction semantics expected will be:

- Atomic transactions
- Long-running transactions

Atomic transactions are similar to the database or Application Platform transactions, where a transaction boundary starts, say at the beginning of a Business process, and at any point the process ends the transaction is committed. At commit, all operations performed as part of the transaction will commit their changes, honoring the ACID properties. In a distributed setup such as in SOA, this will be performed using the two-phase commit (2-PC) protocol, where each service or resource that is participating in the transaction will need to support the protocol. Here, the COMMIT now involves a two-step process, first PREPAREd and the COMMITted.

In the PREPARE step, that is propagated to all the service/resource containers, the changes that were made as part of that transactions are taken to an intermediate persisted state in such a way that the changes still remain private to that transaction, but can survive a crash of the service/resource/container. Once all the participating services have confirmed this state, then the transaction coordinator will issue a final COMMIT on each of the resources. Should any of the services/resources come up with an error on the PREPARE state, then all the services are instructed to roll back. Should, after the PREPARE and when COMMITS are underway, any of the services /resources go down or crash, then on its restart the transaction coordinator will "recover" incomplete transactions and issue a COMMIT on those.

Now, in a widely distributed services environment, it is quite likely that some operations take much longer to complete. Say in a Business Process where there is a process step for the "partner confirmation of an order build". This step will complete only when the partner actually manufactures the required part. This may take days, weeks, or months depending on the nature of the part being manufactured. Such transactions are called Long-Running Transactions.

Conventional transaction models will fail or may be sub-optimal in Long-Running Transactions—as they rely heavily on locking resources to ensure concurrency integrity. And for long running, locking resources is a bad model as this will grossly restrict other business processes that need access to the same data/resource from executing. In such cases, a different transaction model is be needed.

A common approach for these is to have the notion of a "compensating" business operation. For every operation performed, there will be its complementary pair that will provide the "compensating" function. Like, if reserveInventory () is a service, there might be an unreserveInventory () service as its compensating operation. These are much more involved than regular transactions.

In normal atomic transactions, most of the housekeeping and transaction management is managed by the infrastructure. The application need only bother about the transaction boundaries—start, commit, and rollback. In a long-running transaction environment though, the compensating functions are to be implemented and made available by the application. Further, the semantics of such compensating operations are also extremely tied-in to the business processing involved. Say, for the unreserveInventory () operation, the call must be made for the exact same part with the exact same inventory count as was used for the original reserveInventory () operation request. The onus for ensuring such integrity now rests with the application developer.

Transaction Strategies for EAI and B2B

Enterprise Integration using any B2B solutions or EAI essentially involves a hub-and-spoke model, where there is a single central server instance that manages all interactions with the service back ends. In this mode, the distributed transactions involving multiple resources and legacy applications can be managed by having the transactions coordinated out of the EAI server instance. Being managed by a single transaction manager, which is most likely running along with the EAI server instance, existing transaction manager solutions will fit in very well. Any transaction manager and existing two-phase commit protocols can be used to provide the transaction boundaries across access to various services from the EAI platform.

In simple B2B solutions, conventional transaction management solutions will not work. This is primarily because, over an unreliable WAN or internet network, having a tight wire protocol for transaction management is not practical. Here, alternative transaction management solutions such as those that depend on compensating business transactions are warranted. In such solutions, unlike the normal commit and rollback, undoing a transaction's operations is realized by invoking "compensating" business operations. The compensating operations are regular business operations that perform the converse of another business operation.

Distributed Transactions and Web Services

Web Services are designed to be available over intranet or Internet, over high bandwidth networks or loosely coupled networks. When the services are built on EAI or Application platforms, the transaction capabilities of the platforms come into play. These will generally support the atomic transactions semantics, either simple local transactions or per the two-phase commit protocols for distributed transactions across multiple resources. In a more involved distributed-services infrastructure such long-running transactions also can be supported.

Web Service Transaction Standards

Transaction requirements in an SOA platform are addressed by WS-* specifications. The Web Services Transactions specifications describe an extensible coordination framework (WS-Coordination) and specific coordination types for both short-lived ACID transactions (WS-AtomicTransaction) and long-running business processes (WS-BusinessActivity). This provides transaction solutions for the short-lived ACID-enabled business-process coordination within the enterprise as well as the more extended long-term transaction coordination across the partners and the supply chain.

The WS-* standards provide a framework for transaction boundaries to span heterogeneous service environments. In the case of ESB, this becomes a little simplified as there is a homogenous layer introduced by the service containers. The WS transactions specifications are designed to enable interoperability of distributed, recoverable transactions.

The WS-Transaction specifications are defined by the Web Service Interoperability Organization (WS-I Organization), which is an industry-wide effort at standardizing how Web Services are requested and delivered. This includes WS-Coordination, WS-AtomicTransaction, and WS-BusinessActivity.

WS-Coordination: This specification is a generic extensible framework for describing protocols that coordinate the actions of distributed applications. Such coordination protocols are used to support a number of applications, including those that need to reach consistent agreement on the outcome of distributed activities. The distributed activities could be transaction coordination, audit logging, or any other distributed activity that requires central coordination and housekeeping. The WS coordination is generally itself a service in the platform, thus ensuring easy access.

This specification describes a definition of the structure of context and the requirements for propagating context between cooperating services—a mechanism for an individual Coordination service to participate in another Coordination service enables extending the Coordination domain. In effect one SOA or ESB domain, could integrate its coordination space into that of another ESB domain that has its own Coordination service.

WS-AtomicTransaction: This specification provides the definition of the atomic transaction coordination type that is to be used with the extensible coordination framework described in the WS-Coordination specification. The specification defines three specific agreement coordination protocols for the atomic transaction coordination type: completion, volatile two-phase commit, and durable two-phase commit. Developers can use any or all of these protocols when building applications that require consistent agreement on the outcome of short-lived distributed activities that have the all-or-nothing property.

WS-BusinessActivity: This specification provides the definition of the business activity coordination type that can be used to effect compensating business activities for long-lived transactions. The specification defines two specific agreement coordination protocols for the business activity coordination type: one involving the participants to drive the coordination and the other involving a transaction coordinator. Developers can use any or all of these protocols when building applications that require consistent agreement on the state or outcome of long-running distributed activities.

Architecture: The architecture for WS-transaction is not too different from that for conventional transactions. There is a Transaction Coordinator, and transaction-enabled services. Each transaction-enabled service will need to register with the transaction coordinator. As part of this registration, the compensating business operation is also specified. Each business process will register the process instance with the transaction coordinator and, on successful completion, will again notify the transaction coordinator. The TC will do the needful to ensure all services that participated in the transaction have completed their parts. Likewise, if a fault occurred then the process will notify the TC of the same, and the TC will do the needful to roll back all services that participated in the transaction. The rollback may involve triggering the corresponding compensating business operations.

Realizing Transactions in ESB

The transaction models in Web Services-related transaction specifications form the core of typical ESB transaction support. These are extended to leverage the infrastructure capabilities like the underlying messaging infrastructure.

ESB Transactions Built on the Messaging Layer

ESB platforms may provide support for the emerging WS-* standards or could provide transaction support more natively. The primary use case for transactions in an ESB system might be local to the enterprise and it could be unlikely that they will be long lived. Hence regular atomic transactions with a commit and rollback model might suffice most cases. There is the likely standard WS-AtomicTransaction-based implementation.

With messaging being the actual transport layer for the services, the more proprietary solutions may leverage the transaction handling available at the Messaging layer.

Process Driven Local Transaction Semantics

In any SOA application, processes are the primary access points for services. The services are orchestrated in a process. The processes perform the aggregate business functions that involve access to multiple services in the enterprise. It is quite likely that these processes themselves form the transaction boundaries. In cases where the process accesses the services in a local process space, there could be transaction optimizations possible where the distributed transaction now becomes managed from a single process space.

This could use regular two-phase commits, with an in-process transaction manager that manages the transaction coordination and the resource interactions per the two-phase-commit protocols.

Reliability, Scalability, and Management

ESB enables enterprise-grade reliability and scalability through its inherently distributed platform. Having services abstracted behind "endpoints" as opposed to explicit IP and port and specific URLs of each container is the primary enabler for high-end reliability and scalability.

While reliability is described in terms of the availability and service delivery guarantees, scalability is the ability to service higher loads without disrupting the environment or needing major reconfiguration. The reliability is required to ensure that each request to a service is delivered accurately and predictably. And scalability ensures that a large number of such requests are handled by the ESB platform.

Unlike simple Web Services or even platforms such as EAI, ESB is inherently a distributed infrastructure. It is not single-server-centric as in EAI or handling libraries as in simple Web Services. Reliability can be built into the transport and messaging layers of the ESB infrastructure.

Reliability Concepts

Reliability is essentially at the level of reliable communications and high availability of the whole ESB platform. Reliable communication is at a base platform level where there is an expectation that all communications are guaranteed to complete and be failsafe. Additionally, reliability with regard to communication expectations in a widely distributed ESB domain may also be specified by the SOA application. There are standard mechanisms available like WS-ReliableMessaging that allow specifying the reliability expectations.

High platform availability is an attribute of the platform. The only expectation from the application is that the platform be available all the time. Sufficient redundancies via clustering and fail-over have to be built.

There have been several analyses and studies that touched upon how widely Services will be used in the rapidly evolving SOA landscape. The inter-application and cross-application accesses will increase drastically with:

- SOA becoming more easily available
- Services exposed by all applications and legacy systems easily accessible from other applications
- Business processes easily composable from these services

This is much like how DB accesses have become omnipresent in applications today. Even today, if when processing a sales order, the programmer could easily access the customer database maintained by the CRM application to get the latest info on the customer, he or she would do that. But given that such accesses are expensive today, most often there would be a discreet "upload" of customer info from the CRM application to the Order Processing Application—with the info duplicated. And then, there are the Business processes.

The BPM tools have gained in popularity as Business Processes help integrate the IT-Solution Islands that currently exist in enterprises. And these solutions are all interconnected in the functioning of the enterprises. In the absence of any integration solutions, the end user is the integration point: the user accesses multiple applications from multiple windows, and performs the "Business Process".

With SOA, both ends of the integration are targeted well. Each legacy solution/ application can easily expose services, and Business Processes can be composed and executed easily. Unlike traditional BPM solutions that are more focused on just the "process" and service access is more from the process environment, in ESB, services are accessed from a generic framework that is agnostic to the processes or accesses. In effect, there are no synchronous invocations of services. The service invocations are always dependent on typical asynchronous mechanisms such as messaging. This imposes potential reliability issues that need to be addressed by the ESB infrastructure.

Reliable Messaging Basics

What constitutes Reliable Messaging? In short it has to ensure that a message is delivered. This is not exactly a new concept. It has been in existence since the EDI days. EDI in fact solved this very well for information exchanged as files. It had sufficient redundancies and communication protocols and extensive acknowledgement and confirmation mechanism to ensure reliable message delivery.

Reliable messaging could include:

- Ensuring messages are delivered
- Ensuring non-duplicate message delivery
- Ensuring a sequence of messages
- Ensuring sufficient bookkeeping to help with non-repudiation

To ensure the above, additional management of the communication will be needed in the communication layers of the ESB. This includes the notion of sequence IDs, message numbers, acknowledgements of communication packets, and persisting messages to ensure delivery even when intermediate infrastructure components fail or crash.

Sequences—Each message set sent from a source to a destination is given a sequence reference ID. The messages sent from the source to the destination are scoped using a sequence. Sequences are distinguished using a unique identifier (a URI) for each sequence. The sequences only ensure that the messages are delivered in the same sequence as that they were emanated at the source. Sequences are controlled declaratively without the service implementation or the integration application that is accessing the services having to program for managing sequences. The sequences are generated and processed by the communication layers of the ESB infrastructure.

Message Numbers—Messages form the lowest level of a communication. In an ESB, each communication packet typically represents one service invocation. Every message sent in the context of a sequence has a unique identifier in the context of the sequence. This identifier is a serially incremented number, with each message in the sequence getting the next number in the sequence. This identifier is a monotonically increasing integer number, starting with 1 and increasing by exactly 1 for each message. Managing the message numbers would be a responsibility of the communication layers of the ESB infrastructure. The source generates the message numbers within a sequence and the destination ensures that the messages are delivered in the right sequence.

Acknowledgements—One important consideration in ensuring reliable communication is to acknowledge the receipt of messages. An acknowledgement is an indication that a message was successfully delivered to the destination. Messages are acknowledged using acknowledgement ranges. Any missing acknowledgement at the source is an indication of a missed message. This is then processed as per the retry specifications at the source. An acknowledgement does not necessarily indicate that the message was processed. This responsibility rests with the application, and will need to use the Fault and Error response mechanism provided by the service bus to report such processing errors.

Message persistence becomes a necessity when needing to ensure reliable message delivery even when any of the intervening infrastructure components crash. Such durability considerations are beyond the basic wire protocol for the communications. As mentioned above (in the discussion about acknowledgements), WS-RM ensures transfer, not processing. Persistence requirements have to do with the storing of the message on the destination until it is processed, and are thus the responsibility of the implementation.

Since persistence is a common aspect of reliable systems, an implementation of WS-RM would typically provide it (at least, as an option). If provided, a typical implementation would only acknowledge transfer after the transferred message was persistently buffered.

It is interesting to note that because persistence is not related to the wire protocol, applications can be programmed with the same simplified communication error-handling model regardless of the persistence capabilities of the system.

WS-Standards for Reliability

Web Services are dependent on communication, even if primarily peer-to-peer, and as with everything else around Web Services the vendor community has come together and defined the ReliableMessaging standards. Any compliant Web Services processing stack, both on the client side and on the service provider side, can process reliable messaging protocols. WS-ReliableMessaging defines the reliability semantics that can be expected and processed in a Web Services environment and the WS-RM Policy specification describes the language to describe the ReliableMessaging requirements.

WS-ReliableMessaging: This specification describes a protocol that allows messages to be delivered reliably between distributed applications in a communication using the SOAP-based protocols. WS-RM is described in a transport-neutral manner allowing it to be implemented using different network transport technologies. To provide for reliable messaging in Web Services, a SOAP binding is defined within this specification.

WS-RM Policy: Reliable Messaging involves the two ends involved in a services communication describing and understanding the requirements well. For example if sequences have to be used or if acknowledgements are required, accordingly, the infrastructure on both ends will ensure the corresponding handshakes and processing happens when sending and receiving the messages. WS-RM Policy is a specification that describes the policy assertions that leverages the WS-Policy framework to enable an RM Source and Destination to describe their requirements for a given reliable message exchange.

The Policy Assertions supported are:

- Spec Version
- Sequence Creation
- Sequence Expiration
- Inactivity Timeout
- Retransmission Interval
- Acknowledgement Interval

The specification also specifies a good mechanism to handle RM faults.

WS-Addressing: WS-Addressing defines a mechanism for identifying generic Web Services addresses that could be used for replies and fault responses. Basically this is a variant of a Web Service, which is meant as an address to send an arbitrary response or fault or message back to a well defined location. WS-Addressing provides a mechanism to describe such locations.

Reliable messaging is one area of Web Services where there is no unanimity yet among the technology vendors and other stake holders. There are standards in place like:

WS-ReliableMessaging: WS-Reliable Messaging is a standard spearheaded by Microsoft, BEA, IBM, and TIBCO. **WS-Reliability** is encouraged by Sun, Sonic, Fujitsu, Hitachi, NEC, and others. WS-Reliability is part of OASIS RM TC. There are efforts underway to try and get the best out of both.

Achieving Reliable Communication through ESB

In an enterprise scenario, the reliability and scalability of an ESB platform (service providers, service consumers, and the ESB communication layers) is extremely critical. Scalability is an attribute of the platform and configured by the deployer. Reliability, though, is an attribute that could be expected by itself from the platform, and also an application could have reliability expectations to service SLAs. The reliability expectations will be specified by the application developer using standards such as WS-ReliableMessaging. The ESB platform will honor these expectations. Additionally, an ESB platform should support the scalability expectations from any deployment.

While reliability expectations can be specified in a standard manner by the SOA applications, ensuring reliability itself is an internal implementation aspect of the ESB platforms. One common implementation approach for ESB platforms is to have a high-performance messaging backbone as its lowest level infrastructure. Messaging platforms offer message delivery guarantees. An ESB services platform built on such messaging platforms can leverage the message delivery guarantees for service communication reliability as well.

The messaging layers of ESB platforms have a high level of message delivery reliability already built in, as shown in the following figure. This would be available even when WS-RM-based assertions are not set. The WS-RM becomes more important when the same service needs to be accessed from outside of the ESB domain as regular web service. Such accesses will happen through an HTTP gateway that is normally a part of ESB platforms.

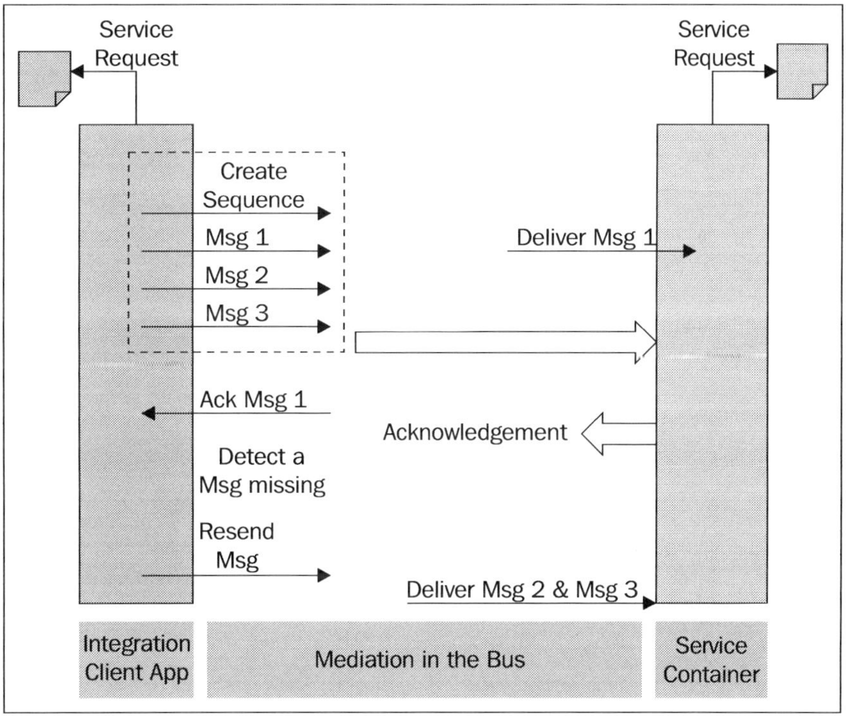

Message platforms have very well defined delivery semantics that include persistence of messages when needed. The message layer includes mechanisms to handle acknowledgements, once-and-only-once delivery semantics, built-in retry mechanisms when a delivery fails, persistence of messages to survive crashes, and such. These will all be implicitly available for the services and service access available on the ESB infrastructure that is built on a messaging platform.

High Availability in ESB—Leveraging the Messaging Platform

ESB platforms being built on messaging backbones have leveraged the high availability capabilities of the messaging system. Most commercial Messaging platforms like TIBCO, Sonic, and IBM MQ Series have strong high availability built into the platform. Some messaging solutions even support failing-over a session when there is an active transaction.

High availability would include ensuring the availability of all parts of the ESB infrastructure: the messaging layer, including the message brokers, client tiers, and the communications among clients, brokers, and destinations. This is in addition to guaranteeing the messaging and reliability semantics such as delivery-exactly-once message reliability under both normal and failure conditions.

The high availability solutions may also include hardware and OS-level capabilities such as RAID, OS clustering software, or third-party HA frameworks in the messaging layer. The expectation from the platform is that the in-process operations/transactions continue to their processing destinations without any costly rollback or recovery time.

Given that ESB platforms leverage the "document flows and gets processed" paradigm, the key infrastructure components will be the documents and their delivery to their destinations. Documents here are delivered as messages in the messaging layer. Any service request is now broken down to a document-type and a delivery address. If these addresses can be logical, with physical resolution itself resolved via late binding just at the time of the actual execution of the request, then this "hiding of the actual address" allows for some creative high availability solutions.

Location Transparency at the Core

In ESB, the services are configured on endpoints. Endpoints have a binding to a specific message destination. The discovery of the specific message destination is made very late at the time of actual invocation of a service, automatically by the infrastructure. The process or a service consumer invokes a service only by using its logical service endpoints. Only when the infrastructure needs to actually "ship" the request to the service, are the actual message destination and other specific details located and used to actually communicate.

The infrastructure would use some domain service or manager in the ESB to locate the "physical address" of a service endpoint—the "logical address" that the process or integration application uses. The address in the ESB will be a destination for the message/document to be delivered. The actual address of any service is registered at the time a service instance is started. And whenever the service needs to to be accessed, the same registry is used to get the physical address for the endpoint.

Smart high availability handling is built into this resolution process. The possible location transparency abilities include:

- The service can be available on any container at any point in time.
- If the current container goes down, a new one could be started and service made available.
- When the load increases, additional containers can be configured.
- The implementation of the service can change and it can be redeployed. This can be done without affecting any of the processes or integration application that access this service.

In such cases, the domain manager, would keep track of the various containers and the services running in each container. (The message/document address is essentially the lowest-level resolution for any service. This is again an infrastructure function, to map a service to a destination/address). Each time a service is accessed, the logical service name is resolved to a physical location and the request is sent to that address. This forms the basis for ESB High Availability.

Multiple, Configurable Interaction Models

Given the location transparency of the services, the interaction models between services and between process and services is extremely loosely coupled. The minimal coupling that exists is also based on interaction configurations. When a service is configured, the endpoint is defined and its bindings to the underlying physical layers such as messaging are also configured. The service consumers though, use only the logical endpoint for the services. This ensures that the service consumers are agnostic to the physical bindings of the service. And for the service itself, at any point the actual runtime or execution environment for the service can be changed—declaratively by just changing the bindings—without in any way impacting the consumers and applications that access the service. The service consumption is configurable in that it needs only the endpoint. And the service itself is also configurable by virtue of the bindings being modifiable at any point.

Even the actual service artefacts are also configurable. When configuring a service, the service artifacts such as class names and JARs are provided. And this could also be modified at any point, again, without affecting any of the consumers and integration applications.

In short, an ESB platform provides for multiple configurable interaction models.

Apart from the location transparency, by abstracting the transport ESB provides for other mediated interaction models including synchronous and asynchronous invocation, publish-and-subscribe-based multi-cast invocation, intelligent routing, and stateful services orchestration.

The location transparency and the flexible interaction models form the basis for the scalability and load balancing capabilities in ESB, even as this builds on the message-oriented middleware models.

Scalability and Performance of ESB

Services and processes in ESB platforms are abstracted behind the ESB domain services. Any consumer of ESB services or processes will only connect to the "domain" and not directly to specific services or processes. This indirection will form the basis for the Reliability and Scalability offerings from an ESB platform.

The location transparency offers Scalability possibility in ESB environments. This could also result in Utility Computing where service can be made available on demand on any container. This requires a high level of configurable service definitions and interactions that ESB anyway offers. While SOA seems to have got a very firm footing in IT organizations, it remains to be seen how the high scalability that Utility Computing offers will be available in ESB. With the advent of SOA, there is a new framework possibly in the making that will accelerate Utility Computing. But one impeding factor, though, is that while SOA provides a very powerful abstraction to provide a common integration fabric for the organization, it still doesn't take away the actual business application execution environments that sit behind this fabric. This is a problem that cannot easily be solved in the case of IT environments with very many application infrastructure platforms (like Java EE, .NET, mainframes, ERP apps, custom applications and more). With the ESB's neutral services framework and the location transparency, this is made possible, though. Someday, ESB will also make possible services grids—very highly scalable and dynamically configurable and reconfigurable services environments.

Something to think about—Application Grids:

- A grid of generic App Server cells (Java EE or .NET)—Each cell is an out-of-the-box Java EE server—with any OS and VM vendor. The application server grid component will run on each cell. Cells can go down and come up at will—grid will be unaffected.
- The work units that run on the grid will be Java EE applications. The grid presents one logical processing environment with a bunch of loosely coupled cells.
- Load distribution and fail-over will be dynamically managed by the grid.
- No single point of failure in the grid. The application server will manage the grid abstraction. Applications available on the grid Distribution are strategy specifiable (what application is available on how many nodes).
- Scheduling and Provisioning managed by the grid.

Implicit Service/framework components:

- Grid-aware naming service
- Application repository—what and where
- Distributed Administration service—for remote administration
- Cluster service—self-organizing, app management, failover++

Missing Pieces:

- Smart Provisioning
- Ease of Management/Administration of the Grid
- Binary management of all nodes on the grid
- We need a Federated Naming Service and a Federated App naming service

Load Balancing and Load Scaling in ESB

We have seen how the abstract address of a service in an endpoint-driven service ESB environment helps with balancing load for any given service. The service can be configured on multiple containers and allow taking on higher number of requests for the service.

ESB offers another interesting possibility with regard to parallel processing. ESB systems being message (document flow)-oriented, a service request is essentially a message sent to the service's endpoint. And at that endpoint, there will be some infrastructure component that waits for the response message from the service. This would mean that by sending multiple messages (for service requests) at any given time, concurrent execution of services is processing. Enabling parallel processing of parts of a given process is as shown in the following figure.

The parallel branches can be triggered one after the other and then the process could wait for the response messages from the invoked services. If a program is managing the concurrent parallel execution of the parts of a common process, then this program will need to have the logic for collating the responses and determining when the process could continue in its path—after ensuring that all parallel parts have completed. In processes engines, this could become more implicit. The process engine when detecting parallel branches in the defined process can trigger the service requests from each branch and then wait on the responses.

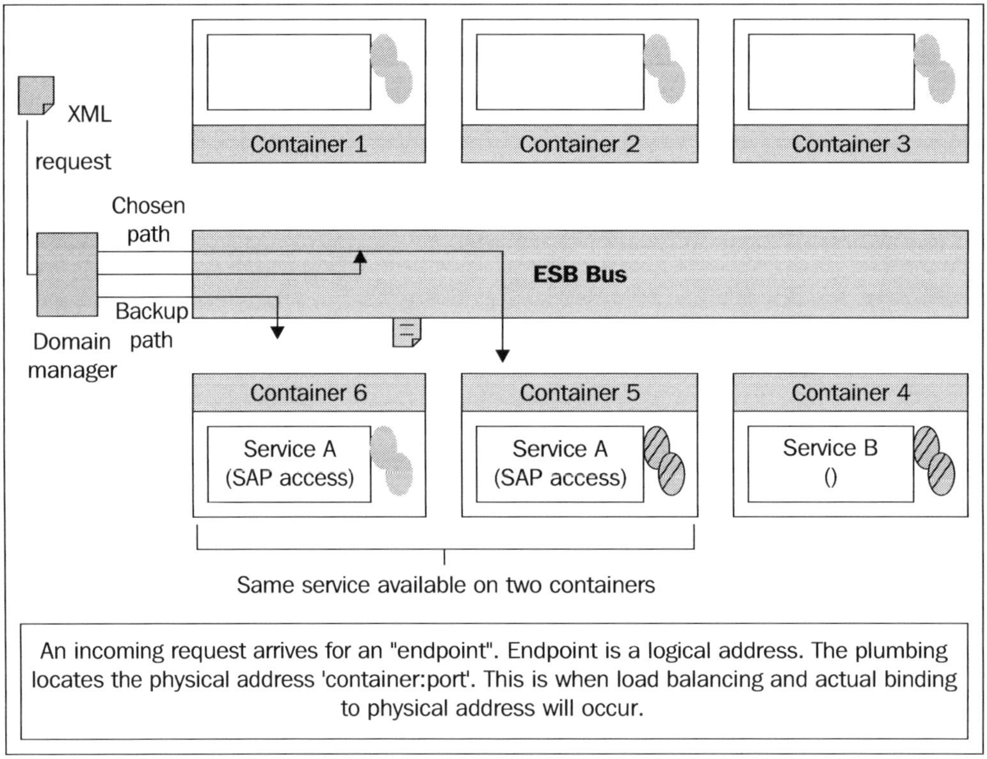

With Load Balancing as the basic functionality, a complete scalable infrastructure is made possible in an ESB. This includes reliable guaranteed message delivery, clustering of the various individual components such as the domain server or the services registry, continuous and high availability of the whole platform, high performance built into every component of the infrastructure with the most critical components of service containers and the messaging and communications infrastructure at the core. Additionally high-performance federated messaging domains play a key role in ensuring reliable and performing interactions in a multi-geography widely distributed enterprise.

Looking at one of the leading players in the space, some of the functionality provided is:

- **Continuous availability**: Provides high availability and transactional fault tolerance. Completely transparent to services, in-process transactions continue without recovery process delay or rollback. Eliminates operational risk of lost data without expensive RAID, OS clustering software, or third-party HA frameworks in the messaging layer.
- **High performance**: Industry-leading high-throughput and low-latency communications, including high-volume/high-availability scenarios (durable, persistent) and high QoS scenarios (durable, persistent, transacted). Provides fast service response at a lower cost of hardware for a given throughput requirement.
- **Clustering**: Scales service throughput and ensures constant response time by load balancing over clustered servers. Also, allows deployments to scale to support large numbers of messages, users, and applications.
- **Dynamic Routing (DRA)**: Supports global service namespace across large, distributed deployments. Routes data and process flows across clusters and sites without manual gateway reconfiguration. The specific load-balancing algorithms are specific to the ESB platforms. Typically, they will support round-robin balancing or available-resources-based balancing.

Control and Management of ESB

ESB being an infrastructure platform targeted at enterprise usage, control and management of the platform are necessary functionality that would be expected. Managing ESB infrastructure includes managing the domain, containers, and services, and monitoring and configuring the reliability, security, and performance of the platform.

Broadly, the management and control involves:

- Configuring the domain and the containers
- Managing the lifecycle of service types, services and processes, from deployment through configuring and monitoring the service and process instances
- Monitoring the business processes and services activity and operational statistics
- Securing the platform
- Tuning and optimizing the platform

The manageability starts from setting up and configuring the domain and containers to be able to set up service types and service instances and managing the lifecycle of a container or a service. As the ESB platform is still emerging with any standards required yet to be defined, in general ESB will follow the Web Services standards, including management. With Java being one of the implementation choices for building ESB infrastructure, Java management standards including JMX may also be relevant. Other existing distributed management technologies such as SNMP will also bring managing Web Services and ESB into their fold. Let us take a quick overview of the relevant management standards and then understand the specifics of managing an ESB platform.

Controlling and Monitoring the Services

Control is essentially the management power made available to the users and systems administrators. Given the inherently distributed nature of SOA applications, if to this mediation power is also made available, then this puts quite some challenge in managing the services, processes and the instances. This will require that the service containers be configured remotely. It will require that a given container configuration be "replicated" quickly to create more "instances" of the containers to take on additional load. It will require that the services and processes be configured separately, and declaratively be made available on multiple containers. And over and above everything, it will require that all the administration be done remotely.

Good "Control" implementations will rely on a logical deployment model that defines the containers, their operating environment, and the service to be made available on the containers. Once defined, these can then be "bound" to physical runtime environments without any additional configuration. Once bound, all the services and operating environment defined in the logical model are available in the physical container.

The model could be extended to individual services as well, where the services are configured once. They are given a name and an endpoint and any initialization or environment parameters are defined once. Once this service with a name is defined, instances can be deployed onto any number of containers.

In addition to the goal to automate management as much as possible, it will also be necessary to enable humans to investigate problems, find root causes, and take action to correct the issues that are discovered. Where the management infrastructure is automated, it codifies the rules that drive simpler diagnosis/action scenarios in a form that is machine readable. This infrastructure may also log and/or warehouse request content for later analysis or auditing.

Management Information Standards

Three generic multi-platform management standards are Java Management Extensions (JMX), SNMP (Simple Network Management Protocol), and Distributed Management Task Force (DMTF). SNMP is a standard to be aware of given its very wide acceptance in the management domain over the years and also extensive existing management infrastructure that uses SNMP—though SNMP may not have anything specific for the management of Web Services and distributed services over ESB.

The Java Management Extensions (JMX) technology is a technology standard developed by the Java Community Process for management and monitoring of infrastructure and applications using Java to build the management solutions. JMX is domain independent and can be used to build management solutions for platforms ranging from legacy systems to those that may come up in the future. JMX management architecture provides for three layers—Instrumentation, Agent, and Remote Management. Instrumentation is the lowest level of management operation layer that collects data and manages any administered unit or entity. Agent is a proxy for the management tools and front ends to work with the instrumentation tier. Remote Management is an extension or mechanism for tools to be able to access the agents and the instrumentation remotely.

The managed resources or entities such as applications, devices, or services, are instrumented using Java objects called Managed Beans (MBeans). MBeans expose their management interfaces, composed of attributes and operations, through a JMX agent for remote management and monitoring. The main component of a JMX agent is the MBean server. MBean server is the repository of all MBeans—kind of like the boot-strap for the management domain. A JMX agent includes a set of pre-defined services for handling MBeans.

Remote Management is provided via Protocol Adaptors. Protocol adaptors and standard connectors make a JMX agent accessible from remote management applications outside the agent's Java Virtual Machine (JVM).

As with most other aspects of Web Services, OASIS is spearheading the standards definition activity in the area of Web Services management. Interestingly, there are two very different views to Web Services and Management:

1. Management of the Web Services
2. Management of any distributed infrastructure/applications/domains using Web Services

The OASIS Web Services Distributed Management TC is defining two sets of specifications, one for each of these aspects: Web Services Distributed Management: Management Using Web Services (MUWS) and Web Services Distributed Management: Management of Web Services (MOWS) specifications.

Another organization spearheading management technologies is DMTF (Distributed Management Task Force), via its working group formed out of the member companies, it develops various documents, guidelines, and standards specifications for Distributed Management. These include CIM (Common Information model) and Web-Based Enterprise Management (WBEM). These are standards for distributed management using Web Services—though the view is one of managing any distributed infrastructure, and there is no specific description of capabilities for managing web services themselves. However, as these are by and large domain independent, the same approach could be used for managing web services and their operating environments and infrastructure as well. DMTF is adopted by many distributed application infrastructure vendors including Oracle, Microsoft, and Sun.

CIM is a common data model of an implementation-neutral schema for describing overall management information in a network/enterprise environment. WBEM is a set of management and Internet standard technologies developed to unify the management of enterprise computing environments. WBEM is built on other DMTF standards including CIM. The Common Information Model (CIM) provides a common definition of management information for systems, networks, applications and services, and allows for vendor extensions. CIM-XML is an extension of CIM, and as a part of WBEM, provides the Representation of CIM using XML. WBEM Discovery using Service Location Protocol (SLP) and WBEM Universal Resource Identifier (URI) mapping are two standards that provide a way for applications to identify and interact with WBEM management systems, capitalizing on existing standards and protocols to enable rapid development and deployment of management solutions.

Infrastructure for ESB Management

ESB is a distributed services infrastructure. To be able to deliver such a platform, a distributed management framework will be an inherent part of such platform. The platform will include a domain manager and the containers that will need to be configured and managed by the management solution that is part of the platform. The management solution will include tools and agents. The tools part offers the management front end for the users and administrators, and the management agents and utilities will be part of each container and infrastructure component that provides the necessary management functions pertinent to that component.

Some of the common management functions that can be expected from an ESB platform will include centralized management support, remote administration of the domain and the containers, configuration of the components, deployment of the application artifacts, configuration of the services, monitoring, and qudiing and logging. While there are no mandated standards yet, the more the standards in any ESB platform, the greater the flexibility in managing the platform. Best-of-breed tools from other vendors could be used for managing the platform and also enterprise-wide multi-infrastructure management tools such as Tivoli or Unicenter could be used to administer the ESB platform along with the other infrastructure such as database servers in the organization.

Let's look at some of the management functions that will be expected from an ESB platform, highlighted in the following figure.

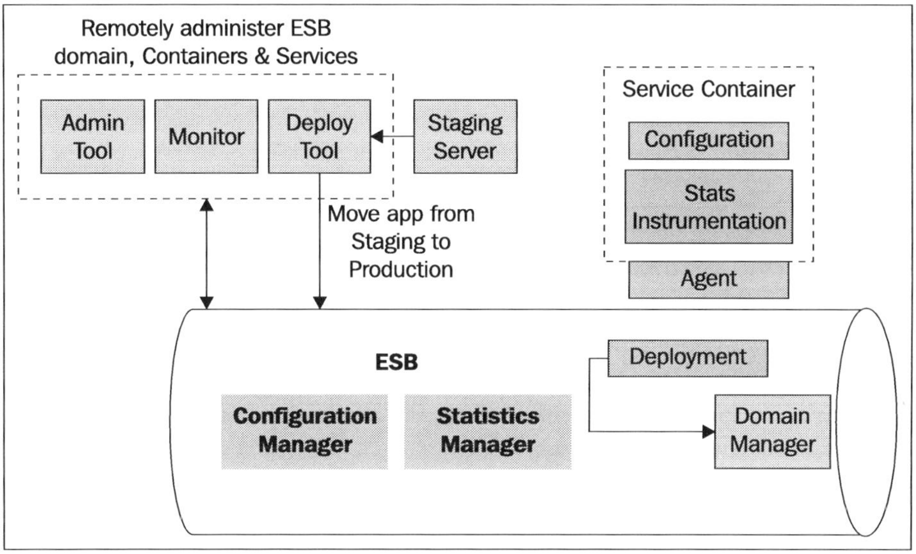

Centralized Configuration: Built-in framework for managing ESB infrastructure and services. Supports management of a large deployment from a single console. This starts from being able to remotely configure the various components of an ESB infrastructure. Once configured, it manages the containers and service lifecycles from starting and stopping through configuring and optimizing.

Monitoring: Information on the status of various parts of the infrastructure and the service containers and services is imperative to effective upkeep of the ESB platform. This includes the availability stats and statistics on various parts and their accesses. Number of active sessions on the platform, number of services accessed, average service times, uptime of various containers and components and such would form the monitoring data of an ESB platform.

Service Interactions: Configurable control of service interaction. This allow modification of data and process flow without re-coding or shutdown of running services. It provides flexibility to adapt SOA to changing business requirements.

Distributed, Dynamic Deployment: Supports distributed deployment of services and their configuration. It provides the ability to independently scale, reconfigure, and redeploy individual services without disrupting other operations.

Staged Deployment: In an enterprise-wide services platform, updating the services and various application artifacts without bringing the whole platform down becomes a major functional requirement. This will need good support for taking an application into production through a staging area. Utilities to simplify this process will be necessary to support deployment and migration of ESB services and processes from development to test and deployment environments. This solves the problem of service and process upgrade management for large-scale SOA deployments.

Centralized Auditing and Logging: Central logging and auditing of services, faults, process status, etc. This provides the ability to monitor and diagnose behaviors of complex distributed systems.

Security and Reliability: Managing Security involves configuring the secure communication channels, security certificates, and user repositories.

Management standards that ESB could use depend on the specific technologies used in the platform. In Java-based environments, the underlying management infrastructure is most likely based on JMX. Additionally, to fit into generic SOA monitoring and QoS solutions, support for simple Web Services management standards may be required.

Application Development Considerations

In this chapter, we have taken a comprehensive look at various aspects of an ESB infrastructure. For an organization adopting SOA, both the infrastructure and the application are equally important.

Integration Application Constituents

Solutions on ESB, or for that matter any SOA application, essentially involve developing the services and the business processes that use the services. In some cases, there could be custom integration applications that may access services from outside of business processes. The list of typical application artifacts includes:

- **Service Types**: A generic handling or program provided for a class of services. This is defined once, and multiple services can be configured. Each service of a given type is differentiated by some initialization properties or parameters for that service. These parameters are provided when defining the service.
- **Services**: Services are the business functions that are made available on the bus for consumption by the integration applications and business processes. These services may be self contained, or an instance of a reusable service type.
- **Service Interfaces (WSDL)**: Each service in ESB will have a well-defined interface. These may be standard interfaces such as WSDL or could be proprietary platform-specific interfaces. The service name, its operations, and the signature (inputs, outputs, faults), its protocol bindings and the access address/IP-port/URL.
- **Adapters**: Services typically may access other applications or systems in the enterprise. This needs adapters to be able to connect to these systems. Adapters provide a common API or interface using which many different systems and application platforms such as mainframes, SAP, BAAN, Java EE, etc. could be accessed.
- **Document Schemas (XSD)**: In an XML-centric environment, applications will also benefit by using XML to describe elements, provide information and transfer information. It is preferable that all business data is represented in XML. In this mode, the structure of these XML documents needs to be described. This is done using XSDs. Any project will have a set of well defined schemas that is used to define service interfaces and to describe the documents that are interchanged between various application components.
- **Transformations**: XSLT and Xquery; as we saw, ESB environments have powerful support for document transformations in the bus. Whether the documents are transformed in the bus or explicitly in a process, this will require the definition of the transformation rules. The standard way of doing this is using XSLT or XQuery.
- **Content-Based Routing**: These are like mini-process files. These define the routing rules based on the content of a document. The CBR files are typically configured on endpoints themselves.
- **Business Processes**: Next to services, the Business Processes are the application artifacts that hold direct business processing logic and rules. The business processes are the primary purpose of any SOA environment. Everything else essentially enables this ultimate goal.

- **Deployment Configuration Map/Plan**: Based on the application artifacts and the physical distribution of the organization, a deployment configuration needs to be defined. Unlike other artifacts, this is not a physical project "file". This is just a description of how all the project artifacts will be taken into the runtime production environment.

ESB—Application Design Approach

ESB being a technology instance for SOA, all the SOA design approaches will come in handy here.

Some of the common SOA design patterns include:

- **Business Patterns**: The interaction between users, businesses, and data. Includes Information Aggregation, Process workflow, and Extended-Enterprise (Business-to-business) patterns.
- **Integration Patterns**: Tie multiple Business patterns together. This includes the Data Aggregation and Process aggregation (workflow) patterns.
- **Composite Patterns**: Commonly occurring combinations of Business Patterns. Examples include Buy-side-hub, Sell-side-hub and other E-Commerce patterns.
- **Application Patterns**: Conceptual layout describing how the application components and the data within the business pattern and integration pattern interact. Includes Asynchronous Services, Publish-Subscribe Services, Synchronous Services, Component Services, and Serial Service Orchestration.
- **Runtime Patterns**: Logical middleware structure that supports an Application pattern. Depicts the middleware nodes, their roles and the interfaces between the nodes.

ESB patterns, while building on the SOA patterns, have few specific considerations. The primary consideration is that ESB is based on a document-flow-based paradigm towards Services, Service Orientation, and Processes. Given this, design of any ESB based application will need to completely ingrain this into the design psyche—that there are documents and document flows. This warrants that any design exercise should start with a complete understanding and design of the data and data flows. Analyze the data in various systems and services and model the data via well described schemas.

In an ESB application, all Components are Services with a WSDL interface, either Custom Services or Generic Services—to ensure reuse with all services maintained in a Central Repository of Service. The application must use Routing and Transformation Logic, which also must be implemented as generic reusable services. Like any other SOA application, ESB applications will also have a Services Orchestration Layer above the ESB layer to automate business processes—but in ESB the processes may run in the "fabric" as opposed to running in a central Orchestration Server or Process Engine. This will require few additional design considerations.

Data Transformations: Once there are well-defined data structures that capture the business data in various systems and departments in the organization, given that departmental systems existed in "isolation" first, this could very well mean that similar business data is represented differently in different departments or systems. This begets the need for common "translation" of data from one department's representation to another department's.

Considering that integration applications essentially start with existing enterprise applications and solutions that need to be integrated into enterprise wide business processes, getting the existing applications onto the ESB platform would be the first task. To enable this, there are design patterns such as the *Service On-Ramp* and *Service Off-Ramp* patterns.

The ESB process model, where the process runs in the fabric as opposed to running in an orchestration server or process engine, offers interesting design possibilities. In this mode, while there may be a well-defined definition of the process much like what is needed in a process server, the process does have a strong document-flow-based processing flavor. In such processes, the focus is a "single" document that is supposed to be flowing through the service steps and getting updated. From a solution design standpoint, this approach is different from a conventional "procedure"-like approach to business processes, where the process expects inputs, has process state and variables to manipulate through the process steps, and at the end there is a return/output from the process. In the ESB process case, the design is essentially around a document that needs to "flow" through various steps.

Security and Transaction Considerations: Ensure that there is very little programmatic handling of both. Use the standard approaches where possible to ensure that there is no vendor lock-in. Integration applications in an SOA environment should ideally separate the logical security model from the physical security. The SOA artifacts, processes, and services shouldn't be programmed for specific security and transaction handling. The security and transactions should be managed outside of the actual service program code, either declaratively as configuration options when setting up the service and process instances, or via the more standard approach of specifying the Security and Reliable Messaging assertions via WS-S and WS-RM.

Comparing ESB with Other Technologies

ESB provides the flexible connectivity and description that Web Services offers, the legacy systems access that EAI provides, and the manageability and performance that Application Platforms provide. Beyond this, ESB provides the enterprise-wide high-performing massively distributed platform, services mediation, and control in such a distributed environment.

ESB—Improves upon Web Services

ESB and Web Services are very complementary. ESB never contradicts Web Services; it only extends it. XML-based wire exchanges are designed for remote access across heterogeneous systems; WS-* standards are used for reliability and security.

XML-Based Data Easily Exchanged

As we saw earlier in this chapter, XML-based data interchange leverages the extensively well-defined XML document structure and semantics via the plethora of widely accepted standards in this space, and by the omnipresent XML-handling utilities and infrastructure. Both ESB and regular Web Services rely quite extensively on XML, both to represent the business data and also for the internal plumbing data interchanges. Requests and responses are typically represented in XML. The service interfaces are represented in XML. System configuration data is represented in XML. The actual middleware exchanges are represented in XML (SOAP). XML is everywhere.

Designed for Remote Access, Across Heterogeneous Platforms

Both ESB and Web Services are inherently designed for access from remote environments—the service and its consumer will be on different machines, and often accessible via a WAN with no assumptions whatsoever on the operating environments on either of the two ends. ESB takes this a step further by even abstracting the ends themselves. Unlike regular web services where the connection is directly established from the client (consumer) to the machine where the service is running, in ESB the connection is established to some intermediary (the ESB mediation layer). And the mediation then performs value-added infrastructure services before routing the request to the right service endpoint, which could again be anywhere in the network (accessible on the ESB domain).

Leverage WS-RM for Reliable Interoperability

WS-RM is a rapidly emerging standard that defines reliable communications. Given that most service accesses may happen via unreliable links in the WAN or still worse over the public Internet, specifying and actually providing the reliability semantics becomes imperative. An aggravating factor is cases where a series of documents/ messages are required to perform a business process, and there are sequencing expectations. Reliability could also mean time criticality—where if a message doesn't arrive by a certain time, there may be a certain "staleness" to the data and the business processes might warrant that that request not be processed. So, some timeout mechanisms need to be specified. In case of communication failure, retries could be attempted. This again is to be specified based on the business expectations from the system. It may be OK to retry just once, or a few times or several times. This is a business requirements-based decision.

WS-RM provides for specifying all of these as "expectations" from the service. The requesting end (consumer) and the service end, it they support WS-RM, will ensure that these reliability requirements are met, with sufficient handling when they fail—like aborting the request and notifying the requester of the failure. Both ESB and WS platforms fully support WS-RM.

Security using WS-S

While ESB platforms may have own proprietary security models, they do fully support the WS-Security standards. This ensures that Web Services and ESB both have a common security model.

Where does ESB better Web Services?

Interestingly, the application's view of a simple Web Services-based integration application and an elaborate ES-based application environment need not be too different. As the business processes may be defined per the BPEL standard, and services described using WSDL, standards based adapters used to connect to legacy systems, and so on. The difference essentially is in the configuration, deployment, manageability and, the internal scalability and performance.

Web Services, being more about the wire protocols, do not have any definition of a services container as such. There is no notion of a set of service containers forming a "bus". This is where ESB steps in and provides this abstraction—without in any way modifying the base application models using BPEL and WSDL. ESB provides the constructs to configure and manage the environment and more importantly, provides a simple mechanism to deploy the services and processes and monitor them. In the Java world, there are standards that are leveraged to build the service containers, as shown in the following figure.

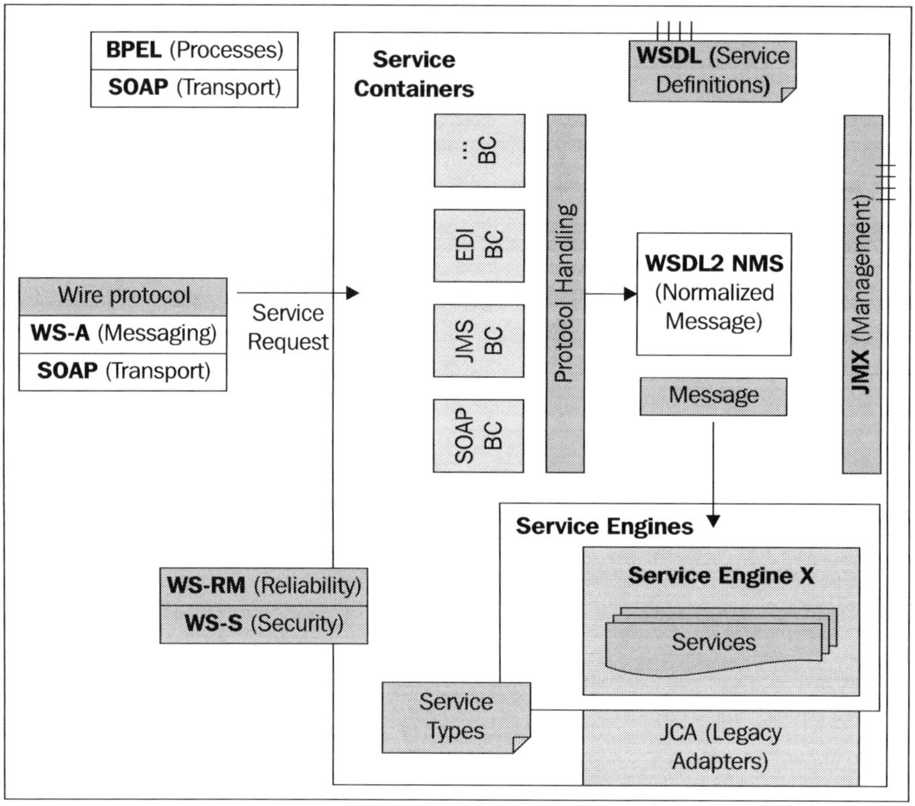

Given that ESB is a platform that has control of all parts of an interaction between the service consumer or process and the service itself, mediation services are possible. In a simple Web Services model, this is not possible, as there is no infrastructure component sitting between the service consumer and the service. Therefore, value-added mediation and control capabilities such as late binding of service physical address, transformation of data on the wire, or content-based routing are not possible in Web Services—while they are inherently supported in ESB platforms.

In Web Services, as there is no intermediary platform as such, there will not be any internal scalability or performance capabilities. ESB being based on a high performance communication backbone, with elaborate service containers and mediation framework can provide a high level of scalability and performance.

Higher Level of Abstraction in ESB

One aspect of services is to abstract out as much of the actual implementation as possible to ensure that the service can be easily be reconfigured, redeployed, and internal implementations changed without affecting any of the "consumers" of the service. This is possible by having a well-defined contract via its WSDL interface and having a simple endpoint URL that is NOT the actual service. The URL should point to a plumbing infrastructure component that does the actual routing. Conventional web services do not support the model; the endpoint is generally directly accesses the service implementation. That makes a hard binding to the deployed and configured service instance. ESB systems typically abstract the actual endpoint behind an elaborate back-end service bus.

This makes the service consumers and service endpoints very loosely coupled—providing a much greater flexibility. This is not that easily possible in simple Web Services, where the binding port directly refers to the service itself, and not to any abstract logical endpoint or address.

EAI: Cannot Span Integration Brokers

EAI solutions are based on Integration brokers. The primary purpose of EAI platforms is to provide simple connectivity to legacy systems. These are typically deployed inside a single company—inside the firewall. Services and processes cannot seamlessly span integration brokers. While some EAI vendors now do talk about federation of Integration Brokers, they would still suffer from the primary focus being on programmatic connectivity to legacy systems than to provide access to services.

Application Servers: Hub-and-Spoke Model Limits Scalability

Application platforms such as Java EE and .NET are primarily targeted to host applications and data- and UI-intensive business applications. Such applications are quite likely to be providing the services that are integrated in an SOA environment. The application platforms are exceptionally good for hosting business logic in a component model and serving web pages. Scalability is well addressed within the context of one server instance via clusters. But these form a very tightly coupled cluster that will most likely depend on intense back-end housekeeping communications either among the cluster nodes or with a data repository.

In a widely distributed enterprise, the application platform instances cannot form a functional single cluster. This would mean that there will be multiple application server instances in the enterprise, and for this to provide a single SOA environment, the instances will need to interact with each other. Application servers do not do a good job at providing a good communication infrastructure for such interactions.

Further, there is no single services namespace that Application Servers offer. Each server instance may have its own services registry. Though technically there could be shared registries, again owing to protocols that were more designed for server LANs, these would not work very well over a WAN.

The Application Platforms have an elaborate deployment and configuration process to get an application up and running. This also means that updating the Services would require disruptive re-configuration and re-deployment.

ESB—Helps Avoid Vendor Lock-Ins

In an ESB environment, there is the infrastructure provided by the vendor and then there is the application. Typical ESB application artifacts will include: services (most likely wrappers that access some legacy system), XML schemas and transformations, and processes. A few off-the-shelf service types may be available like the transform service or a database service as in the case of Sonic ESB. While there are standards to describe a service and to invoke a service, there are not standards yet on implementing services. In the Java world, standards such as JBI are emerging that may help; but this has to gain some traction. So, vendor lock-ins can occur essentially in the implementation of services and processes, wherein the same services and processes will not work in another SOA environment.

This lock-in for the services can be minimized with some good practices. The services' implementation programming code may be in popular languages such as Java, C#, or VB.NET. If designed well, a thin layer that implements any vendor-specific interfaces will alone have the vendor lock-in. When porting from one vendor's platform to another, this thin layer alone will need to be re-written. The rest of the application artifacts can be reused as is.

It is often said that by writing Web Services they become reusable and can be made to run on any platform. One has to understand that just by having a WSDL that describes a service, a Web Service does not just happen. In addition to the plumbing that processes the SOAP requests, there will be the actual service implementation that is sitting behind the plumbing. And this will be platform dependent.

The other major application artifact, the Business Process, has much stronger standards traction. Either the vendor already supports these standards or can at the least be easily exportable to standard BPEL. So vendor lock-in can be kept very minimal here. Again, in the absence of absolute support for standards, good practices will need to be established to try to avoid using vendor-specific capabilities provided in the proprietary process models.

The XML schemas and transformations used in an application are all absolutely standard. Though vendors may support some extensions, say to the standard XSLT, these can easily be avoided to ensure that there is no lock-in. These are probably the easiest to migrate from one vendor's platform to another vendor's.

Of course, in the absence of key standards in the ESB platforms, today there is no out-of-the box portability from one ESB vendor to another. Come to think of it, there are no common definitions of what an ESB is. Even so, with ESB, a good amount of it is possible today. More would be possible in the next few releases as WSDL2 and JBI gain more traction. Even today, with some simple design considerations, the ESB application can be kept as vendor neutral as possible, minimizing the porting effort needed when moving onto a different vendor's.

Standards being the key enabler to minimize vendor lock-ins, it is interesting to note the power of standards here. Just as Open Source does offer alternatives to commercial vendors, Standards enable each commercial vendor being an alternative to the others. To the users and enterprises, both offer the same benefit of rapid "commoditization" of the space. The standards adoption is driven largely by the uptake from the consumers (developers and infrastructure decision makers). So, if there is a push on standards from the developers and IT managers, all ESB vendors will rapidly adopt the same. At least in the case of ESB, there are two key standards that have decent traction—JBI (with WSDL2) and BPEL. This would make it possible for a complete ESB application to move from one ESB platform to another—just as Java EE did in the Application Server space.

Messaging Platforms: ESB Extends the Message Model

ESB platforms typically rely on a messaging-based communication backbone. Messaging platforms are used for delivering messages to destinations and they do not prescribe nor assume the nature of processing involved on the messages. ESB systems, however, have the service execution as their primary objective. That there is a message underneath is incidental and internal to the platform. The ESB infrastructure interacts with the messaging layer and will direct the request to the service by invoking the service operation requested. The messaging layer here is just a means to the end objective—of providing a services infrastructure to host and invoke services.

Extending ESB to Partners

With the highly simplified connectivity that the Internet ushered in, enterprises are rapidly engaging with partners and vendors electronically. In this landscape, once an enterprise adopts ESB for integrating the various systems and solutions in the enterprise, it would be a very logical next step to get even the partner interactions into the same enterprise integration fold. In determining operational needs for partner interactions, there are three levels and areas to include. The first level is the overall operational approach to solving large enterprise-level interactions, then enterprise to small business interactions, and small business to small business interactions.

The typical partner interactions are document-centric rather than remote-procedure-centric. ESB would fit in very well in such partner interactions by its document/ message-based interaction models, as shown in the following figure. This can easily be extended to support the conversational interactions that are common in B2B space. Here, any partner interaction is defined by business processes and agreements between the partners. These will typically involve a series of exchanges, spread over an extended interval, for any given trade transaction.

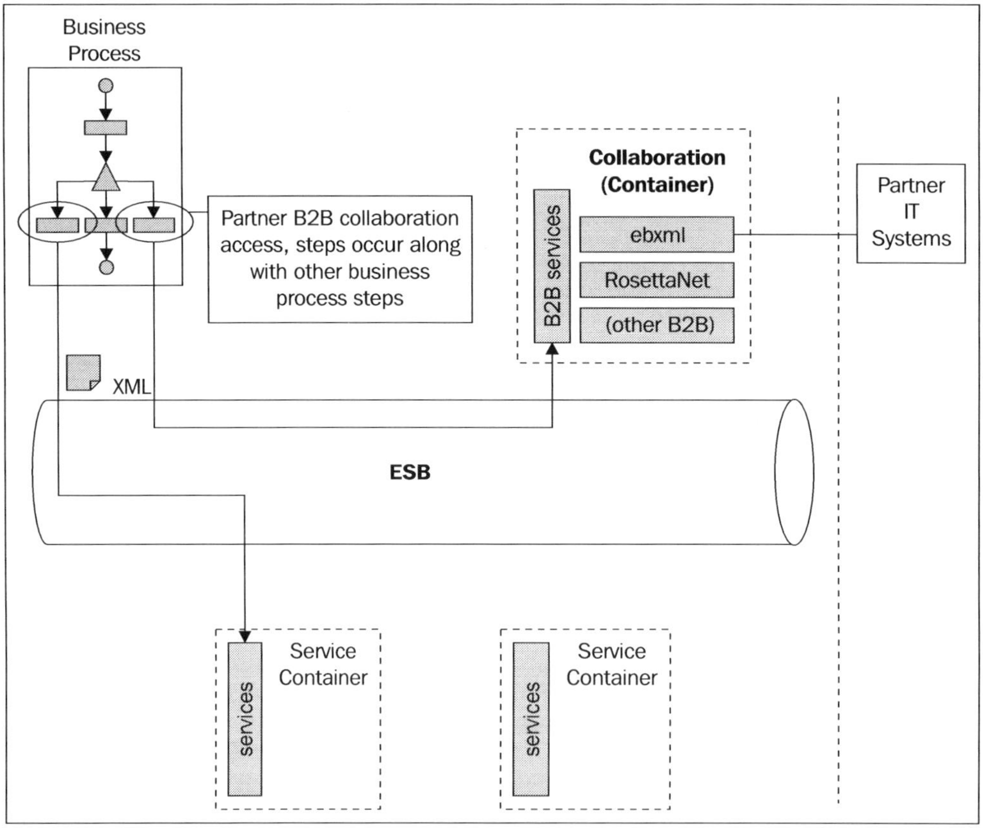

Just looking at a business-to-business interaction, there may be multiple technologies that may be available ranging from the EDI and AS2 type interactions, to Web Services, to a more modern Collaboration Framework such as RosettaNet and ebXML. While Web Services provide a simple interactive point-to-point solution that can address the case of atomic exchanges between two partners, when there are multiple partners and complex business interactions and collaborations to be modeled, simple Web Services will be found lacking. In such cases, more evolved electronic business platforms such as ebXML will be needed. These provide secure, reliable business-to-business exchanges through open eBusiness architecture. They provide for well-defined interchange framework, that supports clearly and unambiguously describing the interactions, including the document structures for the exchanges, the protocols for the interactions and the sequence of interactions in any business conversation.

ebXML as a representative B2B technology includes:

- Business Processes—defined as models in UMM, scripted in XML
- Business Messages—content agnostic - exchanged using ebMS
- Collaboration Protocol Profile and Agreement—specifies parameters for businesses to interface with each other—expressed in XML
- Messaging Layer—moves the actual XML data between trading partners—ebMS
- Core components—library of pre-defined business vocabulary artifacts
- Collaboration Registry—provides a "container" for process models, vocabularies, assembly templates, partner profiles and discovery

One aspect in these interactions is that they are focused on documents flowing between partners. This fits in very nicely with ESB. In ESB messages and documents flow through the bus and get processed. This can easily be extended to include documents being sent to a partner as a part of a bigger business process. Now if the ESB process environment can be made aware of the B2B specifics, such as the specific interaction types in an ebXML or RosettaNet exchange, then the steps in a business process can be more integrated into the ESB. Like for example, as part of an order processing step, can actually include B2B calls to a supplier to supply parts, and the process can actually wait for the confirmation of shipment before proceeding further, say with a build work order handling step.

Summary

In this chapter, we saw how ESB provides a concrete infrastructure for SOA, extending the simple services model to include a robust service bus with extensive mediation functionality.

ESB extends the omnipresent P2P model of Web Services. We saw how ESB provides the middleware functions for SOA via its communication backbone, mediation services, and its services infrastructure. ESB leverages Web Services standards where possible—though standards are yet to come up in the ESB service runtimes space. Until then there will be limitations in terms of portability of applications from one vendor's ESB platform to another.

In summary, ESB is pre-built SOA infrastructure, with enterprise-grade capabilities, generalized support for variety of integration tasks, implementing and reinforcing architectural best practices, suitable for individual projects or massively distributed integration projects. ESB allows enterprises to integrate applications across the extended enterprise using a standards-based, service-oriented architecture (SOA).

11
Loosely Coupling Services

In this chapter we will explore how service virtualization through the Service Bus of the Oracle SOA Suite can be used to deliver more loosely coupled services.

Coupling

Coupling is a measure of how dependent one service is upon another. The more closely one service depends on another service, the more tightly coupled they are. There have been a number of efforts to formalize metrics for coupling and they all revolve around the same basic items. These are:

- **Number of input data items**: This is basically the number of input parameters of the service.
- **Number of output data items**: It is the output data of the service.
- **Dependencies on other services**: It is the number of services called by this service.
- **Dependencies of other services on this service**: It is the number of services that invoke this service.
- **Use of shared global data**: It is the number of shared data items used by this service. This may include database tables or shared files.
- **Temporal dependencies**: Dependencies on other services being available at specific times.

Let us examine how each of these measures may be applied to our service interface. The principles below are relevant to all services, but widely reused services have a special need for all of the items.

Number of input data items

A service should only accept, as input, the data items required to perform the service being requested. Additional information should not be passed into the service because this creates unnecessary dependencies on the input formats. This economy of input allows the service to focus on only the function it is intended to provide and does not require it to understand unnecessary data formats. The best way to isolate the service from changes in data formats that it does not use is not to require the service to be aware of those data formats.

For example, a credit rating service should only require sufficient information to identify the individual being rated. Additional information such as the amount of credit being requested or the type of goods or services for which a loan is required is not necessary for the credit rating service to perform its job.

> Services should accept only the data required to perform their function and nothing more.

When talking about reducing the number of data items input or output from a service, we are talking about the service implementation, not a logical service interface that may be implemented using a canonical data model. The canonical data model may have additional attributes not required by a particular service, but these should not be part of the physical service interface.

Number of output data items

In the same way that a service should not accept inputs that are unnecessary for the function it performs, a service should not return data that is related only to its internal operation. Exposing such data as part of the response data will create dependencies on the internal implementation of the service that are not necessary.

Sometimes a service needs to maintain state between requests. **State** implies that state information must be maintained at least in the client of the service, so that it can identify the state required to the service when making further requests, but often the state information in the client is just an index into the state information held in the service. We will return to this subject later in this chapter.

[Services should not return public data that relates to their own internal processing.]

Dependencies on other services

Generally reuse of other services to create a new composite service is a good thing. However dependencies on other services does increase the degree of coupling because there is a risk that changes in those services may impact the composite service and hence any services with dependencies on the composite service. We can reduce the risk that this poses by limiting our use of functionality in other services to just that required by the composite.

[Services should reduce the functionality required of other services to the minimum required for their own functionality.]

For example, a dispatching service may decide to validate the address it receives. If this functionality is not specified as being required, because for example all addresses are validated elsewhere, then the dispatching service has an unnecessary dependency that may cause problems in the future.

Dependencies of other services on this service

Having a widely used service is great for reuse but the greater the number of services that make use of this service then the greater impact a change in this service will have on other services. Extra care must be taken with widely reused services to ensure that their interfaces are as stable as possible. This stability can be provided by following the guidelines in this section.

[Widely reused services should focus their interface on just the functionality needed by clients and avoid exposing any unnecessary functions or data.]

Use of shared global data

Shared global data in the service context is often through dependencies on a shared resource such as data in a database. Such use of shared data structures is subversive to good design because it does not appear in the service definitions and so the owners of the shared data may be unaware of the dependency. Effectively this is an extra interface into the service. If this is not documented then the service is very vulnerable to the shared data structure being changed unknowingly. Even if the shared data structure is well documented, any changes required must still be synchronized across all users of the shared data.

[Avoid use of shared global data in services unless absolutely necessary. If it is absolutely necessary then the dependency needs to be clearly documented in all users of the shared data. A services data should only be manipulated through its defined interface.]

Temporal dependencies

Not all service requests require an immediate response. Often a service can be requested and the response may be returned later. This is a common model in message based systems and allows for individual services to be unavailable without impacting other services. Use of queuing systems allows temporal or time decoupling of services, so that two communicating services do not have to be available at the same instant in time, the queue allowing messages to be delivered when the service is available rather than when the service is requested.

[Use asynchronous message interfaces to reduce dependencies of one service on the availability of another.]

Reducing coupling in stateful services

A **stateful service** maintains context for a given client between invocations. When using stateful services, we always need to return some kind of state information to the client. To avoid unnecessary coupling, this state information should always be opaque. By opaque we mean that it should have no meaning to the client other than as a reference that must be returned to the service when requesting follow on operations. We will examine how this may be accomplished later in this section.

A common use of state information in a service is to preserve the position in a search that returns more results than can reasonably be returned in a single response. Another use of state information might be to perform correlation between services that have multiple interactions such as between a bidding service and a bidding client.

Whatever the reason, the first question when confronted with the need for state in a service is to investigate ways to remove the state requirement. If there is definitely a need for state to be maintained then there are two approaches that can followed by the service:

- Externalize all state and return it to the client.
- Maintain state within the service and return a reference to the client.

In the first case it is necessary to package up the required state information and return it to the client. Because the client should be unaware of the format of this data it must be returned as an opaque type. This is best done as an `<any>` element in the schema for returning the response to the client. An `<any>` element may be used to hold any type of data from simple strings through to complex structured types.

For example if a listing service returns only twenty items at a time then it must pass back sufficient information to enable it to retrieve the next twenty items in the query.

In the XML Schema example below we have the XML data definitions to support two operations on a listing service. These are:

- `searchItems`
- `nextItems`

The `searchItems` operation will take a `searchItemsRequest` element for input and return a `searchItemsResponse` element. The `searchItemsResponse` has within it a `searchState` element. This element is a sequence that has an unlimited number of arbitrary elements. This can be used by the service to store sufficient state to allow it to deliver the next twenty items in the response. It is important to realize that this state does not have to be understood by the client of the service. The client of the service just has to copy the `searchState` element to the `continueSearchItemsRequest` element to retrieve the next set of 20 results.

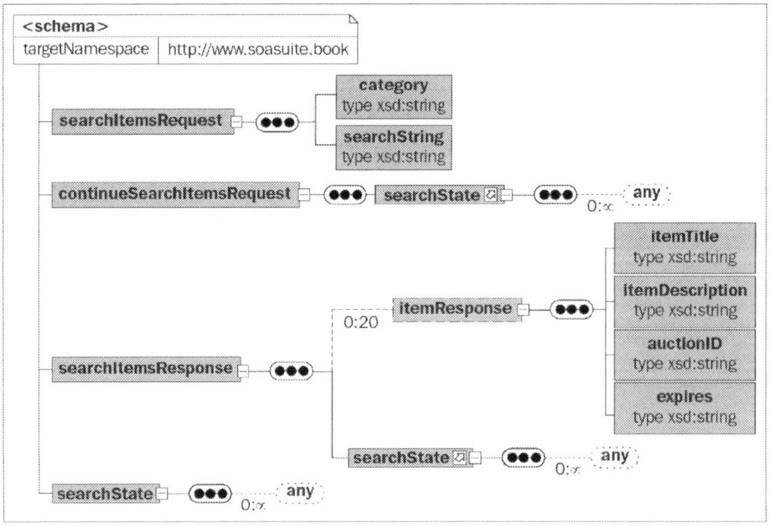

The approach above has the advantage that the service may still be stateless, although it gives the appearance of being stateful. The sample schema shown in the following figure could be used to allow the service to resume the search where it left off without the need for any internal state information in the service. By storing the state information (the original request and the index of the next item to be returned) within the response, the service can retrieve the next set of items without having to maintain any state within itself. Obviously the service for purposes of efficiency could maintain some internal state, such as a database cursor, for a period of time, but this is not necessary.

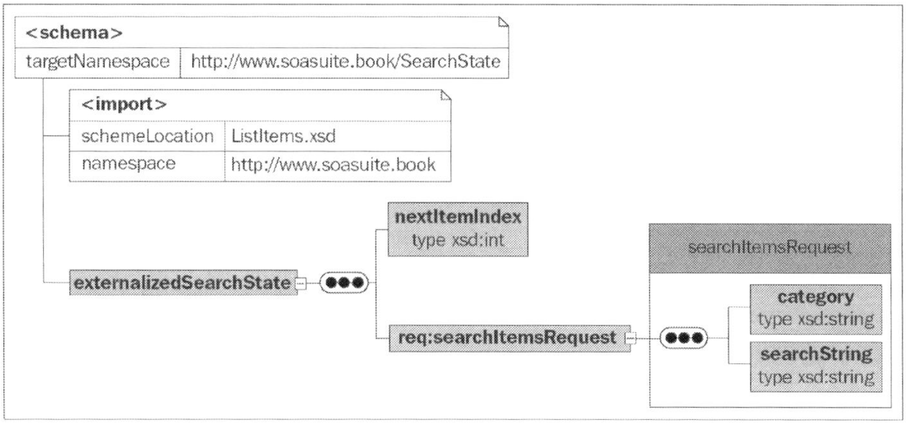

An alternative approach to state management is to keep the state information within the service itself. This still requires some state information to be returned to the client, but only a reference to the internal state information is required. In this case there are a couple of options for dealing with this reference.

One is to take state management outside of the request/response messages and make it part of the wider service contract, either through the use of WS-Correlation or an HTTP cookie for example. This approach has the advantage that the service can generally take advantage of state management functions of the platform, such as support for Java services to use the HTTP session state.

Use of WS-Correlation

It is possible to use a standard correlation mechanism such as WS-Correlation. This is used within SOA Suite by BPEL to correlate process instances with requests. If this approach is used, however, it precludes the use of the externalized state approach discussed earlier. This makes it harder to swap out your service implementation with one that externalizes all its state information. In addition to requiring your service to always internalize state management, no matter how it is implemented, your clients must now support WS-Correlation.

The alternative is to continue to keep the state management in the request/response messages and deal with it within the service. This keeps the client unaware of how state is managed because the interface is exactly the same for a service that maintains internal state and a service that externalizes all state. A sample schema for this is shown in the following figure. Note that unlike the previous schema there is only a service specific reference to its own internal state. The service is responsible for maintaining all the required information internally and using the externalized reference to locate this state information.

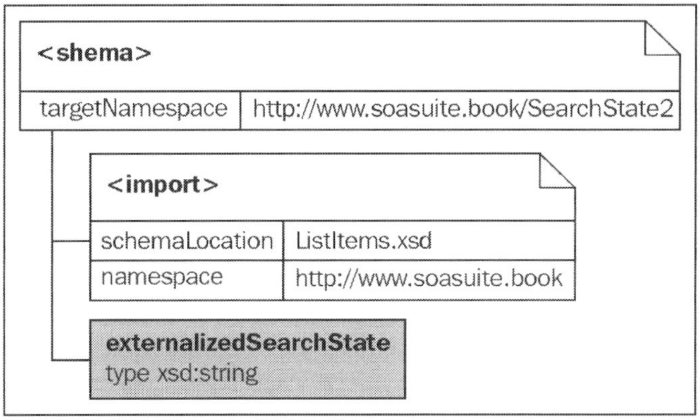

The OSB (Oracle Service Bus) in SOA Suite enables us to have services use their native state management and still expose it as service specific state management that is more abstract and hence less tightly coupled to the way state is handled.

Some web service implementations allow for stateful web services, with state managed in a variety of proprietary fashions. For example, the **Oracle Containers for J2EE** (**OC4J**) used cookies for native state management, other platforms can use different mechanisms.

We want to use native state management when we internalize session state because it is easier to manage, and the container will do the work for us using mechanisms native to the container. However this means that the client has to be aware that we are using native state management because the client must make use of these mechanisms. We want the client to be unaware of whether the service uses native state management, its own custom state lookup mechanism, or externalizes all session state into the messages flowing between the client and the service. The latter two can look the same to the client and hence make it possible to switch services with different approaches. However, the native state management explicitly requires the client to be aware of how the state is managed.

To avoid this coupling we can use the OSB to wrap the native state management services as shown in the following diagram. The client passes a session state element of unknown contents back to the service façade which is provided by the OSB. The OSB then removes the session state element and maps it onto the native state management used by the service, such as placing the value into a session cookie. Thus we have the benefits of using native state management without the need for coupling the client to a particular implementation of the service. For example, an OC4J service may use cookies to manage session state, by having the OSB move the cookie value to a field in the message we avoid clients of the service having to deal with the specifics of OC4J state management.

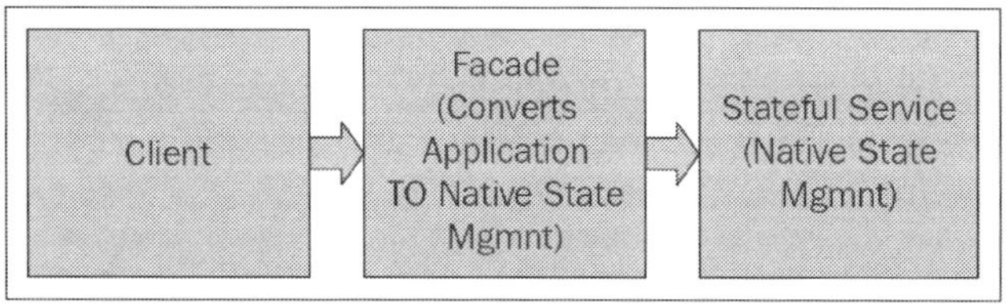

Oracle Service Bus design tools

The Oracle Service Bus can be configured either using the Oracle Workshop for WebLogic or the Oracle Service Bus Console.

Oracle workshop for WebLogic

Oracle Workshop for WebLogic provides tools for creating all the artifacts needed by the Oracle Service Bus. Based on Eclipse, it provides a rich design environment for building service routings and transformations for deployment to the service bus. In future releases it is expected that all the service bus functionality in the Workshop for WebLogic will be provided in JDeveloper. Note that there is some duplication functionality between JDeveloper and Workshop for WebLogic. In some cases, such as WSDL generation, the functionality provided in the Workshop for WebLogic is superior to that provided by JDeveloper. In other cases, such as XSLT generation, the functionality provided by JDeveloper is superior.

Oracle Service Bus Console

Oracle Service Bus Console provides a web-based interface for creating, managing, and monitoring all service bus functions. In this chapter we will focus on using the Service Bus Console. Changes to a service bus configuration are grouped together in a session using the change center. Before any changes are made, it is necessary to **Create** a session from within the change centre. When the changes are complete, they are applied by clicking **Activate**. Clicking **Discard** will cause the changed state to be discarded.

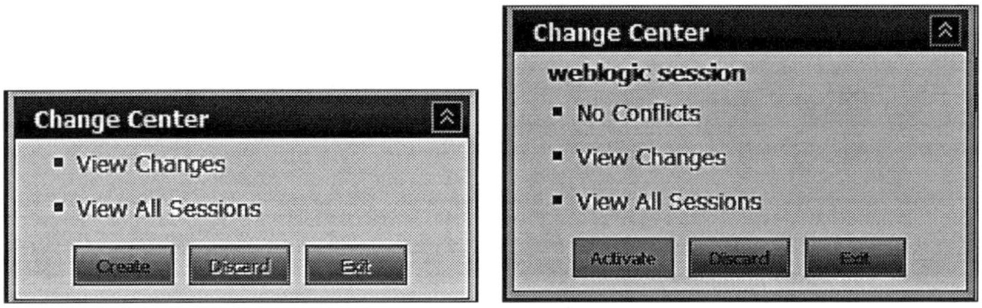

Service Bus overview

The Oracle SOA Suite includes the Oracle Enterprise Service Bus which runs on multiple vendors application servers, and the Oracle Service Bus which in the current release only runs on Oracle WebLogic Server. In the future the Oracle Service Bus may also run on other vendors' applications servers. If you plan on deploying SOA Suite onto non-WebLogic applications servers, then you should use the Oracle Enterprise Service Bus. Most users however run the SOA Suite on Oracle application servers and would be better off using the Oracle Service Bus as it is more functional than the Oracle Enterprise Service Bus and is the stated strategic service bus for Oracle SOA Suite.

Service Bus message flow

It is useful to examine how messages are processed by the service bus. Messages normally target an endpoint in the service bus known as a proxy service. Once received by the proxy service, the message is processed through a series of input pipeline stages. These pipeline stages may enrich the data by calling out to other web services, or they may transform the message as well as providing logging and message validation. Finally, the message reaches a routing step where it is routed to a service known as a business service. The response, if any from the service, is then sent through the output pipeline stages which may also enrich the response or transform it before returning a response to the invoker.

Note that there may be no pipeline stages and the router may make a choice between multiple endpoints. Finally note that the business service is a reference to the target service which may be hosted within the service bus or as a standalone service. The proxy service may be thought of as the external service interface and associated transforms required to make use of the actual business service.

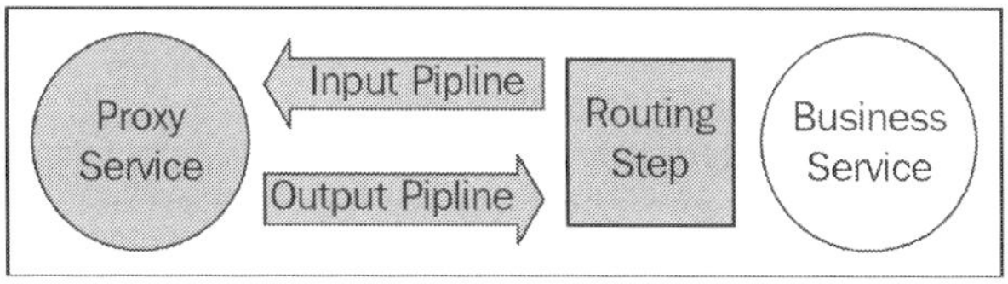

Virtualizing service endpoints

To begin our exploration of the Oracle Service Bus, let us start by looking at how we can use it to virtualize service endpoints. By virtualizing a service endpoint we mean that we can move the location of the service without affecting any of the services' dependents.

We will use an address lookup service as our sample. To begin we create a new **Service Bus Project**. After logging onto the console and before we start making changes in the console we need to create a new session, as described in the previous section. We can then select the **Project Explorer** tab and create a new project by entering a project name and clicking the **Add Project** button. This creates a new Service Bus Project within the console.

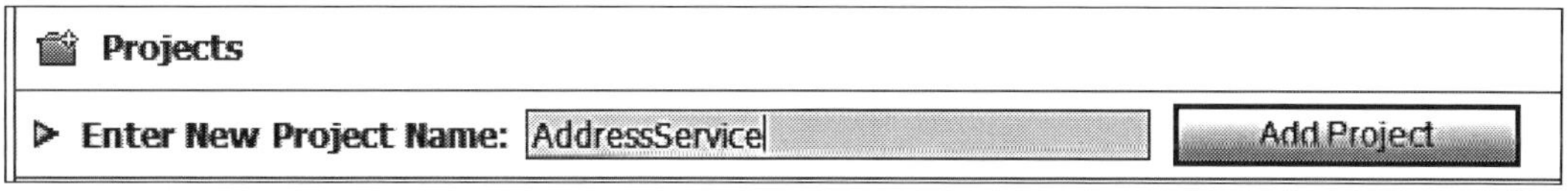

We can now start adding items to our project by clicking on the project name either in the **Project Explorer** tab or in the list of projects under the project creation dialogue. Before adding any items to the project, it is considered good practice to organize the items into folders reflecting their type. So we will use the **Add Folder** dialogue to create folders for the various artifacts we require. We will create a **ProxyService** folder to hold the externally callable service provided by the service bus, a **BusinessService** folder to hold the backend services called by the service bus, and a WSDL folder to hold service definitions (WSDL) files.

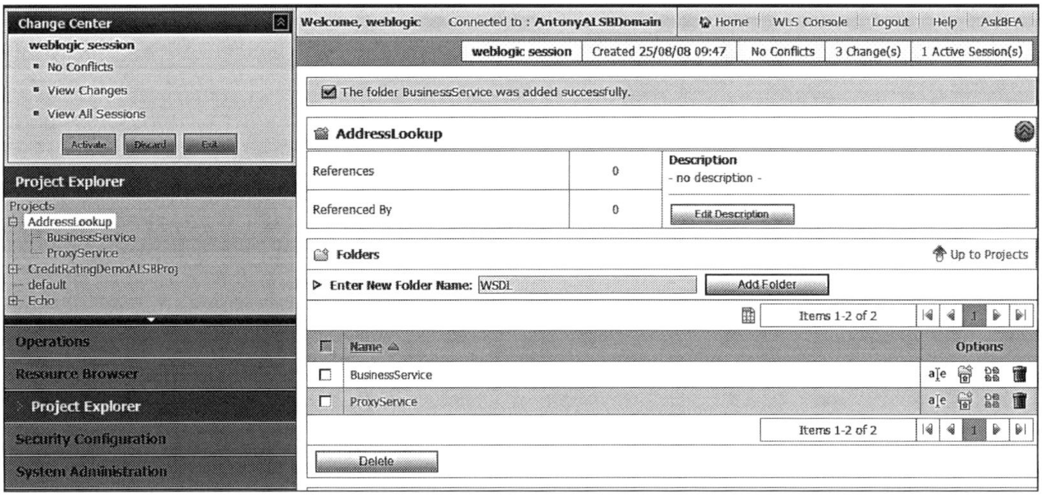

Moving service location

To virtualize the address of our service we first need to add the service definition to the project. In this case we will be adding a web service so we start by adding a service description (WSDL file) to define the service. Before adding the WSDL file, we select the WSDL folder in our project. We then select the appropriate resource type from the **Create Resource** dialogue. We select the **WSDL** resource type from the **Interface** section and are presented with a dialogue enabling us to load the WSDL into the project. We then browse for the WSDL definition and then select **Save** to add it to the project. This registers the WSDL with the internal service bus repository.

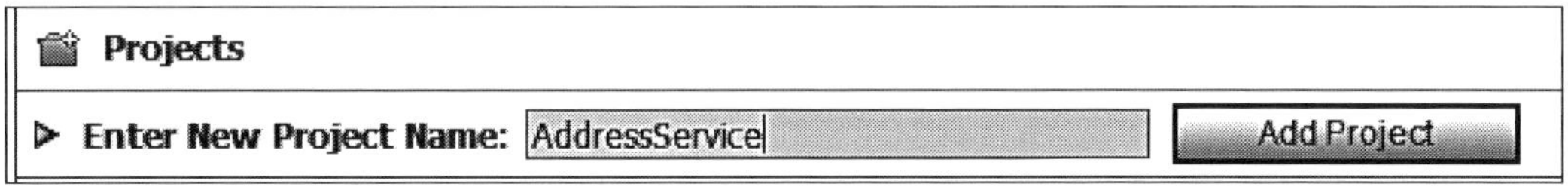

Note that the dialogue requires us to provide a name for the WSDL file and optionally a description. The large blank section in the dialog is used to display the current WSDL file details and is only populated after the WSDL file has been saved.

> **Endpoint address considerations**
>
> When specifying endpoints in the service bus, it is generally not a good idea to use localhost or 127.0.0.1. Because the service bus definitions may be deployed across multiple nodes there is no guarantee that business service will be co-located with the service bus on every node the service bus is deployed upon. Therefore it is best to ensure that all endpoint addresses use actual hostnames.

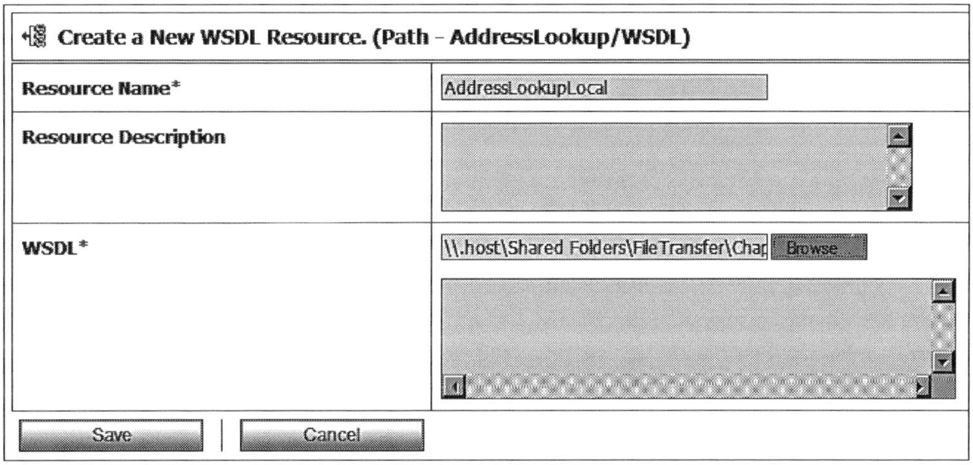

Now that we have a service definition loaded, we can use this to create the business service, or ultimate endpoint of the service. We do this by changing directory to the `BusinessService` directory and creating a resource of type **Business Service**. This brings up a screen allowing us to configure the business service.

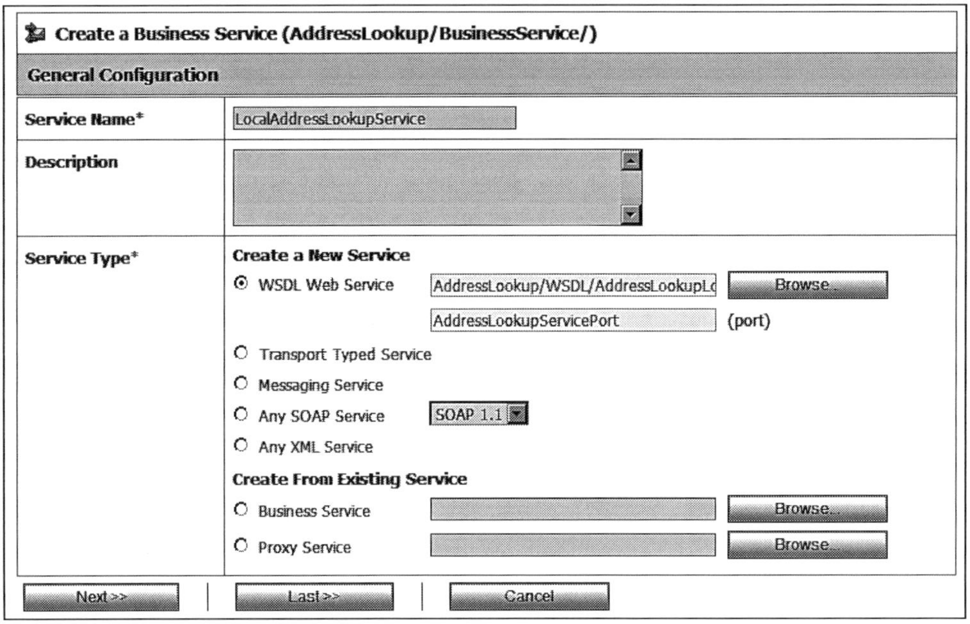

We provide a name for the service and identify the type of service to be accessed. Note that we are not limited to services described by WSDL. In addition to already defined business and proxy services, we can base our service on XML or messaging systems. The easiest to use is the WSDL web service. Browsing for a WSDL web service brings up a dialogue listing all the WSDL documents known to the service bus. We can search this list to select the WSDL document we want to use.

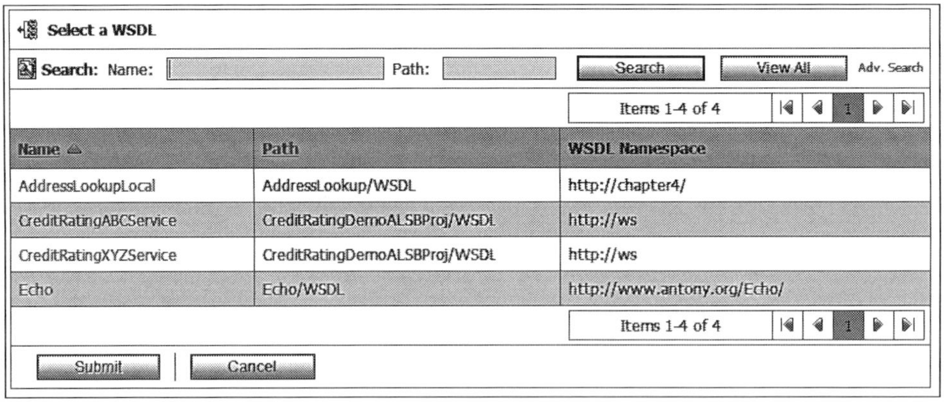

When we select the WSDL name that we want to use, we are taken to another dialogue that introspects the WSDL, identifies any ports or bindings and asks us which one we wish to use. Bindings are mappings of the WSDL service onto a physical transport mechanism such as SOAP over HTTP. Ports are the mapping of the binding onto a physical endpoint such as a specific server.

Note that if we choose a port we do not have to provide physical endpoint details later in the definition of the business service, although we may choose to do so. If we choose a binding, because it doesn't include a physical endpoint address, we have to provide the physical endpoint details explicitly. Once we have highlighted the port or binding we want to use we hit the **Submit** button.

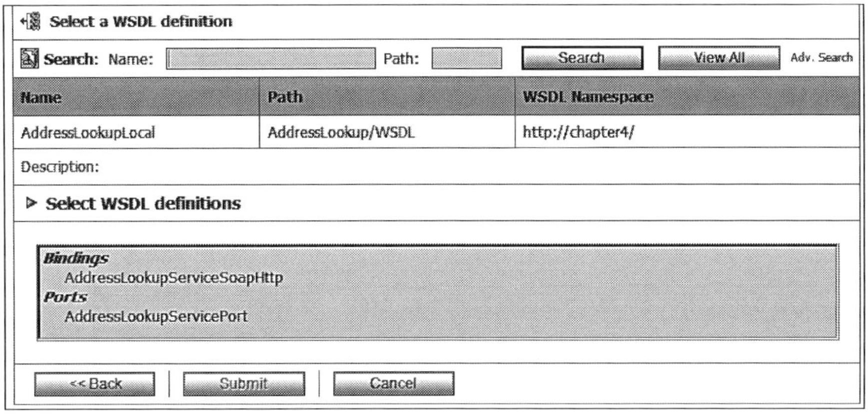

At this point if we have chosen a binding, we can hit last to review the final configuration of the business service. If, however, we chose a port or we wish to change the physical service endpoint, or add additional physical service endpoints, then we hit the **Next** button to allow us to configure the physical endpoints of the service.

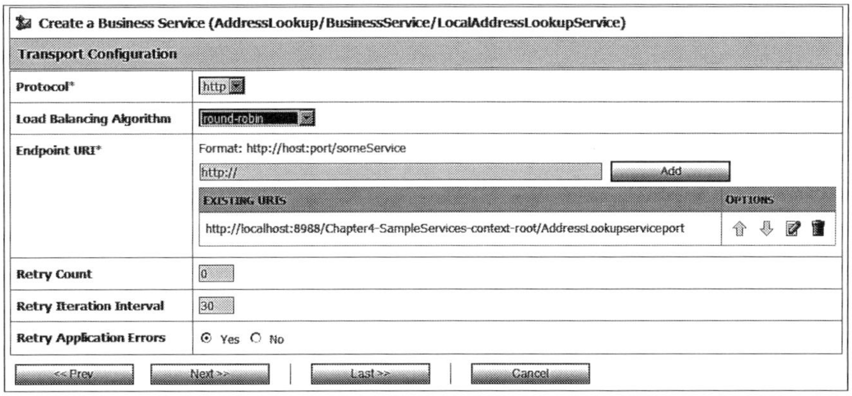

This dialogue allows us to do several important things:

- Modify the **Protocol** to support a variety of transports.
- Choose a **Load Balancing Algorithm**. If there is more than one endpoint URI then the service bus will load balance across them according to this algorithm.
- Change, add, or remove **Endpoint URIs** or physical targets.
- Specify retry logic, specifically the **Retry Count**, the **Retry Iteration Interval** and whether or not to **Retry Application Errors** (errors generated by the service called, not the transport).

Note that the ability to change, add, and remove physical endpoint URIs as well as change the protocol used. This allows us to change the target services without impacting any clients of the service, providing us with virtualization of our service location.

Clicking **Last** enables us to review the configuration of this business service and if we are happy with it, then clicking **Save** will create or update our business service.

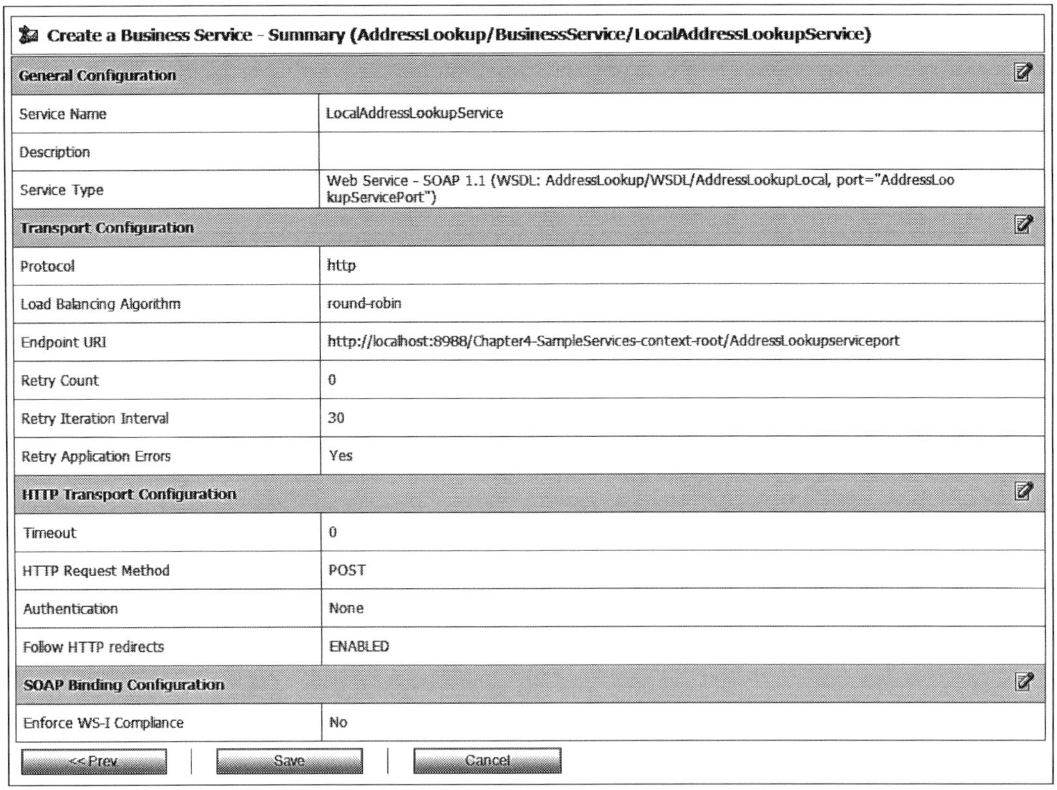

Now that we have created our business service we need to expose it through the service bus by adding a proxy service. We do this in a similar fashion to creating the business service by creating a resource of type proxy service in the `ProxyService` folder. If we are only virtualizing the location of a service then the proxy service can use the same WSDL definition as the business service. Again we can choose to use either a port or a binding from the WSDL for a service definition. In either case the endpoint URI is determined by the service bus, although we can change its location and transport. Once we have created the new proxy service we then need to link the proxy service to the business service.

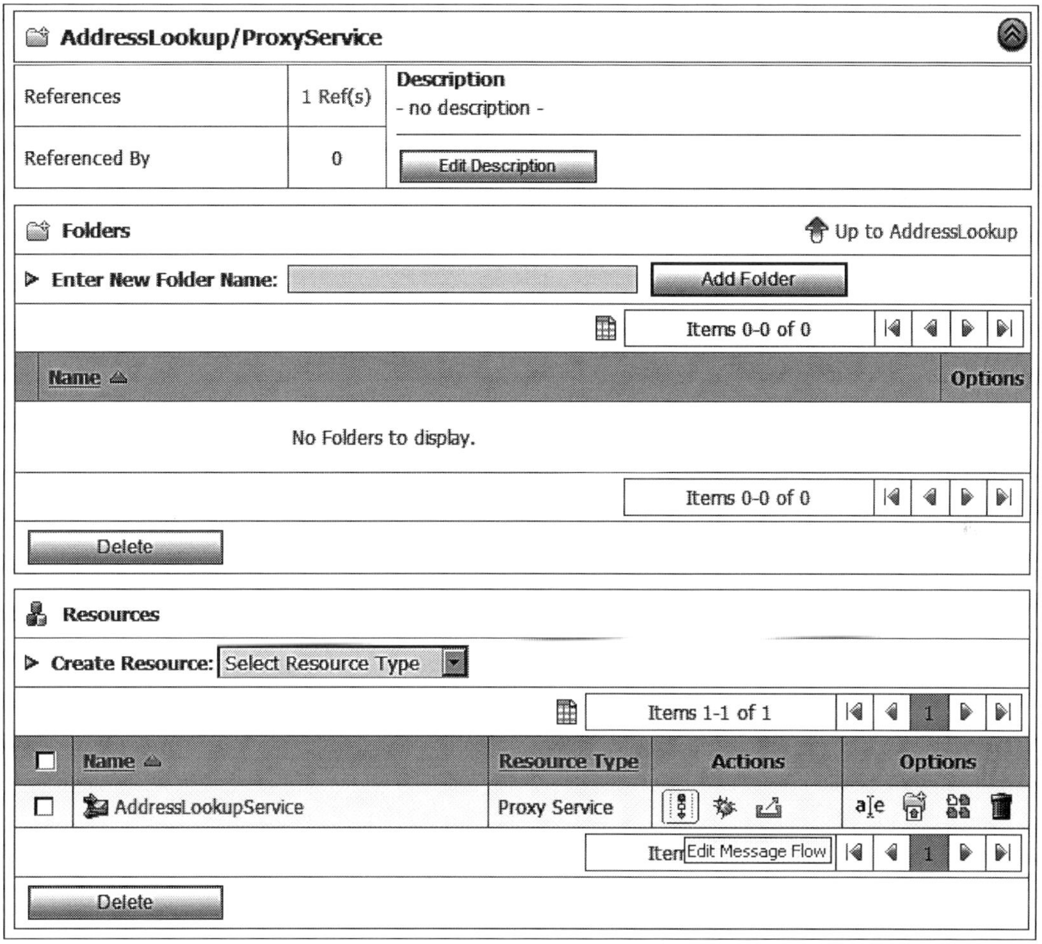

We link the proxy service to business services by selecting the newly created proxy service and clicking on the message flow icon to activate the message flow editor. Within the message flow editor we want to create a routing to the business service so we click on **Add Route**. This creates a new route entry in the message flow.

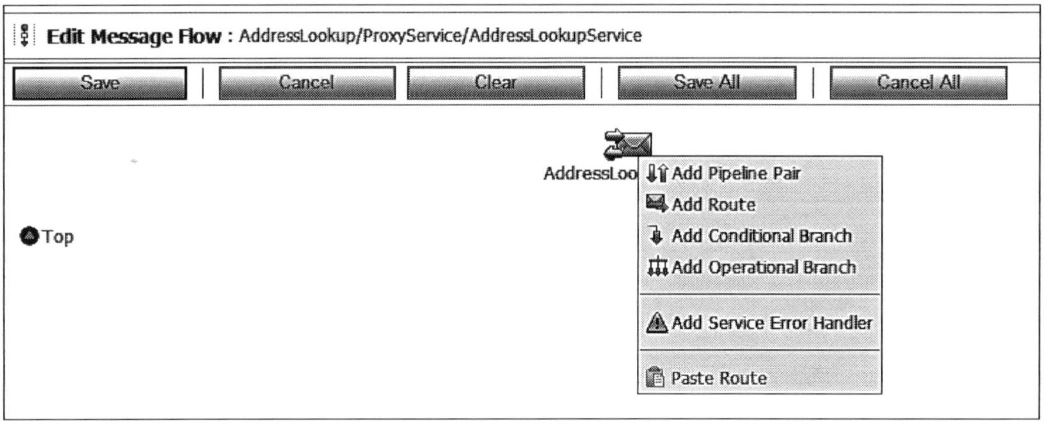

Having created the new route node we can now edit it by clicking on it. We can choose to edit the name of the node and, more interestingly, we can choose to edit the routing details.

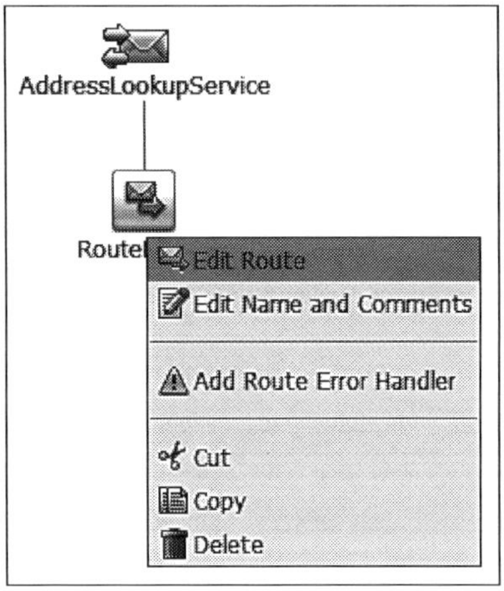

Selecting **Edit Route** brings up the route node editor which allows us to configure the routing details. Clicking on **Add an Action** allows us to choose the type of **Communication** we want to add. **Flow Control** allows us to add `If` ... `Then` ... logic to our routing decision. However in most cases the **Communication** items will provide all the flexibility we need in our routing decisions. This gives us three types of routing to apply:

- **Dynamic Routing**: It allows us route to the result of an XQuery. This is useful if the endpoint address is part of the input message.
- **Routing**: It allows us to select a single static endpoint.
- **Routing Table**: It allows us to use an XQuery to route between several endpoints. This is useful when we want to route to different services based on a particular attribute of the input message.

For simple service endpoint virtualization we only require the **Routing** option.

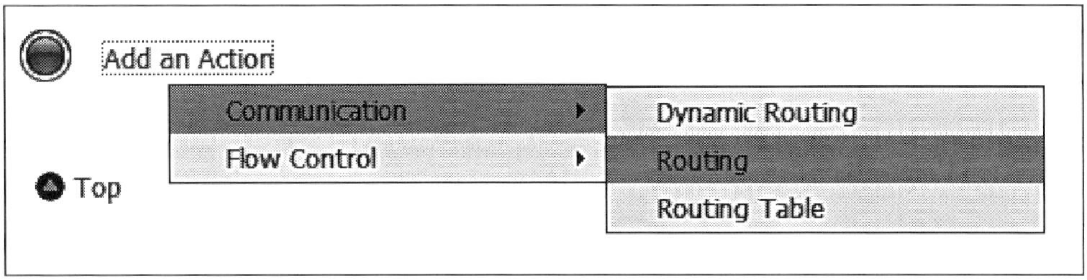

Selecting the **Routing** option then enables us to configure the route by first selecting a service by clicking on the **<Service>** label. This brings up a dialog from which we can select out target endpoint, usually a previously defined business service.

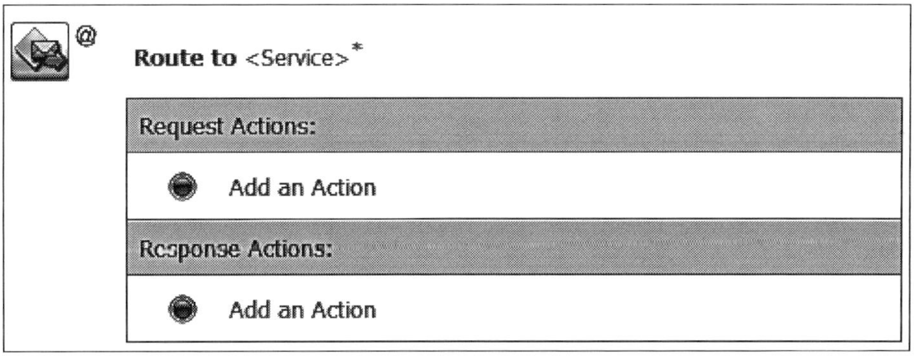

Having selected a target endpoint, we can then configure how we use that endpoint. In the case of simple location virtualization then the proxy service and the business service endpoint are the same and so we can just pass on the input message directly to the business service. Later on we will look at how to transform data to allow virtualization of the service interface.

To provide a simple pass through function we can check the **Use inbound operation for outbound** checkbox. This means that the operation that is requested on the proxy service, the inbound operation, will be invoked on the business service, the outbound operation. Because there is no need to transform the data or perform additional operations we can now save our message flow and activate our changes by clicking **activate** in the session dialog.

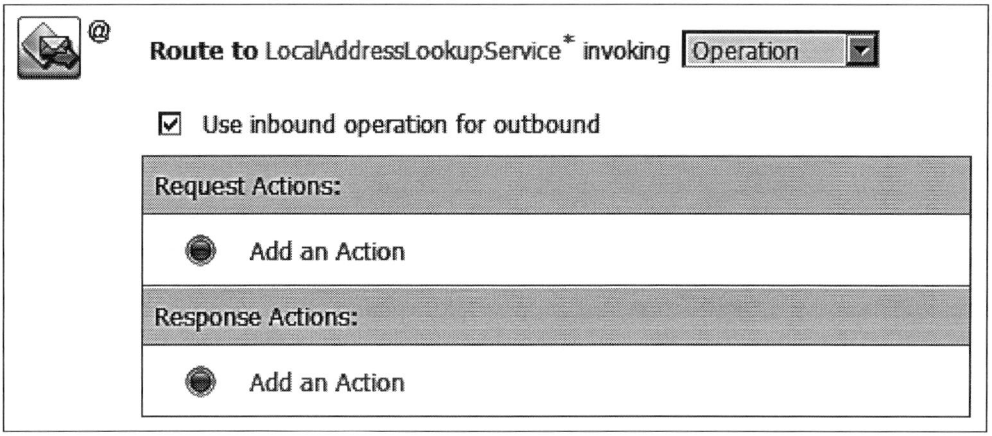

Selecting a service to call

We can further virtualize our endpoint by routing different requests to different services, based upon the values of the input message. For example, we may use one address lookup service for addresses in our own country and another service for all other addresses. In this case, we would use the routing table option on the add action to provide a list of possible service destinations.

The routing table enables us to have a number of different destinations and the message will be routed based the value of an expression. When using a routing table all the services must be selected based on the same expression, the comparison operators may vary but the actual value being tested against will always be the same. If this is not the case then it may be better to use `if … then … else` routing. The routing table may be thought of as a `switch` statement and as with all `switch` statements, it is good practice to add a default case.

In the routing table we can create additional cases, each of which will have a test associated with it. Note that we can also add the default case.

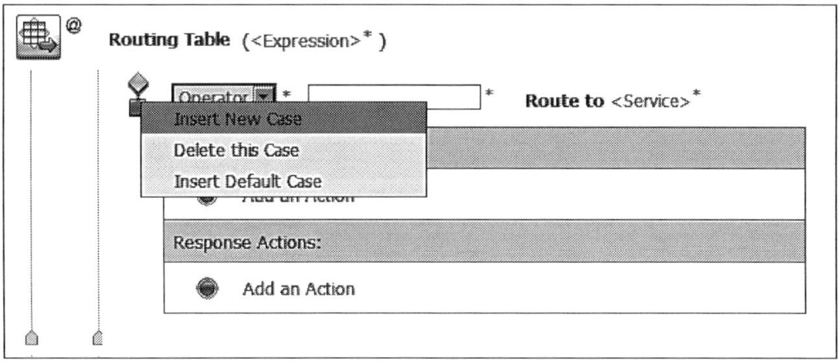

We need to specify the expression to be used for testing against. Clicking on the **<Expression>** link takes us to the **XQuery /XSLT Expression Editor**. By selecting the **Variable Structures** tab and selecting a new structure we can find the input body of the message which enables us to select the field we wish to use as the comparison expression in our routing table.

When selecting in the tab on the left of the screen the appropriate `xpath` expression should appear in the **Property Inspector** window. We can then click on the **XQuery Text** area of the screen prior to clicking on the **Copy Property** to transfer the property `xpath` expression from the property inspector to the **XQuery Text** area. We then complete our selection of the expression by clicking the **Save** button.

In the example we are going to route our service based on the country of the address. In addition to the data in the body of the message, we could also route based on other information from the request, or by using a message pipeline, we could base our lookup on data external to the request.

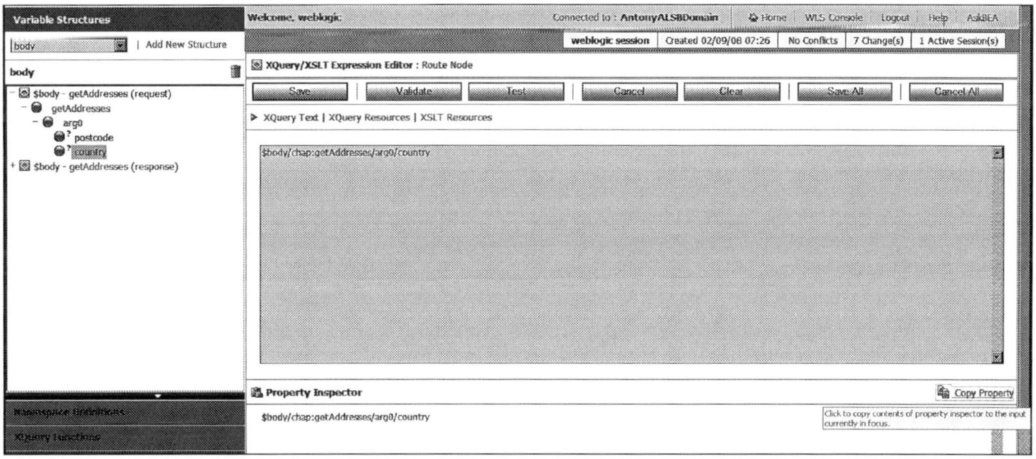

Once we have created an expression to use as the basis of comparison for routing then we select an operator and a value to use for the actual routing comparison. In the example below, if the country value from the expression matches the string **uk** (include the quotes) then the local address lookup service will be invoked. Any other value will cause the default service to be invoked, as yet undefined in the following example:

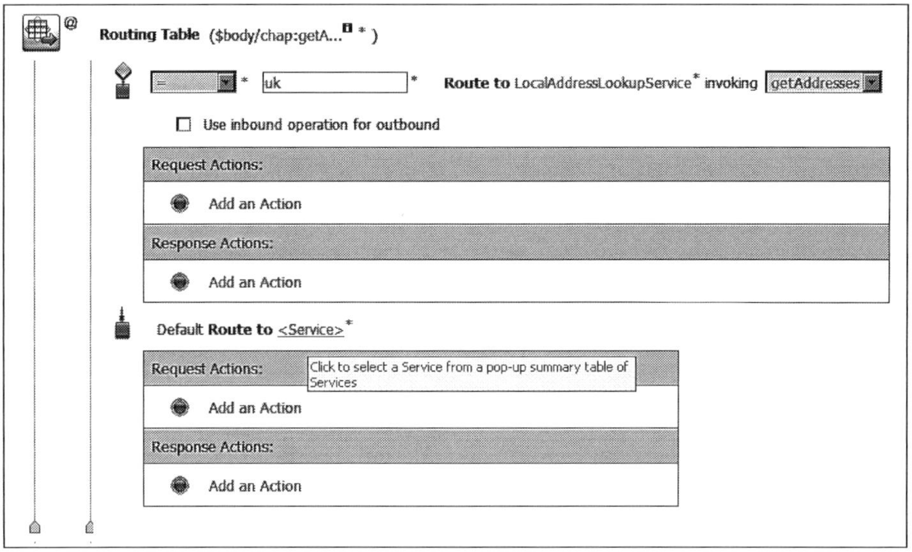

Once the routing has been defined then it can be saved as shown earlier in this chapter.

Note that we have shown a very simple routing example. The service bus is capable of doing much more sophisticated routing decisions. A common pattern is to use a pipeline to enrich the inbound data and then route based on the inbound data. For example a pricing proxy service may use the inbound pipeline to look up the status of a customer, adding that status to the data available as part of the request. The routing service could then route high value customers to one service and low value customers to another service, based on the looked up status. In this case the routing is done based on a derived value rather than on a value already available in the message.

In summary, a request can be routed to different references based on the content of the request message. This allows messages to be routed based on geography or pecuniary value for example. This routing, because it takes place in the composite, is transparent to clients of the composite and so aids us in reducing coupling in the system.

Virtualizing service interfaces

We have looked at how to virtualize a service endpoint. Now let us look at how we can further virtualize the service by abstracting its interface into a common format, known as canonical form. This will provide us further flexibility by allowing us to change the implementation of the service with one that has a different interface but performs the same function. The native format is the way the data format service actually uses, the canonical format is an idealized format that we wish to develop against.

Physical versus logical interfaces

Best practice for integration projects was to have a canonical form for all messages exchanged between systems. The canonical form was a common format for all messages. If a system wanted to send a message then it first needed to transform it to canonical form before it could be forwarded to the receiving system who would then transform it from canonical form to its own representation. This same good practice is still valid in a service-oriented world and the Service Bus is the mechanism SOA Suite provides for us to do this.

The benefits of a canonical form are that:

- Transformations are only necessary to and from canonical form, reducing the number of different transformations required to be created.
- Decouples format of data from services, allowing a service to be replaced by one providing the same function but a different format of data.

This is illustrated graphically by a system where two different clients make requests for one of four services, all providing the same function but different implementations. Without canonical form we would need a transformation of data between the client format and the server format inbound and again outbound. For four services this yields eight transformations, and for two clients this doubles to sixteen transformations.

Using canonical format gives us two transformations for each client, inbound and outbound to canonical form; with two clients this gives us four transformations. To this we add the server transformations to and from canonical form, of which there are two per server giving us eight transformations. This gives us a total of twelve transformations that must be coded up rather than sixteen if we were using native to native transformation.

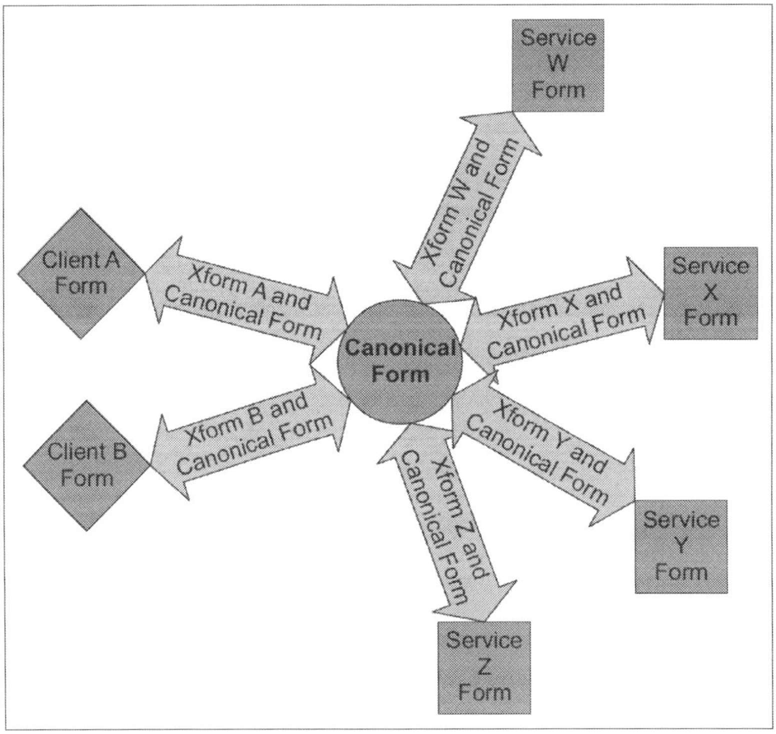

The benefits of canonical form are most clearly seen when we deploy a new client. Without canonical form we would need to develop eight transformations to allow the client to work with the four different possible service implementations. With canonical form we only need two transformations, to and from canonical form.

Let us look at how we implement canonical form in Oracle Service Bus.

Mapping service interfaces

In order to take advantage of canonical form in our service interfaces, we must have an abstract service interface that provides the functionality we need without being specific to any particular service implementation. Once we have this we can then use it as the canonical service form.

We set up the initial project in the same way as we did in the previous section on virtualizing service endpoints. The proxy should provide the canonical interface, the business service providing the native service interface. Because the proxy and business services are not the same interface we need to do some more work in the route configuration.

We need to map the canonical form of the address list interface onto the native service form of the interface. In the example, we are mapping our canonical interface to the interface provided by a web-based address solution provided by Harte-Hanks Global Address (`http://www.qudox.com`). To do this we create a new service bus project and add the Harte-Hanks WSDL (`http://webservices.globaladdress.net/globaladdress.asmx?WSDL`). We use this to define the business service. We also add the canonical interface WSDL that we have defined and create a new proxy with this interface. We then need to map the proxy service onto the Harte-Hanks service by editing the message flow associated with the proxy, as we did in the previous section.

Our mapping needs to do two things:

- Map the method name on the interface to the correct method in the business service.
- Map the parameters in the canonical request onto the parameters needed in the business service request.

For each method on the canonical interface we must map it onto a method in the physical interface. We do this by selecting the appropriate method from the business service operation drop-down box. We need to do this because the methods provided in the external service do not match the method names in our canonical service. In the example we have mapped onto the **SearchAddress** method.

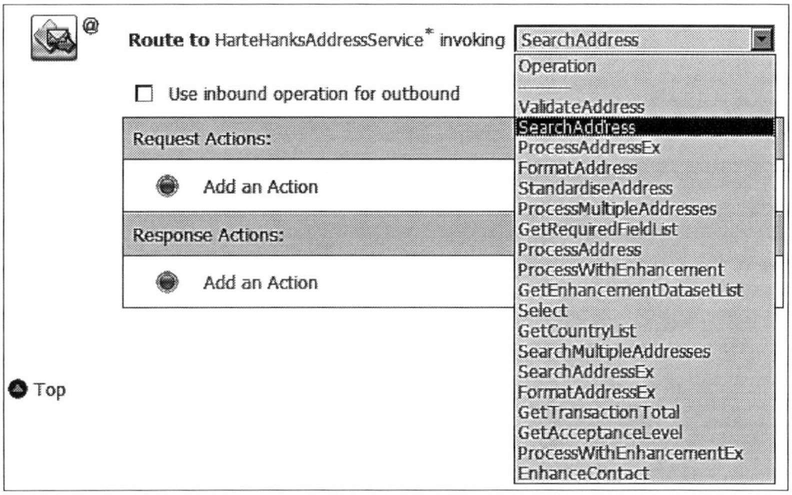

Having selected an operation we now need to transform the input data from the format provided by the canonical interface into the format required by the external service. We need to map the request and response messages if it is a two-way method, or just the request message for one-way methods. The actual mapping may be done either by XQuery or XSLT. In our example we will use the XSLT transformation.

To perform the transformation we add a messaging processing action to our message flow, in this case a replace operation. The variable body always holds the message in the service bus flow; this receives the message through the proxy interface and is also used to deliver the message to the business service interface. This behavior differs from BPEL and most programming languages where we typically have separate variables for the input and output messages. We need to transform this message from the proxy input canonical format to the business service native output format.

Be aware that there are really two flows associated with the proxy service. The **request flow** is used to receive the inbound message and perform any processing before invoking the target business service. The **response flow** takes the response from the business service and performs any necessary processing before replying to the invoker of the proxy service.

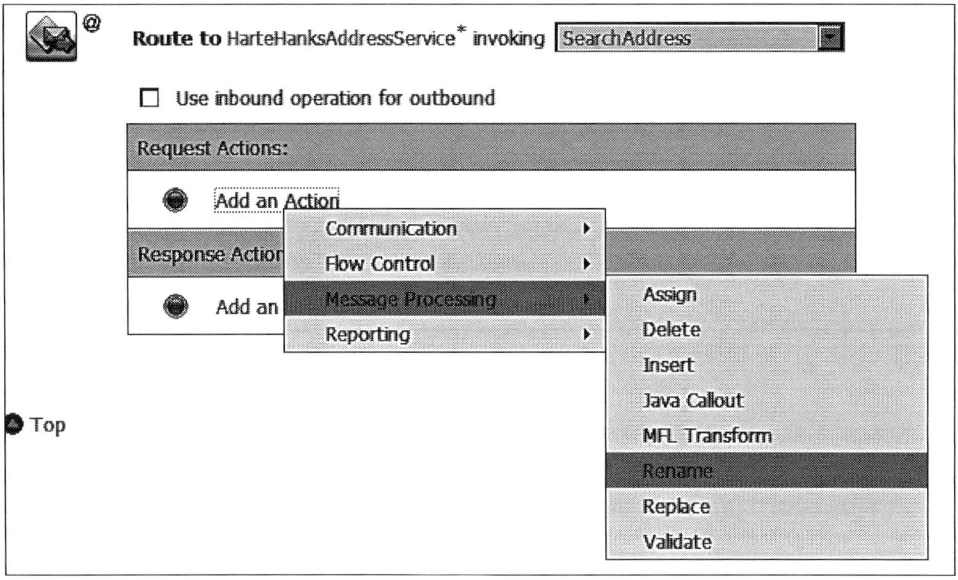

On selecting replace we can fill in the details in the replace action dialogue. The message is held in the body variable and so we can fill this (body) in as the target variable name. We then need to select which part of the body we want to replace.

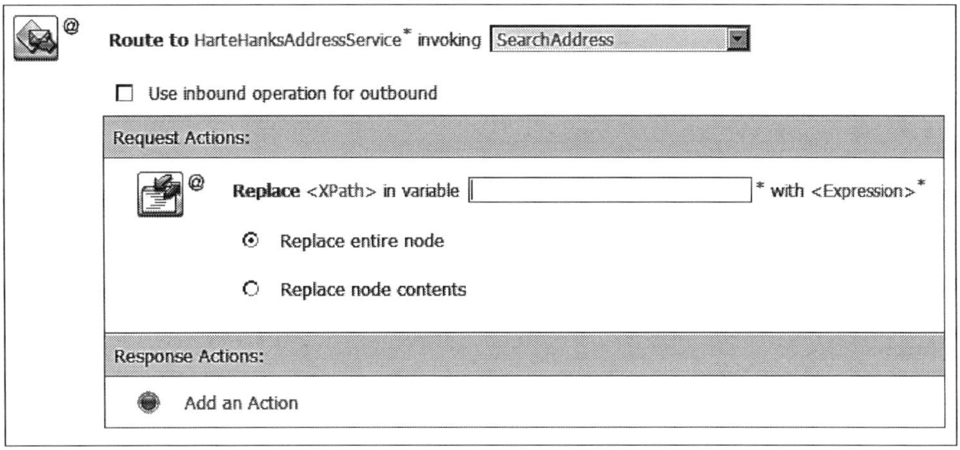

Clicking on the **XPath** link brings up the **XPath Expression Editor** where we can enter the portion of the target variable that we wish to replace. In this case we wish to replace all the elements so we enter `./*` which selects the top level element and all elements beneath it. Clicking **Save** causes the expression to be saved in the replace action dialogue.

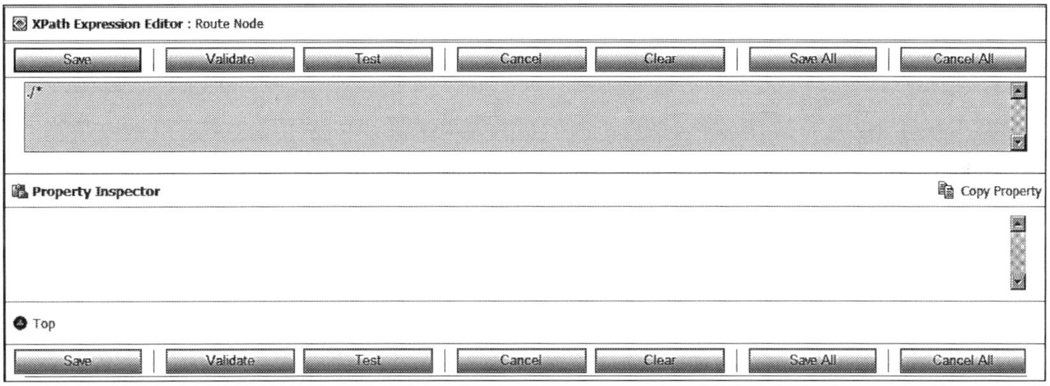

Having identified the portion of the message we wish to replace, all of it, we now need to specify what we will replace it with. In this case we wish to transform the whole input message, so we click on the **Expression** link and select the **XSLT Resources** tab. Clicking on **Browse** enables us to choose a previously registered XSLT transformation file. After selecting the file we need to identify the input to the transformation. In this case the input message is in the body variable and so we select all the elements in the body by using the expression **$body/***. We then save our transformation expression.

Having providing the source data, the target, and the transformation we can then save the repeat the whole process for the response message, in this case converting from native to canonical form.

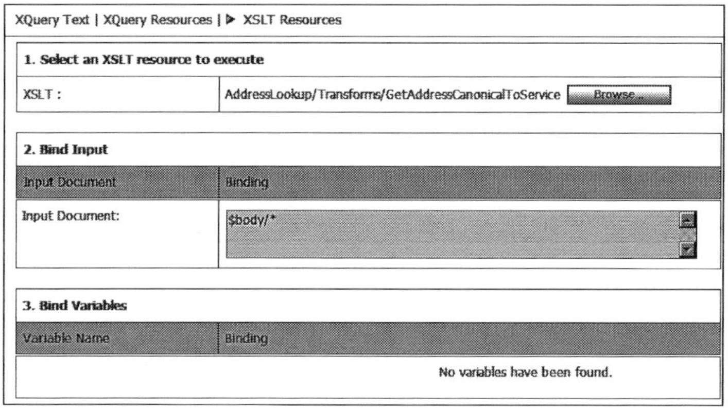

We can use JDeveloper to build an XSLT transformation and then upload it into the service bus; a future release will add support for XQuery in JDeveloper similar to that provided in Oracle Workshop for WebLogic. XSLT is an XML language that describes how to transform one XML document into another. Fortunately most XSLT can be created using the graphical mapping tool in JDeveloper, and so SOA Suite developers don't have to be experts in XSLT, although it is very useful to know how it works. Note that in our transform we may need to enhance the message with additional information, for example the Global Address methods all require a username and password to be provided to allow accounting of the requests to take place. This information has no place in the canonical request format but must be added in the transform. A sample transform is shown that does just this.

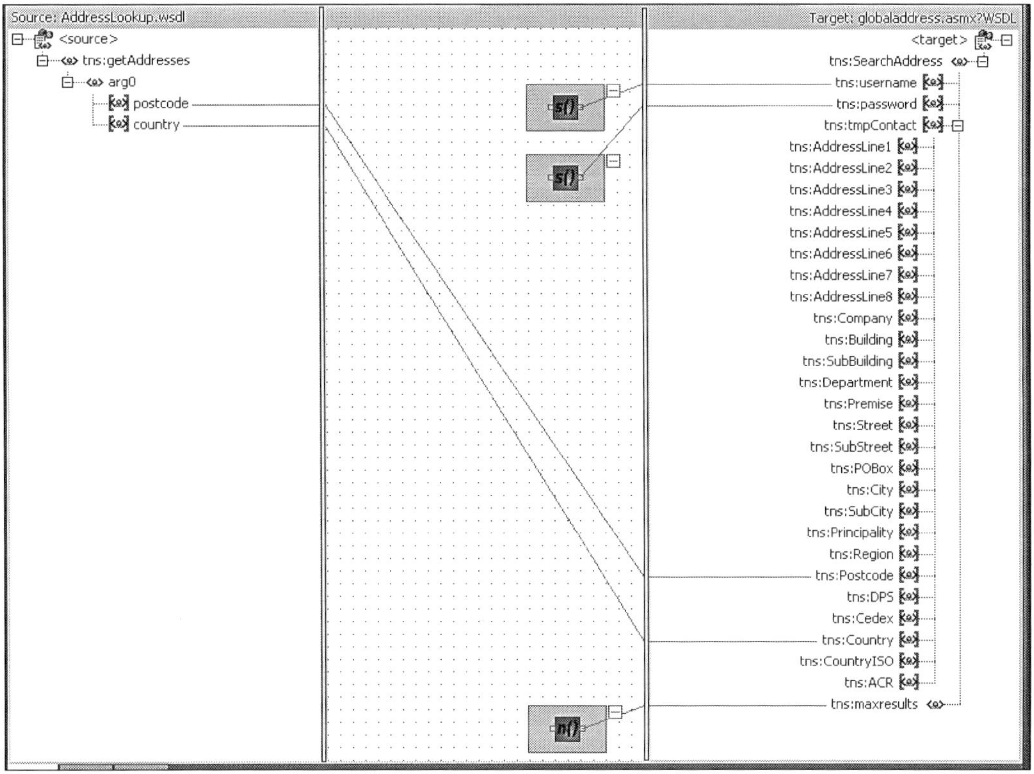

Note that we use `XPath` string functions to set the username and password fields. It would be better to set these from properties or an external file as usually we would want to use them in a number of calls to the physical service. XPath functions are available to allow access to composite properties. We actually only need to set five fields in the request, a country, postcode, username, password, and maximum number of results to return. All the other fields are not necessary for the service we are using and so are hidden from end users because they do not appear in the canonical form of the service.

Applying canonical form in the service bus

When we think about canonical form and routing, we have several different operations that may need to be performed. These are:

- Conversion to/from native business service form and canonical proxy form.
- Conversion to/from native client form to canonical proxy form.
- Routing between multiple native services, each potentially with its own message format.

The following diagram represents these different potential interactions as distinct proxy implementations in the service. To reduce coupling and make maintenance easier, each native service has a corresponding canonical proxy service, which isolates the rest of the system from the actual native formats. This is shown in the following figure in the Local-Harte-Hanks-Proxy and Local-LocalAddress-Proxy services that transform the native service to/from canonical form. This approach allows us to change the native address lookup implementations without impacting anything other than the Local-*-Proxy service.

The Canonical-Address-Proxy has the job of hiding the fact that the address lookup service is actually provided by a number of different service providers each with their own message formats. By providing this service we can easily add additional address providers without impacting the clients of the address lookup service.

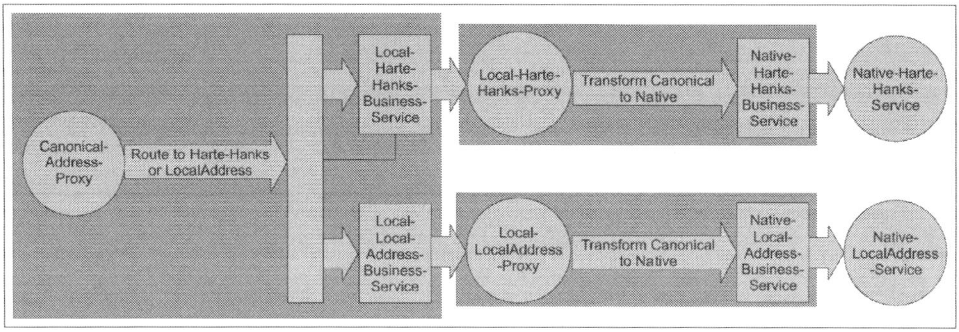

In addition to the services shown in the figure we may have clients that are not written to use the canonical address lookup. In this case we need to provide a proxy that transforms the native input request to/from the canonical form. This allows us to be isolated from the requirements of the clients of the service. If a client requires its own interface to the address lookup service we can easily provide that through a proxy without the need to impact the rest of the system, again reducing coupling.

An important optimization

The above approach provides a very robust way of isolating service consumers and service requestors from the native formats and locations of their partners. However there must be a concern about the overhead of all these additional proxy services and also about the possibility of a client accessing a native service directly. To avoid these problems the service bus provides a **local** transport mechanism that can be specified as part of the binding of the proxy service. The local transport provides two things for us:

- It makes services only consumable by other services in the service bus; they cannot be accessed externally.
- It provides a highly optimized messaging transport between proxy services, providing in-memory speed to avoid unnecessary overhead in service hand-offs between proxy services.

These optimizations mean that it is very efficient to use canonical form, and so the service bus not only allows us great flexibility in how we decouple our services from each other but it also provides a very efficient mechanism for us to implement that decoupling. Note though that there is a cost involved in performing XSLT or XQuery transformations; this cost may be viewed as the price of loose coupling.

Summary

In this chapter, we have explored how we can use the Oracle Service Bus in the SOA Suite to reduce the degree of coupling. By reducing coupling, or the dependencies between services, our architectures become more resilient to change. In particular, we looked at how to use the Service Bus to reduce coupling by abstracting endpoint interface locations and formats. Crucial to this is the concept of canonical or common data formats that reduce the amount of data transformation that is required, particularly in bringing new services into our architecture. Finally we considered how this abstraction can go as far as hiding the fact that we are using multiple services concurrently by allowing us to make routing decisions at run time.

All these features are there to help us build service-oriented architectures that are resilient to change and can easily absorb new functionality and services.

12
Integrating BPEL with BPMN using BPM Suite

BPMN process models modeled with Oracle BPA Suite have to be converted into BPEL skeletal code before we can implement them and deploy to the runtime environment. This approach has some drawbacks, as the resulting BPEL code can sometimes be very hard to understand. Oracle SOA Suite 11*g* PS2 introduces an interesting new feature—BPMN 2.0 execution engine. BPMN 2.0 engine is provided by the **Oracle BPM (Business Process Management) Suite 11*g***, which is layered on top of the Oracle SOA Suite. Oracle BPM Suite provides full support for all stages of the business process development lifecycle, including business process modeling, process simulations, business process implementation, deployment, and execution. As BPMN processes can be directly implemented and deployed, there is no need to transform them to BPEL. The result is a much shorter and simplified development cycle. However, in order to be executable, BPMN models have to be modeled with much more detail. With Oracle BPM Suite, BPMN Process is a new type of service component in SOA Composite Editor. This means that we can use it together with other service components (BPEL Process, Human Task, Business Rule, Mediator, and Spring Context) inside a single SOA composite application.

In this chapter, we will get familiar with the Oracle BPM Suite 11*g*. First, we will look at the Oracle BPM Suite architecture and features. Then we will demonstrate how to model and implement the BPMN business process using Oracle BPM Studio. The main focus of this chapter will be to show how both, BPMN and BPEL processes, can be used inside a single SOA composite application. We will demonstrate this on our TravelApproval process example. We will use a BPMN process for defining the top-level process flow, which will include human interaction and will invoke two BPEL processes: one for retrieving flight ticket offers and one for making the ticket reservation. Finally, we will deploy the composite and initiate a new instance to test the application and see the instance audit trail.

> In general, BPMN processes are more appropriate for human-centric flows, while BPEL processes are well suited for automated service orchestrations.

In this chapter, we will discuss the following:

- Oracle BPM Suite architecture and features
- Modeling and implementing business processes using BPM Studio
- Integrating BPEL with BPMN inside a single composite application
- Deploying and testing BPMN processes

Oracle BPM Suite architecture and features

Oracle BPM Suite provides a unified environment for designing, implementing, executing, and monitoring processes. It provides full support for the **Business Process Modeling Notation** (**BPMN**) version 2.0. High-level architecture of BPM Suite is shown in the following figure:

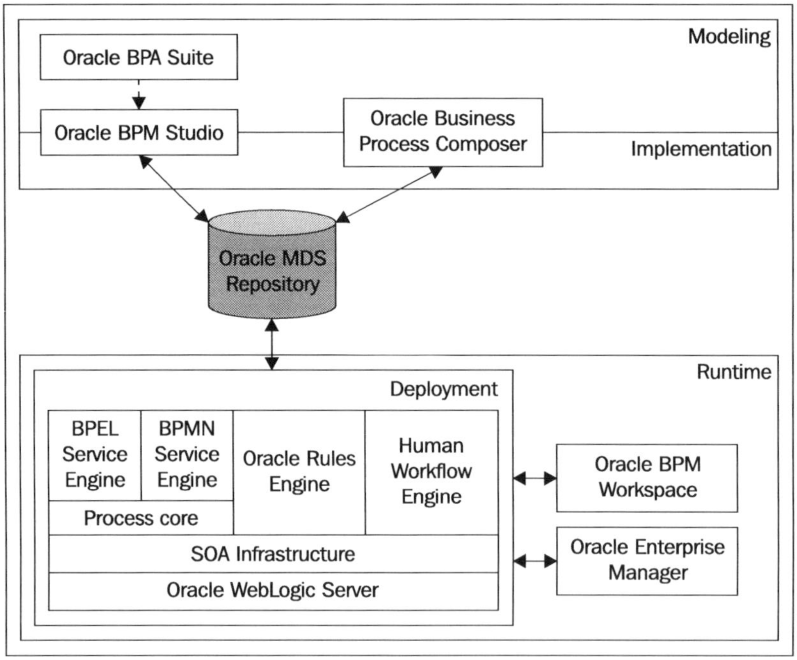

The first stage of every business process lifecycle is process modeling. Business analysts can model business processes using one of the following tools:

- Oracle BPM Studio runs in JDeveloper and provides a user-friendly environment for business process modeling and implementation. Business analysts can use a BPM role, which enables them to use a simplified version of JDeveloper by hiding all unnecessary technical functionality. Using BPM Studio, they can also perform process simulations.
- Oracle Business Process Composer is a web-based application for business analysts. They can model business processes and save the projects to the common metadata repository (MDS). They can also create projects based on predefined project templates, edit them, and deploy them directly to runtime. Using Business Process Composer, business analysts can also edit Oracle Business Rules at runtime.
- Oracle BPM suite enables us to import business process models from Oracle BPA Suite and implement them using Oracle BPM Studio.

Before a business analyst can start with process modeling, they have to create a new Oracle BPM project. Projects are some sorts of containers for business processes and related data. When the business analyst finishes with modeling, they save the project into the common MDS (Meta Data Service) repository, which enables collaboration between business analysts and developers. Using BPM Studio, process developers are able to connect to the repository and open the project to add implementation details. During implementation, developers can also use other components, such as Adapters, Business Rules, Human Tasks, BPEL Processes, and so on. Oracle BPM projects are deployed at runtime as SOA composite applications. The most important component of BPM runtime is the Oracle BPM Engine. Oracle BPM Engine provides support for BPMN and BPEL processes. The engine consists of three separate components: a BPMN service engine, a BPEL service engine, and a common process core. Oracle BPM Suite also uses product components provided by Oracle SOA Suite, including Business Rules, Human Workflow, and so on.

When an SOA composite application created using Oracle BPM is deployed, it can be managed and configured with the use of Oracle Enterprise Manager Console. Another important runtime web-application is Oracle BPM Workspace, which embeds a lot of task list functionality and enables human interaction with SOA composite applications created using Oracle BPM. Using Oracle BPM Workspace, users can act on tasks assigned to them, view process instances, and monitor business processes using the dashboard. Oracle BPM also enables collaboration by providing integration with Oracle Process Spaces, which is a collaborative workspace built on top of WebCenter Spaces.

Demonstration scenario

We will demonstrate the use of Oracle BPM Suite on our TravelApproval business process example. To be able to show how BPMN and BPEL processes can be used inside a single composite application, we will restructure the process into two levels. We will use a BPMN process for defining the high-level process flow, which will include human interaction and will invoke two BPEL processes: one for retrieving ticket offers and one for making the ticket reservation. Finally, we will deploy the composite application to the BPM runtime and test it.

Business Process Modeling and implementation in Oracle BPM Studio

> To be able to create and deploy BPM projects, we first have to install the Oracle BPM Studio 11*g* extension for JDeveloper, which is an extension on top of the Oracle SOA Composite Editor JDeveloper extension. It can be accessed at `http://www.oracle.com/technology/products/jdev/101/update/fmw_products.xml`.

Creating a BPM application and project

Let us open the Oracle BPM Studio using the **Default role**, so that we will be able to model and implement the process at the same time.

We create a new application and select **BPM Application** for **Application Template**.

> We can also create an SOA Application and add the BPM technology scope later.

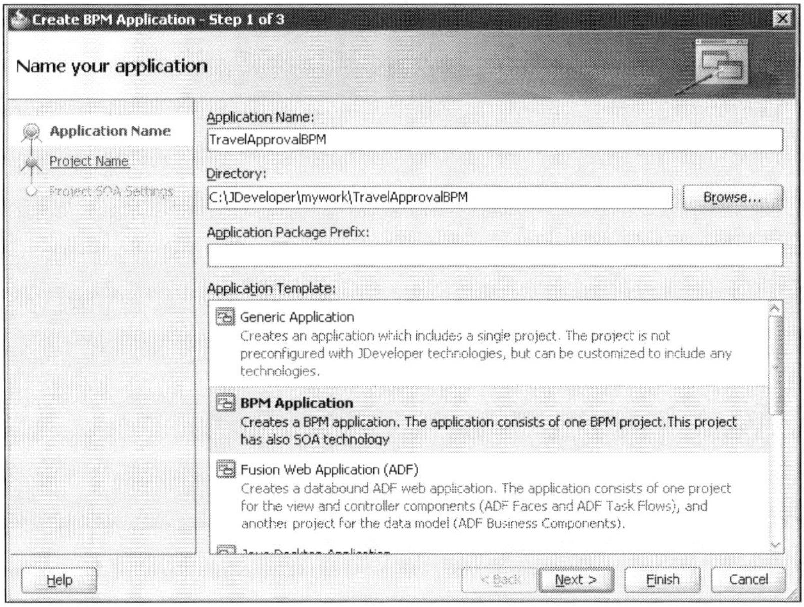

We click **Next**. On the next screen, we set the name of the project to `TravelApproval` and click **Next** again. On the **Configure SOA settings** screen, we select **Empty Composite** from the **Composite Template** list, as we want to show how to create a BPMN process using the SOA Composite Editor.

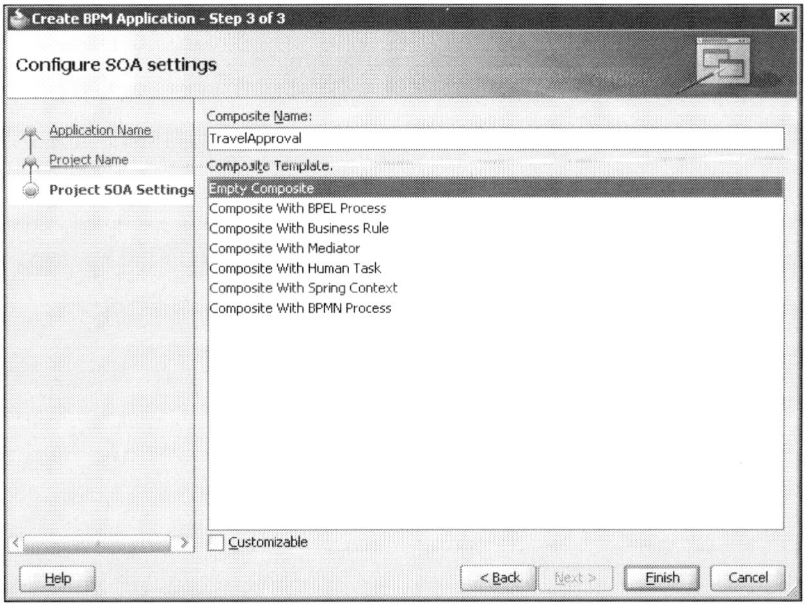

We click **Finish**. The SOA Composite Editor opens. If we look at the **Component Palette**, we can see the **BPMN Process** on the list of available service components.

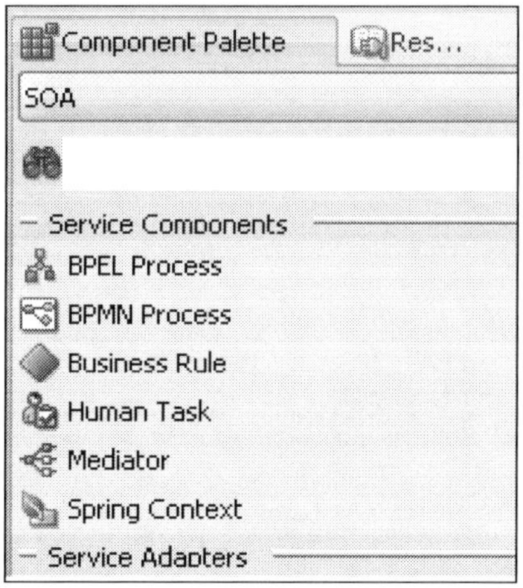

Creating a BPMN process

We drag-and-drop a **BPMN Process** service component from the **Component Palette** to the **Components** swim-lane of the composite diagram. The **Create BPMN Process** wizard opens.

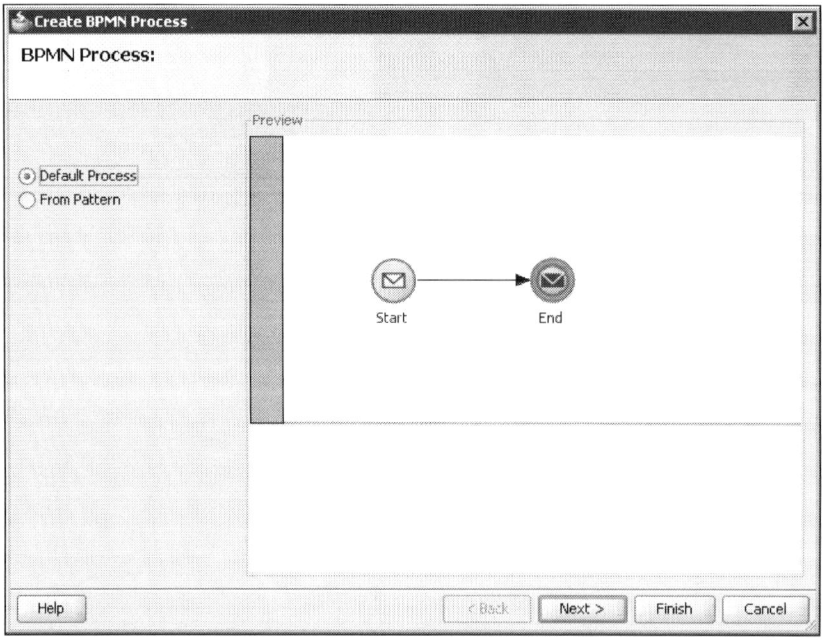

Here we have to select the process type. If we select **Default Process**, a BPMN process with a message start and end event is created. The process is also exposed as a service and can be invoked from other service components inside the same composite and from other composite applications. The exposed service is asynchronous, meaning that it defines two port types (interfaces): the request port type is used by the client to invoke the composite and the callback port type is used by the composite to perform the callback to the client. If we click on the **From Pattern**, we can choose between **Manual Process**, **Asynchronous Process**, and **Synchronous Process**. Manual process is a special type of process that requires human interaction. It starts and ends with one start and end event and is not exposed as a service; however, it can be invoked from other BPMN processes inside the same composite.

We select **Default Process** and click **Next**. On the next screen, we set the process name to `TravelApproval`. We can also enter a process description and an author here.

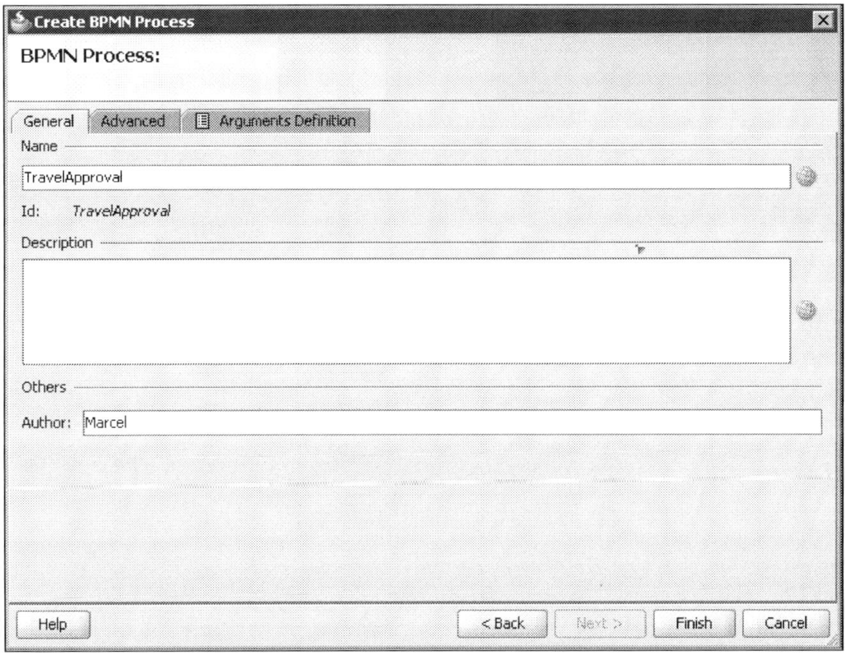

Then we click on the **Advanced** tab. Here we can set process sampling points and the namespace. Process sampling points are used for collecting information about the performance of flow objects. The generated data is stored into BPM, pre-defined cubes, which enable advanced process analytics. Using BPM we can also define Business Indicators and send data to Oracle BAM. Process analysts can then view these metrics using Oracle BPM Workspace Dashboards or Oracle BAM.

We leave the **Inherit project default** option selected. We set the namespace of the BPMN process to `http://packtpub.com/bpmn/travel/`.

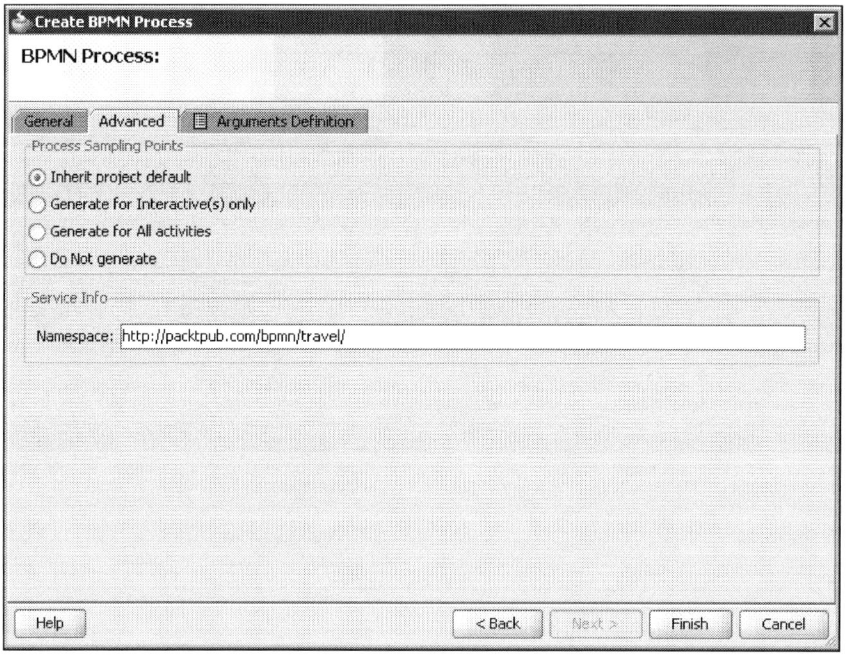

Then we click on the **Arguments Definition** tab to set the process input and output. We will use the same input and output as for the `TravelApproval` BPEL processes. First, we click on the green plus icon to add an input argument. We name the argument `TravelRequest`.

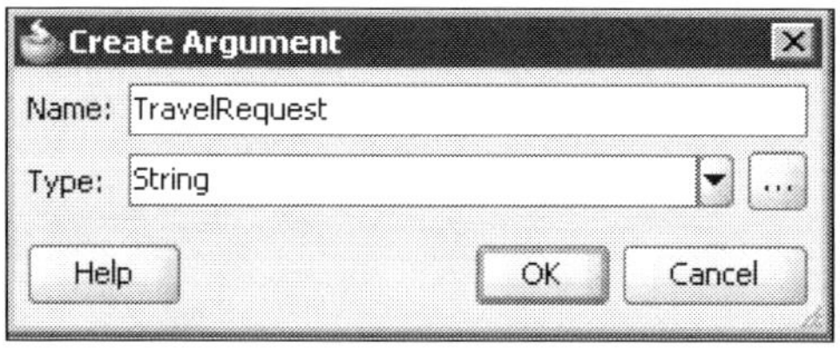

As the argument will be of complex type, we click on the three dots icon to open the **Browse Types** dialog. From the **Type** drop-down, we select **<Component>**.

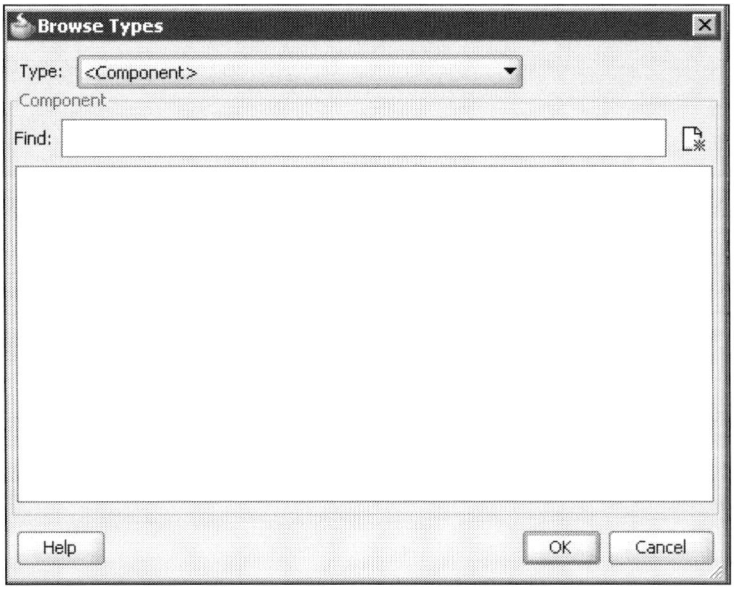

Then we click on the **New** icon next to the **Find** search field. The **Create Business Object** dialog opens, as shown in the following screenshot. We name the business object `TravelRequest`.

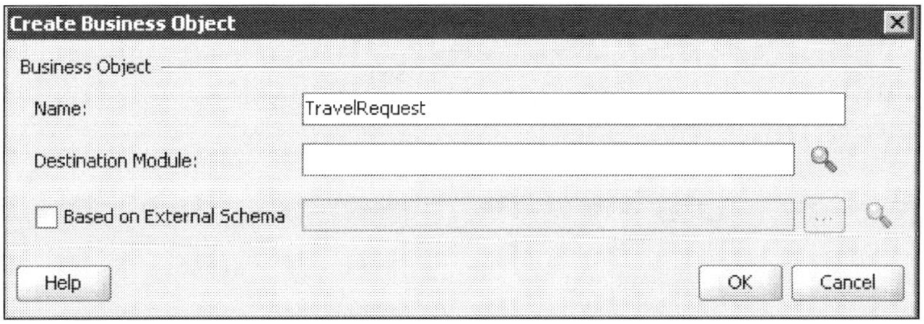

We also have to set the **Destination Module** in the catalog. We click on the magnifying glass icon to open the **Browse Modules** dialog. We create a new module and name it **Data**.

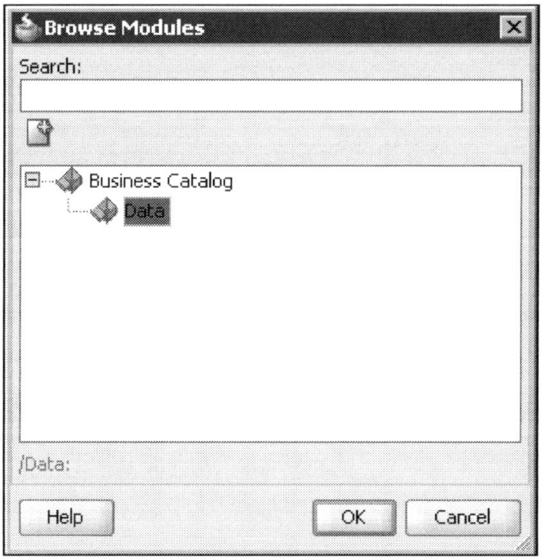

We click **OK** to close the dialog. As our new business object will be based on an XML Schema, we check the **Based on External Schema** checkbox and click on the magnifying glass icon on the right. We import the schema using the **Type Chooser** and select the type or element we want to use. The **Create Business Object** dialog now looks like shown on the following screenshot:

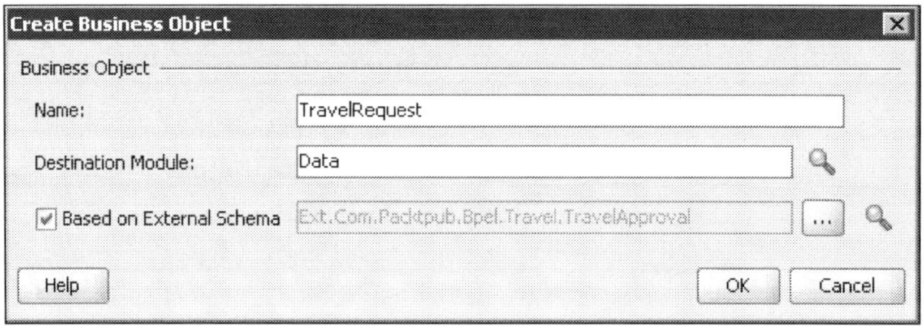

We click **OK**. Back in the **Browse Types** dialog, we select `TravelRequest` business object and click **OK**.

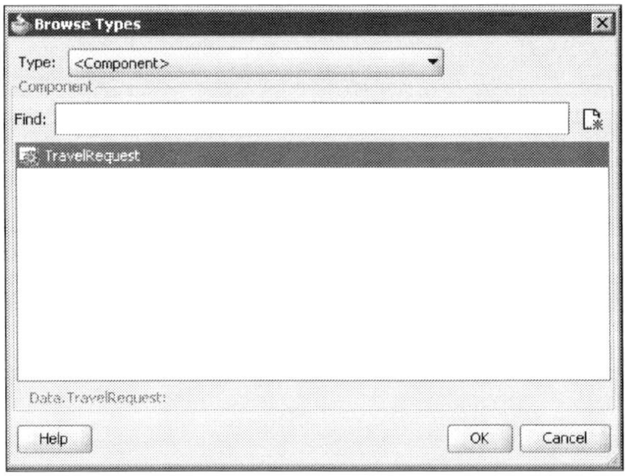

The **Create Argument** dialog now looks as shown on the following screenshot:

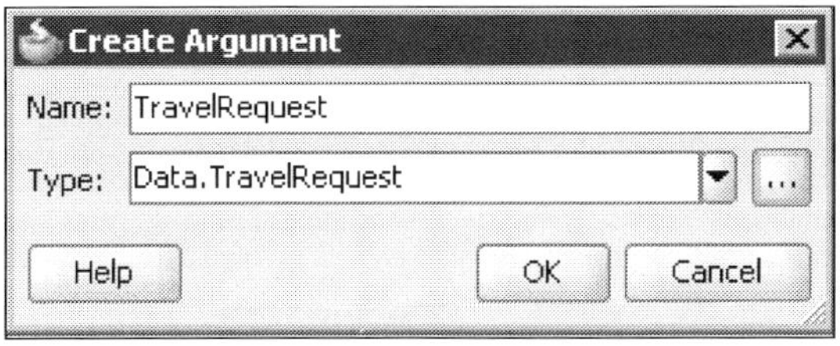

We click **OK** to return to the **Arguments Definition** tab of the **Create BPMN Process** wizard.

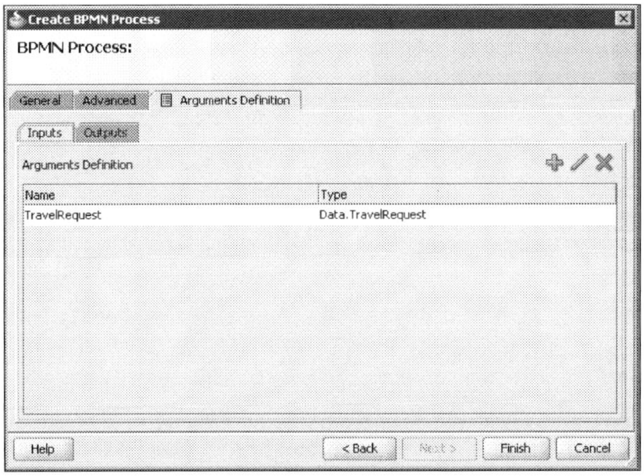

In the same way, we also set the process output and click **Finish**. Our composite application opened in SOA Composite Editor now looks like this:

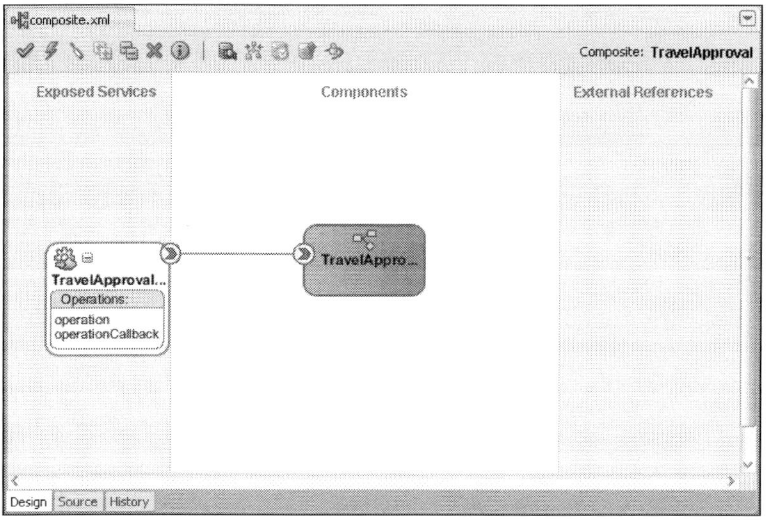

Overview of Oracle BPM Studio

In the SOA Composite Editor, we double-click the `TravelApproval` BPMN process to open the Oracle BPM Studio.

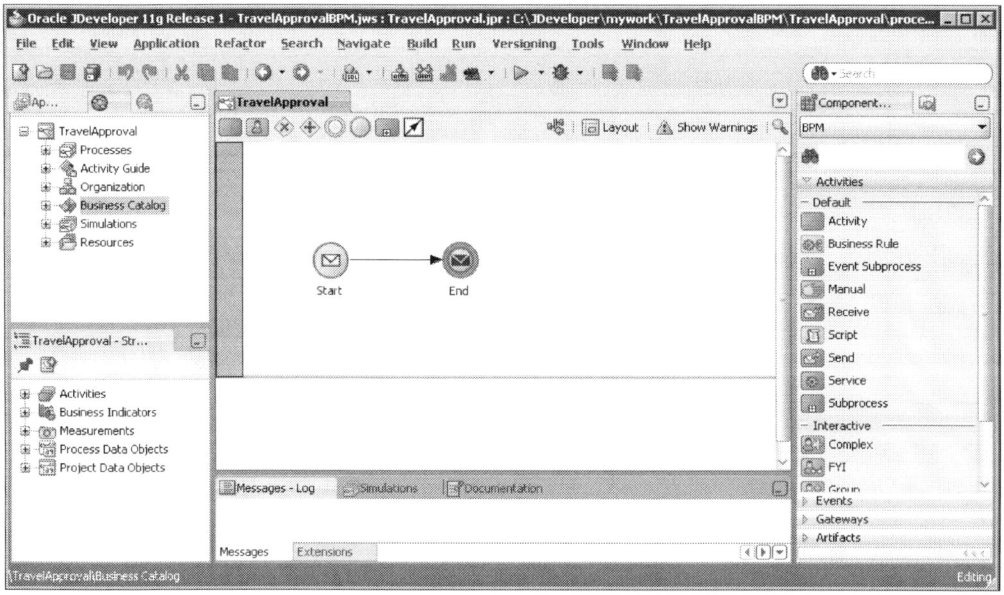

In the middle of the screen, we can see the BPMN Process Editor, which enables us to model business processes by dragging and dropping BPMN components (called flow objects) from the **Component Palette**. If we look at the **Component Palette** on the right-hand side, we can see the list of supported BPMN flow objects. Flow objects are divided into four groups: **Activities**, **Events**, **Gateways**, and **Artifacts**.

In the upper-left corner, we can see Oracle BPM Project Navigator, which shows the hierarchical content of the BPM project.

The **Processes** component contains all BPMN and BPEL processes inside the project. **Activity Guide** contains information about defined milestones for the project. **Organization** contains organizational elements, such as Roles, Organizational chart, Holidays, and Calendar. **Business Catalog** is a repository for storing components we use to implement a BPMN process, such as Errors, Events, Human Tasks, Business Rules, Business Objects, Business Exceptions, and so on. Business Catalog is organized using modules. It provides the following predefined modules: Errors, Events, HumanTasks, References, BusinessRules, Services, and Types. Predefined modules cannot be removed or renamed, because the components stored in them are dynamically generated, based on the SOA composite. These components are also called synthesized components. However, we are able to create custom modules. Modules can be also nested, which allows us to create a hierarchical structure. Organizing components using modules significantly improves the readability of the project and it makes it easier to locate a specific component. The **Simulations** component contains simulation models.

Oracle BPM MDS Browser allows us to access projects and project templates stored in the Oracle BPM MDS Repository. We can check out, lock, export, and delete projects.

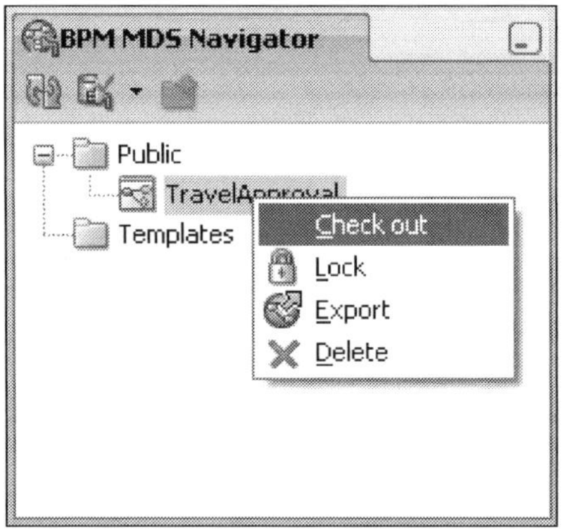

The **Structure** window displays a structural view of the components selected in the BPM Project or Application Navigator. Using the Structure window, we can edit process properties, create data objects, create simulations, convert BPMN process to BPEL, and so on.

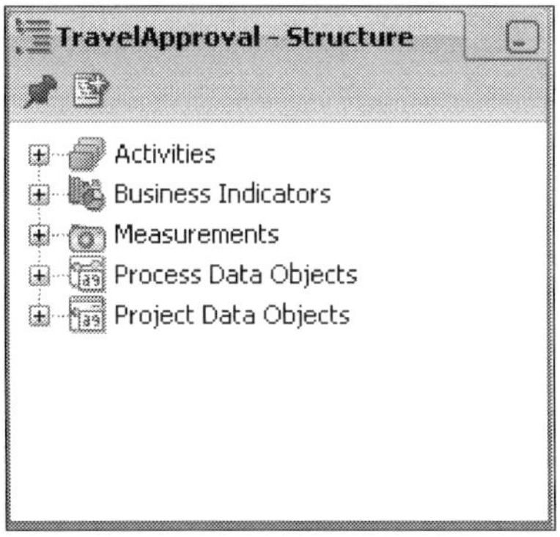

Implementing a BPMN process

Now we will demonstrate how to implement a simple BPMN business process using Oracle BPM Studio. First, we will create a variable (data object) which will store information about the received travel request.

Creating data objects

Oracle BPM supports two types of data objects: process data objects and project data objects. The difference between the two is that the scope of a process data object is limited to the process within which it is defined. On the other hand, the definition of project data object is shared across all processes within the same project (actual values of data objects may be different for every instance). The main benefit of using project data objects is that when changing the definition of the data object, we do not have to make those changes in all the processes that define the same data object. In our simple example, we will use only process data objects. We right-click on the **Process Data Objects** in the **Structure** window and select **New**. We name the data object `travelRequest` and use the previously created `TravelRequest` business object for the data type.

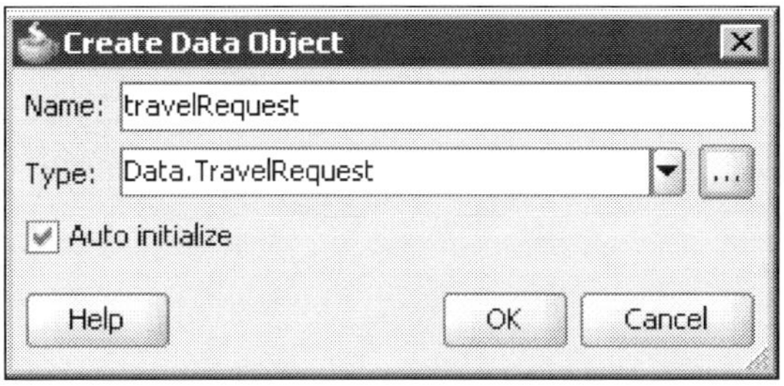

We click **OK**. In the same way, we create another data object for storing the result of the process. We name it `travelResponse` and use the `TravelResponse` business object for the data type.

Configuring start and end events

We double-click the start event. On the **Basic** tab, we change the name of the event to `Receive travel request`. Then we click on the **Implementation** tab.

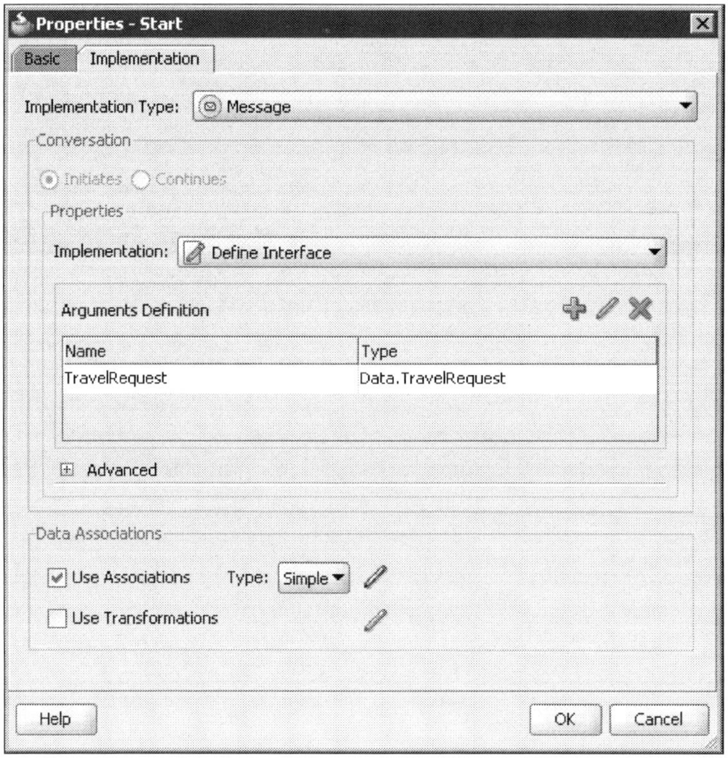

Here we have to configure the mapping between the received input and the `travelRequest` data object, which will be used throughout the process. Remember that in BPEL, we have to use **Assign** and **Transform** activities to define the mapping. In BPMN processes, this can be easily done using **Data Associations**. We can use data associations to define the input and output from a flow object to an external service or process. To define expressions, we use the **Data Association Editor**. To open the **Data Association Editor**, we select the **Use Associations** checkbox and then click on the edit icon on the right. Here we can simply drag-and-drop the `travelRequest` data object from the data objects list on the right-hand side to the **Outputs** field, as shown in the following screenshot:

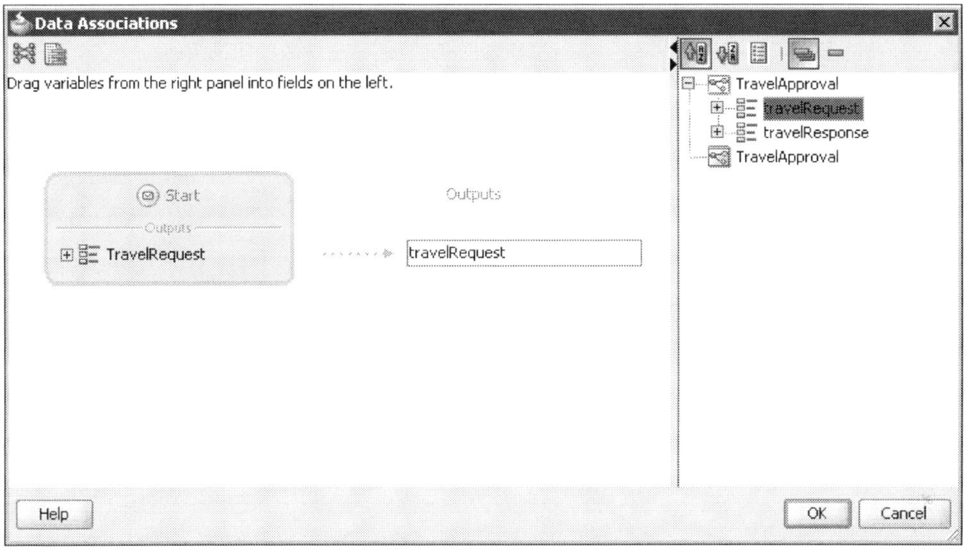

We click **OK** to close the **Data Associations** editor. In a similar way, we configure the end event. However, this time we have to map the data from the `travelRequest` data object to the process output.

Invoking synchronous service

The next step in the process requires invoking the `EmployeeTravelStatus` service to retrieve the employee travel class. Synchronous service can be invoked with the use of the **Service** task. However, before we are able to invoke an external service, we have to add it to the business catalog as a reference. To do that, we have to open SOA Composite Editor and add a reference binding component on the composite diagram. We drag-and-drop a **Web Service** from the **Component Palette** to the **External References** swim-lane. In the **Create Web Service** dialog, we name the reference `EmployeeTravelStatus`, enter WSDL URL, and select Port Type. Then we click **OK**. In the **Customize Adapter Settings** dialog, we click **Cancel**. Our SOA composite application now looks as shown in the following screenshot:

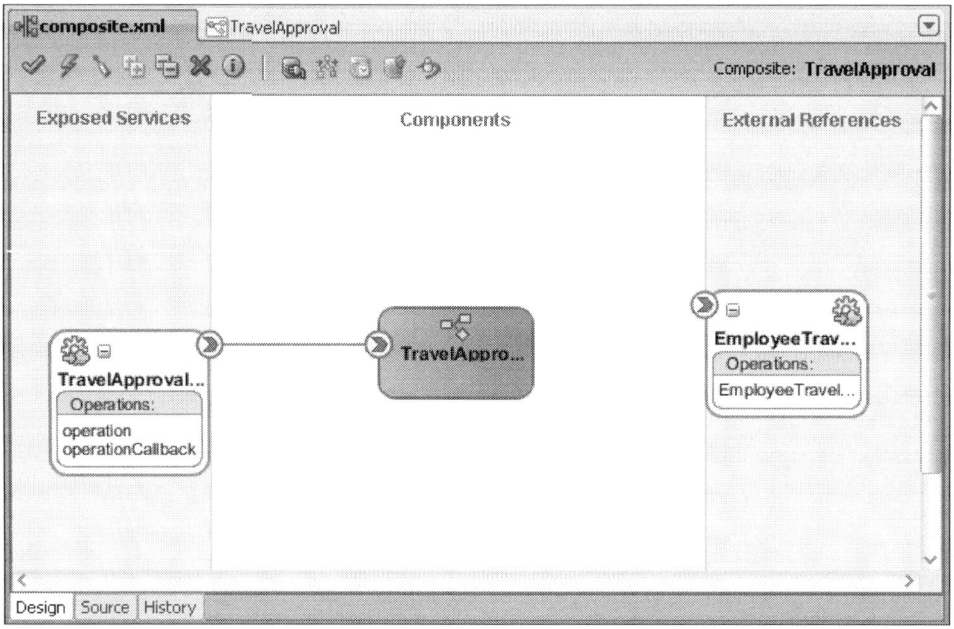

[We cannot wire a BPMN process with other binding or service components using the SOA Composite Editor. However, when we add a new component, it is automatically available in the business catalog. The wire on the composite diagram is automatically added when we configure the BPMN flow object for invoking the component.]

We double-click the `TravelApproval` BPMN process to open the Oracle BPM Studio. We drag-and-drop the **Service** flow object from the **Component Palette** to the process. The **Properties - Service Task** dialog opens. On the **Basic** tab, we set the name to `Retrieve employee travel class`. Then we open the **Implementation** tab. From the **Implementation** drop-down, we select **Service Call**. Then we click on the magnifying glass icon next to the **Name** field. In the **Type** dialog, we select `EmployeeTravelStatus` and click **OK**.

Now we have to define input and output for the service call. We select the **Use Associations** checkbox and click on the edit icon. In the **Data Associations** editor, we first set the input by dragging and dropping `employee` from the `travelRequest` data object to the **Inputs** field. Before setting the output, we have to create an appropriate data object for storing the returned travel class data. This can be done by simply right-clicking the `TravelApproval` process on the right and selecting **Add**.

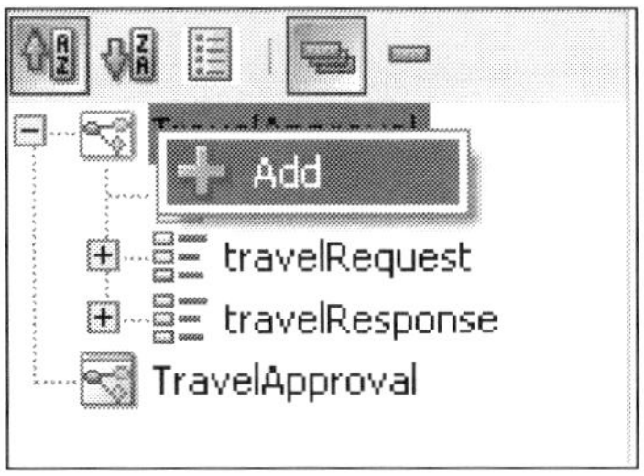

In the **Create Data Object** dialog, we name the data object `travelClass` and set the type to `TravelClass`.

> The `TravelClass` business object has been automatically added to the catalog when we created the `EmployeeTravelStatus` reference binding component.

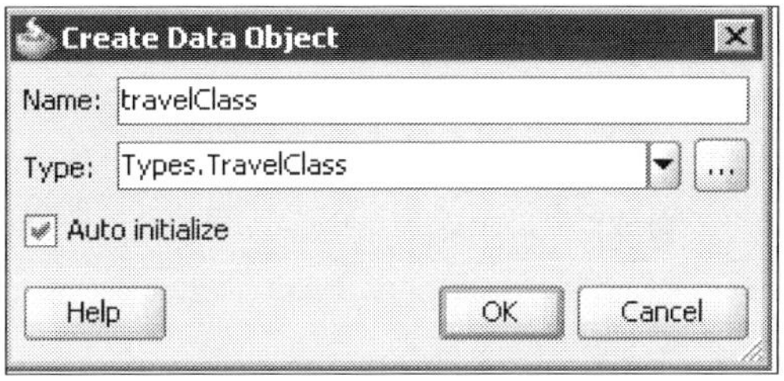

We click **OK** to close the dialog. Now we can drag-and-drop the `travelClass` data object to the **Outputs** field, as shown in the following screenshot:

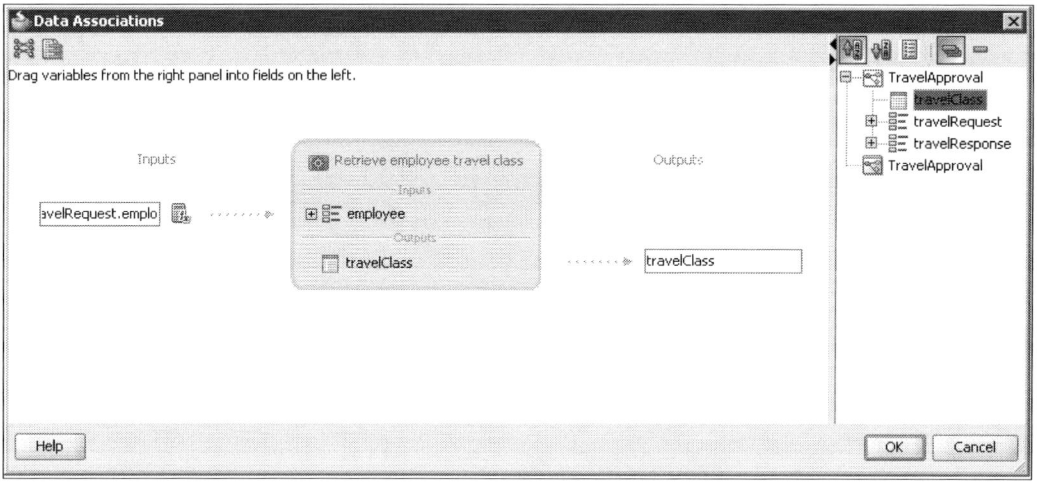

We click **OK** to return to the **Properties - ServiceTask** dialog.

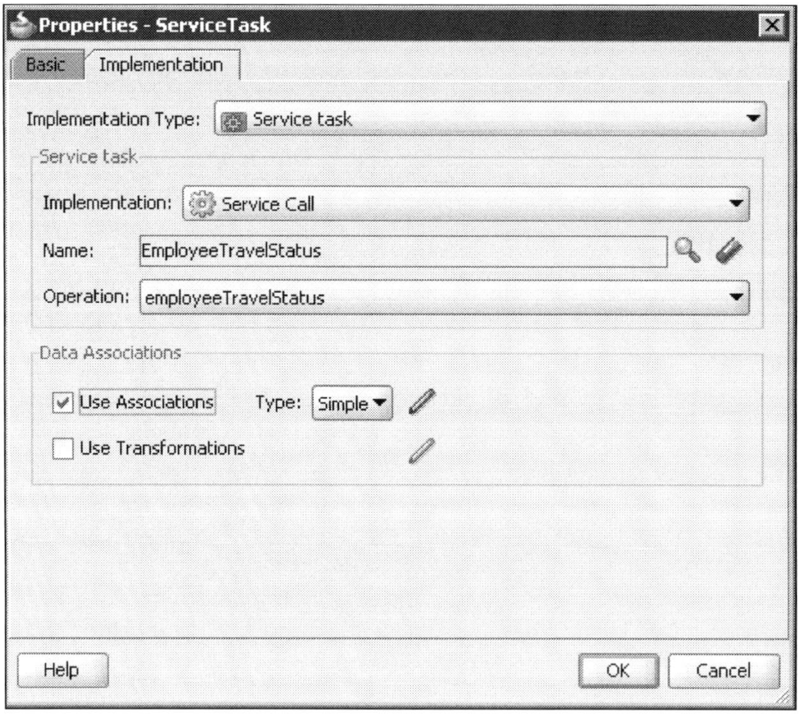

We click **OK** again to return to the BPMN process.

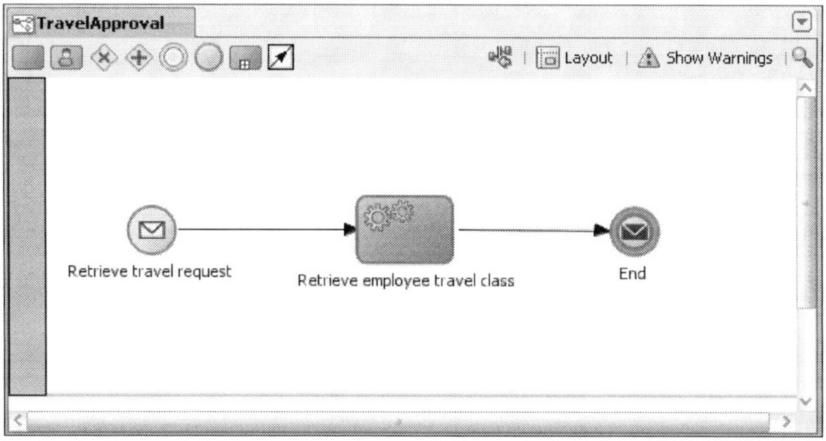

If we open the SOA Composite Editor, we can see that the wire between the `TravelApproval` BPMN process and `EmployeeTravelStatus` reference has been added automatically.

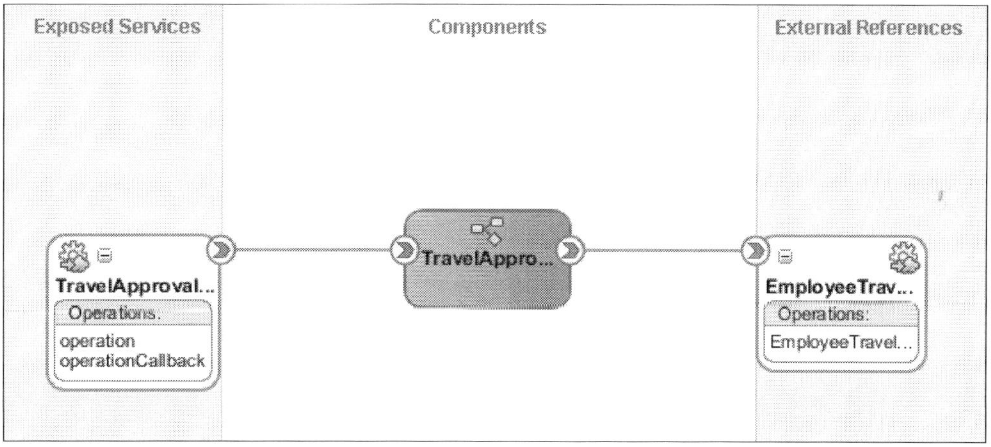

We save the project.

Adding the first BPEL process

Now we will create a BPEL process, which will be used for retrieving flight ticket offers. The process will also compare the offers and return data about the selected flight ticket and the selected airline. We open the SOA Composite Editor and drag-and-drop the **BPEL Process** service component to the **Components** swim-lane of the composite diagram. The **Create BPEL Process** dialog opens.

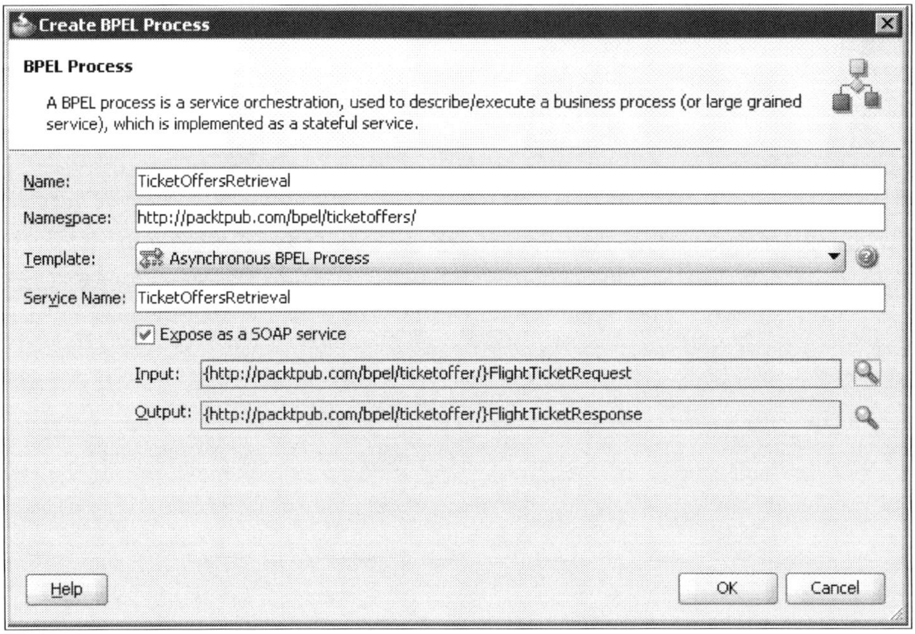

We set the name the process name to `TicketOffersRetrieval` and the namespace to `http://packtpub.com/bpel/ticketoffers/`.

> A BPEL process has to be exposed as a service to be able to invoke it from a BPMN process.

We also set the process input and output. The process input is defined by the `FlightTicketRequestType`, which contains data about the desired flight and the employee travel class:

```
<xsd:schema xmlns:xsd="http://www.w3.org/2001/XMLSchema"
            targetNamespace="http://packtpub.com/bpel/ticketoffer/"
            xmlns:tns=" http://packtpub.com/bpel/ticketoffer/"
            xmlns:emp="http://packtpub.com/service/employee/"
            xmlns:aln="http://packtpub.com/service/airline/"
            elementFormDefault="qualified">
...

  <xsd:complexType name="FlightTicketRequestType">
    <xsd:sequence>
      <xsd:element name="flightData" type="aln:FlightRequestType"/>
      <xsd:element name="travelClass" type="emp:TravelClassType"/>
    </xsd:sequence>
  </xsd:complexType>
</xsd:schema>
```

The process output is defined by the `FlightTicketResponseType`, which contains data about the selected flight ticket and the airline:

```
<xsd:schema xmlns:xsd="http://www.w3.org/2001/XMLSchema"
            targetNamespace="http://packtpub.com/bpel/ticketoffer/"
            xmlns:tns=" http://packtpub.com/bpel/ticketoffer/"
            xmlns:aln="http://packtpub.com/service/airline/"
            elementFormDefault="qualified" >

...

<xsd:complexType name="FlightTicketResponseType">
    <xsd:sequence>
      <xsd:element name="flightData" type="aln:FlightConfirmationType
      "/>
      <xsd:element name="airline" type="xsd:string"/>
    </xsd:sequence>
  </xsd:complexType>
</xsd:schema>
```

Then we add references for two airline services and wire them with the BPEL process, as shown next.

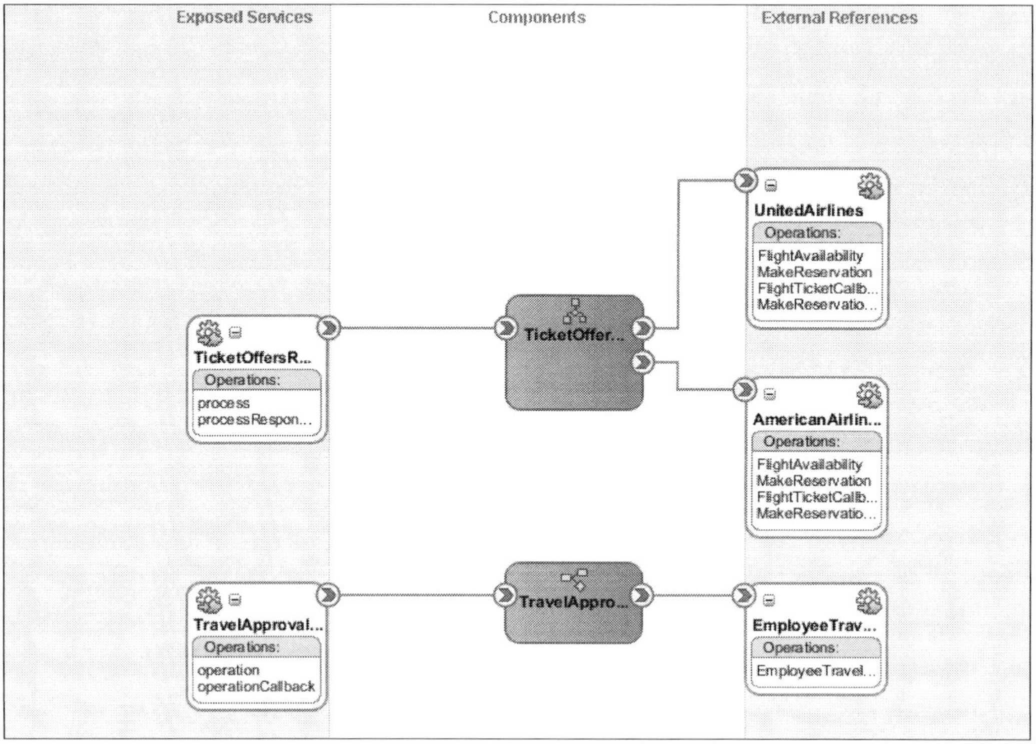

In this chapter, we will not explain how to implement the BPEL process. The following screenshot shows the implemented BPEL process.

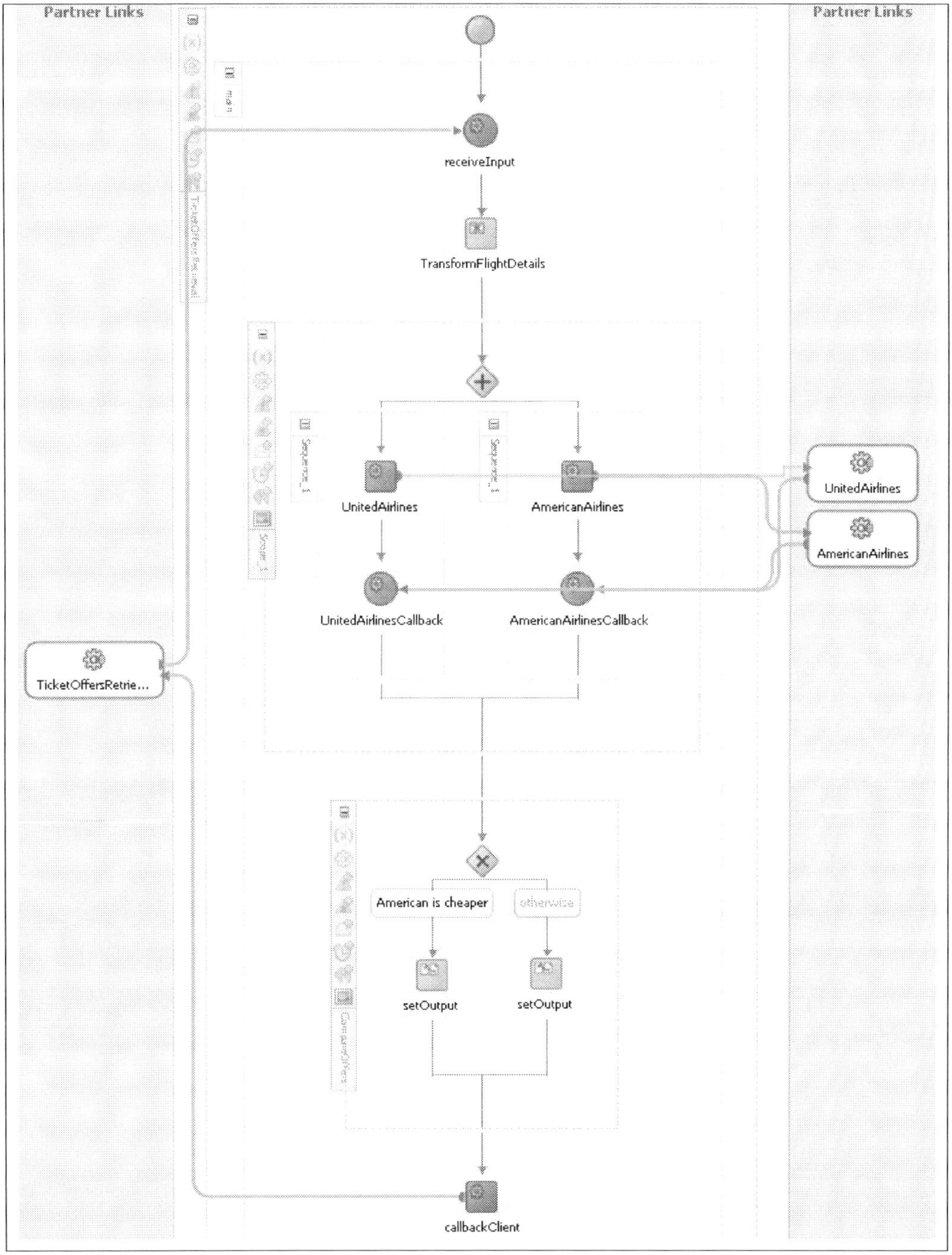

Invoking a BPEL process from BPMN

We open Oracle BPM Studio again. As the BPEL process is asynchronous, we need two flow objects to be able to invoke it (the first for invoking the process and the second for receiving the response). In general, we have two options when invoking asynchronous services or processes:

- We can use a **Message Throw** event to invoke the process or service and a **Message Catch** event to receive an asynchronous response
- We can use **Send Task** to invoke the process or service and **Receive Task** to receive an asynchronous response

Both approaches perform similar functionalities. However, we cannot use the message throw event to invoke a BPMN process that is initiated with a message receive task. Similarly, we cannot use the send task to invoke a BPMN process that is initiated with a message start event. When invoking an asynchronous BPEL process we can use both presented approaches. In our example, we will use the latter approach. First, we drag-and-drop a **Send Task** flow object to the process. The **Properties-SendTask** dialog opens. On the **Basic** tab, we set the name of the object to `Retrieve offers`. Then we open the **Implementation** tab. We select **Service Call** from the **Implementation** drop-down list and select the `TicketOffersRetrieval` BPEL process.

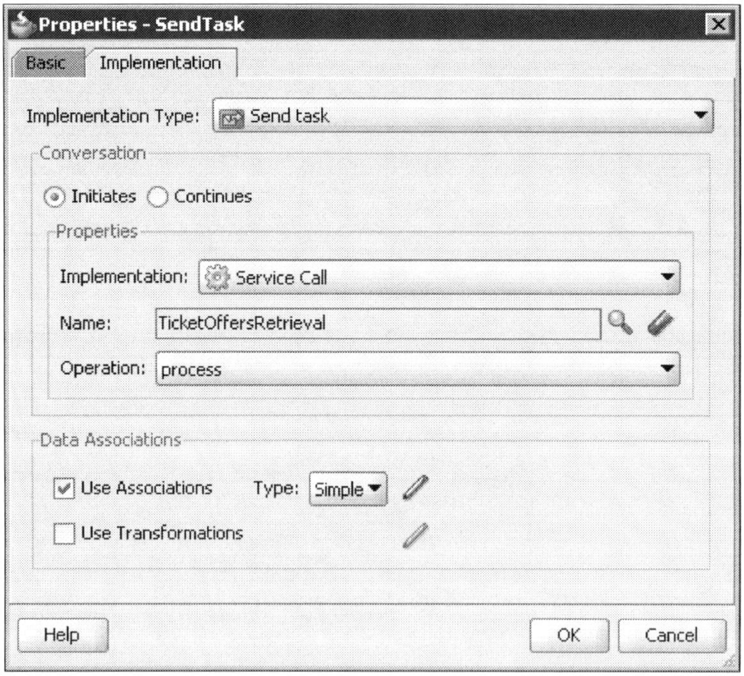

We also configure data associations.

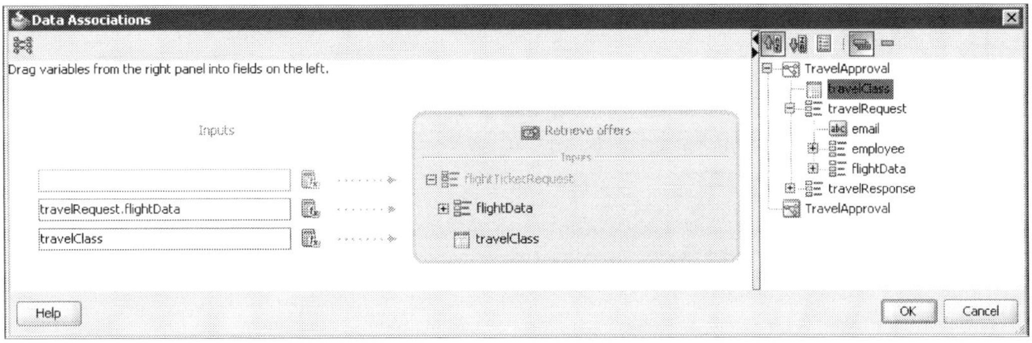

We click **OK** to close the close both dialogs.

Next, we drag-and-drop a **Receive Task** flow object and place it just after the **Send Task.** We name the object `Retrieve offers callback`. On the **Implementation** tab, we select **Continues** for the conversation type, and select `Retrieve offers` from the **Initiator Node** drop-down list. We also configure data associations. In the **Data Associations** dialog, we have to create a new data object to store the result from the BPEL process. We set the name of the new data object to `selectedTicket` and the type to `FlightTicketResponseType`.

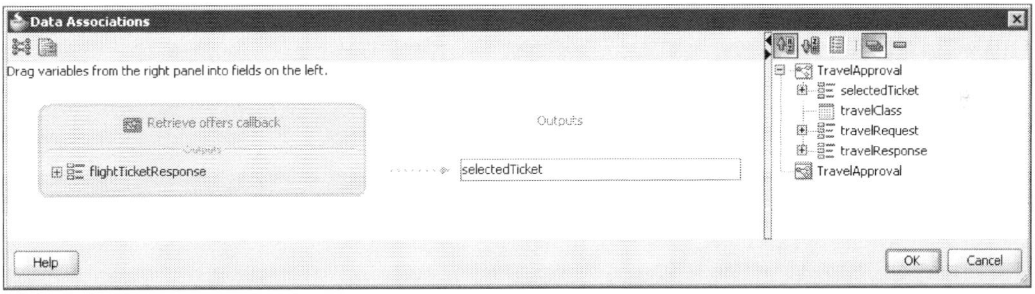

We click **OK**. The new **Receive Task** flow object is now configured as shown next.

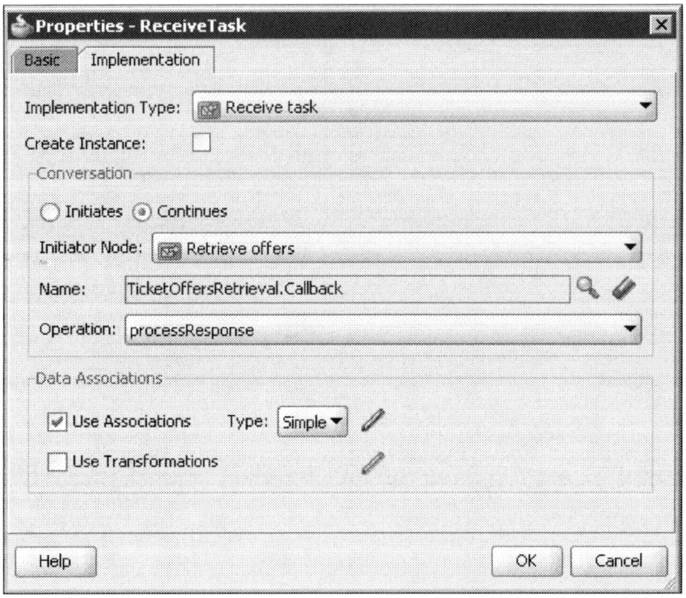

We click **OK** to close the dialog. Our `TravelApproval` BPMN process now looks like this:

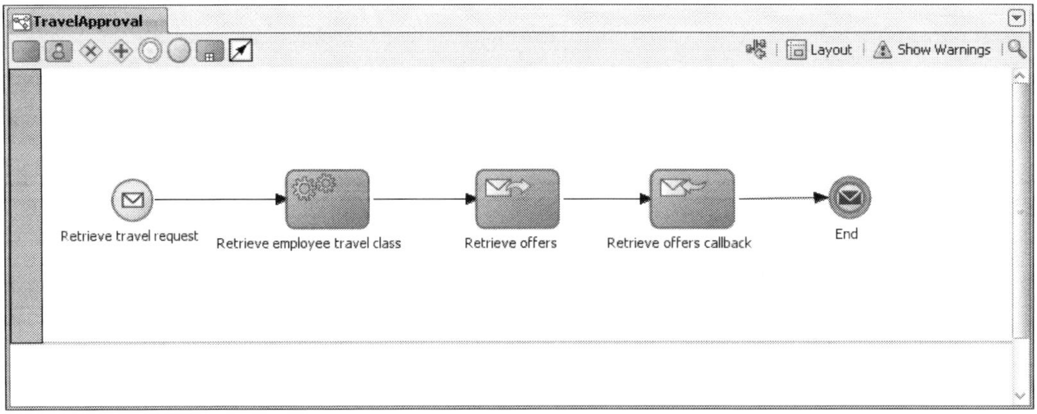

If we open the SOA Composite Editor, we can see that a wire between the `TravelApproval` BPMN process and the `TicketOffersRetrieval` BPEL process has been added automatically.

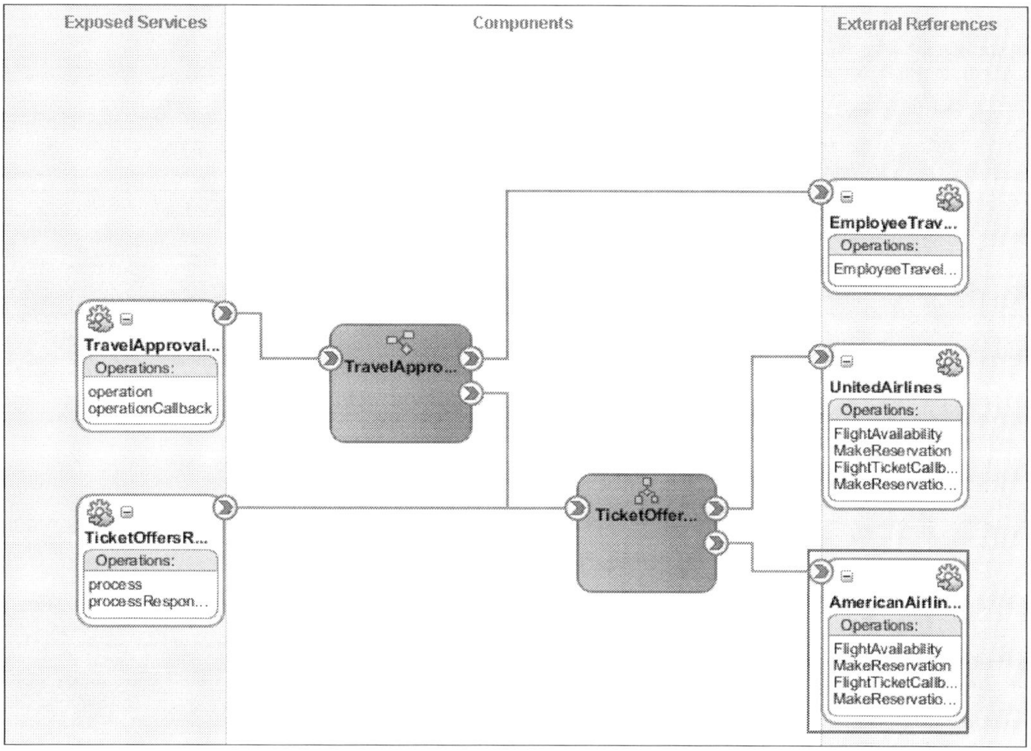

Adding a human task

The next step in the `TravelApproval` process requires human intervention, as the Approval Manager has to approve or reject the selected flight ticket. When creating human tasks in BPM project, we can follow two approaches:

- We can create a human task using the SOA Human Task Editor
- We can use the simplified interface that Oracle BPM provides

We will demonstrate the latter approach. We open Oracle BPM Studio and drag-and-drop a **User** interactive flow object from the **Component Palette** to the process diagram.

> Oracle BPM Suite enables us to use interactive activities, which are shortcuts to different workflow patterns supported by the Oracle Human Workflow.

The **Properties - UserTask** dialog opens. On the **Basic** tab, we set the name of the object to `Flight ticket approval`. Then we open the **Implementation** tab.

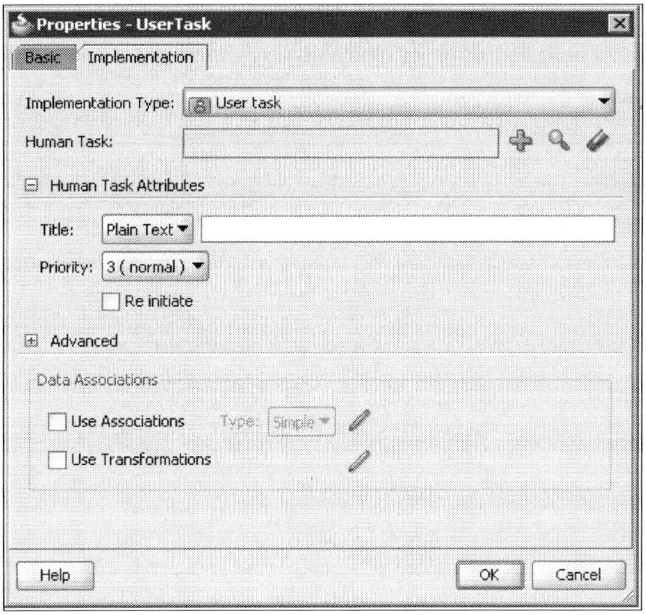

We click on the green plus icon to create a new human task definition. The **Create Human Task** dialog opens. This is a simplified version of the SOA Human Task Editor that we are already familiar with.

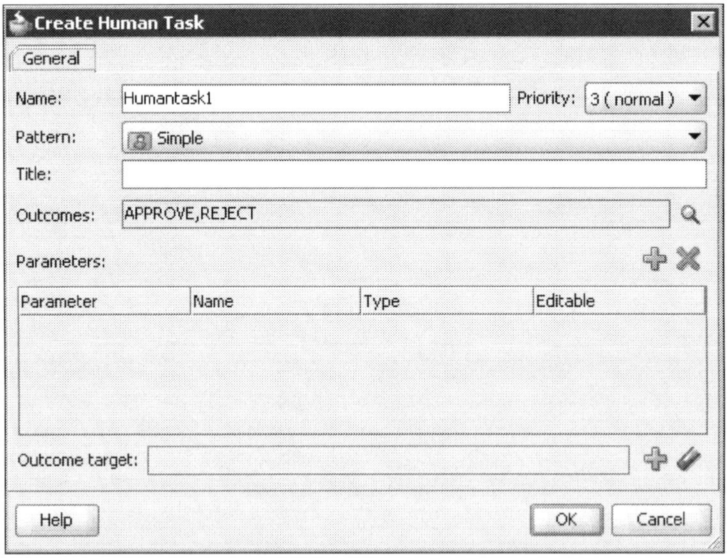

We name the human task `FlightTicketApproval`. We use the default workflow pattern. Then we set the title to `Flight ticket approval`. The title will be displayed in the Oracle BPM Workspace during runtime. We accept the default outcomes (`APPROVE` and `REJECT`). Next, we have to set human task parameters. To add a parameter, we click on the green plus icon. The **Data Objects** window appears on the right side. We simply drag-and-drop the `selectedTicket` data object to the **Parameters** list on the left. Now we have to create a data object to store the human task outcome. We right-click the `TravelApproval` process in the **Data Objects** window and select **Add**. We name the data object `taskOutcome` and select **String** from the **Type** drop-down menu. Then we drag-and-drop the new data object to the **Outcome target** field. The `FlightTicketApproval` human task is now configured as shown in the following screenshot:

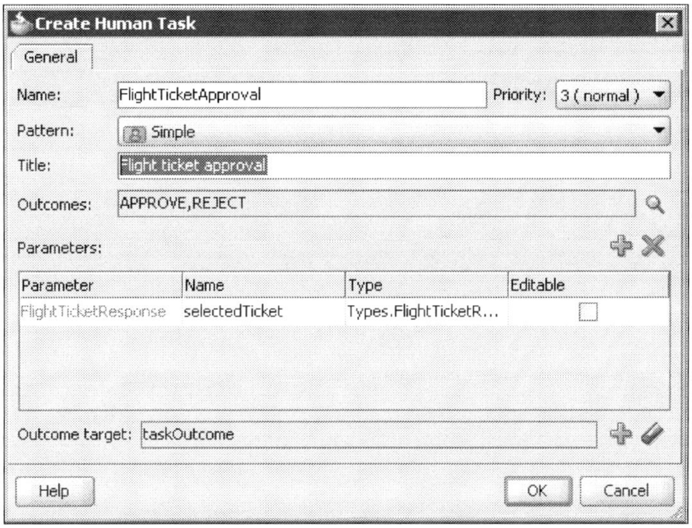

We click **OK** twice to close both dialogs. The **Role properties** dialog is displayed. We create a new logical role and name it **Approval Manager**.

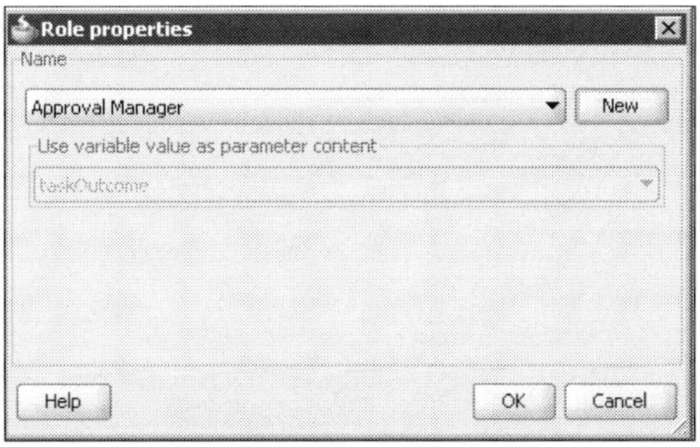

We use roles to model who is responsible for performing the human task. These roles are automatically mapped to the corresponding LDAP roles during runtime. We click **OK** to close the dialog. Notice that a swim-lane with a role name has been automatically created. Our `TravelApproval` BPMN process now looks like this:

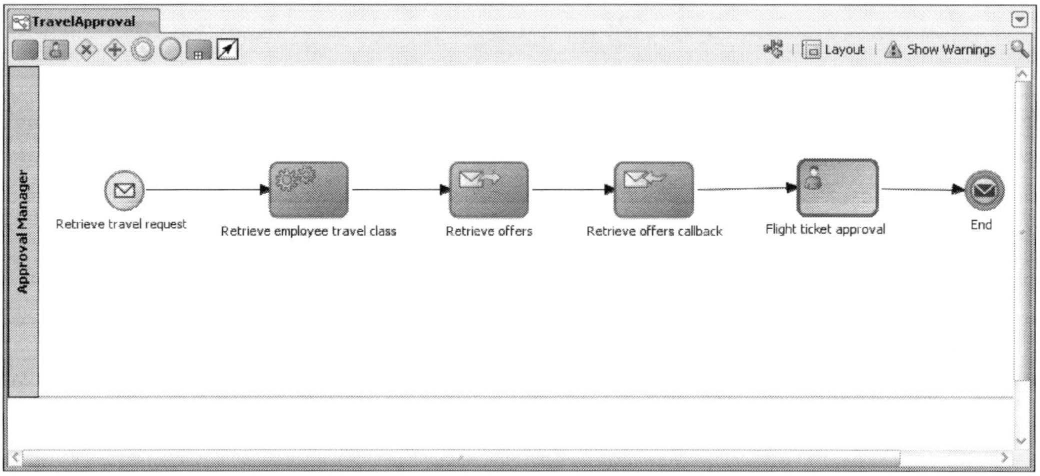

If we open the SOA Composite Editor, we can see that the `FlightTicketApproval` human task is wired with the `TravelApproval` BPMN process.

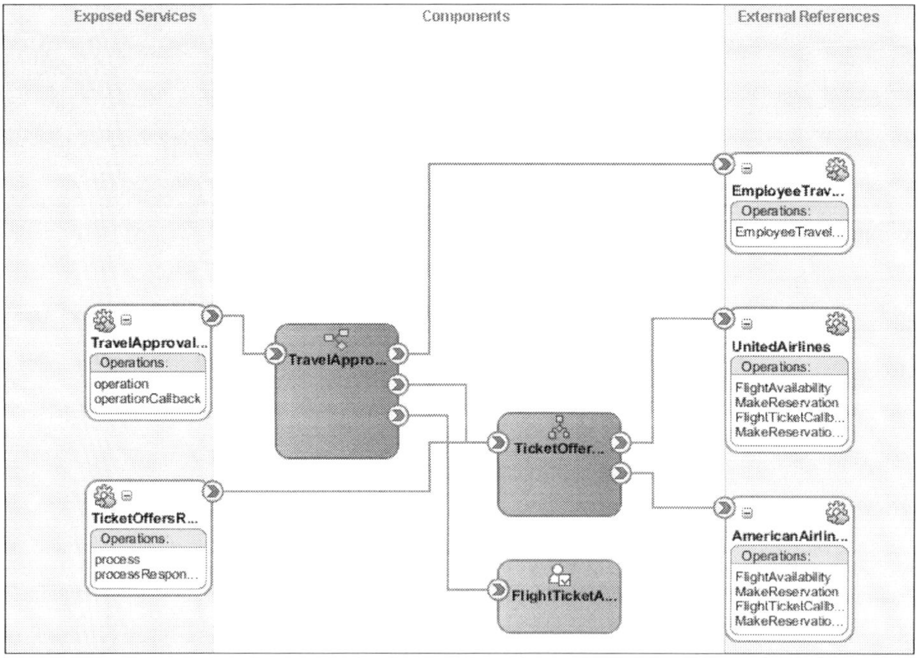

Now we double-click the `FlightTicketApproval` human task to open the SOA Human Task Editor. Then we click on the **Assignment** tab and edit the stage to assign the task to a static user `weblogic`.

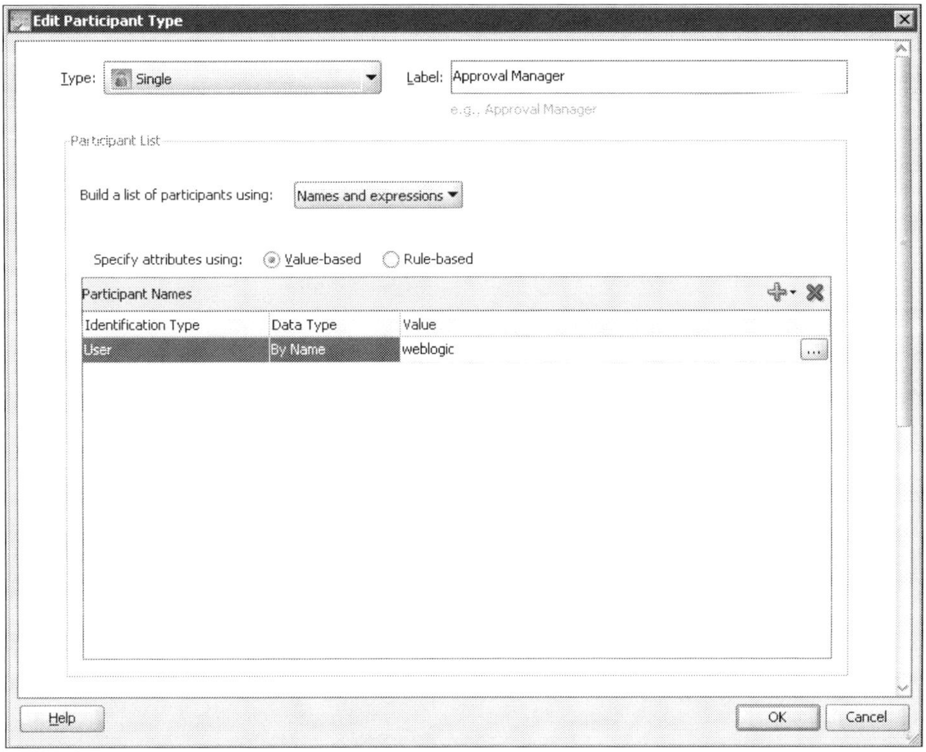

We click **OK** to close the dialog. We also close the SOA Human Task Editor and save the project.

Adding a second BPEL process

If the Approval Manager approves the selected flight ticket, the next step of the process is flight ticket reservation. For this, we will create another BPEL process. We open the SOA Composite Editor and drag-and-drop a **BPEL Process** service component to the **Components** swim-lane of the composite diagram. The **Create BPEL Process** dialog opens.

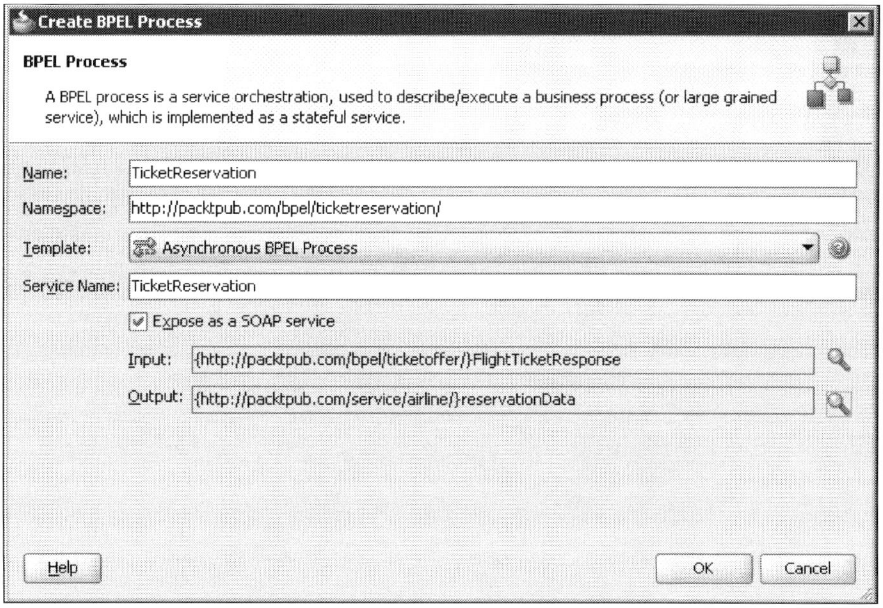

We set the process name to `TicketReservation` and the namespace to `http://packtpub.com/bpel/ticketreservation/`. We also set the process input and output. The process input is defined by the `FlightTicketResponseType`, which was used to define the result of the `TicketOffersRetrieval` BPEL process that we are already familiar with.

For the process output, we use the `FlightReservationType`, which contains data about the selected flight number:

```
<xsd:schema xmlns:xsd="http://www.w3.org/2001/XMLSchema"
            xmlns:tns="http://packtpub.com/service/airline/"
            targetNamespace="http://packtpub.com/service/airline/"
            elementFormDefault="qualified">

<xsd:complexType name="FlightReservationType">
    <xsd:sequence>
      <xsd:element name="FlightNo" type="xsd:string"/>
      <xsd:element name="Confirmed" type="xsd:boolean"/>
```

```
        </xsd:sequence>
      </xsd:complexType>
    </xsd:schema>
```

Then we wire the new BPEL process with both airline services using the SOA Composite Editor.

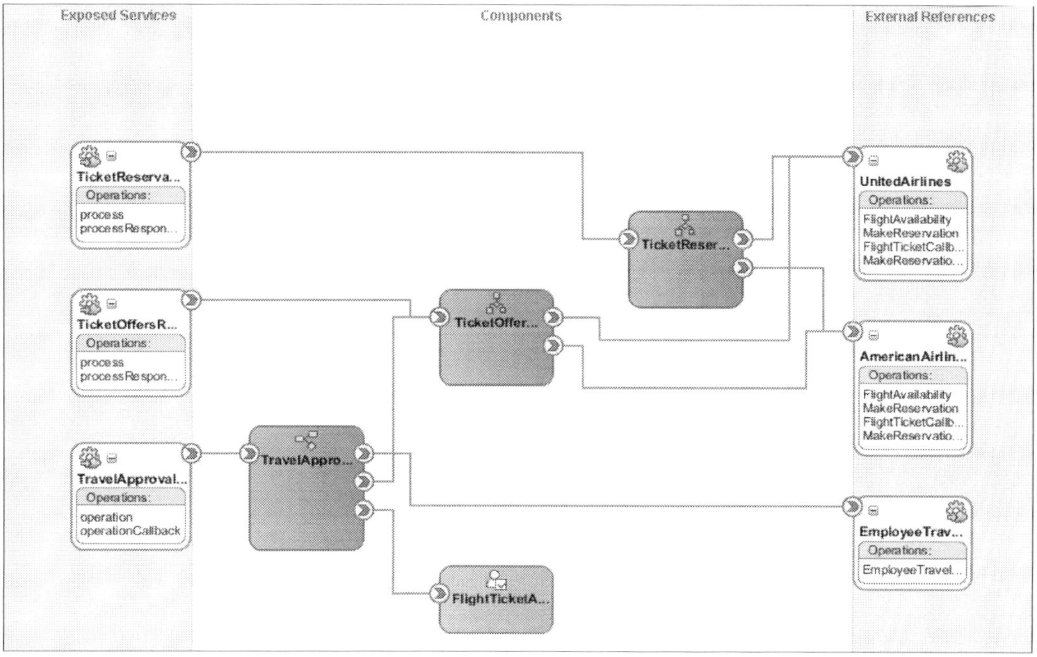

In this chapter, we will not explain how to implement the BPEL process. The following is a screenshot of the implemented BPEL process.

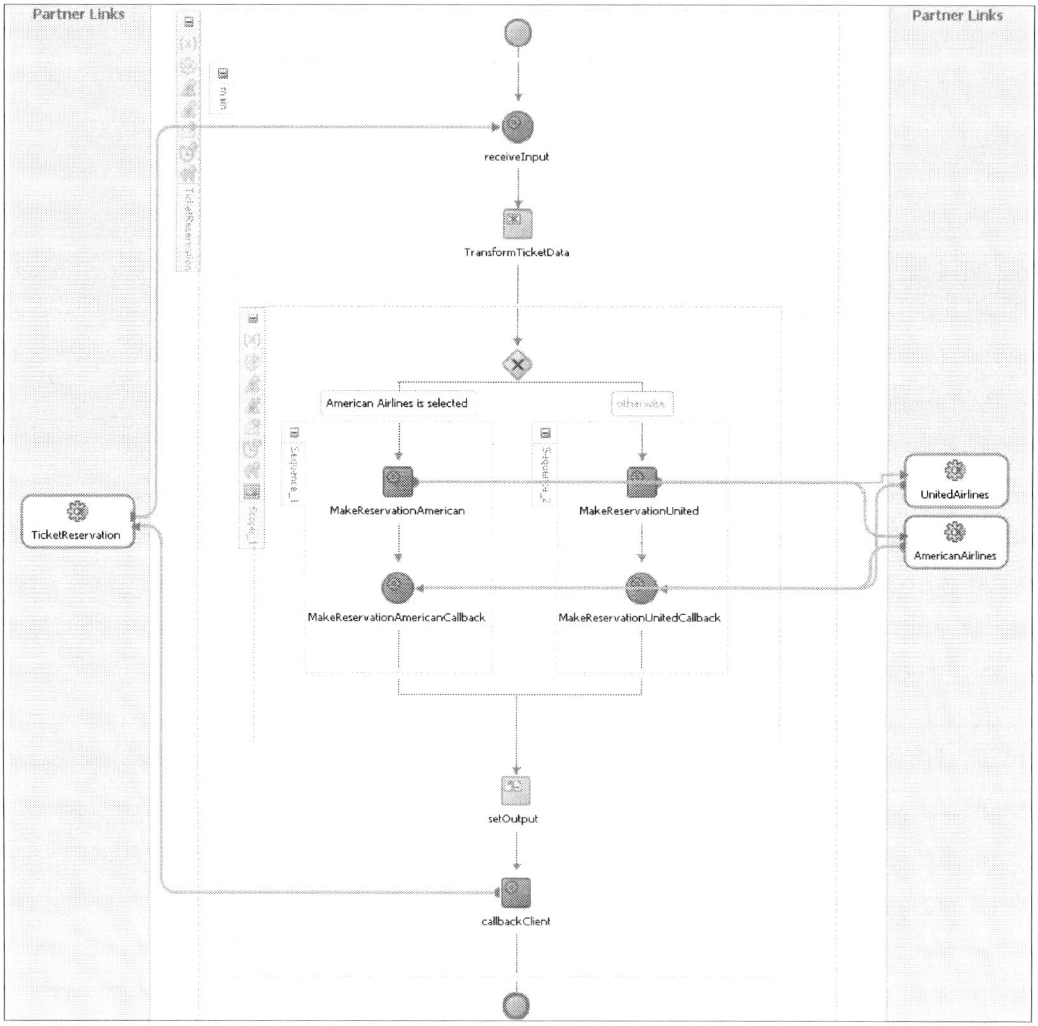

We close the BPEL Editor and save the project.

Completing the process

We open Oracle BPM Studio. As the human task defines two possible outcomes (`APPROVE` or `REJECT`), we have to add an **Exclusive Gateway** flow object to handle the outcome by taking the appropriate path. We drag-and-drop an **Exclusive Gateway** from the **Gateways** category of the **Component Palette** to the process diagram after the `Flight ticket approval` human task. We set the name of the gateway to `Task outcome?`. Then we add **Send Task** and **Receive Task** flow objects and configure them to invoke the `TicketReservation` BPEL process in a similar way as we invoked the `TicketOffersRetrieval` process. We also add another **Exclusive Gateway** flow object to merge both paths.

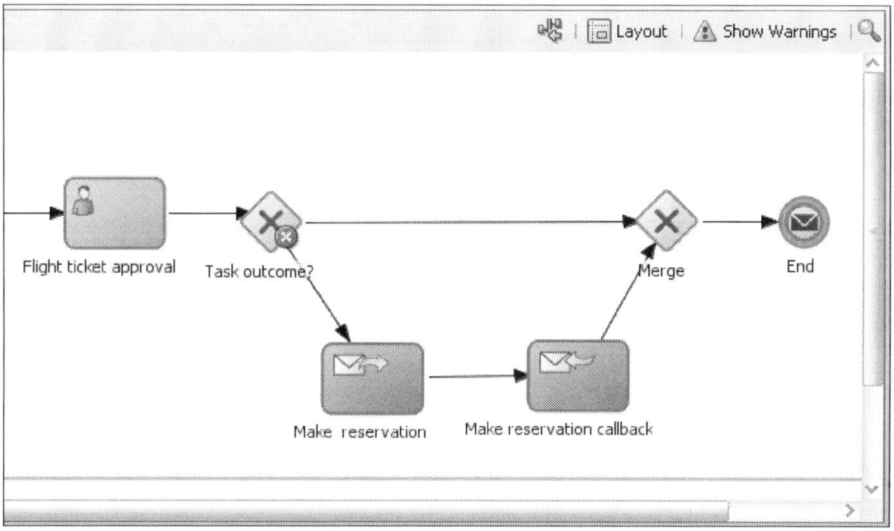

In the previous screenshot, we can see an error icon indicating that conditions for the **Exclusive Gateway** flow object are not set. We double click the transition that connects the gateway flow object and the `Make reservation` **Send Task**. In the dialog, we open the **Properties** tab and select **Condition** from the **Type** drop-down menu.

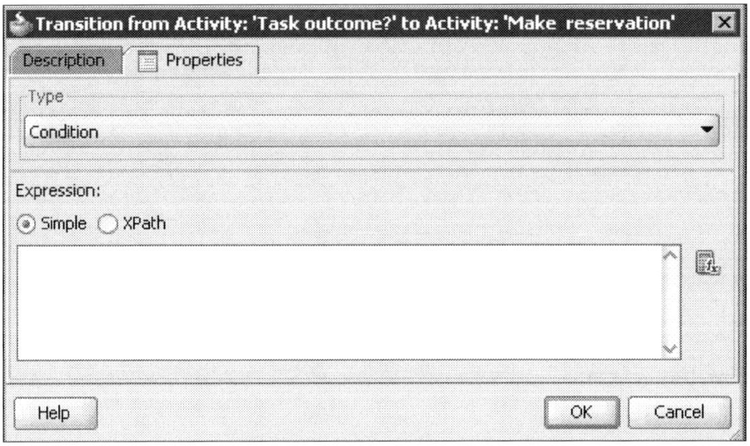

Here we can select whether we want to define simple a condition expression or use the XPath. We select **Simple** and click on the calculator icon on the right to open the Expression Editor. We enter a simple condition expression, as shown next:

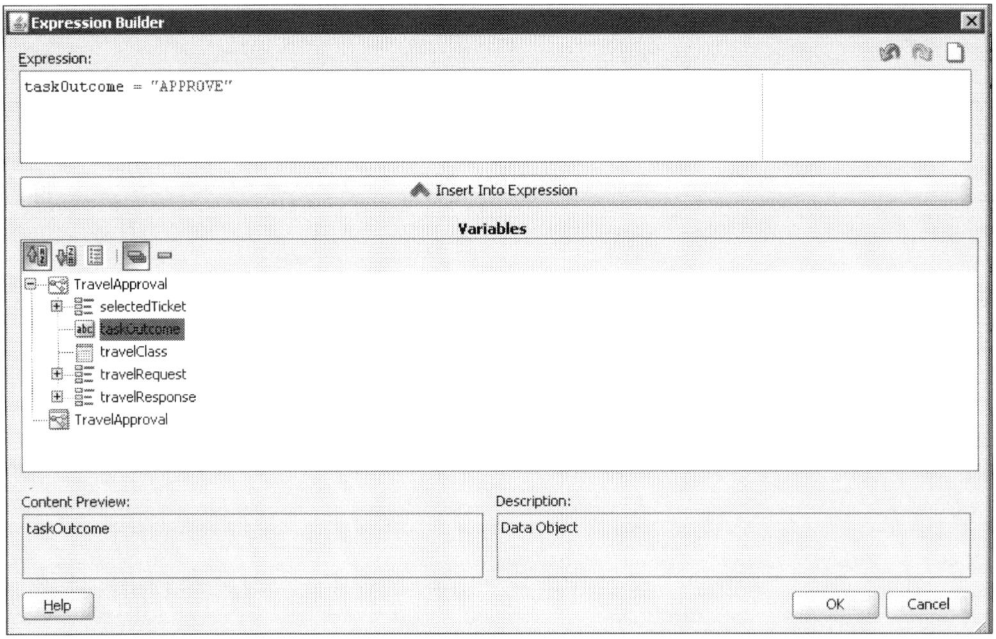

We click **OK** twice to close both dialogs. Our BPMN process is now implemented and is ready to be deployed.

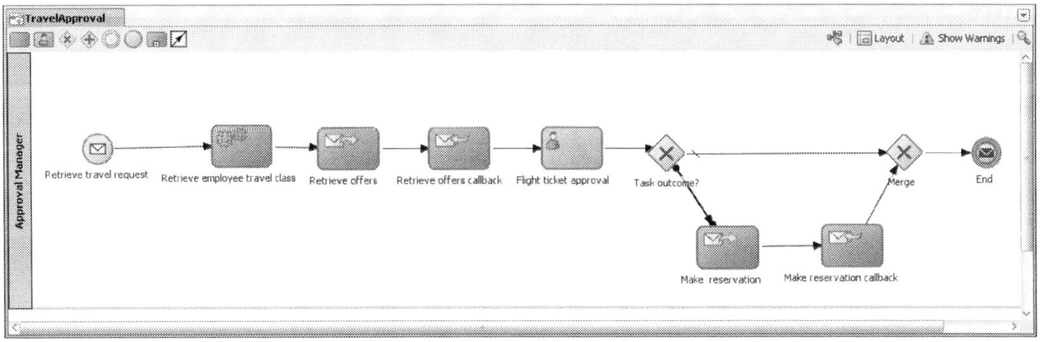

We open the SOA Composite Editor. We can see that our composite application contains four service components. The `TravelApproval` BPMN process is on the top level and uses two BPEL processes (`TicketOffersRetrieval` and `TicketReservation`) and a `FlightTicketApproval` human task. As both BPEL processes are exposed as web services, they can also be invoked from the outside world.

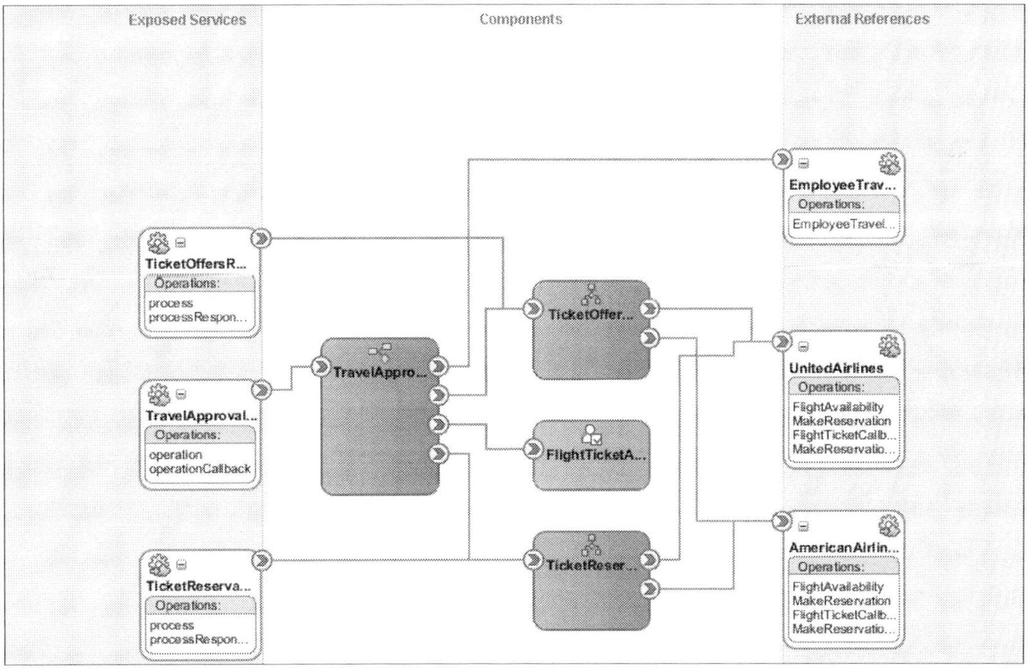

We save the project.

Deploying a BPM project

Now we can deploy our BPM project to runtime. BPM projects can be deployed in the same way as regular SOA projects. We open Application Navigator, right-click the project, and select **Deploy | Project_name**.

Testing an SOA composite application

Now we are ready to test our SOA composite application using Oracle Enterprise Manager Console.

Initiating an SOA composite instance

We open Oracle Enterprise Manager Console and initiate a composite instance. Then we open the instance flow trace.

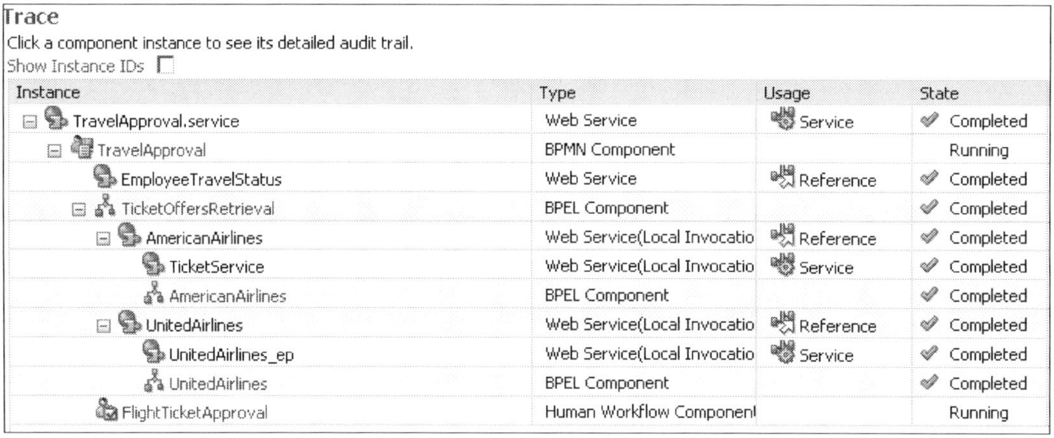

We can see that the instance is still running, as it is waiting for the Approval Manager to complete the `FlightTicketApproval` task. If we click on the **TravelApproval** link, we are able to see the audit trail of the BPMN process.

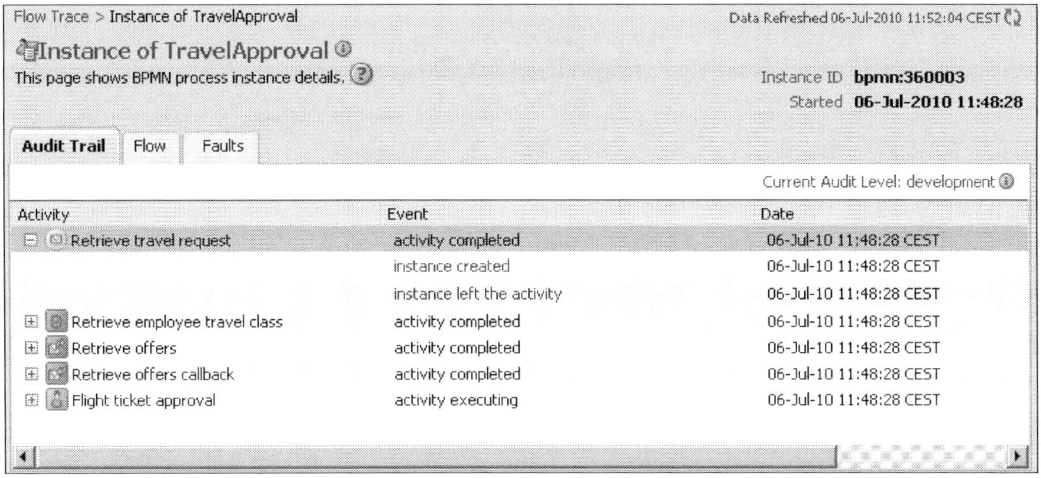

By clicking on the links in the **Event** column, we can see the values of BPMN data objects.

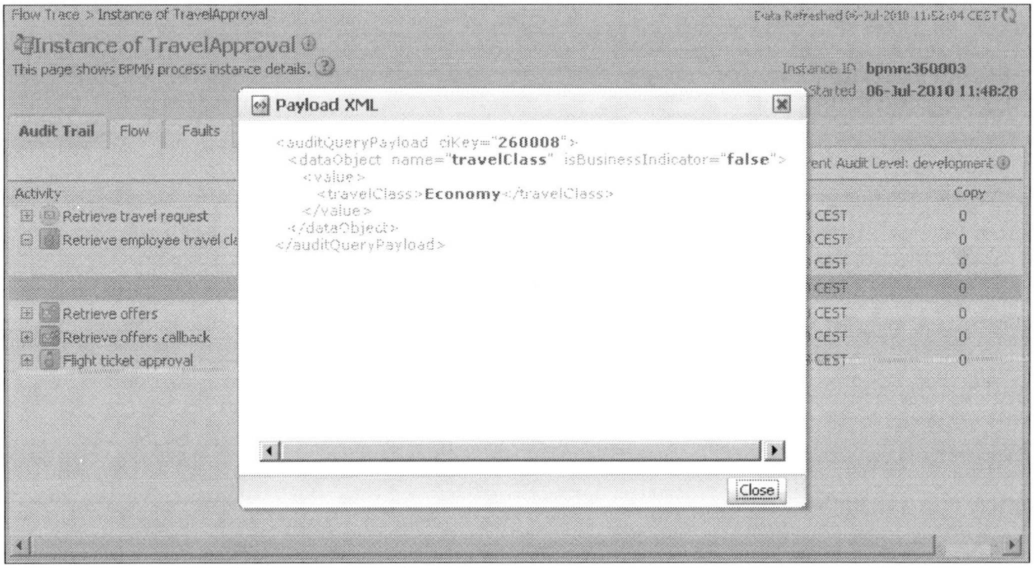

If we click on the **Flow** tab, we can also see the visual flow of the instance. All flow objects that have already been executed, or are currently running, are highlighted with green.

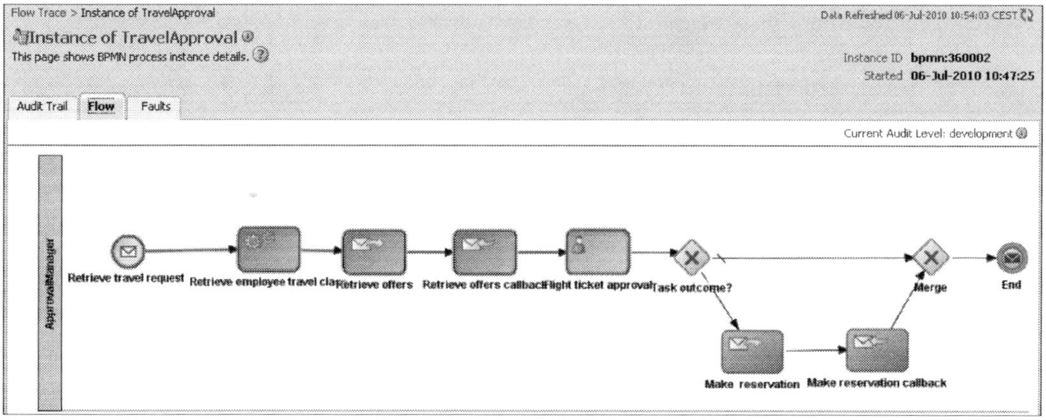

We can also view the audit trail and visual flow of both BPEL processes. The following screenshot shows the flow of the `TicketOffersRetrieval` BPEL process.

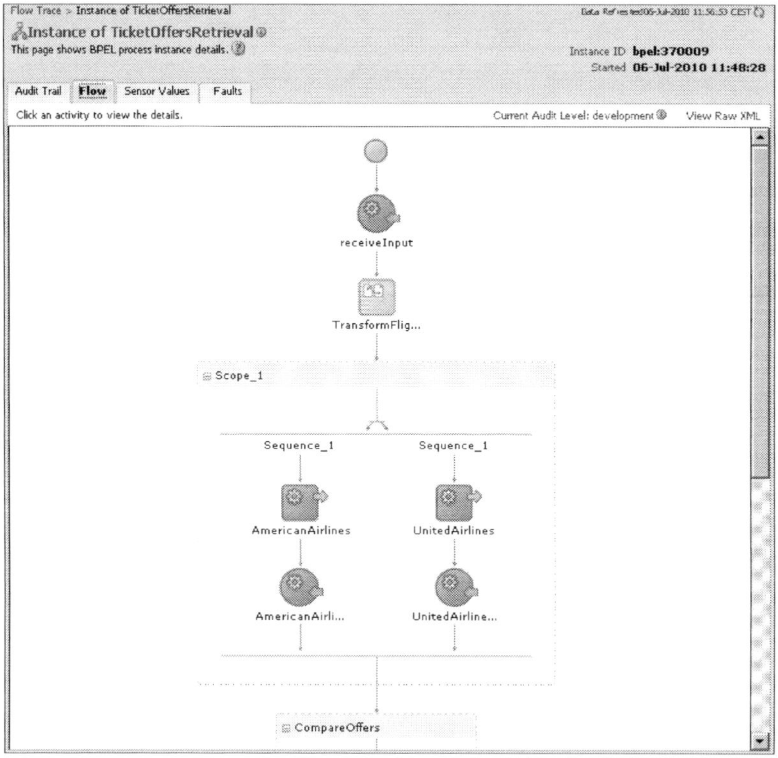

Now we open Oracle BPM Workspace to complete the human task.

Completing the human task using Oracle BPM Workspace

To complete the human task, we have to log into the Oracle BPM Workspace web application using the following URL: `http://host_name:port/bpm/workspace/`, where `host_name` is the name of the host on which Oracle BPM Workspace is installed and `port` is the port number of the SOA managed server (default is 8001). Oracle BPM Workspace is a very powerful application, allowing users to not only act on tasks, but also use the following functionality:

- Customizing the visual appearance and behavior
- Reassigning tasks to other users
- Escalating, renewing, withdrawing, and suspending tasks
- Setting the vacation period to automatically reassign tasks during absence
- Creating reports on task productivity, time distribution, and so on
- Viewing process and custom dashboards to monitor effectiveness
- Sending of notifications and alerts

In this chapter, we will not discuss Oracle BPM Workspace in detail. We will just show how to complete the task. We log into the BPM Workspace as the user `weblogic`, as the task is assigned to him. The BPM Workspace opens as shown in the following screenshot. By default, the **Inbox** view is selected and the user can see all tasks assigned to him in the **My Tasks** list. In our case, there is only one active task: `Flight ticket approval`. Remember that this is the name of the human task that we set during the creation of the human task definition.

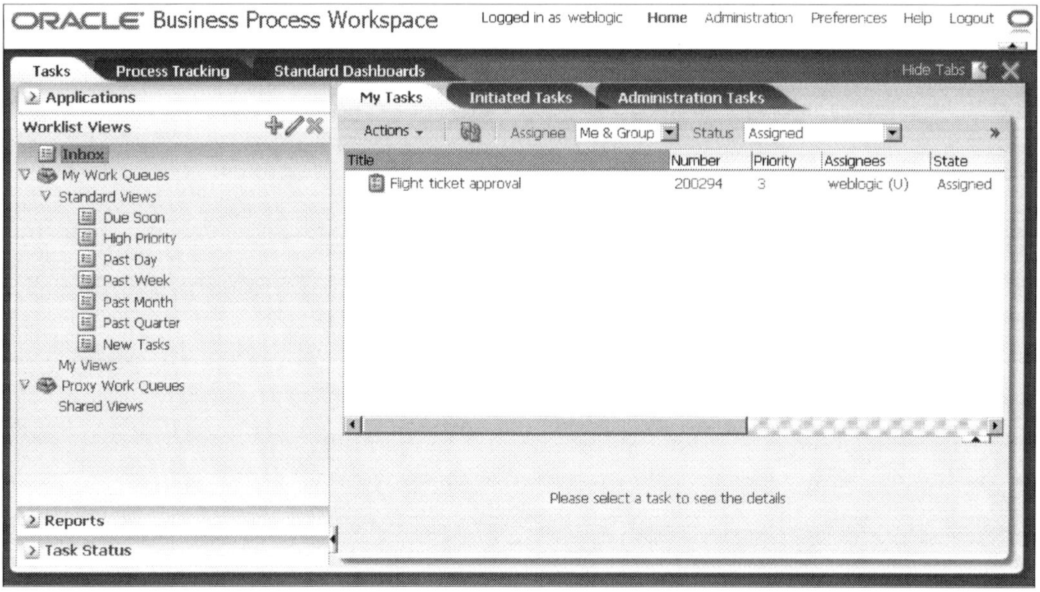

> Notice that a Oracle BPM Workspace application looks very similar to a Oracle BPM Worklist, which we are already familiar with. However, BPM Workspace provides some additional functionality, like monitoring process performance using the Dashboard.

Now we select the `Flight ticket approval` task. Notice that the human task form is not displayed at the bottom of the screen, as we did not create it. We complete the task by selecting **Approve** from the **Actions** drop-down menu. The task is completed and is removed from the **My Tasks** list.

Now we open the flow trace of the instance again. We can see, that all flow objects are highlighted, meaning that the instance has successfully completed.

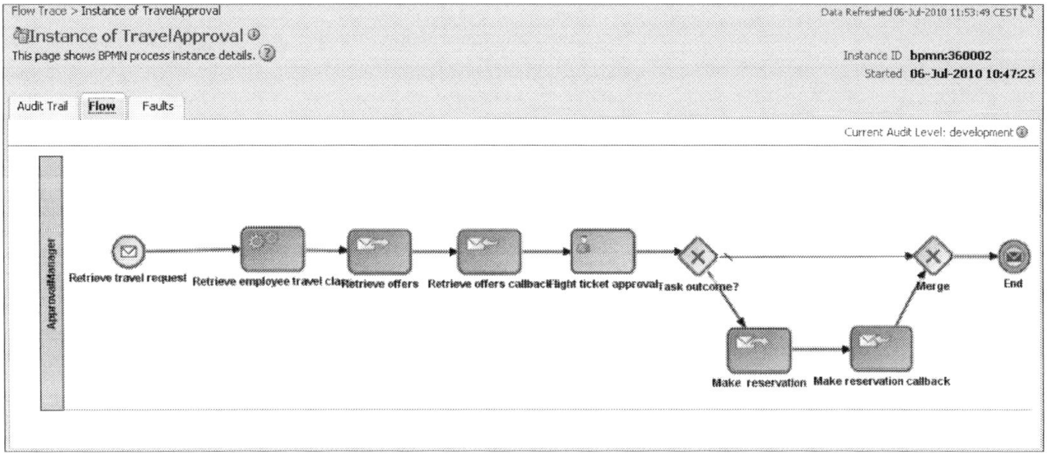

Summary

In this chapter, we have become familiar with Oracle BPM Suite 11*g*. We have described the Oracle BPM Suite architecture and features. We have discussed the importance of being able to directly implement and deploy BPMN processes, without the need to transform them to BPEL.

We have shown how to use Oracle BPM Studio, how to create a new BPM project, and how to model and implement business processes using BPMN 2.0. We have also demonstrated how a BPMN process and BPEL process service components can be used inside a single SOA composite application.

We have also shown how to deploy a BPM project and how to debug a process instance by opening the instance audit trail and the visual flow. Finally we have become familiar with the Oracle BPM Workspace application.

13

SOA Integration—Functional View, Implementation, and Architecture

Let us not expect this chapter to be a primer on Services-Orientated Architecture (SOA). The focus of this chapter is to place SOA in the context of Modernization. SOA can be over hyped and has been, in some cases, exploited by IT vendors as the 'holy grail' of software architecture. However, in the context of Legacy Modernizaton, an SOA Integration architecture can bring your legacy environment into the world of the World Wide Web, Web 2.0, and all the other latest Internet-based IT architectures. Within days, a legacy system can be accessed via a web browser. This is one of the biggest advantages Legacy SOA Integration has over other types of Legacy Modernization. Your time-to-market in weeks, instead of months or years.

Although not a primer, let's first make sure we are all talking the same language when we talk SOA. Though the concepts behind SOA are not new, SOA is also not yet mature. SOA in it current form has really been around only five years now. The concepts of standards-based protocol handlers, pre-defined communication schemas, and remote method invocations have been around for decades. To get a better understanding of SOA, let's see what SOA is, and what SOA is not:

What SOA is	What SOA is not
SOA is an architectural blueprint, a way of developing applications, and a set of best practices. SOA is a journey to a better way of doing business and the technology architecture to support it.	SOA is not an 'out of the box' solution you buy, install, and then have up and running in a matter of months.
SOA architectures can be implemented using Java EE CA, XML file transfer over File Transfer Protocol (FTP), or Remote Procedural Call (RPC) over TCP/IP, Remote Method Invocation (RMI), or other protocols. SOA is a concept and can be implemented in many different ways, some very rudimentary, such as transferring flat files between applications.	SOA is not the same thing as Web services. Web services imply the use of standards such as Java/JAX-RPC, .NET, or REST. Web services also imply the use of a WSDL, SOAP, and/or Java EE Connector Architecture (Java EE CA), and HTTP. In other words, Web services are a very specific set of technologies.
SOA will make your business more agile, increase business visibility, reduce integration costs, and provide better re-use.	SOA will not solve all your IT legacy technology, human, or cultural problems.
SOA is also a broader set of technologies including more then just Web services. Technologies such as an Enterprise Service Bus (ESB), Business Process Execution Language (BPEL), message queues, and Business Activity Monitoring (BAM) all are part of the SOA architecture.	Web services will probably be a part of your SOA architecture, but they are not mandatory. How, when, and where to use the technologies mentioned in the left-hand column is not defined in a manual. You pick and choose the SOA technologies that will be part of your SOA architecture.

Legacy SOA Integration is one aspect of an IT architecture called **Enterprise Information Integration** (**EII**) and **Enterprise Application Integration** (**EAI**). EII is a more data-centric approach to information integration, and EAI is a process or application approach to information integration. EII and EAI include data consolidation, data federation, shared data access, and remote method invocation:

- **Consolidation**—Data consolidation moves all disparate data sources into one central database. This is akin to a data warehouse, and in many ways it can use the same approaches and tools, but with update, insert, and delete capabilities. In many cases, the first stage of data consolidation involves creating a data warehouse, as migrating all the existing applications that access the data can take years or even decades.
- **Federation**—Data federation leaves the data in the individual data source where it is normally maintained and updated, and consolidates it on the fly as needed. In the case of Legacy Modernization, multiple data sources, many of which are non-relational, will appear to be integrated into a single virtual database. The platform will mask the number and different kinds of databases behind the consolidated view.

- **Shared Data**—Shared data integration actually moves data and events from one or more source databases to a consolidated resource, or queue, created to serve one or more new applications. Data can be maintained and exchanged using technologies such as messaging queues and ESBs.
- **Remote method invocation**—The first three options focused on the data side, or EII. The last option is focused on the processes and business logic, or EAI. This is integration at the application layer instead of the data layer.

SOA Integration is a combined data federation and remote method innvocation approach to solve EII/EAI in a Legacy Modernization project. Traditionally, EII has been achieved using Extract, Load, and Transformation (ETL) products. With the advent of SOA technologies such as ESBs, more customers are willing to use ESB products for information integration. ETL vendors have not been standing still and have introduced Web services, and standards-based transformation and workflow engines instead of proprietary software. This means that the differences between ETL and ESB technologies are blurring. In addition, the capabilities of **Business Intelligence** (**BI**) and **Business Activity Monitoring** (**BAM**) technologies are converging. BI tools are becoming more real time, and BAM technologies are offering reporting capabilities.

A major component of an EII/EAI infrastructure is **Master Data Management** (**MDM**). MDM is a single version-of-truth for your information, which is maintained in a central repository. MDM is all about sharing, reusing, and enabling maximum interoperability of your core master reference data. This allows your applications to access the data through a common object or model and a common set of access schemas. Therefore, it does not matter where that data might reside. Your application can access the data through a virtualized access layer.

Now we know what Legacy SOA Integration is, and why we are going to do it. We must now embark on the journey of how we are going to get from a monolithic mainframe to a SOA-enabled mainframe. Before we can just start calling our mainframe or midrange systems, we must first understand the following from a technical perspective:

- What does our business community really want to see?
- How are they going to see it?
- When and where do they want to get the information?
- What should my first project be?
- What will our architecture look like?

We will answer all these questions in this chapter.

The fundamental question many business people ask today is, "Why can't enterprise IT architectures be as straight forward and easy to use as Google, MySpace and other web sites?". This is a valid question, to which the answer is, "IT systems don't have to be and should not be".

As any good IT architect knows, you must balance the combination of cool products, time-to-market, maintainability, ease of use, and cost of the technology. We have not even begun to build the architecture and we are talking of costs for a very good reason. Cost, as in **total cost of ownership (TCO)**, is something every IT decision maker must consider. TCO is not just the upfront cost of the product, but also the cost to maintain, enhance, and manage the environment.

Just placing Web services on an already unwieldy mainfame architecture that does not scale when interfacing to other systems is not the answer. The SOA Integration architecture must be fully secure (in terms of access and data), capable of replication, scalable, and performant. The architecture must also take into account the legacy system that will need to be both a source, and a consumer of Web services.

Unfortunately, most companies with systems older then ten years are starting with an architecture that is appropriately called the Accidental Architecture. This architecture probably looks something like this:

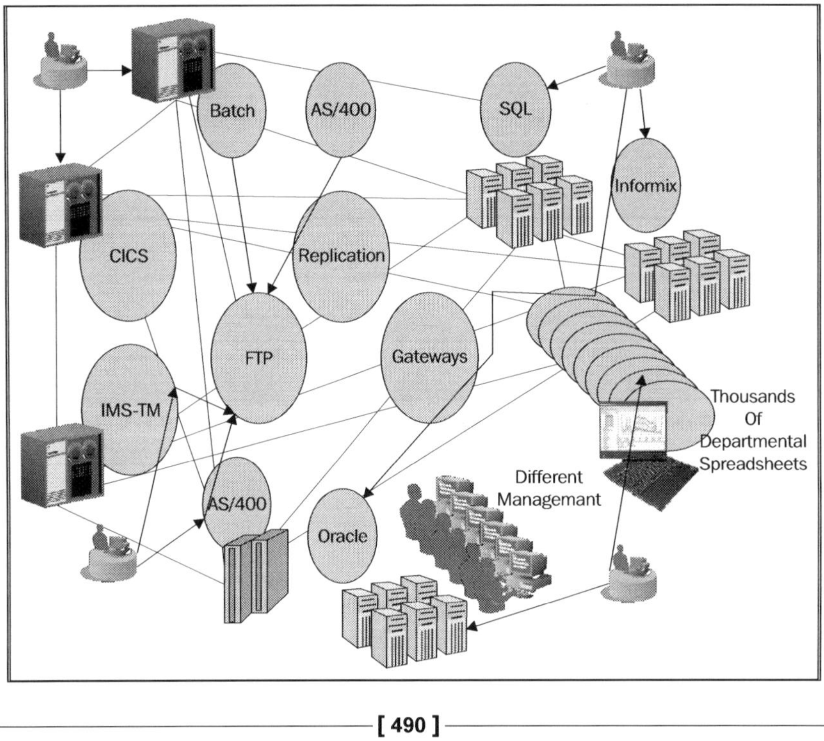

> These lines should cross, go every way, and make a complete mess. The accidental architecture diagram above shows a simplistic view of the integration points in the mainframe systems. Most mainframe systems have far more complex infrastructures with more database vendors, more hardware systems, and systems communicating with each other. As the real diagram would most likely be complex to follow, we have used a simpler version here.

The idea in modern SOA architectures is to eliminate this complex IT architecture. Back in the old days, business IT infrastructures were rigid and complex because memory was expensive, the mainframe disk was small, few people knew about technology, not many technologies or vendors existed, and most IT infrastructures had to be custom coded.

The other thing to consider when developing a Legacy SOA Integration Architecture is that in most cases business processes and workflow are likely to change. Changed business processes entail mapping business services, while taking into account the current business flows, to the new business use cases and creating a business process workflow to implement these use cases.

SOA cannot be discussed without discussing the topic of accessing internal and external Web services. When Web services and SOA were first conceived, the grand idea of developers and users dynamically discovering and using Web services from all over the Internet was at the forefront of the discussion. In reality, this idea was way ahead of its time. Although, almost all SOA implementations leverage internal services, they do so on a very limited basis. Therefore, this chapter will focus on the internal legacy services.

According to the Aberdeen Group: "Organizations that are SOA-enabling their legacy applications on the legacy platform are outperforming those that are using any other approach. They report better productivity, higher agility, and lower costs for legacy integration projects". This is one IT analyst's perspective but it does highlight the importance of SOA integration in any company's legacy modernization strategy.

> **Keeping It Real**: The most difficult aspect of building a new architecture that is completely SOA-enabled is the vast amount of business logic that exists on the mainframe, mostly in COBOL code. A Legacy SOA Integration architecture preserves that legacy business logic but incorporates it into the new world of relational databases, SOA, and Web 2.0.

SOA Integration: Functional View

The business community is not concerned with IMS, VSAM, CICS, IMS-TM, 3270, and other legacy technologies. Business users think in terms of the applications they use, the business processes they execute, and the information they need access to. Their view of the world looks like this:

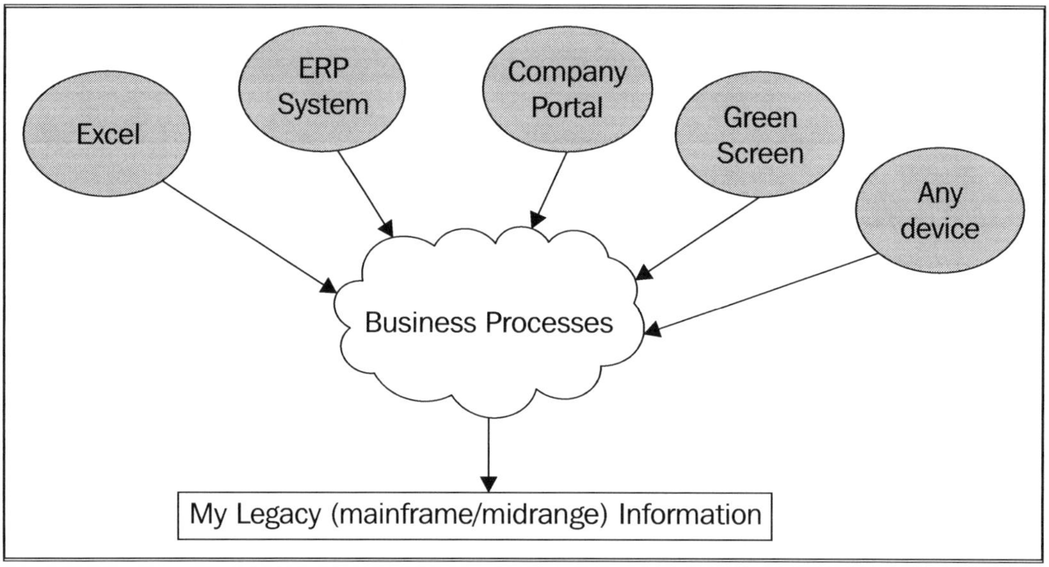

The business community sees the business processes/services as a cloud, something they can see but is far from their world, and not something they can touch or feel. The information they need is like a mysterious 'black box'. It resides somewhere in a dark corner of the IT department.

The business community's functional view of the world consists of four things:

- Applications—This is their interface with the legacy systems. These applications are typically accessed via archaic 3270 (IBM mainframe), 7561 (Fujitisu mainframe), UTS, T27 (Unisys mainframe), and 5250 (IBM iSeries/ AS400) 'green screen' terminals. The users don't necessarily like these interfaces, but this is what they deal with today. They would prefer to get access to information like they do at home, through web browsers and cell phones. They wonder why they can do online banking at home from a nice browser interface, but when they go to work they must use a 'green screen' to look up account information for a client.

- Legacy business processes/services they access—Create new account, check account status, check payment information, submit purchase order, and so on. These are some of the business processes and services the user community executes every day. Most of these transactions ultimately take place on a legacy system.
- Legacy information they need—The user does not care where the information resides. It may be in relational databases on mainframes, hierarchical database, network database, flat files, and so forth. They just want access to the data now and in a fashion that is flexible, adaptable, and easy.
- To an IT person, the business community's view of the world is way too abstract. The IT community will look at SOA Integration in a more technical context and include things like transformation services, legacy connectors/adapters, and types of legacy artifacts. The functional view from the technical perspective looks like this:

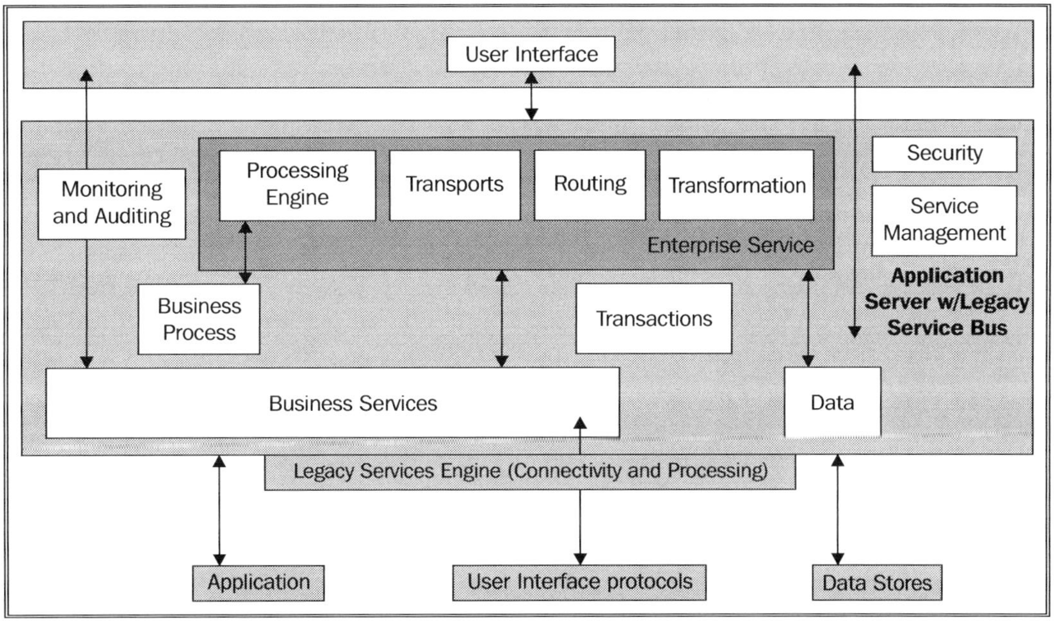

The view consists of four basic components:

- **User Interface** – In the legacy world, these are most likely to be CICS transactions that are executed from COBOL applications and rendered on character-based 'green screens'. The most widely used mainframe 'green screen' is a 3270 device that was manufactured by IBM. These devices have long gone the way of the dinosaur. However, there are many software packages that emulate the 3270 device protocol on modern hardware such as the PCs.

  In the modern world of IT, the user interface could be a PC-based web browser, Java, or .NET application, a browser enabled PDA or cell phone, or any device that understands HTTP.

- **Legacy Service Bus (LSB)** – LSBs have existed for decades. Traditionally, they have taken the form of FTP, mainframe CICS to CICS calls, custom COBOL applications, TCP/IP and/or SNA socket communication, messaging queues, and the list goes on. IBM has done an incredible job of getting IBM MQSeries to be the backbone of most legacy service buses. Most mainframe shops use MQSeries to integrate legacy systems with open systems, internal systems, and packaged applications.

  The world of IT service bus integration moved to RPC, DCE, Corba and others in the late 1980s. Most of the technology has still not become commonplace with FTP and queuing still ruling the legacy world, even today.

  Today, **Enterprise Service Bus (ESB)** products have become the common means to integrate systems. LSB is a specialized ESB that allows you to expose the mainframe artifacts. The component that makes the LSB a superset of an ESB is the legacy connectivity software.

- **Legacy Services Engine (LSE)** – Business users don't see this piece of the architecture and really don't care about it. But it is central to the legacy SOA integration architecture. This technology/software stack is where the magic happens. The magic is making legacy hierarchical and network data stores appear as relational data (and mainframe DB2 accessible from open systems), legacy business transactions look like Java or .NET transactions, and legacy interfaces as accessible as just another Web service. The LSE also provides features such as governance and security that the business users are concerned about. There are other features such as scalability and performance that are transparent to the business user, but are expected to be in the platform. Lastly, features like adaptability, flexibility, auditing, and management are not the domains of business users, but are an IT management concern. Adaptability and flexibility could be argued as transparent business user features, but we put them in IT domain features because business users don't care how rigid or nonrigid that infrastructure is, they just want what they want right away.

- **Legacy Artifacts**—These are the data, application processes, and the user interface. Application processes could be actual COBOL modules, transactions, stored procedures, or even dynamic SQL. To the user, they just want to see the information that is important to them. To you as the IT person, the decision, which legacy artifacts to base your Legacy SOA Integration platform on, is a very crucial one. In most cases, a hybrid, or a combination of the above is what your architecture will require. Typically, IT will not have a comprehensive or corporate SOA plan, let alone a plan for their LSB. So they will take the 'easy path' and expose legacy 'green screens' as Web services. As we will learn later in this chapter, this may not be the best approach.

> **Keeping It Real**: It is possible to call legacy services directly from a script, Java application, or an HTML page. However, your overall SOA architecture becomes even more chaotic than your legacy 'Accidental Architecture' was earlier. A complete Legacy SOA Integration platform provides services such as orchestration, messaging, presentation and data access services, service management, central control, transformation, security, and monitoring in one easy to use solution stack.

SOA Integration: Technical View

This section will describe all the products and technologies that are available to complete your middleware architecture. This may include an LSB, Java EE application server and security infrastructure. Don't get overwhelmed by all the choices and technologies. Your specific business and technology drivers will quickly narrow down the set of products and technologies in your LSB and Java EE application server to a handful mentioned in this section. However, before you buy anything specific, it is important you understand the entire set of products and technologies that make up the LSB and Java EE application server. Otherwise, you run the risk of solving a specific use case but not building an agile middleware architecture that will meet both tactical and strategic business objectives.

The technical view adds aspects to the architecture that are very important from an implementation perspective: performance, scalability, reliability, security, management, end-to-end testing, and governance. It is not that these attributes are not important to the business community. Business users just assume that the IT infrastructure will be easy to use, will always be on, will run fast, are secure, and will run without errors.

Governance must be considered in terms of both design time (developing, controlling, and managing) and runtime (security, control, monitoring, and managing). Questions that are typically asked are: Who is running my services? How are they being used? What are the impacts to current business processes?

Something else that has not been discussed is the mainframe as both a provider and consumer of Web services. In most situations that we encounter, the requirements are that the legacy system will call a Web service (provider), and will also call Web services that are Java or .Net based on open systems (consumer). Your technical architecture should take into account both inbound and outbound Web services support (the legacy system can act as a Web service server, or a Web service client).

Sometimes, we are asked, "Do I really need an LSB or application server? Can't I just call my legacy Web services from an HTML page?". In other words, is an application server and/or SOA suite of products really needed? You could create a LSB without using a SOA product. However, if you thought your legacy architecture was a 'hair ball' to start with, it will now have more lines and points of entry crossing each other. Remember, the idea is to create an infrastructure that is less rigid and more agile then your current system.

The technical view consists of the four basic components from the functional view. Although this is represented as a two-dimensional model, it is actually a three dimensional model. The third dimension includes the aspects of functionality, performance, and governance that cuts through the three layers represented here. The complete set of technologies (once again, don't panic as you will not need any of these) looks like this:

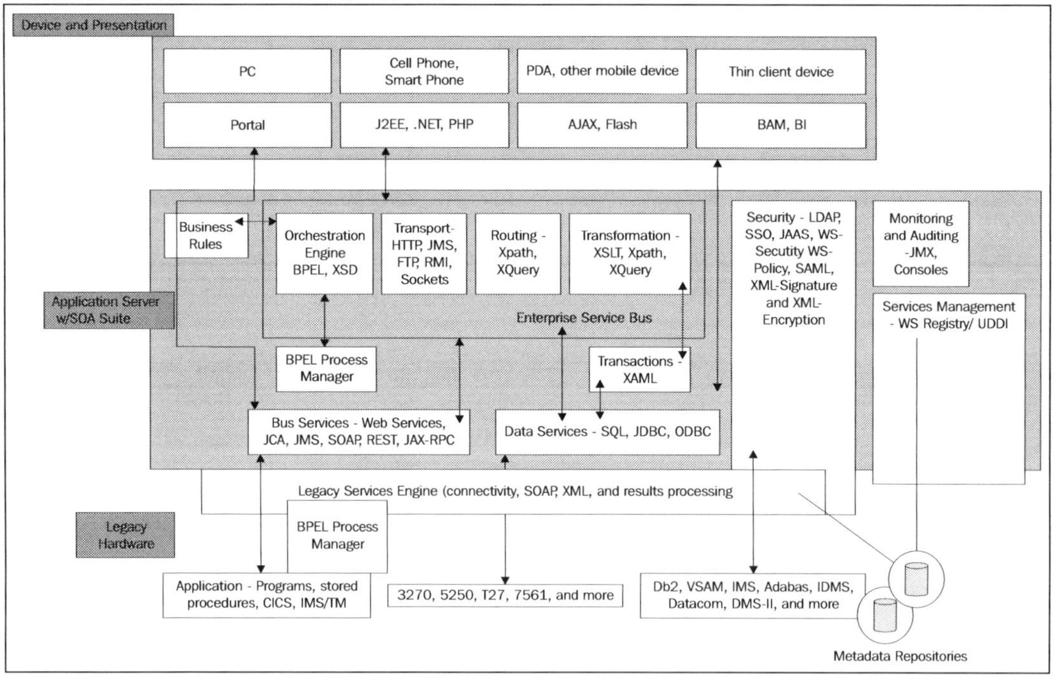

User Interface

In the legacy world, the device and presentation layer are very tightly coupled, for example, a 3270 device displaying a 3270 presentation data stream. In the new world of IT, the user interface device and presentation layer are not tightly coupled, and the devices become much broader. The user device could be a PC, PDA, cell phone, thin client terminal or any device that supports HTTP, and a browser. The presentation layer could be a Java Applet, Java Server Page (JSP), or Java Server Faces (JSF), AJAX, PHP, or .NET application residing in a Portal. Since the device is not fixed, and new devices will emerge that did not exist five years ago (like smart phones and iPhones), the presentation-tier should be capable of display in any channel. This is often called multichannel delivery.

Legacy Service Bus (LSB) and Application Server

The LSB is a component of your middleware stack. Middleware can be anything from a crude, homegrown, internally developed XML data transfer and transformation, to an all-inclusive SOA Suite. Middleware in the open systems realm has advanced from HTTP servers, Java applications, Portals, data integration servers to a complete integrated stack of application server and SOA software. The term SOA Suite has become commonplace in the IT industry. An SOA Suite consists of the following components:

Functionality	Description
Enterprise Service Bus	A multiprotocol server to connect applications and provide a common bus for data integration
BPEL-based Process Manager	An orchestration and workflow engine to compose and execute services within a business process
Business Rules Engine	Capture, centralize and automate business policies and application logic
Business Activity Monitoring	End user graphical dashboard to gain real-time visibility into the operation, and the performance of business processes and services
Web Service Management	A security solution to enforce authentication, authorization and runtime policies on services
Connectivity	Adapters to connect to virtually any data source including applications, databases, queues, RFID and other physical devices
SOA Data Integration	A high-volume, high-performance SOA data integration server
Event processing	A message based system that applications subscribe to which they use to send and receive event alerts and messages

The interesting aspect of SOA Suites in the Legacy SOA Integration space is that some of the components can either reside on the open systems middle-tier, or on the mainframe-tier or on both. These components (as shown in the above picture) include BPEL, Security, Management, and the ESB (normally the queue). This is important because in some cases, it may make sense to do the BPEL process orchestration on the mainframe. So the processing is closer to the application and data. This will reduce network traffic and boost services response time. However, it could increase the MIPS usage of your mainframe, which is typically what you try to reduce.

Legacy Services Engine (LSE)

Talk to any of the legacy connectivity vendor and they will quickly avoid the conversation of gateways and screen scraping, and for good reason. Screen scraping is an old method of exposing the legacy presentation-tier as Web services. It relied on the field position (row/column), and the type of terminal stream. Both these restrictions make it very inflexible. A big problem occurs when a screen map changes. The application that receives the screen scraped stream is most likely to fail. Gateways are taboo because they imply heavy weight, and are difficult to manage products. Most legacy SOA companies will refer to their products as adapters or servers. We will use the term Legacy Services Engine (LSE) believing it incorporates everything that this engine does, all the way from mainframe connectivity to results processing.

The LSE is where the real action happens. This is where the bridge between the legacy system and the middle-tiers takes place. This engine also has features such as security, monitoring, caching, and management. As this is such an important and broad area, we will break this into LSE components, development, and implementation/deployment areas. We will start with the LSE Components.

LSE Components

We will cover the key LSE components in this section—the connectivity and processing engine for mainframe connectivity and information processing of mainframe screens, logic, and data.

Connectivity and Processing Engine

The processing engine has a protocol server, SQL engine, XML parser, and transformation processer. The typical protocols supported are SOAP (HTTP and XML), JMS and Java EE Connector Architecture (Java EE CA). SOAP requires neither an adapter, nor a process on the middle-tier to handle the results on the client. When Java EE CA is used, you hear the term adapter being used. An adapter implies that there is a piece of software on the middle-tier to handle the processing of the results. The Java EE CA adapter will communicate through SOAP messages. JMS is not typically used in a synchronous online transaction environment.

This engine is where the results are processed, and the request sent back to the client. The client could be an HTML page, a BPEL process, or a Java application or some other process residing on the middle or client-tiers. As mentioned earlier, the engine needs to be both a provider and consumer of services. For a provider of Web services, the standard processes are as follows:

- Receive a service request from the client—The LSE has a protocol and request handler to receive the request from the client.
- Map the request to the appropriate legacy artifact—The request is then processed using the metadata repository to map the call to the correct mainframe call and do any data type conversion. If the request is a database call, the SQL engine will transform the call into the appropriate legacy data store access scheme.
- Call the appropriate legacy artifact—The application, transaction, program, stored procedure, 3270 screen, or a data store is called.
- Process the results—The results are returned to the processing engine. The metadata repository is used once again to perform any data transformations, data type mapping, or cleansing. The results are formatted into a SOAP response.
- Send the request back—The results are put back on the communication network and sent back to the client.

SQL Engine

The SQL Engine is required for data-enabled services. The SQL engine will evaluate subqueries, joins, and aggregate functions when possible. It is best for these operations to happen closest to where the data is stored, so the engines will typically do this type of processing before sending the results set back to the client. The SQL engine has minimal work to do when a request is made via SQL, and the database source is an SQL compliant database engine such as IBM DB2. However, differences do exist despite vendor's compliance with industry standards such as SQL. Data type translation is typically more intensive as there are no industry standards on how data is stored. The situation gets exponentially more complicated when you bring non-relational data stores (such as, VSAM, IMS, IDMS, Adabas) into the mix. These databases do not support SQL natively and the database calls in the application are not likely to be SQL. The automated transformations required to solve this problem are fourfold:

- **SQL translations**—SQL translation takes into account the differences between Oracle's implementation of SQL and each participating non-Oracle databases data store call interfaces. In the case of DB2, the differences are minimal, and easy to discover. For nonrelational data stores, SQL is not the native calling method. So SQL will need to be translated into the native call. The SQL statement passed to the engine will look like this:

  ```
  Exec :Bind-variable := value;
  Select column1 from table-name where id = :bind-variable;
  ```

  The corresponding VSAM read statements looks like this:

  ```
  MOVE value TO key1.
          READ file-name RECORD [INTO ws-field]
              INVALID KEY do something
              NOT INVALID KEY do something else
        END-READ.
  ```

- **Data Dictionary translations**—The data dictionary holds the information to map the source tables to the native files or record sets, the column/field mappings, the data type mappings, and other information necessary to transform the calling SQL to the native call interface. IT developers must have the capability to query the metadata of the remote, non-Oracle database in order to diagnose problems. In Oracle, the data dictionary is stored in an Oracle table. The data dictionary translation information on the mainframe is typically in a flat file, sequential file, or in a relational database.
- **Indexing**—Anyone who has done relational database SQL coding knows the importance of indexes. Have the right ones, and your application runs fast; don't have the right ones or have too many wrong ones, then performance suffers. Indexing must include the ability to create indexes on legacy non-relational sequential data sets such as the VSAM files. This means you can have direct indexed access, even to data that does not have a native index. Where native indexes exist, they should automatically be used to optimize query performance. This support becomes more important as you get more sophisticated with your SOA data sets and start joining relational and non-relational data sets. Joining data sets without indexes becomes painfully slow.
- **Data type translation**—Legacy data types must often be converted when viewing the data in a relational format. These data types need to be translated transparently. There are many data type translations that need to happen for date and time, floating point, pic x, and pic n fields. These data types map easily to relational data types. Three common data types in legacy environments that do not map easily to relational databases are: Comp-3 (packed decimal), redefines, and occurs. In COBOL, these data types look like this:

- Packed decimal

```
05  BALANCE-DUE   PIC S9(6)V99 COMP-3.
```

- Redefines

```
05 a pic s9(4) comp-5.
  05 a1 redefines a pic x(2).
```

- Occurs

```
05  MONTHLY-SALES OCCURS 12 TIMES   PIC
    S9(5)V99.
```

The corresponding Oracle data types looks like this:

- Packed decimal

```
BALANCE-DUE      DECIMAL(8,2);
```

- Redefines

```
a BINARY;
a1 CHAR(2);
```

  The redefines becomes two separate columns in the relational table.

- Occurs

```
        MONTHLY-SALES-JAN NUMBER(7,2);
. . .
        MONTHLY-SALES-DEC NUMBER(7,2);
```

  The relational table has 12 columns, one for each month in the year. You will have 12 separate columns coming back in the resulting SOAP message.

> We don't want to turn this into an XML parsing and transformation book, but it is important to mention this briefly. XML processing—parsing and transformation—is both a memory-intensive and a processor-intensive activity. It is an important part of the LSE, as all service requests will come as XML streams, and all responses will go out as XML streams. Therefore, it is critical that the LSE has a highly performant XML engine.

Optional LSE Components

The next components of the LSE we will discuss are often part of (although they don't need to be) the LSE. They can be separate processes that reside on in the middle-tier, on mainframe, one or the other, or even both. There are pros and cons to each of these configurations that we will discuss in the implementation/deployment section of this chapter. For now, we will review each of these components:

Orchestration

Orchestration supports execution of a business process. The business process can consist of a number of steps, transactions, decision points, and other business processes. Orchestration is really just a fancy word for traditional workflow. What is different is that orchestration engines have a common, standardized execution language and run time engine. Most workflow engines are built upon proprietary languages (T-SQL, PL/SQL, VB Script), and run in proprietary runtime engines. The execution language for orchestration is BPEL, and the runtime engine is Java. BPEL supports both human and automated orchestration. In Legacy SOA, BPEL is important because in many instances, the legacy services will be integrated with other Java, .NET, or REST based services that reside on open systems. For example, a web based shopping cart is mostly open systems based, but it needs to communicate with a mainframe based inventory management system to fulfill the order.

Security

Security is a broad topic and includes everything from basic authentication and authorization, data encryption on the network to repudiation (you are who you say you are) and integration with mainframe security. Mainframe security includes, amongst others, **Resource Access Control Facility** (**RACF**) and **Access Control Facility 2** (**ACF2**). Everyone thinks technologies such as RACF and ACF2 make mainframes secure, but in reality, they are secure because of their physical nature—the hardware is in one location and hosted in a locked, physically secure location, and all communication happens over a private network. RACF or ACF2 don't do anything to enhance this locked down hardware environment. In open systems, as the infrastructure and user community is geographically dispersed and public networks are used, the LSE should consider including these technologies:

- **Java Authenticate and Authorization Service** (**JAAS**): As the name implies, JAAS is for determining whether the user or device is authorized to access the service and has the correct privileges. The authentication and authorization information is typically stored in a **Lightweight Directory Access Protocol** (**LDAP**) server.
- **Secure Sockets Layer** (**SSL**)—SSL has become the defacto standard for securing HTTP traffic over the Internet. SSL is very simple to deploy, and all application server vendors support SSL traffic. In most cases, SSL as the security mechanism will do just fine.

- **WS-Security**—WS-Security is a set of standards for ensuring the integrity and confidentiality of data transmitted via Web services. The specific standards that are most important to your LSB are: WS-Policy, Security Assertion Markup Language (SAML), XML-Signature, and XML-Encryption. These standards are constantly evolving and changing, so the best place to find more information is OASIS (`http://www.oasis-open.org/`); the standards board responsible for WS-Security.

  LSEs will also typically integrate with RACF and ACF2 since the services reside on the mainframe. Check with your LSE vendor to see what type of 'out of the box' mainframe security integration they provide.

Caching

Caching may seem like it should be discussed along with performance. Perhaps, but performance is a broad topic while caching is a specific technology that most LSE vendors use to increase end-to-end response time. Caching basically involves storing data in memory. The data may be from a database, a screen, a transaction or any other legacy artifact. An LSE that does not have some type of caching is not going to perform as well.

LSE Development

Just like end user interfaces, the latest trend in development environments is thin client, web-based. There is also a trend towards power users (tech savvy business users) being able to use the design tool on their own. A combination of these two methods would involves the end user using a web-based application to define his or her own Web services. It is up for you to decide which is the best LSE design/development environment for your company:

- Thick or thin—Thick clients (high powered PCs with heavy graphics) have more 'bells and whistles', and are usually much more graphic intensive. However, they require a more expensive workstation for the developer. Obviously, with thin (web-based) client tools, the development environment can be accessed from anywhere. To use the thick client, the user needs to have the PC or laptop with them, or have the PC software installed on all the machines they use. This can lead to a maintenance nightmare, as all workstations need to have the latest development software loaded on them.
- COBOL/Legacy or Java EE/open systems centric—This choice comes down whether you have more COBOL developers or more Java EE developers. Some tools emphasize that a COBOL developer can easily develop and deploy mainframe-based Web services. However, if all your developers know Java EE, or if the groups responsible for the middlware platform are all open systems developers, this may not be the best choice.

- Power users or developers—You may want your business users to define Web services on their own. They are ultimately the customers, and know what they want. However, they don't know the entire ramifications of the services they are creating, and the load they will put on the IT infrastructure. I am sure we have all heard of the horror stories when power users are allowed to write their own ad hoc database queries.

LSE Implementation/Deployment

LSE implementation and deployment must take into consideration the LSE server location, the legacy artifacts, and the metadata repository. LSEs can all be run on the mainframe, run off the mainframe, or in some cases run with part of the server on the mainframe and part off the mainframe. In cases where the LSE is part of the CICS region, it will of course run on the mainframe. The legacy artifacts are the components on the mainframe that we are going to expose as services. The metadata repository contains the mapping and transformation information.

LSE Server Location

It is not just a matter of deciding to run the LSE on the mainframe or off the mainframe but also whether to run the process on the mainframe in a CICS region or not. For the most part, the vendor will decide this for you. Most vendors run outside the CICS region, but a few run in the CICS region.

- **Within CICS region**—The most obvious limitation here is that you must be accessing artifacts (CICS transactions, BMS maps) that are CICS-based. The advantages are that you are closer to where the processing is happening, and the process takes up less memory.
- **Outside CICS**—Outside the CICS region, you can perform any type of screen, transaction/application, or data SOA integration that you want.
- **Off mainframe server**—In some cases, it is not practical, or it is not allowed to run any new processes on the mainframe. **Distributed Relational Database Architecture** (**DRDA**) servers are processes that run off the mainframe and access DB2 on a mainframe server. Some LSE vendors architect their solution to be able to run off the mainframe.

- **Hybrid**—This is dependent on the vendor. Some of the LSE processes, which make sense running closer to the legacy artifacts, run on the mainframe and other LSE components run on open systems if most processing takes place there. BPEL is an example wherein it makes sense to run some of the processing—orchestration of CICS transactions—on the mainframe and then run it on open systems when integrating to Java EE or .NET Web services. Oracle has built in middleware JCA adapters for CICS, IMS/TM, IMS/DB, and VSAM. These adapters are actually OEMed technolgy from Attunity. Oracle also offers DRDA servers for access to DB2 on mainframes and iSeries/AS400. As they are DRDA servers, no footprint is required on the mainframe or the midrange server. Oracle partners with companies that offer LSE solutions: Attachmate, DataDirect, GT Software, Hostbridge, Seagull Software, Micro Focus, and Treehouse. These companies have solutions that either compliment what Oracle offers out of the box, or provides support for presentation or data-tier not offered directly by Oracle such as 3270, 5250, Natural, Adabas, Datacom, and others.

Legacy Artifacts

Legacy artifacts are the actual pieces of logic, screen, or data that reside on, and are processed on the mainframe. The legacy artifact is what the business users want to get to. Since these artifacts were already described in detail earlier in the chapter, we will focus on why you would chose one Legacy artifact/access method over another:

- **Presentation-tier**—This refers to mainframe 3270 or VT220 (DEC) transmissions, iSeries transmissions (5250), and others. Remember, this is not terminal emulation and screen scraping. These techniques were inflexible and tightly coupled to the device. This solution uses the actual field name in the screen map.

  Why choose presentation-tier over applications, data, and others? The simple answer is that none of the application source is available. Other reasons may be that the data stores cannot be accessed directly because of security or privacy restrictions, or that no stored procedures or SQL exist in the application. SOA enablement of the mainframe application is as simple as running and capturing the screens, menus, and fields you want to expose as services. This is fast, simple, and for the most part, easy.
- **Application**—Application service enablement is more than wrapping transactions as Web services. This is all about service enabling the behavior of the system, and includes CICS/IMS transactions, Natural transactions, IDMS and ADS/O dialogs, COBOL programs, and batch processes. This also includes the business rules, data validation logic, and other business processing that are part of the transaction.

Why application based legacy SOA? The application is at the core of most systems. The application contains the screens that are run, the business logic, business rules, workflow, security and the overall behavior of the legacy systems. Transactions on mainframe systems are the way that IT users interact with the system. So using the application layer makes the most sense when you want to replicate the functionality that the legacy system is currently using. This approach allows you to leverage all the behaviors (rules, transaction flow, logic, and security) of the application without having to re-invent it on open systems.

- **Data**—The data can be relational or nonrelational on the legacy system. In most cases, the legacy system will have a nonrelational data store such as a keyed file, network database, or a hierarchical file system. While accessing data in a legacy system, the SOA Integration layer will use SQL to provide a single, well-understood method to access any data source. This is important as some customers will prefer to have SQL-based integration as opposed to SOA-based data integration. The IT architect may decide that having a SQL statement in an open systems database is easier than putting in place an entire SOA infrastructure.

  Why data? This is ultimately the source of the truth. This is where the information that you want is stored. If you are using any of the other three artifacts, these methods will ultimately call the data store. So, it seems very reasonable that most of your services act directly against the data. Sometimes, security and privacy concerns will not make this possible. Sometimes, the data needs to have business logic, business rules, or transformation applied before it is valid. However, if these things are not applicable, going right to the data source is a nice way to proceed.

- **Other**—Stored procedures and SQL are the way most distributed applications get results from a data store. Stored procedures also provide major benefits in the areas of application performance, code re-use, application logic encapsulation, security, and integrity. Why stored procedures and SQL? You are making a move to distributed, open systems, and relational databases so you should use technologies that work well in this environment. There is also the people and skills aspect. Your open systems developers will be very familiar with stored procedures, and will find them easy to develop.

> **Keeping It Real**: An architect who is well experienced in SQL access and relational databases may be tempted to perform Legacy SOA Integration using direct access (SQL instead of Web services) to the mainframe data. There are a couple of fundamental flaws with this approach:
>
> In some cases, the programs may not be available, and the legacy system owners may not allow direct access to the data, or the data does not exist in a clean format.
>
> In many instances, mainframe data is not readily usable until the appropriate business logic or business rule transforms it into meaningful information. On a mainframe, the business rules and business logic are frequently implemented as a program, or as part of a transaction.
>
> In these cases, the user interface or application approach is the one to take for your SOA architecture.

Metadata Repositories

The various combinations of products being used will result in multiple repositories. The objective is to have the least amount possible, and the ones you do should be able to share information with each other. We could have one for LSE, BPEL, ESB, application server, security, services management, and other products that are part of the middleware will have their own repositories. At a minimum, you will have two repositories, one for the application server and one for the LSE. If the best-of-breed approach is taken, you could end up with a handful of repositories.

Other Technical and Business Aspects

The third dimension mentioned earlier will be discussed across all of the components just covered. This dimension is a combination of technical, business, and human nature—yes, human nature in a technical book.

Scalability

Scability is important because legacy personnel are accustomed to mainframe technologies such as Sysplex and CICSplex, which provide scalability on the mainframe. Some questions to ask an LSE vendor are: Does the engine take advantage of Sysplex and/or CICSplex? Can the engine be distributed across multiple mainframe LPRs?

Performance

Usually, performance is determined by the developer's application code. You can tune the operating system, network, and database, but the performance issues will usually come down to an SQL statement, or a poorly written piece of Java code. In the case of SOA Legacy Integration, the biggest areas of concern are not just the developer's application code, but also the performance of the LSE. On the developer side, the results coming back (is there a qualifier—where clause—on data results set) and the number of requests to the legacy system to get all data required are the biggest areas of concern. Having course grained legacy services, instead of fined grained services, can control the number of requests. Course grained (service bundled together) services will eliminate unnecessary network traffic, and back and forth 'chatter' with the legacy system. The performance of the LSE can be addressed through caching, SQL optimization, and high-speed XML processing. These are questions you will need to ask of your potential LSE vendors. Workload Management (WLM) and load balancing can also help.

Failover

If your application server and/or LSE goes down, this can cost you large sums of lost revenue, lost credibility with your business users, negative impact on your entire IT operation, and more. Therefore, application server and LSE failover is key to the success of your SOA Legacy Integration architecture. The simple approach, and actually the one most commonly used in mainframe environments, is to have a duplicate system configured at another location. However, this can be expensive, difficult to manage, and take hours to bring the remote site online. This is an area where open systems have made advances because Internet-based applications are 24X7. Most LSB vendors offer the capability to automatically and transparently fail over to another configuration. The vendors also offer the capability to do **active-passive** or **active-active**. In active-passive, the failover configuration will do a cold failover. In this case, the environment will need to start-up at the time of failover, and the transactions in process will be required to return. In active-active, a hot failover to a configuration that is up-to-date with all the transactions in progress will be made. Therefore, the transactions will automatically be restarted, and in some cases, picked up where they were left off.

Transaction Processing

When you first embark on your journey to Legacy SOA Integration, it is quite likely that most services will not require transactions processing (insert, update, and delete). They will be query or read only. As Legacy SOA matures, we will begin to see more OLTP-based legacy SOA environments. The next phase of SOA Legacy architecture requires high-speed transaction processing across multiple systems, mainframes, mid-range, and open system environments.

While Web services can be based on any transport, they typically use stateless HTTP communication. In addition, not all data sources can support the common commit procedures. For example, an Adabas data source is capable of supporting only one-phase commit, and cannot participate in a two-phase commit coordinated infrastructure. While these would seem to limit transaction support in a SOA integration environment, they are not really a concern as long as the underlying application server and LSE have transactions support. One method of transactions support is the use of the industry standard XA (eXtended Architecture). XA is a very mature distributed transaction manager. Some would argue, just because it is mature does not make it the right technology to use. They see OASIS **Web Services Transaction** (**WS-TX**) or vendor-lead WS-Transaction as better because they are Web services centric. However, as of today, XA is supported in all transaction processors (CICS, Tuxedo), application servers (Oracle, BEA, IBM), and database servers (Oracle, IBM, Microsoft). XA transactions can be used to support the transaction needs of your SOA Integration architecture.

Governance

SOA governance is about managing the portfolio of services, planning development of new services and updating current services, managing the service lifecycle, using policies to restrict behavior, and monitoring performance. SOA Governance is spoken about by industry pundit as being very important to SOA architecture. In reality, when you are just starting off and creating internal Web services, or read-only external services, the need for governance is limited. You will have less then twenty services, so there is no need for a sophisticated service management tool. When you create a new version, or release an existing service, you will probably just delete the old service and put the new service into production. No need for a crazy scheme to make sure all existing transactions use the old service, and new requests use the new services. When you get more services and many consumers of your legacy Web services, something like version or change management control will be important. What if all your customers (Web services consumers) cannot upgrade to the latest release of your Web services? You will need SOA Governance products to handle requests for different versions of the same services from different clients. Monitoring performance is something that should be implemented immediately.

Human Factors

The human factor is a mix of the type of resources, company culture, and adaptability. What type of resources do you have? Are they mostly proficient at Java/.Net, COBOL, JCL, or some other language? Do they work on UNIX, Linux, Windows, or z/OS? These variables play a heavy role in the implementation process and target Oracle architecture.

People don't like change. Don't think your older COBOL programmers have a corner on the "I don't like change market". I have been involved in BEA to Oracle Application Server, and Sybase to Oracle Database migrations, with younger developers and DBAs that resist change. They say, "I am a Sybase DBA", and not "I am a DBA". Well, any form of Legacy Modernization involves change, and in most cases big time change. Both the company culture and the adaptability of the people involved can make or break a project. Over the years of managing IT projects, it has become obvious that technology does not make or break an IT project, but people and company culture do.

Agility and Adaptability of Architecture

We saw how systems developed over 30 years became fragile with different people, and constantly changing business initiatives, technologies and people. With limited resources of money, time, and people, we end up developing an architecture that is not agile. What staggers me is the number of companies that, given a chance to start fresh with modern technologies, develop Legacy SOA Integration architecture that are not flexible, are cobbled together with nonintegrated components, use proprietary technologies, and are different across organizations within the same company or division.

Host Support

It is important to understand the extent of support that the LSE vendor has for operating systems, presentation-tiers, transactions, languages and databases that are supported. Common operating systems support includes IBM zSeries (S/390), IBM iSeries (AS/400), UNIX, and Unisys. Not so commonly supported operating systems include IBM VSE, HP OpenVMS, and HP e3000. Before you choose an LSE product, you must make sure it supports the legacy presentation-tier, data, transactions, and/or languages that you have. Some may support only the presentation-tier, or only the CICS transactions. Keep in mind all the different combinations of host support as we decide on the implementation options in the next section.

SOA Integration

Here, decisions will have to be made on how we move from a rigid, fragile architecture to a more flexible, 'business ready' architecture. In other words, how do we get from source to target? You may think that the quickest and the most flexible option is to build it yourself. Although this is an option many consultants love as they can charge endless hours for doing just that. The products and technologies available today make it much easier and quicker than having to 'reinvent the wheel'.

Implementation Options

Let's have a look at your options. There are basically three options for the implementation of your Legacy SOA Integration solution. You can build it all yourself, buy products from different vendors, and 'glue' everything together, or purchase an end-to-end solution from one vendor. Each option has its strengths and weakness, and your company culture will definitely play a role in the option or options you chose. One of the options can be to choose a mix of the different options. The end goal is to choose an option that is easy to implement, is adaptable and maintainable, and has the lowest cost of total ownership.

Roll My Own

Architects and developers hear about things such as REST, XML, Java messaging, TCP/IP connects to mainframes, and MQSeries. Why can't we just build something? That would be very cool. Using Java EE CA, JAX-PRC, and other APIs, we can build a connector to the mainframe that calls a COBOL program and gets XML results back. We can then process these results, and return the results back to a web page that we develop in JSP. There are many drawbacks to this solution. You have to hand-code the solution while taking into account security, performance, reliability, governance, scalability, and service management. You also need to code and maintain low-level infrastructure software such as a data and SQL translation engine and a high-speed XML parsing and transformation engine.

Buy a Bunch of Products and become an Integrator

You or someone you hire becomes the 'general contractor'. Have you ever tried to be the general contractor for a house project such as finishing a basement, or putting an addition onto your house? You end up doing most of the work. You have to find an electrician, plumber, framer/drywall installer, painter, and research all the materials you will need, and also go out and buy them. It is the same thing here; you have to research all the products, negotiate contacts with each of the vendors, then buy, install, and configure the products. You then get the job of integrating the solution. Chances are that they use different repositories (with different RDBMS as there data store), different caching mechanisms, and different APIs. You also don't know who to go to if the end-to-end process does not work. It could be the fault of the application server, mainframe adapter, security provider, or someone else. This makes it difficult to do 'root cause analysis'.

One Pre-Integrated Stack

SOA Suites have become the latest IT technology rage in the last few years. SOA Suites are for the middleware industry what ERP systems are for the business applications world. They take a number of related but loosely coupled products, and make them tightly integrated but maintain the loose coupling. This gives you the best of both worlds, an integrated solution that does not rely on the other components but shares a common platform across all SOA Suite components. Not only are the SOA Suite components tightly integrated, the LSE is also integrated with the application server. This gives you end-to-end SOA Legacy Integration.

> **Keeping It Real**: You can build your own TCP/IP and/or HTTP communication to the mainframe with custom Java (Java EE CA) adapters that talk to custom code on the mainframe. You can even create your own message queuing system that resides on the mainframe or open systems. But why would you do this? There are many products from Oracle and its partners that bring you bundled, 'out of the box' Legacy SOA Integration solutions to you.

Implementation Approach

Not surprising, the approach we are going to take is pre-integrated stack using as many tools as possible in the development, deployment, and management of the solution. We want the target architecture to be as 'out of the box' as possible, and the development environment to be as much of a 'drag-and-drop' as possible. In this chapter, we will also introduce you to Oracle products and technologies for development and run time/production. We will use the Oracle products to get from Accidental Architecture to SOA Integration architecture. The transformation from Accidental Architecture to an agile architecture looks like this:

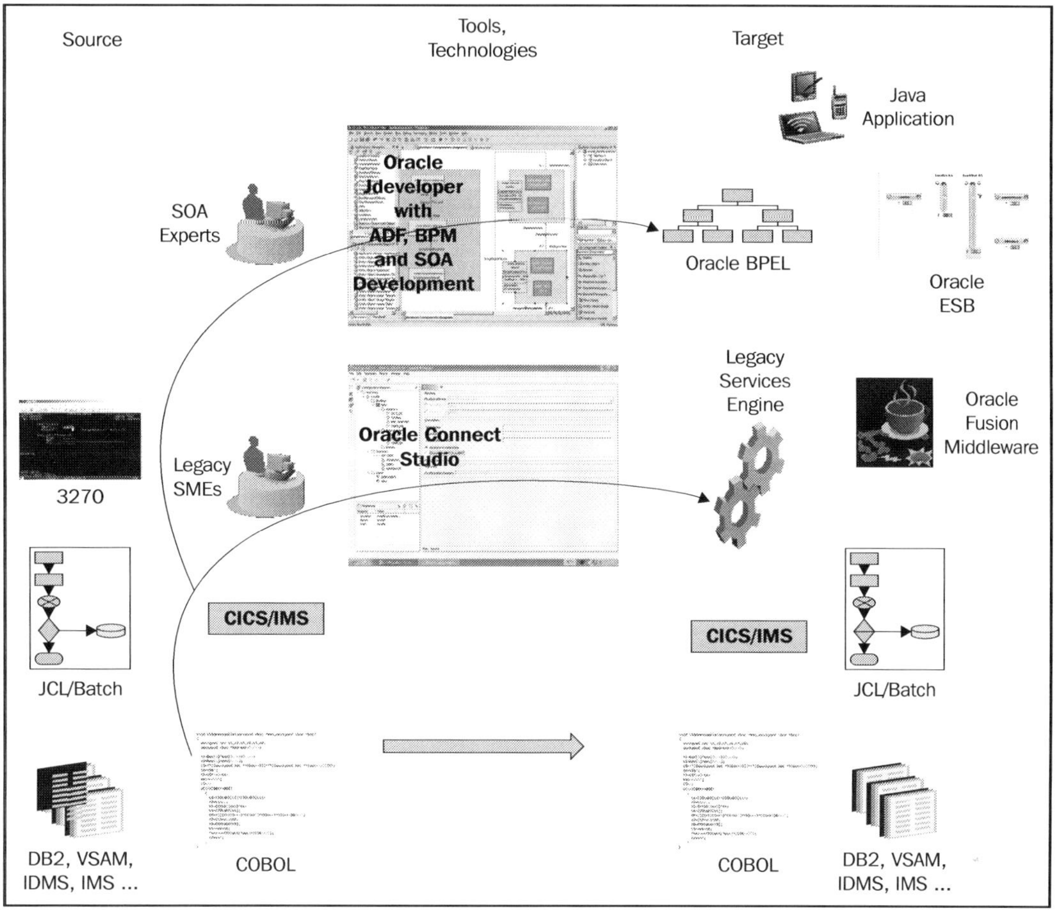

The diagram does not explain the steps or sequence of events. It is not intended to do so as we will cover them next. First, let's examine the overall approach, the tools, products, and technologies used. We will start from the bottom as this follows the high level approach that will be taken.

The big red arrow indicates the COBOL and other legacy languages. JCL/Batch, data stores, and transaction monitors stay as they are today. SOA Integration does not change anything that exists on the legacy system. If you are on the mainframe, you stay on the mainframe running COBOL, Pl/1,JCL, VSAM, IDMS, and other legacy artifacts.

The next level up on the diagram is the LSE development tool. This tool will allow the person responsible for exposing legacy artifacts as Web services to do this in a GUI, drag-and-drop based **Integrated Development Environment** (**IDE**). These tools will typically make it very easy to expose presentation, transactions, or data as Web services. In the case of presentation and transactions Web services, the tool will allow the developer to view the actual legacy interface, and choose the screens, menus, transactions, and fields that will be part of the Web service. The reason for the Legacy Subject Matter Expert(s) listed, as the person(s) doing the work, is that they are best suited to identify, design, develop, and deploy legacy SOA-enabled artifacts. Although these are GUI tools, it is important to have a person adept in legacy technologies performing this process. In this step, we will actually deploy services to the legacy system and/or the open systems platform.

The highest level is where the legacy Web services are incorporated into the SOA Suite and/or open systems presentation tier. In some cases, you may just want to access the services from a Java Server Page, Java Server Faces, or AJAX presentation-tier application. In other cases, you may integrate the services with other services using Oracle BPEL, or you may want to use an ESB when some of the legacy services need to be transformed or passed onto another application. Any of these application types can be monitored using Oracle BAM. The tool used for this development is Oracle JDeveloper. Oracle JDeveloper is Oracle's Java Model Driven Development Environment. The tool contains a Business Process Analysis Suite (BPA Suite) from IDS Sheer. This provides you with the option to start modeling the SOA architecture with business users, and Legacy SMEs using the Unified Modeling Language (UML) and other user-friendly diagrams. The modeling done in the BPA Suite can then be used by Oracle JDeveloper/BPEL Designer to fill in the missing details or incorporate additional elements such as service definition, monitoring elements etc. in the business process (BPEL). Oracle JDeveloper also includes Oracle's Application Development Framework (ADF) to develop standard Java-based Java Server Faces, Struts, and EJB 3.0/Toplink-based applications. ADF is a GUI drag-and-drop based environment to create Java/Java EE-based applications rapidly.

> **Keeping It Real**: Having worked with Independent Software Vendors (ISVs) for years, I can tell you that it is less costly and easier to manage a complete integrated stack of products than a custom-built solution or the best-of-breed architecture. Legacy architectures contain custom developed messaging, integration, interface, rules engines, workflow, and even business applications (inventory, order entry, accounting) for a reason. These pre-packaged solutions did not exist years ago. The great thing about being a Modernization architect is that legacy IT groups get to take advantage of SOA, and the 'out of the box' messaging, workflow, security, integration, management, and even the business application it brings to the table.

Phases in the Implementation Cycle

The implementation lifecycle to create your modern Legacy SOA Integration architecture looks like this:

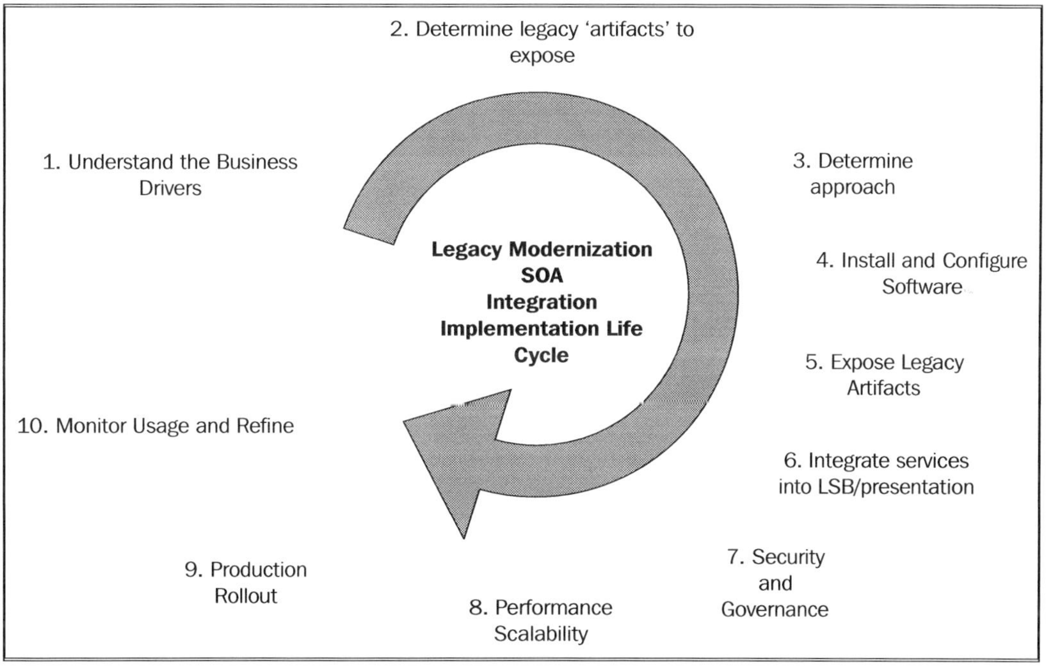

The implementation life cycle is an iterative approach. There will be multiple iterations of the same or similar process. Let's dive down into each of the phases or steps in the implementation life cycle:

Understanding the Business Drivers

Understanding business drivers is an overused mantra. I have seen entire chapters in books dedicated to the importance of business drivers. In the end, we all know that you must understand the business drivers, as technology for technologies sake doesn't make sense. A few of the common business drivers for Legacy SOA are:

- Web enabled applications for internal customer service—In today's 'flat world', many of your customer service agents work either from a home in Idaho, or in a call center in India or Philippines. Imagine trying to put a 3270 terminal at someone's home office or in offices around the world. No way! The answer is a thin application that runs in a browser.
- Customer self-service applications—Fedex was one of the trendsetters in this area. First they gave you the ability to track your packages online. Then, they allowed customers to create their own shipping manifests. What a great way to reduce your customer support costs- get the customer to do it and feel good about it! Today not only do we have the ability to check into our flights from home, but also make our own hotel, airline, and car reservations online using the Web. Believe me, most of these self-service airline reservations are communicating with a mainframe somewhere in the booking process. Online banking is another great example of Legacy SOA integration.
- Alignment with the corporate SOA strategy—This is the grand daddy of them all. This is big because you are operating at a strategic level. If you have a corporate SOA strategy, chances are very good that legacy systems integration will be a part of the architecture.

Products and Technologies Used in this Phase

The choice here is to use a repository based modeling tool, or a simple word processing document. The advantage of the modeling tool (Oracle BPA Suite) is that multiple users can contribute and information in the repository can be used to actually generate code for the implementation.

- Oracle BPA Suite—Oracle Business Process Architect (a component of the Oracle BPA Suite) using an Event or Business Process (BPMN) diagram.

  And/or

- Open Office Writer or PDF document—Business drivers can also be simply captured in a document. It is more difficult to show business requirements in a picture or a diagram format, but text may do just fine.

Determine Business Processes to Expose

Get this phase correct, and you are in good shape. Get it wrong, and you have technology for technology's sake. During this phase, you need to align the business drivers with those legacy technology artifacts. This means finding the correct transaction, screen/fields, or data store in an application that was written over 30 years back containing millions of lines of application code. This can be a daunting task without a tool that can help you identify and document the code or data that is important. Modernization vendors, OpenConnect and Relativity have technologies that discover legacy artifacts to expose. Relativity does static analysis of code and discovers the legacy processes to wrap as services. OpenConnect does real time analysis to do the same thing. These tools also provide additional functionality:

- Proactive performance identified—A focused, automated analysis reveals where the application's existing architecture could lead to a failure of the service or performance issues. The tool will also tell you how you can eliminate these potential performance or service issues.
- Artifact classification—Classification of artifacts makes the next step much easier. Classification also provides you with an application program and/or the screen communication flow and the data stores that the applications access.
- WSDL generation—These tools can even generate the WSDL that can be used in integrating the Web services into the application server or the presentation tier.

Of course, you could always complete this phase using a combination of manual discovery and design using the Oracle BPA suite. This would involve getting the legacy SMEs in a room and doing whiteboarding, modeling in Oracle BPA Suite, and writing the technical specifications.

Products and Technologies Used in this Phase

The choice of tools to use for discovering business processes is really a choice between a tool specifically built (Relativity or OpenConnect) to handle legacy SOA artifact discovery or a generic BPA tool (Oracle BAP Suite).

- Oracle BPA Suite—Oracle Business Process Architect UML Use Case or Activity diagrams.

  And/or

- Relativity—Parses the application sources and performs understanding of the application source code. The information from this analysis is used to determine the application and the data flow.

OR

- OpenConnect Comprehend—Combines real-time interaction with process execution static data from existing system interfaces (logs, batch job output, CICS transaction logs), so a full end-to-end business process can be determined.
- Determine the approach—I believe we covered this sufficiently earlier in the chapter. Now you know what the process is, you need to decide if presentation, application, data, and/or stored procedures are the best approach. The approach identifies the specific use cases/scenarios that you will be implementing. As the integration points in the system may vary with the use cases, you may have a combination of these approaches.

Install/Configure the Software

Remember, this is where you need to be nice to the legacy system data center team. Installing and configuring software on a mainframe is not like doing it on a local Linux box. You also probably need to give them plenty of time to get the appropriate approvals, software and hardware upgrades, and legacy system configured. You will also need to install and configure the Oracle software required for your application server and presentation-tier. We discussed the LSE configuration in the previous section. As I mentioned, the LSE configuration depends upon the vendor. In the case of the Oracle LSE, it is a hybrid configuration where some of the processing takes place on the middle-tier, and some on the mainframe.

Products and Technologies Used in this Phase

These products and technologies are not choices but the products you will need to use. It includes the application server and LSE.

- Oracle SOA Suite—The Oracle SOA Suite is bundled with the Oracle Application Server. The Oracle Application contains the Java EE runtime, Web services support, and HTTP Server among other components.
- Oracle Internet Directory (OID)—Oracle has a number of identity management products, and OID is one of the products in the suite. OID is an industry standard, Lightweight Directory Access Protocol (LDAP) repository. We are going to keep it simple and use LDAP for authentication and authorization.
- Oracle Integration Adapters—This is your LSE from Oracle. You must first install the Oracle SOA Suite. Then, you can install the Oracle Legacy Integration Adapters.

Expose Legacy Artifacts

The GUI development tools from LSE vendors make it easy to expose legacy artifacts as Web services. They will generate the corresponding WSDL, so the legacy Web service can be integrated into the Oracle Application Server. The three most common types of legacy Web services are generated in the following manner:

- Presentation-Tier—Most screen integrations can be done by executing the application using the transaction ID on the mainframe in the LSE development tool, and capturing the screens and fields you want to expose. Developers gather application metadata (screens and fields) from the existing host application, and in most cases, modify the legacy metadata to be more user-friendly.
- Application—Web services access to business rules and business logic can be administered through a simple three to four step process:
    - Specify the name of the program to be invoked
    - Specify the region where the program is to be executed
    - Specify the interface to the program using the COMMAREA of the COBOL module
    - An optional fourth step is available, to handle the transformation from legacy standards to modern SOA standards. The limitations of mainframe naming conventions generated standards that are incompatible with the flexibility offered today.
    - Most tools supports the ability to transform element names in COMMAREAs to comply with the Web services naming standards, and make them more readable.
- Data access—Data access integration is all about exposing relational and nonrelational data stores as SQL, and then publishing the SQL interface through a WSDL. The steps to do this are:
    1. Select the type of data source you will be exposing
    2. Connect to the legacy data source
    3. Select the legacy files or tables you will be accessing
    4. Write the SQL for the queries you will be making
    5. Expose the SQL as a Web service

- Products and technologies used in this phase—Oracle provides a tool in order to expose your legacy transactions and data as Web services.
- Oracle Studio—Oracle Studio comes bundled with the Oracle Integration Adapters you installed and configured earlier. It is a GUI tool that is based on IBM Eclipse. The tool has support for introspecting the metadata in COBOL copybooks, and SQL modeling of IMS/DM and VSAM, and automatically generating the XSD and WSDL schemas.

Integrate Services into the application server

This is a key phase as it makes the Web services we expose on the mainframe accessible to the end users. The end goal of Legacy SOA Integration is to get the mainframe to be part of your SOA infrastructure. We will achieve this goal in this phase. In many cases, the services are exposed in the presentation-tier. The presentation-tier may be a simple JSP or JSF application, Oracle WebCenter (portal framework) or Oracle BAM. It is also common to see these services integrated into an Oracle ESB, Oracle BPEL, or Oracle Data Integrator (ODI) process.

Products and Technologies Used in this Phase

Oracle JDeveloper is the development tool for Java EE and most of the Oracle SOA products. Oracle BAM and Oracle Data Integrator are not required.

- Oracle JDeveloper—A great thing about Oracle JDeveloper is that it can be used for Java EE (JSP, JSF, or ADF), ESB, BPEL, and Oracle WebCenter development.
- Oracle BAM—Developing a BAM dashboard can be done using the Oracle BAM development tool.
- Oracle Data Integrator—Oracle Data Integrator will be used if you are going to include your mainframe Web services as part of your Enterprise Information Integration architecture.

Security and Governance

As we are just getting started, we will be adequately secure using Oracle Internet Directory for authentication and authorization, and SSL for securing the Web services network traffic. For now, we are not going to implement a full-blown governance solution. The auditing and tracking capabilities built into the Oracle Application Server and Oracle Enterprise Manager products should be adequate for your first implementation.

Products and Technologies Used in this Phase

Security and management will become more sophisticated as the Web service number of legacy Web services grow. The products listed below are adequate as you first start Web service enabling your mainframe:

- Oracle Internet Directory(OID)—Autherization and authenticate can be provided through username/passwords and Access Control Lists (ACL) using OID.
- Oracle Application Server—Auditing and logging of Web service usage is automatically done by the Oracle Application Server.
- Oracle Enterprise Manager—Monitoring of Web services can be done using the Oracle Enterprise Manager web-based console.

Performance and Scalability

Just because I have placed this in the latter part of the process, it does not mean you don't take the performance and scalability into account earlier. It means that it is the first opportunity to do real performance and tuning work. Not until the complete environment is installed, configured, and deployed can you determine where your bottlenecks reside.

Products and Technologies Used in this Phase

The Oracle BPA Suite allows you to proactively manage your systems performance and scalability. The Oracle Enterprise Manager Diagnostic pack allows you to manage application performance during production.

- Oracle Business Process Simulator—This technology is part of the Oracle BPA Suite. The tool simulates the process models based on a set of discrete events to do 'what if' analysis.
- Oracle Enterprise Manager (OEM) with Diagnostics Pack—OEM is an end-to-end system management and performance monitoring tool for your database, application server, and the supporting infrastructure. Oracle Application Diagnostics For Java (Oracle AD4J) is a monitoring solution to improve the availability and performance of Java EE application.

Production Rollout

Production rollout is a large and complex area. Production rollouts also tend to vary across company to company. Since most companies already have detailed production rollout plans in place, I will not try to cover different aspects of production rollout here. This will depend on an organization's IT governance standards and culture, which is unique to each company and each department within a company.

Products and Technologies Used in this Phase

Keeping all of your hardware platforms running the same release and patches of software is done through provisioning software.

- Oracle OEM with Provisioning Pack—This tool makes it easier to rollout your application to the production environment. It also assists with new software releases.

Monitor Usage and Refine

Monitor the legacy Web services that your users are taking advantage of. Legacy SOA Integration is not 'build it, and they will' come. People don't like to change. You may have built the best Legacy SOA Integration solution ever, but if business users are still logging into their 'green screens', it does not matter. The general area of business process identification and optimization has become so important to companies that OpenConnect has created a product to not only identify services to wrap, but also to understand how services are being used. In addition, Gartner has created a new concept called **Business Optimization Support System** (**BOSS**) that is focused on just this area.

Products and Technologies Used in this Phase

OpenConnect is uniquely positioned as one of the few companies that provides the software to monitor the usage of your newly web enabled mainframe.

- OpenConnect Comprehend—Comprehend can be used to tell you who is using the new interface and how often, and the usage pattern. This tool graphically displays the usage of the new Web service interface, as compared to the number of people who are still using the old 'green screen' interface.

> **Keeping It Real**: I am a big believer in the 80/20 rule. It applies to your job: 80 percent of the success of an organization is attributed to 20 percent of the people. It applies to life: 80 percent of your happiness is dependent upon the 20 percent of the things you do each day. More importantly, for this book, it applies to Legacy SOA Integration: 80 percent of the business benefits you will derive from Legacy SOA Integration will come from 20 percent of all the possible services you can create from legacy artifacts. Keep this in mind, and you will find that you just need to focus on a small set of services once you identify the top 20 percent.

SOA Integration—Top Four Scenarios and Oracle Solutions

This section is not really about the final product. How can it be, when we have no idea what your environment looks like, what your business drivers are, what your strategic direction is, what tactical solutions you have already thought about, or what your biggest pain point with your current legacy system is today. It has been said a number of times in the technical journals and by IT analysts that SOA is not a product or solution but a journey. If SOA is a journey, then modernization is a journey where you 'pack extra clothes'. This is because your modernization journey will take unexpected twists and turns, and you may go to unexpected places as business objectives, key personnel, and technologies change during the journey. By the end of this section, if we have done our jobs, you will have answers to the questions, when, where, and how to start.

SOA Integration has been chosen for our first book and as the first approach, because it is often the first approach in your modernization journey. It gives you the ability to deliver something tangible quickly. This will make you happy, your bosses happy, and more importantly your IT users and customers happy. SOA projects typically last three to four months and deliver high customer value. This is far from the legacy project of yesterday that involved three to five year efforts. We now live in a world of short attention spans, and instant gratification; we don't read the morning newspaper but get it on the Internet. So our modernization journey needs to reflect these changing times.

In this section we will focus on why specific products and technologies, as opposed to what they are. We will also use a set of common situations we have come across, as we help customers and partners on their journey to a modern IT platform. These situations will be put in the context of a scenario. We will then use a design pattern that we have found successful in that scenario. Design patterns have been around for decades, but have gained a lot of popularity recently and are commonly used in the world of OO and Java. The term design pattern can be overloaded, overused, and be made overly complex. For our purposes, a design pattern should provide an effectively implemented solution to address a recurring problem (in legacy systems).

Oracle Products Included in the Solution

Before we get started, let's cover why these particular products make the most sense, and explain why other products were left out. The Oracle Fusion Middleware family of products contains all the necessary components for your SOA Integration architecture.

- Why Web services?

  Web services are the foundation of our communication and results processing of the mainframe artifacts. Without Web services, you really don't have a Legacy SOA Integration. Enough said.

- Why Oracle Legacy Adapters?

  The Oracle Legacy Adapters are what we have been referring to as your Legacy Service Engine. You need this as it makes the flow of information from your legacy environment to your open systems environment happen in a seamless fashion.

- Why Oracle BPEL Process Manager?

  Business process orchestration and human workflow are key to communicating with your mainframe, internal services, and external services. To align business with IT, applications must become more process-driven. In today's world, users do not have to remember all the activities that need to be done. Instead, workflow engines place tasks that need their attention in workflow inboxes.

  Oracle BPEL Process Manager allows SOA service implementations, human interaction, and system workflow to be orchestrated quickly and easily using graphical 'drag-and-drop' techniques that allow users to be involved in orchestrating their own systems, thereby reducing the amount of custom code required, and increasing an application's agility by allowing users a more direct interaction with their systems.

- Why Oracle Enterprise Service Bus?

  BPEL will provide you with business and human workflow for your business services. However, there are also a number of services that are generic to many applications. A service bus provides these generic services by implementing standard facilities such as messaging or integration capabilities often by encapsulating different existing technologies that implement the generic services and making them appear as one.

  Oracle ESB provides a messaging and integration layer for directly connecting applications and Web services through a common infrastructure. Oracle ESB combines an asynchronous messaging backbone with intelligent message transformation and routing, to ensure messages are passed reliably. Using Oracle ESB, integrating applications becomes a drag-and-drop exercise using prepackaged ESB adapters for file, database, message queue, and COTS access. The mainframe is known for its quality of service and reliability. Oracle ESB makes use of Oracle Application Server's grid capabilities to allow the formation of an ESB grid that crosses multiple platforms.

- Why Oracle Enterprise Manager (OEM)?

  You don't need a specialized Web Services Manager or Web Services Registry at this point in your journey. However, it does make sense to make use of the technology in the Oracle Enterprise Manager product that your company is going to use, to manage your SOA middle-tier and perhaps at some point your Oracle Database Grid. The Oracle Enterprise Manager 10g SOA Management pack integrates with Oracle BPEL Process Manager Console and Oracle BAM. This allows administrators to view service levels for key business processes, and SOA infrastructure components. The SOA Management Pack also provides a means to monitor Web services both from an end user perspective as well as request based monitoring. Administrators can define SOAP tests for one or more partner links of a BPEL process, any hosted Web service, or an external service.

  The OEM plugin Application Diagnostics for Java has interactive transaction tracing feature for the web transactions (legacy Web services) defined as part of web applications. Application Web Transactions can be easily created using a simple, intuitive transaction recorder. Once an application performance problem is identified, Web Transactions can be executed on demand to immediately trace problems to specific application tiers. Transactions are played back interactively, and in-depth breakdowns of response times across all tiers of your application server provide for quick problem diagnosis.

- Why Oracle Identity Management?

  Any IT environment would need some form of security. We will start our SOA Legacy Integration journey with security that is strong but not overwhelming to implement and maintain. Identity Management is a very broad topic when it comes to Oracle. This includes everything from single sign on to provisioning, federated identity, directory services, certificate authority, and more. In the immediate term, we will use Oracle Internet Directory (remember this is called OID and is an LDAP compliant directory) and Oracle Enterprise Single Sign-On so that all applications (Web services) can be logged at once.

- Why Oracle WebCenter Portal?

  A portal provides a single web-based entry point into a variety of applications. Using a portal allows an organization to create a unique user experience that combines many of the functional components of the SOA applications into a single point of access.

The introduction of the Internet and web-based computing is one instance where even users will agree that technology has changed business in a positive fashion. The ability of the users around the world to easily access systems via web-based thin client technology has eliminated the need to have applications executed on a client machine, thus opening the door to self-service applications that have clearly changed the way business is done. Incorporating the use of the Web is fundamental to any modern application using Oracle WebCenter Portal.

- Why Oracle Data Integrator?

  Oracle Data Integrator (ODI) allows users to extract data from many legacy and nonlegacy sources—including those on the mainframe—using web services that are part of your application server and load and transform the data into a number of data sources. Often we times find that flat file information sharing is a corner stone of legacy information integration. Replacing this custom processing with a product such as ODI makes the processing of the flat files more centralized, agile, and adaptable. Also, enhancing the system for new flat file types or changes to current structures is much easier.

- Why Oracle Business Activity Monitoring (BAM)?

  Modern systems do not require you to wait until a report, query, or lengthy batch process is complete before you can get information on business activity. Instead, real-time information is viewed via graphical dashboards that can send out alerts through a variety of communication mechanisms when user-defined 'thresholds of importance' are met. Oracle (BAM) will be used to provide this real time feedback for our Web services, BPEL, and ESB processes.

- Why Oracle Business Intelligence?

  Instead of relying on hard copy reports, real-time business intelligence and data mining tools can be used to "slice and dice" data to determine key performance indicators and discover data trends without having to wait for IT. This increases the overall agility of the organization, allowing end users to react more quickly to ongoing business changes.

Oracle Products Not Included in the Solution

What is equally important is identifying the components that may apply but will not be included in this architecture. The components mentioned here will play a significant role in re-architecture. The following section discusses the products not included and why they are not part of the architecture.

- Why not Oracle Business Rules?

  Business Rules Engines can be used to store business logic and business rules for BPEL processing. For example, what is the credit limit based upon the customer's credit rating? For SOA enablement, a majority of the business rules will continue to be embedded in the legacy COBOL application.

- Why not Oracle Web Services Manager?

  Oracle Web Services Manager (WSM) is a comprehensive solution for securing and managing service-oriented architectures (SOA). It allows IT managers to centrally define policies that govern Web service operations such as access control (authentication, authorization), logging, and content validation, and then attach these policies to one or multiple Web services, with no modifications required for existing Web services. In addition, Oracle WSM collects runtime data to monitor access control, message integrity, message confidentiality, quality of service (defined in service-level agreements—SLAs) and displays that information on graphical charts. Oracle WSM brings better enterprise control and visibility over their SOA deployments. As discussed earlier, a combination of SSL, OID, Oracle Single Sign On, and OEM can provide you the security, governance and monitoring that is required for this phase of our modernization journey.

- Why not Oracle Web Services Registry?

  Oracle Web Services Registry is an industry-standard UDDI-compliant Web services registry. As mentioned earlier, the limited number of services and the fact that these will mostly be consumed internally make the use of a Web Services Registry something of an 'over kill' at this time.

- Why not Oracle ADF?

  Oracle JDeveloper is packaged with Oracle Application Development Framework (ADF), which provides a rich set of templates for developing business applications. For example, using Oracle ADF Faces—a set of user interface components based on industry standards—a developer can quickly develop web-based presentation layers from legacy screens with limited coding. Re-architecting is the best place to implement the full features of ADF.

  Each scenario defines a situation or situations that we have encountered while working directly with our customers. For each scenario, we define the problem, context of the problem, forces (business, human, and technology) and the Oracle product solution set. The design pattern is a combination of the scenario and the recommended Oracle architecture.

Before we get started with the scenarios, a few disclaimers are in order:

- The scenarios are not in any particular order or sequence
- The scenarios described next are not phases, but could be put into any order that fits your technical and business drivers
- The scenarios may not fit your particular situation exactly, but you are most likely to find a fit in one of the four scenarios listed here.

Scenario One—Enterprise Information Integration

Also known as: Data Integration, file sharing, file messaging

Problem

My current Infrastructure for information integration is fragile, expensive, and hard to maintain.

The problem is often characterized by issues with no common work-flow approach, lack of data quality, and data profiling capabilities, customized transformation logic unique to each data feed, lack of real time monitoring capability, and inability to quickly add new data feeds.

Context

Data needs to be shared with new systems developed on open systems and other mainframe systems, both internal and external to the company/organization we work for.

Almost all legacy systems (I have not seen one that doesn't, so I would like to say all, but once you say all, someone will find the exception) have data feeds coming into them or going out of them.

Forces

Applications and organizations were standalone in the past. Now there is a big need to share information between application and businesses.

Solution

The solution includes Oracle ESB, Oracle BPEL, Oracle Legacy Adapters, Oracle Ebusiness Suite Adapters, and Oracle OEM as depicted here:

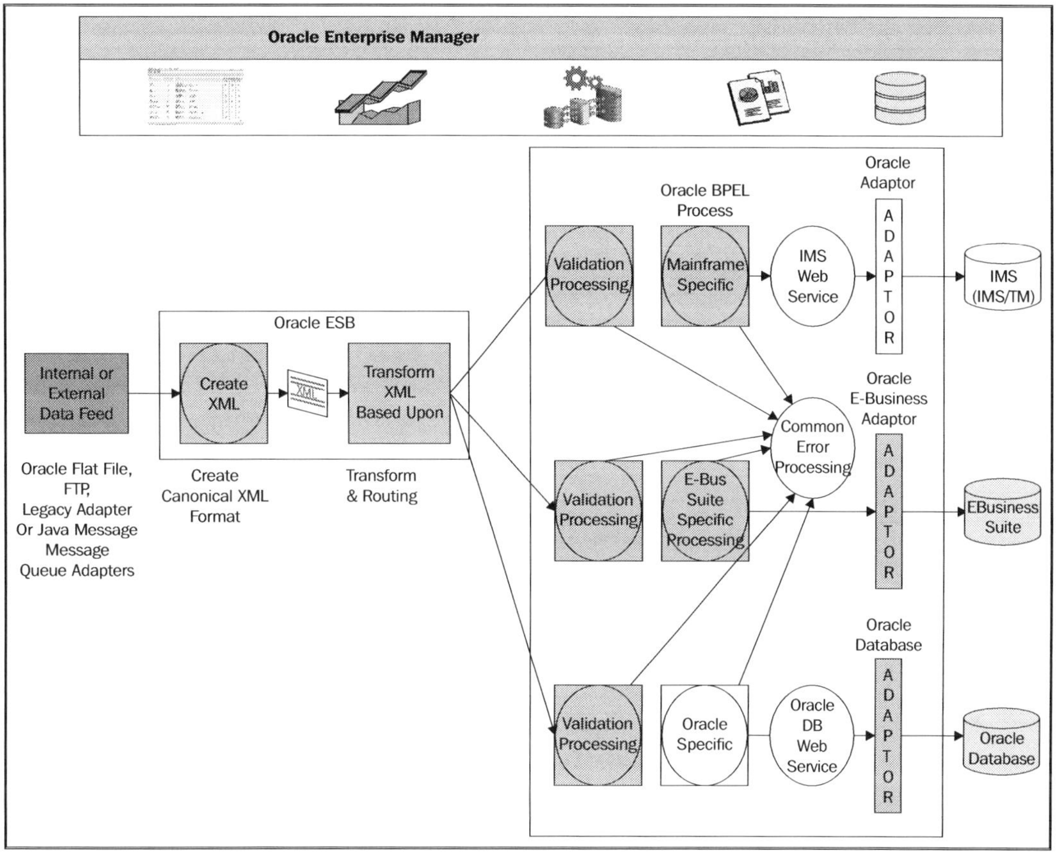

Scenario One Summary

The objective of Legacy SOA Integration is not to disrupt the current business processing and legacy system. We hold this to be true by keeping the same data feed the same. Attempting to perform even minor changes to data feeds are near impossible because:

- If a third party or even an internal organization outside your control is involved, the ability to get the change completed can take months.
- Even internally owned data feeds impact the source systems, current processing, and target systems so that even a small change has a ripple effect that causes the change to take months.

The current data feed will remain and download FTP to a directory and will most likely remain batched. The diagram shows technologies such as Legacy Adapters and Oracle Messaging as these can be adopted when changes to business processes are made.

- Oracle ESB—The Oracle ESB will use the file or FTP adapters to read the flat file and then transform the flat file to a common (canonical) XML file format. Based on the source of the data feed, the message will be routed to the appropriate Oracle BPEL process.
- Oracle BPEL—This is where the workflow and processing that we discussed earlier comes in:
    - Oracle BPEL will call a Java or Web service process to perform any validation processing. This validation processing will probably call out to the Oracle database to validate information based upon the data in the database.
    - After validation, file type specific processing takes place. This is basically 'business rules' being applied to the input data file. This business processing could call the Oracle Rules engine.
    - Common Error Processing—Validation and/or business rule processing errors will be passed to an error-handling route. The BPEL worklist will be populated, so a human may correct the problem file or records.
    - Data persistence Web service—The data will be persisted in the Oracle database, IMS database, and/or the Oracle Ebusiness Suite.

Scenario Two—Web Enablement

This is also known as Screen Scraping, or Re-interfacing.

Problem

My customer support people, sales representatives, customers, and partners would like to access our system through the Web. Why can't I have one interface to update both my legacy system and the Oracle system?

Old 'green screen' technologies have many limitations. A big one is that they are not very intuitive. You have to access several screens or systems to get the information you need, and there is no 'point and click'. In addition, many times, users may have to go to multiple systems to either query or update the same or similar data.

Context

Users want their data now, wherever they are, and at any time of the day or night. Users also want their legacy systems and new Oracle environments to work together.

A business process that requires a user to have to query multiple systems, and then update multiple systems makes everything move slower, and in many cases may cause data inconsistencies.

Forces

We are seeing the ranks of users who were online and on the web at a very young age. Technologies providing better application interfaces have been in the market place for years.

Solution

The solution includes Oracle WebCenter and/or JSF/JSP, Oracle Legacy Adapters and Oracle OEM as depicted below:

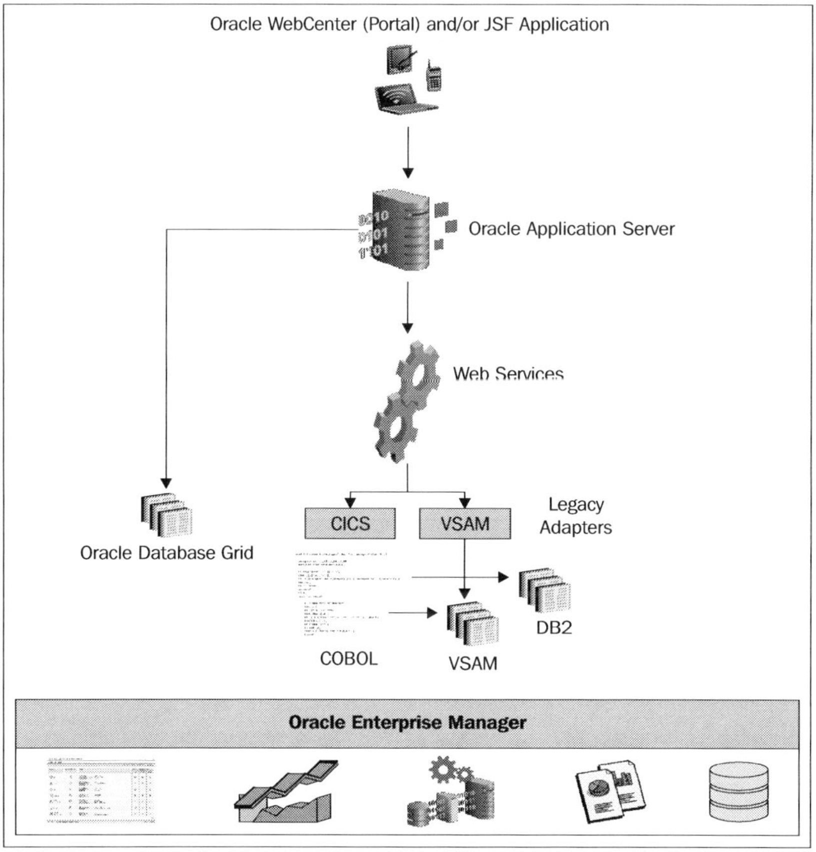

Scenario: Two Summary

The key to this scenario is the interface. Therefore, Oracle WebCenter and/or JSP/JSF will be used. For the first iteration of this scenario, JSP and/or JSF can be used to keep development simple and deployment quicker. A more sophisticated interface would be to use JSF to develop JSR-168 portlets, and deploy them using Oracle WebCenter.

Scenario Three—Report Off-Load Using Data Migration

This is also known as Data migration, Legacy Operational Data Store, or Reporting Modernization

Problem

IT Perspective—My legacy reporting infrastructure is costing me millions to run and I have a six month back log of report requests.

User perspective—I already have 100 green bar reports but I still cannot make business decisions with the information I have.

Context

Users need access to information in a variety of formats and dimensions. They also need to be able to easily do 'ad hoc' and 'what if' scenarios.

It is not uncommon for a mainframe-centric organization to have strategic sales forecasting to be done on all spreadsheets.

Forces

Reporting on the mainframe is expensive, and business users cannot access the information they need to make decisions. So a typical organization will find that users have created their own reports using Excel, SQL, and other desktop tools. Data then gets duplicated throughout the enterprise.

Solution

The final solution includes Oracle Data Integrator, Oracle BPEL, Oracle Legacy Adapters, Oracle BAM, Oracle BI Suite and Oracle OEM as depicted here:

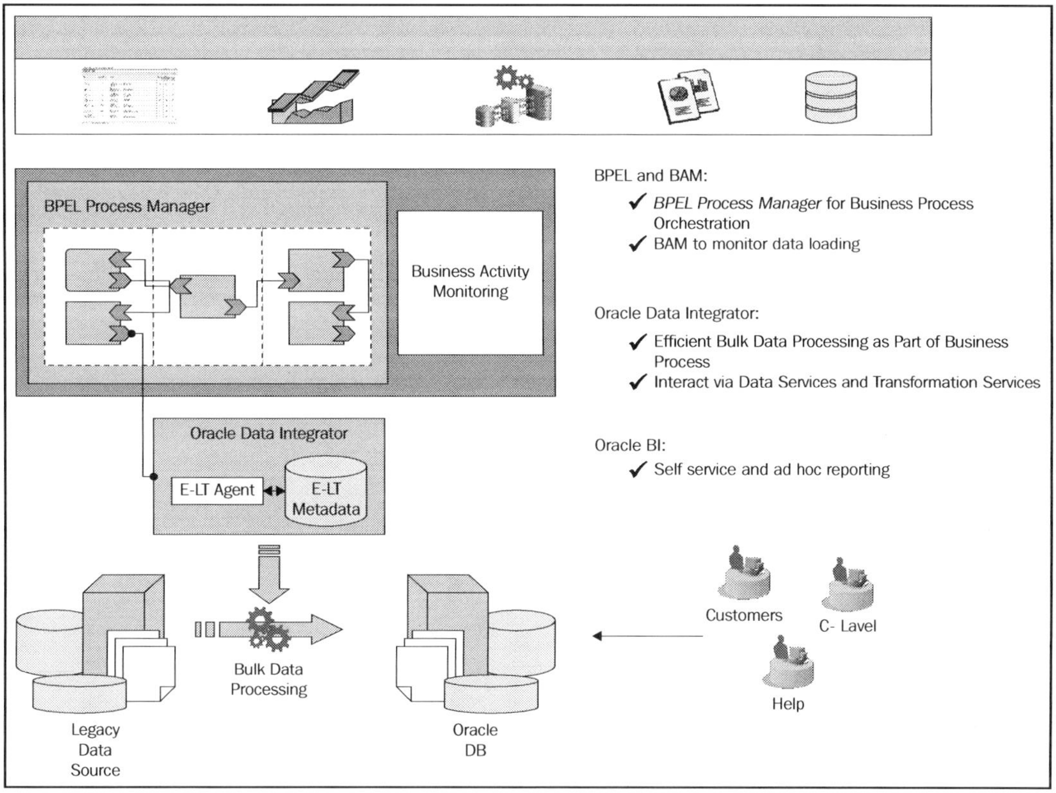

Scenario Three: Summary

In the summary of this scenario, we will discuss why we choose certain Oracle products.

Oracle BAM

In Oracle BAM, both the end user decision makers and IT management see the real time flow of information into the reporting system. End user decision makers can make real-time decisions based upon the most current information. IT management can get immediate alerts if a data load is running slow, alerts on the amount of data being loaded each minute, or the average response time of user ad hoc reports.

Oracle BPEL

Oracle BPEL is used to orchestrate the flow of information into the Oracle database. Oracle BPEL can be used to schedule data loads based upon the time of arrival, or the arrival of a specific file or by constantly looking for the data extracts to load.

Oracle Data Integrator (ODI)

Oracle Data Integrator provides a fast method to bulk load data into the Oracle reporting database. It provides access to data transformation, data cleansing, and data management services. As ODI is fully Web service-enabled, any ODI component can be consumed by Oracle BPEL, Oracle ESB, or any other Web service-enabled tool or product.

Oracle BI

The products we just discussed are all infrastructure products to support the end objective that was to move reporting off the mainframe, and make it accessible to all users. Using Oracle BI tools will hopefully reduce or at least stop the proliferation of Excel spreadsheets and customer SQL reports on user desktops.

Scenario Four: End-to-End SOA

This is also known as Software as a Service, or Legacy SOA Integration

Problem

My legacy system is a 'black box'. Getting information into it is painful and getting information out is worse. I also have no idea of the business processes that run my business.

Context

Your mainframe system does not reflect how business is done today. The legacy system is difficult to maintain, enhance, or rollout new services (product offerings) to internal and external customers.

Forces

The user community demands information to be processed in real time and results to be available immediately. Information integration interfaces into the system are changing every week, and new trading partners wish to interface with you business in days, not months. The system interface needs to be personalized, so that internal power users can see all the information, internal sale people see only sales data pertinent to them, customers only see their data and orders, and company executives have a real time insight into the business as it stands right now, and not what it looked liked three weeks ago.

Solution

The final solution includes Oracle WebCenter, Oracle PBM, Oracle BPEL, Oracle Legacy Adapters, Oracle BAM, Oracle ESB, Oracle OID and SSO, and Oracle OEM as depicted here:

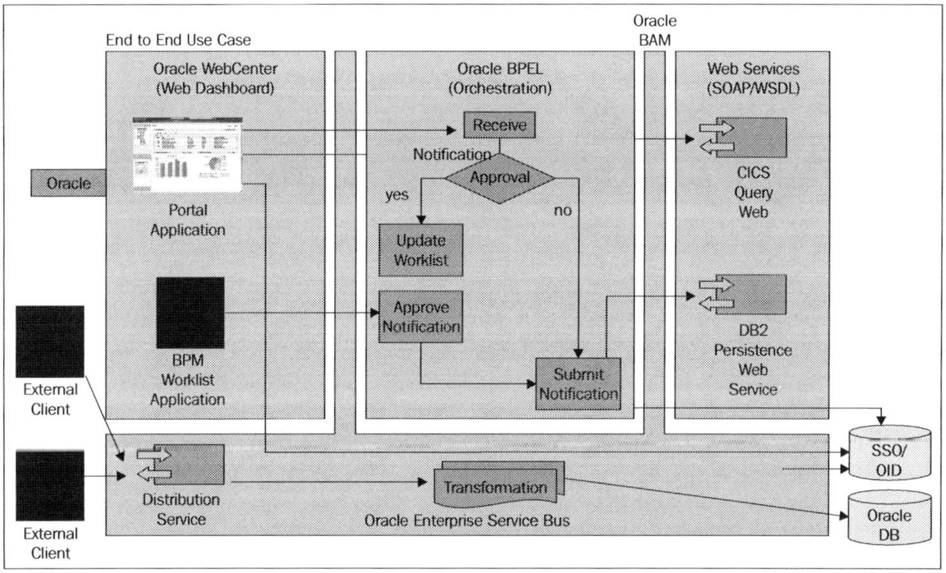

Scenario Four: Summary

As we did with scenario three, we will discuss why we chose certain Oracle products for this scenario.

Oracle WebCenter

Since we want to offer user-personalized views into the system, Oracle WebCenter is the easiest and quickest way to do this. Also, WebCenter provides integration to OID and SSO for user authentication and authorization as well as the ability to verify security to all parts of the system the user will be accessing with one login. Gone are the days of logging into multiple systems. Also, gone are the days of looking between two 'green screens' to verify data. Now all the data is in one web dashboard.

Oracle BAM

BAM plays a big role here, as the amount of processing increases. BAM will make it much easier to monitor all these business process and services in one screen.

Oracle ESB

Just as the ESB was used to help migrate data from other systems and provide an integration bus earlier, ESB is used here to accept two different input file formats and process them in a single workflow.

Oracle OID and SSO

OID is used across all of SOA products (BAM, ESB, and BPEL) to provide a common security repository. SSO makes life easier by allowing access to all applications with a single log on to which a user has access to.

SOA Integration—Final Product Summary

The idea is what you are building in this chapter will become the foundation of your SOA environment moving forward. The SOA architecture you are building is not 'throw away technology' but a quick and hopefully painless way to get you started on the modernization journey.

> **Keeping It Real**: It may seem like 'everything plus the kitchen sink' was thrown in. In a way, it was. SOA is a broad architecture and each scenario is a bit different. The idea here was to show some of the options available. At a minimum, you will require the Oracle Legacy Adapters and a Java-based interface to call the legacy artifacts. Oracle Enterprise Grid Control, Oracle BAM, Oracle BPEL, and Oracle ESB are the next most common components. Next in line comes Oracle Web Services Manager and WS-Security. Most Legacy SOA Integration solutions don't require a Web Services Registry (UDDI register) like Oracle Service Registry as there are not enough services to merit this, and no one really does dymanic/runtime look up of Web services today.

IBM and Legacy SOA Integration

No chapter on Legacy SOA Integration can be written without considering the IBM mainframe hardware and software that have an impact on Legacy SOA integration. In fact, most independent vendors in this space view IBM as their biggest competitor, as well as one of their biggest partners. IBM hardware and software have six capabilities. There are more, but we will focus on those that have an impact on Legacy SOA integration:

- Native IBM Mainframe Integration—WebSphere **Host Access Transformation Server** (**HATS**) can be used to transform existing 3270 and 5250 screens into a Web-browser interface. This is presentation layer SOA integration.
- CICS Transaction Gateway—A user of CICS Transformation Server, Version 3 or greater, has the option of using CICS COMMAREA to expose transactions as Web services. The CICS Transaction Gateway is part of IBM CICS and uses Java EE Connector Architecture (JCA) Version 1.5 to allow CICS transactions to be exposed as Web services.
- IMS SOA Integration Suite—This provides direct access to IMS data stores and IMS transactions from open systems. IMS TM resource adapter and IMS Connect (data services) are part of this bundled suite of middleware, adapters, and mainframe components.
- DB2 Connect—This provides direct access to DB2 data from client/server or web-based applications. This access layer can be exposed as Web services.

- Enterprise Generation Language (EGL)—EGL is a 4GL that has been around for years under various names: Cross System Product (CSP), VisualGen, and VisualAge. IBM promotes 3270 and 5250 SOA enablement using EGL, as EGL includes the notion of a service. EGL is integrated with IBM Rational Business Developer Extension for defining, testing, and deploying the service to all supported platforms, including automated services generation from models.
- zIIP and zAAP processors—Basically, a licensing/pricing configurations to reduce the cost of running Java and DB2 workloads off traditional z/OS partitions on the mainframe. The zIIP and zAAP processor releases followed the release of another specialty processor in 2000, Integrated Facility for Linux (IFL). zAAP is intended for Java and XML. zIIP is intended for DB2 processing. This difference is IFLs are used under z/Linux, and zIIP and zAAP under z/OS. These processors provide significant cost savings over traditional z/OS workloads. The Legacy SOA Integration vendor DataDirect has taken advantage of these processors in the latest release of their product.

IBM's offerings, although complete, continue to be complex. Its Host Access Transformation Server, IMS Connect, and Customer Information Control System (CICS) Transaction Gateway offer a variety of solutions, with or without WebSphere. In addition, IMS, and CICS offer integration capabilities in the form of support for WebSphere MQ, IIOP and Web services. The limitations with the IBM Legacy SOA options are:

- No off host solution—All these products have a footprint on the legacy system. It is not possible to run part of the infrastructure in open systems.
- Limited legacy language and database support—These solutions offer no support for the Natural language or the Adabas database. There is also no support for CA data stores such as the Datacom and IDMS.
- Complex to configure and manage—IBM SOA is really a bunch of point solutions-some for free, such as the CICS with built-in SOA support, and most that are priced separately.
- Different products for screen, transaction, and data access—In order to accomplish SOA legacy across different artifacts and different languages and data stores, you must use a number of different products.
- Need to upgrade to the latest releases of operating systems and CICS—Most of these products require that are on a fairly current release of IBM operating system or transaction monitor.
- More MIPS needed on mainframe—CICS SOA, DB2 Connect, HATS, and IMS SOA Suite require a process on the mainframe and consume more of your MIPS.

Summary

You now have a complete understanding of the source, target, and source to target technical architecture, products and tools involved in Legacy SOA Integration. We learned about some new technologies called the Legacy Service Bus (LSB) and Legacy Services Engine (LSE). We concluded the chapter by applying the product and process knowledge we gained by covering four of the top scenarios.

14
SOA Integraton—Scenario in Detail

We are now going to show an example in detail for—Web Enablement. We will use JSP, JDBC, the Oracle Legacy Adapter, Oracle Application Server, Java EE Connector API, and XA transaction processing to show a two-phase commit across an Oracle database and VSAM on the mainframe.

Why access legacy data instead of CICS, or presentation-tier integration? This is ultimately the source of the truth. This is where the data you want is contained. If you are using any of the other three artifacts, these methods will ultimately call the data store. We have access to the COBOL copybooks and actual VSAM file so there is no need to perform presentation tier integration.

Another reason for choosing VSAM with Java EE is that there is a tutorial on Oracle BPEL using CICS. The Oracle CICS BPEL Legacy SOA integration tutorial can be found here: `http://www.oracle.com/technology/products/integration/adapters/pdf/adapter-Tutorial2-InvokingCICSTransaction.pdf`. This tutorial integrates the BPEL Process Manager with CICS through the Oracle Application Server Legacy Adapter. The Adapter uses **EXCI** (**EXternal Call Interface**) to invoke CICS transactions and uses COMMAREA transactions to exchange message buffers. The Adapter creates a metadata schema for CICS by importing COBOL copybooks and transforming them into mapping definitions for Oracle Connect for CICS on the z/OS machine, and then associating the metadata structures with specific physical files. You may find a review of this tutorial beneficial. Remember that we are using JSP/JDBC/VSAM instead of BPEL/CICS.

Assumptions:

- Oracle software is downloaded and installed using the instructions from Oracle.
- No tutorials on Oracle Application Server and Oracle JDeveloper are included in this chapter because there are many of them on `otn.oracle.com`.
- There is no duplication of Oracle Legacy Adapter tutorials that already exist.

Prior to this release, 10.1.3 Oracle Containers for Java (OC4J's) transaction manager required an Oracle database to perform the two-phase commit protocol when using global transactions that span work in multiple databases. The 10.1.3 release includes a two-phase commit coordinator embedded in OC4J that can perform recovery, and no longer requires the database commit coordinator. The new coordinator may be used with resource managers from any vendor that exposes an XA resource as defined in the JTA specification. More information on JTA can be found here:

- `http://www.oracle.com/technology/tech/java/oc4j/1003/how_to/how-to-midtier-2pc.html`
- `http://java.sun.com/products/jta`

The challenging part here is to configure your mainframe environment with Oracle Connect. Data center folks do not like new products on their mainframe. The most challenging part for us, therefore, is the two-phase commit because Oracle Connect will be installed on the mainframe for us. The remaining work—of exposing legacy VSAM data services via Oracle Legacy Studio, Oracle database access objects, and JSP user interface—is simpler.

We believe that this example has never been demonstrated before. Someone may have done it, but we are sure that there are no documented examples of a Java EE application doing a two-phase commit across Oracle and VSAM using the Oracle Legacy Adapters. So we hope you enjoy getting your 'hands dirty' with a fresh look at SOA Legacy Integration.

We cannot possibly take you through all the steps and show you all the code in this chapter. Therefore, we have posted the Oracle JDeveloper project file including all documentation, source code, and diagrams here: `http://www.packtpub.com/files/code/4060_Code.zip`.

> **Keepin It Real**: The objective of this chapter is to show you how to get started with a two-phase commit Legacy SOA Integration project. We don't want to re-invent what is already available at the **Oracle technology Network (OTN)** website `otn.oracle.com`. So, when information and instructions already exist, we will point you to the appropriate location on OTN.

Oracle Software Required

The software required is often referred to as the bill of materials. The bill of materials for this Legacy SOA Integration scenario is listed here. As URLs change, and the software is constantly updated and re-packaged, you may want to check the Oracle web site to make sure you have the correct software to complete this use case on your own.

- Application Server 10*g* Release 3-Version 10.1.3.3 `http://www.oracle.com/technology/software/products/ias/index.html`
- Application Server Adapters for Legacy Applications with Oracle Connect Mainframe component `http://www.oracle.com/technology/software/products/ias/htdocs/101310.html`
    - Oracle Applications Adapter 10g
        - Installs Application Explorer.
        - Oracle Studio for Legacy Adapters on Windows for the design-time.
        - Runtime components—deploy the following runtime components automatically:
            - J2CA deployment for packaged applications.
            - BSE deployment for packaged applications.
            - Legacy adapters for CICS, IMS/TM, IMS/DB, and VSAM.
            - Java EE Connector Legacy Adapter for connecting with Oracle Connect engine running on legacy platforms.
            - Oracle Connect—The mainframe Legacy Service Engine component, called Oracle Connect, comes with adapter software. It is under the "Oracle_Connect" directory under the staging area of the Legacy Adapter software. There are a couple of files that need to be **ftp**'d to the mainframe, and you will need to follow the installation guide for completing the mainframe configuration steps.
- Oracle JDeveloper—Version 10.1.3.3 `http://www.oracle.com/technology/software/products/jdev/index.html`
- Oracle Business Process Analysis Suite—Version 10.1.3.4 `http://www.oracle.com/technology/software/products/bpa/index.html`

- Oracle pre-packaged tutorials to download and use. We don't want to create material that is already available on the Web:
    - Oracle database invoice schema creation using SQL Developer: `http://www.oracle.com/technology/pub/articles/luttikhuizen-esbcase-setup.html`
    - Oracle Studio step by step to create CICS adapter: `http://www.oracle.com/technology/products/integration/adapters/pdf/adapter-Tutorial2-InvokingCICSTransaction.pdf`

> More information on creating VSAM adapters can be found here: `http://download.oracle.com/docs/cd/B31017_01/integrate.1013/b31002/toc.htm`

The legacy and mainframe adapters (CICS Adapter, VSAM Adapter, IMS/TM Adapter, IMS/DB Adapter, and Tuxedo Adapter) have a design-time component—Oracle Studio for Legacy Adapters that can be installed on Windows and Linux.

The **Legacy Services Engine** (**LSE**) from Oracle has two run-time components:

1. Oracle Connect that gets installed on the mainframe.
2. Java EE Connector Legacy Adapter component that gets deployed on the Oracle Application Server.

There are different flavors for Oracle Connect depending on the mainframe application that you are connecting to:

- Oracle Connect for CICS
- Oracle Connect for IMS/TM
- Oracle Connect for VSAM (The one we are using in this example)
- Oracle Connect for IMS/DB
- Oracle Connect for Tuxedo

The Java EE Connector Legacy Adapter component that gets deployed on the Oracle Application Server is the same for all flavors of Oracle Connect.

> **Keeping It Real**: Modern software change rapidly. In order to ensure that this example will work in your environment, be sure to use the mentioned versions.

UML and Database Diagrams

UML is often the language used to describe configurations, process flows, and event sequences in an SOA-based development. So we will use UML deployment, use case, activity, and sequence diagrams to describe the scenario being implemented in this chapter. We will use a database diagram to illustrate the Oracle Database and mainframe data stores.

Deployment Diagram

The UML deployment diagram depicts a static view of the run-time configuration of processing nodes and the components that run on those nodes. The diagram shows the hardware for your system, the software that is installed on that hardware, and the middleware used to connect the disparate machines to one another. The following UML deployment diagram was created in Oracle BPA Suite using the Oracle Business Process Architect:

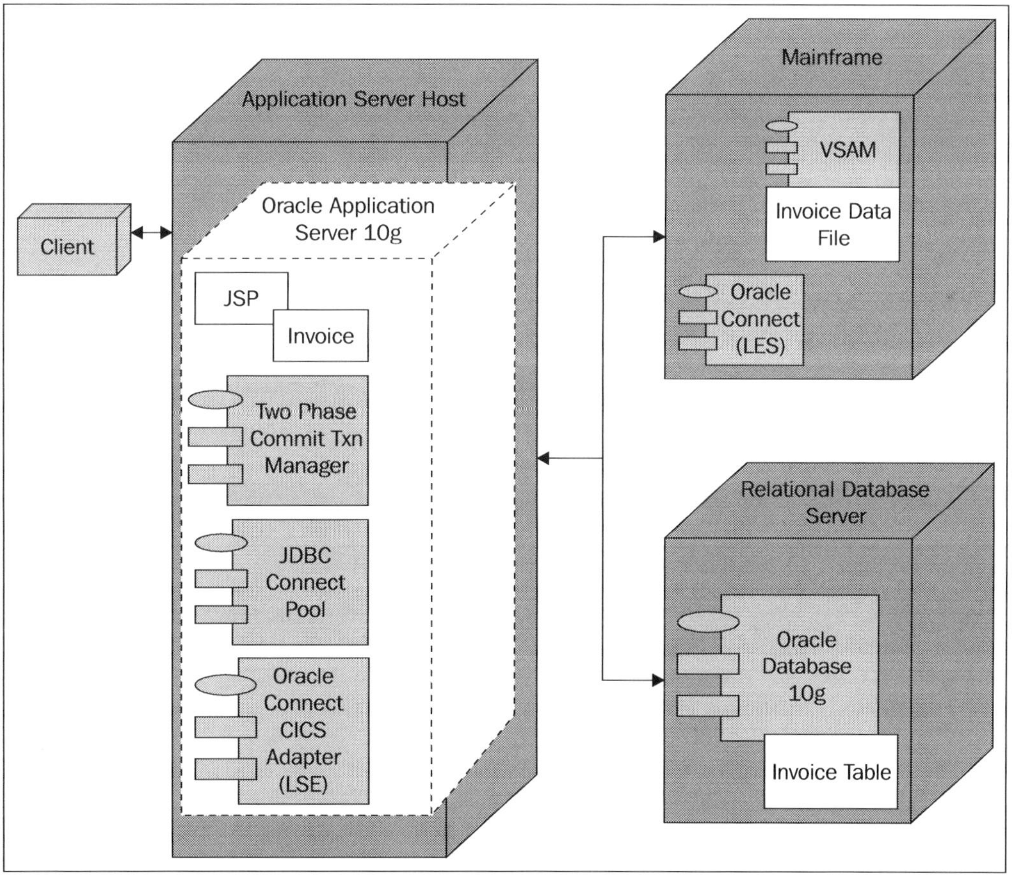

Use Case Diagram

UML use cases are fundamentally in text form. We see the stick figures and oval shaped entities and assume this to be the core of a use case. What many people don't understand is that a 'fully-dressed' use case includes a form at the backend that contains all the important information. This includes scope, stakeholders, primary actors, conditions, scenario, and other detailed information. Our use case, as illustrated in the following figure, is very simple:

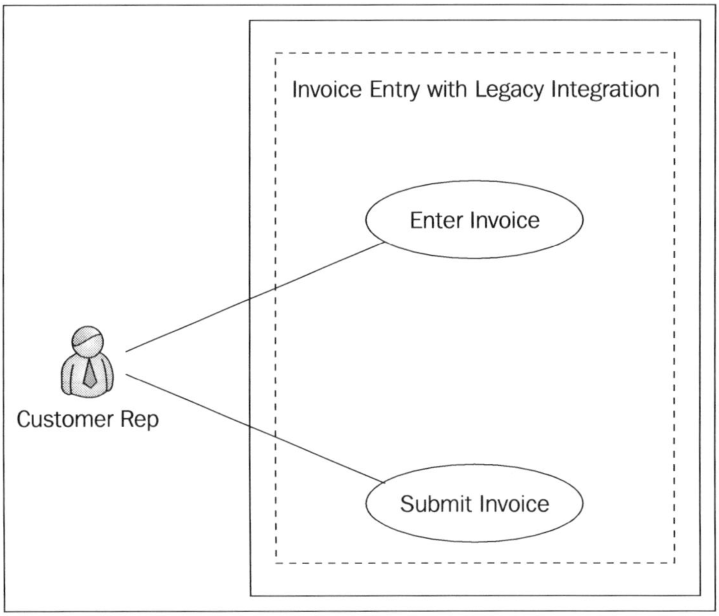

The focus will be on the two-phase commit across Oracle and VSAM. The use case itself is a simple example of an invoice entry screen. In the real world, the invoice is generated by the order. But in our case, we will enter an invoice directly as we don't want to go through the entire order entry process. The use cases are data entries via a Web form. The data being entered is the invoice information to be stored in an Oracle Database and mainframe VSAM data store. The submit invoice use case will then commit one transaction across both databases.

Activity Diagram

The following activity diagram shows, in a top to bottom flow, the state of each database persistence object for the Oracle Database (Invoice), the VSAM database (Legacy Service), and the two-phase commit transaction object in the Oracle Application Server:

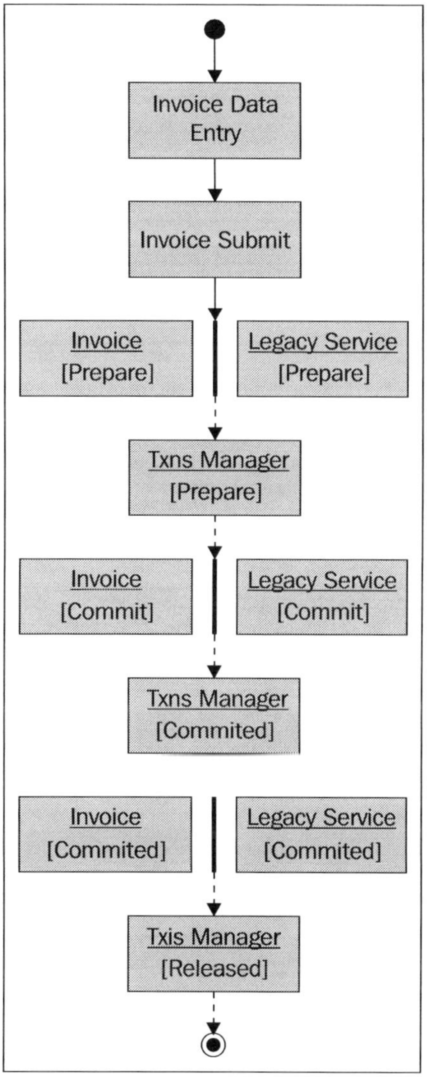

All user activity happens in the first part of the process. The remaining activities are related to coordinating the database persistence objects with the transaction manager, and insuring a successful two-phase commit.

Sequence Diagram

The sequence diagram will focus on the sequence of the two-phase commit as this is the core of your example.

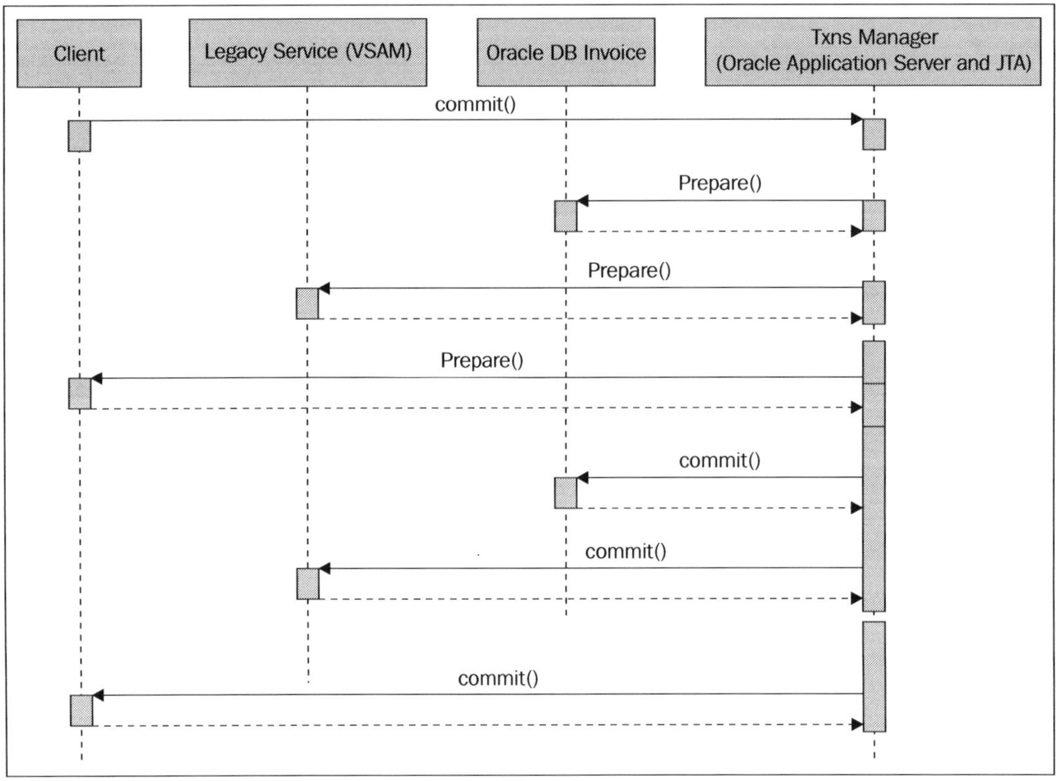

This sequence diagram is representative of any two-phase commit scenario. The only difference is in the object lifelines (client, legacy service, invoice, and transaction manager). The client, invoice, and transaction manager are typical of any two-phase commit sequence diagram. The Legacy Service object lifeline is the only difference here. Typically, in the open systems environment, this would be a data access object that would commit a row to an Oracle or other relational database. In our Legacy SOA Integration example, it is a service that commits a record to the VSAM database.

Data Model Diagram

Let's also take a look at the data model for this application. Remember, we have a table on the open systems Oracle Database 10g instance and on the mainframe in VSAM. As this is a logical data model, it appears as though these two entities are tightly coupled and are on the same Oracle database. As we know, they are on separate databases, and even on separate machines, possibly hosted miles apart. The Oracle Invoice table (INVOICES) and mainframe invoice file (`MF_INVOICE_DATA`) are also loosely-coupled as there is no **foreign** key relationship for the physical implementation of this data model.

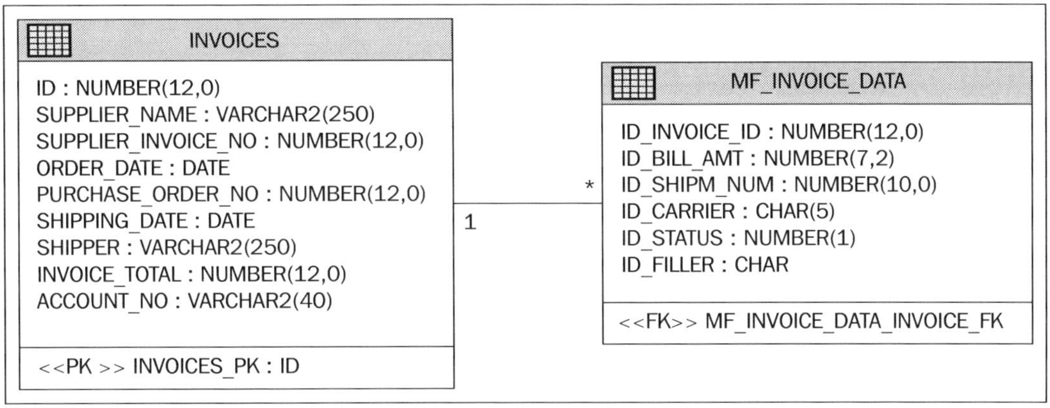

Some interesting things to note when you look at this simple data model:

- Duplication of data—It is not uncommon to find duplication of data when you begin to SOA enable your legacy systems across both the open system Oracle Database and mainframe data store. In this case, invoice total (bill amount), shipper (carrier), and of course invoice ID are present in both the systems. Depending on whether the Oracle or VSAM database is the master database for this information, there may be replication between the two (Oracle Database and VSAM) to keep them in sync. This is typically called **Change Data Capture** (**CDC**). If both of them can be updated, then there needs to be bi-directional replication (some times called write-back).
- Some data in Oracle and some on mainframe—The other case is where some of the data is in Oracle and some in the VSAM file on the mainframe. This happens very often, and is the reason why some users have to go to several systems to get the information they need before Legacy SOA Integration modernization is done.
- Data type mismatches—The data types between the two systems may not match identically.

We discussed these anomalies in the previous chapter, but think it really hits home when you see it in an example.

> **Keeping It Real**: Although developers and 'techies' often like to use the "So let's code" (SLC) development methodology, it is best to start with UML and data model diagramming to get a clear picture of the final deliverable. Even for this simple example, the diagrams shown previously can help the developer, IT architects, managers, and even business people have a clear understanding of the solution set.

Which Legacy Artifacts Should I Expose?—Using the Relativity Product Set

The SOA Integration Scenario starts with a detailed technical example on how to discover the VSAM file to be expose, as well as the components that facilitate access to them. Before we do that, we must get introduced to the Relativity tool set, terminology definitions, and tools overview. The Relativity tool set is used heavily in our example.

The complexity of existing legacy applications makes the task of identifying potential services for exposure in an SOA architecture quite difficult. The difficulty varies based on the **layering** degree of the application. We will discuss layering in more detail shortly. It is simpler to identify and expose legacy artifacts as Web services for a well-layered application and more difficult for a non-layered application. It is simpler to identify and expose legacy artifacts as Web services when programs use simple communication areas, and more difficult when these communication areas are complex and consist of a large number of unused fields.

To expose a service, we must solve a number of problems:

- Which programs are suitable for exposure?
- Which programs contain the desired functionality?
- What is the best level of granularity for the service exposure?
- How to proceed when the desired functionality is intermixed with other functionality?
- How to select the essential fields in the communication areas?
- How to perform minimum intrusive changes to the application code, if such changes are needed for service exposure?

To solve these problems, we will use a number of specialized tools:

- RMW Application Analyzer (`http://www.relativity.com/pages/applicationanalyzer.asp`) will be used to parse the application sources and perform some initial understanding of the application
- RMW SOA Analyzer (`http://www.relativity.com/pages/soaanalyzer.asp`) will be used to discover potential services and define them
- RMW Architect (`http://www.relativity.com/pages/applicationarchitect.asp`) will be used to perform certain remedies on some programs so that they can be exposed as services
- RMW Business Rule Manager (`http://www.relativity.com/pages/businessrulemanager.asp`) will be used to discover validation rules relevant in an SOA enablement project

We will start with a discussion of the application layers, which is relevant for all subsequent points.

Application Layers—Understanding Relativity Terminology

Building an application with distinct layers is not a new concept. Even for old applications, architects have understood the benefits of placing the artifacts in well-defined layers. In a perfectly layered application one may distinguish the following layers:

- Layer 0—User interface layer
  This layer consists of screens which would be visible to the users. This is the user interface.
- Layer 1—Client layer
  This layer consists of all programs that communicate directly with the screens. This is the presentation tier and/or the navigation tier.

  Such programs would contain all the logic for capturing users' requests, validating the input data, invoking the appropriate "service" programs from the lower layers and formatting the output that responds to the user's request.

  In this layer, the execution moves to the lower layers via CALL or LINK operations, and moves to other programs of the same layer via exclusive transfer of control, which in CICS could be accomplished by XCTL or RETURN TRANID statements.

In fact, this layer may contain two types of programs:

- "Client programs" that receive and send screens
- "Transitional programs" that make navigation decisions

Transitional programs are sometimes used as traffic dispatchers. A program CPROG1 may receive a screen, SCREEN1 and pass exclusive control to a program TPROG that analyzes the user request in order to decide the next screen to be presented to the user. TPROG may pass exclusive control back to CPROG1, which in turn may present the same screen, SCREEN1, with additional data that satisfies the request. TPROG may also decide to transfer control to a program CPROG2, which in turn may present the screen SCREEN2.

The benefit of transitional programs is that they encapsulate the navigation logic. The client programs are confined to screen logic, while the transitional programs are confined to navigation logic.

- Layer 2—Service layer

  This layer consists of all programs that satisfy a request, without any screen communication or regard to screen logic. Most programs in this layer interact in one way or another with application's persistent data, but they may also perform certain pure logic related to computation, or formatting. As an example, one "service" program may retrieve invoice information based on an invoice number, or it may simply compute the number of business days between two dates.

  Service layer programs may be also classified based on their position in the calling hierarchy, resulting in three categories:

  - Layer 2A: Frontier programs that are called directly by Layer 1 programs
  - Layer 2B: Indirect data access programs, which access data through some other called service programs, or perform computations or formatting
  - Layer 2C: Direct data access programs, which access the persistent data from VSAM files, or from databases

- Layer 3—The database persistence tier.

A classification of assets in a perfectly layered application is illustrated in the following hierarchy, as displayed by the Relativity's SOA Analyzer tool:

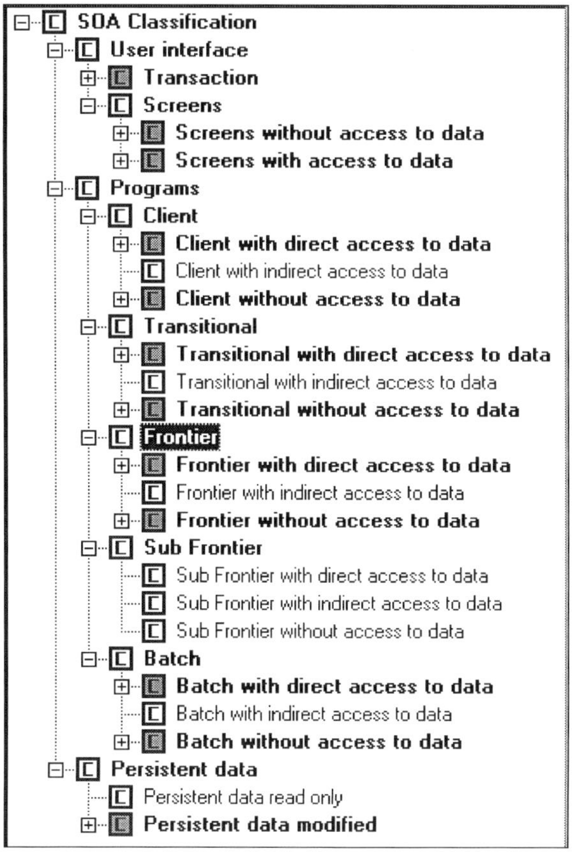

In the case of a well-layered application, programs in each layer will have well-designated business functions:

- Client programs contain screen logic
- Transitional programs contain navigation logic
- Frontier programs contain business level data manipulation logic
- Sub-frontier programs contain both business logic and technical data manipulation logic

The layering of the application is of immediate importance in an SOA enablement project. As we try to expose services that execute discrete requests, we will look at the client and transitional programs only for the purpose of identifying the location of potential services. In themselves, they do not offer services, as they do not execute any server type logic. Their functionality will be replaced in an SOA architecture with new technical artifacts that are "end-user facing", and implemented practically on an application or web server.

The service programs are the ones offering "service" capability, and we can create Web services based on their functionality.

> **Keeping It Real**: Classification and layering of your application assets is valuable in itself. For many organizations, it is the first time they take a complete inventory of their applications, including a classification of all their application artifacts.

Understanding an Artifact's Place in the Architecture

The simple classification of application artifacts does not give us a full understanding of how they are used. The SOA Analyzer provides a more detailed picture when we ask for 'vertical' and 'horizontal' slices that show the context in which the artifact is used. Such 'slices' are very useful, as a complete diagram of the application may be exceedingly complex and hard to understand.

A vertical slice shows "usages", that is, how an artifact is used (for instance via a call or a file access), and how it uses other artifacts. Vertical slicing is the method used to determine the modules that access data files. Vertical slicing is also used to determine 'frontier programs', programs that contain business logic. Both these modules make great candidates for enabling as services. A 'horizontal' slice shows how the control passes between artifacts, usually through exclusive change of control, or through screen navigation. Horizontal slicing is a great way to determine the modules that can be exposed from your presentation-tier (client layer).

Vertical Slices

We can obtain the vertical and horizontal slices by a right-click on an artifact in the **Classification** pane, followed by the selection of the **Show vertical slice** or **Show horizontal slice** menus. Now, let us look at certain examples.

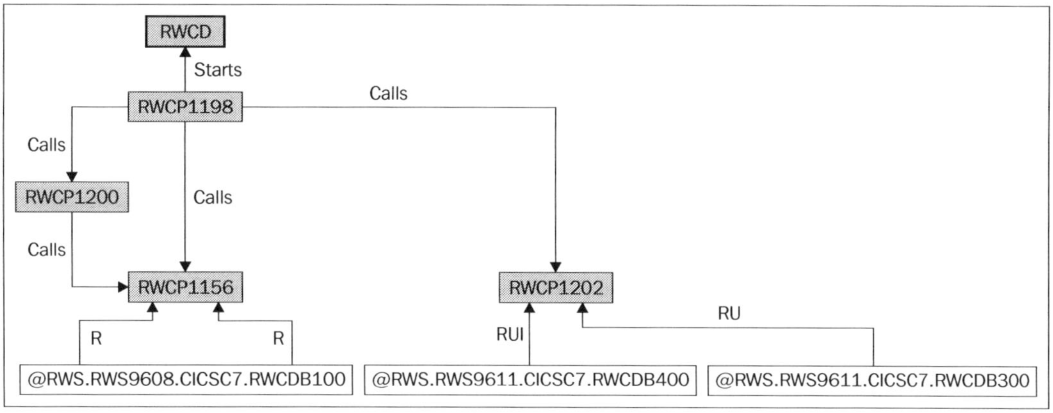

As a CICS transaction appears in the highest layer of the architecture, it is not itself "used" by any another artifact. In the above figure, we can see that transaction RWCD is started by program RWCP1198, which calls RWCP1200, RWCP116, and RWCP1202. In turn, the last two programs access certain files (shown at the very bottom of the diagram) in read mode (R), Read/Update (RU), or Read/Update/Insert mode.

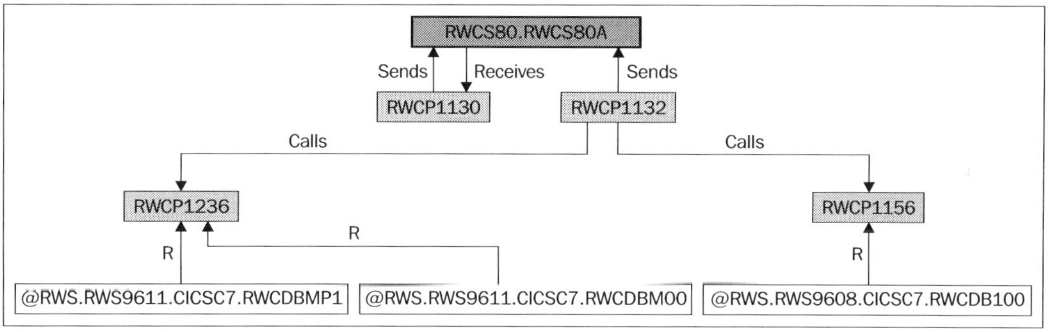

The preceding figure shows a vertical slice of the screen RWCS80A, which is sent and received by the program RWCP110, and sent only by program RWCP1132. These programs then call programs RWCP1138 and RWCP1156 to read data sets.

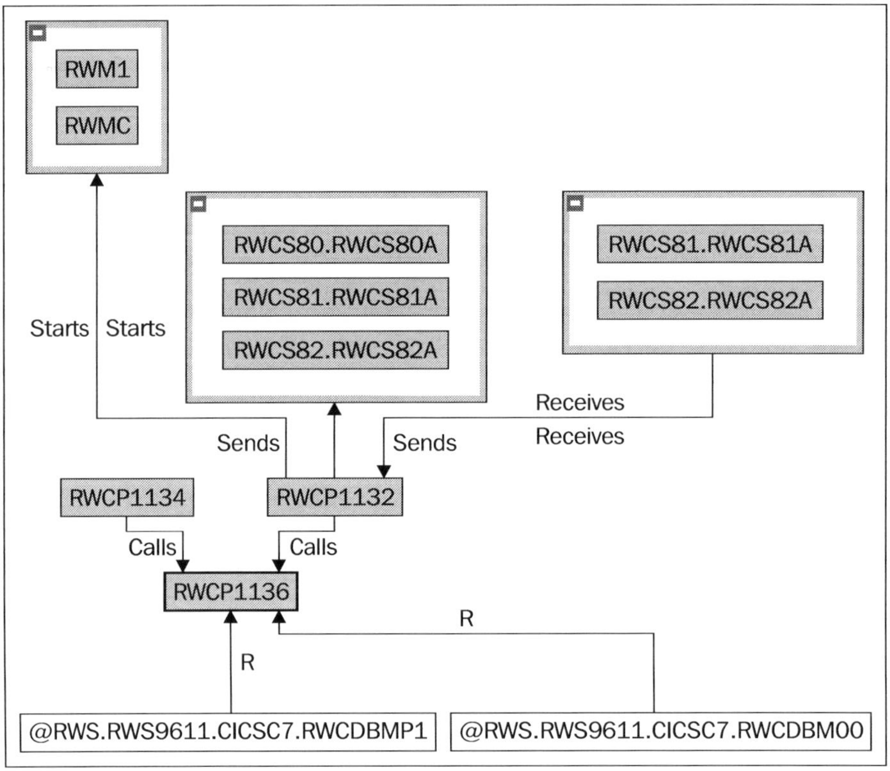

The above figure shows a vertical slice of program RWCP1136. We can immediately notice that this happens to be a 'frontier' program, according to the classification that we have described earlier, as it does not access screens and is called directly by programs that access screens. This special position in the architecture would make it a good candidate for exposure as a Web service.

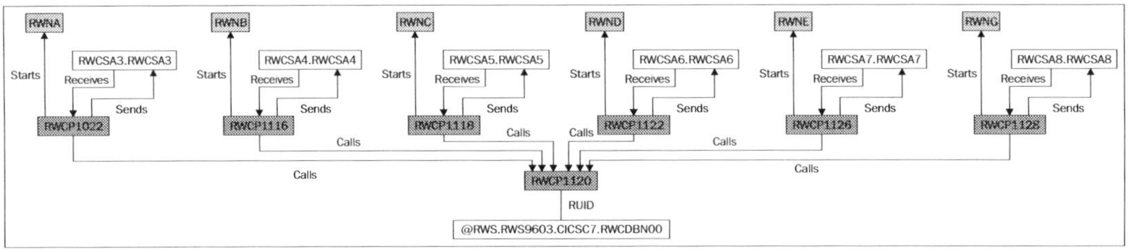

From the preceding figure, we can discover a fact that is relevant in the effort to extract services—all operations against the selected file (seen at the bottom, in a white box) are performed via a single program, RWCP1120. This makes the program ideal as a service, as it certainly contains all the logic needed to access the file from outside.

> **Keeping It Real**: Vertical slicing shows the usage of modules from the presentation-tier through the business logic, down to the data files, and to the modules that access these data files. Vertical slicing is therefore incredibly useful in identifying business logic and data access module to expose as services.

Horizontal Slices

While vertical slices through the application's architecture show usage scenarios, horizontal slices show the processes or workflow performed by the operator. Horizontal slices do not make sense for files or tables of other persistent data artifacts, as they do not represent processes or actions triggered by the user. For programs, horizontal slices show the exclusive change of control from one program to another, as for example via XCTL operations in CICS. For screens, they show the possibilities for the operator to move from one screen to another.

We can look at some examples of horizontal slices.

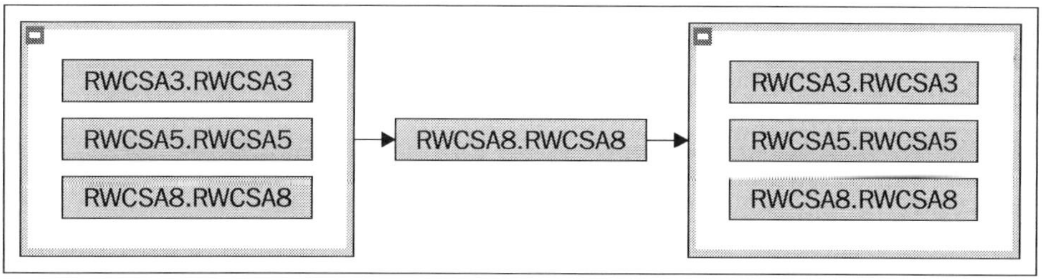

The preceding figure shows a horizontal slice for the screen RWCSA8. The block on the left shows all the screens from which the operator can potentially move to this screen, while the block on the right shows all the screens to which the operator can potentially move from this screen.

I have intentionally used the word "potentially", because not all these transitions may happen at runtime. The simple reason is that the static analysis cannot always discover the exact transitions, due to the fact that they may be controlled deep in a program or even in a file or table. In some legacy applications, the **traffic** between screens is recorded in a table which a **traffic cop** program reads in order to figure out how to process a user request. The preceding figure should be interpreted as "from screen RWCSA8 one can possibly move to screens RWCSA3, RWCSA5 and RWCSA8." In reality, the program that controls RWCSA8 may contain additional restrictions, which prevents, for example, a move to screen RWCSA8.

> **Keeping It Real**: Horizontal slicing shows the modules usage from the perspective of the client and the transitional layers (screens and navigation tiers). Horizontal slicing is therefore incredibly useful in identifying the points or steps in the process where certain services are invoked.

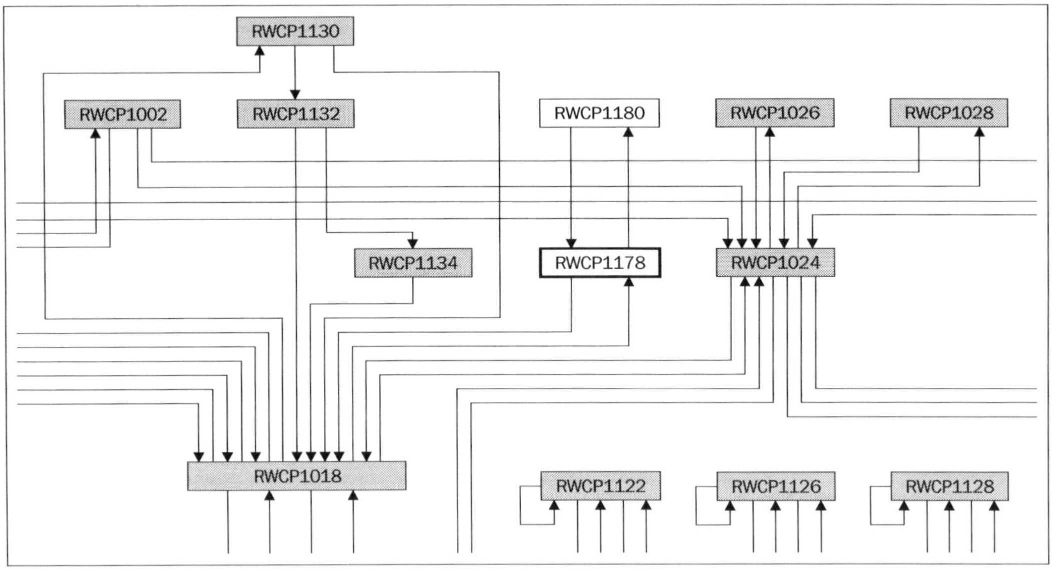

The preceding figure shows a horizontal slice of programs. Every edge in the graph indicates an exclusive change of control from one program to another program.

Together, horizontal slices and vertical slices offer a good picture of the role of a particular artifact in the application architecture.

Understanding Anomalies

In the real world, many legacy applications exhibit various exceptions from the layering scheme described earlier. The SOA Analyzer tool will identify these exceptions, which sometimes need to be addressed in one way or another to allow an SOA enablement by exposing all potential services offered by the legacy application.

We are going to call such exceptions "anomalies", and it is important to notice that they do not represent errors or mistakes. Programs with anomalies (as they are understood here) may function perfectly as they were originally intended, but present difficulties when it comes to a transition towards to an SOA architecture, as you will see.

In all the diagrams presented by the SOA Analyzer, programs with anomalies are shown with a red background. A click on a node for such a program will display the properties pane, where the anomaly is clearly stated, as shown in the following figure:

Name	CUSTINQ1
Type	Program
Layer	Client
Access type	None
Access mode	Direct
Anomaly	Client with data access

There are four types of anomalies that the SOA Analyzer identifies.

Client Programs with Data Access

In a perfect architecture, all programs that belong to the client layer should only deal with screen logic and navigation. Data access should be accomplished through the programs belonging to the frontier and sub-frontier layers, which in turn should be called by the client programs. This is the case in a well-layered application. But in real life, this restriction is not always enforced. In some cases, where no strict architectural discipline is enforced, programmers may take shortcuts and combine the screen access and data access in the same programs, as it is shown in the following vertical slice for program CUSTINQ1:

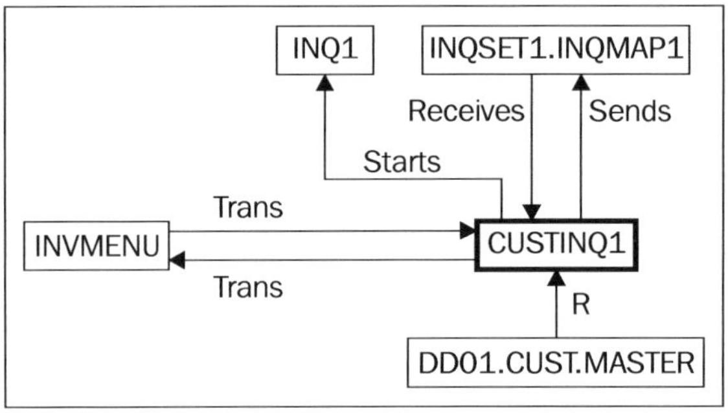

As I have already stated, although a program like CUSTINQ1 may function very well, it may present some limitations when it comes to the mining of services. Let us suppose that this program contains some very special logic that interprets the data read from the Customer Master file. It is possible, for example, that the program reads the date of birth of a customer and calculates the age, which is then displayed on the screen. Many such derivations are possible. We would like to have a service that does not just read a record from the Customer Master file, but also interprets and derives new data items. Unfortunately, while CUSTINQ1 does the interpretation and the derivation, it cannot be simply made into a service, as it is also conversing a screen (by definition, a service cannot do that). We will discuss later what can be done in such a case.

Keeping It Real: Legacy applications are not the only ones that contain database access in client facing modules. Often, Web developers will include JDBC calls directly in JSPs. We will be found guilty of this later on in this chapter. Our example has JDBC calls in a JSP, which is not a recommended practice for production systems, but we will use the excuse that this is just sample/example code!

Calling Client Programs

It is tempting to look at all programs that are called as potential services. In principle, a call is a request to the called program to perform a task, and that is also the nature of a service. However, in real life applications, we will, encounter situations where a called program cannot be made into a service for a simple reason that it also converses a screen, as can be seen in the following figure, with program SYSTEM.PCITN100:

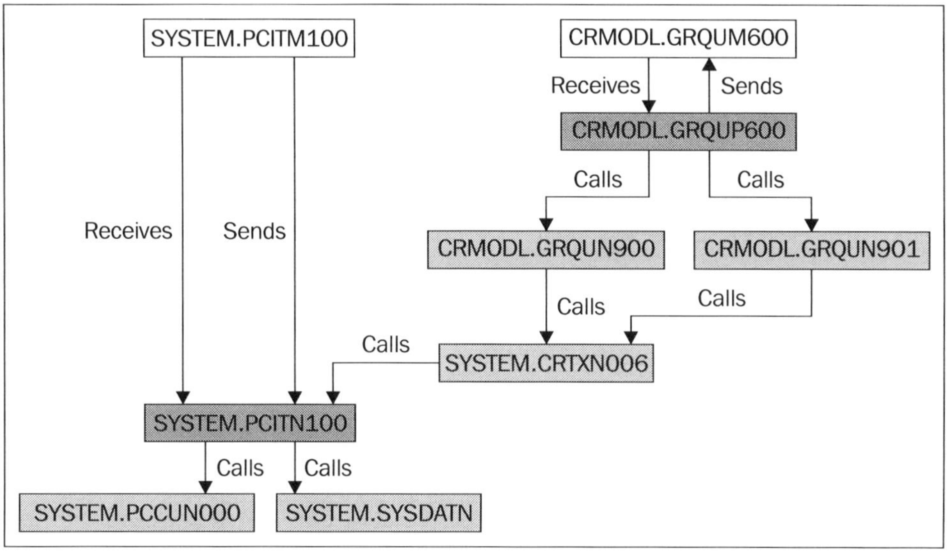

There can be many reasons why the original application included this anomaly. Perhaps the most common reason is that when a "service" program is written the programmer finds it convenient to report an exception immediately to the operator by sending a screen with a message. By writing the program in this style, the programmer simplifies the code, but renders it unfit to become a Web service (which by definition cannot converse with a user interface).

If the program in question is desired as a service, it should be modified such that instead of sending a screen in case of an exception, it should return to its caller with a special return code signaling the same exception.

Calling Transitional Programs

This anomaly is mostly theoretical, as transitional programs are not usually candidates for services. However, it signals a strange situation, in the sense that usually transitional programs (as defined above) are mostly dedicated to directing the screen navigation, and not to the fulfillment of a task (typical for called programs).

Impure Service Programs

This is a generalization of the "Client programs called" anomaly. It happens when a client program calls a "service" program, which in turn calls another client program. Although the one in the middle seems to be a perfect service (because it is called, and does not converse a screen), it is impossible to turn it into a service, as during the execution one of its called programs converses a screen.

In the figure under the heading *Calling Client Programs,* this is the case with the program CRMODL.GRQUN900, which is "almost" a service. This program is called by CRMODL.GRQUN600, but in turn calls SYSTEM.CRTXN06, which calls SYSTEM.PCITN100, which is actually a client program conversing the screen SYSTEM.PCITM100.

Other Anomalies that Need Remedial Action

There are some other challenges we need to overcome in order to expose services from a legacy application. Programs that appear as perfect candidates for services may display certain characteristics that need remedial action.

Data Validation Problem

A perfect CICS service program may not become a perfect Web service due to the fact that it fails to perform data validations. That may not be a problem in its original environment as it relies on its caller program to perform such validations. Let's have a look at the following figure:

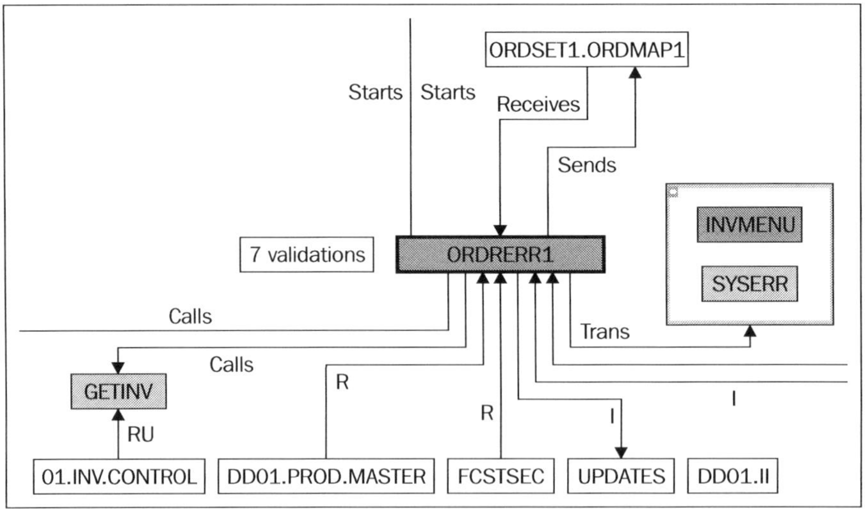

Next to the ORDERR1 program, you can see a label with the text, "7 validations". This label appeared automatically after:

- We used Relativity's Business Rule Manager, where we made a request to automatically detect all screen validations in program ORDERR1.
- We pressed the **Tools | Intersect Validations** menu in the SOA Analyzer.

The "7 validations" label indicates that as ORDERR1 converses the screen ORDMAP1, it performs 7 validations against the data entered by the operator on this screen. Such validations check if the data is numeric, properly formatted, or entered in the mandatory fields. When program GETINV is invoked to perform an operation against the INV.CONTROL file, it assumes that all data is already valid (otherwise ORDERR1 would have issued a warning message to the operator). GETINV can now fulfill the requested tasks without the danger of running into some data that does not make sense.

Although GETINV is otherwise a good candidate for a service, here is the caveat! If this service is invoked from another environment other than its original one, there is no guarantee that the data it receives is valid. What worked perfectly in CICS may not work properly in SOA architecture.

There are various remedies we can apply to resolve this issue. One of them could be that the application server or even the client facing programs in the new architecture perform the validations and ensure that GETINV does not receive anything else other than correct data. Another remedy is to repeat the same validations in GETINV as they exist in its caller, ORDERR1, and have GETINV return with a special return code, should these validations fail.

> **Keeping It Real**: Placing the data validation in your new JSP, JSF, or AJAX application is easily achievable. However, it defeats the purpose of using Legacy SOA Integration as a 'limited coding' modernization approach. However, if your strategic direction is to re-architect your system, you may see writing the data validation in Java EE as your next step toward moving off the mainframe.

The Problem of Transient or Temporary Data Queues

One would usually expect the caller and called programs in a CICS environment to communicate through the CICS COMMAREA. This is the most common way, but not the only way, in which CICS programs pass data. It is also possible that the called program writes the data into a temporary storage queue that the caller reads. As most CICS adapters are equipped to deal only with data passing through COMMAREA, this creates a major difficulty.

We need to discover if such situations exist. It is in fact quite simple. After we display a vertical slice through the architecture (see the description of vertical slices above), we press on the **Tools | Intersect Queues** menu. This will add labels next to the programs that operate with queues, as shown in the following figure:

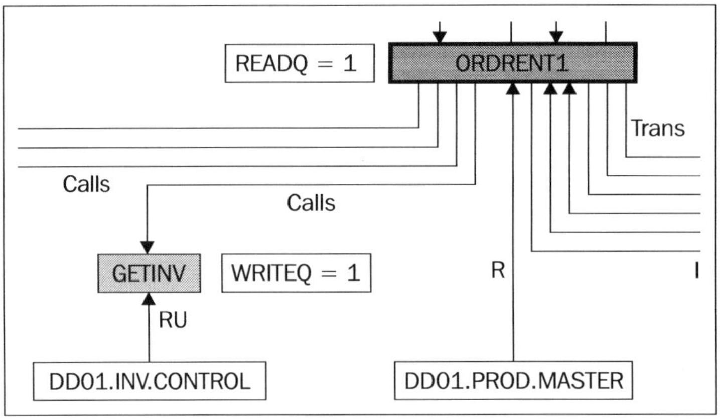

This diagram tells us that GETINV writes to a queue and ORDENT1 reads from a queue. It is just a **red** flag at this point, enough to determine us to investigate. If we really find that the data passes from GETINV to its caller via the queue, then we know that normal service adaptors would not be able to create a good service out of GETINV. When the program is called as a Web service in SOA architecture, the service consumer will expect to collect all the data from the service interface that describes the COMMAREA, while the data actually resides in a queue.

The remedy is to either modify GETINV to pass the data exclusively through the COMMAREA, or to create a special 'service' program that reads the queue and passes it through the COMMAREA. Finally, it is possible that some vendors offer service adapters that are capable of getting the data from CICS queues.

Finding the Service Functionality—Relativity SOA Analyzer Product

As service programs capable of exposure are themselves placed in sublayers, the question is which one to choose. Given that we may look for a particular service function (for example, "retrieve claim"), we need to narrow the search to those that are related to this function, in one way or another. The development team maintaining the application may simply know which are the programs implementing the function. In the absence of such direct knowledge, we can use other methods to find the functionality we want to expose.

Starting from Screens

One such method is to start with the screens that suggest the functionality that we are after. By inspecting the screens, for instance, we may discover that one of them helps the operator perform an **Order Entry** function. Screens may be viewed in the SOA Analyzer by selecting the **View Source** menu visible when we right-click on a screen mode. Our **Order Entry** function will display as follows:

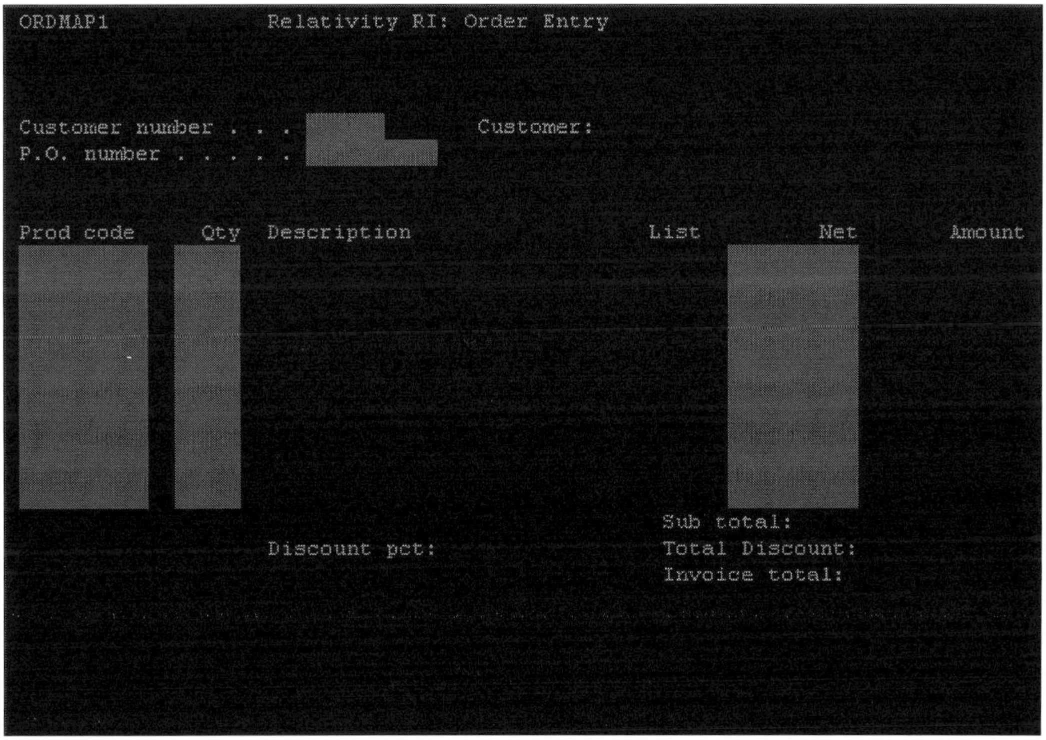

Once we discover the screen that deals with the service function, we can look at its "vertical slice" through the application. The vertical slice, as displayed by the SOA Analyzer, shows a cut through the layers, which includes the screen as well as all the programs that service it, as shown in the following figure:

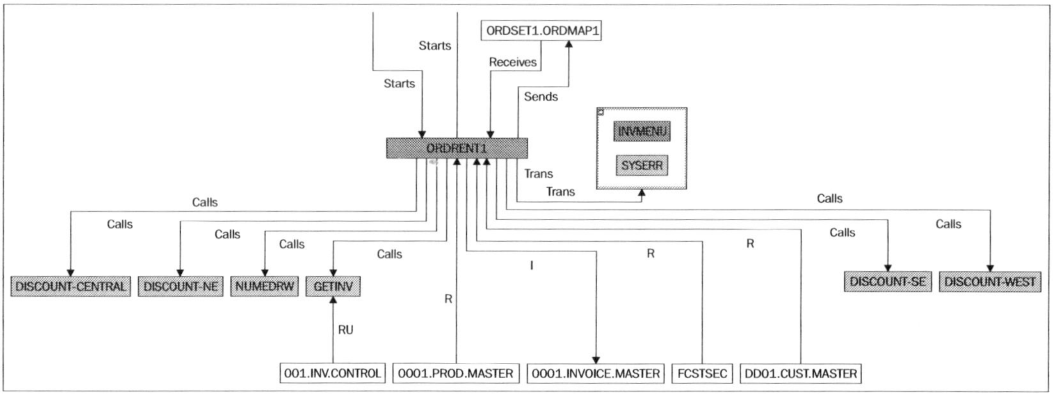

In this diagram, we can see that the screen ORDMAP1 (which appears on the top) is accessed by the program ORDENT1, which in turn calls other programs to fulfill a request. All these called programs are candidates for services. Together, they could become operational in a Web service that would be consumed when one makes a request to create a customer order in the new SOA architecture.

As we look for potential service programs, we should give special attention to the frontier programs. Indeed, they encapsulate the most complete functionality. They not only know which data to access, but also know how to assemble it in a manner consistent with business requirements. If lower-layer programs are selected, then some of the data assembly must be performed on the application server, opening the possibility of erroneous implementations that differ in functionality from the original application. Choosing frontier programs for exposure makes the task simpler and eliminates the possibility for further errors.

Looking for Special Program Constructs

Another method to find the services with a particular functionality is to look for special patterns in the code. This can be accomplished from the Relativity's Application Analyzer with the aid of the so-called clipper queries.

To run a clipper query, we'll go through the following steps:

1. Select a program in the SOA Analyzer, right-click on it, and press the **Show Source** menu. The source of the program appears in a pane of the tool, as shown in the following figure. If you press on the top-right button, a menu appears where you select **Clipper**.

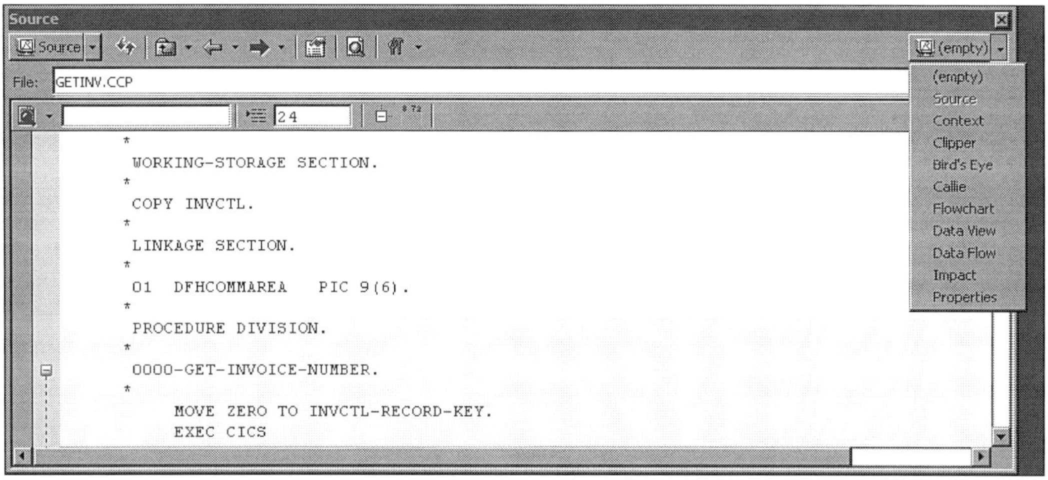

2. A new pane opens up in the **Source** pane. Press the corresponding toolbar button to create a **New list** (this is where the results of the query will be deposited).

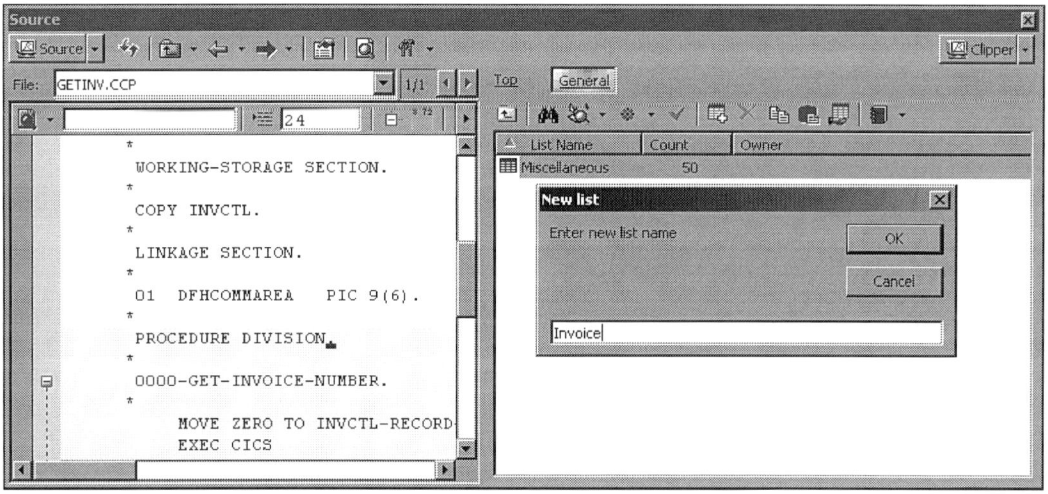

3. A new pane opens up in the source pane, on which you can locate the search button and select **Cobol File** sources as the space where we are going to search, as shown in the following figure :

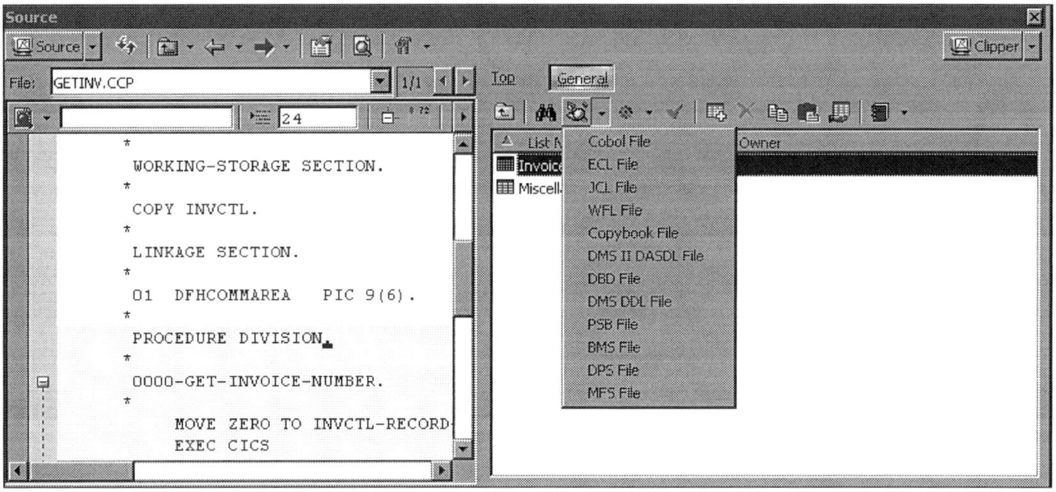

4. We get a new window on which we can build our query. Clipper queries allow us to interrogate any type of program construct as well as combinations of such constructs. In this case, we can build a very simple query that looks for variables containing the string INV, hoping to find the places where an invoice is updated. The intention is to isolate the program that maintains invoice data. The query appears as shown in the following figure:

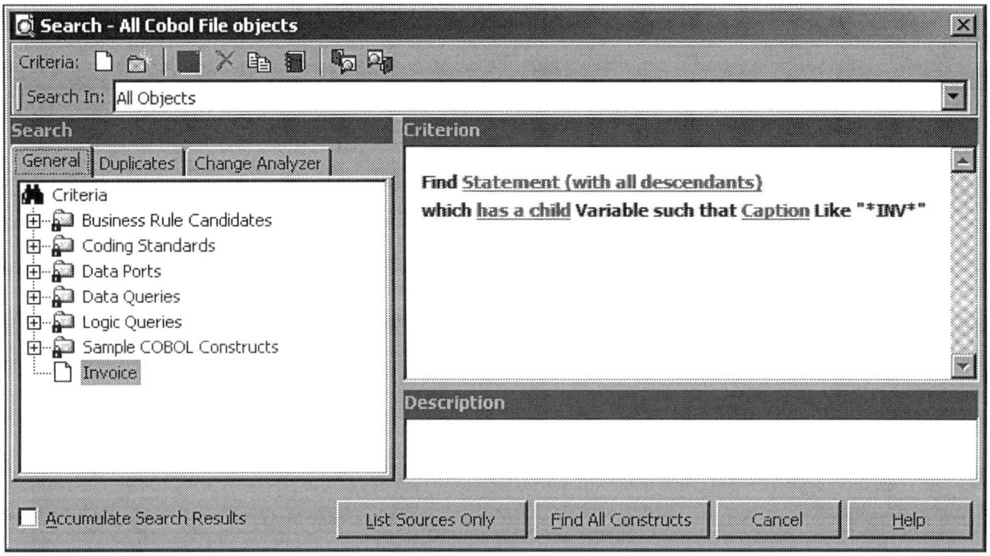

5. After we press the **Find All Constructs** button, a search is performed, and the results are stored in the new list that we have created, called **Invoice**. We can, at any point in time, inspect this list and visit all occurrences of the INV string in a variable name. We can, of course, write down the name of the programs that contain such occurrences, but can also ask the SOA Analyzer to "intersect" any diagram with this list. This will show which programs included in a diagram contain occurrences from the list.
6. In order to intersect a diagram with a list of program constructs obtained from a Clipper query, we first display the diagram, and then select the **Tools | Intersect list** menu. We are prompted with a list of all existing lists, as shown in the following figure, of which we select one (in this case, the one called **Invoice**, which we have just created).

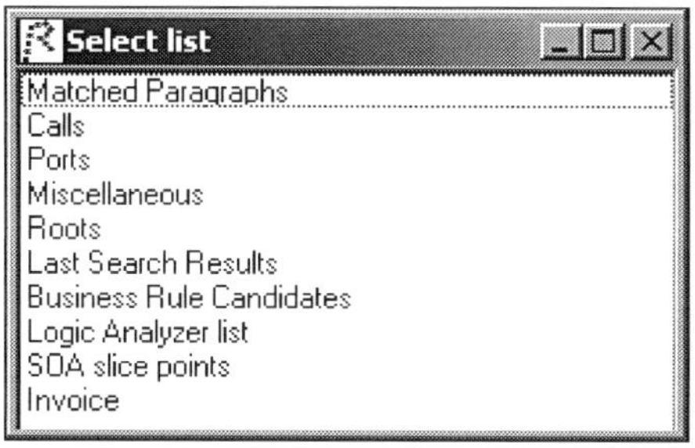

7. As a result of a selection, SOA Analyzer creates labels for all programs in the current diagram that contain items from the list. The text of the label indicates the number of occurrences, as shown in the following figure:

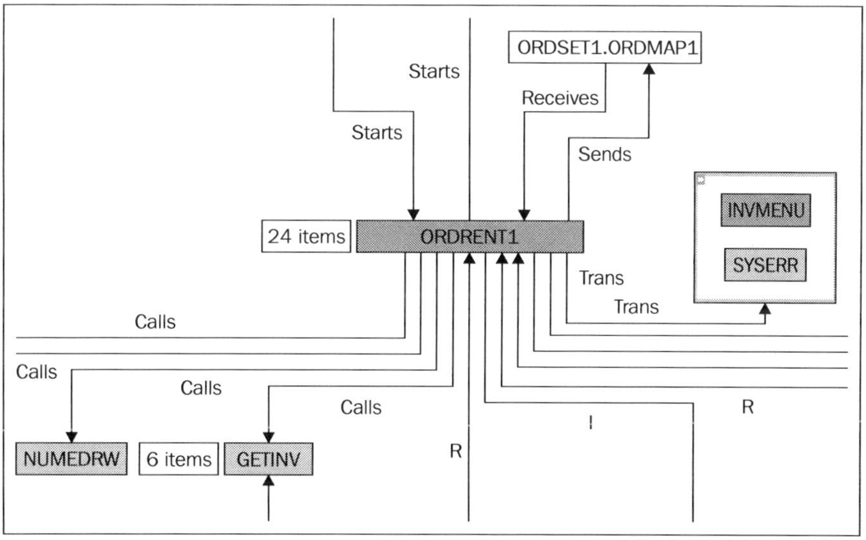

This entire search points to GETINV as a good candidate for the desired service. It performs some operations with the Invoice, and it is a service type program that does not converse any screen.

> **Keeping It Real**: The Clipper query is also very useful while doing a modernization re-architecture project. Often, you will want to determine all the modules that access a particular data element or data file. This is done in order to get an idea of how isolated a particular data element is from access by other systems.

The Case of Mixed Programs—Program 'Slicing'

Sometimes, the functionality we want to expose is found in a client program. Unfortunately, the client program cannot be called as a service as it contains screen communication as well as screen logic that does not make sense in a service call.

There are at least two solutions to this problem:

1. Modify the program by removing all screen interaction and screen logic
2. Split the program into two separate programs, one containing the screen interaction and logic, and the other containing the service function

The first solution has a number of disadvantages:

- It requires a massive modification of the code, which may result in errors
- It results in duplication of code (supposing the original program is kept in production), hence requiring synchronized maintenance of the original and modified versions

The second solution, the one we recommend, avoids the pitfalls of the first. It uses a slicing technique, which could be achieved either manually or by the use of a specialized tool such as Relativity's Application Architect product.

Slicing could be described as follows. Given a program PROG with a paragraph PARA, two programs are created, PROG1 (main) and PROG2 (service), such that:

1. PROG1 calls PROG2
2. Paragraph PARA no longer exists in PROG1, but appears in PROG2
3. PROG1 (which includes the call to PROG2) functions in a manner identical to the original PROG

Program slicing may be employed in order to separate the client functionality from the service functionality. In a simple case, suppose that a program communicates with a screen on which the user requests the content of an invoice with a particular invoice number. The program receives the screen, validates that the invoice number is correctly formatted, determines which program key was pressed by the user, invokes a paragraph GET-INVOICE to obtain the data, formats it, and displays it on the same screen. In this case, paragraph GET-INVOICE may be sliced out of the program. The resulting main program will now contain the screen logic, while the resulting service program will access the persistent storage and return the content of the invoice. Since this second program has the characteristics of a service, it could be exposed to the outside world as a Web service. Furthermore, the application will function just as it used to before the slicing.

If slicing is used to separate screen logic from service logic, the question is, which paragraph should be used as the basis for slicing?

Here, we face a situation similar to the one described earlier, wherein we must decide the level of the granularity offered by the service. If we aim too low in the paragraph **call map,** we risk obtaining services that are too granular and we are losing some of the business logic that prepares the data. If we aim too high, we risk including undesired screen logic. The best choice is to again select a **frontier** paragraph, which sits on the border of the screen and service logic. Such a paragraph would be the highest in the hierarchy of service type paragraphs.

In order to find the best slicing point, and to extract a slice that could be later used as a service, we proceed as follows:

- Once we locate the program that requires slicing, we right-click on a node that represents it, and select the **Show internal** menu. As a result, we can see a new diagram that displays the relationships between paragraphs, as shown in the following figure:

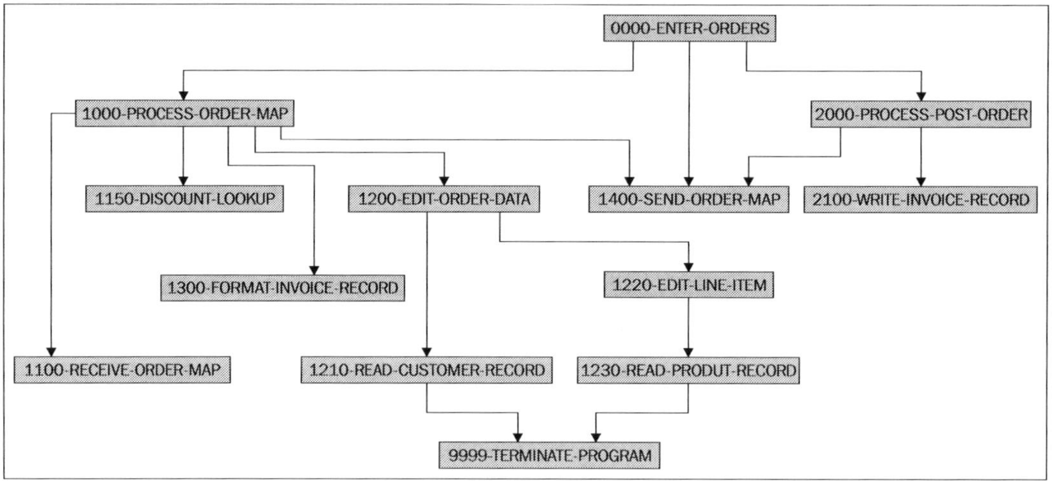

- We must find the paragraphs which can be "sliced out" in the form of separate callable programs. We must select only paragraphs that:

    1. Do not access screens
    2. Do not call other paragraphs that access screens

    In the preceding figure, we can see that 000-ENTER-ORDERS cannot be sliced-out, as it calls 1400-SEND-ORDER-MAP, which contains screen operations. The same is true for other paragraphs, for instance, 2000-PROCESS-POST-ORDER or 1000-PROCESS-ORDER-MAP.

    There are other paragraphs that are good candidates for slicing. It is to our advantage to select one that is as high as possible in this call hierarchy, as that would provide maximum functionality. One such candidate is 1200-EDIT-ORDER-DATA, which accesses both the customer and the product files. Another one is 2100-WRITE-INVOICE-RECORD. If we create slices of these two paragraphs, we obtain two programs, which together offer the functionality needed to create an invoice.

- To mark the selected paragraphs for slicing, we right-click on them and select the **Create slice item** menu. As a result, two things happen:

1. The paragraphs are marked on the diagram indicating that we have selected them as candidates for slicing (as you can see in the figure)
2. A list is created that contains information about these slicing points

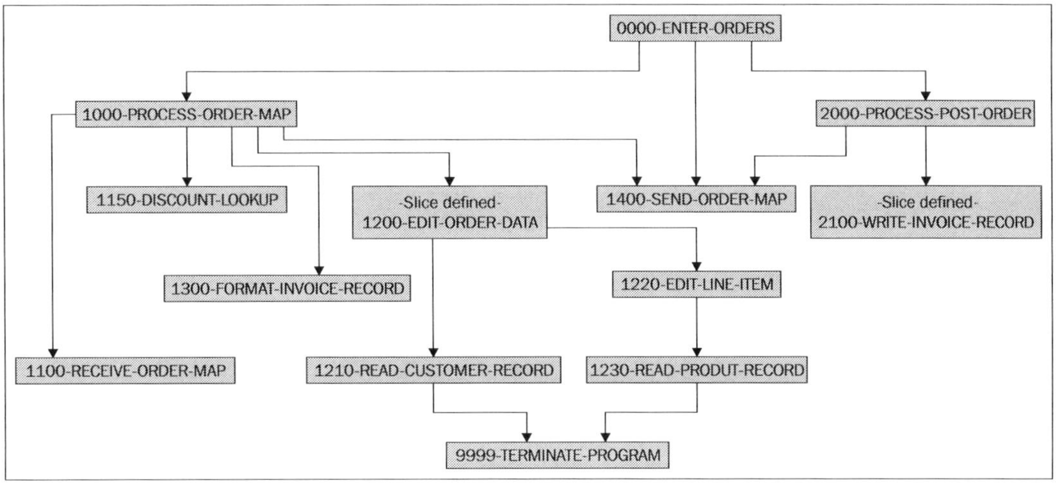

- We switch now to the Application Architect in order to perform the actual slicing operation. We will find two slicing points in a list under the category, **Architect**. As we click on any item in this list, the **Source** pane will automatically select the corresponding paragraph for slicing, as shown in the following figure:

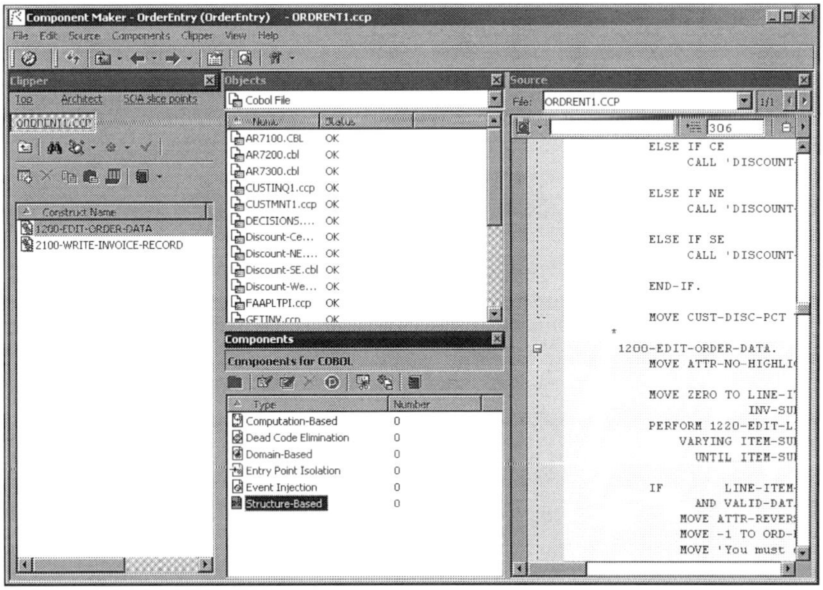

- We right-click **Structure-Based** in the **Components** pane, and then select the **Define new** menu, which opens up another pane, where the parameters of the slice are defined. We only have to point it to the paragraphs in the list created from SOA Analyzer to create a correct slicing definition, as shown in the following figure:

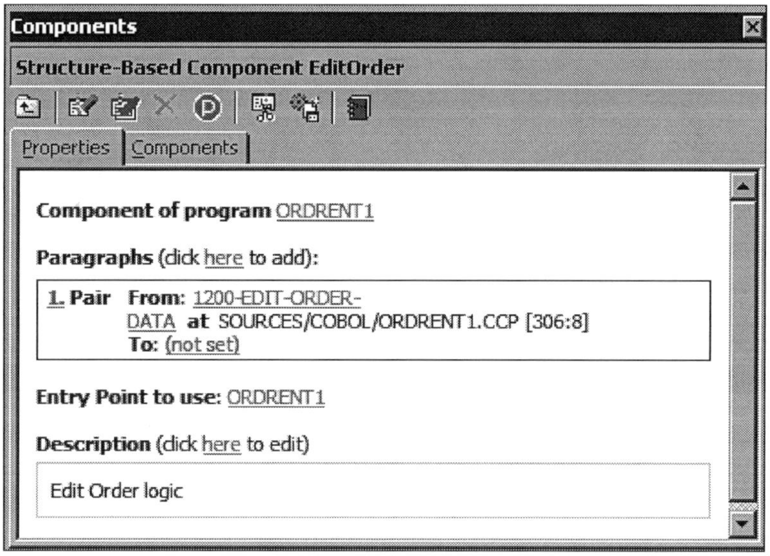

- We press the **Extract** button (represented by an icon showing scissors). We have to specify the number of parameters, say that we want the resulting program to be a CICS callable program. As a result, a new program is created, which contains the intended functionality, and could be exposed as a Web service.

> **Keeping It Real**: Slicing is a technique used by many application portfolio analysis tools. Slicing has been used for years to track back to the source of a problem in code, and was used heavily to help solve the Y2K. Slicing is useful in Legacy SOA Integration as it gives you the capability to look at the legacy artifacts embedded in an application as discrete components that can be exposed as services.

Determining the Data Interface

After we have found the right programs that can be exposed as Web services, we need to define their data interfaces. This is not a trivial task, for a number of reasons.

Let us take the case in which we want to expose the service that retrieves an invoice based on an invoice number. It would be great if:

1. The definition of the COMMAREA of the service program could be stored in a copybook
2. The COMMAREA could have a very simple definition, as in:

```
01 COMMAREA.
        05 INVOICE-NUMBER    PIC 9(7).
        05 INVOICE-CONTENT.
              10 INVOICE-DATE.....
```

In reality, we come across two problems:

1. The definition of the COMMAREA may not reside in a copybook
2. The COMMAREA defined in the LINKAGE section of the program may be very simple, as in:

```
01 COMMAREA PIC X(30000)
```

thus, obscuring the actual fields that appear in another structure to which COMMAREA is moved in the program.

The SOA Analyzer will help us determine the correct interfaces and even create a complete WSDL definition for the service.

We will proceed as follows:

- In SOA Analyzer, we select the **Service | New** menu, and give a name to the service. (We will call it **Invoice**.) This service will appear on a new pane of the tool.
- Having selected this service, we select a proper program (which was found in the previous step), right-click on the node representing it and select the **Add to Service** menu. SOA Analyzer will analyze the program and detect its COMMAREA that will form the basis for the service interface. In the **Service** pane, the SOA Analyzer will display the following:

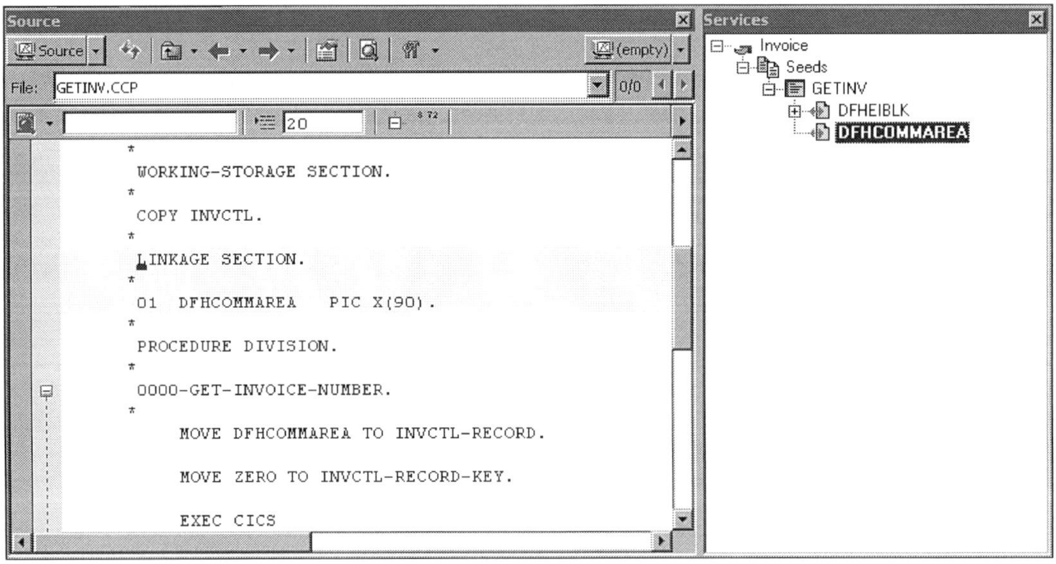

- In the **Service** pane, under the service called **Invoice**, we have a tree with a node called **Seeds**. Under this node, we find the specification for the program that we added to the service, including the COMMAREA that is used as in the interface. However, there is a common problem in that the COMMAREA appears as a single block of 90 bytes, which would not allow us to derive sensible and useful fields for the service interface.

We solve this problem by designating a synonym for **DFHCOMMAREA**. A synonym is another data structure, which either redefines or is moved to DFHCOMMAREA, or DFHCOMMAREA is moved to that structure. Such synonyms are easy to find with the following procedure:

- We select the **DFHCOMMAREA** in the **Source** screen and right-click on it
- We select the **Instances** menu, which will show a list of all usages of this data structure and whether it is moved, or redefined
- As we inspect the list, we select a convenient synonym

- In this example, we notice that **DFHCOMMAREA** is moved to **INVCTL-RECORD**, which may supply a better definition of the interface. We select this data area in the **Source** pane, then select **DFHCOMMAREA** in the **Service** pane, and press the **Import synonym** menu. As a result, the definition of the interface in the **Source** pane changes to what we can see in the following figure:

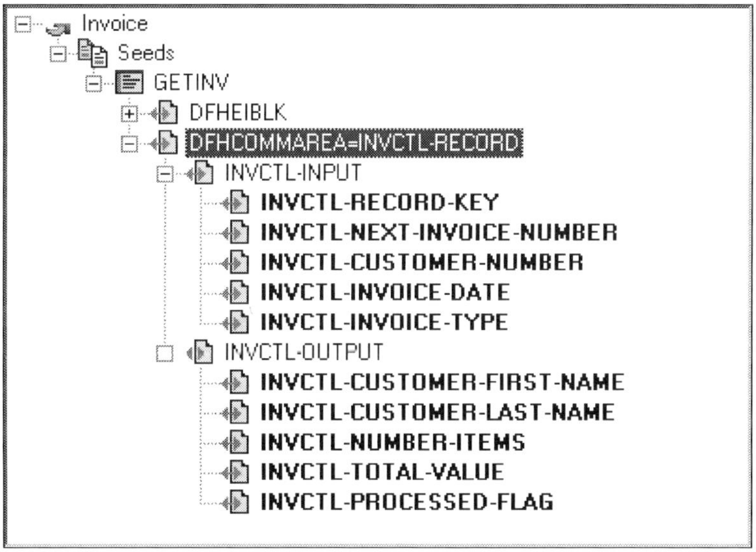

- We now have a detailed specification for the COMMAREA. One last task that we should perform, before creating the WSDL, is to indicate the inputs and outputs of the interface. Although, all fields are both input and output by default, it would be nice to separate them if possible. In this case, it is quite easy, since one substructure contains INPUT and the other contains OUTPUT. We can right-click on **INVCTL-INPUT** and select the **Make Input** menu. In the same way, we select the **INVCTL-OUTPUT** and select the **Make Output** menu. As a result, the specification now looks as shown in the following figure, in which the arrows for the adjacent icons indicate the usage as either input, or output:

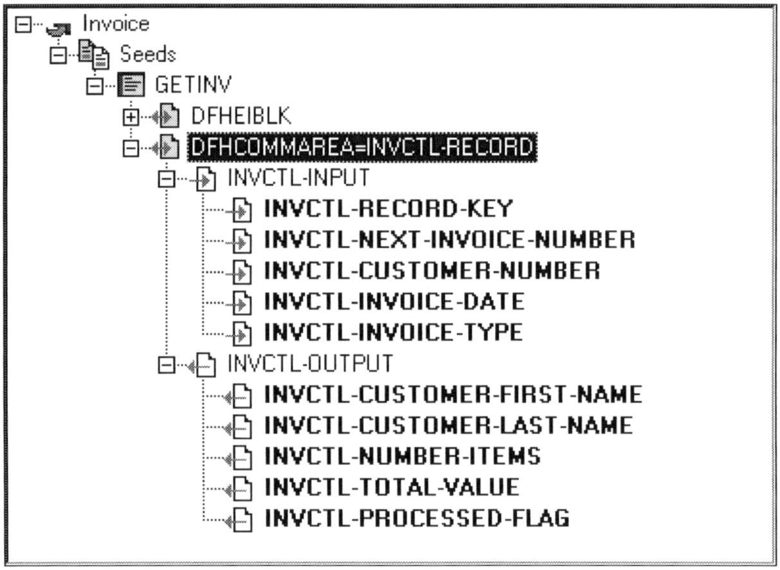

- We have come to the last step, that of creating a service definition. We right-click on the service and press the **Generate WSDL** menu. As a result, a WSDL definition for the service is generated and displayed as shown in the following figure:

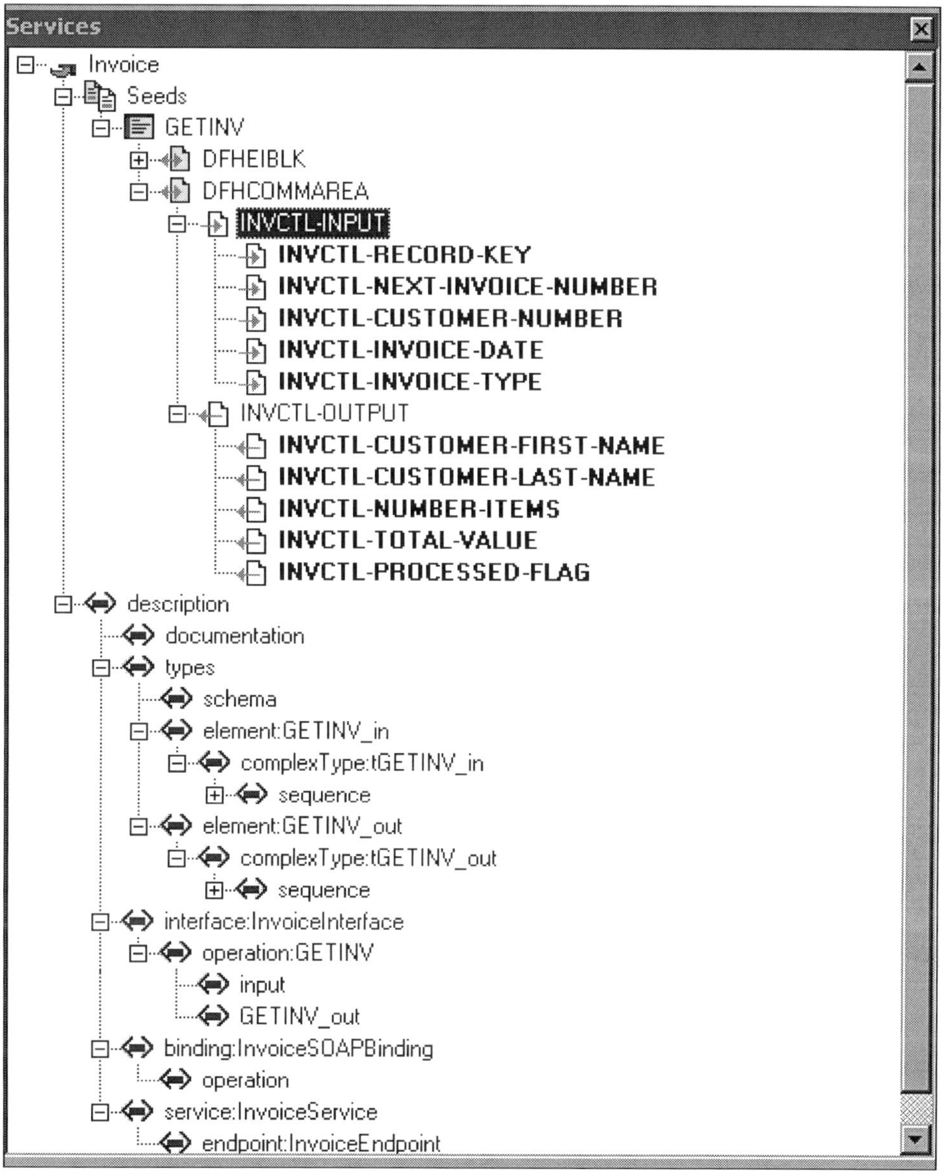

- We can add more then one program to the service. In this case, each program will generate a service operation, while its COMMAREA will define an interface. The resulting WSDL can be exported to an outside file, by using the **File | Export WSDL** menu of the SOA Analyzer tool.

> **Keeping It Real**: In a perfect world, it would be nice to expose a COBOL COMMAREA (that is CICS transaction) area as a service easily. However, in the real world, the COMMAREA definition is not readily available, or it may contain unnecessary fields.

Summary Legacy Artifact Discovery Using Relativity

In the perfect world, you may be able to find the VSAM call to the invoice file that you wish to service enable easily. In reality, you will find that using tools like those offered from Relativity makes the task much easier, especially when faced with millions of lines of code that are poorly documented, or not well understood by your current staff. The last section showed you how to discover the data interface for the service to be exposed. In the next section, we will show how to expose this data access artifact, which we have just discovered.

Exposing the Legacy VSAM File Data Access

Oracle Connect is a component that resides on the mainframe platform. It consists of native adapters for communicating with the mainframe application and data stores. The design-time configuration of Oracle AS Adapter for Legacy and mainframes consists of two steps. The **first step** involves using Oracle Studio for configuring the Oracle Connect engine and the metadata is stored on a file system at the Oracle Connect end. The **second step** consists of exposing the metadata obtained in the first step through a WSIL servlet. Oracle JDeveloper Web service has a WSIL browser which in turn connects to the WSIL servlet. The WSIL servlet communicates with Oracle Connect and exposes the metadata as WSDL with JCA extensions. The WSIL servlet is deployed in the Oracle Application Server Java EE container, and so it needs to be up and running at design time.

Connecting to Oracle Connect on Mainframe and Setting Connection Properties

Before anything is done, you must connect to your mainframe and set the properties for your connection as follows:

1. The Oracle Studio connects to Oracle Connect running on the mainframe. Oracle Connect for VSAM needs to be installed and configured on the OS/390 machine. The steps are detailed in the Adapter User Guide.

   Go to the **Configuration Explorer** view, and select **Machine** folder. Right-click and select **New**. This will bring up the connection panel on the right-hand side. Specify the connection parameters as shown here:

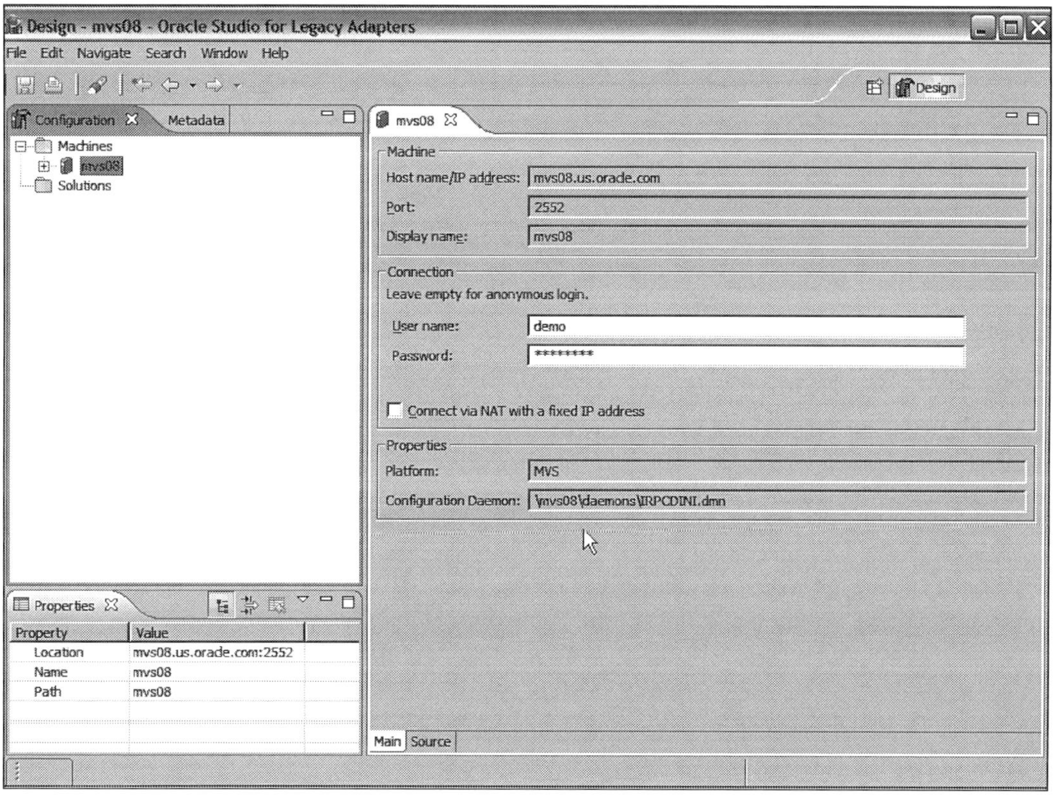

[Your connection parameter will be different based on your mainframe machine name, port number, user name, and password.]

2. Expanding the connection object shows a **Bindings** folder for defining workspaces (domains) and a default workspace called **NAV**. Expanding the **Bindings** folder shows an **Adapters** and **Events** folder. The **Adapters** folder is used to define JCA outbound interactions (request-response services), while the **Events** folder is used to define JCA Inbound Interactions (event services).

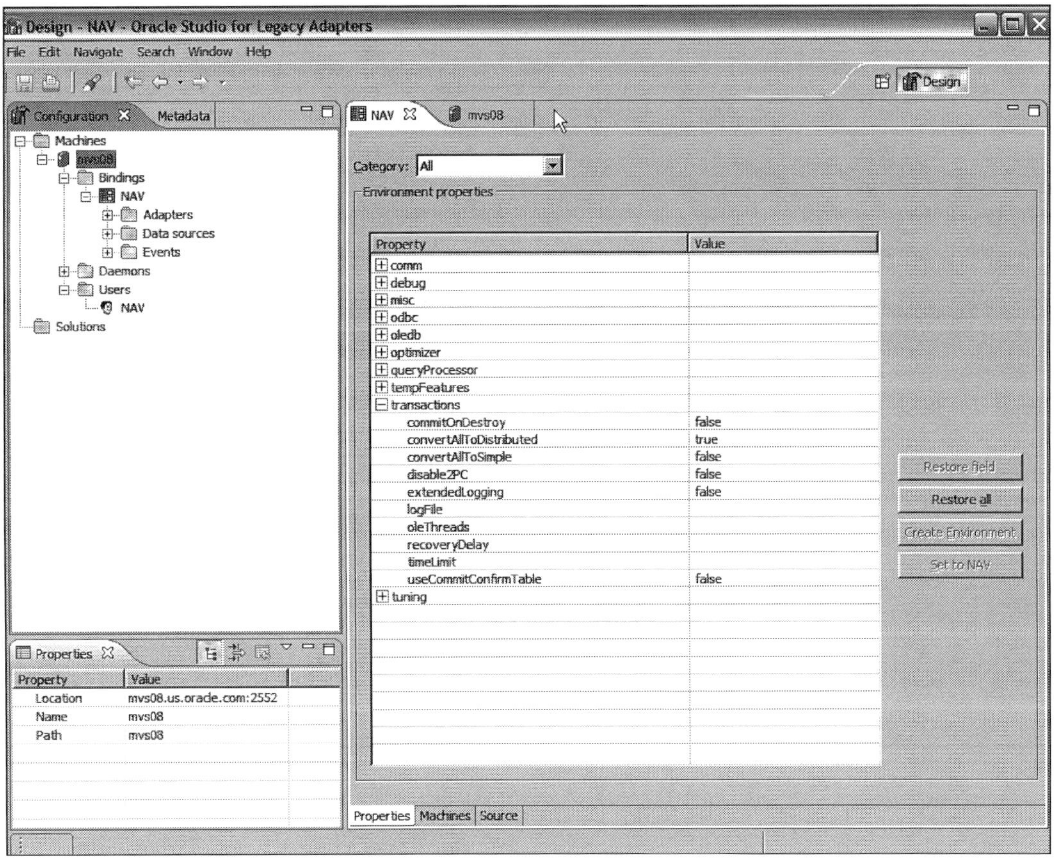

Two important property settings are:

- The property **disable2PC** needs to be **false** in order for the two-phase commit to work.
- To work with global transactions, set the **convertAllToDistributed** transaction environment property to **true**.

More information on the Oracle VSAM Adapter setup in the Legacy Studio can be found here: `http://download.oracle.com/docs/cd/B31017_01/integrate.1013/b31002/vsam_install.htm#i1008132`.

> **Keeping It Real**: Once the Oracle Connect mainframe component is installed, connecting to your mainframe system through the Oracle Studio for Legacy Adapters is simple. The difficult task is to install Oracle Connect on the mainframe system because of the processes and procedures, people's resistance – 'not wanting new things on the mainframe', or even a lack of additional mainframe cycles.

Oracle Connect Data Source

Since we have so much to cover in this chapter and we want to focus on aspects such as the adapter, two-phase commit, and calling the adapter from Java, we will not create a new data source. Instead, we will take a look at an existing data source to keep screenshots to the minimum.

1. The **Data sources** folder contains the VSAM data source. We will be using a data source called **DS_VSAM**.

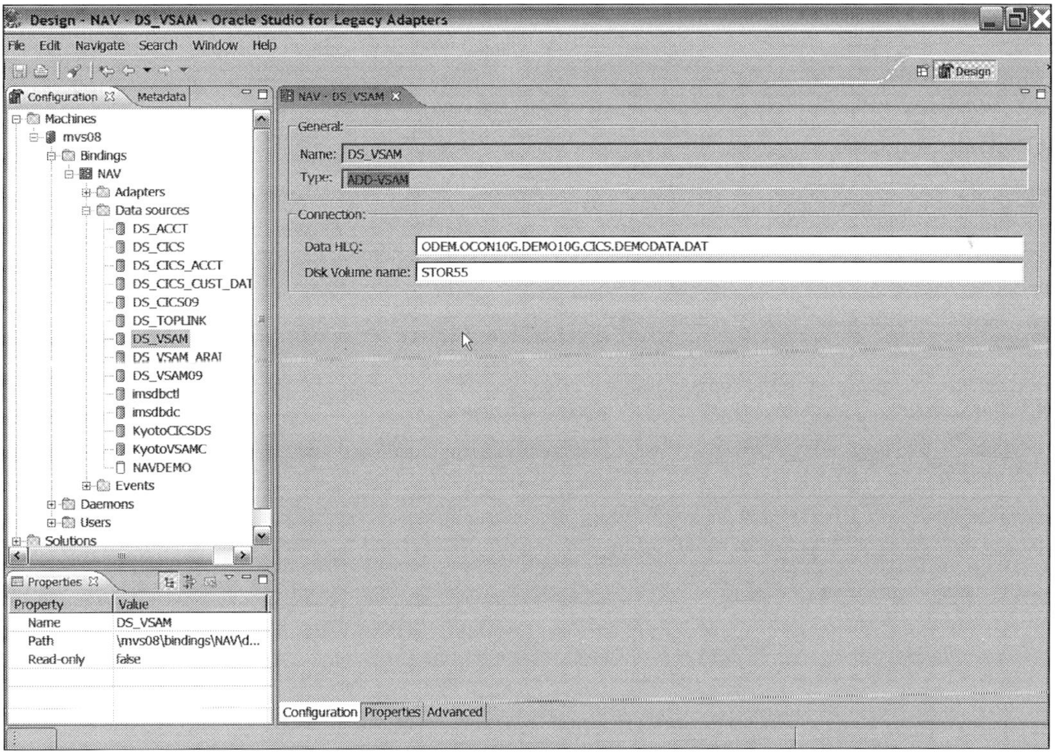

Note that this is a **ADD-VSAM** type of data source.

2. Click on the **Advanced** tab as shown in the screenshot. Click on the drop-down box for the **Transaction type** field. Change the transaction type to **2PC**. This enables two-phase commit for this data source. Your screen should appear as follows:

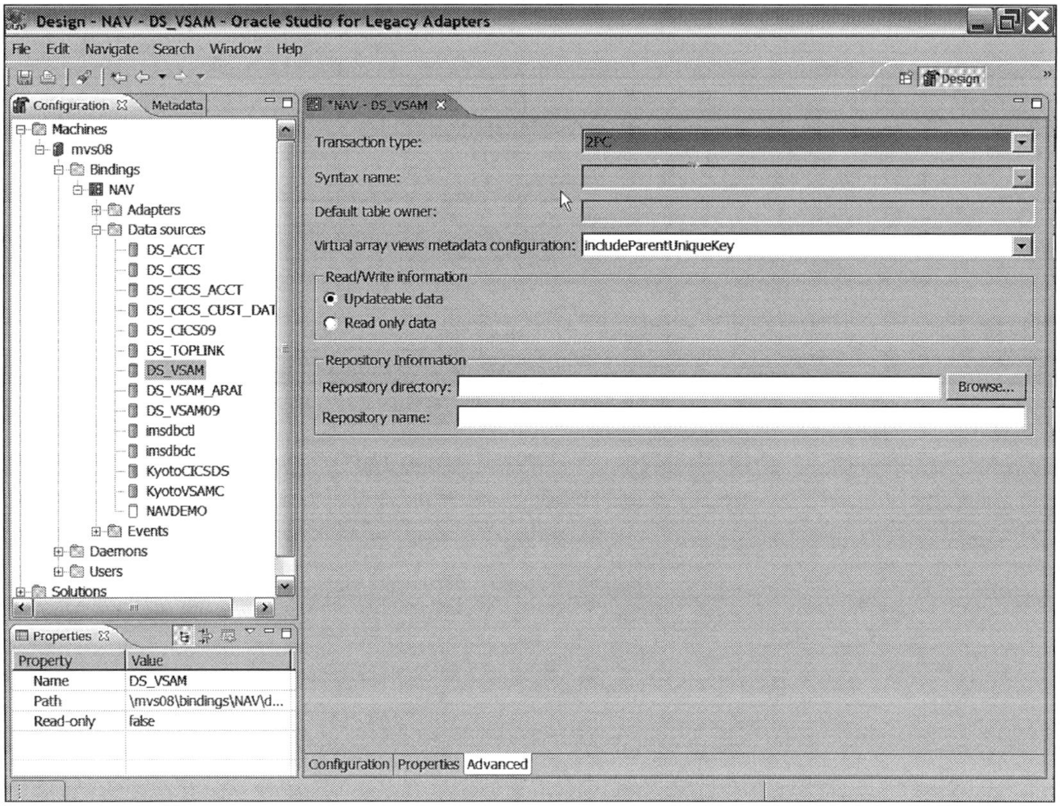

3. Right-click on the **DS_VSAM** data source and select the **Edit Metadata**. Expand the **DS_VSAM** entry (click the **+** sign) under the **Data sources** folder in the **Metadata** tab. Next, expand the **Tables** folder. Lastly, double-click on the **INVOICE_DATA** table entry. Your screen should appear as follows:

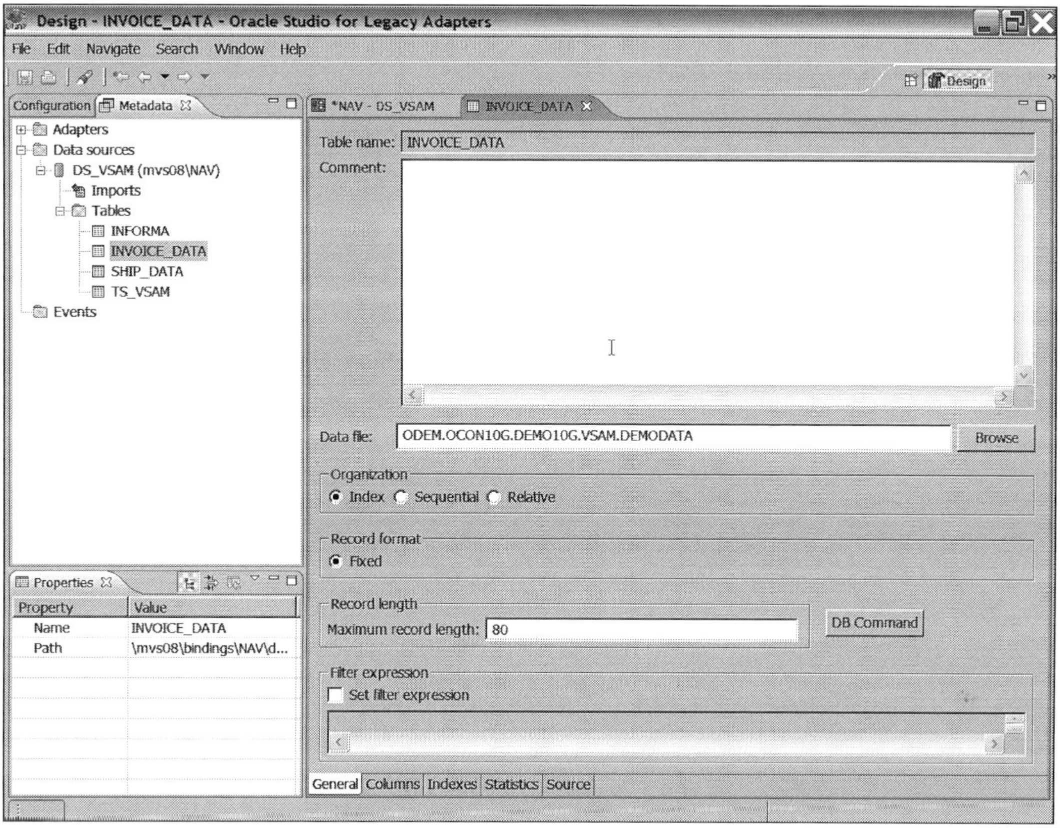

A couple of things to note on this screen:

- **Data file** field—This is the physical location of the VSAM data file on the mainframe.
- **Maximum record length**—The maximum length of each record is **80**.
- **Columns** tab—This tab displays the columns (or in VSAM terms, fields) that make up the **ODEM.OCON10G.DEMO10G.VSAM.DEMODATA** VSAM file.

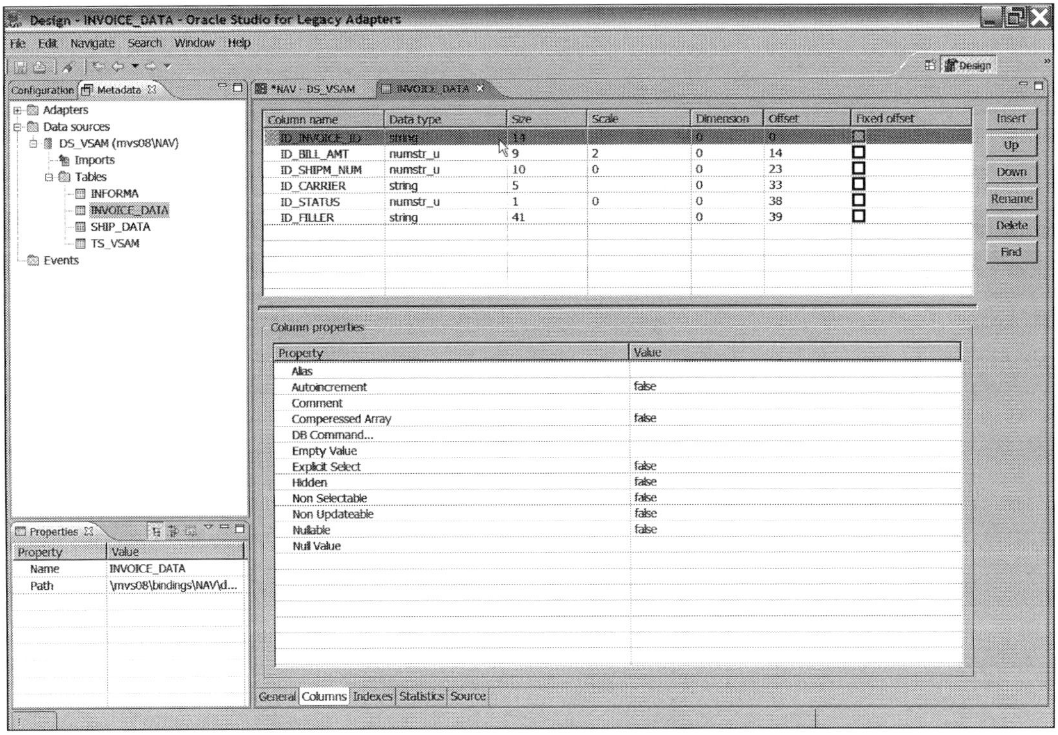

> **Keeping It Real**: Creating the data source is the first step. Most of your legacy services at some point will need to interact with a data source at some point whether they are presentation, transaction, or program-based services. Therefore, exposing the data source as a Web service is a common approach.

Oracle Connect Adapter

The adapter is what you will be talking to from your Java application to insert the VSAM record into the mainframe system using CICS. We will be using an existing adapter called **AD_VSAM**. This adapter uses the **DS_VSAM** data source created in the previous section. The adapter has select, insert, delete, and update interactions associated with it. 'Interactions' are the fundamental methods that Java EE, Oracle BPEL, or other applications interface to the legacy artifacts on the mainframe. Oracle Studio has a test run capability that can be used to test the interactions.

1. The Adapters folder is used to define and modify a VSAM adapter. Right-click on the AD_VASM adapter in the Adapters folder and select Edit Metadata. The Metadata tab appears as follows:

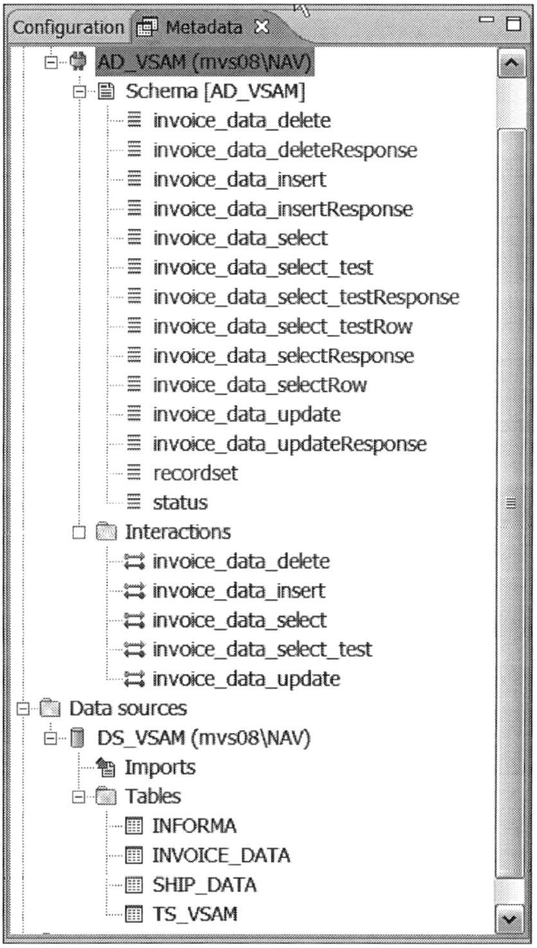

The important thing to note here is that an adapter can have more then one type of interaction. As you can see in the above screenshot, five different interactions are associated with this one adapter.

2. Double-click on the **invoice_data_insert** entry under the **Schema** entry, and you will see the following:

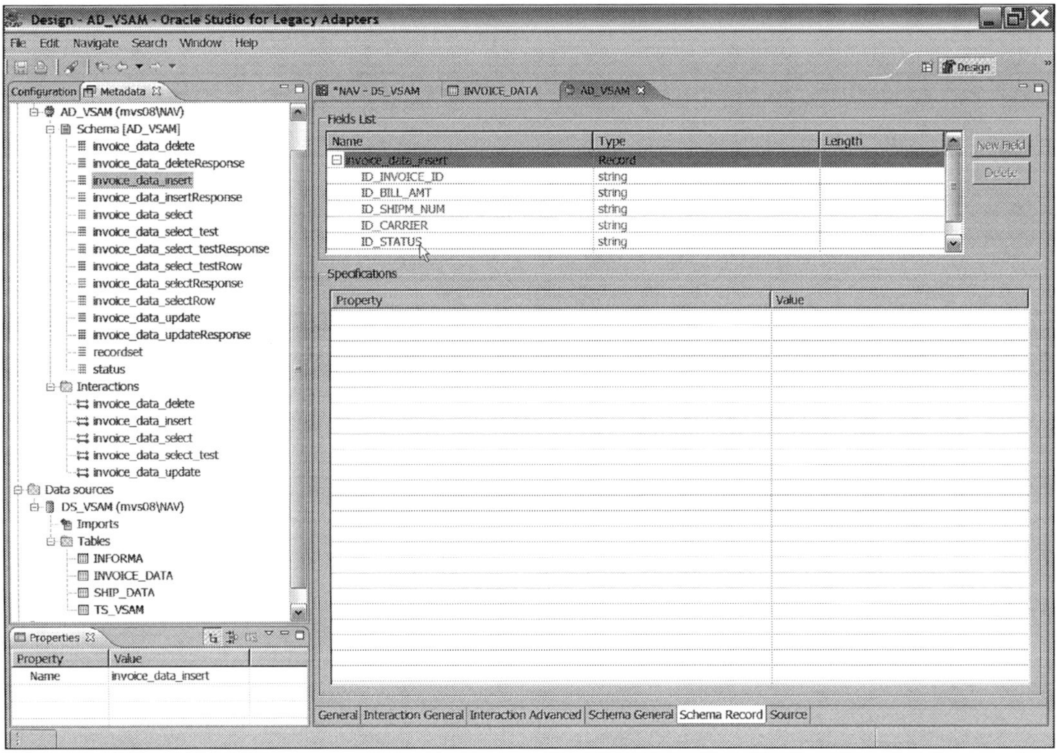

3. The **Schema Record** tab shows the fields that will be passed to the **AD_VSAM** adapter to be inserted into the **INVOICE_DATA** VSAM file using the adapter. The XML payload expects all fields to be character strings so that is why all the fields for INVOICE_DATA_INSERT are string. Double-click on the **invoice_data_insert** entry under the **Interactions** entry, and you will see the following:

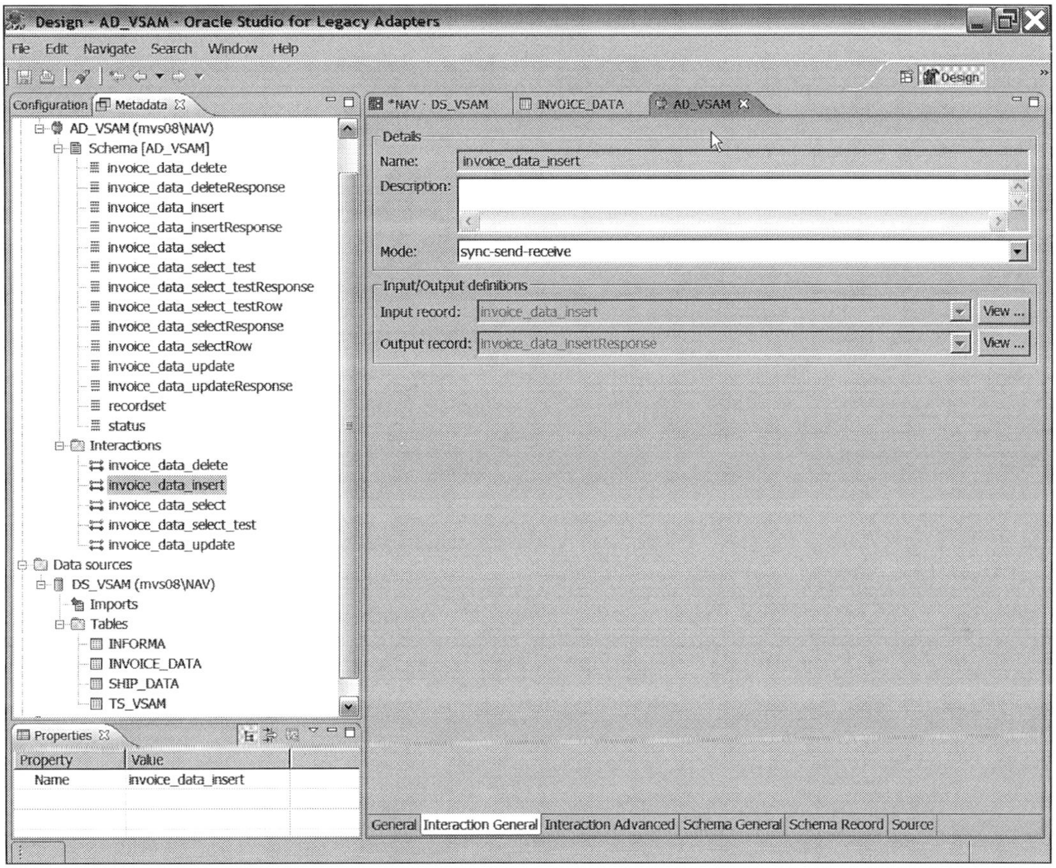

4. The Input record is the **invoice_data_insert** schema we just looked at. The output record is the **invoice_data_insertResponse** schema. The response schema is basically the status of the insert and appears as follows:

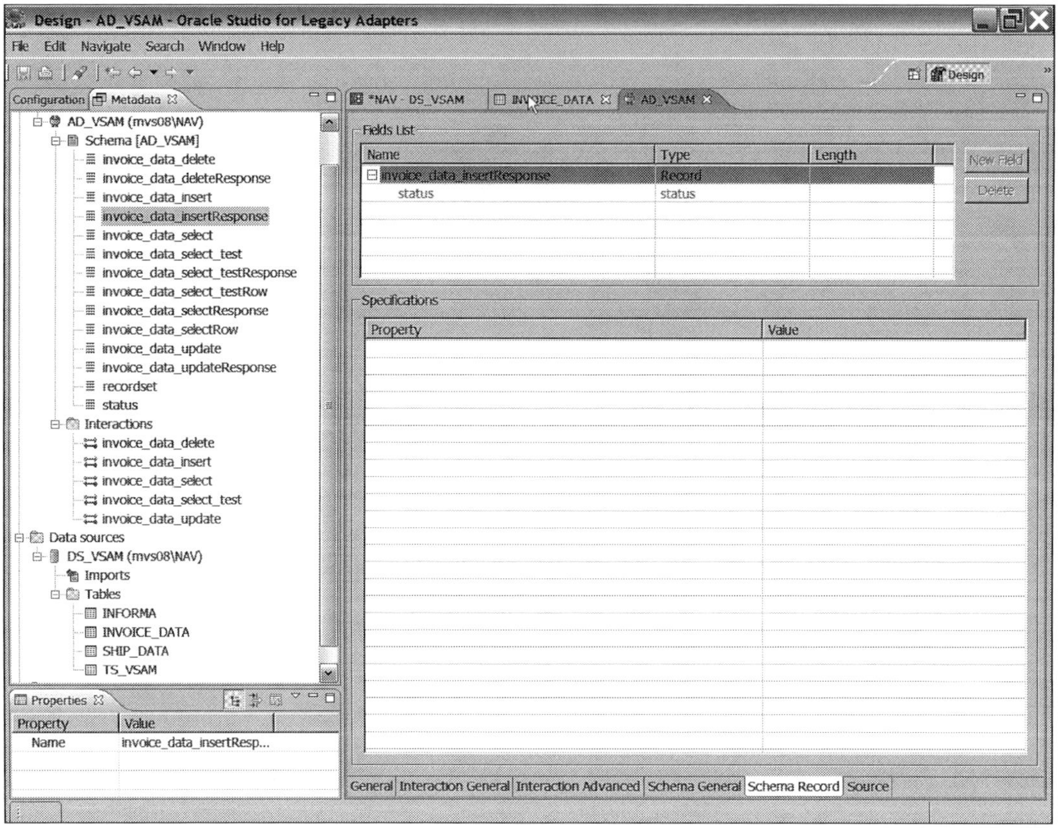

> **Keeping It Real**: The **Interactions** created in this step are the services that we will interact with from our Java EE application. These services are different from the standard SOAP/WSDL based Web services. These services will be accessed using the Java EE Connector API.

Development Using Oracle JDeveloper

Oracle JDeveloper will be used for the all Java EE/Java SOA enabled development. JDeveloper is Oracle's free IDE (Integrated Development Environment) for for Java EE, Web services, Oracle WebCenter, Oracle BPEL, Oracle ESB, mobile devices, database persistence, and UML modeling and development. You can write your Java EE code using **code coach** (which will show you the methods and parameters associated with a class), or use many of the **drag-and-drop** capabilities of JDeveloper. JDeveloper has testing, profiling, debugging, and tuning built into the tool. JDeveloper also has an open-standards-based framework called **Application Development Framework** (**ADF**) which is a visual and declarative approach for quickly developing and deploying applications.

JDeveloper is open-source friendly, and includes built-in integration with Struts, Ants, Junit, XDoclets, and CVS. If you have your own tool, or want to extend the functionality of JDeveloper, you can do so by using the Extention SDK.

Our development processes using JDeveloper will flow as follows:

- Inital setting up, which we will call **prework**. This includes creating the database connection, creating the project file, and including the Java EE libraries we will need for our application.
- Creating the presentation-tier and UI navigation modules.
- Writing the code to access our Legacy Java EE Connector Adapters that reside on the mainframe.
- Configuring the Oracle Application Server for the two-phase commit
- Writing the Oracle Database persistence module.

Before we start developing, we will have a look at how to set things up.

Prework

Build the Oracle database schema—Create the Oracle Data Model in JDeveloper (shown above in the UML and Database Diagrams sections and under the Data Model Diagram subsection). This is as simple as using JDeveloper, creating a new database diagram, and dragging and dropping the invoice table on the diagram. The Oracle database schema is a simple two-table invoice schema with invoices and invoice line items. For this example, we will use only the invoice table. Complete preliminary setup by performing Oracle Database (Steps 1 and 2) activities as per the instructions available at this link:

`http://www.oracle.com/technology/pub/articles/luttikhuizen-esbcase-setup.html`

More on creating database diagrams using JDeveloper can be found here:

`http://www.oracle.com/technology/obe/obe9051jdev/ide1012/dbmodelling/lesson_dm.htm`

* Create the workspace and project to hold the application—To start building the application, we can use the **Application Workspace** wizard to generate a new workspace and an empty project, **File | New | General | Application**. Or just create an **empty** project in any existing workspace. We will work with an application named **BookLegacySOAIntegration**. JDeveloper creates a workspace for each application you create. The workspace created on the local files system for this application will be called `BookLegacySOAIntegration.jws`. The project name given for this application will be called `LegacyOracle2PC.jpr`.

  More on getting started with JDeveloper can be found here:

  `http://www.oracle.com/technology/obe/obe9051jdev/ide1012/firststep/firststep.htm`

* Include standard Java EE libraries required for the application—Include all the libraries required for this example. The Oracle JDeveloper Project requires these libraries to be added by creating new library entries:
  * Attunity libraries for connecting, processing, and executing the services on the mainframe:

    i. Directory: `<OC4J_HOME>\j2ee\home\connectors\jca-legacy-adapter\jca-legacy-adapter`

    ii. Libraries: `attunityCoreResourceAdapter.jar`, `AttunityResourceAdapter.jar`, and `log4j-1.2.8.jar`
  * The XA transaction manager library classes for the two-phase commit processing:

    i. Directory: `<OC4J_HOME>\j2ee\home\lib`

    ii. Libraries: `connector.jar`

These libraries are already part of the standard JDeveloper and will simply have to be added to the project:

* JSP Runtime—As we are using JSPs for this application, we will need the JSP runtime libraries
* Java EE—Used for JSPs and Servlets

Perhaps because this is a basic Java EE development task, there is no information on how to do this in JDeveloper. However, we do find that newer Java/Java EE developers can struggle with this task. To locate libraries for JDeveloper projects, right-click on your project file name. Select the **Project Properties** entry. You will then see this screen where you can add and create new library entries:

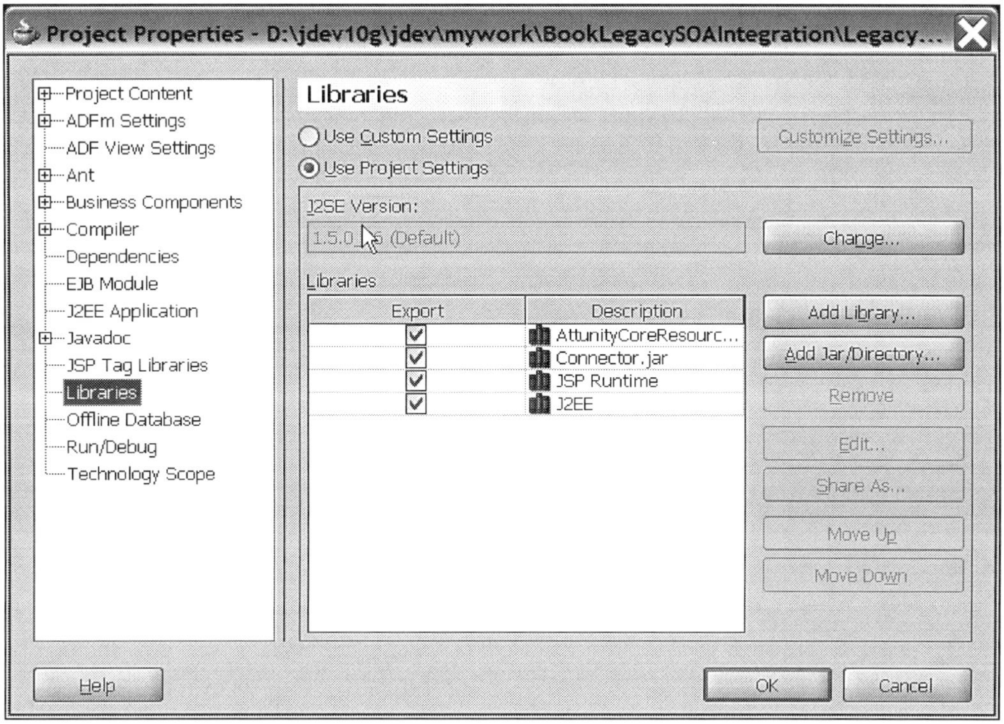

Application Modules

We will demonstrate the separation of the presentation and database access tiers in this example. We will demonstrate the separation of the presentation and database access tiers in this chapter. There is no business logic in this application since we are doing simple two-phase CRUD against the Oracle and mainframe VSAM data stores. Screen navigation is so basic that it is included in the DAO JSPs.

These are the four application modules that make up this example:

- `Index.html`—This is the presentation-tier for the application. It is a simple HTML form page.
- `Create.jsp`—This JSP is used to create **Database Access Objects (DAOs)** that use JDBC to insert a new invoice into the VSAM file on the mainframe. It also has the two-phase commit logic.
- `Verify.jsp`—This JSP uses DAO with JDBC to query the Oracle database invoice table and VSAM invoice file on the mainframe to verify whether the insert has been completed.
- `Remove.jsp`—This JSP uses DAO with JDBC to delete the Oracle invoice table and the VSAM invoice file on the mainframe.

Typically, the DAO modules are **Plain Old Java Objects (POJOs)**. Perhaps, a POJO implementation like Oracle TopLink will be used for the DAO. In order to keep the example simple, we will use JDBC embedded in JSPs. This is not recommended for production systems. But as this is an example, we are 'cheating' a bit. The JDBC calls could also be in a Java Bean. A Java Bean would separate the presentation-tier from the database access-tier.

Presentation-Tier/User Interface—HTML Page

The presentation-tier for this application is contained within one HTML page:

```
<html>
<head>
  <title>SOA Integration - Mid-tier 2PC Oracle DB and VSAM </title>
  <h1>SOA Integration - Mid-tier 2PC Oracle DB and VSAM </h1>
  <LINK href="../blaf.css" type=text/css rel=stylesheet>
</head>
<body>
      <h3>Create an Invoice in Oracle and also
          create an  invoice in VSAM</h3>
This sample demonstrates two-phase commit scenario involving an Oracle
DB and VSAM. Please enter the invoice details and click on Submit and
the invoice record will either be created in both Oracle and VSAM DBs,
or will be rolled back
            <br>
<FORM ACTION="create.jsp" METHOD="POST" >
   <b>Invoice ID :<INPUT TYPE="text" NAME="invoiceID" SIZE="12"
                            MAXLENGTH="12" >
   <br><br>Supplier Name<b>:</b><INPUT TYPE="text"
                                     NAME="supplierName" SIZE="40"
                                     MAXLENGTH="40" >
   <br><br>Shipper<b>:</b><INPUT TYPE="text" NAME="shipper" SIZE="40"
                               MAXLENGTH="40" >
   <br><br>Invoice Total<b>:</b><INPUT TYPE="text"
```

```
                                        NAME="invoiceTotal" SIZE="12"
                                        MAXLENGTH="12" value="0" >
      <br><br>Purchase Order Number<b>:</b><INPUT TYPE="text"
                                                NAME="purchaseOrderNo"
                                                SIZE="12"
                                                MAXLENGTH="12" >
      <br><br>Account Number<b>:</b><INPUT TYPE="text" NAME="accountNo"
                                        SIZE="12" MAXLENGTH="12" >
      <br><br>Shipment Number<b>:</b><INPUT TYPE="text"
                                         NAME="shipmentNo" SIZE="10"
                                         MAXLENGTH="10" >
      <br><br>

   <INPUT TYPE="Submit" VALUE="Submit Invoice">
   <INPUT TYPE="reset" VALUE="Clear">
   </FORM>
   </body>
   </html>
```

The user enters all the information required to create the invoices in the Oracle and VSAM databases. Not the best of practices to show here, but in this example the navigation logic is in the same module as the presentation code. The embedded navigation logic is the calling of the JSP `create.jsp` when the **Submit** button is pressed.

Legacy Web Service—VSAM Adapter Service

The legacy service can be executed as a Web service or through the Java EE Connector API. The Oracle Legacy Adapters uses Java EE Connector architecture to access the legacy services. The contract between the OC4J client application (in this case a JSP) and the resource adapter is defined by the **Common Client Interface (CCI)**. More information on CCI can be found here:

`http://download.oracle.com/docs/cd/B31017_01/integrate.1013/b31002/vsam_oc4j.htm`

Create the Java code using CCI methods to insert into the mainframe VSAM file:

```
Context ic = new InitialContext();
//Legacy Adapter VSAM lookup
AttuManagedConFactory amcf = new AttuManagedConFactory();
amcf.setConnectTimeout("99999999");
AttuConnectionFactory acf;
javax.resource.cci.Connection jcaConnection;
amcf.setEisName("AD_VSAM");
amcf.setServerName("mvs08");
amcf.setPortNumber("2554");
amcf.setUserName("demo");
```

```
amcf.setPassword("use4demo");

acf = (AttuConnectionFactory)amcf.createConnectionFactory();
jcaConnection = acf.getConnection();
         AttuInteraction ix = (AttuInteraction)jcaConnection.
createInteraction();

try {
       // Add an interaction spec
AttuInteractionSpec iSpec                  = new
                          AttuInteractionSpec("invoice_data_insert");

       // Create a record via record factory
       out.println("Create a record via record factory.. \n" );
       AttuRecordFactory recordFactory =
                           (AttuRecordFactory)acf.getRecordFactory();
       CoreMappedRecord input = (CoreMappedRecord)recordFactory.
                           createMappedRecord("invoice_data_insert");
       out.println("Created input record of type = " + input);

       // Add data to input record
       out.println("Add Legacy Data to input record..");

       input.put("@ID_INVOICE_ID", invoiceIDString);
       input.put("@ID_BILL_AMT", Double.toString(invoiceTotal));
       input.put("@ID_SHIPM_NUM", Integer.toString(shipmentNo));
       input.put("@ID_CARRIER", shipper);
       input.put("@ID_STATUS", Integer.toString(status));
       input.put("@ID_FILLER", filler );

CoreMappedRecord output    = (CoreMappedRecord)ix.
                             execute(iSpec, input);
       out.println( "Inserted Invoice Data Successfully \n");

       } catch (ResourceException re ) {
            out.println("Error creating an Insert interaction:");
            out.println(re.getMessage());
            re.printStackTrace();
            ut.rollback(); //if there is an error
            return;
        }
```

The VSAM invoice file COBOL copybook file definition looks like this:

```
01  INVOICE-DATA.
    02  ID-INVOICE-ID    PIC X(14).
    02  ID-BILL-AMT      PIC 9(7)V99.
    02  ID-SHIPM-NUM     PIC 9(10).
    02  ID-CARRIER       PIC X(5).
    02  ID-STATUS        PIC 9.
    02  ID-FILLER        PIC X(41).
```

Although the actual data file has character and numeric fields, the CCI code given here uses only string data types. This is because the Oracle Connect on the mainframe receives an XML payload with string data fields.

Two-Phase Commit

The transaction manager in OC4J can coordinate two-phase transactions between any type of XA resources, such as databases Oracle or DB2, Oracle Legacy Adapters, and JMS providers such as MQSeries.

A transaction manager capable of doing recovery in a two-phase commit scenario needs to perform logging at the middle-tier. OC4J provides two ways to log transactions: in the local file system, or in an Oracle database table.

The `server.xml` must contain the following to enable logging by the transaction manager:

```
<transaction-manager-config path="./transaction-manager.xml"/>
```

In this example, we will use file-based logging in the mid-tier. To enable file-based logging, certain changes must be made to the configuration files in OC4J. This includes the type of logging and the location/directory where log files will be stored. We recommend that you use the default location for logging. However, you can modify the location for log files. For example, you have the following in your `transaction-manager.xml`:

```
<transaction-manager
  xmlns:xsi="http://www.w3.org/2001/XMLSchema-instance"
  xsi:noNamespaceSchemaLocation="http://xmlns.oracle.com/ias/schemas/
  file:transaction-manager_1_0.xsd">
<commit-coordinator retry-count="4">
<middle-tier>
<log type="multi-file" location="d:\debu\tpclogs"/>
</middle-tier>
</commit-coordinator>
</transaction-manager>
```

The Java code for the two-phase commit looks like this:

```
Context ic = new InitialContext();
       UserTransaction ut =
             (UserTransaction)ic.lookup("java:comp/UserTransaction");
// Start Transaction
    ut.begin();
```

```
...(code for Oracle database and VSAM insert)
    ut.rollback(); //Issued any time an error is encountered
ut.commit(); //Issued at end if everything is successful in both the
  Oracle and VSAM databases
```

More information on using two-phase commit with the Oracle Application Server can be found here:

```
http://www.oracle.com/technology/tech/java/oc4j/1003/how_to/how-
to-midtier-2pc.html
```

Oracle Database Persistence

We are using a data source that is defined in the Oracle Application Server configuration file called `data-sources.xml`. We will take a closer look at this file in the Oracle Application Server configuration section shown here. For now, the connection string looks like this:

```
DataSource ds1 = (DataSource)ic.lookup("jdbc/OracleInvoiceDB");
Connection conn1 = ds1.getConnection();
```

The close connection command is as simple as:

```
conn1.close();
```

The insert statement (in the `create.jsp` page) uses the values entered in the `Index.html` page to insert the invoice into the Oracle database. As this is a two-phase commit, we need a preparatory step which is in the `prepareCall` method:

```
PreparedStatement  ps1 = conn1.prepareCall("INSERT into invoices(id,
  supplier_name, supplier_invoice_no, order_date, purchase_order_no,
  shipping_date, shipper, invoice_total,account_no) VALUES (?, ?, ?,
  sysdate, ?, sysdate, ?, ?, ?)");
        ps1.setDouble(1,invoiceID );
        ps1.setString(2,supplierName );
        ps1.setString(3,supplierInvoiceNo );
        ps1.setDouble(4,purchaseOrderNo );
        ps1.setString(5,shipper );
        ps1.setDouble(6,invoiceTotal );
        ps1.setString(7,accountNo );
        ret1 =ps1.executeUpdate();
```

> **Keeping It Real**: Relational database access methods such as ODBC and JDBC have been around for years. Therefore, there is no need to go into great detail on how to insert a row into an Oracle database.

Deploying to the Oracle Application Server

The last step before we can run our application is deploying the application to the Oracle Application Server. We will be using Oracle JDeveloper to deploy our application. Before we can do this, we need to add a couple of the Oracle Application Server XML configuration files and the Oracle Application Server connection to JDeveloper. Now, we are set to use the JDeveloper wizards to create the deploy descriptor, and deploy the application to the Oracle Application Server we just created a connection for.

Configuring Oracle Application Server for the Legacy Adapter

The connection factory for the Oracle Legacy Adapter is defined in the `oc4j-ra.xml` configuration file. This file is located in the `<OC4J_HOME>\j2ee\home\application-deployment\default\jca-legacy-adapter\directory`. The entry looks like this:

```
<connector-factory location="eis/legacy/AD_VSAM"
 connector-name="Attunity Connect Legacy Adapter">
      <config-property name="userName" value="demo"/>
      <config-property name="password" value="use4demo"/>
      <config-property name="eisName" value="AD_VSAM"/>
      <config-property name="serverName"
                       value="mvs08.us.oracle.com"/>
      <config-property name="workspace" value="Navigator"/>
      <config-property name="portNumber" value="2552"/>
      <config-property name="persistentConnection" value="true"/>
      <config-property name="keepAlive" value="true"/>
      <config-property name="firewallProtocol" value=""/>
      <config-property name="connectTimeout" value=""/>
      <config-property name="encryptionProtocol" value=""/>
      <config-property name="encryptionKeyName" value=""/>
      <config-property name="encryptionKeyValue" value=""/>
      <config-property name="fakeXa" value="false"/>
      <config-property name="useNamespace" value="true"/>
```

```
        <config-property name="networkXMLProtocol" value="binary"/>
        <config-property name="exposeEventStreamMetadata"
                         value="true"/>
        <connection-pooling use="none">
        </connection-pooling>
        <security-config use="none">
        </security-config>
    </connector-factory>
```

You can also add this adapter using the **Oracle Enterprise Manager**. The Legacy Adapter connection factories in OEM are found in the **OCJ Home | Application: default** area as follows:

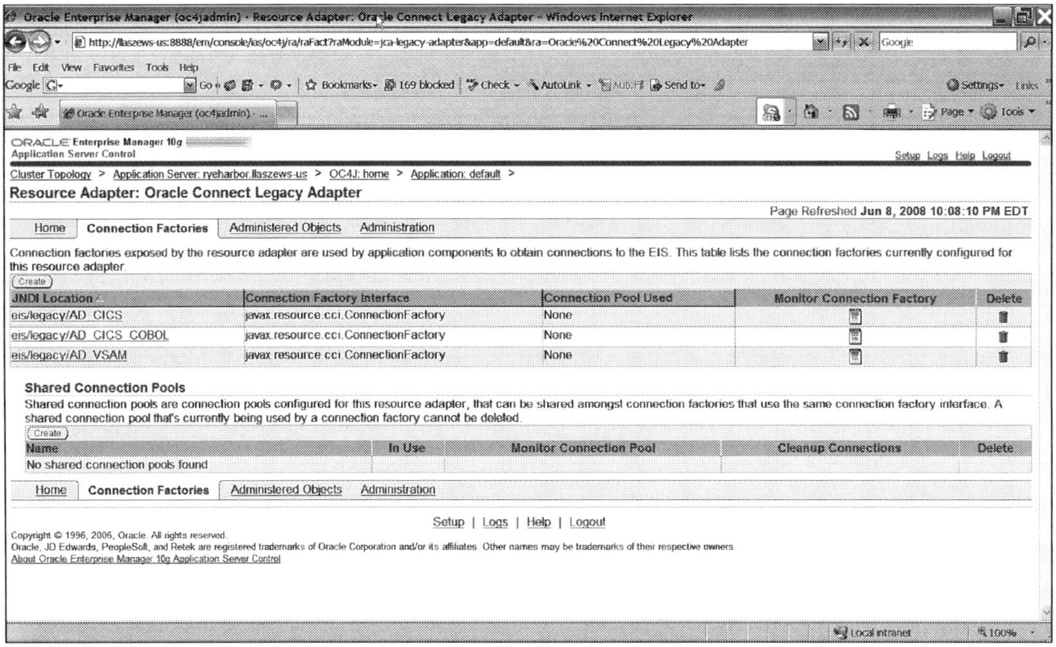

Configuring Oracle Application Server Oracle Database Connection

We will use a connection pool for the Oracle Database. The following is an example of the DataSource that can be used for the Oracle Database to access the Invoice table:

```
<managed-data-source connection-pool-name="OracleInvoiceDB"
  jndi-name="jdbc/OracleInvoiceDB" name="OracleInvoiceDB"/>
<connection-pool name="OracleInvoiceDB">
```

```
<connection-factory factory-class="oracle.jdbc.pool.OracleDataSource"
                    user="invoice_demo" password="oracle"
                    url="jdbc:oracle:thin:@localhost:1521:xe"/>
  </connection-pool>
```

From this connection factory configuration, you can see the following:

- Using the Oracle Express Edition Database (XE)
- Running the Oracle database on our local machine
- Connecting to the schema `invoice_demo`
- The JNDI data sources lookup name—`OracleInvoiceDB`

The data sources connections are defined in the `data-sources.xml` configuration file. This file is located in the `<OC4J_HOME>\j2ee\home\config` directory.

Deploying to Oracle Application Server Using JDeveloper

Before you can deploy the application to the Oracle Application Server, you need to create a connection using the **Connections Navigator**. The connection we have set up for this example is as follows:

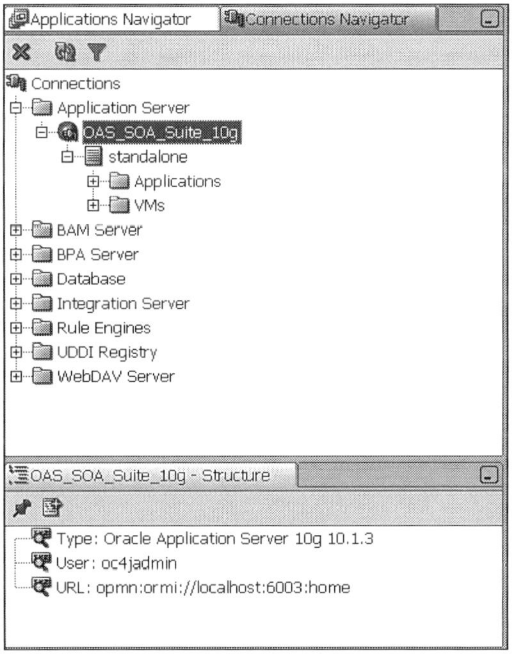

The name of our connection is **OAS_SOA_Suite_10g**. More on setting up connections can be found here: `http://www.oracle.com/technology/obe/obe1013jdev/10131/deployment/deployment.htm`

Next, you create the deployment file in the **Applications Navigator**:

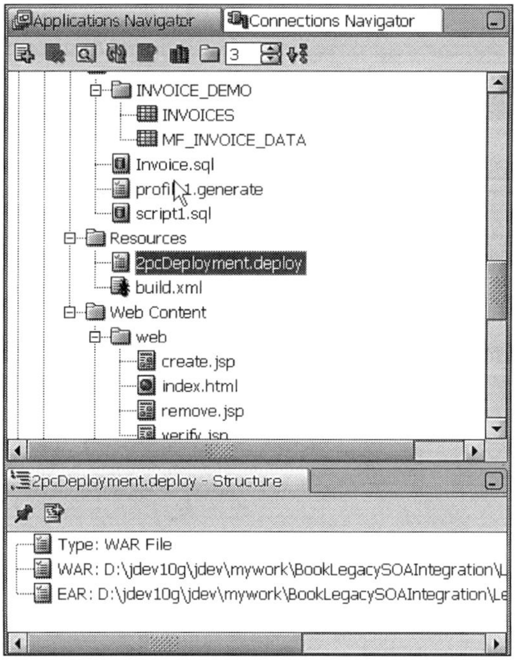

Right-click on the highlighted **2pcDeployment.deploy** file and select **Deploy to OAS_SOA_Suite_10g**. A step-by-step tutorial on setting up JDeveloper Deployment Profiles can be found here: `http://www.oracle.com/technology/obe/obe1013jdev/10131/deployment/deployment.htm`

Deploy the application to Oracle Application Server using JDeveloper. You could also use Ants. More on Ants can be found here:

`http://download-west.oracle.com/docs/cd/B32110_01/web.1013/b28951/anttasks.htm`

> **Keeping It Real**: Deploying Java EE applications to the Oracle Application Server is easy using JDeveloper. However, in a production environment, you will probably not be deploying applications directly from JDeveloper. In this case, you will probably create scheduled nightly executable batch files that will use Ants to deploy the application to your Oracle Fusion Middleware production environment.

Running the Example

Running the Legacy SOA Integration application in a web browser for the first time in front of users who have been dealing with green screens for years or decades is typically an awe inspiring event. They are usually more than happy to get rid of their difficult to view, bulky 3270 terminal. They also cannot believe the rich graphics and colors presented in the browser. IT personnel, both mainframe and open systems staff, are typically amazed that the mainframe and relational database worlds with so little development effort can co-exist.

Running the application

Test the application by accessing the web app at the URL: `http://localhost:8888/LegacyOracle2PC/web/index.html`

The `index.html` page is displayed where you can enter the invoice information:

Although the Invoice **ID** is alphanumeric in the VSAM file, it is an integer in the Oracle Invoice table. Therefore, only numeric Invoice IDs are allowed. This slight difference shows you one of the many situations (different data types between legacy and open systems worlds) that you will run into during your Legacy SOA Integration projects.

Click on the **Submit** button, and you will see that the Invoice Oracle Database and VSAM file have been successfully processed:

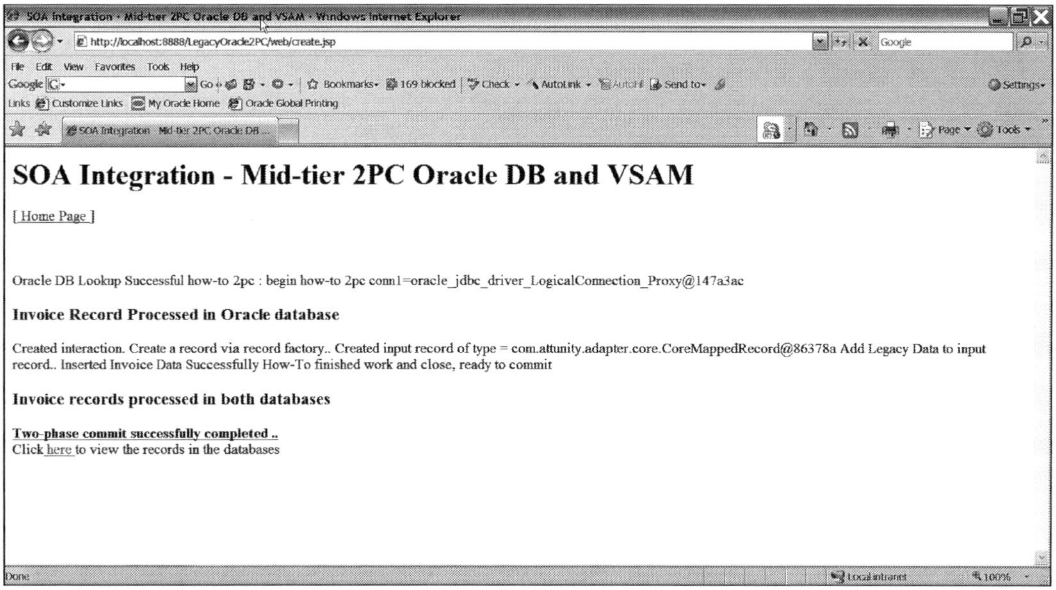

Oracle SQL Developer will be used to verify the row that has been inserted into the Oracle **INVOICES** database table:

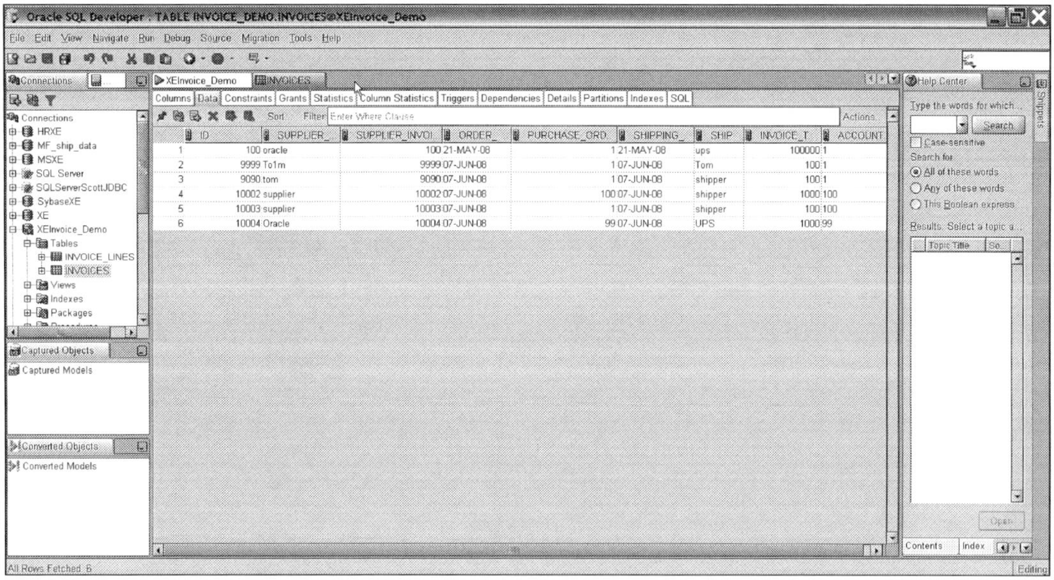

You can see that the row with the Invoice **ID** of 10004 has been added to the **INVOICES** table.

To verify the insert into the mainframe VSAM file, we will use the Oracle Studio for Legacy Adapters. Right-click on the **AD_VASM** adapter in the **Adapters** folder and select **Edit Metadata**. Right-click on the **invoice_data_select** interaction and choose **Test**. In the **Test Wizard**, enter the invoice number, **10004**. We can see that the VSAM file was populated with the same information:

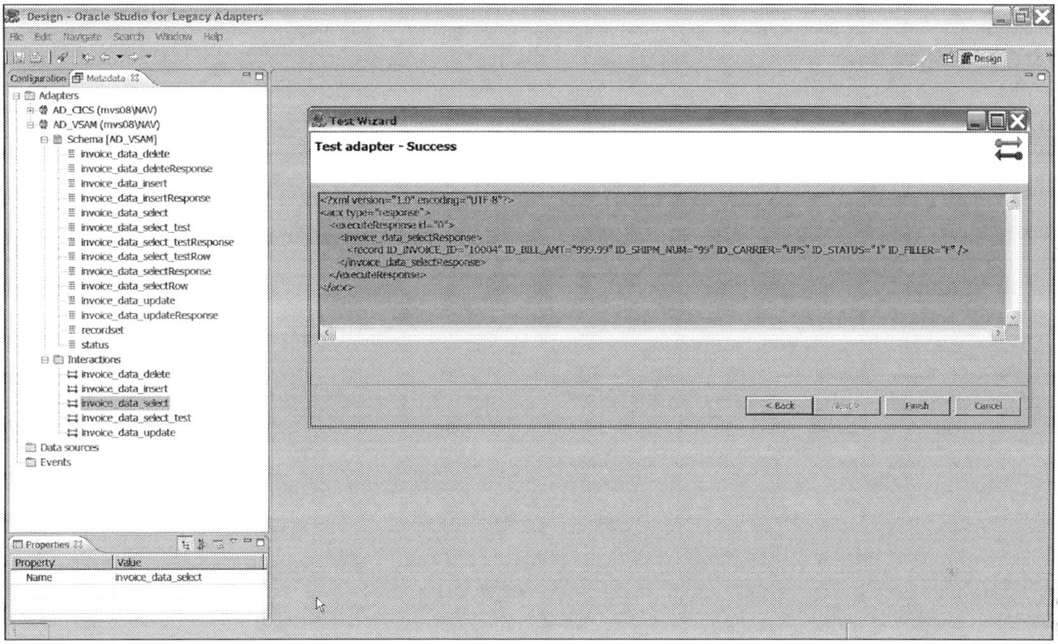

> **Keeping It Real**: What you accomplished was one small step in your Legacy SOA Integration journey, but one giant step forward in your first tactical project. By seeing an example that is not just a basic query from a DB2 or VSAM database, we believe you are now much better prepared when you do this for real. We have also given you an example that is not based on BPEL, as enough of those exist already.

Summary

We covered significant ground in this chapter. Starting with a sample legacy COBOL/CICS/VSAM application, we went on to discover the legacy artifact that is the best candidate for enabling SOA using the Relativity tools set. Then we used Oracle Studio for Legacy Adapters to expose the legacy VSAM artifact. We used Oracle JDeveloper to create the web-based Java EE frontend for our application. Next, we created the Java module to invoke the Oracle Connect Legacy adapter on the mainframe using the Java EE Connector standard. We deployed our application to the Oracle Application Server, and showed it running. Not bad for one chapter. You now have everything you need to execute a Legacy SOA Integration pilot project.

A
Establishing SOA Governance at Your Organization

The adoption of SOA can represent a fundamental change in the way you deliver technology solutions. While many books have been written on the technical aspects of SOA, it is the cultural aspects that can pose the biggest challenge. An organization must learn how to break down the boundaries that have built up over time, and leverage the assets available to them in a more effective manner. SOA governance is about establishing the appropriate structure to guide an organization through this change with people, policies, and process. While it can begin as an extension to the normal project governance process to include appropriate use of service technologies like XML, SOAP, or REST, it must go beyond the core technology guidance and into changes in how development teams interact with each other across the organization, changes in how services and their consumers are managed at run-time, and changes in how an organization determines what solutions will be built in the first place.

Every company is unique with its own corporate culture. A Center of Excellence may be required for success at one organization, while another organization may not need to establish that level of formality. One company may get significant benefit out of a commercial Registry/Repository product while another company may achieve the same benefits by utilizing an open-source wiki. Factors such as company size, IT structure, IT locations, business goals, and competition are some of many that play a role in determining the right approach. In all cases, if your company does not clearly articulate its desired behavior, have people responsible for establishing the policies that will elicit the behavior, have consistent policies throughout the organization, and establish processes for education, communication, measurement, and enforcement, you will struggle.

This chapter will walk through the three major components of a successful SOA governance effort: people, policies, and processes. Various areas will be covered that a company must consider when adopting SOA. Some may be areas that are not applicable; some may be areas that are very applicable. Use it as a cookbook for determining the right SOA governance approach for your organization.

People

There are many different people that can play a role in your SOA governance efforts. This section will go over the various roles and their responsibilities within SOA governance, whether it be in establishing policies, or in the processes associated with education, communication, measurement, or enforcement. It will also call out how these various roles can be organized and the various engagement models that can be utilized.

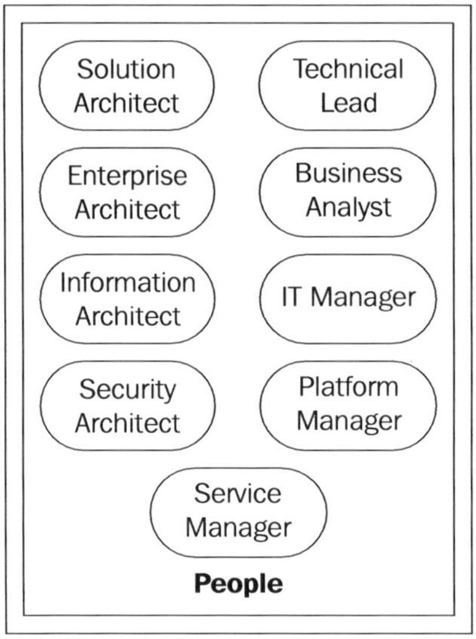

Solution Architect

The solution architect is the person responsible for the technical leadership and decisions on a project or program. Being the technical decision maker, this person is responsible for the project's compliance with the technical design-time policies. This includes both the solution's architecture, for which the person likely has direct responsibilities, as well as the solution's design, for which the person will be working with the developers and other project staff. Typically, the solution architect has a larger role in ensuring that services are built the right way. In ensuring that the right services get built, the solution architect must work closely with the lead analyst on the project.

The solution architect is also responsible for ensuring that the appropriate run-time governance policies are established. If the project delivers a service consumer, the solution architect must work with the lead analyst to determine the expected usage for all services. If the project delivers a service provider, the solution architect must determine the resource consumption associated with a service invocation.

It is important to remember that the solution architect is a role. Your organization may not have a formal job title of solution architect, but someone will play this role on each and every project.

Business Analyst

The business analyst is the counterpart to the solution architect on a project, focusing on the functional aspects of the solution. They frequently perform requirements gathering activities, create use case diagrams, and may also be responsible for business process modeling. A more senior business analyst will have a significant amount of domain knowledge and may have key relationships within the organization outside of IT.

Within the SOA governance effort, business analysts play a key role in determining the appropriate functional boundaries for services. If you are able to move beyond the boundaries of projects and pursue the development of business architecture models, business analysts may be a significant part of the effort. If your enterprise architecture organization is focused on technology architecture, an effort to establish business architecture will require the domain knowledge of your most senior business analysts.

Technical Lead/Domain Architect

The technical lead and/or application architect is typically the job title associated with individuals that act as solution architects. Frequently, however, these individuals also have domain architecture responsibilities. That is, they may have oversight over several projects within a particular domain, or a role in establishing reference architectures within a particular domain outside of the context of any particular project.

Clearly, these individuals have a role in the many of the governance policies discussed earlier in the book. If an organization chooses to establish a SOA Center of Excellence, it is very likely that the domain architects will play a significant role. The domain architecture provides context for all of the projects that are executed within that domain. This can include business process analysis or business architecture development, as discussed earlier. It may also include guidance for particular technologies that are only used within that domain, such as ERP modules.

A particular challenge for this role is that these individuals frequently come from a development background, rather than an analyst background. The differences in architecture from domain to domain are typically not in the technologies utilized, but the functional domains involved. If these individuals do not have the proper functional knowledge of their business domains, they need to work closely with the key analysts in their organizations.

Finally, the technical leads must have clear and open communication with each other. It is likely that the current organizational structure does not reflect the boundaries between service consumers and service providers, meaning that there is significant redundancy across those domains. In the early stages of SOA adoption, these domain architects must work together to provide assistance to the IT managers in determining appropriate ownership.

Enterprise Architect/Technology Architect

The enterprise architect plays a very similar role to that of the domain architect. The key difference is that enterprise architects normally deal within domains that are applicable to the entire enterprise. This tends to include all of the pure technology domains, as well as security. Recently, enterprise architecture is expanding into the business architecture space, being seen as a key to aligning IT with the rest of the company. Organizations that are embracing business architecture will likely include domain architects as part of their enterprise architecture team.

In terms of SOA governance, the enterprise architect, like the domain architect, is typically in an oversight position, rather than being an active project team member. Enterprise architects are frequently responsible for strategies, roadmaps, reference architectures, and patterns that project teams are expected to implement and utilize. Therefore, enterprise architects are clearly well-positioned to provide governance. A reference architecture or design pattern is nothing more than a collection of policies that ensure solutions are built the appropriate way.

Enterprise architects that are more focused on technology architecture are responsible for the infrastructure strategy. Earlier in the book, a number of alternatives were presented for implementing policy-driven infrastructure. If enterprise architecture handles technology architecture, then it is their responsibility to set the direction in this space. This also includes ensuring that application teams use the infrastructure properly. This is an especially important concern in the SOA space primarily due to the emergence of the Enterprise Service Bus. No two ESBs are alike, as products marketed as an ESB come from **EAI** (**Enterprise Application Integration**) technology, **MOM** (**Message-Oriented Middleware**) technology, network appliances, and even products that are built from scratch. It is up to the enterprise architect to provide clarity on how an ESB should be utilized, if even at all. One of the questions that SOA governance must address is how to ensure that services are built the right way; clearly, the policies that ensure this behavior are the domain of the enterprise architect.

Enterprise architects that have business architecture responsibilities have an even larger role in the SOA governance efforts. The second major question is how to ensure the right services get built, and the key is business architecture and the creation of appropriate business domain models, possibly including business process models or business capability maps. The enterprise architect that is focused on business architecture has a role in performing the analysis and incorporating the business strategy into these business domain models that ultimately will be used in the project definition process to ensure the right services get built.

Information Architect

The information architect is a role that sometimes may get overlooked in SOA governance. A key challenge in adopting SOA is striving for consistent representations of information on service messages. Frequently, information architects may not be involved in this discussion because the conversation is typically between developers or solution architects. As a result, the representation of the information may be rooted in the processing models of the service consumers and service provider. This is neither good nor bad, but it does not take into account any storage model of the information, or any work that may be done by an information governance council in trying to define a canonical model or data dictionary.

In order for an organization to strive for consistency in the representation of information, it is important to include information architecture in the SOA governance efforts for service design, specifically in providing context for defining the schemas of the service messages.

Security Architect

The security architect is the role associated with ensuring that the technology solutions of the company take appropriate measures to protect its sensitive information, whether for protection of intellectual property, or for privacy protection related to the information maintained by the company. It is very likely that security architects are already involved with governance, whether it is part of broad IT governance related to Sarbanes-Oxley, or more exclusively focused on security policies.

One key area of focus for the security architect with regards to SOA governance is the role of identity in service interactions. Run-time governance techniques, such as traffic shaping/request throttling, are completely dependent on having identity of the consumer. As the degree of interactions between services increases, determining exactly what identity should be passed through these interactions is a challenge, and one that will require the guidance of your security architects.

IT Manager

The role of the typical IT manager is to manage personnel, manage work, and manage budget. This role is absolutely critical to the success of the SOA, because the changes that can be achieved have the most impact on IT management. Developers will still be writing code, but managers will have their entire world changed. IT managers that previously had complete control over their applications now may be dependent on other IT managers, or have other IT managers dependent on them. While most organizations are already dealing with this when it comes to infrastructure dependencies, many are not dealing with application-to-application dependencies.

If we look significantly forward, a successful SOA adoption can lead to significant organizational changes. IT managers may be reluctant to embrace this change as they may feel that their power is being taken away from them. Upper management tends to remain stable, and the people working in the trenches will still be doing analysis, project management, or development, but middle management has no such guarantees.

In order to mitigate this risk, it is important that IT management, specifically the middle managers, take an active role in the early decisions around service ownership.

Service Manager/Owner

The service manager, also known as the service owner, is a new role to most organizations, although if your organization has adopted ITIL and ITSM, you may have some familiarity with the concepts, but focused on services provided by IT operations. The service manager is the person responsible for managing the relationships with service consumers, scheduling and executing the upcoming releases of the service, and establishing relationships and service contracts with new consumers.

The service manager plays a key role in ensuring proper run-time governance is in place. Ultimately, the service manager, as the name suggests, is responsible for the service that is provided to the consumers, and the last thing needed is to have a service outage. The service manager must ensure that all details of the service contract have been established and that the infrastructure has been properly configured to enforce the policies within the service contract.

Initially, service managers may come from IT, but it is entirely possible that service managers may also be placed outside of IT, especially where services are exposed to external partners.

Platform Manager

The platform manager is responsible for the technology platform where services (and consumers, for internal consumers) are hosted. For most organizations that do not have the role of service manager defined, it falls to the operations team, whether an individual engineer or team or their associated manager to ensure that no outages occur in production.

Even when an organization does have a service manager role, the platform manager is still responsible for the underlying platforms, effectively providing a hosting service for the solutions that are deployed on them, whether those solutions represent service consumers or service providers. An individual service manager is primarily concerned about their service, and may not be watching the entire platform. Furthermore, for a service that involves several systems in its implementation, multiple platform managers may be involved, while the service manager is still responsible for the end-to-end performance of the entire service implementation across all systems, as illustrated by the following diagram:

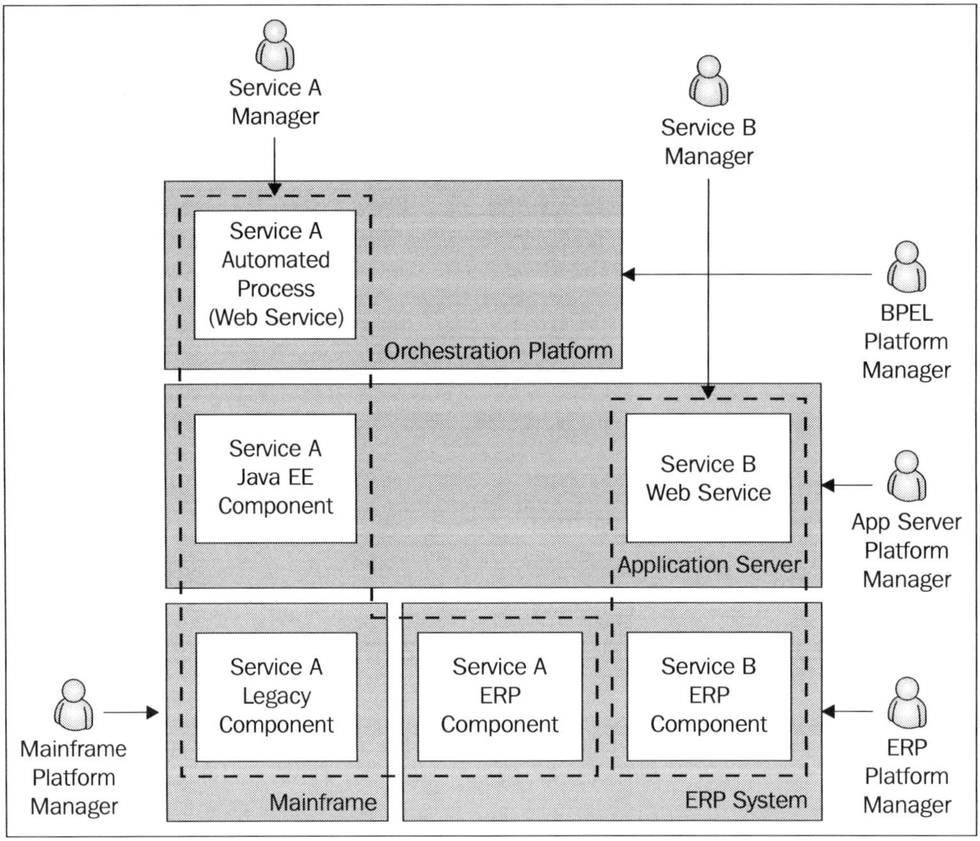

In this diagram, Service A is comprised of components that run on an orchestration platform (BPEL engine), an application server, a mainframe, and an ERP system. The manager for Service A must be concerned with the end-to-end performance across the platforms. Service B is comprised of a Web Service hosted on the application server platform and an ERP component. The manager for Service B is concerned with these two components. In contrast, each of these platforms has a platform manager that is concerned with the overall performance of the platform and each component running on it. The manager of the application server platform is concerned about the performance and capacity of the application server platform and must watch the performance of the Java EE component of Service A, and the web service of Service B, but is otherwise unconcerned about the remaining components that constitute Service A and Service B.

The platform manager is involved with establishing the entry criteria in order for a component to be deployed on a platform in a production environment. For example, if it is determined that a service did not use the appropriate instrumentation framework to allow for operational monitoring, it should not be allowed to go into production, since it can put the entire platform at risk.

Other Stakeholders

Besides the individuals already mentioned, there are other stakeholders that will play a role in your SOA governance efforts. While the majority of the technical governance issues are covered by the existing roles that have been identified, there are additional roles that may be involved with the non-technical governance. These individuals are likely already involved with your normal IT governance efforts, such as members of review boards that approve capital expenditures and project requests. Rather than forming additional committees designed to be involved in the governance process, it is better to ensure that the desired behaviors and goals for SOA are factored into the existing governance process.

Organizing Your People

There are many different organizational approaches that can be leveraged for your SOA governance efforts. SOA adoption is an enterprise initiative, however, which creates a challenge. Of the roles mentioned, only the Enterprise Architect, the Information Architect, and the Security Architect normally operate at the enterprise level. The remaining roles are either focused on project activities, on segments of technology, or on segments of the business. At the same time, many Enterprise Architectures are heavily focused on the underlying technology platforms, and may not have the appropriate functional knowledge to contribute to defining the functional boundaries associated with SOA adoption. As was shown in the Advasco story, both the technology architecture and the functional architecture are key aspects of SOA. Information architects are similar to enterprise architects in that they have broad visibility, but in a narrow area; in this case, the data systems of the enterprise. A similar story holds true for security architects.

Given the plethora of roles available, but the lack of the right role, it is important that the organization determine an approach to ensuring a successful adoption of SOA. There are a variety of different techniques that can be used.

Enterprise Architecture Driven

In this approach, the responsibility for SOA adoption lies solely within the enterprise architecture team. This can be a very good fit for many of the project governance concerns, and even some of the run-time governance concerns, since Enterprise Architecture is frequently tasked with driving strategic technologies into the enterprise. If your Enterprise Architecture team is also responsible for business architecture, then it is in an even stronger position, as it can also handle many of the pre-project governance concerns. The risk, however, is that technology is just a small part of SOA. The greater challenge is the cultural changes both in the way projects are defined and the way they are built. This can be a much more difficult task for Enterprise Architecture, since they are not normally in the management hierarchy with the people who will be most impacted by SOA adoption.

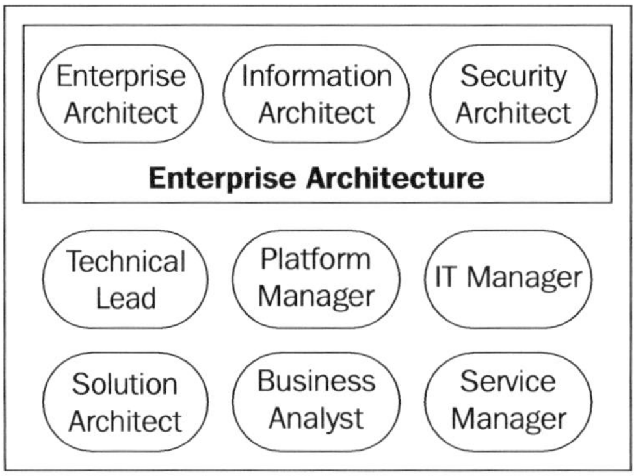

Two key relationships that can be a good litmus test before embracing an Enterprise Architecture driven SOA effort is the relationship with key IT managers, including the ability to influence organizational issues, and the relationship with key business leaders, especially those responsible for business strategy and architecture. If the Enterprise Architecture team is responsible for business architecture, chances are even better that they can drive the effort.

Another factor is the current role of Enterprise Architecture in the educational and governance processes that already exist in the enterprise. If the organization is used to taking direction and learning from Enterprise Architecture, this is a good thing. If the enterprise architects already play a role in the governance process for software development, whether through formal reviews or through less formal project engagements, again, it is not a big stretch to have them include enforcement of some of the SOA policies in their existing activities.

One risk associated with the Enterprise Architecture driven approach is the number of resources that can be dedicated to the effort. While one or more members of the EA group may be dedicated (or partially dedicated) to the effort, they need support from members of other organizations to participate in the effort. Another risk is in the area of run-time governance. An enterprise architect is normally not involved with the run-time management of production solutions. As a result, they are not as well-positioned to provide guidance on the right way to manage the services. Given the strong technology backgrounds of many enterprise architects, however, they usually have excellent relationships with the operational staff that allows for appropriate influence.

Center of Excellence/Competency Center

In this approach, the responsibility for SOA adoption is given to a cross-functional team of people. This has advantages, since it can draw from all areas of the organization and can include as many of the roles associated with SOA governance as desired. There are two factors that can have a large influence in the success of a Center of Excellence: the composition of the team and the engagement model with the organization.

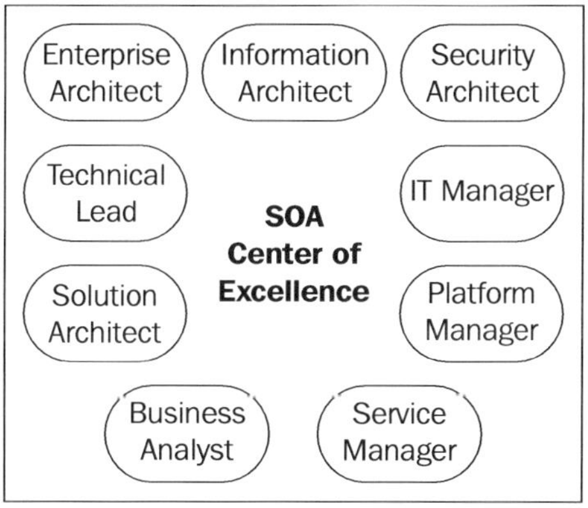

The composition of the team is the first decision that must be made by the organization. As with any virtual team, a common mistake is to choose people who have time to participate rather than choosing people who should be participating. Just as with the Enterprise Architecture driven approach, it is important that the people chosen for the Center of Excellence have the ability to influence the rest of the organization. Choose people that will struggle trying to influence others, and there's a good chance that the entire SOA effort will struggle as well.

The second factor is the engagement model with the rest of the organization. While a permanent organization like Enterprise Architecture may already have a defined engagement model with projects, a new virtual team does not. There are many nuances to the Center of Excellence that must be examined. First, what is the team's purpose? Is it to communicate a message about SOA and educate the rest of the organization? If this is the only focus, there is a risk that the effort will become disconnected from the projects that are realizing the organization's SOA. If the Center of Excellence tries to remain connected by participating on projects, how will that occur? At a minimum, the Center of Excellence can act as a reviewer for projects. A second option is to act as a staffing center for the projects. This is a common approach for Competency Centers, where a goal of the group is to train other staff members by working alongside them. This works well for the more technical areas of SOA, such as teaching staff how to work with XML or Web Services, but it may not be as practical for the non-technical aspects. A third approach is to act as an outsourcing center for service development. This approach has benefits in that the development of key services can be separated from the projects that identified the need, allowing them to be developed in a way that benefits a broader audience. The inherent risk with this approach is that the Center of Excellence may not have the domain knowledge of the functional areas necessary to develop the services properly. Once again, it is likely that a team can be formed with the necessary technical skills, but it is far more difficult to staff a team with the necessary functional knowledge. Furthermore, it is not possible for a small, centralized team to own all services in the organization. Eventually, this approach will not scale. Your goal must be to establish service development and service integration as a standard capability of the entire organization, not just one team.

A successful approach for a Center of Excellence is to initially focus heavily on communication and education, along with providing some amount of resources that assist in staffing initial projects. Rather than have work outsourced to them, they provide staff to projects that can train other people, ensure compliance of the SOA governance policies within those projects, and also bring back feedback to the Center of Excellence on policies that encountered resistance or were problematic to implement. Over time, the need to be a staffing center will go away, but the need for SOA governance will not. The Center of Excellence must still be a source of policies, an arbitrator when policies are conflicting or confusing, a source of consulting for decision guidance, continued education and communication on the SOA efforts, and finally, the group that is measuring the efforts of the organization against the desired behavior and making whatever adjustments are necessary. Eventually, if the organization achieves the desired behavior, the need for the Center of Excellence may go away, as the behavior that they helped encourage has now become second nature for the organization.

Review Boards

Another approach to SOA governance focuses exclusively on the enforcement of the policies that have been outlined through the use of review boards. Many organizations already have formal review processes in place; therefore it makes some sense to extend the policies enforced by the existing review boards.

For example, it is very likely that your organization already has a review board that approves projects. This review board may currently focus on the financial side of the proposed projects in making their approval decisions. That review board can now factor in the business domain models to determine the architectural fit of the proposed project in addition to the financials of the proposal. This may require adding members to the approval process that are familiar with the architectural side of the equation, or it may require educating the existing members on the importance of the domain models.

The same thing holds true for architectural reviews and design reviews. The challenge for these reviews is the opposite of the project approval review. In that review, we needed to augment the process and optionally the people to take more technical issues into account. In the case of architectural and design reviews, the review board likely already covers many of technical issues, but is not properly positioned to handle organizational issues or scoping issues that may arise from applying the policies to the projects.

The biggest challenge with this approach to SOA governance, however, is that there are significant gaps. First, who is responsible for establishing policies in the first place? More often than not, review boards are responsible for enforcing policies but don't normally set them. At best, they may make decisions on the fly where policies don't exist, but even then, the reasons for the decision are unlikely to turn into official policy. In order to address this gap, some other authority in the organization must establish the policies that are enforced by the review boards. This will likely be an existing organization like Enterprise Architecture or a cross-functional group like a Center of Excellence.

Common Challenges

Regardless of the organizational approach chosen, there are several challenges that must be factored into your decisions around your organizational approach. The first is the risk of focusing too much on enforcement, and not enough on education on what the desired behavior is. When people don't understand the reasons why policies exist, they are likely to resist them when they see them as getting in the way of their responsibilities. When educated on the reason for the policies and the desired outcome that they are intended to achieve, they are more likely to be compliant with the policies. As stated earlier, the easiest way to achieve compliance is to make compliance the path of least resistance.

The second challenge is in picking governance processes that are inconsistent with the existing culture of the organization. If your organization is very consensus driven, an enforcement process that places extensive power in the hands of a few, such as with a review board, can be very risky. A strong focus on education, allowing key members to influence and persuade others in the process that establishes consensus may be easier for the organization to digest. If your organization is accustomed to a command-and-control structure, then yielding power to a few individuals and giving them authority to stop projects in their tracks may be possible. This is not to say, however, that matching the existing culture is always a good thing. Sometimes, the existing culture may be the biggest problem. Remember, SOA governance is about achieving a desired behavior in your SOA adoption efforts, and it is very likely that the desired behavior is different from what you are doing today. If the culture needs dramatic change, then dramatic changes in governance may be required. Frequently, however, this may require a change in leadership. It is typically very difficult for existing leadership to make dramatic changes in the behavior of an organization.

The next challenge is remaining relevant. A Center of Excellence is not the only approach that must be concerned about the engagement model with the rest of the organization. Enterprise Architecture is commonly at risk of becoming an ivory tower if they do not remain engaged with project activities. A review board is at even more risk, since they normally may not even meet with each other except when reviews are occurring. The team establishing policies must remain engaged with the teams that are expected to be compliant with those policies. An approach that strives to educate and mentor first, and then reviews and accepts/rejects second is more likely to be accepted, and more likely to have a higher compliance rate.

The final challenge is in matching the needs of all areas of the organization. While smaller companies may be able to have a single approach to SOA, larger companies with multiple lines of business may have different desired behaviors for each line of business. For example, if a company is focused on rapid growth in one line of business, but cost containment in another line of business, embracing policies that require company-wide standardization may help the second line of business cut their costs, but may severely restrict the ability of the first line of business to grow rapidly. Preferably, these goals are captured in the business domain models, however, they might not always be, or more likely, the domain models may not exist until further down the SOA journey. SOA must be business driven, and the behaviors, policies, and processes all must be reflective of those business goals.

Policies

The second piece of SOA governance is policies. Policies are the standards and guidelines that guide the staff associated with SOA towards the desired behavior. There are three key timeframes that have been addressed in the book:

1. During the processes associated with determining what IT projects to fund and execute: These processes are frequently associated with the broader subject of IT governance. While SOA governance should not introduce new governance processes associated with deciding what projects to fund and execute, policies associated with SOA governance should be included in the criteria. Surprisingly, vendors that offer tools in the SOA governance space do not have a term for this timeframe. We will refer to this as pre-project governance.
2. During project execution: In the vendor community, this is frequently referred to as design-time governance, however, the scope of SOA governance is certainly broader than just the design activities of a project. We will refer to this as project governance.
3. During the operation of production systems: In the vendor community this timeframe is referred to as run-time governance. As long as there are services running in your production systems, there is a need to govern the interactions between consumers and providers.

Pre-Project Governance

During this timeframe, the desired behavior is centered on a simple concept: building the right thing. The decision-making process that results in an approved and funded project is what sets the initial scope for the effort. This initial scope has a significant impact in determining the artifacts that will be produced. If the scope incorporates an enterprise viewpoint appropriately, an organization may quickly build up a library of services whose expectations for reuse and agility in times of change have been well thought out. If the scope does not incorporate enterprise viewpoints and needs appropriately, it creates a risk that the artifacts developed will struggle to provide value outside of the initial project.

Artifacts

In order to perform pre-project governance, the following artifacts are recommended:

- Organization Chart
- Business Domain/Capability Models
- Business Process Models

- Application Portfolio
- Service Portfolio

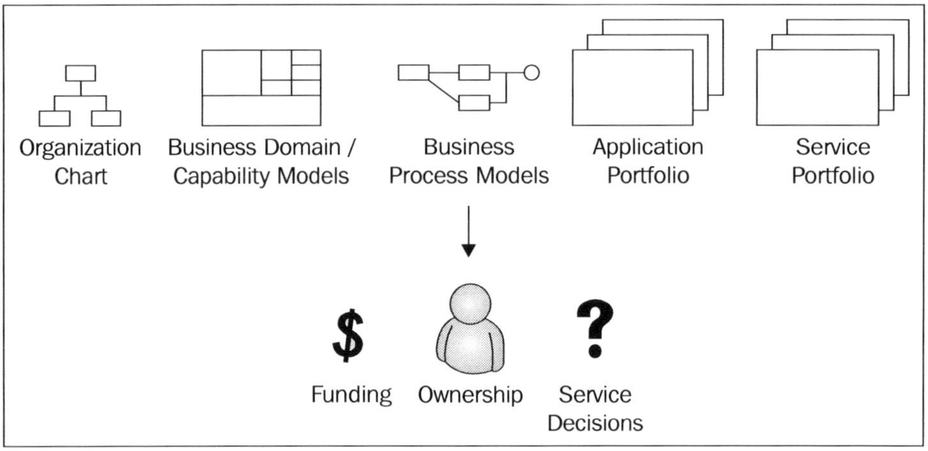

The first artifact, the **Organization Chart**, is a key element in how projects get defined. Normally, relationships with areas of the business outside of IT are highly influenced by the organization of the IT department. Change the organization of the IT department and you may change the way relationships are formed and managed with the rest of the business. The same also holds true with the organization of the rest of the business. Change the organizational structure of the business, and it's likely that the IT organizational structure will change with it.

The reason why the organizational chart is so critical is because there is normally a direct relationship between budget and organization. If a particular department in the business is in control of their own budget, it could be a big barrier to either creating services that will be used by other departments, or in using services that are managed by other departments. In the first scenario, many budget owners may want other organizations to contribute to the cost of development or maintenance of services if they use them. In the second scenario, they may be asked by those organizations to contribute to their costs. In addition, the projects that are proposed may have dependencies that other organizations must deliver in order to be successful. Depending on the state of relationships in the organization, this could be a major hurdle to overcome.

The thing to remember when adopting SOA is that it will likely put pressure on the existing organizational structure. If it doesn't, there are number of possibilities. First, your organization may already be aligned along the concept of service consumers and service providers. Second, your organization may not let organizational boundaries get in the way of doing the right thing. Finally, it may be that your SOA efforts are working too much within the boundaries of the organization and not really creating the type of change possible with SOA.

The next three artifacts, **Business Domain/Capability Models**, **Business Process Models**, and the **Application Portfolio** are closely related. These are analysis artifacts that should be used to guide the decisions on what services should be created. At a minimum, as discussed in the Advasco example, some form of domain/capability models and business processes models should be leveraged. Business process models on their own create a risk for creating process silos; just as many organizations today have application silos based upon their application portfolios. When business process models and application portfolios are combined with a domain/capability model, the resulting combination can be a powerful tool in guiding the decisions on what services should be established.

The final artifact, the **Service Portfolio**, is frequently a catalog of services that have been built and are available in production, but it is much more powerful when it is used as a planning tool. When the organization has taken the time to perform business process analysis and business domain/capability analysis, an outcome should be the definition of key services that the organization needs to create to fully leverage SOA.

Policies for Pre-Project Governance

The following are questions or policies that you should consider in your pre-project governance efforts:

- Has the proposed project identified candidate services?
- Has the proposed project mapped candidate services to the business domains as represented in the business domain/capability models?
- Has the proposed project reviewed the service portfolio against the list of candidate services?
- Has an appropriate team of project stakeholders been identified based upon candidate services?
- Has the proposed program/project been appropriately structured and scheduled to properly manage the development and integration of new and existing services?

- Have all funding details been determined based upon the services proposed and the organizations involved?
- Does the roadmap include the development of services with high potential for reuse?
- Are projects encouraged to reuse existing services, where appropriate, based upon the business domain models and business objectives?
- Are projects allowed to create redundancies, where appropriate, based upon the business domain models and business objectives?
- Have existing systems been taken into account in the definition of the proposed services?
- Is the organizational structure being reviewed on a regular basis based upon continued service analysis?
- Does the organization have a clear approach to resolving service ownership models?
- Are business processes properly leveraging services?
- Does your service portfolio properly account for any globalization impact?
- Does the service portfolio properly account for any planned areas for growth by acquisition?

Remember, this phase is the key timeframe to ensure that the organization builds the right services. If the decisions on what services to build are not investigated until after projects have been defined and funded, constraints will already exist that can be an impediment to building the right services.

Project Governance

During this timeframe, there are two major concerns: building the right services and building those services the right way. While the pre-project governance efforts are supposed to focus on building the right services, all too often, the proper artifacts are not available to make the necessary decisions at the time projects are approved. As a result, the necessary analysis and the decisions associated with the project architecture are performed within the project itself. This creates some risk, because the project does establish constraints that may get challenged by the results of analysis and architecture.

Like the architecture decisions that are made prior to project approval, the architecture and design activities must incorporate enterprise viewpoints and needs appropriately. For this purpose, the artifacts and policies mentioned as part of the pre-project governance all still apply. Besides these concerns, this timeframe is where an organization must ensure that services are built the right way.

Artifacts

In order to perform project governance, the following artifacts, besides those already mentioned in the pre-project governance section, are recommended:

- Service Technology Reference Architecture
- Service Security Reference Architecture
- Service Blueprints and Frameworks
- Standard Information Models and Schemas

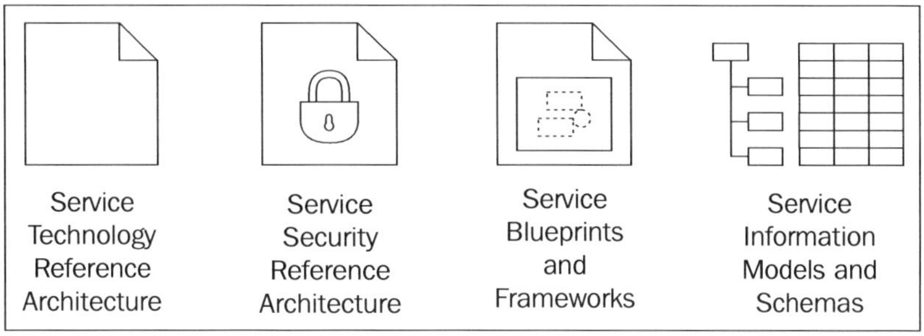

These artifacts are only the ones that have an impact on SOA governance. Clearly, there are many other artifacts that are associated with general development governance, but those that are not specific to service development and integration are outside of the scope of this book.

Service Technology Reference Architecture

The first artifact is the **Service Technology Reference Architecture**. The purpose of this artifact is to ensure that the appropriate technologies are used for the service being developed. The document should first define the appropriate service types for the organization and then map those types to specific service technologies. The document should never have more than one type mapping to the same set of specific service technologies. If multiple types map to the same set of service technologies, it may create more confusion than clarity. While those service types may be useful in determining service ownership, this document is focused on determining service technologies. On the flip side of things, enterprises with centralized infrastructure will also want to ensure that there is only one set of service technologies for each service type. For example, there will always be a catchall type, like "General Business Service" that will map to an application server and its associated service framework. Is it good to have both a .NET platform running on Windows Server and a Java EE application server running on a Linux platform? The correct answer is it depends. If your organization was a Microsoft development shop, but then acquired another company that was a Java development shop, it may make sense to have two general business service platforms. If both these groups still maintain their own data centers and operations staff after acquisition, there aren't too many issues. If, instead, the acquisition results in a consolidation of data centers and reduction in operational staff, justifying the continued operation of both platforms will be much more difficult.

Here are some service types that you should consider. Each one has the potential for being mapped to a specific set of service technologies.

- **Composite Services**: These are services that are built by combining the output of two or more services, and aggregating the respective responses into a single response.
- **Automated (Orchestrated) Processes**: These are services that are built by executing a fully automated sequence of actions as represented in a graphical process model. Technically speaking, a composite service is normally a specialized case of an orchestrated process, but if you choose to leverage very specific technologies for narrow service types, it is possible that you may need to define both service types and their associated service platform and technologies.
- **Integration Services**: These are services whose whole purpose is to service enable some system that does not support the standards required to speak natively to service consumers.
- **Presentation Services**: These are services that provide information in a presentation-friendly format. They don't actually produce the end user interface, but they provide the information in such a way that it is easily consumed by user interface technologies. This may require a slight variation of the standard service platform.
- **Management Services**: These are services that expose management and administrative functionality. In the past, there have been management-specific technologies including SMNP and JMX. Today, there are increasing numbers of products that expose management interfaces as SOAP or XML/HTTP interfaces, however, the use of SMNP and JMX are still far more prevalent.
- **Information Services**: These are services that are used to retrieve information from a variety of data sources, aggregating the results into a single response. Vendors typically market solutions in this space as data service platforms or data integration platforms. These services differ from composite services in that they are specifically designed to talk only to data sources on the back end, rather than any arbitrary web service.
- **Content Subscription Services**: These are services that provide content feeds, typically adhering to feed syndication standards such as RSS and ATOM.

- **General Business Services**: This is the catchall category for any service that doesn't fit into any of the other categories.

When mapping these service types to technologies, the following things must be considered:

- **Service Platform**: The technology decisions start with an underlying hosting platform. Typical choices include a Java Application Server, Windows Server, a Data Integration/Services Platform, a BPEL-based orchestration platform, and some ESB offerings.
- **Service Communication Technology**: The communication technologies are the protocol used to interact with the service. This includes both the message format used, such as POX, SOAP, or RSS, and the underlying message transport (HTTP, WebSphere MQ, or Tibco JMS).

For example, using the service types listed, a mapping to service platforms and communication technologies could look like this:

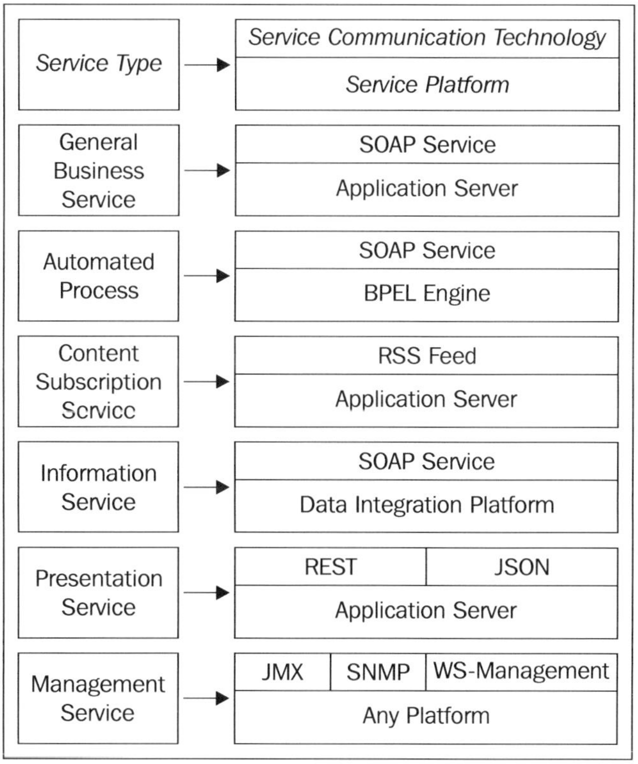

Beyond the mapping of service types to service technologies, the service reference architecture must also address policies associated with the message itself that go beyond the core communication technology. This can include naming conventions for URLs, namespace conventions for the XML messages, references to a canonical model, or more. It must also provide policies on how the non-functional capabilities associated with services interactions will be provided by the underlying infrastructure. This includes:

- Security (see Service Security Reference Architecture)
- Routing and load balancing
- Transport and mediation
- High availability and failover
- Monitoring and management
- Versioning and transformations

These non-functional capabilities are a key aspect of SOA, because they are the foundation of run-time governance. At the same time, they must be factored into the design-time decisions, because if the development teams don't utilize the technology appropriately, the ability to enforce run-time governance policies will disappear. If a team chooses to build its own security implementation or hard code rules for versioning into the implementation, it will likely require a code change and the associated release process to implement and enforce the policies in a service contract for a new consumer, increasing the time and effort required to bring new consumers online. We want to strive to implement these non-functional capabilities through policy-driven infrastructure that is configured, rather than coded.

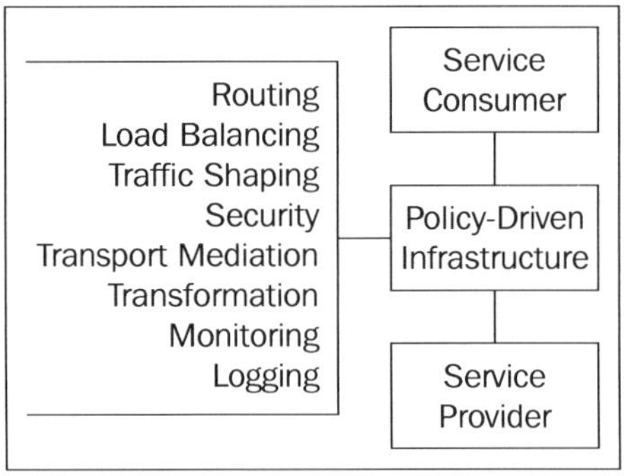

Service Security Reference Architecture

The next artifact is the **Service Security Reference Architecture**. This can be included as a subset of the Service Technology Reference Architecture, or created as a standalone artifact. Regardless of the approach, there are two questions that must be answered by the reference architecture:

1. What security policies must be enforced?
2. What technologies are used for enforcing those policies?

The first question must guide the developers of services and their consumers on security policies for authentication, authorization, encryption, digital signatures, and threat prevention.

There are two components to authentication. The first is a simple policy that states whether or not identity is required on all service invocations. It is strongly recommended that this is the case. With this policy in place, your organization must then specify what constitutes identity. It can be a user's name, an application's name, a company's name, or any combination of them. It may include additional attributes such as group membership or more. The one thing it should not be is anonymous. Companies must assume that in the future many services will comprise a particular interaction, with multiple teams involved. If identity on messages does not exist, it makes it extremely difficult to enforce run-time governance, since identity is what ties an interaction back to a service contract, as well as making the debugging process much more costly should problems occur in production.

With this identity specified, the next step is to decide when authentication is required on service invocations. Unlike a web application that faces an end user, one cannot assume that a simple challenge can be issued to allow a consumer to specify credentials on demand. When dealing with system-to-system interactions, it is very unlikely that the service consumer has access to the password of the user associated with the current thread. If passwords are not issued, then there needs to be a way to ensure that the credentials passed on the request have not been forged. For internal consumers, many organizations choose to only validate that credentials are from a trusted source, rather than performing an authentication on every request. This, of course, assumes that an authentication was performed at the user interface of the system.

Authorization, on the other hand, should always be performed on all service requests. Besides stating this policy, the reference architecture must also cover whether role-based or user-based authorization will be leveraged. Role-based authorization is generally preferred, as the management of policies associated with individual users can quickly become an impossible task for large organizations.

At first glance, you may first think that encryption is only concerned with the protection of sensitive data from systems that have no need for accessing it, but the certificate exchange associated with bi-directional SSL communications can also be leveraged to ensure that service endpoints only accept connections from authorized points on the network. For example, if you are leveraging an XML appliance as a policy enforcement point, it is possible for a rogue consumer to circumvent the appliance by entering the hostname or IP address of the service endpoint directly. By forcing a bi-directional certificate exchange between the XML appliance and the service endpoint in order to exchange service messages, these rogue consumers would be prevented from accessing the service, since they would not have the certificate required.

Digital signatures are a means of ensuring that the service messages have not been modified en route. While this is typically not used with internal consumers, it is frequently used when dealing with external consumers or external service providers, especially when those requests are sent over the open Internet. It may also be required on internal messages to ensure that some portion of the message, such as identity credentials, is coming from a trusted source.

Finally, threat protection is concerned with preventing consumers from exploiting a variety of techniques that can compromise the security of the service provider. Common examples include checking for SQL injection or detecting harmful XML messages, such as ones that are compliant with the XML schemas involved, but exploit recursion or buffer overflows to attempt to crash the server that will process the message.

The second question deals with the specific technologies associated with enforcing those policies. This begins with the service messages themselves. While the reference architecture has previously specified what constitutes identity, it must now say how that identity is represented on service messages. Will it be issued in plain text in a standard location? Will it be specified using transport-specific mechanisms (for example, HTTP headers) or as part of the actual message payload? The most flexible mechanism available today is only associated with SOAP messages, and that is the WS-Security framework. This framework establishes a standard location in the SOAP header for credentials, and provides a framework for specifying profiles that allow different token types to be used. Standard profiles include the Username profile (simple plaintext and hashed credentials), the **SAML** (**Security Assertion Markup Language**) Token Profile, the X.509 Token Profile, the Kerberos Token Profile, and the **REL** (**Rights Expression Language**) Token Profile. Not all products support all of the profiles, so be sure to dig deeper when a product claims to have WS-Security support. It may only support one or two of the token profiles, or potentially none at all, since WS-Security also specifies standard ways of handling message encryption and digital signatures.

Once the policies for the messages themselves have been set, the reference architecture must address the specific infrastructure associated with the enforcement of those policies. Will a standalone gateway, such as some ESBs or an XML appliance, be used to enforce authorization policies? If so, then all service traffic must be routed through those gateways, and techniques must be leveraged to prevent rogue consumers from circumventing those gateways. While a policy may say that SAML assertions must be used, how does a developer of a service consumer place those assertions on a message? Are they responsible for writing the code to do so, or will a framework be provided for them? If a framework is used, must the developer explicitly reference it, or will the insertion of credentials happen implicitly? The security reference architecture must provide enough information so that the developers of a service consumer or service provider know exactly what is required of them in their coding efforts versus what must be simply configured as part of establishing a service contract.

Service Blueprints and Frameworks

When trying to guide people to the desired behavior, a very powerful technique is to simply give them examples of it. This is the role of service blueprints. The reference architectures discussed can contain a large number of policies that can seem daunting to a developer, creating the risk that they get ignored. By creating blueprints that show a common pattern, and preferably the simplicity associated with following the pattern, developers are more likely to follow the guidelines.

For example, if your organization will be exposing external services, a challenge may be the propagation of identity to back-end systems, since identity checks may occur in a DMZ or through federation, yet the back-end services have no access to those identity stores. A blueprint can be created that demonstrates how that original identity flows through the connections required, and what code is required at each step (if any) to ensure it happens.

Blueprints also provide a convenient way of demonstrating how to choose within alternate strategies for a given service type. For example, a general business service may be accessible by either asynchronous messaging via message-oriented middleware, or via a synchronous messaging approach over HTTP. When should one be used over the other, and what are the differences in how to leverage them?

The second key piece of this artifact is service frameworks. While the underlying service platforms typically include frameworks for doing HTTP communication, XML message processing, and SOAP processing, it doesn't mean it's easy to use. This is especially true for security. While many frameworks can construct a SOAP message through the use of a wizard or code generator and one or two lines of code, adding a SAML assertion to that SOAP message can be much more complicated. A common theme with governance is that if you make compliance the path of least resistance, you're more likely to get compliance. If you have a policy that all service messages must contain identity, providing a framework so this can be done in one or two lines of code, or zero if possible, will ensure that your developers are compliant with the policy, versus requiring them to research SAML libraries and write many lines of code to make it happen.

Standard Information Models and Schemas

The final artifacts that are imperative for design-time governance are standard information models and schemas. A common goal associated with SOA is reuse, but reuse becomes much more difficult when common information is not represented consistently. For example, if there are two services that both need to deal with Account information, but both services represent that information in different ways, any consumer that needs to use both of those services must now implement logic that translates between the two definitions of Account.

In order to prevent this situation from becoming rampant, an organization must take this decision out of the hands of individual projects, and put it into the hands of a group with broader focus, whether that is the entire enterprise, or some larger domain. It is important that this group (or groups) understands that the goal is not to come up with the one universal representation that everyone agrees on, because odds are it doesn't exist. Rather, the goal is to minimize the number of representations for common information. If it can be one, that's the optimal point, but if it winds up being three or four, and we provide mechanisms for easily translating between them that is a big improvement over leaving it in the hands of every individual service consumer or service provider.

One factor that can play a key role in defining these models is the existence of industry standards for the information domains involved. For example, there are many messaging standards that exist for various verticals, such as financial services (SWIFT, ISO-20022), healthcare (HIPAA), and insurance (ACORD), which have been created for the explicit purpose of information exchange in business-to-business interactions. These schemas can be an excellent starting point for establishing internal standards, and should definitely be leveraged when exposing services externally. A second factor is the organization's use of third-party solutions, such as a major ERP product like SAP or Oracle. These systems often come with information schemas pre-packaged. The more customization to these schemas that you do, the more difficult it may be to upgrade that infrastructure. As a result, these schemas may also be a good starting point for establishing your own standards. The best scenario is where an industry standard exists that is independent of any third-party application, but supported by those third-party applications. That maintains independence from the vendor solution, yet leverages a schema with broad adoption in the industry.

Just as with the security reference architecture, the information models and schemas must make sure that they not only provide the standard models, but sufficient instructions on how to utilize them in service traffic. For example, if there was a common XML schema file for Account information called `account.xsd`, organizations should not allow individual projects to copy that file into their own projects. Rather, their projects should reference that schema file from some location that will be universally available. That allows the schema to be maintained and updated centrally, rather than having to go out to each individual project and update the Account definition one at a time.

Policies for Project Governance

The following are questions/policies that you should consider in your project governance efforts, in addition to all those that were specified in the pre-project governance if not enforced at that time:

- Have all services been mapped to an appropriate type?
- Are the service technologies chosen for each service consistent with the type to technology mapping specified in the reference architecture?
- Does the service use the standard communication technologies specified in the reference architecture?
- Does the service interface comply with all naming conventions for URLs as specified in the reference architecture?
- Does the service interface comply with all namespace conventions as specified in the reference architecture?
- Does the service interface properly reference all external schema definitions, rather than copying them locally?
- Does the service interface use the standard schema definitions properly?
- Do external facing services only expose industry standard schemas, where they exist?
- Is the service interface compliant with industry standards, such as WS-I?
- Does the service require identity on its messages?
- Are all service consumers properly specifying identity on outgoing requests?
- Have appropriate authorization policies been established for the service?
- Is the service communication infrastructure being leveraged appropriately?
- Are all internal consumers properly leveraging the standard service frameworks?

- Are all internal providers properly leveraging the standard service frameworks?
- Is all sensitive information properly encrypted according to the service security policies?
- Have service contracts been established between all consumers and providers?
- Are all aspects of the service contract fully specified including message schemas, versions, delivery schedule, points of contact, and expected usage rates?
- Have all services been thoroughly and adequately tested, with testing results available to service consumers, if required by the service contract? For internal consumers, testing results should always be available to help counter the natural tendency for developers to resist using things they didn't personally write.
- Have service managers been assigned for all new services?
- Are the service boundaries identified in the solution consistent with the business domain models?
- Has the solution incorporated existing services appropriately?
- Has the solution properly published information about new services into the Service Registry/Repository?
- Has the solution avoided creating redundant services that were not appropriate according to the business domain models?

Remember that all of these policies are in addition to policies that are already being enforced as part of your normal project governance process. Policies around coding conventions, project structures, code repositories, unit testing, integration testing, performance and capacity testing, and so on still apply.

Run-time Governance

During this timeframe, the major concern is the correct behavior of service consumers and service providers so that the infrastructure remains operational and in a healthy state at all times. There are two keys to this. The first is an accurate understanding of the role of infrastructure in the run-time environment at the time solutions are built, and second, is the appropriate use of the run-time infrastructure to enforce the policies established in the service contract. Unlike the other timeframes, there is really only one artifact that is used to describe the run-time behavior, and that is the service contract. Before covering that, let's first look at a conceptual view of the infrastructure and the guidance that must be given to teams during their design processes.

Policy-Driven Infrastructure

At its core, the run-time infrastructure consists of three things: infrastructure used to execute the logic associated with the service consumer, infrastructure used to execute the logic associated with the service provider, and infrastructure used to allow communication between the two. Earlier, it was stated that a goal should be to minimize the ways in which a service consumer and a service provider can communicate. Through the use of reference architectures, the policies are created that define these standards. With these standards in place, there are three core principles that should be adopted:

- Service consumers are responsible for ensuring that all messages they send are compliant with the service communication standards.
- Service providers are responsible for ensuring that they expose endpoints that can consume messages that are compliant with the service communication standards.
- The service communication infrastructure will enforce all non-functional capabilities for all messages that are compliant with the service communication standards, including mediation between those standards.

This results in a logical picture like this:

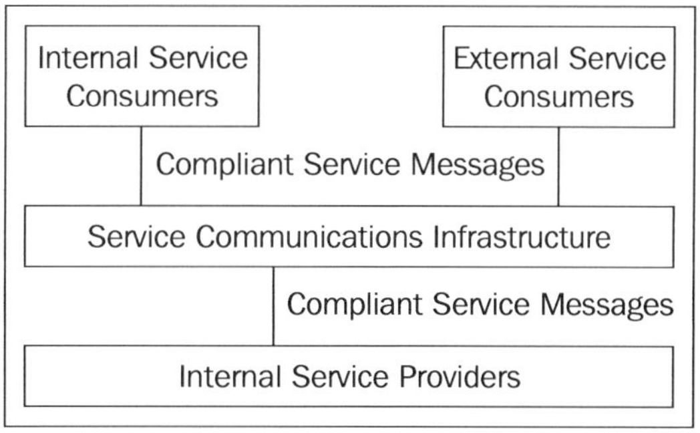

This clearly leads to a simple statement about run-time behavior: all service messages are compliant with the service communications standards. Unfortunately, that is seldom the case. If your organization leverages third-party products, it is unlikely that they will be compliant with all of your standards out-of-the-box. The key principle to follow, however, is that it is the responsibility of the non-compliant party to find a way to be in compliance, not the service communications infrastructure. Previous integration approaches, such as EAI technology, attempted to allow the endpoints to do whatever they wanted, and mediate between all of this in the middle. This quickly ran into problems, as precious CPU cycles were spent doing transformations and other activities to tie systems together which degraded the performance of other transactions that required little in mediation. The right approach is to push these adapters out to the endpoints, in an approach like this:

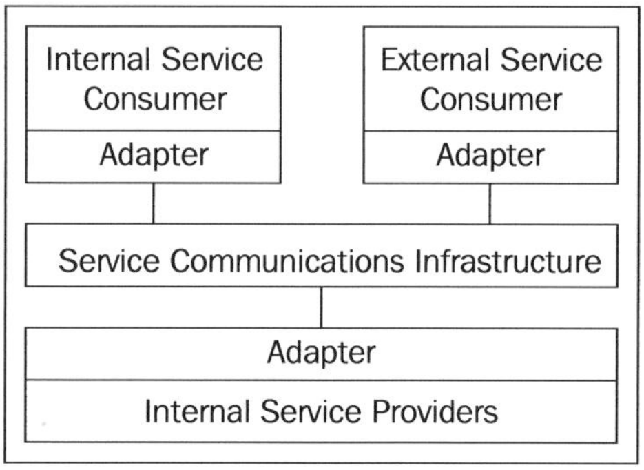

In this approach, it is the responsibility of the service consumer or service provider to put an adapter into their processing path prior to sending messages out through the service communications infrastructure. This can still involve EAI technology, but the use of that technology only accepts message traffic that is associated with the non-compliant system, versus dealing with all message traffic. These adapters can also be leveraged in process at the consumer or provider, such as using a third-party SOAP library within a Java execution environment that doesn't natively provide one.

The final adjustment to this diagram is to understand that the standards may be significantly different when dealing with an external party, whether that party is a service consumer or a service provider. This results in the following picture:

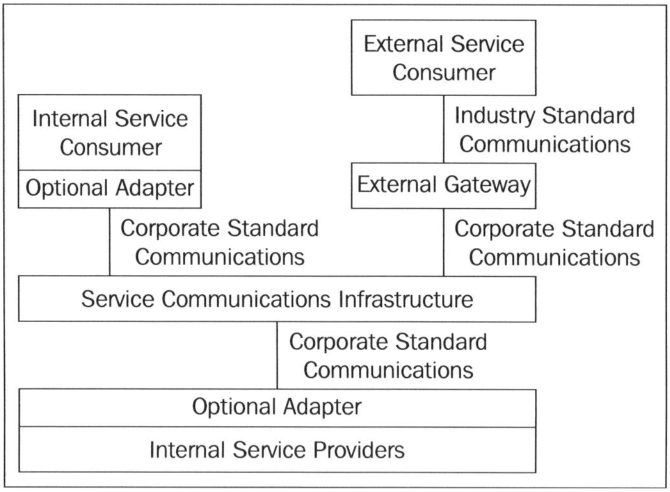

In this picture, an external service consumer communicates with an external gateway using industry standard communications technologies, both for the underlying transport as well as the messaging schemas. It is the responsibility of the external service consumer to be compliant with these industry standards.

The external gateway is responsible for the initial enforcement of security policies, as well as any mediation from the industry standards to the internal standards. Again, this encompasses both transport and messaging schema. If multiple versions of an industry standard exist, and are supported, the external gateway must be capable of transforming any of them into the approved internal corporate standards. If the internal standards are identical to the external standards, clearly this step is unnecessary. As a result, a best practice is to try to leverage industry standards for internal message formats as well, although it is recognized that this may require extending the standard for additional internal information.

Inside the corporate data center, all message traffic through the service communications infrastructure must be compliant with the corporate standards. Mediation within the corporate standards is a capability of the service communications infrastructure. This can include moving a message from an HTTP transport to a JMS-based transport (if both are allowed), mediating between POX/HTTP and SOAP/HTTP, and so on. It also includes mediation required for versioning of those standards. If the schema for an information entity has changed, but the use of a previous version is still allowed, the infrastructure should handle transformations between the two, when it is required.

It is the responsibility of the internal service consumer and the internal service provider to ensure that they are compliant with at least one of the standards for service communication. The endpoints do not need to support all of them, but they must support at least one. Where a service consumer or provider is non-compliant, they are responsible for employing an adapter, whether in process or an external entity for providing a compliant interface. Clearly, native compliance is preferable, as this prevents the proliferation of "glue" infrastructure used to tie everything together. The policies around service communication technologies should be used as part of your technology evaluation process for third-party packages to prevent this need as much as possible.

Service Contracts

With the standards for communication established, the infrastructure can now focus on the enforcement of the policies within service contracts. Some policies may be common to all service contracts, consistent with the policies that are in place in the reference architectures. For example, if the service technology reference architecture states that only XML payloads are allowed, this should be reflected in all service contracts. Any service message received by the communications infrastructure that does not contain an XML payload should be rejected.

While many of these policies can, and should be tested at development time, they must also be enforced at run-time, whether to deal with unknown bugs in the consumer or provider, protection against rogue applications that didn't follow appropriate testing procedures, or in case of external consumers, because we don't know what testing was performed at development time.

In addition, there are behaviors that cannot be handled by development time testing, typically associated with SLA enforcement point. A capacity test can be done to verify that the system behaves properly when 1,000 users of a service consumer are sending simultaneous requests, but this can't account for a mistake in analysis of the user base. If the real number is 10,000 users, how do we prevent the system from being overwhelmed? Each individual message may be fully compliant with all standards, but it's the fact that a much higher rate of message traffic is occurring that can create the problem.

The service contract must specify the expected usage by the consumer in an appropriate level of detail, as well as the expected response time from the provider when the system is behaving as expected. Additionally, thresholds for both usage by the consumer and response time from the provider must be established. Exceeding these thresholds results in notifications, allowing corrective action to be taken before a problem occurs, or a switch to a mode of self-preservation, where requests will be rejected in order to protect the back end service implementation from a complete failure.

The infrastructure must be capable of changing the policies associated with a contract, or establishing new contracts, without requiring a deployment of a new version of the service or the consumer solely for that reason. It is common that a change in contract may accompany an associated functionality change in a service consumer, service provider, or both, but it is the functionality change that drives the implementation change and the contract change. We never want a contract change to require an implementation change.

The service contract must also address reporting policies for service usage. The desired behavior at run-time should never be to deploy a service in production and then ignore it unless the system tells us otherwise. Usage reports should be provided to each consumer, as well as to the service provider. Analysis of these reports may trigger a change in policy, or even a need for a capacity modification, if the reports indicate the usage characteristics are changing.

Policies for Run-Time Governance

The following are questions or policies that you should consider in your run-time governance efforts:

- What is the normal rate of requests for a given service consumer?
- What is the expected response time for the service provider for typical requests from that service consumer?
- What actions are taken when the request rate for a given service consumer exceeds each of the agreed upon thresholds?
- What actions are taken when the response time for a given service consumer exceeds each of the agreed upon thresholds?
- Are there any time restrictions on when a particular consumer can access a service?
- For services with multiple entry points via different technologies (for example, SOAP/HTTP, XML/HTTP, SOAP/JMS), is policy enforcement defined and consistent (if needed) for each entry point?
- Are all security policies configured and being enforced?
- Are service requests routed to the appropriate version for each consumer, or have appropriate transformations been applied, preserving backward compatibility?
- Are all service messages being logged appropriately per any enterprise auditing requirements?
- Are all service messages being logged and preserved for the purpose of debugging?
- Are usage metrics being properly collected?
- Are usage reports being generated and distributed appropriately?
- Are the recipients of these reports properly reviewing them and accounting for any discrepancies in behavior?

- Are all policies associated with message structure being enforced by the run-time infrastructure?
- Are non-compliant messages being logged, rejected, and reported to appropriate personnel?

Remember that while the infrastructure can enforce many of the run-time governance policies, there is still a need to have people involved. If the staff deploys services into production and then forgets about them, there is significant risk of problems down the road. The lifecycle of a service consumer and a service provider must be managed from inception to decommissioning, not just from inception to production deployment.

SOA Governance Processes

Now that people and policies are in place, the focus turns to process. There are four major governance processes that need to be addressed:

- Establishing Desired Behavior and Policies
- Education and Communication
- Policy Enforcement
- Measurement

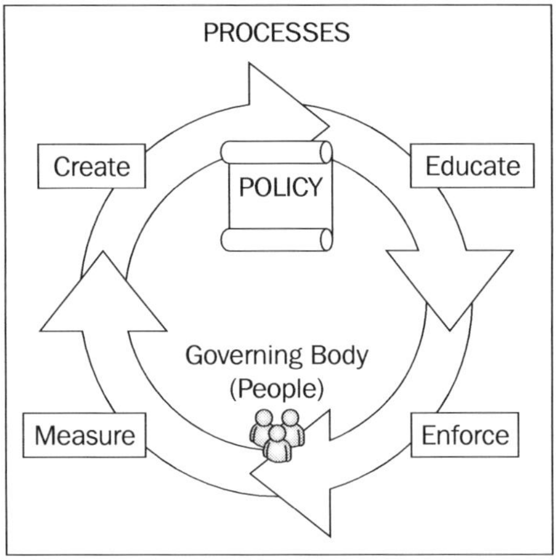

Establishing Desired Behavior and Policies

While most people immediately think of enforcement when they hear the word "governance" in the context of software development, this is not where governance begins. SOA governance begins by establishing the desired behaviors you want to achieve through your adoption of SOA. If there are no desired behaviors, how will you know if your SOA efforts are successful? Likewise, if the desired behaviors cannot be measured, how will you know if your SOA efforts are successful? "Increasing business agility" is not a behavior that can be easily measured. "Decreasing the average delivery time for IT solutions by 20%" is a behavior that can be measured. As you refine your desired behavior, keep in mind that SOA governance includes pre-project activities, project activities, and run-time activities, and your desired behavior should reflect all of these. The earlier behavior that discussed decreasing the average delivery time really only impact project activities. If there is a need to change the way IT solutions are defined, as was the case for Advasco, there needs to be a desired behavior that reflects this. Likewise, what is the driver for policy-driven infrastructure in support of service interactions? This could be a behavior related to the responsiveness of IT to business change, or it could be a behavior associated with the up time of the IT systems.

Once the desired behaviors have been established, then the organization can establish policies that will yield this behavior. In order to establish these policies, the roles described earlier must be considered, and responsibility given appropriately, whether that is through a cross-functional Center of Excellence or in a more decentralized manner where the individuals in those roles work together as needed to establish enterprise policies for pre-project activities, project activities, and run-time activities.

The importance of this step cannot be understated. All too often, the people acting as "governors" are put in place, but the policies (and sometimes even the desired behavior) are never established. This can result in a dictatorial style, where the "governed" can only guess what the governors are looking for, and those guesses are usually wrong. In addition, the outcome is completely dependent on the particular governor involved. Another potential outcome is where the SOA effort slowly fades into the background. Some teams may claim they are "doing SOA," but there's nothing to either support or refute the claim. Over time, people will simply stop paying attention, since the claim doesn't mean anything.

Education and Communication

Now that you have your desired behaviors and policies specified, the next process is still not enforcement, it is education and communication. While the governors may be aware of the policies, the governed may not be. In order to properly educate the staff, the people driving your SOA adoption efforts and establishing policy should also create a formal communication and education plan. The communication plan should include presentations that appeal to a broad audience, as well as presentations that are targeted toward particular audiences or toward a smaller group, such as an individual team. In addition to formal presentations, other communication techniques should be leveraged including whitepapers, blogs, and any other communication resources your organization has at its disposal.

Educational courses should be created for any skill sets the organization may lack, whether that is development technologies, such as Web Services, REST, or XML, analysis technologies, such as Business Process Modeling, or run-time management approaches such as **ITIL** v3 (**Information Technology Infrastructure Library**).

The people involved with your SOA governance effort must get the word out through presentations, documents, blogs, and whatever communication resources your organization has at its disposal. In addition to raising awareness of the effort, it will also build support for the effort such that people want to participate. People that may have questions about it will have the opportunity to voice those concerns, which can either lead to clarification on the reasons behind the policies, or to an adjustment of the policies. These conversations can be very constructive, because the policies must be connected to the desired behavior. If the connection between them is not clear, they should be questioned. If there is disagreement on whether the policy will lead to the desired behavior, alternative policies can be suggested, either by the governors or the governed. The one thing that is not questionable, however, is the desired behavior. For example, there should not be debate around the need to improve the average delivery time for IT solutions; however, there can be debate on the specific policies that will lead to that result.

Once again, there are strong parallels between SOA governance and traditional government. Constituents feel disconnected from their government when there is insufficient education and communication about the activities of the government. At its extreme, it can lead to a complete lack of faith in the government, which can have consequences ranging from revolt to the government becoming irrelevant. The same holds true for SOA governance. If the people involved in your SOA governance efforts are not educating and communicating, the people trying to make SOA a reality may simply ignore them or may be very resistant toward the enforcement efforts. Education and communication processes are the key to ensuring that governance is not seen with contempt in your organization, but rather as the key to enabling change for the better.

Policy Enforcement

The next process that must be addressed is the one that most people associate with governance, and that is policy enforcement. Regardless of how much you've educated your organization and communicated the desired behavior and policies, you still need to ensure that you have compliance with those policies, and that requires enforcement. First and foremost, you must remember the golden rule when it comes to any enforcement process:

> The easiest way to achieve compliance is to make compliance the path of least resistance.

Education and communication are a big part of this, but there are also many opportunities beyond this, especially for project governance and run-time governance. For example, if you have a policy that states that average response time must be collected for all services, the easiest way to ensure this happens is to make it a zero-effort activity for the service development team. Their service needs to be deployed onto an application server in a production environment to be used. If those application servers already have a service management agent deployed on them, that agent will recognize the new service and immediately begin collecting metrics and storing them in the appropriate repository, generating reports, and so on.

There will be policies for which some effort is required, but the burden should be on the people establishing the policies to ensure that the required effort is as minimal as possible. In the Advasco story, a policy was established that required service development teams to seek out potential consumers from outside the project at hand. If the team has to arrange for meetings with every development manager to discuss this, clearly, it's not going to happen. The managers will get tired of the meetings, and the development team will struggle trying to figure out who to talk to, while at the same time, they will be pressured by the project manager who is wondering what is taking so long. Instead, if the act of entering a proposed service into the Registry/Repository kicks off notifications to other development managers, the effort can be significantly reduced. With appropriate analysis of the business domains and capabilities, the effort can be reduced even more by only sending notifications to managers most likely to be interested.

To further emphasize the need for the previous processes, enforcement processes can be streamlined when the people doing the enforcement are trusted to evaluate projects on their own. A possible approach recommended earlier was the use of review boards. Too often, review boards are only used because the policies have not been formally specified, and a room full of smart people is expected to make the decisions during the review process. This process is at risk for turning into a debate over policy between the people performing the review, rather than an effort to review and improve (if necessary) the project under review. By formally stating policies and educating the project teams with solid communication, the focus can get back to where it belongs—making the projects better or simply adding them to the list of compliant efforts and getting out of their way.

Measurement and Improvement

The final process associated with SOA governance is that of measurement and improvement. While policy enforcement can tell you whether your efforts are compliant with the policies or not, policy compliance alone will not tell you whether you're achieving your desired behavior. If you're not, then something needs to change. Your organization is adopting SOA because something needed to be improved. Governance guides the organization through that change. If, however, you don't get there, then something else needs to change, and it could be the governance itself.

At each step along your SOA journey, you should be measuring whether or not your SOA governance efforts are achieving the desired outcome. This includes:

- Ensuring that policies are established and documented.
- Ensuring that education and communication is relevant, understood, and successful.
- Ensuring that policy compliance is on an upward slope toward 100% at the rate desired.
- Ensuring that the measurable desired behaviors are being achieved. You could have 100% compliance, but still not reach the desired behavior.

If your measurements show a problem, then something needs to change. It can be a change in process, policy, or people. If the policy compliance rate is low, one should look at the effectiveness of the communication and education, as well as make adjustments to how policies are enforced. If policy compliance is high, but the desired behavior is not achieved, then perhaps additional policies are necessary. If the effort is in complete disarray, then perhaps new people are needed, or a new organizational approach, such as switching from an Enterprise Architecture-driven approach to a Center of Excellence. This cycle of continuous improvement can also be leveraged by the IT staff itself, to measure the effectiveness of the people providing SOA governance. If policies are causing undue pain for the staff, there needs to be a way to bring attention to it, and either lead to a change in policy or a change in people.

Simply put, if you are not measuring your efforts, there is no way to state whether your SOA adoption efforts are successful or not.

SOA Governance Technologies

There is no shortage of vendors in the marketplace that are marketing their technologies as SOA Governance solutions. It is important to know that you can't buy SOA Governance. What you can buy are solutions that make your governance processes more efficient, especially when it comes to policy enforcement. Policy-driven infrastructure, which has the following key components:

- Policy enforcement points
- Policy decision points
- Policy information points
- Policy management points

Technology can help you in all of these domains, whether it is for pre-project governance, project governance, or run-time governance. The technology solutions that are available today include:

- Service Registry/Repository
- Service Testing Platforms
- Enterprise Service Bus
- XML Appliances
- Service Management Platforms
- Service Invocation and Exposure Frameworks

Service Registry/Repository

The Service Registry/Repository, in addition to tracking services and consumers, can assist you in the management and storage of policies associated with your SOA Governance efforts. It can easily play the role of a policy information point, and some products can also act as the policy management point. It is even possible to have it act as a policy decision point, although this is less common.

Being a repository, clearly the most value offered by a service Registry/Repository is as a policy information point. A core concept of SOA is that of the service contract, which is a collection of policies that govern a relationship between a consumer and a provider. These policies should be captured in the service Registry/Repository, as it needs to capture service consumers, service providers, and most importantly, the relationship between the two.

In addition to the policies that govern the interaction between a consumer and a provider, which are typically more concerned with run-time behavior, the Service Registry/Repository can also be a point where policies that apply at design time are captured. For example, a common policy associated with the design of SOAP-based interfaces is that the interface is compliant with the WS-I Basic Profile. This policy can be captured in the repository as something that must be enforced on all assets that have a type of SOAP Service.

For the pre-project governance phase, once again, the service Registry/Repository can be used to capture services from the moment they are first identified, regardless of whether any implementation of the service exists or any approved project exists to build an implementation. The service can simply be given a status of "planned" or "needed". From that point, new efforts that are seeking funding can take these services into account as they plan out their high-level architecture. Likewise, the repository can be a source of project ideas where a strategic service has been identified and entered into the repository, but no project has been proposed and approved to create it. These services would be entered into the repository as they are identified as part of the analysis efforts to define business domain models.

The service Registry/Repository can also be used to determine when the appropriate time is to decommission a service. By tracking the relationships and versions, and through integration with a service management platform that can assist in attaching actual dollar costs, candidates for decommissioning efforts can be more easily determined.

It is useful to think of the service Registry/Repository as a service lifecycle and portfolio management tool. From the perspective of the service provider, it is a tool for tracking each release of the service, the contracts with all of the consumers, as well as all of the corporate policies that apply to service design efforts. From the perspective of the service consumer, it's a way to easily find services that may be appropriate, keep up with the planned roadmap for services in use, and manage the contracts with each of those services. From the perspective of the enterprise, it provides a complete view of all of the consumers and services that are available, their roadmaps, as well as a view of services that haven't yet been created, but have been identified.

As a lifecycle management tool, the Registry/Repository can also be a trigger for events that cause policy enforcement as part of project time governance to happen. For example, when a service interface is defined and stored in the repository, this should trigger a review of the interface to check for compliance against the enterprise policies associated with service interface design.

The challenge for these tools is that there are very few standards for specifying policies and for interacting with a Service Registry/Repository. Standards such as UDDI and ebXML provide some guidance in interacting with the registry, but each tool is likely to have its own custom information model for how it represents policies. As a result, any policy enforcement point that wants to leverage a Registry/Repository as a policy information point will likely require custom integration work. All in all, the Registry/Repository is really the cornerstone of the infrastructure associated with SOA Governance. If a Registry/Repository does not exist, the individual enforcement points must each maintain their own record of the services involved. This cannot only lead to redundant data stores, but also to gaps in the data coverage where automated enforcement of policies may not currently exist.

Service Testing Platforms

The next piece of technology is a service testing platform. As the name suggests, these tools are focused on testing services. They may be sold as an add-on module or extension of a broader application testing platform, or they may be standalone solutions focused exclusively on services. In addition to being a tool that can automate the project-time compliance checks, they can also be a source of many "out-of-the-box" policies that can be reviewed by the people responsible for your SOA governance efforts and incorporated into the enterprise policies if deemed appropriate.

In addition to checking service interfaces for compliance with interface policies, service testing platforms also play a key role in the definition of service contracts. A service provider needs to provide baseline performance information for capacity planning purposes, the baseline's information can be captured consistently for all services through the use of a standard service testing platform. Furthermore, the testing platform can also be used to test service consumers and assist in the efforts to establish thresholds for notification and throttling. Once again, a standard tool for this purpose can be very advantageous. By preserving test scripts for each individual service consumer (which, incidentally, can be stored in a service Registry/Repository), capacity tests can be executed that include background traffic from other consumers, giving a more accurate picture of the behavior of the production systems.

As is the case with most of the tools discussed here, integration with a Service Registry/Repository is an important factor to consider. In order to automate enforcement of service interface policies, the Registry/Repository must be capable of kicking off compliance tests executed by the testing platform automatically kick of compliance checks against documented policies in at the time an interface definition is stored in the repository.

Enterprise Service Bus

The enterprise service bus, is primarily a policy enforcement point. All service traffic is intended to flow through the bus, making it an excellent place to enforce the policies associated with a service contract. An ESB can also be used to enforce some amount of project-time policies, simply because the ESB must be made aware of the service interface in order to make it available to service consumers. Normally, however, this takes place too late in the development process to be practical.

When evaluating enterprise service bus products, be sure to evaluate them from the perspective of policy enforcement points and service contracts. The product should provide a contextual model that easily allows the configuration of policies for the enforcement of service contracts. In utilizing an ESB, one must also be cautious to define your policies for run-time service interaction first, and then use the ESB to enforce them, rather than opening up the full range of capabilities of the ESB as the default policies for communication. Some ESB products have backgrounds in EAI technologies, and as a result, can still promote and integrate anything-to-anything mentality, which will not achieve any goals of reduced complexity in your environment.

XML Appliances and Security Gateways

XML appliances, are also policy enforcement points for run-time SOA governance. A difference between ESB products and XML appliances is that many ESB products tend to operate more like traditional software middleware. In fact, many ESB products have roots in EAI middleware technology. XML appliances, on the other hand, tend to have an operational model more similar to a network appliance than traditional middleware. Just as was recommended with ESBs, when evaluating these products, keep in mind the policy-driven mantra of configure, not code. Look closely at the contextual model of the appliance and how well it allows for the configuration of policies for the enforcement of service contracts between a service consumer and a service provider.

There is one additional differentiator between most of the XML appliances and the ESB products, and that is in the realm of security. At least two of the major XML appliances available took a path of supporting accelerated XSL transformation first, XML security second, and then full service intermediation third. As a result, the security features tend to be far more robust in the appliances, primarily in the area of threat protection. Threat protection is not normally something associated with a particular service consumer; rather, it is a set of policies that apply to all services, scanning all requests for malicious content, such as SQL injection. There are some consumer-specific policies that this enhanced scanning capabilities can enforce, however, such as a restriction on the size of the message. Two consumers using the same service could easily have very different characteristics in the message sizes. For example, in an ordering service, a key strategic partner may always have many line items per order, thereby increasing the size of a typical message from them, while a smaller partner may typically have one or two line items per order. Most appliances can handle policies on message size quite easily.

For both ESBs and XML appliances, a limitation is in the management capabilities. They typically have some elementary management capabilities, but if you require sophisticated management of the run-time behavior where complicated analytics are performed and then fed back into the enforcement points for SLA enforcement, you may need to look at the next type of product, a service management platform.

Service Management Platforms

Service management platforms, like both ESBs and XML appliances, are involved in run-time SOA governance, providing very similar coverage. These products may have fewer supported transport options than an ESB and fewer security capabilities than an XML appliance, but they typically provide more sophisticated management capabilities. Where ESBs and XML appliances can monitor and collect metrics, they typically only make these measurements available to some other analytics engine and/or dashboard. Service management platforms, however, include the analytics engine and dashboard. This analytic capability can allow the service management platform to inspect messages and track key metrics on a per service level, a per consumer level, per service broken down by consumer, and many other ways. It will also look at metrics from all monitoring points, so if you have a load balanced or clustered environment, you can see the rate of requests across all collection points, rather than seeing the rate of requests at one particular collection point. When enforcing the policies in a run-time service contract, this is an important consideration.

Furthermore, most service management products include both agents and gateways, which create additional flexibility in deployment. For example, most service management platforms include agents for ESBs; some even can work with certain XML appliances. Therefore, it is possible to use all three, leveraging ESBs where a large number of transports need to be supported and XML appliances at the perimeter for enhanced security, while deploying agents from a service management platform on both of them.

Service Invocation and Exposure Frameworks

Service invocation and exposure frameworks are a key part of the policy enforcement mechanism that may be overlooked. When Microsoft finally made a statement regarding products in the ESB space in 2005, they stated that the two key components of their solution were BizTalk and **Windows Communication Foundation** (**WCF**). WCF is a framework for both invoking services and exposing logic as services. The biggest benefit of frameworks in the SOA governance space is that by using them, compliance with certain policies should be automatic. For example, if your organization has a policy on how identity should be represented on service messages, a framework can easily extract identity from the current consumer, format it in the appropriate way, and place it on the outgoing message. Depending on the framework involved, this may only involve a code annotation, a few lines of code, or perhaps nothing at all from the developer writing the service consumer. This certainly makes compliance the path of least resistance.

Summary

SOA Governance is a critical part of the SOA adoption effort. It begins with a concrete definition of what your organization hopes to achieve by adopting SOA, and then sets in place the people who will make the policy decisions that through effective processes, guide your organization to that desired outcome.

There is no one universal approach to SOA governance that works at all organizations, rather, the organization must take into account their own business structure, organizational model, and corporate culture in determining the appropriate way to drive SOA adoption, whether through Enterprise Architecture, a cross-functional Center of Excellence, or by simply relying on the organization as is to modify their individual behaviors to reach the goals desired.

The policy makers must address the desired behavior of the organization in defining and choosing what projects to execute, known as pre-project governance, the desired behavior of the project teams that are building the services and their consumers, known as project governance, and the desired behavior of those services, consumers, and the people that manage them at run-time as they execute in production.

However, stating policies are not enough. The organization must be educated on the desired behavior and the policies that will guide you there, and some amount of enforcement must be put in place to achieve compliance with those policies. Whether it is pre-project, project, or run-time governance, there are many technologies that can increase the efficiency of your compliance processes, whether through automated compliance checks, frameworks that guarantee compliance when used, or by simply raising the awareness through easy access to information about services and their consumers.

Ultimately, governance can only be effective if the organization puts measurements in place to judge whether or not the desired behavior is being achieved. Measuring compliance with policies is easy to capture, but if the wrong policies are put in place, the desired behavior will not be achieved. Governance is first and foremost about achieving the desired behavior. If policy compliance does not yield the desired behavior, then the policies may need to be changed.

As your organization proceeds along its SOA journey, the effectiveness of your governance processes can make or break your efforts. With good governance you can make your SOA efforts, and ultimately your business more successful, whether that represents some small changes in an organization that already works very well with its IT department, or a more fundamental change in the way the IT department works with the rest of the organization.

Index

A

B

D

E

F

G

H

I

J

L

M

N

O

P

Q

R

S

T

U

V

W

X

Z

[PACKT] enterprise
professional expertise distilled
PUBLISHING

Thank you for buying

Do More with SOA Integration: Best of Packt

About Packt Publishing

Packt, pronounced 'packed', published its first book "Mastering phpMyAdmin for Effective MySQL Management" in April 2004 and subsequently continued to specialize in publishing highly focused books on specific technologies and solutions.

Our books and publications share the experiences of your fellow IT professionals in adapting and customizing today's systems, applications, and frameworks. Our solution based books give you the knowledge and power to customize the software and technologies you're using to get the job done. Packt books are more specific and less general than the IT books you have seen in the past. Our unique business model allows us to bring you more focused information, giving you more of what you need to know, and less of what you don't.

Packt is a modern, yet unique publishing company, which focuses on producing quality, cutting-edge books for communities of developers, administrators, and newbies alike. For more information, please visit our website: `www.packtpub.com`.

About Packt Enterprise

In 2010, Packt launched two new brands, Packt Enterprise and Packt Open Source, in order to continue its focus on specialization. This book is part of the Packt Enterprise brand, home to books published on enterprise software – software created by major vendors, including (but not limited to) IBM, Microsoft and Oracle, often for use in other corporations. Its titles will offer information relevant to a range of users of this software, including administrators, developers, architects, and end users.

Writing for Packt

We welcome all inquiries from people who are interested in authoring. Book proposals should be sent to author@packtpub.com. If your book idea is still at an early stage and you would like to discuss it first before writing a formal book proposal, contact us; one of our commissioning editors will get in touch with you.

We're not just looking for published authors; if you have strong technical skills but no writing experience, our experienced editors can help you develop a writing career, or simply get some additional reward for your expertise.

[PACKT] enterprise
professional expertise distilled
PUBLISHING

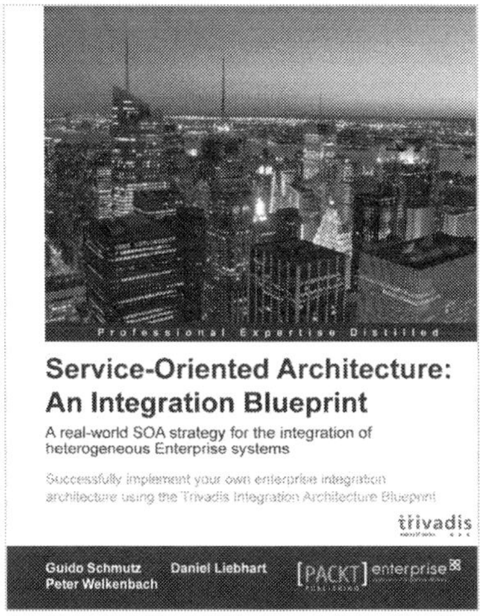

Service Oriented Architecture: An Integration Blueprint

ISBN: 978-1-849681-04-9 Paperback: 240 pages

Successfully implement your own enterprise integration architecture using the Trivadis Integration Architecture Blueprint

1. Discover and understand the structure of existing application landscapes from an integration perspective
2. Get to grips with fundamental integration concepts and terminology while learning about architecture variants
3. Fully comprehend all the individual layers and components that make up the Trivadis Integration Architecture Blueprint

---

Building SOA-Based Composite Applications Using NetBeans IDE 6

ISBN: 978-1-847192-62-2 Paperback: 300 pages

Design, build, test, and debug service-oriented applications with ease using XML, BPEL, and Java web services

1. SOA concepts and BPEL process fundamentals
2. Build complex SOA applications
3. Design schemas and architect solutions
4. JBI components including service engines and binding components

Please check **www.PacktPub.com** for information on our titles

[PACKT] enterprise
PUBLISHING professional expertise distilled

Oracle SOA Suite Developer's Guide

ISBN: 978-1-847193-55-1 Paperback: 652 pages

Design and build Service-Oriented Architecture Solutions with the Oracle SOA Suite 10gR3

1. A hands-on guide to using and applying the Oracle SOA Suite in the delivery of real-world SOA applications
2. Detailed coverage of the Oracle Service Bus, BPEL Process Manager, Web Service Manager, Rules, Human Workflow, and Business Activity Monitoring
3. Master the best way to combine / use each of these different components in the implementation of a SOA solution

---

WS-BPEL 2.0 for SOA Composite Applications with Oracle SOA Suite 11g

ISBN: 978-1-847197-94-8 Paperback: 616 pages

Define, model, implement, and monitor real-world BPEL business processes with SOA powered BPM

1. Develop BPEL and SOA composite solutions with Oracle SOA Suite 11g
2. Efficiently automate business processes with WS-BPEL 2.0 and develop SOA composite applications
3. Get familiar with basic and advanced BPEL 2.0

Please check **www.PacktPub.com** for information on our titles

13312742R00402

Made in the USA
Lexington, KY
09 February 2012